The Economic Societies in the Spanish World
(1763-1821)

5 -

The Economic Societies in the Spanish World (1763-1821)

ROBERT JONES SHAFER, 1915 -
Syracuse University

HC
384
S5

SYRACUSE UNIVERSITY PRESS

1958

Library of Congress Catalog Card Number : 57-12362

*This work has been published with
the assistance of a Ford Foundation grant.*

1958 SYRACUSE UNIVERSITY PRESS

For My Family

Preface

The *Sociedades Económicas de Amigos del País*[1] of the Spanish world in the half century before its political fragmentation were creatures of a minority of the elite, attached to views which were to become those of the majority in the Occidental culture-area, but which penetrated the Spanish world with some difficulty. The history of the Societies illuminates general intellectual change, economic conditions, and attitudes toward economic questions in the Spanish world in the later eighteenth and early nineteenth centuries.

The prime concern of this study is with America. It was first necessary, however, to furnish a picture of the Economic Societies of Spain, since the colonial Societies were founded in imitation of the peninsular, often by Spaniards familiar with the latter. The records of the Spanish Societies may be "equalled by no other scientific material in the light they shed on the situation in Spain and its colonies" in the late colonial era,[2] but those records have not been exploited systematically.[3]

A systematic exploitation of the available evidence bearing on the Spanish and colonial Societies is attempted here. This means that all aspects of the

---

[1] The usual name; but *patriótica* sometimes substituted for *económica*.

[2] Fernando de los Ríos, "The Social Sciences as Disciplines: Spain and Portugal," *Encyclopedia of the Social Sciences*, I, 295-300.

[3] Nor have many aspects of Spain's economic history. Cf. the opening words of Jaime Carrera Pujal, *Historia de la economía española* (5 vols., Barcelona, 1943-47), I, 1: "En la historia de Espana tal vez no haya ningún aspecto menos conocido que el económico."

history, belief, and labors of the Societies have been described. It does not mean that all aspects of the labors and of the doctrine have been fully analyzed. In the case of the Spanish Societies it also means that a vast amount of evidence was not available to the author. The records of the colonial—and even more of the Spanish—Societies thus contain much information suitable for further study. For America this includes, for example, the technicalities of Havana interest in sugar processing, the problem of land ownership in Cuba, and Guatemala interest in indigo.

An effort has been made to provide a framework on which additional studies may be built, by providing: (1) not only a description of the character of the Societies' efforts, but quantitative data on the numbers of members, finances, and the size of operations; (2) precise chronological information; (3) abundant citation as a guide to sources; (4) a topical organization; and (5) plentiful generalization on the evidence available.

This is the first large-scale account of all the known colonial Societies. Societies not mentioned here may have been suggested for America, or even tentatively organized, but it is unlikely that they could have been of such importance as to contradict seriously the picture here presented.

The history of the American Societies is carried to 1821, but most of the data relate to the years before 1814; most of that thereafter relates to Havana. In its American aspects, therefore, this study deals with the last years of the colonial era. The colonial Societies show creole and Spanish concern for the economic state of the realms; the vacillating and harmful Spanish policy with regard to colonial discussion of economic problems; the considerable number of Spanish officials in America who, imbued with the ideas of the Enlightenment and with a sense of the economic deficiencies of the Spanish world, were in favor of some degree of economic change and experiment; the extent to which new ideas and a taste for rationalism had penetrated the ranks of creoles and of Spanish officials in America; and specifically the stimulating effect of optimism and belief in progress, which led them to praise effort and condemn sloth and passivity.

Some of these moderate liberals (or liberal conservatives) became conservatives in republican Spanish America, others remained moderate liberals in Spain or the surviving colonies. The Societies in the late colonial era, therefore, provide a picture of moderate opinion, largely directed to economic interests. The concentration on economics and avoidance of politics was in itself moderate; but the coming age in America was to be both political and in some measure revolutionary.

This study probably displays a bias in favor of the revisionists as opposed to traditionalists in the Spanish world. But it must be emphasized that the revisionists involved in the Societies were moderate liberals. These moderate liberals could only be considered radicals by those traditionalists opposed to almost any effective effort to accommodate Spanish thought and institutions to the realities of modern economic, technological, and diplomatic competition. The author confesses a conviction, also, that not all traditionalists were moved primarily by principle, but often were simply or largely influenced by consideration of their personal or class interests.

My thanks are due to the staffs of the Library of Congress, the Bancroft Library, the American Philosophical Society, the New York Public Library, and the Syracuse University Library; to the Director and staff of the *Biblioteca Nacional* of Guatemala; to the staff of the *Biblioteca* of the *Sociedad Económica* of Havana; and especially to Señor Joaquín Pardo, Director of the *Archivo General* of Guatemala, and his staff. Thanks are due also for the kindly extended advice of Drs. A. P. Whitaker and D. W. McPheeters; and for the stimulating aid of Dr. R. D. Hussey, who first turned my attention to the Economic Societies. Financial assistance for research in Latin America was provided by the United States Office of Education.

Abbreviations used often in the following pages: AGG—*Archivo General de Guatemala;* BAGG—*Boletín del Archivo General del Gobierno,* Guatemala; ASGH—*Anales* of the *Sociedad de Geografía e Historia,* Guatemala; BAE—*Biblioteca de Autores Españoles;* RBC—*Revista Bimestre Cubana;* HAHR—*Hispanic American Historical Review; Revue Basques—Revue internationale des études Basques;* BHPR—*Boletín Histórico de Puerto Rico.*

Contents

PART THREE

Aims and Activities of the Colonial Societies

PART ONE

The Economic Societies of Spain (1763-1821)

CHAPTER ONE

Spain in the Eighteenth Century

Political economy was the vital fluid of the Economic Societies of Friends of the Country, however diluted with the whey of philanthropy. Their economic interests were central to all others, though mingled with concern for political and social objectives, military strength, and the over-all security and vigor of the Spanish world. Ofttimes, alas, the members seemed unable to soar to that noble antipathy for economic thought and action reputedly a feature of the Spanish cultural medium. They even seemed aware that the history of the Spanish does not unequivocally show an inherent distaste for wealth; that several Spaniards have devoted thought and ink to economic questions;[1] that numerous non-Spaniards have concentrated on the study rather than the acquisition of wealth; and finally, that the results of such de-emphasis of economic motivation as has in fact existed in the Spanish world are far from clear, even in the pastures of the spirit. The common

---

[1] Cf. the five volumes of Carrera Pujal, *Economía española*, for voluminous discussion of Spanish writers on economics from 1500 to 1808, and especially I, 84-85, that nineteenth-century students, preferring to consider the 16th and 17th centuries barbarous, spread the notion that Spain lacked writers on economics then; José Canga Argüelles, *Diccionario de hacienda, con aplicación a España* (2d ed., 2 vols., Madrid, 1833-34), "Economistas Españoles," for a list of 350 works on economics; Manuel Colmeiro, *Biblioteca de los economistas españoles de los siglos XVI, XVII y XVIII* (Madrid, 1861), for 405 items; Colmeiro, *Historia de la economía política en España* (2 vols., Madrid, 1863); Gabriel Alonso de Herrera, *Agricultura general* (4 vols., Madrid, 1818-19), IV, 353-61, an account of its 28 editions, from 1513 to this one by the Madrid Economic Society.

sense of the Societies was typical of men of the Enlightenment, who applied rationalism to everything but their own cherished beliefs. But not all facets of Spanish development in the eighteenth century were typical of the period in the rest of western Europe.

Politico-Economic Conditions

The Spanish Bourbons inherited in 1700 from their Hapsburg predecessors a nation suffering from a diseased economy, however sound the other national organs may have been. On this the commentators nearly agree, while arguing the cause of the malady.[2] At least it was clear then, as now, that a cure for the economic ailment would be useful. All governments of eighteenth-century Spain yearned to fatten the fisc by improving the general economy; but their efforts had ambiguous results at best.[3] Revenues were perennially insufficient. Efforts were made to revamp the administration and increase taxes, but the best statesmen knew that the real necessity was an increase in wealth, perceiving the Spanish economy decayed, the wealth of her rivals increasing.

As always with national economic decay, the Spanish decline had not issued from simply economic causes. Other causes were centralized government and a series of inferior monarchs; a foreign policy that lavished wealth on the pursuit of imperial ends in Europe, to the detriment of the Spanish economy; and the rising force and aggressiveness of the rivals of Spain complicated and made costly her plans and system of control.

In addition, the eighteenth century inherited problems of currency inflation and rising prices; an emphasis on stockraising at the expense of agriculture; the holding out of production of vast lands held by communes, nobility, and Church; a decayed commerce, internal and external; a long enfeebled

---

[2] Spanish writers have for centuries exaggerated the absolute decay of the Spanish economy, yearning for a supposed earlier golden age, and thus have tended to somewhat underplay the decline of Spain relative to other powers. Cf. Carrera Pujal, *Economía española*, I, 79 *et seq.*, for an expression of this view, including the assertion that there simply was no great Spanish industry in the 16th century; Earl J. Hamilton, "The Decline of Spain," *Economic History Review*, VIII (1938), 168-79, to the effect that the economic decline of Spain in the 17th century is clear, if difficult to measure.

[3] The essential conclusion of the well-balanced studies of Carrera Pujal, *Economía española;* Rafael Altamira y Crevea, *Historia de España y de la civilización española* (3d ed., 4 vols., Barcelona, 1913-14), IV; Antonio Ballesteros y Beretta, *Historia de España y su influencia en la historia universal* (9 vols., Barcelona, 1918-41), V-VI; G. Desdevises du Dézert, *L'Espagne de l'ancien régime* (2d ed., 3 vols., in *Revue Hispanique*, 1925-28, hereafter cited by titles of the volumes: *La Société, Les Institutions, La Richesse*).

industrial production; and a social bias against manual labor. None of these was unique to Spain, but in their detail, and even more in their combination, they contributed to economic difficulties which were both absolute and relative to the growing strength of other powers. The problems of America were of course unique. Finally, it may be that the insistence on orthodoxy and the relative rigidity of intellectual control in the Spanish world inhibited the capacity to make use of novelty in the face of altering conditions.[4]

Although more and better literature on economic questions was produced in Spain in the eighteenth than in earlier centuries, Spaniards in Hapsburg times did not lack interest in the things of this world. Indeed, so numerous were the fantastic schemes for profit presented to the court by the *arbitristas* of the late sixteenth and the seventeenth centuries, that the Cortes wished them expelled from the court, and they were satirized by Quevedo, Cervantes, and other writers. Statesmen and serious writers of the seventeenth century devoted considerable thought to economic matters,[5] tending to emphasize the importance of excluding foreigners from the Spanish system, although they were not always the simple-minded exponents of mercantilist notions that the traditional interpretation suggests.[6]

Early in the century, Sancho de Moncada, insisting upon the study of government as a science,[7] found the fundamental cause of the lowered state revenues in the intrusion of foreigners into the Spanish economic system,[8] and suggested cutting them off from all sources of income in Spain.[9] He wanted to prohibit exports of raw materials in order to stimulate industry,[10] lamented the sparse population,[11] and pointed out that the Indies

---

[4] For an excellent discussion of various interpretations of Spain's economic troubles, see Carrera Pujal, *Economía española*, I, 57 *et seq.*

[5] *Ibid.*, I, 52-53, for a good comment on this; and all of vols. I-II for economic writers of the 16th and 17th centuries.

[6] Cf. Robert S. Smith, "Spanish Anti-Mercantilism of the Seventeenth Century," *Journal of Political Economy*, XLVIII (1940), 401-11; Javier Márquez, "El Mercantilismo de Saavedra Fajardo," *El Trimestre Económico*, X (1943-44), 247-86, for a seventeenth-century mercantilist who attributed importance to diverse elements of the economic structure—money, industry, population, commerce.

[7] *Restauración política de España, y deseos públicos, que escrivió en ocho discursos* (2d ed., Madrid, 1746), "Discurso Octavo." Campomanes, *Apéndice a la educación popular* (4 vols., Madrid, 1775-77), Parte Primera, p. L, noted that in 1619 Sancho de Moncada had proposed a "cátedra de política," and that Felipe IV created one in 1625, but it did not do all the good that it might have (p. xliv).

[8] Moncada, *Restauración política*, "Discurso Quarto."

[9] *Ibid.*, "Discurso Primero," including such comments as. "Los estrangeros, como más diligentes que los Españoles, usan en España casi todos los oficios."

[10] *Ibid.*

[11] *Ibid.*, "Discurso Segundo."

had not enriched Spain. But he also noted that the only value of money consisted in what was bought with it.[12]

Much of this was reflected later in the century in Francisco Martínez de Mata, who inveighed against the Spanish practice of concentrating on silver to the neglect of manufacturing,[13] asserted that kings needed *vasallos industriosos*,[14] pointed out that all the different sorts of economic activities tied together into a *harmonía general*,[15] and disapproved of consumption of foreign goods.[16] Campomanes, in reprinting Martínez de Mata in the eighteenth century, noted that the latter's method was essentially that of Sancho de Moncada, attributing depopulation and weakness to the abandonment of manufactures and the introduction of foreign goods.[17] Campomanes had difficulty locating copies of Martínez de Mata,[18] a fair measure of the failure of the Spanish to make good use of their writers in the field.[19]

It has been asserted of seventeenth-century Spanish economists that "history records few instances of either such able diagnosis of fatal social ills by any group of moral philosophers or of such utter disregard by statesmen of sound advice."[20] Their list of the worms eating at the Spanish economy included primogeniture, mortmain, vagabondage, deforestation, redundance of ecclesiastics, contempt for manual labor and arts, indiscriminate almsgiving, monetary confusion, and oppressive taxation. Their suggested reforms included technological education, importation of artisans, monetary stability, extension of irrigation, and improvement of internal waterways.[21]

The numerous decrees of the seventeenth century aimed at economic improvement, including creation of *juntas de comercio* late in the century,

---

[12] *Ibid.*, "Discurso Tercero."
[13] "Epítome de los discursos que ha dado á su Mag. Francisco Martínez de Mata ... ," in Campomanes, *Apéndice a la educación popular*, I, 433-500, at 434.
[14] *Ibid.*, 436.
[15] *Ibid.*, 470-71. Campomanes found this a particularly praiseworthy idea (*ibid.*, 471 n.).
[16] *Ibid.*, 479 *et seq.*
[17] *Ibid.*, I, vii-viii, of Campomanes' "Advertencia a los lectores patriotas." Cf. *ibid.*, IV, 1-431, eight discourses of Martínez de Mata, in which he dealt at greater length with the ideas expressed in the "Epítome," blaming the Indies in part for the depopulation and unsatisfactory economic condition of Spain.
[18] *Ibid.*, I, 435 n.
[19] His reprint enabled the Economic Society of Valencia in 1777 to cite Martínez de Mata against the "brutality" of consuming foreign goods even when they were cheaper than Spanish wares (*Instituciones económicas de la Sociedad de Amigos del País de la ciudad, i reino de Valencia* [Valencia, 1777], 97, citing the *Apéndice* to the *educación popular*.
[20] Hamilton, "Decline of Spain," *loc. cit.*, 179.
[21] *Ibid.*, 178-79.

had little result.[22] Efforts were continued in the next century to renovate various aspects of the Spanish system,[23] and to introduce new features, the latter often owing their impulse to French ideas brought into Spain by the Bourbons. Some ministers of the century were foreigners by birth, and they and statesmen of Spanish origin alike tended to accept extrapeninsular thought. Some of their revisionist effort aimed at administrative efficiency, primarily in terms of centralization and simplification. Their appreciation of the needs of Spain was, however, superior to their capacity to secure improvement under the burdens of war or in the face of vested interest and belief and the national distaste for change.

The efforts of the regalist ministers tended to increase friction between civil and ecclesiastical authority, and the spirit of the age encouraged the pretensions of the former. The influence of the Church was attacked by a number of measures, of which the expulsion (1767) of the Jesuits was merely the most spectacular. The Church cast a sour eye upon the revisionists, nor was it reconciled by knowledge that other governments in the Age of Enlightened Despotism were enacting similar measures. There were few liberal ecclesiastics, and the general population of Spain was never enthusiastic about the aims of the civil government in its quarrels with the Church.[24]

For the Spanish government the eighteenth century was one long fiscal crisis. Many expedients were adopted to stimulate economic production, that this might swell the fisc. With the accession of Philip V in 1700 the influence of Colbertian mercantilism grew apace. The generally quickened interest

[22] Desdevises, *La Richesse*, ch. iii, sec. i; Roland D. Hussey, *The Caracas Company 1728-1784* (Cambridge, 1934), 8 *et seq.*, 23, 31, for seventeenth-century suggestions for trading companies, the *Junta de Comercio*, and the judgment that Spanish trade was in such an "abyss" that the ministry clung to any "glimmer of hope"; Carrera Pujal, *Economía española*, II, 62; Antonio L. Valverde, "La Creación de las Sociedades Económicas," RBC, XXI, No. 1 (January-February, 1926), 38-51.

[23] Carrera Pujal, *Economía española*, often insists (e.g., I, 88) on the continuity of politico-economic policy between the late Hapsburgs and the Bourbons.

[24] Ballesteros, *Historia*, VI, ch. i, for government in eighteenth-century Spain; Desdevises, *Les Institutions;* Modesto Lafuente y Zamolloa, *Historia general de España* (25 vols., Barcelona, 1887-90), especially vols. 14-15 for the period 1749-1802; François Rousseau, *Règne de Charles III d'Espagne 1759-1788* (2 vols., Paris, 1907), ch. x, "Réformes intérieurs"; Altamira, *Historia*, IV; Amilio Marichalar and Cayetano Manrique, *Historia de la legislación y recitaciones del derecho civil de España* (9 vols, Madrid, 1861-72), IX 419-755, "Casa de Borbón;" Emile Gigas, "Un voyageur allemand-danois en Espagne sous le règne de Charles III," *Revue Hispanique*, LXIX, No. 156 (April, 1927), 341-519, for sketches of Spanish statesmen late in the reign of Charles III. Cf. Hamilton, "Decline of Spain," *loc. cit.*, 175-76, that Spanish economists of the 17th century almost unanimously agreed that the growth of the Church was harmful to the Spanish economy.

in political economy was reflected in renewed attention to earlier Spanish writings on the subject, and led also to the production of many new works.[25]

Gerónimo de Ustáriz, a disciple of Colbert, and author of *Teórica y práctica del comercio y de la marina* (1724), was the most influential Spanish writer on political economy in the first half of the century. His interest was in practical measures rather than in theory. He advocated the revival of internal manufactures and of external trade, a stronger army and navy, the advantage of "active" trade (balance of exports, handled by nationals), and the necessity of hoarding coin in the Peninsula as a stimulant to production.[26] A better industry, combined with a reduction of duties on colonial trade, and with discrimination against foreign merchants, he thought would enable Spain to undersell contrabandists in America. His interest, of course, was the improvement of the financial condition of Spain, and the situation of America was incidental to that aim.[27] Ustáriz expected agricultural prosperity to flow from commercial and industrial survival. This mercantilist emphasis may be contrasted with the Physiocratic emphasis on agriculture by the revisionists who were active in the Economic Societies in the second half of the century. Each group had, to be sure, some interest in both agriculture and industry.

While many—probably most—Spanish writers on political economy after Ustáriz clung to bullionism and to mercantilist notions of regulation and protection, doctrines with a laissez-faire tinge—such as suggestions for freer trade—gained increasing currency. By the time of the foundation of the Economic Societies, criticism of the older notions was neither novel nor rare.

Bernardo de Ulloa in 1740, much under the influence of Ustáriz, and primarily concerned with the transformation of Spanish trade from its "passive" to an "active" condition, devoted most of his well-known treatise to the necessity of reviving industrial production in Spain. This was to be

---

[25] Cf. Hussey, *Caracas Company*, 30, on expanded interest in monopolistic trading companies; *Memorias de la Sociedad Económica* (5 vols., Madrid, 1780-95), I, xvii-xix of the "Discurso Preliminar," to the effect that Spain had many writers on economics, but that their chief defect was the inexactitude of their data.

[26] *Théorie et practique du commerce et de la marine* (tr. fr. Span., Hambourg, 1775), 446 *et passim*.

[27] Cf. Andrés V. Castillo, *Spanish Mercantilism : Gerónimo de Uztáriz Economist* (New York, 1930); Earl J. Hamilton, "The Mercantilism of Gerónimo de Uztáriz: A Reëxamination," pp. 111-129 in *Economics, Sociology and the Modern World, Essays in Honor of T. N. Carver*, ed. Norman E. Himes (Harvard University Press, 1935); Javier Márquez, "Gerónimo de Uztáriz como Economista," *El Trimestre Económico*, XI (1944-45), 471-94.

done primarily by means of improved transportation, and the reduction of taxes and imposts so as to free production from burdens that made it impossible for Spanish goods to compete in price with foreign goods.[28]

José Campillo y Cosío in the 1740's lamented that not a twentieth of the consumption of the Spanish Indies was of the products of Spain,[29] whereas "commerce maintains the body politic, as the circulation of the blood the natural."[30] The advantage of foreigners lay in good government, giving vassals the means of enriching themselves, the only means of enriching also the treasury and the State, lightening taxes, freeing commerce.[31] He would allow colonial manufacture of goods not easily made in Spain;[32] integrate the Indians into the economy by persuading them to speak Spanish and wear European-style clothes;[33] allow free commerce to the colonials, as other powers did;[34] and admit foreign Catholics into Spanish America.[35]

Bernardo Ward, in the next two decades, argued—with Campillo, and most other revisionists of the second half of the century—that the only advantage other nations had over Spain lay in their using their governments to promote their interests.[36] Other colonial nations, starting with the restrictive principle still followed by Spain, had learned that to enrich the metropolis it was necessary to loosen the fetters of the colonies so the latter could enrich themselves.[37] He thought, also, that no nation could be rich with agriculture alone, needing crafts, factories, and commerce, for "the union of the four is what makes the wealth and power of a state."[38] He advocated juntas or societies of "zealous patricians" to work for improvement of the economy, on the model of such bodies then existing in other European countries.[39] Both Campillo and Ward, therefore, advocated a mixed system of freedom

---

[28] *Restablecimiento de las fábricas, y comercio español* (Madrid), 4-6, for passive condition of trade; 117, for a statement incorporating many of his basic ideas; 118, for advantages gained by freeing some aspects of foreign commerce.

[29] *Nuevo sistema de gobierno económico para la América ...* (Madrid, 1789), Part I, ch. i, sec. 16.

[30] *Ibid.*, Part I, ch. i, sec. 19.

[31] *Ibid.*, Part I, ch. v.

[32] *Ibid.*, Part I, ch. ix.

[33] *Ibid.*, Part I, ch. ix, secs. 25 *et seq.*

[34] *Ibid.*, Part II, ch. ii.

[35] *Ibid.*, Part II, ch. viii.

[36] *Proyecto económico, en que se proponen varias providencias, dirigidas á promover los intereses de España ...* (Madrid, 1779, but written more than a decade earlier), Part I, ch. xxi.

[37] *Ibid.*, Part II, ch. i, ii, iv.

[38] *Ibid.*, Part I, ch. xvi.

[39] *Ibid.*, Part I, ch. iv, "Junta de Mejoras," mentioning societies in Sweden, Tuscany, and France, but especially celebrating the Dublin Society.

and regulation.[40] The introduction to the 1779 edition of Ward suggested that the Economic Societies should be interested in his work.[41] They were. He was perhaps more often referred to in the five volumes (1780-1795) of the *Memorias* of the Madrid Society than any other writer on political economy save Campomanes.

The colonial trade law was considerably liberalized in the second half of the century, for by mid-century it was difficult to be satisfied with a system that left so much of the commerce of the Spanish world—European and American —to foreigners. This dissatisfaction increased interest in new economic doctrine. The modification of the mercantilist emphasis went so far that Campomanes and Jovellanos—both members of the Madrid Economic Society—have been described as "tacit Smithians," since they repeatedly attacked some aspects of the regulatory system.[42] Jovellanos believed that: "Industry is natural to man, and scarcely requires other stimulus on the part of the Government than the liberty to grow and prosper." Liberty, with enlightenment and good economic techniques, was for him sufficient.[43]

Even more important than the advance of free-trade doctrines for the overseas traffic was the extension of the spirit of criticism to domestic institutions and practices which the vested interests were bound to defend grimly. The revisionists charged the guilds with impeding industrial progress, and the sheep-raisers' organization with damaging agriculture.[44] And their consideration of the effect of law and custom upon agricultural production led them to condemn such institutions as the mortmain of the Church, the seignioralty, and the practice of entail. Traditionalists in rebuttal noted that this sort of revision, hacking at the economic roots of privilege, had large social and political as well as economic implications.[45]

---

[40] Cf. Hussey, *Caracas Company*, 195, on Campillo, and other discussions of economic theory at pp. 8 *et seq.*, 36-37, 168, 196, 227; Colmeiro, *Historia economía política*, II, 221 *et seq.*, *et passim*, on laissez-faire doctrines in Spain in the second half of the 18th century.

[41] *Proyecto económico*, p. v.

[42] Ballesteros, *Historia*, VI, 163.

[43] Seventh letter to Antonio Ruiz, in *Obras escogidas* of Jovellanos (*Clásicos castellanos*, vols. 110-111, 129), III, 218, written sometime after 1790. Cf. Jean Sarrailh, *L'Espagne éclairée de la seconde moitié du XVIIIe siècle* (Paris, 1954), ch. v, "L'économie nouvelle," for discussion of economic doctrine in Spain, emphasizing that the primary interest in agriculture is indicative of Physiocratic influence in Spain.

[44] Cf. Julius Klein, *The Mesta* (Cambridge, 1920), 97, 132 *et seq.*, *et passim*. The campaign against the Mesta in the second half of the 18th century is a good lead into the attitudes and objectives of the revisionist statesmen and economists.

[45] Cf. Colmeiro, *Historia economía política*, II, 250 *et seq.*, *et passim*, on attacks on the regulatory system by Campomanes, Jovellanos, and others.

The Spanish political economy in the eighteenth century was a combination of the old and the new, for, though new doctrines were much discussed and some implemented, action lagged well behind suggestion. Efforts in Philip V's reign to improve commerce bore small fruit. His minister Patiño could not implement the suggestions of such men as Ustáriz because the immediate demands of government dictated a hand-to-mouth policy.[46] Nor did Philip follow the suggestion of Melchor Rafael de Macanaz that *Sociedades Patrióticas* and popular industries be established in towns of sufficient size.[47] These suggestions prefigured the Economic Societies of half a century later, established in three-score Spanish towns, with one of their prime interests the promotion of popular industry. Macanaz wrote at length on many subjects, including political economy, and many of his attitudes were similar to those of the members of the later Economic Societies.[48]

In the second half of the century, as the revisionists gained influence in the reign of Charles III, the gap between discussion and action somewhat narrowed. By 1777 the Economic Society of Valencia could quote Campomanes to the effect that Spanish laws favored commerce and industry, though the editors simultaneously found that the economy of Valencia was susceptible of much improvement.[49] It was a favorite claim of Campomanes that the laws of Spain encouraged economic advance, but that they were not properly enforced. Campomanes was possibly the most talented and influential of all eighteenth-century Spanish writers on political economy. Most influential of his writings were his discourses on popular industry and education,[50]

---

[46] *Ibid.*, I, 250; Joseph Addison, *Charles the Third of Spain* (Oxford, 1900), 57, for evidence that Grimaldi said that Spain lived from hand-to-mouth; Hussey, *Caracas Company*, 37; and see Jean O. McLachlen, *Trade and Peace with Old Spain, 1667-1750* (Cambridge University Press, 1940), 152.

[47] Antonio Ferrer del Río, *Historia del reinado de Carlos III en España* (4 vols., Madrid, 1856), III, 231-32, citing Macanaz, "Representación ... desde Lieja ... al ... Felipe V, expresando los notorios males que causan la despoblación de España, y otros daños aumamente atendibles y dignos de repara, con los generales advertimientos para su universal remedio"; and see Lafuente, *Historia*, XIV, 313.

[48] Cf. *Auxilio para bien gobernar una monarquía católica, o documentos, que dicta la experiencia, y aprueba la razón, para que el Monarca merezca justamente el nombre de Grande. Obra, que escribió, y remitió desde París al rey nuestro señor Don Felipe Quinto Don Melchor de Macanaz, & c.*, in *Semanario Erudito* [Madrid], V (1787), 215-303, in which he deprecated the emphasis on mining, called commerce "the main nerve" of the monarchy, inveighed against the large numbers of religious, attacked the Jesuits, called for more manufacturing, and a variety of other economic improvements, and for the establishment of academies of arts and sciences.

[49] Valencia Society, *Instituciones económicas*, 33, citing from the appendix to the *Educación popular* of Campomanes the Royal Instruction of July 30, 1760, applying the liquid surplus from taxes on spiritous liquors to the development of agriculture, public works, or popular industry.

[50] *Infra*, 49 *et seq.*

and the four-volume appendices to the latter, which seem to have been the *vade mecum* of the Economic Societies, and are a mine of information on the historical and contemporary political economy of Spain.[51] Campomanes noted that the treatises of Spanish writers in the field were not sufficiently attended to when published,[51] and that recent improvement was partly due to the illumination of the nation by the reading of *escritores económicos*, who had been protected by recent monarchs.[53] Though this class of author had been criticized as *proyectistas*—that is, too theoretical—he found them useful and necessary.[54] All nations knew "eclipses and decadence," due largely to lack of proper study and reflection and planning. *Gacetas de comercio*, and *diarios económicos*, and other periodicals were necessary; monopolies were undesirable.[56] A nation must study to advance, and the estimation that the English and French gave to writers in political economy helped explain the flourishing state of their industry.[57] Campomanes' conviction that ignorance was the worst barrier to the improvement of the Spanish economy he asserted by claiming that until good principles were adopted the country could scarcely expect economic improvement,[58] and in the statement that "in our nation it is more important to remove certain fallacies, adopted without inquiry, than to produce new discoveries."[59]

Criticism of the national political economy attained new proportions after 1775 in the discussions and publications of the Economic Societies. It was stimulated, also, by the relaxation of the censorship in the later years of the reign of Charles III. The potentially great influence of the periodical press for the stimulation of interest in the deficiencies of the national political economy was exploited on a somewhat larger scale than earlier. The *Espíritu de los mejores diarios* carried considerable criticism of politico-economic conditions. A series by Valentín de Foronda, a member of the Basque Society of Friends of the Country, criticized the guilds and the tax system,[60] praised

[51] Probably more important than the reprints of works by other authors, and the royal decrees and acts, were his extensive footnotes, and his long introductory treatises (*Apéndice a la educación popular*, I, iii-lii, 1-6; II, iii-cclxiv; III, iii-cclx, 1-15; IV, iii-xcii).

[52] *Ibid.*, I, iv.

[53] *Ibid.*, v.

[54] *Ibid.*, x.

[55] *Ibid.*, xxii.

[56] *Ibid.*, xxiii.

[57] *Ibid.*, xxix *et seq.*

[58] *Ibid.*, xlvii.

[59] *Ibid.*, xlvi. But cf. Carrera Pujal, *Economía española*, I, 90-92, *et passim*, for criticism of Campomanes' views on the promotion of industry. And see, infra, 49 *et seq.*

[60] Nos. 158-159, 164 (December 8 and 15, 1788; January 19, 1789).

Descartes, and lamented that the study of politics was on a bad footing in Spain, where the great writers on the subject, Spanish and foreign, were insufficiently studied, whereas Spain needed more study of

politics, that profound science which understands how to distribute with equity the imposts of a State, which is acquainted with the resources of commerce, of industry, of agriculture and the means of making a nation opulent.[61]

Such men as Campomanes and Jovellanos—so important in the history of the Economic Societies—not only thought and wrote on political-economic subjects, but as officials and ministers helped to institute reforms.[62] Florida-blanca, long chief minister of Charles III, and in some respects not so thorough-going a revisionist as Campomanes and Jovellanos, was nevertheless much concerned with the economic changes to which they devoted so much energy.[63]

The economic situation of the Spanish world improved in some respects in the eighteenth century,[64] but the basic problem of increasing agricultural and industrial production was far from solved, and the differential between Spain and her rivals continued to grow. The population, declining in the seventeenth century, rose in the eighteenth, a social phenomenon often interpreted as indicating a betterment of economic conditions. All the political economists of Spain desired an even greater increase of the hands available for work.

The royal revenues—another yardstick of sorts—rose, but expenditures more than kept pace. The government, in peace and war, was forced to unusual—sometimes brutal—expedients to keep abreast of the situation. None of these measures had by the end of the century got effectively at the basis of the problem in the corruption, excessive privilege, absurd regulations, and generally outmoded arrangements of the national social economy.[65]

---

[61] No. 179 (May 4, 1789).

[62] Cf. Earl J. Hamilton, *War and Prices in Spain 1651-1800* (Cambridge, Massachusetts, 1947), 190 *et seq.*, for Campomanes studying the domestic grain trade as a fiscal of the Council of Castile.

[63] For extensive evidence of this, see "Instrucción reservada que la junta de estado, creada formalmente por mi decreto de este día, 8 de julio de 1787, deberá observar en todos los puntos y ramos encargados a su conocimiento y exámen," 213-72 in *Obras* of Floridablanca (BAE, LIX). The *Juntas de estado* provided a new, regular system for all ministers coming together in council (Addison, *Charles the Third*, 105 *et seq.*).

[64] Carrera Pujal, *Economía española*, I, 87, maintains that the improvement of the 18th century, like the decadence of the 16th and 17th, has been exaggerated. Cf., for a somewhat different view, Earl J. Hamilton, "Money and Economic Recovery in Spain under the First Bourbon, 1701-1746," *Journal of Modern History*, XV, No. 3 (September, 1943), 192-206.

[65] Ballesteros, *Historia*, VI, ch. ii; Vera Lee Brown, *Studies in the History of Spain*

Neither commerce, nor agriculture, nor industry flourished to the satisfaction of government or revisionists. The economy at the beginning of the nineteenth century seemed as unsatisfactory, and for the same reasons, as at the beginning of the eighteenth.[66] The usual imbalance of trade was still large at the end of the century, while much of the trade of Spain and of America was in the hands of foreigners.[67]

Land was poorly used, and the proportion of proprietors to population was too low for a sound economic or social situation, with Church and nobility together holding twice as much as the rest of the populace,[68] an evil recognized by most of the later eighteenth-century revisionists. Much land was burdened with feudal dues, and efforts to reduce them had small success.[69] At the same time the country suffered from underpopulation and from inflated land prices due to so much land being permanently withdrawn from the market in inalienable holdings. These things the Economic Society of Madrid inveighed against in the strongest terms. Even Andalusia, often reputed the Eden of Spain, was only rich by comparison with some other provinces. Laws of the eighteenth century designed to correct or alleviate the abuses of the *latifundium* had little effect.[70] The agricultural industry was the most important in Spain, the greatest source of wealth; but it was corrupt, inept, and susceptible of enormous improvement.[71]

Spanish manufacturing was much less important than agriculture, both in terms of value and of the persons involved.[72] Furthermore, it was far inferior

---

in the Second Half of the Eighteenth Century (Northhampton, 1929-30), 30, 56, *et passim*, for some of Charles III's financial difficulties; Desdevises, *La Société*, ch. i, sec. i, for information on population, and *Les Institutions*, 263, for the opinion that by the end of the 18th century Spanish finances were a complete ruin, and p. 347 *et seq.* for information on the failure to improve the revenue system.

[66] Cf. Canga Argüelles, *Diccionario*, article "Amiens," including the "Memoria que el ministerio de Hacienda de España pasó al de Estado en 1802 ...," por D. José Canga Argüelles," of which a part is "Punto I. Estado actual de la población, agricultura, industria y comercio de España."

[67] Desdevises, *La Richesse*, ch. iii, sec. viii.

[68] Ballesteros, *Historia*, VI, 132.

[69] *Ibid.*, 48.

[70] Desdevises, *La Richesse*, ch. i, sec. i.

[71] Cf. Sarrailh, *L'Espagne éclairée*, ch. i, "La Douloureuse Existence de la Masse Rurale."

[72] Canga Argüelles, *Diccionario*, "Estadística," gives a breakdown of the 10,541,120 of the 1797 census, living in 21,120 pueblos: 168,248 secular and regular clergy; 181,321 employees in civil and military departments; 1,677,172 peasant farmers; 533,769 artisans; 25,685 merchants; 174,095 servants; 13,507 sick in public hospitals; 11,902 poor in hospices. In 1799 the value of manufactures as compared with the value of agricultural products ranged from two-thirds in Cataluña, to considerably less than one-half in Madrid, one-quarter in Guipúzcoa, one-ninth in Aragón, a fourteenth in Extremadura, and but one-eighteenth in Zamora (*ibid.*, "Manufacturas").

to that of some other countries. In 1803 wealth produced in Spain by the mechanical arts was less than a fifth of that produced in either England, France, or Germany.[73] The royal establishments for fabrication of hats, textiles, porcelains, and other products did little to correct the fundamental weaknesses of Spanish manufacturing, nor did the fretting of the revisionists add much to its vigor.[74] Spanish production fell far short of supplying domestic demand.

The importation of foreign craftsmen and equipment was useful, but it was also realized that industry and craftsmanship required "the sciences, and especially . . . the exact and natural," and the Crown endeavored to promote them.[75] This effort came late in the century, and had little effect on the Spanish mind.[76] The intellectual climate of Spain at the beginning of the industrial age did not favor the acquisition of new techniques, though such institutions as the Economic Societies promoted their adoption. There was too little interest in science or its practical applications, and mechanical inventions in the Peninsula were rare and of little importance. Spain, it has been remarked, produced no James Watts.[77]

Cataluña was unusual in that by the last decade of the century it had some large factories with English machines, even steam-driven machines (Desdevises, *La Richesse*, 117).

[73] Canga Argüelles, *Diccionario*, "Artes Mecánicas."

[74] *Ibid.*, "Fábricas Reales"; Desdevises, *La Richesse*, ch. ii, sec. ii, "Efforts Tentés par le Gouvernement pour Restaurer l'Industrie Espagnole"; Colmeiro, *Historia economía política*, ch. lxix, "Causas de la decadencia de la industria según nuestros escritores políticos." Cf. Antonio de Miguel, *El potencial económico de España* (Madrid, 1935), 27-28, for a typical twentieth-century assertion that the 18th century was one of the few periods in which Spanish industry flourished. Spanish writers of that day did not think so.

[75] Floridablanca, "Memorial presentado al rey Carlos III, y repitido a Carlos IV ... renunciado el ministerio," dated October 10, 1788, in BAE, LIX, 307-50, at 329.

[76] Antonio Gil de Zárate, *De la instrucción pública en España* (3 vols., Madrid, 1855), III, 314.

[77] Desdevises, *La Richesse*, ch. ii, sec. i. Marcelino Menéndez y Pelayo, *La ciencia española* (4th ed., 3 vols., Madrid, 1915-18), failed to prove the grandeur of Spanish science; the only remaining merit of his work is the bibliographical list, as he predicted (*ibid.*, I, 12). Cf. Américo Castro, "Algunos aspectos del siglo XVIII," in his *Lengua, Enseñanza y Literatura* (Madrid, 1924), 281-334, at 288, that Menéndez y Pelayo's *Ciencia* was "afán pueril," and his methods poor. Santiago Ramón y Cajal, a Spanish scientist, in his *Reglas y consejos sobre investigación científica* (8th ed., Madrid, 1940), ch. x, analyzed many theories as to the historic poverty of Spain's scientific production, and ascribed it more than anything else to intellectual isolation from the rest of the world. Henry T. Buckle, *History of Civilization in England* (2 vols., New York, 1871-73), II, ch. l, in a well-known, but now out-dated discussion of the "history of the Spanish intellect," ascribed much of Spain's economic decay to national ignorance, which in turn he blamed on the aristocratic dispensation and the determination of the Church to stifle intellectual curiosity. *Infra*, 18, 20.

Capital for manufacturing was not forthcoming, partly because the guardians of peninsular wealth were not prepared psychologically for such investment, while the middle class was too puny to produce funds or the concentrated interest in the matter necessary for effective action. As realistic Spanish scholars agree, the bourgeoisie did not remotely approach the real or potential influence of that class in England or France, even though the Spanish Bourbons made some effort, with little success, to break down the barriers between the middle class and the nobility. The nobility did develop some tendencies of a mildly democratic and fuzzily philanthropic nature—the work of the Economic Societies showed this—but the new bourgeoisie of England and France was formed on trade and industry, not on beneficence. It was no accident that the novelists Richardson and Fielding were English, or that they were so widely read in France. The bourgeois snobbishness of Richardson could find fewer kindred spirits in the Spanish world; and Fielding's *Tom Jones* could be seized by Spanish officials in Guatemala,[78] but it could not have much vogue there.[79]

Nor was there in Spain anything comparable to the peasant propietor group of France in wealth, numbers, and psychological capacity for action. Whereas in France in 1789 the entire third estate could at least cooperate in the demand for abolition of aristocratic privilege and the manorial system,[80] no such working alliance of bourgeoisie and peasantry was possible in Spain.

The proletariat, urban and rural, was ignorant, fanatical, generally apathetic, and always poor. Industrial or craft laborers were immensely more numerous than proprietors, though of course Spain was not unique in this. The ordinances of guilds viciously cut competition and production and the opportunity of rising from journeyman to master-craftsman. The condition of agriculture is suggested by the cry for cottage or "popular" industry to supplement the incomes of the rural population. The land teemed with beggars and vagrants, while as usual the impotence of charity was exceeded only by its promiscuity. And in the midst of a social situation so needful of change, the general population hated change and despised foreigners.[81]

---

[78] *Infra*, 143.
[79] Cf. Crane Brinton, *Ideas and Men* (New York, 1950), 375, for a good recent statement of the role of a literate middle class in extending the ideas of the Enlightenment.
[80] Henri Sée, *Economic and Social Conditions in France during the Eighteenth Century* (tr. E. H. Zeydel, New York, 1927), pp. ix, xvi, 208-9.
[81] Ballesteros, *Historia*, VI, 52. Cf. on social conditions. Desdevises, *La Société*, ch. v, secs. iii, v, vi, and *Les Institutions*, 41, 265, 266 *et seq.*

Intellectual Conditions

Political economy and government were not the only interests of men of advanced opinion in eighteenth-century Spain. It is conceivable, if not easily demonstrable, that those of an intellectual, or moral, or esthetic connotation were more important. Even writers on politico-economic subjects were given to disquisitions on the moral import of their projects, and no doubt they usually were sincere. In any event, there was no such compartmentalization of studies as a later age was to know.

Though Spanish culture always was affected by general European developments,[82] the flow of extrapeninsular thought across the Pyrenees quickened with the advent of the Bourbons, who approved an influence which on the whole supported their French-flavored measures. These ideas of the Enlightenment flowed into Spain by many routes. One was by way of the Spanish colony at Paris.[83] Even more influential than Spanish travelers or residents abroad who sent or brought back the new ideas, were: the importation of books written in other languages than Spanish, the preparation of translations, and the diffusion of the Enlightenment by peninsular authors. So far had the last succeeded by the 1780's that a French traveler found that the Spanish "have naturalized in their language" French and English works, so as to accommodate them to Spanish orthodoxy.[84] Discussions of this process of "naturalization" commonly begin with Jerónimo Feijóo (d. 1764), who grappled in many volumes with the new science, superstition, miracles, myths, prejudices, and all manner of false beliefs. The poor development of the natural sciences in Spain he attributed to the national prejudice against novelty, to the improper identification of all modern philosophy with Cartesianism, to the idle fear that philosophy must damage religion, and to personal, national, and factional jealousies.[85] He argued that to combat Aristotle and scholasticism was no heresy against the Church, found no conflict between science and religion, and promoted the critical or rationalistic attitude

---

[82] Cf. Castro, "Algunos aspectos del siglo XVIII," *loc. cit.*, 288 *et seq.*, that there were signs in the 17th century of a desire in Spain to reincorporate its intellectual life with that of Europe at large.

[83] On the Duke of Alba and the Count of Aranda at Paris, see Jefferson R. Spell, *Rousseau in the Spanish World before 1833* (Austin, Texas, 1938), 49 *et seq.*, 57-58; A. Morel-Fatio, *Études sur l'Espagne* (2d ed. of the 2d series, Paris, 1906), 9-10, and ch. iv, "La colonie espagnole a Paris. ..."

[84] Jean François, baron de Bourgoing, *Nouveau voyage en Espagne, ou tableau de l'état actuel de cette monarchie* (3 vols., Paris, 1789), I, 256-57.

[85] *Obras escogidas del Fray Benito Jerónimo Feijóo y Montenegro* (Madrid, 1924, BAE, LVI), 540-49.

generally. He was never gagged, despite opposition to his views and attitude, because his expressions were less drastic than those of the works on which he drew, and because of sympathy in high places for the new ideas.[86]

The direct and indirect influence of Feijóo was considerable in the later Economic Societies.[87] His appeal to revisionists may be seen in a reference in 1777 to the writing on poverty of this "renowned writer of our century."[88] On the other hand, a man sent the Madrid Society an essay in which he rejected Feijóo's view that observation of the moon and stars was useless in agriculture and stockraising, and held to the beliefs of the learned and experienced ancients.[89] But even this note of opposition indicates the stimulating effect of Feijóo's work.

Foreign ideas also penetrated Spain by way of the numerous Frenchmen teaching in Spain in the second half of the century.[90] Many writers noted the accumulation of Gallicisms in the language. The Jesuit father J. F. de Isla ascribed them to four sources: conversations at the court, sermons, French books, and bad translations.[91] Isla also laughed at the orations *a la francesa* of ignorant popular preachers.[92]

Spanish periodicals, as the *Gaceta de Madrid*,[93] imported extrapeninsular thought. The liberal *Espíritu de los mejores diarios*,[94] late in the century,

---

[86] Castro, "Algunos aspectos del siglo XVIII," *loc. cit.*, 299 *et seq.*; Spell, *Rousseau*, 20 *et seq.*; M. Méndez Bejarano, *Historia de la filosofía en España en el siglo XX* (Madrid, 1926), 345-6; Julio Cejador y Frauca, *Historia de la lengua y literatura castellana comprendidos los autores hispano-americanos* (14 vols., Madrid, 1915-22), VI, 48 *et seq.*, finding Feijóo's skepticism pallid; Angel del Río, *Historia de la literatura española* (2 vols., New York, 1948), II, 3-11.

[87] Fernando Ortiz, *Hija cubana del Iluminismo* (La Habana, 1943), 10-11, suggests that Feijóo was the precursor of the Societies because of his opposition to superstition; his criticism of Spanish poverty, which he ascribed to war, emigration to America, and to the expulsion of the Moors; and because of his view that proper economic and political foresight could have prevented many of these ills. Cf. Charles E. Kany, *Life and Manners in Madrid 1750-1800* (Berkeley, 1932), 339, for the view that Feijóo's subjects are eloquent evidence of the cultural backwardness of Spain at the time.

[88] Valencia Society, *Institutiones económicas*, 11.

[89] Madrid *Memorias*, I, 254-87.

[90] Paul Merimée, *L'influence française en Espagne au dix-huitième siècle* (Paris, 1936), 96.

[91] Antonio Rubío, *La crítica del galicismo en España 1726-1832* (Mexico, 1937), 119, 201, *et passim.*

[92] In the first volume (1758) of his *History of the Famous Preacher Friar Gerund* (George Ticknor, *History of Spanish Literature* [4th American ed., 3 vols., Boston, 1872], III, 337 *et seq.*; Angel del Río, *Historia de la literatura*, II, 20).

[93] Valencia Society, *Instituciones económicas*, 122, noted that the *Gaceta* of March 22, 1777, told that the Economic Society of Berne had the main function of promoting physics and agriculture, but also interested itself in criminal legislation.

[94] Madrid, 1787-90.

extracted material from European and American periodicals. Theoretical and practical science loomed largest in its pages, the first issue proclaiming the "eighteenth century . . . the most scientific of all those composing the extensive epoch of seven thousand years."[95] This interest ranged from practical inventions to astronomy, to medicine, and to that favorite Spanish subject of the century, the increase of the population. The periodical contained many notices of academies and societies in Paris, Marseilles, Amiens, Orleans, London, Dublin, Haarlem, Berlin, St. Petersberg, Philadelphia, and other places. It also carried more controversial material, giving space to such names as Hume, Montesquieu, Rousseau, Gibbon, and Raynal, both to praise and to blame them; lauding English-Americans and their services to humanity;[96] condemning that intolerance which assertedly contributed to the decay of Rome, and stating that Spain long had been crippled by ignorance resulting from lack of freedom to write.[97] It also carried considerable criticism of politico-economic conditions.[98]

Foreign ideas imported by all these roads were disseminated the more easily because the censorship was somewhat relaxed, especially under Charles III. Much restrictive law remained in force, of course, and the Index continued to expand its lists, in the middle and later century especially anathematizing the works of the Enlightenment.[99] While the regulations were massively violated and evaded by the small literate portion of the population,[100] no listing of exceptions and violations will alter the main fact that the condition of the printing and book trades was poor in eighteenth-century Spain.[101]

The Spanish revisionists were moderate reformers, not revolutionaries or heretics. Some, as Aranda, were fundamentally political figures, and most of the important revisionists held some sort of official position; others, as Olavide and Cabarrús were in part writers of a doctrinal and ideological bent; another group, including Campomanes, was distinguished by its learning, especially

---

[95] No. 1 (July 2, 1787), "Idea de la Obra."

[96] Nos. 47-48, 61-62, 92-93, 114 (October 18 and 20, November 19 and 22, 1787; January 1, February 2 and 4, 1788).

[97] Nos. 175-177 (April 6, 13, 20, 1789).

[98] *Supra*, 12-13.

[99] Cf. *Indice último de los libros prohibidos y mandados expurgar : para todos los reynos y señoríos del católico rey de las Españas* (Madrid, 1790; and Supplement for 1805), which lists the edicts.

[100] Spell, *Rousseau*, 40, that the more enlightened Spanish thinkers had contempt for the Inquisition which tried to regulate their thinking.

[101] Cf. Kany, *Life and Manners*, 79, *et passim*, on the poor state of the printing trade, and the generally backward intellectual situation of Spain.

historical, and by its practical point of view.[102] They could not turn for advancement of their ideas to the universities, which clung to traditional patterns, much as English universities in the same period. Intellectual fossilization in these cloisters merely resulted in the new ideas being introduced outside them often through specialized institutions formed on foreign models.[103] These included the Royal Spanish Academy (1713), the Academy of History (1738), the Academy of Fine Arts of Saint Ferdinand (1774), special colleges of surgery and pharmacy, the School of Mines at Almadén, and a Museum and Garden of Botany at Madrid. These and other institutions bespoke the interests of the governing group and their confidence in the capacity of human reason, acting upon information, to secure the progressive improvement of the individual and the State. Not least of these new, liberal, extra-university centers of enlightenment were the sixty Economic Societies of Friends of the Country organized between 1775 and the dawn of the new century.

Despite these advances, there were more restrictions on intellectual life in Spain in the later eighteenth century than in England, France, Holland, or perhaps even in Prussia. The control of publication and thought in Spain was clearly in part responsible for the inferior Spanish science.[104] The Economic Societies were in no doubt as to the lag in Spain's intellectual achievement. Their publications often lamented that other lands, notably England, were forging ahead. The reaction of the Inquisition to Jovellanos' report on agrarian reform for the Madrid Economic Society was illustrative of Spanish reactionary obscurantism.[105]

Nevertheless, at the death of Charles III in 1788 some aspects of the Enlightenment were influencing ideas and institutions in Spain. The new notions were admired there, as elsewhere, both for their supposed rational excellence and because they appealed to interests—especially in change of

---

[102] Del Río, *Historia de la literatura*, II, 24-25, for this summarization; cf. Andrés Muriel, p. 21 of the "Introduction" to the French translation of Floridablanca's "Instrucción reservada," published at Paris in 1839 under the title *Gouvernement de Charles III, roi d'Espagne; ou, Instruction réservée transmise a la Junte d'état par ordre de ce monarque*, for a comment on the fashion in which Spanish ministers were protecting advanced opinion.

[103] Desdevises, *La Richesse*, ch. iv, sec. iv, opined that the statesmen of the period never expected anything of the universities, only began to reform them in response to the dictates of their revisionist consciences, and depended always on extra-university influences to spread the new learning.

[104] Desdevises, *La Richesse*, ch. v, "La Science," including a low opinion of Menéndez y Pelayo's fantasy that the Inquisition did not hurt Spanish science, and noting one of Menéndez' typical phrases regarding the "purity" of the Inquisition as a national institution—a verbalism scarcely suited to the discussion of social history.

[105] *Infra*, 58-59, 98-99.

various sorts—whose genesis had no necessary direct relationship to the new currents of thought.

While it was a flaw in the revisionist program that so few people were reached, it could scarcely have been otherwise, given the social structure of Spain. It would be naive to expect the nobility as a class to embrace learning,[106] and the general population had small access to instruction, since the question of public education had never stirred much interest in Spain.[107] So it was that with the illiterate lump of the population the influence of the new ideas could not but be indirect. Between the ignorance of the upper class and the "inopia" of the masses were a few intellectuals, "a numerically unappreciable fraction in comparison with the national mass," isolated from the nation by their critical perception of its deficiencies.[108]

Educated men who accepted with enthusiasm at least some of the new ideas did not always examine the implications for their own position of such notions as the rational approach to government and to the socioeconomic order. Some of these fashionable liberals found upon reflection—especially after 1789—that the new ideas were at bottom iniquitous, un-Catholic, un-Spanish, and apt to turn things quite topsy-turvy. Still, while some were faddists, their views often dilettante, and their attitude paternalistic, they did stimulate the spirit of critical analysis.[109]

This activity led those who were satisfied with the social structure to suppose that their interest and privilege or their ancient beliefs stood in mortal peril, so they gilded custom and apotheosized the status quo. Having isolated the commonalty in ignorance, the conservatives could use its prejudice in favor of the habitual as an emotional bulwark against the intellectualism of the

---

[106] Cf. Henry Swinburne, *Travels through Spain, in the Years 1775 and 1776* (2 vols., London, 1787), II, 212-13, for an unflattering picture of the intellectual status of the court nobility, albeit by a man who found little to admire in Spain, and seemed unaware of the notoriously unsatisfactory habits of much of the English nobility; Mario Méndez Bejarano, *Historia política de los afrancesados* (Madrid, 1912), 94-95, on the dullness of upper-class social life; Gigas, "Un voyageur," *loc. cit.*, 452, 493-94, *et passim*.

[107] So wrote Gil de Zárate, *Instrucción pública*, I, vi-vii; cf. Desdevises, *La Richesse*, ch. iv, "L'Enseignement Public."

[108] Méndez Bejarano, *Los afrancesados*, 69-70; cf. Desdevises, *La Société*, ch. v, sec. vi, "L'Esprit Public," which finds the "bourgeois routinier et somnolent," and "la plebe restait ignorant et fanatique," and for all that there were enlightened figures in eighteenth-century Spain, they had little effect on the general population.

[109] Cf. Kany, *Life and Manners*, 340, that the majority of the enlightened in Spain just considered the new ideas the fashion, this being indicated by the fact that the illustrious men of the century mostly came from the middle class and from the clergy rather than from the aristocracy of blood.

advocates of change.[110] At a later day this would drive liberals to anticlericalism, and lead to a demand for the "complete secularization of education."[111] The clerical reaction to Olavide's colonization work indicated how a liberal with connections with the founders of the Economic Societies could antagonize conservatives as soon as he began to act on the implications of his beliefs.[112]

After 1789, the problems of war and fear of French revolutionary ideas hardened the conservative temper and caused a revulsion among the mildly-, the fashionably-, and the pseudo-liberal. Floridablanca turned from his earlier liberalism, and Jovellanos after 1808 deplored the tendency to move too rapidly toward a new order. But by the time of the French Revolution the ideas of the Enlightenment were part of the intellectual stock-in-trade of the educated Spaniard. His stock might be small. He might approve them in part or wholly, or simply wish to condemn them out-of-hand. In any case, the new ideas could be fought over; they could not be legislated out of existence.[113] Indeed, restrictions were enforced primarily against the most obnoxious of the new ideas, while others were tolerated. Thus, as the climax of the French Revolution passed, Rousseau seemed preferable to Voltaire and the Encyclopedists, because of his religious beliefs and his denunciations of the philosophers.[114] The Economic Societies continued to operate in the period from the French Revolution to the French invasion of Spain in 1808, though hampered by the new spirit of suspicion and repression and by the dislocations of wartime.

During the War of Liberation, and under the irregular resistance governments of 1808 to 1814, chance inflated the opportunities of men of radical views. Their failure was due primarily to inability to carry along either the vested interests—especially Church, higher nobility, and entrenched officialdom—or the masses in support of their scheme of constitutional monarchy, representative government, and reduction of antique privilege. This indicates

---

[110] Altamira, Ballesteros, and Desdevises note intellectual advance in eighteenth-century Spain, but point out that it was less effective than in other countries; e.g., see Desdevises, *La Richesse*, iv-vi, for a clear view of the influence of the new thought, tempered with the judgment that it acted upon a very small part of the population. Cf. Méndez, *Los afrancesados*, ch. vi, "El Reverso," for an account of the forces in Spanish life which resisted innovation.

[111] Gil de Zárate, *Instrucción pública*, I, 116, in the middle of the 19th century made this demand.

[112] *Infra*, 72.

[113] Juan Andrés, *Orígen, progresos y estado actual de toda la literatura* (tr. from Italian by Carlos Andrés, 8 vols., Madrid, 1784-99), is an example of the sort of literature carrying a heavy freight of the new ideas across the bridge of the revolutionary year 1789. Andrés included science as a branch of literature; also history, nor did he omit discussion of Voltaire (VI, 171 *et seq*.) and Raynal (VI, 175-79).

[114] Spell, *Rousseau*, 143 *et seq*.

how shallowly the revisionist temper had penetrated the layers of Spanish society by the nineteenth century. The government of Ferdinand VII after 1814 was unsympathetic to change, and impeded, if it could not entirely prevent it. The ineffective liberal revolt of 1820 is of no interest to the present study, since by that time America was irretrievably lost.

So Spain by the opening of the nineteenth century was still a land of the aristocratic dispensation, with a feeble middle class and few of the marks of bourgeois egalitarianism which was to distinguish the coming age in the Occident. The old regime was decaying in Spain, but not so rapidly as in England and France. The tragic, even if admirable, irresolution of Spain was powerfully to determine her history even into the twentieth century. In the eighteenth century the government and part of the educated class became interested in the ideas of the Enlightenment and made open use of the new rationalism in dealing with problems of ancient date. But the intellectuals and members of the upper class who went over to the new dispensation in some of its aspects were heavily outnumbered. Spain remained conservative, traditionalist. The story of the use of the new ideas and method by the Spanish Economic Societies, their successes and their frustration, is the subject of the following chapters.[115]

---

[115] Cf. Antonio Ramos Oliveira, *Politics, Economics and Men of Modern Spain 1808-1946* (tr. Hall, London, 1946), for a vehement view, after the Civil War of 1936-39, that the irresolution of Spain in the 18th century was not at all admirable, that what Spain has needed and still needs is a bourgeoisie, that much of the literature dealing with Spain is "incomprehensible and absurd" (p. 17), and that the history of Spain can be explained without reference to any science other than History (p. 16). This last is a view, as he says, shared by too few men of the Hispanic culture. No doubt they can dismiss him as a gross (Latin) materialist. For an excellent discussion of liberal and conservative historiography of eighteenth-century Spain, see "The Spanish Enlightenment," in *The Times* [London] *Literary Supplement*, March 15, 1957.

CHAPTER TWO

Basque Society of Friends of the Country
(1763-1800)

Origins of the Spanish Societies

The Economic Societies were founded on the dual interest of the revisionist temper: in Spanish affairs, and in the ideas of the Enlightenment. The founders were influenced by their knowledge of domestic and foreign academies and societies, by their education, their personal associations, their interest in specific problems, and by faddism. There is no question but that the ultimate origins of their characteristic interests were those of the Enlightenment generally, lying especially in the development of experimental science, philosophical rationalism, faith in progress, and popular philanthropy.[1] There has been some speculation, however, as to the ultimate institutional prototype of the Spanish Economic Societies. Suggestions that this prototype was the Society of Solomon's House in Francis Bacon's *New Atlantis* (1627), or perhaps the Society of Friends or Quakers,[2] are interesting but unprovable. On the other hand, it is indisputable that the Spanish Economic Societies were directly influenced by the Royal Society of London, the Society of Dublin, by the royal academies in Paris, Berlin, and St. Petersberg.[3] And these

---

[1] Cf. Ortiz, *Hija cubana*, 19.

[2] *Ibid.*, 20-22. Cf. Havana *Memorias 1817*, 150, that Bacon recommended Societies.

[3] *Infra*, ch. iii, foreign influence in Campomanes' treatises proposing foundation of the Economic Societies; the petition, May 30, 1775, asking a Society for Madrid, after the example of those elsewhere; Madrid Society statutes, which praised European literary societies and various royal academies; Madrid Society *Memorias*, I (1780), "Discurso Preliminar," xiii-xiv, academies in London, Paris, Berlin, St. Petersburg;

contemporary institutions certainly influenced the founders of the Basque Society more importantly than did other organizations.[4] Spaniards resident in France in the last three or four decades of the century must have known of the numerous agricultural societies of that country.[5]

Other possible influences can be advanced, since the eighteenth was an organization-founding century. The men of the new temper were everyplace driven by the sort of impulse to communication and discussion displayed by Benjamin Franklin upon the fringe of the Occidental culture-area. Again, the suggestion of Macanaz,[6] that Patriotic Societies be founded, may have had some influence. And the *Junta de Comercio* of Cataluña, created by royal order in 1755, was not only mercantile, but interested in the propagation of ideas, especially applied science, and operated schools similar to those of the Economic Societies.[7] Various other groups can be put forward, without proof of influence on the Societies, as having preceded them in time.[8]

It is certain that freemasonry in Spain helped prepare the ground for other organizations of liberal temper; but its influence cannot be measured. The

Valencia Society *Instituciones económicas*, 65-66, 128, xliii, 36, showing that in 1776 it had access to literature referring to Societies in several foreign countries; Havana *Memorias*, t. XIX (Habana, 1844), 56, for the assertion, in an article on the history of the Societies, that the "principal bases" of the Berne and Dublin Societies were copied to create the Basque and Madrid; *supra*, 8, for Ward and foreign societies in the 1760's; Sarrailh, *L'Espagne éclairée*, 225-28, for Spanish knowledge of foreign societies. In Scotland the Honourable Society of Improvers of the Knowledge of Agriculture was in existence by 1723; in 1731 was founded the Dublin Society for the Improvement of Husbandry, Agriculture and other Useful Arts (Basil Williams, *The Whig Supremacy 1714-1760* [Oxford University, 1942], 260-88. Economic Societies were created at Zurich in 1747 and at Paris in 1761 (*Enciclopedia Ilustrada Universal*, XVIII, 2a. Parte, p. 2832).

[4] *Infra*, sec. 2 of present chapter, for Peñaflorida's knowledge of the work of the Royal Society of Dublin at a date earlier than his organization of the Basque Society in 1764-65; sec. 3, for foreign Societies mentioned in the *Extractos* of 1771-76.

[5] Cf. Arthur Young, *Travels in France during the Years 1787, 1788, 1789* (3d ed., London, 1890 [1st ed., 1792]), for many references to these.

[6] *Supra*, 11.

[7] Rafael María de Labra y Cadrana, *El instituto de derecho internacional* (Madrid, 1907), 250-51, without indication of date for the schools.

[8] Carrera Pujal, *Economía española*, suggests some precursors of the Economic Societies as having some influence on the foundation of the latter: III, 466-69, that the periodical writer Francisco Mariano Nifo in 1761-62 defended the creation of "Academias científicas y Sociedades económicas para promover la enseñanza y el fomento público, como se practicaba en otros paises," and was thus a precursor of the plan of Campomanes; IV, 9; IV, 96, the Academia de Agricultura del Reino de Galicia, established at La Coruña in 1765. See Sarrailh, *L'Espagne éclairée*, 224-25, on scientific and literary societies in Spain before the Economic Societies were formed. Hamilton, "The Mercantilism of Uztáriz," *loc. cit.*, 121, that Ustáriz in 1724 advocated an academy of arts and sciences, modeled after those established in France by Colbert, to facilitate the imitation of foreign technology.

Economic Societies were not a "result" of masonic action, which would require us to believe that the Enlightenment could penetrate Spain by none other than a masonic route and appeal to none other than a masonic interest. What we come back to finally is that the Economic Societies used current ideas for the solution of local problems. No doubt the same could be said of *Pithecanthropus erectus.*

Foundation and History of the Basque Society

In the Basque provinces of northern Spain circumstances favored reception of extrapeninsular thought, and encouraged interest in economic development. The area was relatively prosperous, although the need of improvement was obvious to the founders of the Basque Society of Friends of the Country.[9] Long after the foundation of the Society, a member found the region still in poor economic condition.[10] In any event, the active ports of the area facilitated the exchange of ideas, and the commercial interest was susceptible to new economic doctrines offering hope of profits. The vessels of the Guipuzcoan Company for Navigation to Caracas have been called "ships of the Enlightenment."[11]

Proximity to France assisted the penetration of French ideas among nobility and burgesses. In the first half of the eighteenth century many young nobles crossed the Pyrenees to school.[12] Others traveled abroad for other reasons. Rousseau's ideas were first transmitted directly to Spain

---

[9] "Historia de la Real Sociedad Bascongada de los Amigo del País por el Conde de Peñaflorida," ed. from the MS. by Julio de Urquijo, in *Revue internationale des études Basques*, XXI (1930), 317-33, and XII (1931), 442-82, ch. I, "Estado que tenía la nación bacongada antes de este establecimiento"; Guillermo de Humboldt, "Los Vascos o Apuntamientos sobre un Viaje por el país vasco en primavera del año 1801," trans. Aranzadi, in *Revue Basques*, XIV (1923), XV (1924), data on towns and areas; Ballesteros, *Historia*, VI, 52, 120, noting that the 1797 census showed Guipúzcoa with 80 per sq. kil., Vizcaya with 42, Asturias 47, Extremadura 14, Sevilla 29, Cataluña 34; Swinburne, *Travels*, II, 274, raptures on the prosperous appearance of the Basque country, which contrasts strongly with his description of other regions of Spain; José Aralar, *El Conde de Peñaflorida y los caballeritos de Azkoitia* (Buenos Aires, 1942), often insists on the flourishing condition of the region; Desdevises, *La Société*, ch. i, sec. ii, "Les Provinces Basques," largely on political matters; Hussey, *Caracas Company*, 59-60; Carrera Pujal, *Economía española*, V, 32-35.

[10] *Espíritu de los mejores diarios*, No. 185 (June 15, 1789), "Carta de un Guipuzcoano [Valentín de Foronda]."

[11] Ramón de Basterra, *Una empresa del siglo XVIII : Los navíos de la Ilustración* (Caracas, 1925).

[12] Juan Sempere y Guarinos, *Ensayo de una biblioteca española de los mejores escritores del reynado de Carlos III* (6 vols., Madrid, 1785-89), V, 65; Aralar, *Peñaflorida*, *passim;* Marcelino Menéndez y Pelayo, *Historia de los heterodoxos españoles* (2d ed., 7 vols., Madrid, 1911-32), VI, 266.

through a Basque, Manuel Ignacio de Altuna (1722-1762), who knew Rousseau in Venice and Paris in 1743-1744. Altuna returned to Guipúzcoa in 1745, became mayor of Azcoitia and an alderman, and exchanged letters with Jean Jacques.[13]

Altuna shared an interest in new ideas with two other residents of Azcoitia, Joaquín de Eguía,[14] and Francisco Munibe e Idiáquez, Count of Peñaflorida; and these three were important in the intellectual development of the region which led to foundation of the Basque Society. Peñaflorida (1729-1785), the chief mover of the Society, was son of a prominent founder of the Guipúzcoa Company. He received his first schooling from Jesuits in the Basque country, and later studied in France at the Jesuit seminary of Toulouse. Returning home in 1746, he was dissatisfied with the intellectual life of his native province, but it is not clear that he thought at once of an academy or society.[15] By 1753 the young man wrote to Toulouse that the state of letters and the sciences in the Basque country was very low; physics being hardly known, he asked that texts on the subject be sent him.[16] Peñaflorida was a reasonably well-educated man of his day, with a strong interest in the sciences, and some interest in innovation.[17]

Vicente María Santibáñez, a Basque contemporary of Peñaflorida, left an account of the latter's influence. In many towns the local gentry and "enlightened" clergy attended gatherings in the municipal building. Apparently social in character originally, by 1748 they had been transformed into *juntas académicas* at Azcoitia, where the schedule of discussions showed its scien-

---

[13] Rousseau, *Confessions*, Bk. VII, for discussion of Altuna; Julio de Urquijo, *Los amigos del país según cartas y otros documentos inéditos del XVIII* (San Sebastián, 1929), 7 *et seq.*, for extensive comments on Altuna and Rousseau, and on the religiosity and intellectual interests of the former.

[14] Cf. Aralar, *Peñaflorida*, 38-39, for biography of Eguía, later Marquis of Narros.

[15] Martín Fernández de Navarrete, "Elogio Póstumo de D. Javier María de Munive e Idiáquez, conde de Peñaflorida ... fundador de la Real Sociedad Vascongada de amigos del país ...," in *Colección de opúsculos* of Navarrete (2 vols., Madrid, 1848), II, 341, states that Peñaflorida did think of a *Sociedad académica* from the time of his return from France in 1746.

[16] Urquijo, *Amigos del país*, 18, claiming to have the letter in his possession; cf. Aralar, *Peñaflorida*, 14, 36, 131-32.

[17] Menéndez y Pelayo, *Heterodoxos*, VII, 266-67, typically sneered at him as a dilettante dabbling with new ideas without a serious purpose and without understanding the possible consequences of his actions; a man who liked to read, but not to study. This judgment combined the snobbery of the professional scholar with the narrowness of a too-exclusive concern with literature and the bitterness of a traditionalist in a changing world. He also called Peñaflorida "algo erudito a la violeta," and asserted that he admitted as much (*ibid.*), and claimed that the man and his circle had "laical and anticlerical animositites" (*ibid.*, 267-69). Cf. Kany, *Life and Manners*, 157 *et seq.*, for discussion of the *violetas*.

tific bias: Monday, mathematics; Tuesday, physics; Wednesday, history; Friday, geography; Saturday, current events; Thursday and Sunday, music. The group was attracted to the then popular problems of electricity, knew the work of Franklin, and possessed an "electrical machine."[18] This "academy" collapsed before the Basque Society of Friends of the Country was founded.[19] But it is clear that interest in the new secular learning was being exhibited by the most prominent members of the community.

In 1758 Padre Francisco José de Isla, attacking the ignorance and pretentious Gallicisms of popular preachers, also supported the merits of Aristotelean as contrasted with contemporary science.[20] Peñaflorida replied under a pseudonymn in a booklet entitled *The Critical Villagers*, defending science against scholasticism and conservative clericalism. It led to an acerb correspondence between the Jesuit and Peñaflorida, with Isla referring to Altuna, Narros, and Peñaflorida as "the triumvirate" and as the "young gentlemen" (*caballeritos*) of Azcoitia.[21] Peñaflorida continued his interest in science while resident (1758-1763) in Madrid as the representative of his province.[22]

In 1763 a "Project and Plan of Agriculture, Sciences and Useful Arts for Guipúzcoa" was presented to the provincial *Juntas generales* at Villafranca by Peñaflorida and fifteen other "Caballeros Procurados" representing pueblos of the province. The *Juntas* approved the Plan, and had it printed and circulated through Guipúzcoa.[23] This Plan dealt with the proposed organization

---

[18] Sempere, *Ensayo*, V, 152-58, quoting from the eulogy of Peñaflorida by Santibáñez, which was read to the Society in 1785, was printed in the Society *Actas*, and also at Madrid in 1785 with the *Discurso* of Santibáñez for the opening of the *juntas generales* of the Society at Vergara in July of that year (*ibid.*, 152, n. 1); cf. Nicolás de Soraluce y Zubizarreta, *Real sociedad bascongada de los amigos del país* (San Sebastián, 1880), 101 *et seq.*, on what he calls "una instructiva tertulia."

[19] Sempere, *Ensayo*, V, 154-55, that the Society ended with the death of the two most active members; Navarrete, "Elogio Peñaflorida," 341, thought a few years later that Peñaflorida began foundation of the Society in 1754, but that this effort was abortive.

[20] In vol. I of his *Fray Gerundio*.

[21] *Obras escogidas del Padre Francisco José de Isla* (Madrid, 1918, BAE, XV), 367-93, 589, the letters between Peñaflorida and Don Francisco Lobón and Padre Isla. For comments on this controversy see Aralar, *Peñaflorida*, 133-37, 151, accusing Menéndez y Pelayo of juggling the evidence; Spell, *Rousseau*, 15-16; Ortiz, *Hija cubana*, 37; Menéndez y Pelayo, *Heterodoxos*, VI, 268 n.

[22] Navarrete, "Elogio Peñaflorida," 351-54. Peñaflorida mingled with the court aristocracy and with literary figures. In 1760 with three other men he discussed mathematics and experimental physics in the presence of the royal family and the Royal Seminary of Nobles. In 1763, after his return to the north, a patent arrived at Azcoitia making him a member of the Academy of Sciences and Fine Arts of Bordeaux (*ibid.*, 371).

[23] For study and definitive resolution in the next *Juntas*, of July, 1764, at Azcoitia; there it was again approved.

of a "Society," a lottery to support it, and means of improving agriculture, rustic economy, the sciences, the useful arts, industry, and commerce.[24] Another booklet, printed after the *Juntas* of 1764, declared that "this Economic Society is to develop, perfect, and advance the agriculture, rustic economy, the sciences and arts and everything that may be immediately directed to the maintenance, relief and ease of the human species."[25]

Peñaflorida was discussing the Society with friends at Vergara in September, 1764.[26] The putative members met at Azcoitia in December, 1764, and organized the Society.[27] The first of the annual general meetings of the Society was at Vergara, February 6 to 14, 1765, where the members heard numerous papers, especially on science, agriculture, and the theater, and tinkered with pneumatic devices. One of the two discourses on agriculture celebrated the methods of Tull and Duhamel, foreign experts whose names were to echo at meetings of Economic Societies all over Spain after 1774; the other expounded the thesis that industry, commerce, and agriculture all were necessary for economic prosperity.[28] This call for a rounded economy

---

[24] Soraluce, *Sociedad bascongada*, 7-8, upon the basis of a copy of the Plan, printed in 1763 in 63 pages, giving the headings of the pamphlet, and listing the signers; cf. Sempere, *Ensayo*, V, 154-55, asserting that Peñaflorida produced the Plan alone, basing it on work done by the Royal Society of Dublin; Menéndez y Pelayo, *Heterodoxos*, VI, 269, thought that Altuna, Eguía, and Peñaflorida had drawn up the Plan before the death of Altuna in 1762; Urquijo, *Amigos del país*, 27-29. Many accounts of the Plan say flatly that nothing was done about it (cf. Navarrete, "Elogio Peñaflorida," 355). But Soraluce used the records of the *Juntas forales* of the province, and a copy of the printed Plan. Cf. Carrera Pujal, *Economía española*, V, 21 *et seq.* on origins of the Basque Society.

[25] Quoted in Soraluce, *Sociedad bascongada*, 9-10. It had 75 pages, and was headed: Plan and Statutes of the Academy of Agriculture, Sciences, Useful Arts and Commerce of Guipúzcoa.

[26] At a fiesta. Peñaflorida used the occasion, as he recorded, to interest a few caballeros in the Society (Peñaflorida, "Historia de la Sociedad," *loc. cit.*, ch. 2; and cf. Sempere, *Ensayo*, V, 155-57, for an account of Peñaflorida's literary activities at the fiesta, asserting that the young men agreed to meet again, and that this was the beginning of the *Sociedad de Amigos;* Urquijo, *Amigos del país*, 29 *et seq.;* Soraluce, *Sociedad bascongada*, 10). The comic opera by Peñaflorida performed on this occasion is printed in *Revue Basques*, I (1907), 383 *et seq.* The "forward" by the Ayuntamiento of Vergara, August 25, 1764, praises Peñaflorida for his knowledge of various subjects and especially for "aquel admirable Plan de una Academia que para Ciencias, Artes, Agricultura, y comercio debe a V. S. esta Provincia."

[27] Peñaflorida, "Historia de la Sociedad," *loc. cit.*, ch. 3, for account of this *junta preparatoria.*

[28] *Ibid.*, ch. 5 to end. Peñaflorida's "history" is mostly devoted to the events of those nine days, and the present account is compiled from it. Peñaflorida called the meetings *asambleas;* in later years the annual meetings were called *juntas generales.* The 1764 sessions also heard a discourse on hydraulic machines; a long defense of the theater replete with sound arguments and with historical figures of presumed good Catholic character who were fond of the drama; a "philosophical-moral discourse"

was one of the fundamental economic ideas of men of the Enlightenment in Spain.

An order in 1765 gave royal license for the Society, directing officials of the Basque provinces to aid it.[29] Statutes were printed in 1766,[30] but soon changed,[31] the new statutes being approved by the Crown in 1773,[32] and published in 1774.

Although there was opposition to the Society in the Basque provinces, it met regularly for over twenty years, the acts of the general juntas, published annually from 1771 to 1793, marking the chronological limits of the effective life of the Society.[33] But if opposition did not cause the decline of the body, it probably accelerated it once it had set in. Peñaflorida noted the opposition:

> Some painted this respectable body as being dedicated only to profane diversion; others estimated it as directed to a search for shallow applause; others saw it as a school of idleness, and even of libertinism.[34]

The Society no doubt gained some enemies by its support of vaccination.[35] A priest named Ostiz preached a sermon against the Society, and was possibly the author of an anonymous essay claiming that the only aims of the Society were poesy and music, that it was under French influence, and constituted a danger to religion. The *amigos* replied with an essay of their own.[36]

---

on women; a comedy by Peñaflorida entitled *La Tertulia*, which had as one of its aims an attack on enemies of the theater; a tragedy of Horace translated into Spanish from French by a member "in the short space of eight days"; a French comedy translated to Spanish by Peñaflorida; and a discourse on the study and uses of history.

[29] *Estatutos aprobados por S. M. para gobierno de la Real Sociedad bascongada de los amigos del país* (Vitoria, 1774), 1-4, for the order of April 8, 1765.

[30] Soraluce, *Sociedad bascongada*, 13-15, for description of statutes of 1765.

[31] *Plan de la colección general de estatutos de la Real sociedad bascongada de los amigos del país, según de sus juntas generales, celebradas en la Villa de Vergara por noviembre de 1770* (Madrid, 1772).

[32] August 10 (*Estatutos Sociedad bascongada*, 1-4, 132).

[33] Earlier meetings were described in an *Ensayo* printed at Vitoria in 1768 in 352 pages (Soraluce, *Sociedad bascongada*, 20; Urquijo, *Amigos del país*, 36-40). Cf. *Extractos de las juntas generales celebradas por la Real Sociedad Bascongada ... 1771* (Madrid, 1772), pp. [i] - [iv], "Aviso a los Socios," that the *Extractos* were being printed to communicate the Society's activities to members in Spain beyond the Basque provinces, and in the Americas.

[34] "Historia de la Sociedad," *loc. cit.*, ch. 3.

[35] *Infra*, 12.

[36] "Los Amigos del País y un enemigo anónimo," *Revue Basques*, XXIV (1933), 134-37, printing from an eighteenth-century MS. excerpts from the attack ("Apologia de una nueva Sociedad ultimamente proyectada en esta M. N. Y M. L. Provincia de Guipúzcoa con el título de los Amigos del Pays"), ironical in method; and the whole of the until this time unknown reply ("Respuesta de Valentín al Autor de la Apologia"). Cf. Soraluce, *Sociedad bascongada*, 48-49, that criticisms of the Society were printed in 1777 on the ground that it accomplished little, and that the *juntas generales* were expensive and encouraged luxury.

The Society was moribund after 1794, partly because of the French invasion of that year and the sack of Vergara and the complete destruction of the Society's Seminary.[37] But the Society may have been failing before that date. In the earlier 1790's the funds of the body and the number of pupils in the Seminary both were falling off, though the number of members may have been stable.[38] Even more indicative of decay is the possibility that from 1789 the four commissions into which the membership was divided had ceased to function.[39] The attitude of Godoy may have damaged the Society,[40] but it is a much-vexed question whether Godoy's anti-Basque feelings were justified by Basque collaboration with the French in 1794-1795.[41] Though dying after 1794, the Basque Society did not expire until the Bonapartist invasion of 1808. Resuscitation was attempted in 1819, and several times thereafter, under protection of the provincial juntas of Alava and Vizcaya.[42]

Organization, Members, and Labors of the Basque Society

The 127 printed pages of the statutes approved in 1773 were themselves an instrument of propaganda. Members had to be able to pursue the interests of the body stated in the statutes, which eliminated illiterates. The *Amigo* of the name found expression in the purpose of improving the condition of the State, in the equality of members within the body, and in the provision that members from the three Basque provinces were to be equal within the Society.[43] Twenty-four *socios de número* were the controlling membership,[44] a small proportion of the total of several varieties of members. Some meetings were open only to the dues-paying type of members, and the fees were high enough—120 reals per year—to lead a friendly contemporary to call it a

---

[37] *Ibid.*, 55. Many copies of Society publications were burned in these years (Fernando de la Quadra Sa'cedo, Marqués de los Castillejos, *Economistas vascongados y artículos varios sobre problemas destacados de la economía vizcaína* [Bilbao, 1943], 104, and naming the best collections extant in Vizcaya).

[38] Soraluce, *Sociedad bascongada*, 54-55.

[39] *Ibid.*, 54.

[40] *Ibid.*, 60, for the charge, also putting some blame on Charles IV; Aralar, *Peñaflorida*, ch. ix, "Por que Murió la Sociedad Bascongada de Amigos del País," *et passim*, belabors this theme, insisting the Society was not killed by the wars of 1794 or 1808 but by the anti-Basque Godoy, who hated the independent attitude of Basques and their cultural preference for France.

[41] Aralar insists that the Basques did resist the French, the old claim of collaboration being an invention of Castillian scholars ignorant of Basque history and determined to destroy Basque independence and claims to pre-eminence.

[42] Labra, *El instituto*, 253; Soraluce, *Sociedad bascongada*, 63.

[43] *Estatutos Sociedad bascongada*, art. xiv, xv.

[44] *Ibid.*, tit. vii.

prominent fault.[45] But lower dues probably would not have increased its effectiveness, which depended on the influence and ability of the members rather than on their numbers.

The Society enrolled the most important men of the Basque provinces,[46] a number of outstanding men in other parts of Spain, and some prominent foreigners. The Society was dominated by the well-born, well-educated, well-connected, and wealthy. The rolls included nobles; the well-to-do of the middle class; officials and members of government; military men; a few of the learned professions; and many churchmen.[47] The bulk of the membership consisted of Basques not resident in the provinces, but pursuing military, commercial, or other careers in other parts of the Spanish world. The forty-one members in 1766 were largely in the Basque provinces, and none was in America.[48] By 1771 there were 143 members, with 36 residing in the Basque provinces, 92 in the rest of Spain (including 27 at Madrid and 19 at Cadiz), 9 at other places in Europe, and 6 in Spanish provinces overseas.[49] In 1773 there were some 400 members, of which only 47 resided in the Basque provinces, and some 159 in the rest of Spain; while about 190 were resident in America, and some few others in London, Paris, Italy, and Brussels.[50] The membership grew fairly rapidly in succeeding years.[51] By 1776 the accumulative membership reached 1000,[52] but of course by then some of the members had died.[53]

---

[45] Sempere, *Ensayo*, V, 159-60.

[46] As indicated in the "Catálogos" in the *Extractos* for 1771, 1774-75, and in the *Estatutos*. Cf. Altamira, *Historia*, IV, 259, that "most" of the Basque nobles joined, and "not a few" clerics.

[47] Cf. on important members, Aralar, *Peñaflorida*, 59, 99-100, 107-8, 114, 137-38, 177.

[48] Soraluce, *Sociedad bascongada*, 14-18, printing the *Catálogo de Socios* of that year; Urquijo, *Amigos del país*, 36 *et seq.*

[49] *Extractos 1771*, 57-73, "Catálogo ... de los individuos de la ... Sociedad. ..."

[50] "Catálogo general ... de los individuos de la ... Sociedad ..., con expresión de su antigüedad, clases, y ocupaciones; a fines ... de 1773," printed as pp. 134-80 of the *Estatutos* of 1774. Some in addition to those so listed may have been resident in America; the catalogue is not always clear. Since the residence for military members is not indicated in any of the lists, we lump them with Spain outside the Basque area.

[51] Fifty members were added in 1774 (*Extractos 1774*, 106-13, "Suplemento al Catálogo General ..., publicado a continuación de los Estatutos. ..."), of which 36 were in Spain (mainly residing outside the Basque provinces), 1 in the Canaries, and 13 in America. Another 101 members were added in 1775 (*Extractos 1775*, 150-61, "Catálogo. ..."), including 72 resident in Spain (only 19 of them in the Basque provinces apparently), 6 in Paris, Amsterdam, London, and 23 in America.

[52] Soraluce, *Sociedad bascongada*, 39.

[53] The catalogue of members in 1793 showed 1,216 (*ibid.*, 55). Navarrete, "Elogio Peñaflorida," *loc. cit.*, 372, writing in 1785, claimed nearly 2,000 members.

By 1774 the Society had two directors, one at the Spanish court, one in the Basque provinces; vice-collectors at Madrid, Sevilla, and Cadiz; and various agents in America.[54] The absent members subscribed fifty reals yearly, but did not participate directly in the labors of the Society.

The membership in each of the three Basque provinces was divided into the four commissions of agriculture and rustic economy, science and useful arts, industry and commerce, and *buenas letras*. The membership of all provinces met for several days each September in *juntas generales*, in turn at Vitoria, Bilbao, and Vergara. The juntas included both private and public meetings. At least those of 1774 included a public display of manufactures.[55] Discourses were read. Annual reports were made for the commissions, a treasurer's report rendered, and other business transacted. During the year, the Society helped promote manufacturing, fishing, and agriculture; collected books, machines, and mineral specimens.[56] The financial resources of the Society were not great. It spent very little in 1772-1774: an average of little over 8,000 reals each year; but considerably more in 1775-1776, about 70,000 each year. The accounts of expenditures make clear the concentration of resources on the practical improvement of agriculture, industry, and fishing, with the next largest amount (but much less) going for education.[57]

As the financial records suggest, economic development was the main interest of the Basque Society; but many modern studies obscure this by concentrating on its "cultural" activities.[58] Although Peñaflorida's largest

[54] *Extractos 1774*, 114-18, "Socios empleados dentro y fuera de las tres Provincias [sic] Bascongadas." There was a vice-collector at Cadiz at least as early as 1771, being Juan de Eguino at that time (*Extractos 1771*, "Catálogo general. ...").

[55] *Extractos 1774*, 6.

[56] Cf. *Extractos 1771*, 74, that one of the "ideas" of the Society was to gather books, machines, and other curiosities relative to the arts and sciences; *ibid.*, 75-85, "Lista de los efectos, libros, máquinas, y curiosidades que ha tenido la Sociedad de regalo, desde su fundación hasta el presente"; and new lists in *Extractos 1772*, 125-33, *Extractos 1773*, 121-24, *Extractos 1774*, 99-104, *Extractos 1775*, 144-50, *Extractos 1776*, 92-92. A rather large proportion of the books were in French or translated from French. Books included items by societies and academies at Bologna and Amsterdam and in Denmark; a few items in English or from that language; and a number of practical manuals in the arts and crafts. The instruments included such things as microscopes, a theodolite, a pneumatic machine, optical instruments, and models of various sorts of machines. Other items included maps, and samples of ore, stone, and stalactites.

[57] *Extractos 1772*, 116-19, "Razón de lo empleado por las Comisiones de Vizcaya, Alava y Guipúzcoa en fomento de sus respectivos obgetos"; *Extractos 1773*, 111-13; *Extractos 1774*, 90-92; *Extractos 1775*, 135-36; *Extractos 1776*, 109-12.

[58] So with Menéndez y Pelayo's obsession with the heterodox ideas of members, although he recognized that the *Extractos* were "una especie de enciclopedia de conocimientos útiles" (*Ciencia española*, III, 418); or Aralar, *Peñaflorida*, which indicates (e.g., 75-76, 102-3, 105) that the records of the Society show much economic activity,

single interest seems to have been in education and study,[59] this too had an important economic aspect; and Peñaflorida told the members in 1768 that hacienda owners, above all citizens, had obligations to their country, and should study economic and scientific questions; and in 1779 told them that they would have to be more learned than the other Societies in Spain because the Basque soil was less fertile.[60] The original statutes of 1766, and the *Ensayo* of 1768, devoted considerable attention to economic matters,[61] and the statutes as approved by the Crown in 1774 plainly indicated an intent to deal as much with economic matters as with anything else,[62] and even included a request that the members buy and wear only Spanish goods.

Even clearer, however, is the indication of the overriding economic interest of the Society in the published *Extractos* of activities in 1771-1776,[63] a total of over 800 pages reviewing the work of those years, with some reference to 1768-1770. The *Extractos* deal largely with practical questions of production or with the utilitarian aspects of education, being especially notable for reports of experimental or developmental activity, as the trial plantings of new crops or of old crops under new methods of cultivation, distribution of seeds, interest in planters and harrows and plows, support for iron and steel manufacture, promotion of fishing, and the like.[64] Of the four commissions into which membership was divided in each of the three Basque provinces, only the fourth spent much of their effort (so far as the *Extractos* show their work) on things only remotely and ultimately concerned with economics (as education); and the fourth commissions seem to have done

---

but does not try to analyze it; or Soraluce, *Sociedad bascongada*, who devotes only two pages (43-44) to the agricultural and stockraising interests of the Society, and little more to other economic interests, but is interested in every detail of the foundation of the Society.

[59] Peñaflorida, "Historia de la Sociedad," *loc. cit.*, ch. 4, that study was to be the main interest of the members.

[60] Navarrete, "Elogio Peñaflorida," *loc. cit.*, 369 *et seq.*

[61] Urquijo, *Amigos del país*, 40, that the *Ensayo* dealt principally with agriculture, industry, commerce, and civic architecture; Aralar, *Peñaflorida*, 100.

[62] *Estatutos Sociedad bascongada*, art. xv, for the four commissions, which show this intent.

[63] After the first volume was published at Madrid, the others were published at Vitoria.

[64] Cf. *Extractos 1776*, 109-12, for money spent for cattle distributed to farmers; and to pay for the *gaceta de agricultura* of Paris; and the big expense of setting up cutlery and button manufactories; paying for a sloop to be used in hake fishing, and for the costs of curing the fish; and for developing ribbon manufacturing, and other practical efforts. *Extractos 1772*, 116-19, showing over one-half the total expenditures were by the third commissions (industry and commerce).

no more (and possibly less) than one-fourth of the work of the Society, though this is not measurable. Furthermore, the educational work was in large measure inclined to the aid of the economy of the region. The impression of interest in practical economic development is overwhelming in the *Extractos* of 1771-1776, even more so than in the Memorias of, say, Madrid and Havana in later years.[65] The years 1771-1776 were, of course, those of greatest interest to a student of the Americas, since after that time the more numerous Spanish Societies were available to influence the colonies.

This consideration and trial of practical economic development was devoted to the Basque area;[66] there was virtually no interest in the development of the rest of Spain or of America. This was, of course, to be the local interest of the later Spanish and American Economic Societies. The *Extractos* contain a notable amount of reference to foreign economic activity and writing, methods, and devices; they show much interest in instruments, machines, and books on economic subjects; they indicate a great respect for the value of applying science to economic life.[67]

The Society was interested in developing agriculture, industry, and fishing. It did not concern itself with commerce as such,[68] presumably because the strictly mercantile interest was adequately attended to by other institutions. The two most persistent agricultural interests in 1771-1776 were in grain (mainly wheat) and in pasturage and cattle feed—alfalfa, turnips, clover, sweet potatoes, sainfoin, carob beans. It was also interested in a variety of other crops; in methods of seed treatment and planting; in wheeled plows sent by Pablo Olavide of Sevilla; in bees; in the planting of olives and cedars; in fertilizers; and in seeders and harrows. The Society subsidized experimental plantings, collected books on agriculture, had soils tested, and imported seeds from abroad.[69]

The single most important industrial aim of the Society was the improvement of iron manufacture. Aid was given to the cutlery works at Vergara.

---

[65] No doubt partly due to the different type of publication, in the form of short, bare extracts, rather than the sometimes long, eloquent and moralistic essays in the Memorias.

[66] A good indication of this may be derived from the "Acuerdos en Fomento de las Comisiones," summaries of Society actions in the *Extractos* : *1771*, 49-55; *1772*, 119-25; *1773*, 115-20; *1774*, 93-98; *1775*, 137-43; *1776*, 86-91.

[67] And cf. *Extractos 1771*, "Aviso a los Socios," that it is "a Society whose functions require many practical and expensive operations."

[68] Cf. *Extractos 1772*, 90-92, "Theórica del Comercio," for an exception; a dissertation submitted to the Society which was a rhapsody on the value and importance of commerce and the need of fostering it.

[69] *Extractos 1771*, 11-13; *Extractos 1772*, 13-31; *Extractos 1773*, 9-48; *Extractos 1774*, 7-28; *Extractos 1775*, 12-54; *Extractos 1776*, 4-26.

Some consideration was given to the establishment of a wireworks. The improvement of iron manufactures was not only undertaken by the third commissions (on industry and commerce), but by the second (on science and useful arts). Metallurgy and mineralogy were by far the largest interest of the latter. As early as 1767 the second commissions circulated a questionnaire among ironworkers, gathering data on methods used.[70] And the *Extractos* of 1776 included data collected that year from all the ironworks in Guipúzcoa.[71] The *Extractos* show much interest in what was called the "metallic sciences" of chemistry, mineralogy, and metallurgy. The Society collected samples of iron ore; was interested in the ironworks of Sweden and the mines of Germany; in docimasy (the art of tests) as applied to the iron industry; in bellows, trompes, and other technical devices; and in steel. In addition to ironmaking, the Society in 1771-1776 tried to promote button making, the manufacture of cane chairs, fur dressing, table linen, a ribbon works; and showed interest in or printed information on spinning wheels, shoemaking, silk, instruction in sewing, hydraulic engineering, a sawmill, a saltworks, and the manufacture of braid and baize.[72]

The Society's interest in the iron industry led to a temporary connection (1777-1783) with the Spanish Navy Department, which wished to improve the manufacture of guns. The Navy Department secretly paid for the studies abroad of Juan José and Fausto Elhuyar, who were ostensibly fellows of the Society in the field of mineralogy. In 1778 the king, through the Navy Department, agreed to finance the Society's plan for the establishment of a chair of chemistry and metallurgy, and one of mineralogy. These courses constituted the Royal School of Metallurgy, administered separately from the Society's Seminary, until 1783, when they were combined.[73]

The Society tried to promote fishing, both because it was important to the economy of the area, and because it was a means of creating mariners.[74] In 1770 and succeeding years the Society displayed strong interest in improvement of hake fishing and salting, partly in the hope of reducing imports of cod from England. The Society sent to Ireland for information on Irish

---

[70] *Extractos 1771*, 33-39, "Metalurgía."

[71] P. 32, a table showing a total of 94 ironworks in 30 pueblos. Cf. Soraluce, *Sociedad bascongada*, 36, that 18 ironworks were reported for Alava in 1779, and that the Society paid some attention to the ordinances regulating the ironworking trades; Aralar, *Peñaflorida*, 93-96.

[72] The foregoing is widely scattered in the sections of the *Extractos 1771-76* dealing with the Comisiones segundas and terceras.

[73] A. P. Whitaker, "The Elhuyar Mining Missions and the Enlightenment," HAHR, XXXI, No. 4 (November, 1951), 557-85.

[74] *Extractos 1771*, 44-46; and 46 *et seq.*, a suggestion that an "Escuela de Náutica" was needed, and that the merchants of San Sebastián were interested in it.

methods. In 1774 the king approved a Society plan for a fishing company (*Compañía general de la Pesca y salazón del Cecial*), but it was never established. In 1776 the four commissions of Vizcaya were spending all their funds on the hake project, and some was being sold in Madrid, Sevilla, and elsewhere.[75] The Society displayed considerable interest in public health and medicine, especially in smallpox inoculation;[76] in science;[77] in education;[78] and in Basque history, customs, and language.[79] The phrase "national history" as used in the *Extractos* meant Basque history. The Society probably did something to promote the already strong sense of Basque unity and uniqueness.[80] One of the most interesting educational efforts was the decision in 1774 to establish a free school of drawing in each of the three provinces, to teach this useful subject to men of all classes. In 1775 there were some 220 pupils in the classes.[81] The Society pursued an interest in primary education throughout these years,[82] despite the debate of 1772 as to the utility

---

[75] Fishing is treated in *Extractos 1771*, 44-46; *1772*, 80 *et seq.*; *1773*, 85 *et seq.*; *1774*, 62-65; *1775*, 92 *et seq.*; *1776*, 47 *et seq.* The fishing company had not been organized by early 1776 (*Extractos 1775*, 93); and according to Soraluce, *Sociedad bascongada*, 31, never was organized. The *Extractos* show interest in other sorts of fishing in addition to hake, but that is the chief interest in 1771-76.

[76] *Extractos 1771*, 9, a discourse on the subject at the *juntas generales; Extractos 1772*, 54-65, an account of inoculation, one of the longest single items in the *Extractos* of 1771-76. Other items included hydrophobia, agaric, safe methods of baptism, mineral and thermal springs, and epidemic fever.

[77] In addition to metallurgy, mineralogy, and chemistry: botany, electricity, and navigation.

[78] In 1771 a plan for the perfection of "escuelas de menores letras"; and the Society ordered for the use of its *Caballeros Alumnos* the formation of a "compendium of the geography of the three provinces." In 1772 the Society debated whether multiplication of schools was desirable, coming to an affirmative answer; and considered education in Castillian grammar, geography, astronomy, military science, municipal law, and political arithmetic (political economy). In 1773 much of the foregoing, and natural history, experimental physics, *política* (lessons on the population, industry, and natural history of Vizcaya; on ancient and modern Spanish coinage; arithmetic; navigation; tactics).

[79] In 1771 an essay on Basque municipal laws; and an account of the voyage of the Guipuzcoan Juan Sebastián de Elcano. In 1772 the Basque language; the inclusion of the Basque country in ancient Cantabria; the rights of Basques to fish in Newfoundland. In 1773 the treaty of 1481 between Guipúzcoa and England; and an *Obra Histórica Nacional.*

[80] Aralar, *Peñaflorida*, 105, *et passim*, insists on this as a prime function of the Society.

[81] *Extractos 1775*, 113. Cf. Soraluce, *Sociedad bascongada*, 31, 44, that drawing schools were founded in five towns. The evidence of the *Extractos* would seem to indicate as unfounded Carrera Pujal's (*Economía española*, V, 23) suspicion that Soraluce was confused in asserting that the Society founded such schools.

[82] E. g., *Extractos 1775*, 115-17, prizes by the Society to primary schools; *Extractos 1773*, 111-15, prizes for development of primary schools.

of multiplying schools. In 1775 one argument in favor of education was the necessity of sending young men out of the poor Basque provinces to Spain and America with a good understanding of writing and figures.[83]

The most successful educational project of the Society was the Seminary at Vergara; and it was probably the most successful single effort of the Society in any field.[84] The *Reglamento* of the student members (*alumnos*) of the Society was approved in 1765,[85] and a catalogue of the *alumnos* was published in 1766.[86] The Society presented at the provincial juntas of September, 1767, a "Project of a Plan for a Patriotic School," beginning its efforts to take over the building occupied by the Jesuit college at Vergara until the expulsion of that order earlier in 1767.[87] In 1768 Society members were teaching mathematics, algebra, geometry, geography, history, Latin, French, dancing, and fencing.[88] In 1769 the Council of Castile gave the name *Real Seminario* to the school.[89] The Jesuit building was taken over in 1771,[90] and the Society had a library there at least as early as 1773.[91] The royal cedula of permission was issued in 1776, and the school formally opened,[92] bearing the name *Real Seminario Patriótico Bascongado* from that time until 1804.[93]

---

[83] *Extractos 1775*, 122. Cf. *ibid.*, 111 *et seq.*, a project for an *escuela patriótica*, including a curriculum for students not destined for the church, law, or military—embracing commerce, the metallic sciences, politics, and other subjects to serve the business life.

[84] Sempere, *Ensayo*, V, 175, writing in the 1780's, that the greatest feats of the Society were the Seminary and the *Casa de Misericordia;* Aralar, *Peñaflorida*, 54-67, that the Seminary was the "obra maestra" of the Society.

[85] Soraluce, *Sociedad bascongada*, 18.

[86] *Ibid.*, 19, being published with the first statutes and the membership roll of the Society, and listing the ten *alumnos*, two being in Madrid and eight in the north, and including Peñaflorida's son.

[87] *Ibid.*, 21.

[88] *Ibid.*, 22-23.

[89] *Ibid.*, 22. Cf. *Extractos 1771*, 6-7, that the *juntas generales* heard a report on the work of establishing "the Patriotic School or Seminary projected for the Royal College of Vergara."

[90] Navarrete, "Elogio Peñaflorida," *loc. cit.*, 363-64; Aralar, *Peñaflorida*, 57, that the Seminary did not move from the Society's quarters in Vergara to the ex-college until 1779.

[91] *Extractos 1773*, 118-19.

[92] Navarrete, "Elogio Peñaflorida," 363-64, 366; cf. Soraluce, *Sociedad bascongada*, 21, 34, that the *Proyecto* of 1767 was submitted to the government in 1775, and approved in 1776. But *Extractos 1774*, 4, that the *juntas generales* that year received a royal cedula approving the plan for the Seminary, with the name of "Escuela Patriótica." *Extractos 1776*, 90, that an "Escuela patriótica provisional" was established in the College, with teachers of various listed subjects.

[93] Soraluce, *Sociedad bascongada*, 87-88. In 1782 the courses of the Seminary were declared valid for further study in Spanish universities (*ibid.*, 37).

One of the first pupils at the Seminary was Martín Fernández de Navarrete (1765-1844),[94] later a famous historical scholar. In his day it had one hundred pupils, and its direction was divided among the twenty-four *socios de número* of the Society.[95] Badly hurt by the French invasion of 1794, it reopened in 1798 with only four students. In 1804 it became the Royal Seminary of Nobles, falling under the control of the government in Madrid. At this time there were seventy-eight students in residence.[96]

Peñaflorida moved from Azcoitia to Vergara in 1768 to work on the foundation of the school, and he insisted that "useful" sciences receive attention.[97] He stimulated this interest by sending his son Ramón Munibe (1751-1775) abroad to study as the representative of the Society.[98] From 1770 to 1773 Ramón studied sciences in various countries, becoming a member of the Academy of Sciences of Stockholm and of the Institute of Freiberg, and sent letters to his father and to the Society, keeping them in touch with the latest European thought.[99]

Fausto and Juan José D'Elhuyar, native Basques who had studied mineralogy and mining engineering in several countries, taught at the Seminary in the early 1780's. They discovered wolfram in the Seminary's laboratories, which had been inaugurated in 1777, and their findings were published in the *Extractos* of the Society for 1783.[100] The brothers later were sent to

---

[94] Navarrete, "Elogio Peñaflorida," *loc. cit.*, 366; cf. Aralar, *Peñaflorida*, 78, that Navarrete studied there from 1770 to 1780.

[95] Navarrete, "Elogio Peñaflorida," 369 *et seq.*, 372; Soraluce, *Sociedad bascongada*, 61, that the Seminary was at its apogee at the death of Peñaflorida in 1785, with 130 resident and 80 day students.

[96] *Ibid.*, 62.

[97] Aralar, *Peñaflorida*, 57-60, listing the studies at the Seminary (without date) as including experimental physics, chemistry, mineralogy, humanities, mathematics, philosophy, ethics, fundamentals of religion, poesy, drawing, statistics, the *fueros* of the Basque provinces, and various languages; cf. Soraluce, *Sociedad bascongada*, 35, that the "useful" bias appeared in the approved project of 1775, and describing it,

[98] Navarrete, "Elogio Peñaflorida," *loc. cit.*, 359, calling him a *socio viajero*, and claiming that Peñaflorida thought this the best method of enlightenment for the Society; *Extractos 1774*, 88-90, eulogy of the deceased Ramón. The *Extractos* for 1771-73 include several references to information sent by Ramón from abroad.

[99] Urquijo, *Amigos del país*, 42 *et seq.*, on Ramón's travels, with extracts from his letters; Spell, *Rousseau*, 46-47, that the Abbé Cluvier, who went with Ramón as tutor, knew the works of Rousseau, and noting that the tour itself is evidence of Peñaflorida's familiarity with Rousseau's notions of education.

[100] A. Federico Gredilla, *Biografía de José Celestino Mutis* (Madrid, 1911), 151-53, also dealing with the spelling of D'Elhuyar, which leads to the statement that the *Extractos* of the Seminary (presumably meaning the Society) have been called "literariamente ... un modelo de incorrecciones de lenguaje y de descuido y ligereza de los cajistas"; cf. Soraluce, *Sociedad bascognada*, 36, 42, insisting that the Lyuyards [sic] were foreigners; Aralar, *Peñaflorida*, 69.

America as government mining experts.[101] Another distinguished member of the Society who taught in the Seminary was Valentín de Foronda.[102] His articles on political economy in the *Espíritu de los mejores diarios* have been noted.[103] He described the Basque Society as the "mother of all the *patrióticas*" of the kingdom and the Indies.[104] He inveighed against tariffs, preferring trade and fraternity between nations, and individual liberty to buy and sell.[105] He told the Basque Society that: "A nation is not powerful by reason of the space it occupies on the globe, but by reason of its population, its labor, and its industry," claiming Holland and Andalusia proved his point, the former being rich and the latter poor when it ought to be rich.[104] From 1801 to 1809 Foronda was Spanish consul-general and chargé in the United States.[107] He became a member of the American Philosophical Society.[108] Returning to Spain in 1809, Foronda was closely associated with the liberals.[109] If Foronda was not typical of the membership of the Basque Society, at least he is proof that the Society appealed to liberals.[110]

---

[101] Cf. for excellent information on Fausto's long and distinguished career in New Spain, Walter Howe, *The Mining Guild of New Spain and its Tribunal General 1770-1821* (Harvard University, 1949); *supra*, 36.

[102] In 1779 he presented to the Society a parallel between the *Casa de Misericordia* of Vitoria and the Society of San Sulpicio of Paris, praising France for her contributions to beneficence, to good taste, and the exact sciences (printed in his *Miscelánea, ó, Colección de varios discursos* [Madrid, 1787], 32 pp., separately paginated).

[103] *Supra*, 12-13. They were discontinued on the advice of a friend in government, but reprinted with additions in 1795 by permission of Godoy (Spell, *Rousseau*, 114).

[104] *Espíritu de los mejores diarios*, No. 185 (June 15, 1789).

[105] *Ibid.*, No. 162 (January 5, 1789), headed Vergara, August 27, 1788.

[106] *Disertación sobre lo honresa es la profesión del comercio, leída en las Juntas generales que celebró la Sociedad Bascongada en Vilbao el año de 1778*, in his *Miscelánea*, 39 pp., separately numbered. Cf. in *ibid.*, his *Disertación sobre la nueva Compañía de Indias Orientales, leída en la Junta pública que celebró la Sociedad Bascongada en año de 1784, día de S. Carlos en la Villa de Bergara.*

[107] J. R. Spell, "An Illustrious Spaniard in Philadelphia—Valentín de Foronda," *Hispanic Review*, IV (1936), 136-40, for his American residence.

[108] Foronda to John Vaughan, Philadelphia, December 16, 1802—Archives of the American Philosophical Society. The minutes of the Philosophical Society record that he sent several of his own works to the Society, including his *Carta sobre Lo Que debe Hacer un Príncipe que Tenga Colonias a Gran Distancia* (Philadelphia, 1803)— *Early Proceedings of the American Philosophical Society . . . From the Manuscript Minutes of its Meetings from 1744 to 1838* (Philadelphia, 1884), entries for January 21, 1803, and February 3, 1804.

[109] In 1814 at La Coruña his Spanish version of Rousseau's *Social Contract* was published, which entitled him to imprisonment later (Spell, *Rousseau*, 197-98). He was acquainted with Jefferson, and sent him a project for a constitution which the latter praised (Jefferson to Don Valentin de Foronda, Monticello, October 4, 1809, in Ford, *Writings of Thomas Jefferson*, IX, 259-61).

[110] Menéndez y Pelayo, *Heterodoxos*, VI, 270, complaining of the French connections of the Society, mentioned Foronda as the interpreter of the *Logic* of Condillac,

Félix María de Samaniego (1745-1801), nephew of Peñaflorida, and one of the founders of the Society, also did some teaching at the Seminary, where he commenced his famous fables,[111] which Peñaflorida requested as an aid to education at the Seminary.[112] Samaniego was sufficiently enlightened to suffer denunciation to the Inquisition as a reader of prohibited books, but escaped serious punishment.[113] Another teacher was Vicente María de Santibáñez, who taught humanities from 1782 to 1792.[114] Yet another man connected with the Seminary was the eminent Miguel de Lardizabal y Uribe (b. 1744), of Basque descent but born in Mexico, who was director of the Seminary in 1801-1808.[115]

The Seminary turned some young Basque nobles from French schools, and no doubt this increased their interest in their own locality.[116] The Seminary, under its moderately liberal direction, offered modern and traditional subjects, and adopted new pedagogical techniques in place of the maxim that "learning enters with blood."[117] A contemporary writer called the Seminary the first in Spain in which "virtue is united with the sciences most useful to the state."[118] The Seminary was not the first lay school in Spain,[119] and it can hardly have been of prime importance in the growth of secularism in general or of laical education in particular.

Long before 1804, when the Seminary was removed from the control of the Basque Society and put under the Spanish Minister of State, a number of schools had been set up by the Economic Societies of Spain and America. The latter offered a more limited, vocational type of training than the Semin-

---

Samaniego who wrote in the manner of La Fontaine, and Santibáñez, who translated the *Novelas Morales* of Marmontel.

[111] Navarrete, "D. Félix María Sánchez de Samaniego," in *Opúsculos*, I, 365-77. Vol. I (Valencia, 1781) was titled *Fábulas ... para uso del real Seminario ... Publícanse de órden de la misma Sociedad.*

[112] *Ibid.*, 367 n., by editor.

[113] Spell, *Rousseau*, 48.

[114] Aralar, *Peñaflorida*, 70 *et seq.*, combating the notion that Santibáñez was irreligious; Sempere, *Ensayo*, V, 152 n., that Santibáñez' eulogy of Peñaflorida was read to the Society in 1785, and printed thereafter.

[115] Aralar, *Peñaflorida*, 60-61; Soraluce, *Sociedad bascongada*, 62.

[116] Sempere, *Ensayo*, V, 175-77, that the Seminary stimulated "patriotism" by keeping young Basques at home.

[117] Valentín de Foronda, "Carta escrita al censor sobre el Seminario de Bergara," in his *Miscelánea*, apparently written in the late 1780's or the 1790's, noting the abandonment of the old barbarous discipline, and describing examinations, and, incidentally, the curriculum.

[118] Sempere, *Ensayo*, V, 175-76, adding that Vergara was the first pueblo in Spain to have founded chairs of chemistry and of metallurgy.

[119] As Menéndez y Pelayo (*Heterodoxos*, VI, 269-70) would have it.

ary. The Basque Society had of course done some of the latter in setting up free schools of drawing.

Character and Influence of the Basque Society

There is no evidence that the Basque Society had secret purposes in addition to its announced aims; it was not a conspiracy. The members had some interest in novelty; were revisionists at least in the sense of wishing to promote the latest scientific studies; and were materialistic to the extent of wishing to improve the economy of their region.[120] Some scholars have charged, however, that the Basque nobles who were members of the Society were also freemasons. No doubt some were, though the evidence is obscure; but it would not matter in any event were the charge not so often linked with accusations of heterodoxy or irreligion. The founders of the Basque Society were Catholics, but young men of their times, and much of the braying against the body is nonsense.[121] It seems a plausible theory that the legend of the heterodoxy of Peñaflorida and his friends, promoted by Menéndez y Pelayo and Vicente de la Fuente,[122] may have been caused in part by the Society's advocacy of inoculation against smallpox, since in 1791 the community was still divided on the question, whereas the Society had favored it since 1768.[123]

---

[120] *Extractos 1774*, 84-85, "Disertación sobre la utilidad de las Sociedades Económicas," the burden of which is that human culture was once primitive, and then man developed control over nature.

[121] Ortiz, *Hija cubana*, 12-13, 26-28, thinks so; not being sure, and not much caring, whether they were freemasons. Cf. Julio de Urquijo, "Ceremonial del Real Seminario Patriótico Bascongado," *Revue Basques*, XIV (1923), 439-41, copy of MS. showing Society members properly lined up in the processions of the *Día de Corpus* of 1782 and 1783; and editorial note asserting the Seminary was not the first lay school in Spain, and claiming many documents prove that neither the Society nor the Seminary was laical. Aralar, *Peñaflorida*, 138-39, 151-53, 160, 162 *et seq.*, 176, 178, *et passim*, that Peñaflorida got the *Encyclopédie* for the Society, but after it was banned by the Church got permission for its use in 1772, and a renewal in 1793; and criticizing the methods of Menéndez y Pelayo and Vicente de la Fuente in dealing with radicalism and masonry in the Basque country; noting that the government, Inquisition, and ecclesiastics supported the Society. Sarrailh, *L'Espagne éclairée*, 240-45, that most, Society members were not noted for audacious ideas, and that while some had advanced views, they were not heterodox or irreligious.

[122] *Historia de las sociedades secretes antiguas y modernas en España* (Nueva ed., 3 vols., Barcelona, 1933). He shows no interest in or understanding of the activities of the Basque Society, but only in connections between it and masonry.

[123] S. Múgica, "Un caso curioso de viruela," *Revue Basques*, XVI (1925), 306-20, mostly documents of the controversy of 1791, showing the attitude of different sections of society in the Basque country; Julio de Urquijo, "Los Amigos del País y la vacuna," *Revue Basques*, XVI, 321-22, a short sketch of the Society's interest, suggesting that the documents edited by Múgica may be a clue to the legend of the heterodoxy of the *amigos*.

There is no important question as to whether the Basque Society was the first of the Economic Societies of Friends of the Country and the prototype of the others. Two Societies—Baeza and Tudela—were organized after the foundation of the Basque, and before the formation of the Madrid.[124] The Basque Society certainly served as an example for the Economic Society of Madrid, in that Campomanes was a member of the Basque body when he recommended societies for Spain;[125] but he also knew of societies in England, France, and other countries. He might have suggested Economic Societies even if no Basque Society had ever existed. It was in part an "accident" that the first such body was organized in the Basque country. The rapidity with which they were organized after the call went out from Madrid in 1775 indicated a large latent desire for something of the sort. Considering the time it took Peñaflorida to arrange his institution, there is no reason to suppose that someone could not have done as well in Madrid or elsewhere. In any event, there is no question that all the Economic Societies founded after that of Madrid were set up in imitation and upon the example of the Madrid body, and in response to a circular of the Council of Castile.[126]

On the other hand it is an exaggeration to find a great distinction in the absence of the term *económica* from the name of the Basque Society. An "economic society" was spoken of in the Plan of 1763, and the Basque Society emphasized economic matters in its statutes and pursued economic interests throughout its history. The term *Amigos del País* was common to the names of the Basque and the Economic Societies and they had some similarities of organization and method of work. If we are to accept the judgment that the Basque Society was "essentially a cultural association,"[127] of limited membership and influence, something of the sort must be admitted also of the Economic Societies; it is a matter of degree.[128]

---

[124] *Extractos 1774*, 3, the Basque Society heard of the formation of "la Sociedad de verdaderos Patricios de la Ciudad de Baeza y Reyno de Jaen." *Infra*, 52.

[125] *Extractos 1771*, "Catálogo general ...," that Campomanes and Pablo Olavide were members in 1769.

[126] Cf. Sempere, *Ensayo*, V, 135, expressing this view in the 18th century; Altamira, *Historia*, IV, 259; Carrera Pujal, *Economía española*, V, 23 *et passim*.

[127] Aralar, *Peñaflorida*, 90.

[128] Labra, *El instituto*, 234-35, 252, admits some influence from the north, but finds the Basque and Economic Societies different in organization and character; Soraluce, *Sociedad bascongada*, p. [3], calls the Basque the first of the Economic Societies of Spain; Ferrer del Río, *Carlos III en España*, III, 234-36, the Basque Society found no imitators, the Economic Society of Madrid set the tone of the others; Aralar, *Peñaflorida*, 24, 29-30, 60, 85 *et seq.*, 90, points out the differences, but tries to "prove" the Basque the source of all others because the royal license of 1765 hoped the Basque would find imitators in other provinces, hits at Jovellanos for believing Campomanes the founder of the Societies, charges Spanish encyclopedias with bias.

The influence of the Society in the Basque provinces is difficult to estimate. The ideas it promoted reached only a minority—which was receiving the same ideas from other sources; and its influence in the realm of physical action probably was small, in view of its limited budget and the few members residing in the Basque provinces.[129] The amount of heterodox opinion in the region is a moot question [130] and in any event cannot be ascribed simply to the Basque Society.

It is equally difficult to estimate the Society's influence in the rest of Spain and overseas.[131] Alumni of the Seminary carried the Society's influence abroad, as did the numerous members we have seen listed in 1773 as resident outside the Basque provinces, and the prominence of the latter ensured that the organization would not lack force because of the obscurity of its adherents. The publications of the Society certainly influenced some non-members. Some of the Spanish Societies in later years followed the work of the Basque body. The director of the Madrid Society, at the time of its foundation, proposed that the districts aggregated to the Society in the capital be connected with it "on the example of that used by the Basque Society in the three provinces of Vizcaya, Alava, and Guipúzcoa."[132]

We have seen that some members of the Basque Society were resident overseas before the Economic Society of Madrid was founded in 1775. In

---

[129] Cf. Carrera Pujal, *Economía española*, IV, 471, on a memorial approved by the Basque Society in 1792, which noted that the Economic Societies in the capitals of provinces were not influencing the small towns, so that Societies should be established in *pueblos*, under the direction of priests. Carrera Pujal considers this an impractical suggestion.

[130] Cf. Menéndez y Pelayo, *Heterodoxos*, VI, 270-71, for poor evidence, presented with prejudice, on subscribers to the *Encyclopédie* in the Basque country, "collaborators" and "separatists" during the French invasion of 1794, and priests favoring civil marriage there; Aralar, *Peñaflorida*, 138-39, 144 *et seq.*, finding Menéndez y Pelayo's views biased, erroneous, and incompetent.

[131] Aralar, Soraluce, and Urquijo scarcely try.

[132] Madrid *Memorias*, xxxviii, in t. I, of "Discurso del señor Antonio de la Quadra ... 1775." In 1776 the Madrid Society thought the Toledo Society should spread knowledge of the Basque Society's work in metallurgy (*ibid.*, II, Memorias of Artes y Oficios, No. III). An essay of 1778 printed by the Madrid Society on carob beans referred to the treatment of the subject by the Basque Society in 1774 (*ibid.*, III, Memorias of Agricultura, "Informe sobre la plantación de algarrobas. ..."). Floridablanca, in approving erection of the Valencia Society, suggested it remark the experience of the Basque Society (Valencia Society, *Instituciones económicas*, 129-32, "Real órden ... 1777"). The Valencia Society's commission on agriculture discussed the work of the Basque Society, citing its publications (*ibid.*, 72); it knew of the travels of Ramón Munibe, and cited the *Extractos* (*ibid.*, 138-39); and knew of the discussion of the fishing company (*ibid.*, xxx, 117). Peñaflorida and Eguía were made *socios agregados* of the Madrid Society (Madrid *Memorias*, II, Apéndices of Memorias of Artes y Oficios, 307-18).

1771 there were six overseas: a corregidor in Peru who had joined in 1767; Captain General Simón de Anda at Manila, who had joined in 1769; the other four had become members in 1771—two at Buenos Aires, and one each at Jalapa in New Spain and at Havana.[133] The 190 members listed in 1773 as resident overseas included: Mexico City, more than 120; Zacateca, 2; Querétaro, 5; Jalapa, 1; Guadalajara de Nueva España, 1; Valladolid de Nueva España, 3; Vera Cruz, 1; San Luís de Potosí, 5; Oaxaca, 4; Tarija, Peru, 1; Lima, 4; Havana, 14; Cartagena de Indias, 6; Buenos Aires, 5; Manila, 2.[134] The members in America tried to recruit new members, an activity largely confined to the principal trade centers, with Mexico being the most successful field of action.[135] In the poverty-stricken province of Venezuela the propaganda of the Society seems not to have really begun until 1774, and even then did not immediately bring members to the Society.[136] Presumably the same was true of efforts of Society agents in some other parts of America.

The thirteen new members admitted overseas in 1774 included the Commandant General of the Canaries; one man at Havana; the Captain General of Chile; three men at Buenos Aires, including Governor Juan Joseph de Vértiz, and Joseph de Albizuri, Secretario del Gobierno; one at Cartagena; two at Lima, including an *oidor;* at Santa Fe the Viceroy, Manuel de Guirior; and four at Mexico, including Melchor de Peramais, Secretario del virreynato.[137] The twenty-three new members resident in America admitted in 1775 included three in Buenos Aires, three in Popayán, eleven in Havana, two in Lima, two in Cartagena, one in Mexico, and one in Tucumán.[138]

Payments of various kinds by men in the Indies to the Society and to its Seminary at Vergara, from 1774 to 1790 inclusive, totaled almost 1,700,000 *reales vellón*. The sums were well distributed through the twenty-two-year period. More than half the total came from New Spain; next came Peru,

---

[133] *Extractos 1771*, "Catálogo ... de los individuos. ..."

[134] "Catálogo ... de los individuos ... 1773," *loc. cit.* Aralar, *Peñaflorida*, 181 *et seq.*, lists, without date, as members overseas: Archbishop Sancho de Santa Justo of Manila; bishops Moscoso of Tucumán, Alday of Santiago de Chile, and Pérez de Calama of Quito; Martínez Campañón, successively bishop of Trujillo in Peru, Cuzco, and Santa Fe; Francisco Jabier de Eguino, Provisor y Vicario General de Cartagena; and deans, prebendaries, and numerous other ecclesiastics of America. He listed many for Peru and Mexico, but none for Central America or Cuba.

[135] Soraluce, *Sociedad bascongada*, 34, notes the many members admitted from Mexico in the juntas of 1773.

[136] Julio de Urquijo's review of Ramón de Basterra's *Una empresa ...*, in *Revue Basques*, XVII (1926), 129-32, quoting a letter to Peñaflorida in December, 1773, which recounted efforts to recruit members in Mexico, and plans for the same for Caracas. Urquijo notes that in the lists of new members for 1774-76 none appeared for Caracas.

[137] *Extractos 1774*, "Suplemento al Catálogo. ..."

[138] *Extractos 1775*, 150-61, "Catálogo de los Socios. ..."

but much less; and small sums from Havana, Chile, Caracas, Buenos Aires, Cartagena, Popayán, and Manila.[139]

Copies of the *Extractos* of the Basque Society were sent to the colonies through the regular trade channels. Juan de Eguino, vice-collector of the Society in Cadiz,[140] helped to spread the word abroad, and appealed for funds to sustain his work. He distributed 120 of the *Ensayos* of 1768 to Manila, Mexico, Vera Cruz, Havana, Cartagena, Lima, Caracas, Buenos Aires, and Puerto Rico. He even suggested to his correspondents that people give to the Society currently and in their wills. Eguino was also "an enthusiastic propagandist of Guipuzcoan industry."[141] Some years later, Ignacio de Aguirre Arana, another vice-collector of the Basque Society in Cadiz was sending its publications overseas. A shipment of 1788 included 100 examples of the *Extractos* of 1787 for Lima and 50 for Manila.[142]

The Society had vice-collectors in New Spain as early as 1774,[143] and commissioners in Mexico, Havana, Lima, Chile, Buenos Aires, Santa Fe, Tucumán, Cartagena, the Canaries, and Manila.[144] All these representatives were members of the Society. It will be observed that no agent was listed for Venezuela, possibly because of the Caracas Company's presence there; possibly because the Society had lesser connections with that area.[145]

The number and importance of Society members residing in Spain and overseas as early as 1773 is one measure of how knowledge of the Society

---

[139] Soraluce, *Sociedad bascongada*, 55-57, a 1790 report to the Society.

[140] *Infra*, 33 n., that he held this post at least as early as 1771.

[141] All the foregoing is from Julio de Urquijo's review of Basterra's *Una empresa*, *loc. cit.*, in the course of which he quotes from a letter of Eguino to Peñaflorida, Cadiz, 1772, asking for examples of the manufactures of Vergara. Ambrosio de Meabe, native of Vizcaya resident in Mexico, on his death in the latter place in 1781 left 12,000 *pesos fuertes* to the Seminary of Vergara (Soraluce, *Sociedad bascongada*, 34, 47); somewhat later, Pedro Antonio Escuza, resident of the Philippines, left 18,000 pesos to the Society (*ibid.*, 48).

[142] Urquijo's review of Basterra, *loc. cit.*, printing a document from the archives of the ayuntamiento of Vergara, which asked the certification of the Holy Office for the books consigned to Aguirre Arana at Cadiz. Urquijo claims to have other evidence of the publications of the Society being sent to America by Aguirre Arana, in letters of the latter to the Count of Peñaflorida. Since the latter died in 1784, the shipments were made before that date.

[143] All in Mexico City: Antonio de Basoco, Sebastián de Eguía, Ramón de Goya, and Joseph de la Guardia (*Extractos 1774*, "Suplemento al Catálogo ...").

[144] *Ibid.* These included Francisco Leandro de Viana of the Audiencia of Mexico, and Ambrosio Meabe of the same place; the Director General of Mails of Cuba; the Captain General of Chile; the Governor of Buenos Aires; the Viceroy of New Granada; the Bishop of Tucumán; the Governor of Cartagena; the Commandant General of the Canaries; and the Consul General of the Philippines.

[145] Cf. Soraluce, *Sociedad bascongada*, 41-42, for Basque Society representatives in America in 1784.

was carried beyond the Basque provinces. But although this influence was operative before the foundation of the Madrid Economic Society in 1775, no Economic Societies were established in America until after the date of the foundation of the Madrid Society. And while we have just seen that Chile, Mexico, Lima, and Buenos Aires knew of the Basque Society fairly early, the first two never established Economic Societies; and the Lima Society was not founded till the 1790's and was not much like the Basque body; and Buenos Aires never put a Society into operation, though one was discussed early in the nineteenth century.[146]

---

[146] Yet another influence of the Basque Society in America might be through creole alumni of the Seminary. Cf. Havana *Memorias*, t. XVIII (Habana, 1844), 65-70, "Necrología Histórica," Don Juan Montalvo y O-Farrill, born at Havana in 1778 of an old and important family, studied at the Seminary of Vergara for three years in the 1780's, entered the army, returned to Cuba, ultimately was director of the Economic Society, died in 1844. Cf. *Gazeta de literatura de Mexico* (2d ed., 4 vols., Puebla, 1831), that the editor Alzate was a corresponding member of the Basque Society (indicated on t.p.), and mentioned its work at least once (III, 14: issue of October 27 and November 12, 1792).

CHAPTER THREE

Foundation, History, and Organization of the Economic Societies of Spain

(1770-1821)

Some seventy Economic Societies of Friends of the Country were formed in Spain between 1770 and 1820; between 1780 and 1822 at least fourteen were created or suggested overseas. Nearly all these Societies were formed after 1775, in response to recommendations by Campomanes and the Council of Castile.[1]

Foundations of the Spanish Societies

Pedro Rodríguez, Count of Campomanes (1723-1802), was responsible for foundation of the Madrid Society, and for the recommendation of the government that such bodies be set up throughout Spain. Campomanes, one of the most learned and energetic statesmen of the reign of Charles III, retained little of the medieval attitude and interest. The most fundamental of his beliefs were in the rational method as applied to political economy, and in the necessity of a freer economy for Spain. He wrote widely on these questions.[2] He was fiscal of the Council of Castile when his discourse on the

---

[1] The only exceptions known to the present writer were the Economic Society of Tudela, founded in 1770, and the Baeza, founded in 1774.

[2] Cf. his *Tratado de la regalía de amortización* ... (Reimpresión of 1821, Gerona [1765]), ii, calling a large population the greatest wealth, if in the proper economic condition; *et passim*, on the efforts of a number of countries to prevent the accumulation of property under laws of inalienability. Addison, *Charles III*, 102, found him fit for comparison with Adam Smith, though not understood by fellow Spaniards. Swinburn, *Travels*, II, 206, seldom praising Spanish intellectual life, found Campomanes "active," with good ideas, but not solid enough, having recently published "five or six volumes of ill-digested materials for the improvement of his country."

development of popular industry was published in 1774 by order of the Council, with "the desire to banish idleness and promote popular industry,"[3] and sent out to the officials of the realm, including municipal councils. The discourse recommended establishment of Economic Societies, which was quickly done, with Madrid leading the way. The Economic Societies "always considered that work as the precursor of their establishment."[4]

The discourse dealt with the need to improve the study of political economy, to examine carefully the economic problems of the regions of Spain, and to make use of the economic thought and practice of the rest of Europe. It was chiefly concerned with the economic problems of the metropolis though one reference was made to the land problem in the Indies, finding it "incredible" that in the midst of such huge territories many Spaniards and Indians lacked land, and suggesting that the matter deserved "all the attention" of the ministers of the Council of the Indies.[5] Its tone was entirely secular, soberly practical, rationalistic, with a minimal obeisance to the social problems of Spain, and a maximal consideration of those economic shortcomings which he thought the cause of social decay.

He found the state of Spain was so desperate that all nations marveled at its decadence in the midst of fertile land surrounded by the sea. No government could survey the needs of so vast a territory, so Economic Societies in the provinces should study their condition and prospects.[6] Idleness was an evil,[7] but labor should be directed by men who had studied political economy, were familiar with the latest methods, devices, and theories, and could apply them to concrete situations. The Societies should translate foreign writings, supplementing them with notes.[8] European discoveries should be followed through periodicals, and attention given to the memorials of the societies of Berne and Dublin, the latter making "the study of the English language of the greatest importance."

The Societies, without jurisdiction or privilege, would be a "public school of the theory and practice of political economy in all the provinces of Spain," studying Spanish as well as foreign writers. In some provinces existing academies could be used, as the Academy of Agriculture of Galicia. The

---

[3] *Discurso sobre el fomento de la industria popular. De órden de S. M. y del Consejo* (Madrid, 1774), 1-6, the "Advertencia."

[4] Madrid *Memorias*, I, xxxi of the preliminary section entitled "De la Industria Popular." Cf. Basque *Extractos 1774*, 105, for a letter of Campomanes to the Basque Society, enclosing a copy of his *Industria popular.*

[5] *Industria popular*, 118, n. 26.

[6] *Ibid.*, sec. xiv, sec. xix; cf. sec. vi for citation of a Scottish writer in favor of the creation of "political bodies" to promote and perfect agriculture and the crafts.

[7] *Ibid.*, 7, and men are born to toil.

[8] *Ibid.*, secs. vi, xx. Further discussion of the *Industria popular* is based on sec. xx.

Societies should study prices and production, the economic history of their provinces, and the causes of economic decadence. They must take censuses; count mendicants and vagrants, note the causes of their being in that condition, and the means of giving them work; know those who left the country to find work; deal with agriculture, fishing, stockraising, manufacturing, commerce, and navigation; help the government examine "economic projects"; write *memorias* and *actas*, and publish them for the public; teach mathematics, dyeing, machines, drawing, and other things in connection with industry; and set up cabinets of natural history, remembering that the cabinets had an economic interest in view.

The membership dedicated to this ambitious labor was to be composed of the "best educated nobility," since they possessed the richest land and would benefit most from the industry of common folk. The Basque Society, Campomanes wrote, understood the fundamental importance of the education of the nobility, who should be taught by the Societies in provincial seminaries, learning public law and subjects not taught in the universities or schools. Their education should include reading in "economic works," necessary for the formation of a "certain number of cardinal principles." With this theoretical background, economic projects would no longer be chimerical and "founded on monopoly and oppression."

These enlightened nobles, and other members, were to practice equality within the Societies, for rules of precedence had in Spain "destroyed many good things." Personal interests should not be uppermost in a nation, or it would meet disaster. From these exalted principles Campomanes descended to questions of membership, officers, statutes, and even dues or fees, which he approved on the model of the Royal Society of London.

Campomanes continued the argument of the *Popular Industry* the following year in a discourse on the popular education of artisans,[9] again advocating Economic Societies to correct political errors, confer with each other, and suggest remedies to the government. Asserting that such useful laws as existed in this field were not executed because of a lack of educated personnel, he wished to promote instruction, especially of a technical nature, for Spain ought to adopt the latest techniques, collecting works, foreign and Spanish, dealing with the crafts.[10] In pursuit of this end, the Societies should translate

---

[9] *Discurso sobre la educación popular de los artesanos, y su fomento* (Madrid, 1775). Four additional volumes, bearing title *Apéndice a la educación popular*, were published at Madrid, 1775-77. These, of more than 500 pages each, bear testimony to the eighteenth-century interest in the political economists of the 17th. The "Parte Segunda," iii-cclxvi, "Discurso preliminar sobre las fábricas," went over much of the ground on the Economic Societies, but with some new information.

[10] *Educatión popular*, 356-57.

and distribute such treatises, and add to them in such fashion as to contribute to the perfection of the crafts in Spain. Abuses and ignorance were to receive special attention,[11] for the progress of production and consumption had been impeded by such things as guild restrictions.[12] In support of the projected Societies, Campomanes again observed that the Academy of Science of Paris and the Royal Society of London had been doing useful work,[13] and noted the sound practice of the Royal Society of Dublin in offering prizes to stimulate endeavor and interest.[14] In brief, Campomanes examined the economic shortcomings of the realm, pointed out the reasons for them (especially the abuses of the guild organization, and other restrictions on free industry), and indicated a remedy—education.

A petition to the Council of Castile, May 30, 1775, asking permission to form a Society in Madrid, was signed by Vicente de Rivas (director of the Royal Company of Caracas), José Faustino de Medina (*Contador General* of the Inquisition and secretary of the Council of Castile), and José de Almarza (governor of the *Real Sitio* of San Fernando) who signed for himself and eight residents of the court.[15] The petitioners asked for a Society after the example of those in other places, a reference either to the Basque Society or to foreign organizations. They said their request was due to a sense of the common welfare and to the discourse of Campomanes, ordered distributed by the Council, which had prescribed rules for such a Society.[16] Acceptance of the petition cannot have been hampered by the fact that the petitioner Medina was secretary and the author Campomanes was fiscal of the Council.[17] In June the Council licensed the establishment.[18]

The Society began its organization that month.[19] Antonio Quadra (Minister of Posts) became first director, and José Ayala (of the secretariat of the *Despacho de Indias*) was secretary. The statutes of the Society were drawn up by a committee of members, and approved by the government in

---

[11] *Ibid.*, 357.

[12] *Ibid.*, sec. 15, 284-92.

[13] *Ibid.*, 79.

[14] *Ibid.*, 307.

[15] Madrid *Memorias*, II,. 5 unnumbered pp. before the *Apéndice a las memorias de la Sociedad*, entitled "Advertencia"; Ferrer del Río, *Carlos III en España*, III, 236; cf. Hussey, *Caracas Company*, 166, 184-85, 292, for Rivas and the Caracas Company.

[16] Sempere, *Ensayo*, V, 137-38; cf. Labra, *El instituto*, 259; Ferrer del Río, *Carlos III en España*, III, 236.

[17] Madrid *Memorias*, II, Apéndice no. II, 3-4, "Copia de la repuesta del señor Fiscal sobre el propio asunto," June 2, 1775.

[18] *Ibid.*, Apéndice no. I, 1-2, "Licensia del Consejo. ..."

[19] *Ibid.*, I, vii-viii; II, unpaginated "Advertencia" before the Apéndice; Apéndice no. III, 5-7, "Primer conferencia de la ... Sociedad."

November.[20] These statutes—which other Societies were expected to use as a model—stated the Society's objectives as: (1) to confer, and produce memorials for the improvement of industry, the arts and crafts, through instruction; and (2) to promote agriculture and stockraising. In short it was dedicated to *economía universal*, by the method of education, aimed at improvement of the economic understanding of the populace, expecting thus to increase the prosperity and strength of the nation. The educational aim was incorporated in the Society motto: "Assist Education." It hoped to gain accurate information by cooperative effort,[21] using the analytic rather than the syllogistic method, "establishing the Society . . . as a school of economic science."[22] Since it was felt that the district of Madrid would not in itself give sufficient range for the work of the Society, Toledo, Guadalajara, Segovia, Avila, and Villa de Talavera were "aggregated" to the Madrid Society, making them branches of it for some purposes.[23]

All but the Basque and two other Societies were founded after 1775, in response to the recommendations of Campomanes and the Council of Castile. There were at least sixty-eight Societies in all parts of Spain by 1791; then no more were founded until 1814, and only seven from the latter date to 1833.[24] The Tudela Society was founded in 1770;[25] the Baeza in 1774;[26] the Madrid in 1775; then several each year through 1791; but the Cadiz Society was not founded till 1814, whereas many small and unimportant towns had Societies from an early date.[27]

The municipality of Sevilla, receiving the circular of the Council and the discourse of Campomanes on popular industry, appointed a committee to consider methods of promoting agriculture, and this committee reported

---

[20] *Ibid.*, II, Apéndices, No. V, "Segunda representación que hizo la Sociedad al Consejo, pidiendo la aprobación de sus Estatutos"; No. VI, "Real Cedula de S. M. y Señores del Consejo, en que se aprueban los estatutos ...," San Lorenzo, November 9, 1775; *Novísima recopilación de las leyes de España*, Lib. VIII, tit. XXI, Ley I, incorrectly puts 1785.

[21] Madrid *Memorias*, I, xiii.

[22] *Ibid.*, I, xv-xix.

[23] *Ibid.*, I, xxxix-xl of "Discurso ... Antonio de la Quadra ... 27 de Agosto de 1775"; II, Apéndice No. VI, includes the statutes.

[24] "Sociedades Económicas," Havana *Memorias*, t. XIX (Havana, 1844), 56-65, an article assertedly—and obviously—based on research; although the *Guía de Forasteros* was the only source cited, reference was made to other data. Cf. Ballesteros, *Historia*, VI, 144-45, reciting the names of 60 Societies from the *Guía* of 1804; Desdevises, *La Richesse*, 89-90 n. 3, finding 64 in the same *Guía*. Bourgoing reported 44 in the later 1780's.

[25] Carrera Pujal, *Economía española*, IV, 9.

[26] Sarrailh, *L'Espagne éclairée*, 247, citing Basque *Extractos 1774*.

[27] "Sociedades Económicas," in Havana *Memorias 1844*, listing all the Societies by date of foundation.

that a "patriotic society" offered the best hope. The Society was founded in 1775. Its statutes followed the pattern of the Madrid Society, as the Council had ordered. The declared aim of the Sevilla Society was the improvement of agriculture, industry, arts and crafts, and commerce and navigation.[28] Jovellanos was one of its early and energetic members, before moving to Madrid in 1778.[29]

The Valencia Society was initiated early in 1776 by seven men, including a canon of the cathedral, a judge of the audiencia, and two marquises. On petition, the Council of Castile conceded license in a letter to Pedro Mayoral, and instructed that the town council of Valencia be given notice to make ready free space for the Society in the municipal building. With fifty members, the Society was inaugurated in July, 1776, the officers elected and given power to name commissioners to form the statutes. By August the intendant of the province was suggesting to the Society a navigation canal from the sea to the vicinity of the Custom-house, and the Society named a commission to study the idea.[30] By the junta of May 14, 1777, attended by nearly 100 members, the Society had a total of 240 contributing members. The archbishop graced this junta with his presence. The Society met once a week from this time at least to September, 1777.[31] It early cooperated with the Royal Academy of the Three Noble Arts in Valencia.[32] It read works on political economy,[33] had a display of fabrics in the summer of 1777,[34] and began to plan for a "commerce company" to promote industry and commerce.[35] By the end of September, 1777, there were well over 300 members.

A royal order, written by Floridablanca in 1777, approved erection of the Society and the rules suggested for its government until the statutes were ready. The minister suggested that in drawing the statutes it would

---

[28] Sempere, *Ensayo*, VI, 20-22. There is considerable disagreement as to when some of the Societies were founded, the differences being small, and probably in part due to the acceptance of different criteria for the determination of "foundation": e.g., Labra, *El instituto*, 311, that the Sevilla Society was established January 2, 1778; "Sociedades Económicas," Havana *Memorias 1844*, that it was founded in 1777; Sarrailh, *L'Espagne éclairée*, 249, organization began in 1775, but the first general meeting was not until November, 1778.

[29] Cándido Nocedal, "Discurso Preliminar," to the *Obras* of Jovellanos (BAE, XLVI), viii *et seq.*

[30] Valencia Society, *Instituciones económicas*, ii-v, 21. This publication is a mass of references to and quotations from the *Industria popular* and *Educación popular* of Campomanes.

[31] *Ibid.*, v-vii.

[32] *Ibid.*, xix.

[33] *Ibid.*, viii, xxii.

[34] *Ibid.*, xxxiii, *et passim*.

[35] *Ibid.*, xxv *et seq.*

be well to follow the experience of the Basque Society. The king he represented as being pleased to approve the "utilísima idea" of establishing Economic Societies.[36] Campomanes wrote three months later to the director of the Valencia body, praising the prizes it offered, and especially that for fisheries, so important to a coastal province. He suggested a bit more activity, lauded the archbishop for giving money, and declared that their work represented *progresos*.[37] The statutes were approved in 1785.[38] The Society was still active in 1803.[39]

The Economic Society of Mallorca held its first junta in 1778.[40] The institution leaped as rapidly across the greater stretch of sea between the Peninsula and the Canary Islands. That of Las Palmas was promoted by Bishop Juan Severa to a group of distinguished persons who met at his residence in February, 1776. Royal permission was obtained, and with an initial membership of sixty-five they drew up statutes on the model of Madrid, and received definitive approval in 1777.[41] Royal permission was given for establishment of the Society of S. Cristóval de la Laguna in 1778, but the Society was enrolling members the preceding year, under the provisional approval of the audiencia of the Canary Islands and the town council of the city of S. Cristóval. The royal license conceded it the royal protection, and "aggregated" it with the Madrid Society. The membership included well over one hundred names in 1777-1779, including several persons resident in America.[42] A third Canarian Society was founded at Santa Cruz de la Palma.[43]

[36] *Ibid.*, 129-32, "Real órden de su Magd. ... "

[37] *Ibid.*, xl-xliii, for text of letter.

[38] *Real cédula por la qual se aprueban los estatutos de la Sociedad Económica de Amigos del País de Valencia* (Valencia: Benito Monfort, 1785).

[39] *Premios que ofrece la Real Sociedad Económica de Amigos del País de Valencia para el día de diciembre de 1803* (4 pp.; n. p., n.d.). Cf. *Junta pública de la Real Sociedad Económica de Amigos del País de Valencia ... 1799* (Valencia: Benito Monfort, 1800), p. 5 n., that the Society published accounts of *juntas públicas* in 1791, but not in 1792-98. The Society had 161 members in 1799, including the American Philosophical Society—a member since 1796—and Viceroy Azanza of New Spain—a member since 1792 (*Ibid.*, 181-94).

[40] Sempere, *Ensayo*, VI, 27-30; Juliette P. Monbeig, "La Real Sociedad Económica de Los Amigos del País. Une Source de l'Histoire Economique de Majorque au XVIIIe Siècle," *Annales du Midi*, XLV (1933), 163-73, at 164.

[41] Agustín Millares Torres, *Historia general de las Islas Canarias* (2d ed., La Habana, 1945), 366-67.

[42] *Estatutos de la Sociedad Económica de los Amigos del Pays de la ciudad de S. Cristóval de la Laguna, capital de la isla de Tenerife ...* (En Madrid ... Año MDCCLXXIX), 1-2, 25-28, 29-38.

[43] Millares Torres, *Historia Canarias*, 367. Cf. Agustín Millares Carlo, *Ensayo de una bio-bibliografía de escritores naturales de las Islas Canarias (siglos XVI, XVII y XVIII)* (Madrid, 1932), for items relating to the Canarian Societies.

A proposal of 1776 for establishment of a Society at Segovia was approved by the Council, but it was not formed because of opposition in Segovia. In 1780, after a manufacturer had represented to the Council that a Society would aid manufacturing in Segovia, the body was formed, and approved at the end of that year.[44] Campomanes visited the city in October, 1780, and went out of his way to attend a meeting of the Society and exhort it to labor.[45] The weekly juntas of the Society began in April, 1781.[46] Since Segovia was one of the towns "aggregated" to the Madrid Society, it may be that the complaints of the latter influenced the Council to act. In an important memorial on the poor, made by a commission of the Madrid Society in 1778, in response to a request by the Council, it was suggested that more Economic Societies were needed, and that Segovia had held no juntas as yet.[47]

Although several Economic Societies were founded in Cataluña in the early period, the municipality of Barcelona rejected Campomanes' project, partly on the grounds that the city's *Junta de Comercio* was doing the work proposed for the Societies.[48]

History of the Spanish Societies

The history of the Societies falls into chronological periods, with the years 1775-1808—from the foundation of the Madrid Society to the French invasion—being the first. In those years the Societies rendered their greatest service, having little competition in their fields of economic propaganda and study and education. They were more favored in 1775-1789 than from the latter date to 1808. The government of Charles III was more enlightened than that of Charles IV under the favorite Godoy; and events stemming from the wars of the French Revolution and from fear of liberalism created a less favorable atmosphere. During the War of Liberation (1808-1814) the Societies could not operate; after the war various institutions soon were established to handle matters formerly left to the Societies.

Even in the time of Charles III the Societies did not fulfill all the hopes that had been confided in them. Campomanes in 1776 complained that the

---

[44] Real Sociedad económica ... de la provincia de Segovia, *Actas y memorias* (Segovia: Antonio Espinosa, 1785), 1-7.

[45] *Ibid.*, 7-8, n.

[46] *Ibid.*, 8.

[47] Madrid *Memorias*, III, Memorias of Industria, "Memoria sobre el recogimiento y ocupación de los pobres ... 20 de marzo de 1778," 15.

[48] Sarrailh, *L'Espagne éclairée*, 249-50, 262; Carrera Pujal, *Economía española*, I, 112, 121-22. Cf. Labra, *El instituto*, 302, that one was finally founded at Barcelona in 1822; "Sociedades Económicas," in Havana *Memorias 1844*, that the Barcelona Society was formed in 1834.

Madrid Society's classes (into which the membership was divided) scarcely met; those of agriculture and of crafts had held no juntas and had not distributed their work.[49] Jovellanos, on taking office in 1784 as director of the Madrid Society, criticized its condition, noting that it showed signs of decrepitude, with meetings badly attended, and most of the classes of members not working; but he thought that posterity would judge that their efforts had been directed to the public good.[50] Men in other regions were exhorting the nation to support the Societies; Madrid was not alone in its indifference to enlightenment.[51]

The government in 1786 noted the shortcomings of the Societies, in a royal order, sent out with a circular of the Council, recommending that the civil, military, and ecclesiastical authorities protect them and propose ways of making them more effective.[52] In that year Jovellanos reported to the government on the decadence of the agricultural division of the Madrid Society, finding attendance reasonably good, and the Society using its sparse funds to spread enlightenment, since it could not hope to change agriculture immediately and directly. He felt that in the light of the constitution of the Society and its resources, it had done all the government could expect, and merely needed a confinement of membership to those useful to the organization, and government support of its efforts.[53] Floridablanca, in 1788, while acknowledging they had not been equally useful, did feel that most of the Societies had done well.[54]

The Societies were not equally active. The Madrid enjoyed unique advantages, so its activity shows an unmatched continuity and vigor. Some towns apparently opposed the idea of change more vigorously than others, and some could not give effective financial support to a Society. It was difficult to find men of energy, learning, and organizational capacity to serve as Society directors. Some of the bodies frittered away their opportunities in idle rhetoric.

---

[49] Madrid *Memorias*, II, 62-69, "Memoria presentada por ... Campomanes, sobre poner en sólida actividad las tres clases de la Sociedad ... leída en la Junta General de 6 de Abril. ..."

[50] "Discurso ... de tomar posesión del cargo de director ...," in *Obras publicada e inéditas* (2 vols., Madrid, 1858-59, BAE), II, 554-55.

[51] Juan Catalina García, *Datos bibliográficos sobre la Sociedad económica Matritense* (Madrid, 1877), 40, lists: *Discurso sobre la obligación que tiene la Nación de contribuir al fomento de las Sociedades Económicas, por D. Luís García de la Huerta* (Mallorca, 1785); *Sistema para hacer más ventajosa las Sociedades Económicas, discurso leído á la Aragonesa por D. Manuel Aguirre* (Madrid, 1785).

[52] *Novísima recop.*, Lib. VIII, tit. XXI, ley II.

[53] "Dictamen que dió a la clase de agricultura ... para evacuar un informe pedido por el Consejo Real, sobre ... la decadencia de estos cuerpos," in *Obras* (BAE), II, 57-60.

[54] "Memorial presentado al rey," *loc. cit.*, 323.

Some members had the passion of authorship divorced from affection for learning or accuracy. A contemporary declared that some men joined the Societies only to see their names in print, so many Societies did little more than have their establishment announced in the *Gazeta* and the officers listed in the *Guía de Forasteros*.[55] It seems a fair guess that the experience of Murcia, where a Society was formed with some difficulty only to fail to become operative,[56] cannot have been unique in Spain.

The "born enemies" of the Societies were said to be entrenched public officials, especially in subaltern positions. The Societies offended them by influencing the king on public questions and by hitting them in the purse in connection with such questions as mendicancy.[57] Another source of opposition is indicated in the controversy of 1786-1787, due to ecclesiastical objections to the ideas of Lorenzo Normante y Carcaviella, holder of the chair of civil economy of the Zaragoza or Aragonese Economic Society, inaugurated in 1784. Normante had items on the subject published in 1784 and 1786. In the latter year a preaching friar made a violent attack on Normante's ideas, especially his notions that no members should be admitted to the religious profession before the age of twenty-four, that luxury was permissible (hence the production of luxury goods), that usury was admissible, and that ecclesiastical celibacy was prejudicial to the State. Some ecclesiastics supported the Society in this controversy. The Society sent a circular explanation of the affair to other Spanish Economic Societies, and received from them a number of responses supporting the Zaragoza Society.[58] It is clear that some of the opposition to the Societies came from conservative ecclesiastics.[59]

The death of Charles III marks the end of an era both because succeeding kings were of inferior stuff, and because of the difficulties soon to arise from the French Revolution. Perhaps the character of Charles IV and events in France were both in the mind of Jovellanos in November, 1789, when he

---

[55] Sempere, *Ensayo*, VI, 148-49.

[56] Alexandre de Laborde, *Itinéraire descriptif de L'Espagne, et tableau élémentaire des différentes branches de l'administration et de l'industrie de ce royaume* (2d ed., 5 vols., Paris, 1809), II, 236.

[57] Sempere, *Ensayo*, V, 150. Cf. Carrera Pujal, *Economía española*, IV, 14, that officials opposed the Societies as interfering with their own "despotisms"; IV, 15, that the masters of guilds opposed the Societies as offering competition in some fields of economic production.

[58] Sarrailh, *L'Espagne éclairée*, 274-76, based on documentation in the Municipal Archives of Zaragoza, including the replies of 14 Economic Societies; Carrera Pujal, *Economía española*, V, 406 *et seq.*; Menéndez y Pelayo, *Heterodoxos*, VI, 272.

[59] Cf. Sempere, *Ensayo*, V, 151, that ecclesiastics were not always helpful to the Societies.

read to the Madrid Society a eulogy of Charles III the light-bringer, with emphasis on economics and the ancillary studies necessary to its development. Condemning the intellectual tyranny of Aristotle, he spoke of Spain's long experience of a state of "superstition and ignorance," which needed to be relieved by "useful sciences, economic principles, the general spirit of enlightenment." But the long neglect of the study of "civil economy" was rectified, he said, with the coming of the Bourbons.[60]

On the eve of the French Revolution, Floridablanca was praising the work of the sixty Societies, calling them *cuerpos útiles*, and recommending that their labors be extended.[61] And though he disclaimed credit for having invented them, he invited praise for having supported them.[62] The upheaval in France, however, so alarmed Floridablanca,[63] perceiving the possible social and political implications of the ideas he had helped promote in Spain, that in his reaction the minister in 1790 curtailed the Societies somewhat.[64]

The hysterically anti-French ministry of Floridablanca ended with his removal in 1792; the subsequent ministries of Aranda and Godoy were more moderate. The Societies operated throughout the reign of Charles IV (1788-1808). Godoy, minister by virtue of personality rather than talent, at least liked to appear enlightened, and approved some of the objectives of the Societies.[65] But Godoy was vindictive, which may have played some part in his attitude toward the Basque Society, though a statesman devoted to centralization and uniformity would need no other reason for disliking the Basques than their opposition to those ideas. Count Cabarrús, the naturalized Frenchman who was a prominent supporter of the Economic Societies, was imprisoned in 1790; and Jovellanos was exiled to Asturias for defending him. During his years in the north, Jovellanos continued his interest in the Societies, writing for the Madrid Society the great treatise on the agrarian law, based on the treatises published by the Society. This work, the greatest single production of the Societies of Spain in 1775-1820, was denounced to the

---

[60] "Elogio de Carlos III ...," *Obras* (BAE), I, 311-17.

[61] "Instrucción reservada," *loc. cit.*, sec. LIII, "Las Sociedades Económicas fomentan las artes y procuran desterrar la ociosidad."

[62] "Memorial presentado al rey," *loc. cit.*, 322-23.

[63] José Gómez de Arteche, *Reinado de Carlos IV* (3 vols., Madrid, 1893-98), I, 51 *et seq.*, ascribes some of Floridablanca's actions to public reaction in Spain against the excesses of the French Revolution.

[64] Menéndez y Pelayo, *Heterodoxos*, VI, 296-97.

[65] *Cuenta dada de su vida política por D. Manuel Godoy Príncipe de la Paz ...* (4 vols., Madrid, 1908-09), IV, 63, for his comments on the Economic Societies, written in later years, after his fall. Cf. *infra*, 208, for his approval of the Guatemala Society.

Inquisition.[66] Jovellanos and Cabarrús were briefly back in favor in 1797-1798, but in the latter year Godoy again exiled Jovellanos from the court. In 1801 he was arrested, moved to the island of Mallorca, and held there till the fall of the government in 1808 brought his release. The experience of Jovellanos helps to show that the temper of the times was increasingly inimical to the effective operation of the Economic Societies.

Between 1784 and 1804 the American Philosophical Society at Philadelphia elected to membership thirteen Spaniards, including several members of Economic Societies.[67] Some publications were exchanged. But the connection seems not to have been close, since in 1836 the Philosophical Society was just being informed, in answer to its own inquiry, that "Joseph Miguel de Flores died many years ago; his Excellency Don Luís de Urbina followed him some years after & Don Pedro Cevallos is still living and residing in Seville."[68]

In 1789-1808 the Madrid Society did some work, but only one volume of Memorias was published, and the relatively realistic attention to economics shown in published Memorias of earlier years was more and more replaced by philanthropic and cultural interests.[69] After 1790 the Society became less and less like the organization suggested by Campomanes. It recognized the fact on publication of volume five of its Memorias in 1795, seven years after volume four had appeared. The fifth volume was thinner than the others, and mostly taken up with a single item, the long Agrarian Law of Jovellanos, which did not represent new work on the part of the Society. The editors apologized that the Society, though no longer publishing yearly, had been

---

[66] *Infra*, 98-99.

[67] *The American Philosophical Society Year Book 1949* (Philadelphia, 1950), 432-44, "Former Foreign Members." No more Spanish members were elected between 1805 and 1821.

[68] F. de P. Quadrada to John Vaughan, Washington, May 18, 1836—Archives of the Philosophical Society. Campomanes, the first Spaniard elected to the Philosophical Society, sent it books by way of Benjamin Franklin (MS. Minutes of the Philosophical Society, August 15, 1788). Elected to membership in 1796: Joseph de Jaudennes, member of the Valencia Society, and intendant of Mallorca; Luís de Urbina, captain general of Valencia, and director of its Society (MS. Minutes, July 15, 1796). *Supra*, 40, for the election of Foronda. In 1804 Godoy was admitted, and wrote his thanks for the membership and for the 5 vols. of the *Transactions* sent him, and praised the work of the Society as "de la mayor utilidad" (El Príncipe de la Paz to the Sres. Yndividuos de la Sociedad Filosófica de Philadelphia, Madrid, July 9, 1804—Archives of the Philosophical Society). Jaudennes sent several volumes of the publications of the Valencia Society to the Philadelphia body; the latter in 1803 resolved to send a set of its *Transactions* to the "Aragonese Society established in Zaragoza" (MS. Minutes, July 21).

[69] The women members ran the Royal Home for Foundlings (García, *Datos bibliográficos*, No. 84, for year 1804); the Society managed a new school for deaf-mutes, opened in 1805 (*ibid.*, No. 80-83); it took an interest in shorthand writing, continued to offer prizes, experimented with Rumford's *comidas económicas*, and did a bit of publishing (*ibid.*, *passim*).

doing other good work, and was still giving an account of its work in annual general juntas. Funds were so limited that it had been decided to use them "in other objects of more urgent and public necessity" than publication.[70] The French invasion of 1808 entirely interrupted the work of the Societies.[71] Floridablanca died that year, while he held the office of president of the Supreme Governing Junta of the Realms of Spain and the Indies, which was trying to lead the Spanish resistance against the invader. The Society's eulogy praised Floridablanca for cherishing the Patriotic Societies, most meritorious of the learned institutions of Spain, though recently moribund under the long tyranny of Godoy.[72]

When Napoleon lured Charles IV and Ferdinand to France, and then installed his brother Joseph as king of Spain, the usual collaborators appeared in the ranks of the privileged; but most Spaniards would have none of him. The term *afrancesado* later applied to the collaborators, helps indicate one source of the animus against them: as being not only unpatriotic, but foreign, and of a foreignness touched with crimes against the Church and with the deification of Reason. Though Jovellanos was no deist and would not serve Joseph, the term has been applied to him because he had intellectual interests and a belief in certain politico-economic reforms also held by some collaborators and promoted by Joseph Bonaparte.

Many in the resistance government at Cadiz in those years had these ideas as well. The "extraordinary" Cortes there brought to prominence men whose ideas were in tune in many ways with those of the Economic Societies. But they went further—being a political body—and tried to act on some of the political and social implications of the ideas of the Enlightenment and of the infant age of egalitarianism. Floridablanca and Jovellanos and others imbued with the new ideas had helped bring the new age to Spain, partly by way of the Economic Societies. But in 1808 and thereafter these intelligent moderates, these "gradualists," did not quite like the aspects it assumed.

---

[70] Madrid *Memorias*, V, [i-iv], "Prólogo;" Méndez Bejarano, *Afrancesados*, 83, for Seville Society and education to 1808; Gil de Zárate, *Instrucción pública*, III, 348 *et seq.*, Madrid Society and deaf-mute education and shorthand in 1802; Sarrailh, *L'Espagne éclairée*, 248-49, *et passim*, that the Zaragoza or Aragonese Society, approved in 1776, was one of the most active in Spain, and mentioning some of its activity well into the 1790's.

[71] García, *Datos bibliográficos*, lists announcements of Society prizes in the *Gazeta* all through the 1790's, and in the new century up to the supplement to the *Gazeta* of April 26, 1805, then lists the announcement of prizes in the supplement to the *Gazeta* of September 3, 1814. He lists (No. 89) a publication of the Society for 1808, but the next item (No. 90) is for 1814.

[72] "Elogio histórico del serenísimo señor Don José Moniño, Conde de Floridablanca ...," BAE, LIX, 516-17.

The Cortes did many things that the Societies had not discussed, but also enacted measures that the Societies had long favored. The Cortes wished to free industry and destroy the guilds; it favored agriculture over stock-raising; it even tackled, cautiously, the problem of dividing the huge *latifundium* of Church, noble, and town. All these things had been discussed in the Societies. The decree of the Cortes establishing political freedom of the press indicated belief in discussion and in the dissemination of ideas, in the usefulness of information.[73] It has even been claimed that the process of discussion in the Societies, being an exception in the political and intellectual life of Spain in the eighteenth century, made them "the school of our parliamentarians of 1812."[74] In any event, the Societies and the Cortes may not have been interested in freedom of discussion for the same reasons, but each approved it for its own purposes.

Jovellanos did good work for the irregular government in preparing a system of public education, advocating modernization of the curriculum with modern languages and science, and declaring "that liberty to speak, write, and print ought to be seen as absolutely necessary for the progress of the sciences and for the instruction of nations."[75] But he worried lest changes be effected too quickly, and an abrupt break with tradition hamper reform, and opposed the notion of lumping the national population for purposes of political representation, obliterating class lines, and favored calling the deputies of clergy and nobles to the Cortes to represent their estates. He opposed tyranny, but supported the monarchy. And he deplored factionalism in Spain, abhoring the "clubs" of France.[76] In short, he favored educational and economic rather than political change. Thus after his death the Cortes could praise his services to humanity and education, his opposition to despotism, and his treatise on the agrarian law, which it ordered used in the schools.[77] In this connection, the Cortes was approving a line of thought dating back to the first days of the Madrid Society in 1775.

The Cortes in 1810 sent to committee a memorial calling for establishment

---

[73] *Colección de los decretos ... desde ... 1810 hasta ... 1823 ...* (7 vols., Madrid, 1811-23), I, 14-17, Decreto IX, Nov. 10, 1810.

[74] Labra, *El instituto*, 269.

[75] "Bases para la formación de un plan general de instrucción pública," Sevilla, November 16, 1809, in *Obras* (BAE), I, 268-76.

[76] Andrés Borrego, *Historia de las Cortes de España durante el siglo XIX* (2 vols., Madrid, 1885), II, 143-57, 166; cf. G. de Artíñano y Galdácano, *Jovellanos y su España* (Madrid, 1913), 102, calling Jovellanos "reformador, pero moderado," and 128-29, on his individualistic ideas of political economy; Edith F. Helman, "Some Consequences of the Publication of the *Informe de Ley Agraria* by Jovellanos," 253-73 in *Estudios Hispanicos* (Wellesley, Mass., 1952).

[77] *Colección de los decretos*, II, 67, Decreto CXXVII, January 24, 1812.

of *sociedades patrióticas;*[78] in 1811 the proposition was passed to the committee on instruction;[79] in 1812 a member asserted that under the new constitutional system Economic Societies, if allowed in Spain, must be permitted in America, where they would foster a necessary increase in American production.[80] The Regency in 1811 ordered a Society created in Puerto Rico, and in 1814 the Crown approved the statutes of the Society.[81] The Cortes in 1813 ordered the establishment of chairs of *economía civil* in all universities, and *escuelas patrióticas* of agriculture in all principal towns; while existing Economic Societies were to work actively, and new Economic Societies were to be formed in the capitals of provinces and chief towns where there were none. The Societies were to prepare and distribute studies in the fields of agriculture, stockraising, and arts and crafts; pass out seeds and plants; offer prizes; and enlighten the town councils and provincial deputations. They were to elect their own officers, but the Societies themselves were to have no "authority."[82] This definition of the function of the Societies was explained by the projected widening of municipal actions and the development of education by the State, but it has also been suggested that the revisionists of Cadiz felt driven to centralization of their forces in order to battle reaction.[83]

In November, 1813, the Madrid Society sent a discourse to the *Cortes ordinarias* on the occasion of its installation; and it sent the same discourse in January, 1814, to the Regency on the occasion of the removal of the latter to Madrid.[84] The discourse felicitated the Cortes for having adopted the doctrines of the Economic Society, and specified approval of a recent series of reforms, most of which were directed to the destruction of economic privilege.[85]

The government of Spain after restoration of the dynasty under Ferdinand VII in 1814 supported the old regime. Ferdinand swore to defend the somewhat liberal constitution of 1812, and then promptly foreswore himself

---

[78] *Diario de sesiones de las Cortes ... 24 de setiembre de 1810 ... 20 de setiembre de 1813* (9 vols., Madrid, 1870-74), session of Nov. 25.

[79] *Ibid.*, session of March 9.

[80] *Ibid.*, session of June 9.

[81] *Infra*, 247.

[82] *Colección de los decretos*, Decreto CCLXI, June 8. Jovellanos always opposed "authority" for the Societies, in 1781 agreeing that they had none and arguing that it was not necessary for dissemination of enlightenment ("Discurso dirigido a la Real Sociedad ... de Asturias, sobre los medios de promover la felicidad de aquel principado," Madrid, April 22, 1781, in *Obras* [BAE], II, 438-53, at 452). *Infra*, 348, on dispatch of the 1813 decree to Guatemala.

[83] Labra, *El instituto*, 272-73.

[84] García, *Datos bibliográficos*, No. 92.

[85] Labra, *El instituto*, 272, so describes the discourse.

and hounded its partisans. On the whole it may be said that both the opinion of the upper class and the passions of the masses supported him.

Ferdinand encouraged the Economic Societies to some extent, ordering new ones formed, the statutes and operation of all made uniform with the Madrid, and the Societies in provincial capitals to send deputations to reside in Madrid to serve their interests.[86] Evidently this was meant to apply to America as well as Spain.[87] But although the Madrid Society did some work in 1814-1821,[88] it confined itself to relatively innocuous charitable, educational, and cultural work, not picking up the controversial economic questions considered earlier.

So Ferdinand's reign (1814-1834) was a time of decay for the Societies.[89] In 1821 the Madrid Society was castigated for having accomplished little despite many projects and studies relative to the public prosperity.[90] Its sessions stopped entirely in 1823, and did not resume for ten years.[91]

After the liberal failure of 1820-1823 it became ever clearer to liberals that direct political action was necessary, and they moved far beyond the position of the Economic Societies. By 1855 a former Director of Public Instruction could write that Spain needed a completely secularized educational system.[92] This would dispose of most of the educational function of the Societies, which could not hope to compete with the State. The other functions of the Societies also were to be handled in new ways in the nineteenth century. So, although the Societies took on renewed vigor for a time

---

[86] *Decretos Fernando VII*, t. II, 410-13, decree of June 9, 1815.

[87] *Infra*, 196, for response of Havana Society to this decree.

[88] In 1815 it persuaded the government to found chairs of agriculture at several places (García, *Datos bibliográficos*, No. 102), and itself inaugurated a chair in 1820 (*ibid.*, No. 113); but the government of those years did little else for economic education (Gil de Zárate, *Instrucción pública*, III, 318). It got teaching of deaf-mutes started again in 1814, but, lacking funds, accomplished little (*ibid.*, III, 348, *et seq.*). It promoted teaching of shorthand, as it had earlier (García, *Datos bibliográficos*, No. 98); picked up its interest in beggars (*ibid.*, No. 99); the ladies were again at work with their charity for girls (*infra*, 93); it added an interest in music and the printing of music (García, *Datos bibliográficos*, No. 100).

[89] Labra, *El instituto*, 271 *et seq.*, calls the period 1775-1814 in the history of the Societies "that of initiatory acts, enthusiasm, great successes, and splendors."

[90] García, *Datos bibliográficos*, No. 124: *Impulso patriótico a la Sociedad de Amigos del País* (Madrid, 1821; 15 pp.); Garcia calls it a "Philippic."

[91] García, *Datos bibliográficos*, No. 134: *Memoria de las tareas de la Sociedad ... desde 1823 en que suspendió sus sesiones hasta ... 1833 en que fué reinstalada* (Madrid, 1835). Madrid Society membership (resident and corresponding) declined to 265 in 1821, to 206 in 1835, to 192 in 1839 (*ibid.*, Nos. 121, 135, 155). The Society of S. Cristóval de la Laguna, founded with enthusiasm in 1777, was dead by 1820 (Millares Torres, *Historia Canarias*, 423).

[92] Gil de Zárate, *Instrucción pública*, I, 116.

in the mid-nineteenth century,[93] it did not last long, and they have dwindled in importance to the present day.[94]

Methods of the Spanish Societies

The chief methods of the Societies were: discussions, preparation of papers, public meetings, publications, establishment of schools and classes of instruction, and advice to government. They gave many prizes—for essays, and for drawing, spinning, and other physical performances.[95] They collected models of implements and mechanical equipment, and books on political economy.[96] They divided the members into classes, those at Madrid being agriculture, arts and crafts, and industry.[97]

The Societies did little to develop connections with other institutions, or with each other. There were some unorganized relationships,[98] but what

---

[93] García, *Datos bibliográficos*, No. 250, shows the Madrid Society with 381 resident members, 113 Spanish corresponding members, and 21 foreign members, in the year 1863. Cf. "Sociedades Económicas," Havana *Memorias 1844*, that 18 were founded in 1836-44.

[94] Labra, *El instituto*, 317, and that most Societies were (early in the 20th century) in decadence, with other bodies performing their old functions; Fernando de los Ríos, *loc. cit.*, in the 1930's noted that the most important thing about the Societies by that time was their records. Cf. "Sociedades Económicas," Havana *Memorias 1844*, that of the 110 founded in the European realms of Spain to 1844, 31 were extinct, including 27 that had been founded before 1792.

[95] Prizes included publication of winning essays, small sums of money, spinning wheels. The Madrid Society announced its contests in the *Gazeta*. The statutes of the S. Cristóval de la Laguna Society let foreigners into its prize contests, writing in Spanish, Latin, French, English, or Italian (*Estatutos*, tit. XIII). Cf. Valencia Society, *Instituciones económicas*, 149-88, for elaborate plan for prizes.

[96] Madrid, *Memorias*, I, xliii of "Discurso ... Antonio de Quadra ... 27 de Agosto de 1775," on care of the books and machines the Society would acquire; Valencia Society, *Real cedula*, tit. XVII, art. II, calling for collection of economic and political writers.

[97] Madrid *Memorias*, III, i of "Prólogo" at beginning of vol., on the utility of this division. The Valencia Society at first thought of 7 divisions: agriculture; arts and crafts; manufactures; patriotic schools; navigation and seamanship; commerce; and economy, condition, and improvement of the pueblos in particular (*Instituciones económicas*, No. 11, 17-128); but the statutes approved in 1785 called for only classes of agriculture, industry, and arts (*Real cedula*, tit. XIII, art. I).

[98] The Madrid Memorias of 1780-95 show little of this. The Valencia Society thought of corresponding with all the "commercial bodies" in the country, and applauded the good relations between the Basque Society and the Consulados of Bilbao and San Sebastián (*Instituciones económicas*, 77-78); it formed relations with the Royal Academy of the Three Noble Arts in Valencia (*ibid.*, xix); thought the Economic Societies should correspond with each other, in view of the beneficial

they needed was a method of pooling or centralizing information. The Madrid Society helped Sempere y Guarinos collect information for his description of the Societies,[99] but this literary work was of limited practical value.[100] The *Gazeta de Madrid* gave only limited information, mostly simple announcements, on some of the Societies. The Madrid Society did nothing about a proposal made to it in 1797 that extracts of the Memorias of all the Societies be published.[101] Similarly fruitless was the consideration the Society began to give in 1817 to a guide to all the Societies, with a history of each, a relation of each year's work, their educational and charitable institutions, the royal orders for each year touching the Societies, and other data.[102]

The methods outlined were those emphasized by Campomanes and in the statutes of the Madrid Society.[103] The chief results attainable by such methods were: (1) changes in the thought and knowledge of the small but powerful literate portion of the population; and (2) changes in legislation or in its implementation. The Societies had not the resources to educate more than a few, or for directly and immediately altering the economy. The methods of the Societies were thus well suited to their character and resources.

The Societies held regular private meetings of members, and occasional public concourses. The latter were primarily designed to stimulate interest in the general ideas of the Societies, being occasions for the reading of papers and announcement of prizes. The public meetings did, also, somewhat serve the interest in the collection of information. Even when the

---

results of this sort of communication abroad, as in France (*ibid.*, xliii-xliv); heard from and answered, in 1787, the Granada Society on the question of the Seminary of Nobles of Valencia (*Extracto de las actas de la Real Sociedad Económica de Amigos del País de Valencia del año 1786* [Valencia, 1788], 11); had a request from the Society of Motril for information on rice culture (*Extracto de las actas ... Sociedad ... de Valencia ... 1787, hasta ... 1791* [Valencia, 1792], 9); heard about Siberian flax from a Spaniard in Russia (*ibid.*, 63).

[99] It asked the Valencia Society for information on its foundation and work (*Extracto ... actas ... Sociedad ... Valencia ... 1785* [Valencia, 1797], 8).

[100] Years later, the Valencia Society, on request from Sempere y Guarinos, sent him copies of all its printed works for his periodically published *Biblioteca Económica Política* (Valencia *Junta pública 1801*, 17-18). Cf. for Valencia connection with Mallorca Society, Valencia *Junta pública 1799*, 42.

[101] García, *Datos bibliográficos*, No. 67.

[102] *Ibid.*, No. 101. Cf. "Sociedades Económicas," Havana *Memorias 1844*, for a suggestion in 1781 by the secretary of the Segovia Society that all the Societies meet for certain work, especially for the study of climatology, by means of provincial and local observatories run by Society members.

[103] Other methods included the library opened to the public by the director of the Xérez Society (Desdevises, *La Richesse*, 91). Cf. Sarrailh, *L'Espagne éclairée*, 255, insisting that the Societies were uniform in foundation, statutes, and work, but only citing the activities of the Zaragoza Society.

Madrid Society curtailed its publication, it continued to hold an annual public junta.

Publication included information on foundation of the Societies; summaries of their activities; their statutes, apt to be long and instruments of propaganda themselves; discourses by members; eulogies of deceased members; drawings of machines, plants, and minerals; notices on the progress of industry, agriculture, and teaching, in Spain and other countries. The Madrid Society was interested in publishing a periodical,[104] but did not do so before 1820.[105] The S. Cristóval de la Laguna Society did start one in this period. Under the auspices of the Mallorca Society the islands' first periodical was published from 1779 to 1808.[106] The Madrid Society prepared an edition (1818-1819) of Herrera's *Agricultura General* (1513), the first and classic work in Spanish dealing with rural economy; and interested itself in translation of some of the works of Count Rumford.

The published materials dealt mostly with economics or with beneficence, sometimes together. Some authors considered the effects of institutions, habits, and ideas upon economic practice; some the effect of ignorance on economic life, dealing as much with education as with economics. The material is notable for its emphasis on exactitude, the Madrid Memorias advising members not to fill volumes, but confine themselves to specific observations, the method of foreign academies, which often limited themselves to combating those errors and vulgarities which "have checked the progress of the arts and sciences." They were not to deal in sophisms, "monstrous paradoxes," and "vain questions"; but to state principles with clarity, observe "the historic progress of human knowledge," and to prefer the "analytical method to the syllogistic."[107] It is thus not surprising that statistics bulk large in some sections of the Madrid Memorias,[108] or that the members assigned to examine the ordinances of guilds should display such an appetite for detail.

An impressive quantity of publication was due to the Societies. The five

[104] *Memorias*, III, Memorias of Agricultura, "Noticia de las operaciones de la clase de agricultura en el segundo bienio ...," v., note, indicating that a plan for a periodical was considered excellent in 1778, but difficult of execution because the Society lacked the income to support it.

[105] Labra, *El instituto*, 268-69, n., mentions periodicals published by the Madrid Society, apparently later than 1820; García, *Datos bibliográficos*, lists none before 1821.

[106] Monbeig, "La Real Sociedad Económica," *loc. cit.*, 166.

[107] Madrid *Memorias*, I, "Discurso Preliminar."

[108] E. g., I, 129-34, folding tables on production and use of hemp in Valencia; II, Apéndice, No. XXXI, 124-222, "Relación de los pueblos que comprehenden las Provincias de Madrid, Toledo, Segovia, Avila, y Guadalajara con expresión de sus vecindarios," which is a mass of figures.

volumes of Madrid Memorias to 1795 contained over 2,700 large pages.[109] The Valencia Society, between 1777 and 1802 published at least 1,496 pages of material.[110] The Societies of Las Palmas and La Laguna imported presses into the Canary Islands, and the latter brought out the first periodical of the province.[111] Publications of the Societies often were listed in the *Gazeta de Madrid*, and might be noted therein by the educated of all Spain.[112] The publications of the Societies not only were numerous, but some of them were widely disseminated.[113]

Instruction, especially vocational, was an important part of the work of the Societies. Much of this was *educación popular*, techniques suitable to cottage industry, spinning above all.[114] The Societies seemed to have talked about providing other instruction; they did little. The Madrid Society certainly did little to 1820.[115]

The function of rendering advice to the government was set by statute of the Madrid Society. The possible frictions of such an arrangement were reduced by the fact that so many public officials were members of the Society. In its first years the Society was almost a research bureau for government, receiving many things from the Council of Castile for study. The most important response to a Council request was the Society's many years of examination of Spanish agrarian law: the final result was the *Ley Agraria* of Jovellanos, which recommended sweeping changes in legislation.[116] The Society also made for the government a broad study of guild organization, again recommending sweeping changes.[117] And government and Society cooperated to provide work for the poor and to train them for textile work, this resulting in creation of the Royal Gratuity Fund of the Society, financed by the government with sums that went far beyond anything the Society ever

---

[109] *Memorias*, I, vii-viii, royal cedula, December 18, 1777, granting the Society a ten-year exclusive right to publish its memorias; I, "Prólogo," on the arrangement of the *memorias*, and welcoming constructive criticism.

[110] The present writer has seen that much Valencia material.

[111] Millares Torres, *Historia Canarias*, 368, 394. The periodical appeared in 1785-89.

[112] E. g. *Gazeta* of February 13, 1789, that the Tudela Society presented the first tome of its memorias to the royal family.

[113] *Ibid.*, December 29, 1789, for announcement that a publication of the Society of Motril could be bought in Madrid, Málaga, Sevilla, and Granada.

[114] The Madrid Society's most impressive expenditures were for the four "patriotic schools" training women and girls to work flax, hemp, cotton, and wool. The Society spent more than 65 per cent of its funds on this purpose from 1775 to June, 1777 (*Memorias*, II, folding table preceding Memorias of Industria: treasurer's report).

[115] *Infra*, 84 *et seq.*, for the educational work of the Societies.

[116] *Infra*, 98-99.

[117] *Infra*, 105 *et seq.*

saw for any other purpose.[118] The Council presented the Society with many other materials, for study and reference.[119]

Presumably many of the other active Societies, if not all, had some interest in changes in legislation. The Valencia in 1777 observed that laws must change as conditions alter; but when this involved economic matters, the evidence often was poor. It was here that they saw an opportunity for the Society to help educate the government.[120] That advice might drift out of the technical into the political sphere is shown by the pressure exerted by the Society at Ciudad Rodrigo, together with prominent grain merchants at Madrid and Santander, to secure freedom to export grain when the markets of Extremadura and Old Castile-León were glutted.[121]

Membership of the Spanish Societies

The only requirements for membership were an interest in and capacity for the work; that is, a fair education. All men were equal within the Madrid Society, there being no precedence founded on social or official position outside the Society, and the order of members at meetings being that of their arrival. This was common with the other Societies.[122] These were, of course, upper class organizations, joined by "cabelleros of the first distinction,"[123] and not egalitarian simply because the Valencia Society approved the quality of membership in the Paris Society, where a peasant might sit next to a marshal.[124] Its commission on statutes noted that Campomanes

---

[118] *Infra*, 101 *et seq.*

[119] E. g., mines (Madrid *Memorias*, II, Artes y Oficios, No. VI); foreign agricultural treatises (*ibid.*, I, No. V, "Censura ... del Tratado traducido del Italiano ... sobre el cultivo de las viñas. ..."); models and plans of mills for grinding flour and plaster (*ibid.*, IV, Memoria of Oficios, "Informe ... sobre ... varios modelos ... 1778"; "Extracto de tres informes ... sobre las máquinas ... para moler yeso ..."; "Informe ... la máquina para moler trigo, y abatanar paños. ..."); and legislation on *comercio libre* for America, the prohibition of imports for the protection of Spanish industry, the printing and book business, and training for the crafts (*ibid.*, II, Apéndice, No. XXXII, 223-306, printing fifteen such decrees, cedulas, and orders).

[120] *Instituciones económicas*, 10-11; cf. Monbeig, "La Real Sociedad Económica," *loc. cit.*, 166, on privileges obtained by the Mallorca Society.

[121] Hamilton, *War and Prices in Spain 1651-1800*, 196, citing a document of the Archivo Histórico de Colombia, and the *Gazeta de Madrid* of March 7, 1783. Freedom to export had been cut off in 1769; it was restored after the above protest, in 1783.

[122] Bourgoing, *Nouveau voyage*, I, 271, that "a perfect equality is the most sacred law of all these societies," where an archbishop might find himself next to an artisan. The S. Cristóval de la Laguna Society prohibited precedence and personalities (*Estatutos*, tit. III, art. x-xi). In 1777 the archbishop declined a special seat at the Valencia Society (*Instituciones económicas*, v; Sempere, *Ensayo*, V, 224 n.). Cf. Sarrailh, *L'Espagne éclairée*, 225 n. 4, citing the statutes of the Zaragoza Society.

[123] Valencia Society, *Instituciones económicas*, liii.

[124] *Ibid.*, 22-23.

said "repeatedly that the Societies should be composed of caballeros, of ecclesiastics, and of well-to-do and wealthy subjects."[125] The censor of the Society divided the State into: (1) officials, the religious, and the military, composing the highest grade of authority, and entitled to the love and respect of the inferior individuals of civil society; (2) the nobility, the literary profession, the *Gente rica*, and all persons of talent in affairs, this class providing most of the recruits for the first; and (3) the citizens "who work corporally for the physical necessities of society, certainly worthy of the attention and zeal of the other classes who owe them their prosperity and convenience." He supposed that most of the members of the Economic Society belonged to the second class.[126] Floridablanca, who helped promote the Societies, was looking for useful action by the "best citizens," not for mass enthusiasm.[127]

The Societies provided several types of membership, of which the local resident and corresponding were perhaps most important.[128] The Societies divided the local members for working purposes.[129] These divisions worked separately, but the members of all came together regularly at Society juntas.

About a decade after creation of the Madrid Society, the question of admitting women arose. Count Cabarrús, bravely liberal on some questions, argued against it, and received a rough, and public, answer from a Madame Levacher de Valincourt of Paris, who declared that she would prepare her own little daughter to be a useful member of society and mother, by instructing her in botany, drawing, history, geography, and home medical remedies, but that she thought the girl could struggle through life without knowledge of

---

[125] *Ibid.*, 21.

[126] *Ibid.*, No. I (1-16), "Discurso ... por el ... Censor ... 1776."

[127] "Memorial presentado al rey," *loc. cit.*, 323, the Societies served to bring together "los primeros ciudadanos, ocupar el clero y la nobleza dignamente su tiempo y cuidados, y exitarse en todas las clases la emulación y el deseo de hacer algo bueno en servicio de la patria."

[128] The national interest of the Madrid Society appeared in its special treatment of members resident in the five cities aggregated to the Madrid Society to give range for its work in agriculture and silk and wool manufacture, and a type of membership for men residing anywhere in Spain who sent to Madrid information relating to the economy of their areas (Madrid *Memorias*, I, xxxix-xl; II, Apéndices, 307-18). Cf. Monbeig, "La Real sociedad Económica," *loc. cit.*, 171, that the members of the Mallorca Society were large landholders.

[129] The Madrid Society had the *clases* of agriculture, industry (including commerce), and arts and crafts; at various times before 1787 that of industry had 77 members, agriculture 45, and arts and crafts 43 (*Memorias*, III, Memorias of Industria, xvi-xviii; III, xv-xvi of Memorias of Agricultura; IV, Memorias Artes y Oficios, vii-viii). The Valencia Society had classes of agriculture, industry, and arts. The Segovia put members into divisions of manufactures, agriculture, and public instruction (*Actas y Memorias 1785*, 102).

military tactics.[130] Even before this letter was printed, Jovellanos favored admission of women with the requisite knowledge and interests, such as the daughter of the Count of Oñate, Doña María Isidra Guzmán y Lacerda, doctor of philosophy from Alcalá.[131] This lady and the wife of the Duke of Osuna were made members in 1786, and the former delivered an oration to the Society.[132]

Floridablanca soon definitively settled the question of lady members by writing from the court in August, 1787, that the king thought ladies could do useful work in promoting the virtue, education, and industry of their sex. The Society immediately admitted twenty-four more aristocratic ladies; and females of the royal family allowed their names to be enrolled. By 1794 the ladies had their own auxiliary, with separate statutes. They were at first chiefly concerned with vocational education for women. And they showed their fine interest in the objectives of the Society by determining to use no silken goods but those made in Spain.[133] After 1800, however, the ladies seem to have occupied themselves chiefly with direction of the royal asylum for foundlings.[134] The labors of the female members could scarcely become very important in Spain, since there were even fewer educated women than in France or England.[135] And as for the Madrid Society, we may suppose

---

[130] "Carta al Señor ... Cabarrús ... en respuesta al Discurso que pronunció en la Real Sociedad ... en Madrid, contra la admisión de las mugeres en las Sociedades literarias ...," reprinted from Paris in *Espíritu de los mejores diarios*, Nos. 73-77 (December 17, 20, 22, 24, 29, 1787).

[131] "Memoria leída en la Sociedad Económica de Madrid, sobre si se debian o no admitir en ella las señoras," in *Obras* (BAE), II, 54-56, without date, but presumed to be of 1786. The lady was a member of the Royal Academy of History and of the Basque Society.

[132] García, *Datos bibliográficos*, No. 26: *Oración ... que hizo a la Real Sociedad ... Señora Doña María ...* (Madrid, 1786). García says it is little more than a not very notable contrast between the backwardness of the 17th century and the advancement of the late 18th, and that the lady ought to have been able to do better.

[133] Madrid *Memorias*, IV, 364-76 of Apéndices; Sempere, *Ensayo*, V, 212-18; Lafuente, *Historia*, XIV, 317-19, including text of the Floridablanca letter; Sociedad económica matritense, *Catálogo de los libros que forman su biblioteca* (Madrid, 1870), 223, lists: *Estatutos de la Junta de Socias de Honor y Mérito de la Real Sociedad Económica* (Imprenta de Sancha, 1794). Cf. Labra, *El instituto*, 268, that the Junta de Damas was created in 1778, but giving no authority.

[134] García, *Datos bibliográficos*, No. 71, this work in 1801; No. 111, the same work in 1819. Cf. "Sociedades Económicas," in Havana *Memorias 1844*, that the ladies' *sección* of the Madrid Society was still in existence in 1844.

[135] Swinburne, *Travels*, II, 217, a harsh critic, found most ladies of the court unlearned and indifferent to learning; Addison, *Charles III*, 35, that the king's wife disliked Spain partly because she considered the women ignorant and their company insupportable.

that their activity—aside from benevolence—was much on the level of fashionable interest in milking at Versailles.[136]

Members of the Societies were mainly enlightened nobles, reformist ecclesiastics, and persons of the middle class imbued with the current philanthropism.[137] A striking number of public officials enrolled;[138] this was to be notable also of the overseas Societies. The Societies did attract intellectuals,[139] but they were not the dominant element. The S. Cristóval de la Laguna Society had more military than scholarly or academic members.[140] Each Society enrolled the bulk of its membership soon after foundation. There was no attempt in 1795-1808 to widen fundamentally the basis of membership.[141] A minority did most of the Society work, many men having joined merely because it was the fashion. This active minority included Campomanes,[142] though he was less active than Jovellanos in the work of the Societies. Jovellanos (1744-1811) turned from church to secular studies in part because of Pablo Olavide, an enlightened Peruvian living in Sevilla,

---

[136] *Infra*, 117, for the Countess of Montijo and the Society. Cf. Sarrailh, *L'Espagne éclairée*, 252-54, ladies connected with the Madrid and a few other Societies.

[137] Altamira, *Historia*, IV, 259; Menéndez y Pelayo, *Heterodoxos*, VI, 273-76.

[138] Madrid *Memorias*, IV, Apéndices, 364-76, for list of the 324 men admitted in 1775-86, including more public officials and fewer ecclesiastics than the present writer had expected. The Segovia Society, however, included all curates of the province (*Actas y Memorias 1785*, 415-24); and the Valencia emphasized the role of parish priests. The 36 founders of the Madrid included high public officials, merchants, academicians, architects, ecclesiastics, and the director of the Five Major Guilds of Madrid (*Memorias*, II, Apéndice, No. IV, 7-9). Later in 1775 the rolls included the Prince of Asturias and the two Infantes; various Councillors of Castile, the Indies, and War, including José de Gálvez, Minister of the Indies; numerous titled gentlemen; generals; merchants; an engineer; a sculptor; ecclesiastics, including the bishop of Nicaragua. By 1787 the list was longer, but the quality much the same.

[139] The eight members of the Madrid Society who made the additions to the Society's edition of Herrera's *General Agriculture* were all men of learning, five being teachers (*Agricultura general*, "Lista Alfabética" of the authors at beginning of each volume).

[140] *Estatutos*, 29-38, "Lista de los Socios. ..." Cf. Millares Torres, *Historia Canarias*, 367, the members of the Las Palmas Society were "las mas ricas, influyentes e ilustradas personalidades de la isla."

[141] Madrid had 36 members in June, 1775; 91 in September, 1775 (*Memorias*, unpaged "Advertencia" before Apéndice of t. II); 326 in 1780 (*ibid*., II, Apéndices to Artes y Oficios, 307-18; IV, Apéndice, 364-76); no change to 1787; 450 in 1795, but this was probably the peak (García, *Datos bibliográficos*, No. 52, catalogue of 1795; No. 121, catalogue of 1821 showed 265 members). The S. Cristóval de la Laguna Society had 83 in 1777, 111 in 1778, 122 in 1779 (*Estatutos*, 29-38). The Valencia Society had the same experience.

[142] Cf. "Elogio del excmo. señor Conde de Campomanes, leído en junta [of the Real Academia de la Historia] ... 1803 ...," in Campomanes, *Tratado de la Regalía de amortización* (reimpression of Gerona, 1821), at 31, noting Campomanes' aid to the Madrid Society.

at whose salon Jovellanos was encouraged to study science and otherwise broaden his knowledge. Olavide became an honorary member of the Basque Society in 1769; and soon thereafter sent the Society some wheeled plows.[143] Olavide was a man of enlightenment, but of poor judgment in practical affairs. In 1775 he was jailed as a heretic, atheist, and materialist who read prohibited books and corresponded with Voltaire and Rousseau.[144] Jovellanos was a civil official at Sevilla in 1775 when the Economic Society was formed there, and became one of its most energetic members.[145] Moving to Madrid in 1778, he became a member of the Society, its president in 1784. During his exile in the 1790's in Asturias he established the Royal Asturian Institute, and continued to work for the Economic Societies. Recalled by Godoy in 1797 to head the ministry of Grace and Justice, he was banished to Gijón after less than a year in office, perhaps because Godoy could not bear his elevated views.[146]

Another notable member of the Madrid Society was the Count of Cabarrús, native of Bayonne, but a naturalized Spaniard. His opinions on the obstacles which nature, opinion, and the law put in the way of public felicity were much like those of Jovellanos.[147] A link between Rousseau and the Spanish court,[148] Cabarrús was an important figure in the reign of Charles III. Another man of advanced views attracted to the Madrid Society was Juan Sempere y Guarinos (1754-1830), who won a Society contest on poverty. A learned magistrate much like Jovellanos and Campomanes, he was made

---

[143] Basque *Extractos 1771*, "Comisiones Primeras."

[144] Years before, Aranda had secured Olavide's appointment as superintendent of the colonization project in the Sierra Morena, and Olavide had enraged the Church by permitting no religious foundations and placing the schools under control of laymen with compulsory primary and vocational instruction. Aranda protected Olavide from the Inquisition in the 1760's; his imprisonment in 1775 came when Aranda was in France. Olavide escaped to France himself, only returning to Spain in 1798 (Lafuente, *Historia*, XIV, ch. x; Cándido Nocedal, "Discurso Preliminar," *loc. cit.*, viii; Spell, *Rousseau*, 55-56, that Olavide encouraged the Economic Societies). Cf. Basque *Extractos 1771*, "Comisiones Primeras," noting Olavide's attempt as head of the Sierra Morena project to plant Cuban cedars.

[145] Nocedal, "Discurso Preliminar," *loc. cit.*, viii *et seq.*

[146] So says Ticknor, *History of Spanish Literature*, III, 379 *et seq.* On the later troubles of Jovellanos and imprisonment on Majorca, see Spell, *Rousseau*, 164-65.

[147] "Cartas sobre los obstáculos que la naturaleza, la opinión y las leyes oponen a la felicidad pública; escritas por el Conde de Cabarrús al señor ... Jovellanos, y precedidas de otra al Príncipe de la Paz," in *Epistolario español* (2 vols., BAE, XIII, LXII), II, 551-602, written in the 1790's.

[148] Spell, *Rousseau*, 60. Menéndez y Pelayo, *Heterodoxos*, VI, 273-76, condemning him for accepting the "social pact" and opposing the hereditary nobility, for his friendship with Jovellanos; and finding his work "an arsenal of arguments ... for the patriots of Cadiz."

a *socio de mérito* in 1783.[149] He wrote extensively on subjects of interest to the Societies.[150] His *Ensayo* on writers of Charles III's time contained considerable information on the Economic Societies.

How many men belonged to Economic Societies? The Madrid had 450 enrolled in 1795; the Segovia, 116 in 1785; the S. Cristóval de la Laguna, 122 in 1779; the Las Palmas was founded by at least 65 at about the same time; the Valencia claimed over 300 in 1777, but listed only 206 in 1786; the Basque had some 400 members in 1773, and may have enrolled 1,000 between 1767 and 1793. There were sixty-odd Societies in 1803: some did little, some nothing at all. From the foregoing we may speculate that between 5,000 and 10,000 men may have belonged to an Economic Society in 1764-1821. Of course, some were enscribed on the rolls of more than one Society. Some members were honorary, some merely corresponding. We have noted that the working members of the Madrid Society in the early years came to about 150. Perhaps it would be safest to suppose that no more than 5,000 men belonged to Societies between 1767 and 1808. In any event, we are dealing with a few thousand men, and a very few women, as members, and even fewer as frequent participants, but with a considerably larger group more or less influenced by the labors of the Societies.[151]

Finances of the Spanish Societies

Though the free services of members somewhat reduced the need for income, the Societies were handicapped by their small financial resources. The dues of members was the only regular income common to all Societies.[152] The first treasurer of the Madrid Society supplemented the funds out of his own pocket, which may help explain his tenure of sixteen years.[153] We may be sure that dues collections were often slow. In any event the sum would not be great. In its first two years the Madrid Society collected some 50,000 *reales de vellón* in dues; this was hardly more than half the cost of founding and operating the four small spinning schools during the same period, even with

---

[149] Madrid *Memorias*, IV, Apéndice, 364-76.

[150] E. g., *Historia del lujo y de las leyes suntuarias de España* (2 vols., Madrid, 1788); *Biblioteca española de economía-política* (4 vols., Madrid, 1801-21); *Historia de los vínculos y mayorazgos* (Madrid, 1805).

[151] Cf. "Sociedades Económicas," Havana *Memorias 1844*, for an estimate that 2,000 men joined the Spanish Societies in the 18th century.

[152] The Segovia collected some 26,000 *reales vellón* in 1785, of which 25,000 came from the dues, and only 1,000 from donations (*Actas y Memorias 1785*), table between 410-11).

[153] García, *Datos bibliográficos*, No. 68, his eulogy, read in 1799.

the aid of some free rent and materials.[154] Gifts to the Societies came chiefly from the Crown and the ecclesiastical hierarchy. On royal order, the municipal councils gave some help: the Madrid and Valencia Societies had quarters in the municipal buildings.[155]

The Madrid Society got far more aid from the Crown than the others, which helped it accomplish more.[156] Its income of 151,000 *reales de vellón* in the two years to June, 1777, included at least 100,000 from essentially public funds. When the Society in 1778 opened a subscription for expansion of its spinning instruction, the Crown came to its aid with some 322,000 reals, for establishment of the *Monte Pío* to give work to the poor.[157] The capital of the *Monte Pío* rose from 350,000 reals in 1779-1780,[158] to some 588,000 as shown by the inventory of 1786.[159] From January, 1779, to June 30, 1780, alone, the cost of providing work for 1,576 persons came to over 155,000 reals.[160] This gives a fair notion of the limitations imposed on the Societies by the meagerness of their financial resources.[161]

---

[154] *Memorias*, II, treasurer's report, preceding Memorias of Industria.

[155] Madrid *Memorias*, II, Apéndices, Nos. X, XI, XII; Sempere, *Ensayo*, V, 179; García, *Datos bibliográficos*, No. 45; Valencia Society, *Instituciones económicas*, ii. The S. Cristóval de la Laguna Society proposed to raise money by selling its published annual *Actas* (*Estatutos*, tit. X).

[156] Bourgoing, *Nouveau voyage*, I, 269, 271, commented on this; cf. *Novísima Recop.*, Lib. VIII, tit. XXI, nota 3, and tit. XXIV, ley VIII, secs. 7-8, on concession of excise on wool to Economic Societies of Segovia and Soria, in 1782, to aid in the promotion of the textile industry.

[157] Madrid *Memorias*, IV, Apéndices, No. I.

[158] *Ibid.*, No. XXXVII, "Inventario de los efectos y utensilios del Monte Pío."

[159] *Ibid.*, No. XCIII.

[160] *Ibid.*, No. XXXVIII.

[161] Cf. "Sociedades Económicas," Havana *Memorias 1844*, for a calculation based on "unos apuntes económicos que tenemos a la vista," that the 68 European Societies in the 18th century spent over 1,500,000 reals—including government funds supplied them—on the promotion of factories, workshops, and schools; and that while the Societies had more members in the 19th century, they had less money.

CHAPTER FOUR

Ideas, Education, and the Problem of Poverty

The Societies did a poor job of defining their ideas themselves;[1] they were more interested in arousing discussion and stimulating action. Society members were interested in both theory and practice,[2] but seldom separated them carefully. Some of the essay contests of the Madrid Society encouraged theory, but the entries had a high factual and practical content.[3] The practical bias of the Societies is seen even in their seals.[4] Much material was printed on methods of carrying out specific economic operations.[5] The practical

---

[1] Valencia *Instituciones económicas*, xlv-xlix, the five principles of the Society: no jurisdiction, to study and recommend only; use anyone willing to work for its objectives; receive as members natives or foreigners domiciled in Spain; imitate the Dublin Society in printing useful materials; show preference for what pertained to *economía política*, and pursue whatever was for the public good.

[2] E. g., the Valencia Society thought it desirable to combine theoretical and practical studies of commerce, but tended to prefer the former, since "el estudio teórico del Comercio es de suyo muy noble, profundo, y de una amenidad, y extensión prodigiosa" (*Instituciones económicas*, 78).

[3] No doubt entries in a contest (1803) on bankruptcy could be both theoretical and practical (García, *Datos bibliograficos*, No. 77).

[4] That of S. Cristóval de la Laguna included a spinning wheel, painter's palette, drawing instruments, book, anchor, and a plow (*Estatutos*, frontispiece); Segovia showed similar instruments and indications of interest in industry and husbandry (*Actas y memorias, 1785*, seal on t.p.); Valencia included fishing and agricultural gear, overflowing cornucopia, and a ship under sail (*Instituciones económicas*, t.p.).

[5] Cf. Madrid *Memorias*, I, No. XI, 102-4, on use of thermometers in raising silk-worms; *ibid.*, No. IX, 68-98, on the results of the actual cultivation of flax and hemp; *ibid.*, No. XVII, 147-95, a factual account of the cultivation of white mulberry trees.

material in the Madrid Memorias includes statistics, and data on machinery, instruments, botany, and the details of husbandry and craftsmanship. Most of volume one deals with specific agricultural, pastoral, and legal problems, although there is also much petulant and unscientific complaint about the laborer's love of luxury and his use of mules instead of oxen; but this sort of matter is outweighed by complaints of legal abuses and poor methods of cultivation and the unfortunate effects of the wanderings of animals through unenclosed fields.[6]

Ideas in Society publications were derived from foreign and Spanish writings;[7] from knowledge of foreign academies and economic practices; from suggestions of the Council of Castile; from the experience of the members; and even from ancient and medieval history. The authors and editors of the Madrid Memorias very often referred to conditions and practices in England; somewhat less often to France, Switzerland, Denmark, Holland; less often to Russia, Germany, and Italy.

Ideas of the Spanish Societies

MATERIAL PROSPERITY

Wealth—material prosperity—was the pivotal concern of the Societies. This concern had more than one motivation, but to it almost all problems and efforts were related, usually intimately, seldom remotely. Most of the efforts of the Societies had a close relationship to economics. The 2,700 pages of the Madrid Memorias (1780-1795) contain but one small item without an obvious relationship to economic matters.[8] This Society early printed the view that in a State all should be happy, not just a small number possessing all the wealth; and that no one doubted that the Prince had the power to reduce excesses when they blocked this desired universal prosperity of his

---

The systems of cultivation of Tull and Duhamel were referred to especially often (e.g., *ibid.*, No. III, 29-48, "Memoria ... sobre el producto y los gastos de una labranza de 50 fanegas de trigo. ...").

[6] The *Actas y Memorias 1785* of the Segovia Society contain many statistics, some running back into the late 17th century. The *Extractos* (1785-91) of the Valencia Society contain much practical information and suggestion. Even Menéndez y Pelayo, *Heterodoxos*, VI, 265, wrote that the Societies were plainly useful, their usefulness being not speculative but practical; but he feared that this tended to degenerate into materialism and revolutionary change.

[7] So often referred to, that we note them only in connection with the fields of agriculture and industry, in the next chapter. Cf. Sarrailh, *L'Espagne éclairée*, 269-70, that in 1776 Campomanes applied in person to the Inquisition for permission for the Madrid Society to read prohibited books.

[8] T. II, Memorias Artes y Oficios, No. VIII, a report on a case of instruments and remedies for the succor of suffocated or drowned persons.

vassals.[9] The publications of the Societies and the opinions of the active members testify to an overwhelming concern with the conviction that the economy of Spain was decadent—and that was the word they used—and that the nation was not prosperous.

While it is true that the benevolent or philanthropic motive was strong in the Societies, it was usually much mixed with other motives. It was always prominent in the Madrid Society, growing after 1790 when the other work of the Society declined. The Valencia Society promised to show preference for what related to *economía política*, but it also called on the pious ladies (of the upper class) of Valencia to aid in the education of poor women in cottage industries,[10] and talked of "good customs" in such terms as to suggest that there was some thought that Christian ethics would improve production, desirable both for reduction of beggary and idleness and for the provision of more income to the government coffers, augmentation of population, filling the ranks of the army, and providing hands for field and craft.[11] It believed that "the fundament of common prosperity consists in good Christian and civil customs, among which one very necessary is application to honest work," and proposed giving prizes to people for honesty, modesty, obedience to betters, and application to work.[12] The Sevilla Society in 1789 heard a cleric say of education: "Unfortunate the State in which men neither find work, or what is worse, their work does not produce what is necessary to live. . . ."[13] This is a good example of the difficulty of separating motives, beliefs, desires, and effects in connection with the work of the Societies. It matters little whether the cleric's opinion was purely religious in motivation; some of his auditors would have other motives, and all would have to act in the economic realm to improve economic conditions.

The Madrid Society—and no doubt the others—followed Campomanes in minimizing bullionism,[14] defining wealth as production and the exchange of goods by way of improved transport. True wealth for Jovellanos lay in the quantity and value of products, this value being natural or artificial, for raw materials or added by refinement.[15] This involved de-emphasis of foreign

---

[9] Madrid *Memorias*, I, No. XVI, 139-46, "Extracto de la memoria ..., sobre los arrendamientos de tierras."

[10] *Instituciones económicas*, 57-62.

[11] *Ibid.*, 9-10.

[12] *Ibid.*, No. VI. But the Society's volumes entitled *Extracto de Actas* for 1785, 1786, and 1787-91 are filled with unambiguously practical economic material.

[13] *Espíritu de los mejores diarios*, No. 216 (January 18, 1790).

[14] Cf. Carrera Pujal, *Economía española*, I, 98, that eighteenth-century economists in combating earlier notions as to the importance of bullion were guilty of exaggeration themselves.

[15] "Discurso dirigido a la Real Sociedad de Asturias," *loc. cit.*, 433.

trade; the first concern was for interior commerce, which put products into circulation.[16] The Madrid Society emphasized the belief in production in an essay on commerce with the Indies, pointing out that foreigners knew how to look after "true wealth, which consists in the fruits, primary materials, and manufactures, for whose purchase gold and silver are necessary."[17] Of course, a Society at a port city, as Valencia, had a specialized interest in foreign commerce. And the Madrid Society studied *comercio libre*. Still, the main emphasis of the Societies was on production in Spain.

REASONS FOR INTEREST IN WEALTH

The first reason for the interest in wealth was a concern for the national strength and the income of the State.[18] This was aggravated by the under-standing that England, France, and even Holland, were outdistancing Spain in the race for material strength.[19] Nor had England's wealth reduced her martial vigor.[20]

The second reason was concern for the income of individuals as related to the social consequences of poverty, to what was commonly called the decay of "good customs." This motive was doubtless predominant with many individuals, as the friar who looked for useful plants near his convent because of a desire to help reduce idleness, "so opposed to Christian maxims."[21] The question of whether the moral interest was more important than the material in the Societies was not answered by the Madrid Society. When it discussed the question of the "Necessity of establishing the Society of Madrid as a school of economic science,"[22] it said the most ancient writers treated economic matters right after moral and political. This put the Society on the side of the angels, whereupon it proceeded directly to discussion of the great obligation of not neglecting "public necessities or of promoting the common prosperity of the nation." The fact is that while there was reference in the Memorias to moral questions, most of the talk was about means of

---

[16] *Ibid.*, 449.

[17] *Memorias*, III, Memorias of Industria, 262-81, "Memoria que d. Miguel Gijón escribía para la Real Sociedad ... 7 de marzo de 1778," at 271.

[18] Cf. Madrid *Memorias*, I, iii-v, dedication before the "Prólogo," for comment on "the prosperity of the nation."

[19] Cf. *ibid.*, I, "Prólogo" to No. 1, "Noticia del nuevo instrumento para sembrar ...," for comment on the great recovery of English agriculture since 1689.

[20] *Ibid.*, II, Memorias of Industria, No. IV. Cf. *ibid.*, III, Memorias of Industria, 175-77, in the *piezas justificativas* of the preceding memorial on the poor, for the establishment by Christian VI of Denmark of a Council of Commerce and General Economy to examine the whole question of the wealth of a State. The Societies were doing that, in part, in Spain.

[21] *Ibid.*, I, No. XV, 135-39.

[22] Section heading in *ibid.*, I, xv-xix, "Discurso Preliminar."

promoting material prosperity. The members may have preferred moral to material progress, but they seemed bent on achieving the latter—perhaps in order to attain the former.

The third reason for interest in wealth was a prejudice in favor of "progress," which operated together with the notion that the decay of the Spanish economy was correctable. Some members may not have been entirely conscious of this prejudice in favor of progress, but such men as Jovellanos were. We can no more weigh the importance of this factor than estimate the quantitative effect of the Madrid Society's dictum that owners of great estates were obliged to study *las materias económicas* because the *pacto social* required them to look after their holdings properly and to "contribute with their knowledge to the common good."[23]

OPTIMISM ON ECONOMIC IMPROVEMENT

Optimism was strong in the Societies, some coming from the Enlightenment in general, much of it directly from Campomanes' works. There were three reasons for thinking it possible to improve Spain's economy.[24] First, it was argued that it needed only a combination of better laws, and improved educational facilities, together with a general effort to relate them to material prosperity in the modern age. This confidence stemmed from the rationalism of the day—and from common sense. Secondly, the Societies were much affected by the notion that Spain once had been more prosperous,[25] combined with the assumption that conditions were sufficiently unchanged so that this guaranteed recovery of that prosperity if only proper efforts were made. This uncritical appeal to a golden economic age could be linked, furthermore, with the golden age of Spain as a great Power. Thirdly, the Societies felt some optimism on the grounds that Spain had economic advantages, both in peninsular resources and in those of the Indies.

MEANS OF ECONOMIC IMPROVEMENT

Most important were demands for: (1) specific, accurate, detailed information on the economy of Spain; (2) study of the principles of political economy; (3) improvement of economic techniques; (4) improvement of all phases of the economy; (5) expansion and better use of the labor force; (6) government action; (7) exclusion of foreign goods.

---

[23] *Memorias*, I, xxii of "Análisis del sistema y establecimiento de la Sociedad."

[24] The evidence for these three sources of optimism is overwhelming in the Madrid Memorias and the Valencia Society publications.

[25] Society publications are full of this idea: e.g., Valencia Society, *Instituciones económicas*, 62-69, the commissioners drawing the Society statutes, noted that manufactures had decayed.

(1) The thirst for information was asserted in Society statutes and in the discussions of political economy, and was demonstrated by the mass of factual —often statistical—information in the records. The Madrid Society demanded that the analytical method be followed,[26] strongly demanded exact information,[27] opposed hyberbolical and impertinent language,[28] and printed masses of statistics.[29]

(2-3) The interest in the study of political economy flowed naturally from the belief that Spain could be prosperous if only the problem were attacked correctly. The current notion of political-economic study did not clearly distinguish between what would today be considered economic theory on the one hand and the techniques of production and the statistics of output on the other. Members studied political economy individually, discussed it at meetings, and established courses in the subject. In 1784, with royal permission, the Aragonese Society opened the first course in political economy given in Spain.[30] The study was promoted by the government in its insistence that the Madrid Society examine legislation.[31] The interest no doubt also came from the prejudice in favor of study generally.[32] In any case, Campomanes had recommended the study in his discourses on popular industry, and the statutes of the Madrid Society had taken up the cry. Since these two documents were influential in the foundation of all the Societies, it is not to be wondered that the statutes of the S. Cristóval de la Laguna recommended that books on political economy be collected, and read and discussed by the members when they lacked other business.[33]

---

[26] *Memorias*, I, xiii of "Discurso Preliminar."

[27] *Ibid.*, II, Memorias of Industria, No. VII, Campomanes to the Society, 1776. An essay on wheat, well-larded with statistics, could go into the crops planted, the cost of labor, the value of the product, getting down to the cost of a pair of mules and a *mozo* (*ibid.*, I, No. III, "Memoria ... Sarmiento, sobre ... trigo").

[28] *Ibid.*, I, 376-83, "Memoria ... Pedro de Campomanes. ..."

[29] E. g., 100 pages of figures on the towns of the five provinces aggregated to the Madrid Society, supplied by the *Contaduría de Propios y Arbitrios del Reyno*, with the objective, the Society said, of building up exact information on the population, crops, and manufactures, and hoping that the rest of Spain would collect exact data in this fashion (*ibid.*, II, Apéndice, No. XXXI). Antonio Regás of the Madrid Society wanted, in 1814, to set up a system of correspondence to collect information on agriculture in the province of Madrid (García, *Datos bibliográficos*, No. 90).

[30] *Supra*, 57, for contemporary criticism of this course. Cf. Sarrailh, *L'Espagne éclairée*, 272, on the interest of the Palma Society in the *Lessons in Civil Economy* of the Italian Genovesi.

[31] Cf. Sempere, *Ensayo*, V, 139-40, for comment on this.

[32] Cf. García, *Datos bibliográficos*, No. 41, a discourse on the importance of the "natural and exact sciences" to political economy, by Martín Fernández de Navarrete on his admission to the Madrid Society in 1791.

[33] *Estatutos*, tit. XI.

The Madrid Society lamented, late in the reign of Charles III, that in Spain it was generally thought that knowledge of manufactures and commerce was only for its practitioners, whereas in England and Holland it had long been understood that statesmen and even persons of the *primera gerarquia* ought to pay attention to such matters.[34] Jovellanos advised the Asturias Society in 1781 what works on political economy to read, but also pointed out that the country must be known before the Society could do useful work, so recommended that a topographic description be compiled.[35]

The demand for better production techniques led to the formation of schools and classes, importation of instruments and machines, and study of production methods.

(4) The emphasis upon "universal economy" was fundamental to the theoretical basis of the Societies, though the term itself was little used. This idea that agriculture, industry, and commerce all should be promoted, had been advanced by Spanish political economists for years.[36] Part of it was the doctrine that the three elements of the economy were interrelated, that no one could be sound without the concurrent soundness of the others. Agriculture provided raw materials for industry, while commerce provided markets for both the others.[37]

(5) This belief in the use of the whole economic potential of the nation extended to an insistence on the honorable nature of labor, and a condemnation of idleness, not only as conducive to vicious habits but as detrimental to production.[38] Further, all elements of the population, including women and children, were needed as part of the laboring force,[39] and it must be augmented by planned increase of the population.[40] The size of the popula-

---

[34] Madrid *Memorias*, II, Memorias of Industria, No. IV.

[35] "Discurso dirigido a la Sociedad de Asturias," *loc. cit.*, 439-40, 442, recommending the available translations of the works on commerce of Condillac and Cantillon; the work of the Marquis of Mirabeau, some of which had been printed by a member of the Basque Society; the published extracts and memorials of the Madrid, Sevilla, and Basque Societies; and the Spanish writers Ulloa, Navarrete, Moncada, Argumos, Ustáriz, Santa Cruz, Alvarez Osorio, Martínez de la Mata, Ward, and Campomanes.

[36] Campomanes emphasized it: e.g., *Apéndice a la educación popular*, Segunda Parte, "Discurso Preliminar sobre las fábricas," iii *et seq.*

[37] Valencia Society, *Instituciones económicas*, 84, that commerce has an "intimate union" with manufacturing, that one cannot subsist without the other; *ibid.*, 92-93, that commerce, agriculture, industry affect each other.

[38] *Infra*, 88 *et seq.*, for discussion of poverty, labor, and idleness.

[39] Madrid *Memorias*, I, x.

[40] *Ibid.*, I, ii-iii of Prólogo; Jovellanos, "Discurso dirigido a la Sociedad de Asturias," *loc. cit.*, 443.

tion had been a favorite topic of Spanish political economists for years,[41] and the Societies took up the subject with enthusiasm. One man found that the abundance of ancient Spain came from its large population, that depopulation was the origin of the decadence of Spanish agriculture, and that farming could not be successfully developed just by means of instruments and costly machines.[42] Another writer ascribed depopulation to lack of affection for matrimony, voluntary separation, the rights of widows in entailed estates, the large number of these estates, laziness, bad habits, improperly treated contagious disease, and to the bad division of the land.[43]

The Madrid Society deplored that part of the Spanish tradition which made it difficult to accept the belief that labor was honorable; and it also argued that all sorts of labor were equally honorable, that none was vile. In 1782 the Society was told that tanning could be promoted among the peasants of Galicia if the occupation were not unjustly looked down upon. A part of the argument was that only the king could deal with such a "pernicious illusion," and that English prosperity was in part due to the absence of this illusion, and the willingness of men of the upper classes to be connected with economic activity. The Society recommended the thesis to the king, as a result of which a cedula, March 13, 1783, declared that the occupations of tanner, smith, tailor, shoemaker, and others of a similar sort, were both honorable and honest; and that the position of such persons and their families was not to be prejudiced by such labor.[44] The Valencia Society wished to promote economic activity among all classes, advocating harder manual labor for the third order of society,[45] and suggesting that the nobility engage in such economically useful activity as the study of political economy or

---

[41] Cf. Robert S. Smith, "Maltusianismo Español del Siglo XVII: El *Arcano de Príncipes* de Vicente Montano," *El Trimestre Económico*, XXII, No. 3 (July-September, 1955), 350-85.

[42] *Ibid.*, I, 322-33. He put the Spanish population at 20 million in the time of Ferdinand the Catholic.

[43] *Ibid.*, I, 288-321, an essay by a canon of the cathedral of Tarazona. Another essay ascribed depopulation to the wars with the Moors within Spain, and to the expulsion of the Jews and people of Muslim stock (*ibid.*, 333-37). The problem of sparse population is often alluded to in discussions of other matters in the records of the Madrid and Valencia Societies.

[44] *Ibid.*, IV, Memorias of Artes y Oficios, "Memoria anónima baxo el nombre de Don Antonio Filántropo, sobre el modo de fomentar entre los labradores de Galicia las fábricas de curtidos ...;" Ferrer del Río, *Carlos III en España*, IV, 69-70, and f.n. on 70-72; Ortiz, *Hija cubana*, 59-61, for text of cedula and discussion in connection with condition of Cuban peasant at the end of the 18th century. A prize of 1,000 reales, offered in 1784 by a member of the Madrid Society for "application to useful and honest labor," was won by a tailor (García, *Datos bibliográficos*, No. 19).

[45] *Instituciones económicas*, No. VI, Asuntos I-III, all demanding application to work.

participation in commerce.[46] It will be noted that the concern with the honorable nature of labor was linked with the view that much of the idleness and vagabondage plaguing Spain was the result of laziness as well as of lack of opportunity.

(6) The action of the Madrid Society with regard to labor illustrates its role as adviser to government, and its conviction that government action was essential to economic improvement. The call for government action was tied to support of the removal of restrictions on the economy. This laissez-faire attitude was expressed in recommendation of abolition of the restrictive features of the guild organization.[47] It was expressed in an impressive mass of opinion in the Madrid *Memorias* for the alteration of legal practices restrictive of agricultural production, on the ground that studies of soil, climate, methods of work, and the like, would be of little avail if the laws themselves needed changing.[48] This material was reworked by Jovellanos into the great *Informe* of the Society to the Council of Castile on the agrarian law, published in the Memorias of 1795.[49] A paper in 1778 on the liberty of commerce for South America just conceded by the king, gave the same view, finding that the ignorant and the interested opposed free trade, which should be enjoyed by all (that is, in the Spanish system). It declared that an examination of the facts put the matter beyond argument, and that the cry that had gone up a few years earlier when the internal grain trade was freed was indicative of the opposition to such measures.[50] The Valencia Society publications carried much less than the Madrid on the necessity of government action. Probably no Spanish Society approached the daring of the Madrid in advocating changes in legislation; certainly the American Societies did not.

(7) The Societies hoped to reduce importation of foreign goods by increasing Spanish production. This was implicit in most of their discussions of industry and crafts. Foreign workers might be imported, but the objective was invigoration of Spanish industry.[51] Valencia favored the laws against foreign wares, but found these wares plaguing the city, drawing money from Spain, and driving craftsmen out of work.[52] The fact was, of course, that Spain could not get along without foreign goods.[53]

---

[46] *Ibid.*, 72-73, 78-79, *et passim.*

[47] *Ibid.*, I, xxv *et seq. Infra*, 104 *et seq.*, for a full discussion.

[48] Cf. *ibid.*, III, iii-iv of "Prólogo," for a good discussion of this.

[49] *Infra*, 98.

[50] *Ibid.*, III, Memorias of Industria, 282-94, "Discurso sobre la libertad de comercio ... por don Francisco Cabarrús. ..."

[51] Valencia Society, *Instituciones económicas*, 68, favoring imitation of the French and English policy of permitting foreigners in domestic manufacturing.

[52] *Ibid.*, 86, 97, 147-48, *et passim.*

[53] *Infra*, 117, for recognition of this by the Countess of Montijo.

EMPHASIS ON LOCAL PROBLEMS

The Societies emphasized their own local or regional problems, as Campomanes had intended. The Madrid Society was an exception in its interest in Spain as a whole; but most of its studies dealt with limited localities and subjects. The activities of the other Societies were strongly colored by the local economy. The Crown ordered the S. Cristóval and Las Palmas Societies to attend to local plants and fisheries.[54] The Valencia Society was interested in navigation and a commercial company to serve as an outlet for local manufactures;[55] the Sevilla in improved navigation;[56] the Mallorca in commerce and commercial companies.[57]

The Societies gave little attention to America, in this following Campomanes' works on popular industry and education. The statutes of the Spanish Societies showed no concern for America. The Madrid Society paid little attention to America in its Memorias, and that little only incidentally,[58] in connection with the supply of raw materials for Spanish industry or the like. The Madrid Society's edition of Herrera's *General Agriculture* remained a treatise on Spain, containing much less on America than a creole might have hoped in this twenty-eighth edition. A creole might be interested in the methods and ideas of the Spanish Societies, but they did not deal with most of his problems.

The Spanish Societies and Education

The schools and classes of the Societies constituted their most important effort to improve techniques and increase production. This was almost the only interest in education shown in the Madrid Memorias of 1775-1795; probably the same was true of the other Societies, since they were founded on the basis of the *Industria popular* of Campomanes and the statutes of the Madrid Society, both of which recommended education aimed at improvement of the economy. This was the clear intent of educational activity in the early years, despite allusions to the superior importance of the moral

---

[54] S. Cristóval *Estatutos*, 27; Millares Torres, *Historia Canarias*, 367.

[55] Sempere, *Ensayo*, VI, 224-26; *Instituciones económicas*, xxxiii, 195-206.

[56] Sempere, *Ensayo*, VI, 20-22.

[57] José de Jaudenes y Nebot, *Sobre la excelencia y utilidades del comercio, y las que pueden resultar a Mallorca del establecimiento de una Compañía, Discurso ... de la Real Sociedad Mallorquina ... 30 de Julio de 1797 ...* (Palma: Imprenta real, 1798), asserting that all nations have found companies the best way of promoting commerce, and discussing the history of commerce, finding the United States a "nación toda commerciante." Jaudenes was a member of the Philadelphia Society.

[58] An exception was the *comercio libre* of 1778.

ends to be attained by such work.[59] The extent of their accomplishments is a moot question.[60] In the course of time the interest of the Societies became more generalized, and more afflicted with a philanthropic rather than an economic intent.

The educational efforts of the Societies had two aspects: that of enlightening the upper classes, and that of improving the techniques and encouraging the industry of the masses. This dual role Jovellanos stated to the Asturias Society, advising it to found a school for the nobility like the Seminary of Vergara, where the "useful" sciences would be emphasized; and to pursue *educación popular*, setting up "patriotic schools" for the people.[61] The Sevilla Society received much the same advice from another source in 1789. The Sevillans heard that education for some classes must be designed to promote their enlightenment; but for others it must be vocational, meaning especially *educación popular* for artisans. Also, that education was useless without improved economic conditions, and that the lack of popular education in Spain was such that only the government could correct the situation, a fact which the Economic Societies ought to keep pressing upon it. Furthermore, *educación popular* would give only a "momentary and apparent progress, without National education; for it is impossible to accomplish the education of one class without developing with equal measures that of the others." Finally, the nations of Europe which led in industry and commerce also led in the sciences and *conocimientos útiles*.[62] Some Societies did not have— or heed—such counsel; their discussions of popular education were often unrealistic.

The term "patriotic school" suggests the concern for the economic life of the entire nation, and the voluntary, nonprofit, unofficial character of the

---

[59] Cf. for such an allusion, Jovellanos, "Discurso pronunciado en la Sociedad Económica en 16 de julio de 1795, con motivo de la distribución de premios de hilados," in *Obras* (BAE), II, 32. Ballesteros, *Historia*, VI, 145, that the Madrid Society favored technical schools; Labra, *El instituto*, 267, that the Societies' educational work was the "origin" of the later schools of arts and crafts and of industrial engineering.

[60] Altamira, *Historia*, IV, 320-21, called them "a vast network of establishments, whose persistence ought to have resulted in great accomplishments." Gil de Zárate, *Instrucción pública*, III, 314 *et seq.*, that the general value of the Societies as a stimulant was more important than their schools; that of their educational work the most important was that for industry and the crafts, the necessity for which was little understood in Spain till the end of the 18th century, apprenticeship being thought enough.

[61] "Discurso dirigido a la Sociedad de Asturias," *loc. cit.*, 452.

[62] *Espíritu de los mejores diarios*, No. 216 (January 18, 1790), "Sevilla. Discurso sobre la educación, leído en la Real Sociedad Patriótica ... en la Junta General ... por el Doctor Joseph Isidoro Morales, Presbítero."

training offered. Instruction in spinning, mathematics, and drawing or draughtsmanship were the most common. Classes in reading and writing were at least discussed. The largest single educational effort of the Madrid Society in 1775-1795, in the form of organized classes, was in connection with spinning and clothmaking, chiefly the former. The purpose of this work was partly economic, to improve techniques, and partly beneficent, to provide work for the poor—mainly girls and women—so as to enable them to maintain good habits.[63]

The Madrid Society heard from its director on "patriotic schools of practical machinery," meaning on the one hand schools teaching how to make instruments needed for common tasks—as flax combs, spinning wheels, looms—and on the other more numerous schools teaching the use of those instruments. The director lamented that the term "*mecánica* is poorly understood in our ordinary language."[64] The Madrid Society heard a project for teaching arithmetic, reading, and writing to artisans;[65] gave prizes for drawing and geometry;[66] and heard a suggestion that the bad state of the mechanical arts might be improved by the development of clockmaking.[67]

The Valencia Society showed interest in draughtsmanship.[68] The Las Palmas Society opened a school of drawing late in the eighteenth century.[69] The Segovia Society proposed the teaching of primary letters.[70] The Sevilla Society provided instruction in primary letters and mathematics early in its history;[71] and Sevilla may have established spinning schools before Jovellanos

---

[63] *Infra*, 101 *et seq.*, for the spinning schools.

[64] *Memorias*, II, Memorias of Industria, No. I, 1-14, "Memoria ... sobre Escuelas patrióticas de Maquinería práctica," Junta of September 3, 1775. He explained it by quoting from an English book dealing with machines, mechanics, geometry, and movement. The director thought one instrument-making school in Madrid would be enough, drawing pupils from the five places aggregated to the Madrid Society, from each Madrid parish, and from each guild of artisans. The records do not show that the school was established.

[65] *Ibid.*, IV, Memoria of Oficios, "Prospecto de un curso ...," in 1777.

[66] *Ibid.*, Apéndices, 268-71, in 1779.

[67] *Ibid.*, IV, Memorias of Oficios, "Memoria de ... Felipe y d. Pedro Charost ... maestros reloxeros ..."; "Reflexiones ... sobre la memoria de los señores ... Charost ..."; in 1782.

[68] *Instituciones económicas*, xix, 13-14, 45-46, and Número VI, Asunto VI, "Dibujo para las Artes." Cf. Floridablanca, "Memorial presentado al rey," 322, that the Societies had established many schools of drawing.

[69] Millares Torres, *Historia Canarias*, 394.

[70] *Actas y Memorias 1785*, 43-44, 131 *et seq.*, 138 *et seq.* Cf. Sarrailh, *L'Espagne éclairée*, 266, that the Societies of Palma, Valladolid, and Vera also were interested in primary letters.

[71] "Prospecto y Plan de una Clase de Humanidades que Establece la Real Sociedad Económica de Sevilla," in Méndez Bejarano, *Afrancesados*, 117-32, Apéndice II to Libro Primero; Godoy, *Cuenta dada*, IV, 63.

left the city in 1778.[72] The Mallorca Society in the 1780's established schools of engraving, mathematics, primary letters, and an Academy of Political Science.[73] The Aragonese or Zaragoza Society in the 1790's supported instruction in agriculture, botany, chemistry, mathematics, millinery, and the making of artificial flowers.[74] The Zamora and Xerez Societies established schools.[75] The Valladolid Society taught mathematics and civil and agricultural economy early in the nineteenth century, before the French invasion.[76] The Valencia Society in its publication of 1777 talked of the need for various sorts of instruction, and claimed to have instituted cooperation with the Royal Academy of the Three Noble Arts in the city, for the promotion of drawing, noting that the Academy was too small to provide it for all the craftsmen of Valencia. The Society also wished to teach women and girls the techniques of simple cottage industry.[77]

The Madrid Society's interest in the education of deaf-mutes, and in shorthand, seem to date from 1801-1802.[78] The Royal College of Deaf-mutes, run by the Society, opened in 1805.[74] The Society in 1803 opened a Pestalozzian school at Madrid, under direction of an army captain of Swiss origin, José Döbley, who had been using the method of Pestalozzi with the children of soldiers of a Swiss regiment at Tarragona. The results so pleased the Society that it sent Döbley to revise the methods of its school at Santander, and he opened a normal class there in 1805.[80] The government set up a Pestalozzian school at Madrid in 1806, but Godoy had it closed in January, 1808, on the grounds that some parents objected to it. News of the Pestalozzi enthusiasm appeared in periodicals, and was reprinted as far distant as Havana. The Economic Society of Havana sent someone to Spain to study the method.[81]

The Sevilla Society, shortly before the French invasion of 1808, proposed to establish a class in humanities, feeling that in a populous city a Society

---

[72] Nocedal, "Discurso Preliminar," viii-ix, calling them "escuelas patrióticas de hilazas"; Labra, *El instituto*, 311, that in its early years the Sevilla founded "escuelas gratuítas de hilazas y tinturas."

[73] Sempere, *Ensayo*, VI, 27; Monbeig, "La Real Sociedad Económica," *loc. cit.*, 165, 167, 169.

[74] Desdevises, *La Richesse*, 90, citing *Diario de Zaragoza*; Sarrailh, *L'Espagne éclairée*, 263-66.

[75] Desdevises, *La Richesse*, 90-91.

[76] Godoy, *Cuenta dada*, IV, 63.

[77] *Instituciones económicas*, 43-46, 57-62, 149-88, *et passim*.

[78] Gil de Zárate, *Instrucción pública*, III, 348 *et seq.*, 355; García, *Datos bibliográficos*, Nos. 98, 103, on the Real Escuela de Taquigrafía.

[79] *Ibid.*, Nos. 80-83, 86-87, 105-6, on the college, its curriculum, and the work in Madrid of the Parisian, Rouyer.

[80] Spell, *Rousseau*, 182.

[81] *Ibid.*, 183-84. *Infra*, 194, on the Havana venture.

could do little for agriculture, but should do something for what it called the big city "rabble," "the dregs of humanity," who were vicious because of their poverty, miserable because of their idleness, and condemned to both "by the luxury of the wealthy." This situation could not be corrected "by a junta of men with no other power than their beneficent desires." The poor would have to remain in their current condition, or get a better education. The plan went on to try to demonstrate the necessity of studying the fine arts and languages as well as the sciences. Students in the two-year course in humanities were to learn the "general precepts of poetics and oratory"; receive lessons in ancient geography and mythology; and be exempted from a knowledge of Latin, since so many translations from that tongue into French were available.[82] It is hard to believe that the "rabble" of Sevilla could be influenced much by such an effort.

The educational work of the Societies perished in the wars of liberation after 1808; nothing remained when Ferdinand VII came to the throne in 1814, and the latter took little interest in economic education.[83] In any event, only work accomplished or suggestions made before 1808 could have had importance for America.

The Problem of Poverty

The Societies were interested in poor relief, considering poverty a social and an economic problem, as did the government, while also concerned about the police problems arising from widespread vagrancy. Of course, countries other than Spain were plagued by the problem. England had many miserable poor, and those—including John Locke—who considered the problem tended to think in terms of half-right generalities and platitudes, combining a moiety of Christian beneficence with a modicum of under-standing of economic realities. In France the situation worsened in the eighteenth century, especially in rural areas, where vagrants robbed and pillaged, and idleness contributed to misery and to poor moral conditions. Neither the noble proprietors nor the ecclesiastical tithe-owners of France

---

[82] "Prospecto y Plan de Una Clase de Humanidades," *loc. cit.*; cf. Méndez Bejarano, *Historia de la filosofía en España* (Madrid, 1926), 344, for general information on the educational activity of the Sevilla Society.

[83] Gil de Zárate, *Instrucción pública*, III, 314-19, for this judgment, and that at the end of the war the only industrial education in Spain was in Barcelona; and Ferdinand did no more than establish six chairs of theoretical practical agriculture under the direction of Economic Societies. Cf. García, *Datos bibliográficos*, Nos. 102, 110, 113, 115, on the chairs of political economy, that of Madrid being inaugurated in 1820.

were notably philanthropic. And the State's alms-stations, workhouses, hospitals, orphanages, and kitchens for the poor were but feeble palliatives.[84]

Early in the eighteenth century clerics of San Vincente de Paúl founded *casas de misericordia* in Barcelona and Mallorca. A priest established the *Monte de Piedad* of Madrid in 1702; it was soon taken up by the Crown. In mid-century even more was done, including formation of maternity houses, refuges for the needy, and orphanages. An ordinance of 1749 was designed to put vagabonds not serviceable as soldiers or labor into houses of mercy.[85] Bernardo Ward in mid-century opined that indiscriminate almsgiving made the poor more of a problem in Catholic than in Protestant countries. He favored strict enforcement of the laws against vagabondage and begging, separation of the true poor from the lazy, and creation of workhouses on the model of those he had inspected abroad for the Spanish government.[86] These ideas of a favorite author of the Societies summarize their opinions on the poor. How far these ideas had penetrated may be indicated by the opinion of Floridablanca that the wrong sort of charity impeded the work of the Economic Societies, meaning that personal almsgiving ought to be abandoned. He noted that some church groups had set up the right sort of poorhouses, separating the true poor from the lazy, and making them work, thus avoiding the evils flowing from the giving of daily alms.[87]

In 1778 the Crown ordered vagabonds to return to their place of birth or to the capital of their bishopric to be taken care of; those of Madrid were to be put in hospices.[88] But this and subsequent measures had little effect, and the census of 1797 showed the continuing inadequacy of care for the poor.[89] Beggars, estimated by Campomanes at 140,000 men, women, and children, were not reduced markedly in the reign of Charles III; nor was beneficence made more effective by the decree of 1798 making use of the funds of public beneficent institutions to satisfy the debts of the State.[90]

---

[84] Sée, *Economic and Social Conditions in France*, 42-43, 46-48, and ch. xi, "Poverty and Its Relief."

[85] Ballesteros, *Historia*, VI, 210-11.

[86] *Proyecto económico*, Parte I, ch. xix, and suggesting financing the workhouses with lotteries in Spain and America.

[87] "Memorial presentado al rey," *loc. cit.*, 323, 325.

[88] Ballesteros, *Historia*, VI, 210-11; and cf. *ibid.*, 213, for later efforts.

[89] With a population of 10,541,221, Spain had 2,262 hospitals for the sick, with 13,507 patients; and 101 hospices, with 727 employees, and giving asylum to 11,796 of the helpless poor (Canga Argüelles, *Diccionario*, "Hospicios," "Estadística").

[90] Ballesteros, *Historia*, VI, 213, would concede some success to the ministers of Charles III, but offers no statistics. Cf. Desdevises, *La Société*, ch. v, sec. v, "Le Jeu, la Mendicité, la Débauche."

Probably many Societies did something for the poor, since Campomanes recommended it. The Valencia Society in 1777 stated that persons of "our condition" (of the upper class) could help the other classes through the Society by promoting good Christian and civil customs, which would result in an end to idleness and beggary. Beggars were said to swarm in Valencia, many being healthy men and women of all ages, and children of both sexes, and "many of these with the title of students, when they scarcely know how to read." These, "raised in this bad school . . . will be voluntary idlers, and true delinquents all their lives."[91] In 1771 when so many silk manufactories shut down in Valencia, some 1,600 families had been thrown into poverty, and the community had experienced considerable difficulty seeing them through.[92] Some towns had too many fiestas, taking men from work. *Monte píos* might be erected to aid peasants, but the main aid should be *industria popular*.[93] But *monte píos* might aid fishermen, and work in connection with hospices and *Casas de Misericordia*.[94]

The director of the Madrid Society told a junta that beggars should be put in hospices and reduced to some sort of authority; that there was no hope of stopping begging and vagabondage so long as it paid better than "laborious application"; and that the success of this sort of effort depended on all sources of alms being turned into it, and on enforcement of the laws against begging. Too much money was wasted on such superfluities as fiestas, *cofradías*, and alms. Curates and *alcaldes de barrio* should aid in educating the poor for popular industry.[95] Many women in the city were unemployed; perhaps 25,000 of them were employable. In the director's view the spinning of flax offered an answer to the problem of easing the poverty of Madrid families.[96] The Society's division of industry noted in 1778 that Ward had called men the most precious resource of monarchies, if made use of; but that idle

---

[91] *Instituciones económicas*, 9-10.
[92] *Ibid.*, 87-88.
[93] *Ibid.*, 34-35, 40-42.
[94] *Ibid.*, 117, 120-22. The Segovia Society noted proposals for a hospice (*Actas y Memorias 1785*, 45-47, 109 *et seq.*, 117 *et seq.*). The Zaragoza and Tarazona Societies did something before 1808 (Ballesteros, *Historia*, VI, 216: Colmeiro, *Economía política*, II, ch. liii, 17-42; Sarrailh, *L'Espagne éclairée*, 262, citing Zaragoza Society *Memorias 1789*). The Sevilla in 1789 heard that "to seek to augment the population . . . other . . . than [by] increasing the means of subsistence, is to believe that the number of men is increased when it is only the number of the miserable" (*Espíritu de los mejores diarios*, No. 216 [January 18, 1790]). The Tudela Society founded a hospice (Sarrailh, *L'Espagne éclairée*, 262, citing Tudela Society *Memorias 1787*). Cf. Colmeiro, *Economía política*, 41-42, n. 2, on the Tarazona Society and beggary.
[95] Madrid *Memorias*, II, Memorias of Industria, No. I.
[96] *Ibid.*, No. II. He offered figures as to the possible quantity and value of their production.

hands were worse than useless since the State had to support them and their bad habits corrupted others.[97] The editors of the Madrid Memorias found it unfortunate there were fewer members of the division of industry than of agriculture, since the former should be providing "ocupación honesta y útil" for the women and girls of Madrid, especially by spinning yarn on wheels.[98]

The Council of Castile suggested that all the Economic Societies examine the problem of the poor, bearing in mind Ward's views.[99] In response to this, in 1778 a commission of the Madrid Society reported that attempts to control begging extended back to the time of Charles V, that current conditions did not permit a good solution, which lay in improvement of the economy. Government *hospicios* and *Casas de Misericordia* were poor devices, because women were not trained properly in them, the collection of poor in hospices diminished the population since the inmates did not marry, and the development of skills could be achieved in hospices only by a miracle. New hospices, with machines and instruments, would be costly. Hospices in provincial capitals were satisfactory, if confined to people too old to work. But separate houses of correction were needed for those who were idle by choice.

The report asserted, further, that reason and experience showed that reward and punishment governed men's actions, and that the former was the more appealing. By the most moderate calculation, two million persons were completely idle because of lack of *industria;* they would not need to produce much income to equal the value of all the goods imported into Spain. Suggestions for action included a discount bank; more Economic Societies; and a change in the guild organization, to improve the lot of apprentices, and to provide funds for crises affecting the masters and their families, and to cut down the monopoly of the guilds, which "have waged a cruel and destructive war" against consumers. Finally, more manufactories were needed, but they were impeded by taxes, by the exclusive privileges of certain companies, by the entrance of foreign goods, and by use of the *palmeo* in the commerce of the Indies, for this aided the fine goods of foreigners since they were less bulky than the rougher Spanish products which suffered from this bulk tax.[100]

---

[97] *Ibid.*, III, Memorias of Industria, 184-203.

[98] I, x of "Prólogo."

[99] Sempere, *Ensayo*, V, 203-5; Lafuente, *Historia*, XV, 22. The Madrid and Murcia Societies, responses to this order were published at Madrid in 1781 (García, *Datos bibliográficos*, No. 59).

[100] *Memorias*, III, Memorias of Industria, "Memoria sobre el recogimiento y ocupación de los pobres ... leída ... 1778." This forty-three-page report was

In 1781 Juan Sempere y Guarinos received a prize from the Madrid Society, in competition with more than thirty authors, on the subject of mendicancy and the poor. Working upon a basis of sacred literature, the saints, canon law, and Spanish legislation, he concluded that the poor were not those without money, but those who refused to work. He felt that all attempts to end mendicity failed because of false notions of the virtues, and especially objected to popular notions of piety and beneficence as contained in the maxim favoring blind contributions: "To give properly without looking to whom." He opposed giving mass aid to the poor in *Casas de Misericordia*, suggesting they be given work instead. Sempere's essay, and a number of others, were published by the Society.[101]

The Madrid Society early discovered that the poor were too numerous for it to take care of. The Council, taking note of this, provided funds for making yarns of flax, hemp, wool, and cotton. This was the origin of the Pious Fund, set up in the Royal Poorhouse of Madrid under direction of the Society.[102] Beginning with a capital of 350,000 reals in January, 1779, by 1786 the fund's capital was some 588,000.[103] No Society could finance such an operation with its own funds. The *Monte Pío* was devoted to training in work connected with textile making. From the beginning of operations on January 19, 1779, to June 30, 1780, a total of 1,576 persons was given work.[104] Fewer were involved in subsequent years, with only 808 receiving work in 1786, the last.[105] Most of the people involved were women, some were girls; only a few men were served. A good share of the funds went for materials rather than for payment to the students. Five thousand seems a fair estimate of the total number served in the eight-year period 1779-1786. In 1786 the editors of the Memorias noted that the Society deserved credit for working hard with a project plagued by difficulties such as short funds, the unskillfulness of the operators, high wages in Madrid, the uncertainty

---

accompanied by 140 pages of *piezas justificativas* (*ibid.*, 44-183), dealing mostly with the manufacture of textiles, and with the importation of foreign stuffs. This material was linked to the problem of poverty by its location, but the material itself is concrete, statistical, and intends to be nothing but utilitarian—i.e., deals with economics, not philanthropy.

[101] Sociedad económica matritense, *Colección de las memorias premiadas. ... Tratan del excercicio de la caridad y socorro de los verdaderos pobres, corección de los ociosos, destierro de la mendicidad voluntario, y fomento de la industria y aplicación* (Madrid: La Imprenta real, 1784), "Asunto Primero," 1 *et seq.*, for Sempere's essay. Cf. Sempere, *Ensayo*, V, 200-204; Ferrer del Río, *Carlos III en España*, IV, 64-67, and note on 67-68; Carrera Pujal, *Economía española*, IV, 24 *et seq.*, on the Societies and poor relief.

[102] *Memorias*, IV, Apéndices, "Advertencia."

[103] *Ibid.*, Nos. I, XXXVII, XCIII.

[104] *Ibid.*, No. XXXVIII.

[105] *Ibid.*, Nos. LIX, LXI, XCIII, XCV.

of the price of raw materials bought for the *Monte Pío* and of the finished goods sold, and the continuous and laborious effort of dealing with small quantities of materials.[106]

The beneficent work of the ladies' junta of the Madrid Society[107] looms the larger in the later years because the typical work of 1775-1795 had by then been drastically reduced. It supervised the Royal Asylum for Foundlings, which had 1,020 children at the end of 1800,[108] continuing this work to the end of our period.[109] Another philanthropic effort of the Madrid Society was in connection with the "economic meals" (*comidas económicas*) of Count Rumford. The Society translated and published some of his works. For a short time early in the nineteenth century the Society distributed meals according to Rumford's plan.[110] The Valencia Society also tried this plan.[111]

---

[106] *Ibid.*, "Advertencia" to the Apéndice. The *Monte Pío* was presumably the "hospice" observed in the early 1780's by the Dane, Daniel Gotthilf Moldenhawer, who called it a workhouse of "les petits mendiants et petites mendiantes, de jeunes garçons et de jeunes filles." He said the usual term of "detention" was three months, after which inmates were sent out of the Madrid district (quoted in Gigas, "Voyageur," *loc. cit.*, 415-16).

[107] *Supra*, 70.

[108] García, *Datos bibliográficos*, No. 71. During 1800, 1,137 had been admitted, and 936 had died. Over 100 subscribers contributed nearly 60,000 reals to the asylum in 1801 (*ibid.*, No. 72).

[109] *Ibid.*, Nos. 78-79, 111, 120, showing 1,198 foundlings at the end of 1819, while during 1820 1,080 entered and 834 died.

[110] *Ibid.*, No. 69; *Ensayos políticos, económicos y filosóficos del Conde de Rumford, traducidos de órden de la Real Sociedad Económica ...,* t. I, 375 pp., Madrid, 1800, t. II, 491 pp., 1801; No. 75: *Reglamento que se ha de observar en la distribución de las comidas económicas á la Rumford*; No. 88: *Aviso al público* (1807 ?), on suspension of distribution of the meals by the Society at the end of the winter season.

[111] Cf. Valencia *Junta pública ... 1800*, 48 et seq., "Socorro de Mendigo," discussion of Rumford's ideas, and tables of amounts and costs of salt, flour, etc., used in making "Sopa económica."

CHAPTER FIVE

Branches of the Economy

Agriculture

The Societies considered agriculture the richest source of wealth, but related its prosperity to that of industry and commerce, believing the nation should promote all three.[1] This was one reason for their strong interest in industrial crops.[2] Agriculture was considered decadent, but since it had been prosperous in the past, and the climate had not changed, why should it not bloom as before?[3] This decadence they hoped to correct was ascribed to bad techniques and to hindrances due to law and custom. These things were correctable.[4] Their correction required the application of art to the agrarian industry, and the perfection of this art required investigation and the application of

---

[1] Cf. Madrid *Memorias*, I, No. XVI, and many other places in the volume. Sarrailh, *L'Espagne éclairée*, 257-59, insists on the Physiocratic emphasis of the Societies on agriculture, but does little to analyze their activity, and less to relate it to their interest in industry. Monbeig, "La Real Sociedad Económica," *loc. cit.*, 163, that the appearance of the Economic Societies in Spain was connected with the introduction of Physiocratic ideas after 1750.

[2] Cf. Madrid *Memorias*, I, 110-34, a report from Valencia on hemp cultivation, with tables showing production costs and the value of products in various parts of Spain, and drawings of instruments and methods.

[3] *Ibid.*, I, xxv of editorial summary "De la Clase de Agricultura."

[4] Cf. Jovellanos, "Discurso dirigido a la Sociedad de Asturias," *loc. cit.*, 446, combating the vulgar notion that cultivation could not be improved.

the latest methods, including those of foreign origin.[5] The history of the Hebrews, Greeks, Romans, Chinese, and Carthaginians showed the need of agricultural science.[6] So they needed investigation, statistics, experiment, study, and science for the physical aspects of agriculture.[7] The Madrid Society proposed that the Council of Castile direct justices and parish priests of villages of the Madrid district to answer a questionnaire on agriculture drawn up by the Society.[8] From one source and another the Madrid Society collected considerable information.[9] It printed suggestions for "patriotic schools" to teach peasants "the theoretical art of agriculture";[10] a book of instructions for peasants, explaining the latest methods and instruments;[11] and farm schools (*escuelas de labranza*), at least in the capitals of provinces, to teach, among other things, "intensive cultivation."[12]

All the obstacles to agriculture noted by the Societies had been perceived in the seventeenth century and earlier in the eighteenth.[13] The novel factors were the vigorous campaign by the Societies against these obstacles, and the government's support of their efforts. Of course this Spanish effort was not unique. There was unhappiness in France that English agriculture was more progressive, and the government, under the influence of economists, tried to correct the situation, partly by promoting societies. The agricultural society founded by the Estates of Brittany in 1757 was often referred to in the publications of the Spanish Societies.[14]

Many of the Madrid Society's views on agriculture were summed up in

---

[5] Madrid *Memorias*, I, iii of "Prólogo," xiii *et seq.*, *et passim*. The authors of the Madrid Memorias referred often to progress in other parts of Europe, especially France and England.

[6] *Ibid.*, I, xxiii-xiv of editorial essay "De la Clase de Agricultura." Cf. Valencia *Instituciones económicas*, 12, in 1776 advocating study of the science of agriculture.

[7] Madrid *Memorias*, I, xxx, of editorial summary on agriculture.

[8] *Ibid.*, I, "Noticia ... de ... la clase de agricultura," unnumbered pp. between "Discurso Preliminar" and Memorias of Agricultura, in junta, April, 1776.

[9] Cf. *ibid.*, I, No. X, an essay carrying the passion for classification and description to the length of 39 types of land in Extremadura alone, from *tierras inútiles*, to *tierras negras* (good for vegetables), to *tierras valdías* of villages, a mixed classification.

[10] *Ibid.*, I, 345.

[11] *Ibid.*, I, 251.

[12] *Ibid.*, I, 352-54. As late as 1807 the Economic Society of Valladolid obtained from the king a royal park for establishment of "a practical school of agriculture" (Desdevises, *La Richesse*, 34).

[13] Colmeiro, *Historia economía política*, II, 110.

[14] Cf. Sée, *Economic and Social Conditions in France*, 29-33. An attempt was made, starting in 1761, to establish an agricultural society in each generality of France; but they had little effect, and on the eve of the Revolution most of the work of agricultural reform remained to be done.

an essay contest of 1776 on the improvement of agriculture.[15] The essays tended to agree on many points, perhaps partly due to editing. All but one essayist thought farmers needed more knowledge; that one simply wanted them to work more. The main repeated themes were: the decadence of agriculture; need for more population;[16] intensive as opposed to extensive agriculture, ascribing wasteful methods to the use of mules rather than oxen,[17] and to large landowners for leaving too much land idle, imposing unfair rents, not residing on the land, and lacking interest in agriculture; effective reform—giving the farmer land nearer his house, more or different animals, better rents, better crops—required government action, and also required knowledge and investigation; the latter included foreign writings,[18] an interest in all sorts of details of economic activity from butter to fertilizer,[19] in artificial meadows and forage crops,[20] in plowing and plows and clod-

---

[15] *Memorias*, I, 197-287, prints the winner and another; 288-350, extracts from four more; 350-56, summaries of six more; 357-66, summarizes two ineligible essays. The problem was: "Quales son los medios de fomentar sólidamente la agricultura en un país, sin deterioro de la cría de ganados, y el modo de remover los obstáculos que puedan impedirla."

[16] *Ibid.*, 288-321, 322-33, for two essays that relate agricultural depression to the sparse population, find peasants idle and poor, advocate popular industry for rural cottages.

[17] *Ibid.*, 338-50, that "this modern practice is a species of the most prejudicial vanity: it is . . . a luxury introduced among peasants for their destruction"; that this destroyed peasant ambition; that they even competed for possession of the best mules; oxen were cheaper initially, cheaper to maintain, and useful for meat; their use would encourage more intensive agriculture, since the fast pace of mules encouraged inefficient extensive cultivation; most prosperous farmers in Spain had small plots and a very few animals. *Ibid.*, 333-37, advocating more draft animals, but oxen, not mules. *Ibid.*, 352-54. *Ibid.*, V, "Memorias sobre las ventajas ... de bueyes o mulas ...," harking back to Feijóo's consideration of the question, and finding the speed of mules an advantage when so many peasants lived far from their land, but in the end considering them so undesirable that they should be taxed out of existence.

[18] The English agricultural writer Jethro Tull and the Frenchman Duhamel appeared especially often in the Madrid *Memorias* (e.g., I, No. III). The editors advised use of the *Gazetas* of agriculture and commerce published in Paris (I, unumbd. pp. between "Discurso Preliminar" and Memorias of Agricultura, entitled "Noticia resumida de ... la clase de agricultura").

[19] *Ibid.*, I and II are especially rich in practical details on such matters as wheat, barley, flax, hemp, sesame, herbs, gums and resins, sainfoin or forage plant, mulberry trees, olives, grapes; threshing devices, sowers, harrows; thermometers for silkworm production; cultivation of unwatered land, and the relationship between pasturage and tillage; land leases, tithes, oxen and mules. Cf. I, 22-25, a good example of the practical interest, a memorial of 1776 by a regidor of Toledo on "el modo de sacar el aceyte a costal"; or I, 147-95, a long "Memoria ... sobre el cultivo de moreras ...," being simply technical and economic, designed, as the author says, to help peasants, expand Spanish manufacturing, and increase the royal revenues.

[20] Cf. *ibid.*, III, Memorias of Agricultura, "Memorias sobre los prados artificiales ... 1778"; *ibid.*, "Memoria sobre los prados ... Juan Pablo Canals ... 1778,"

breakers,[21] in a planting drill,[22] better communications,[23] weights and measures,[24] and new crops and plants.[25]

Presumably all the Societies had some interest in agriculture, both because of its importance in Spain, and because Campomanes emphasized it; but the interest must have varied according to the economic interests of the areas. The Valencia Society showed more interest in commerce and industry than in agriculture, and most of its interest in agriculture related to the notion of supplementing peasant income by promoting cottage industry.[26]

The Madrid Memorias often complained—explicity and implicity—of the "political" abuses of agriculture. All writers seem to have agreed on the abuses of concentrated land ownership by private proprietors, by the Church, and uncultivated town lands, since in all three cases much land lay unused.[27] There was strong sentiment in favor of agriculture as against stockraising as practised under the *Mesta* system. Contestants in the Society's first essay contest (on aiding agriculture without hurting stockraising) seemed to think that stockraising would not be damaged by enclosures, and the reduction of stockraising to small-scale enterprise in combination with farming.[28] Complaint was made that *hacendados* lived in town, paying little attention

---

noting work by the Society of Brittany. It is not clear whether the members understood that little of this was actually done in France (cf. Sée, p. 30).

[21] Several authors in the Madrid *Memorias* advocated deeper plowing. Cf. *Memorias*, I, 48-51, for description and illustration of a clodbreaker consisting of two rollers; *ibid.*, III, Memorias of Agricultura, "Descripción del arado inglés. ..."

[22] *Ibid.*, I, 1-25, on the seed drill of the 17th century Carinthian, Josef Lucatelo, designed to plant seeds at the proper depth and with adequate and even distances between each other and between the rows. Illustrated. Lucatelo got royal privilege to manufacture and sell it in Spain. The English, especially Tull, approved Lucatelo's ideas, and the latter assertedly founded his system on the Carinthian's.

[23] *Ibid.*, I, 288-321.

[24] *Ibid.*, V, "Memoria sobre si convendría o no la venta de los granos a peso, y no a medida. ..."

[25] *Ibid.*, I, 104-7, on pipirigallo or sainfoin; I, 108-10, on "la planta anthoxantum," edible by stock; V, "Disertación sobre la planta de sésamo. ..."

[26] Most of the Society's prizes were proposed for industry, commerce, and fishing (*Instituciones económicas*, No. VI, 149-88).

[27] III, Memorias of Agricultura, "Extracto ... Josef Cecilia Coello ... 1778," for enclosure of lands and confinement of use to owners and cultivators, and prohibition of common pasturage; *ibid.*, V, "Memoria sobre arreglar la legislación para conseguir el cómodo precio de los granos, sin perjudicar la libertad de los propietarios ... 1795," for the subdivision of land, and combating entail and mortmain; *ibid.*, I, 288-321, by a canon of the cathedral of Tarazona, against the bad division of land; *ibid.*, I, 333-37, that many lands in *mayorazgos* and *capellanías* were not cultivated; *ibid.*, I, 358-66.

[28] Madrid *Memorias*, I, 355-56, a cleric's view that the separation of agriculture and stockraising had ruined farming; I, 358-66, another view, attributing the decadence of agriculture to the lack of hedges, to keep stock from cultivated fields.

to agriculture, whereas people might be more influenced by a good example on their part than by the activities of literary societies.[29] One solution for inflated land rents was for the government to require proprietors to offer equitable contracts, since the proprietors mistook their true interest in lower prices rather than in higher rents.[30]

Twenty years after the foundation of the Madrid Society, the agricultural problem was summarized by Jovellanos in the name of a Society committee.[31] This was the famous *Report of the Economic Society . . . to the Council of Castile on the . . . Agrarian Law*, printed in 1795 in the Madrid *Memorias* (V) and numerous times thereafter, one of the greatest works produced by the eighteenth-century revisionists in Spain.[32] The work examined the influence of laws upon agriculture and recommended that they be altered where they hindered production. Hindrances were divided into three classes: (1) those that were political or derived from legislation, as uncultivated public lands, the rural holdings of municipalities, or the *Mesta;* (2) those derived from opinion, some being due to the government and some to the agriculturalists themselves, and the cure being instruction for both proprietors and peasants; and (3) those of a physical origin, or derived from nature, involving such topics as aridity, poor communications, and faulty ports. If carried out, the recommendations of this report would have revolutionized not only the agriculture but the social arrangements and the government of Spain. The Inquisition condemned Jovellanos' views on mortmain, and urged condemnation of the *Ley Agraria* both because it was inimical to the interests of the Church and because it might awaken people to the idea of equality in property rights. Although the Council of Castile decided in favor of Jovellanos in 1797, he had many troubles in succeeding years because of his liberal ideas,

---

[29] *Ibid.,* I, 354-55.

[30] *Ibid.,* I, No. XVI, "Extracto de la memoria ... sobre los arrendamientos. ..." The censor of the Valencia Society noted that most cultivators in that province were renters and in miserable condition (*Instituciones económicas,* 12).

[31] Madrid *Memorias,* III, Memorias of Agricultura, v-vii, the class of agriculture, September, 1777, named 7 members to examine the mass of data in the "informe sobre el expediente de ley agraria" which the Council had received from the intendants, *corregidores,* and various justices of the provinces of Castilla, Andalucía, and Extremadura. The 7 members examined the material during the rest of 1777, 1778, and till April, 1779. Jovellanos was not one of the 7, though he was assigned to the class of agriculture at the time. Cf. Sarrailh, *L'Espagne éclairée,* 277 *et seq.*

[32] *Informe de la Sociedad Económica de esta corte al Real y supremo consejo de Castilla en el expediente de ley agraria, extendido por su individuo de número el Sr. D. Gaspar Melchor de Jovellanos, á nombre de la Junta encargada de su formación, y con arreglo á sus opiniones.* The 149 pages of the *Informe* in *Memorias,* V, comprise more than half the volume.

as we have seen.[33] We have seen also that the radicals of Cadiz in 1808-1814 approved much of the report on the agrarian law, but accomplished none of its objectives. Nor was the problem solved during the next century and a half.

Industrial Interests

INDUSTRY, ARTS AND CRAFTS

The Societies found industry in as parlous case as agriculture. The Madrid and Valencia Societies were shocked to find so few craftsmen in their cities, certain crafts absent entirely, and total ignorance of some sorts of fabrication.[34] The Madrid Society thought Spain must accept the importance of industry to the economy, and must free it of some restrictions.[35] It was claimed that the need of Spain for more *fábricas* was impeded by taxes, monopolistic privilege, foreign goods, and the *palmeo* which deprived Spanish industry of what ought to be an advantage in traffic with America.[36] The Madrid Society found the textile industry in that area handicapped by the lack of materials for making thread, and suggested means of promoting cultivation of flax and hemp.[37] The Valencia Society in 1777 found difficulties to include: small-scale enterprise, the need of considerable capital in such industries as silk, and poor transportation; and it decided to concern itself with the flow of raw materials to factories.[38]

Probably all the Societies frowned on imports. The Madrid editors ascribed much of the decadence of the crafts to excessive importation contrary to law, and recorded that the Society had recommended to the government that it be stopped.[39] Somewhat related to the objection to foreign goods was the hope of using American raw materials in Spanish industry. This ancient

[33] *Supra*, 58-59; Helman, "Some Consequences of the *Ley Agraria*," *loc. cit*.. for an excellent account, based on good documentation—including Inquisition records—of Jovellanos' troubles in connection with the *Ley Agraria*.

[34] Madrid *Memorias*, I, xxxv-xxxvi, "De la Clase de Oficios," noting that this resulted in importation of goods they wished the poor of Madrid might make; Valencia *Instituciones económicas*, 62, 66.

[35] This appeared in the work on the guild ordinances (*infra*, 106, 108); also in the Society's dubiety regarding the desire of the town council of Oviedo to discriminate against goods made outside the town, and against artisans moving there (Madrid *Memorias*, II, Memorias of Artes y Oficios, No. IV).

[36] *Ibid.*, III, Memorias of Industria, "Memoria sobre ... los pobres ... 20 de marzo de 1778."

[37] *Ibid.*, unmbd. pp. at beginning of t. II, "Noticia ... de ... la clase de industria."

[38] *Instituciones económicas*, 84, 99, 106.

[39] Madrid *Memorias*, II, Memorias of Artes y Oficios, unmbd. pp. at beginning, "Noticia resumida. ..." Cf. Valencia *Instituciones económicas*, No. V, that imports were deleterious to the local economy.

plank of the mercantilist platform had not been properly supporting the economy of the Spanish world. The Madrid Society found that the cotton usually used in Cataluñan cloth manufacture came from the Levant; the region had used Spanish American cotton, but the Levantine price was better.[40] This did not prevent the Society from printing an assertion that Spain could get cheap cotton from America, which would give the former an advantage in cotton manufacture.[41]

It was recognized that industrial advances abroad were leaving Spain behind. Since England at the end of the seventeenth century had opened her eyes to her true interest and improved her economy, Spain should do as much, and understand as well as England and Holland that the most important persons in the nation must devote attention to manufactures and commerce.[42] Distinguished Englishmen, even "Lordes," did not disdain to be listed as members of London guilds in order to be able to aspire to the lord mayoralty; King William was listed with the clothiers, and one of his predecessors with the grovers. The Spanish sovereign would have to change the national attitude on this.[43]

The Madrid Society, in dealing with industry, insisted on the necessity of careful investigation, the collection of factual material, the value of study, the need for improvement of production techniques. This would involve treatises on the crafts and on instruments, the use of foreign works, and comparison of Spanish crafts with foreign.[44] It required adoption of the latest and best equipment,[45] and a class in machinery was needed.[46]

---

[40] *Memorias*, II, Memorias of Industria, No. XI.

[41] *Ibid.*, III, Memorias of Industria, 139-40 of the "piezas justificativas." Cf. *ibid.*, II, Memorias of Industria, No. VI, an author, after looking into prices for cotton in America and at Cadiz, suggested that a certain amount of raw cotton be brought to Spain for the Society on warships free of freightage charges.

[42] *Ibid.*, II, Memorias of Industria, No. IV.

[43] *Ibid.*, IV, Memorias of Oficios, "Memoria anónima ... sobre ... curtidos ... 1782." Cf. *ibid.*, III, Memorias of Industria, 189, an essay of 1778 calling on Spain to put as much effort into manufacturing as had other nations.

[44] *Memorias*, II, Memorias of Artes y Oficios, No. I, noting also that the Academy of Sciences of Paris was interested in crafts; cf. *ibid.*, III, 44-183 of "piezas justificativas," for a fair amount of data on foreign textiles, including costs.

[45] *Ibid.*, III, Memorias of Industria, i-ix, "Noticia de las operaciones de la clase ...," noting superior qualities of Swiss spinning wheels; *ibid.*, I, 102-4, for use of thermometers, as in France, to inform peasants raising silkworms when the windows should be adjusted.

[46] *Ibid.*, I, xxxvi-xxxvii, "De la clase de machinería," noting that an *Escuela teórica y práctica de machinería* has been announced, that the notably backward Spanish artisan needed instruments and machines before the crafts could advance, and that the Society needed teachers for this school, and models of machines, some of which would have to be brought from abroad. Cf. Jovellanos, *Obras escogidas* (*Clásicos castellanos*), III, 225-26, that the Economic Societies could have no real success

The industrial efforts of the Madrid Society revolved around textiles. The schools of popular industry and the *Monte Pío*, both of which served this interest, are discussed below. Interest in production other than textile seems to have been informed by no directive principle. The Madrid Society printed a description of a Turkish carpet shop,[47] and an essay on clock-making.[48] The Valencia Society was interested in buttonmaking.[49]

The three Societies in the Canary Islands at some time in their history may have tried to improve cloth and hat making, tanning, and the fabrication of pottery.[50] Jovellanos wished to promote flax and hemp, and wood and leather work;[51] and such rustic "industries" as cheesemaking.[52] The Valladolid Society wished to restore the ancient but then decadent linen industry; the Palma Society published memorias on oil making and silk manufacture; the Zaragoza had some industrial interests; the Tudela wished to revive the decadent linen industry.[53]

"POPULAR INDUSTRY" AND THE MONTE PÍO OF MADRID

The Societies founded "patriotic" schools of popular—or cottage—industry, with the essential function of giving instruction in spinning,[54] though some other operations of textile manufacture were occasionally included. The first two decades of Madrid publications show that popular industry was one of the Society's three largest interests, together with the guild organization and agriculture. Cottage industry was prominent in England at this time, though beginning to shudder under the blows of the coming industrial revolution. Rural industry also expanded in France during the century.

The motive for the Spanish schools was both economic and beneficent or moralistic. Thus Jovellanos could emphasize the great economic importance

---

promoting industry since the root difficulty in Spain was the lack of mathematicians, physicists, chemists, mineralogists, and draughtsmen. *Supra*, 86, on efforts of the Societies to promote draughtsmanship and geometry.

[47] *Memorias*, II, Memorias of Artes y Oficios, No. VII. The shop was established at Madrid with royal aid early in the 18th century, and was still operating in 1776.

[48] *Ibid.*, No. II, finding it a fine introduction to mechanical devices, and including a short history of clockmaking to the 10th century.

[49] *Instituciones económicas*, No. V, *et passim*. Cf. *ibid.*, xxx-xxxiii, on the Company of Commerce suggested by the Valencia Society in 1777; despite its name, its task was to be more the development of industrial production than anything else.

[50] Millares Torres, *Historia Canarias*, 367.

[51] "Discurso dirigido a la Sociedad de Asturias," *loc. cit.*, 448.

[52] *Obras escogidas* (*Clásicos castellanos*), III, 210 *et seq.*

[53] Sarrailh, *L'Espagne éclairée*, 260, 261.

[54] Cf. García, *Datos bibliográficos*, No 3: *Instrucción para las Escuelas patrióticas* (Madrid, 1776; 29 pp.), noting that "la enseñanza de las escuelas se reducía a prepración é hilado de cáñamo, lino, algodón y lana. Eran exclusivamente para mujeres."

of spinning, "without dispute the most important and profitable of all that have been invented by the industry of man," and immediately assert that it was above all important "for the influence it has on public customs," contributing to the moral improvement of women by rescuing them from idleness and poverty.[55] With the Madrid Society the philanthropic was more important than the economic motive in the foundation of the schools, the editors of the Memorias in 1780 praising the Society's class of industry as curator of the schools and of the Pious Fund, for the class had[56]

> labored with incessant zeal and intelligence in discovering the means capable of establishing in Madrid popular industry with the praiseworthy object of assuring honest and useful occupation to the women and girls of the vicinity.
>
> When are compared the total abandonment which this art had in Madrid, the general idleness of its population, and the eagerness with which women and girls now search for yarns, the Society ought to hope that the public may be grateful for and aid its zeal. In what can alms be used more beneficially than in supplying wheels and yarns?

But the community seemed slow in the exercise of its beneficence or in the perception of this new economic opportunity. As early as March, 1777, a general junta of the Society was informed that although women had been trained in the patriotic schools, they now had insufficient materials to work with at home. It had been hoped that merchants or other private citizens would aid this work, but they had not. So until the idea caught on, the Society was setting up a subscription system, the proceeds of which were to go for the purchase of materials. The first objective was to give employment to those taught to spin,[57] but the main problem was finding a market for the products turned out by the women.[58]

The Madrid Society recognized that the need of extending rural industry stemmed in part from the insufficiency of agricultural production, and the need of adding to the income of peasants.[59] In 1780 the editors of the Memorias wrote:

> Popular industry is that type of lucrative occupation which neither pertains to agriculture nor to crafts, and results in those minor and easy products which men can make in unoccupied seasons, days, and hours without slighting their primary

---

[55] *Obras* (BAE), II, 32, "Discurso pronunciado en la Sociedad Económica en 16 de Julio de 1785, con motivo de la distribución de premios de hilados."

[56] T. I, "Prólogo," ix-xii.

[57] *Ibid.*, II, Memorias of Industria, No. X. They meant to aid those using the distaff for spinning, as well as those using the wheel.

[58] García, *Datos bibliográficos*, No. 4, "Aviso al público," probably of 1776 or 1777, informing the public that linen shirts were for sale.

[59] Cf. Sée, *Economic and Social Conditions in France*, 34-36, for the same motive in France.

obligations. It mainly comprehends yarn, embroidery, lace, all sorts of linens, ribbons, twine, garters, stockings, nets, and in a word all the minor fabrics in which it is advantageous to employ women and girls, without admitting among them a guild of men, which ought to be reserved for the more arduous arts and crafts.

They thought that where popular industry had been domiciled, the State and the families involved received great benefits. And the Madrid Society had pushed women into popular industry by opening four "patriotic schools of wool, flax, hemp, and cotton," in different parts of the city, providing teachers and distributing spinning wheels; and by teaching the preparation of yarns so as to give them the required fineness and consistency, "in spite of the wastage which this precise instruction produced in the funds of the Society." They claimed that prizes—mostly wheels—given at these schools had stimulated the girls of Madrid, the girls preferring them to money payments; and recommended that the public distribution of prizes be extended to hospices and educational establishments.[60]

The four schools were initially financed by the Society, contributions from members, and a royal grant of 2,000 reals from the lottery. The Society provided supervisors, found and paid teachers and a "director of spinning," and worried about the scarcity of materials. This last led to offers of prizes for flax and hemp cultivation. The pupils in the spinning schools received a small daily sum, in accordance with the work they performed,[61] and prizes for superior performance.[62] In 1780 three schools dealt with the spinning of flax and hemp, and one with wool.[63] The main purpose of the Society with regard to spinning was the encouragement of the use of wheels instead of distaffs.[64] Other Societies than that of Madrid were interested in popular industry.[65]

---

[60] T. I, xxxii-xxxv, "De la industria popular."

[61] *Ibid.*, II, unmbd. pp. at beginning, "Noticia ... de ... la clase de industria."

[62] *Ibid.*, III, Memorias of Industria, 295-310, "Noticia de los premios ... 1778," including the first period of 1779. The prizes in 1778-79 went largely to very young women or girls, mostly under eighteen, and often ten or eleven years old and occasionally younger still.

[63] *Ibid.*, II, Memorias of Industria, No. XI.

[64] *Ibid.*, III, Memorias of Industria, i-ix, "Noticia de las operaciones de la clase de industria en el segundo bienio," noting the superior quality of Swiss wheels. The Society was interested in the price and quality of wheels, including the wheel adopted by the Society of Dublin (*ibid.*, II, Memorias of Industria, No. XI).

[65] That of Sevilla was interested in a spinning school as early as 1778 (Sarrailh, *L'Espagne éclairée*, 263), and some time in its early years established free schools of yarns and dyes (Labra, *El instituto*, 311); the Valencia in 1777 noted the need for promotion of popular industry among poor peasants (*Instituciones económicas*, No. VI); the statutes of the S. Cristóval de la Laguna noted the necessity of establishing patriotic schools (*Estatutos*, títulos XII, XIV); the Segovia operated spinning schools

The impact of the schools of popular industry upon either economics or morals cannot have been great.[66] Twenty prizes distributed by the Madrid Society in the first *semestre* of 1778[67] could scarcely be expected to have much effect. The Society itself realized that giving spinning equipment to girls was useless unless they had materials to spin and a market. Perhaps this was the best method open to the Societies for the simultaneous promotion of textile production and provision of employment for idle females.

The establishment of the *Monte Pío* of the Madrid Society was the direct result of the recognition that the resources of the body were insufficient for the relief of the poor by means of instruction in spinning. The subscription fund did not extract large sums of money from the public, but it led Campomanes to induce the Council to set up the *Monte Pío* in 1779, with a capital of more than 300,000 reals. Established in the Royal Poorhouse, under the direction of the Economic Society, it taught spinning and weaving, and engaged in dyeing and other operations of the textile manufactory. From 1779 to 1786 it seems never to have provided work for as many as 1,000 persons in any one year. Most of those served were women. Despite Floridablanca's report that the king was pleased by some muslins produced in the establishment, we must not suppose that it transformed the textile industry. Most of the work consisted in the spinning operations.[68]

GUILDS

Campomanes recommended that the Societies study the guild organization as a barrier in the way of economic progress.[69] This was an attitude in accord

---

(*Actas y memorias 1785*, 93 *et seq.*, giving statistics of their work); the Zaragoza in the early 1790's established a spinning school (Sarrailh, *L'Espagne éclairée*, 27, 263); the Zamora had a spinning school in the 18th century (*ibid.*, citing Desdevises). Cf. Madrid *Memorias*, I, 384-431, for an article "On the development of popular industry in Salamanca," in fact a description of the actual condition and history of Salamanca from the economic—and some other—points of view, rather than a discussion of popular industry.

[66] Cf. Sempere, *Ensayo*, V, 211-12, that they had considerable success in promoting spinning.

[67] Madrid *Memorias*, III, Memorias of Industria, 295-310.

[68] *Ibid.*, IV, Apendices, over 300 pages of the records of the *Monte Pío*. The editors noted that the smallest papers from the secretariat of the Society had been included so the public could see how the *Monte Pío* operated from 1779 to 1786. Cf. García *Datos bibliográficos*, No. 20: *Reglamento para la Escuela de Encaxes, establecida en virtud de Real Orden de S. M. en el Monte Pío de la Real Sociedad Económica de Madrid* (Madrid, 1784).

[69] E. g., in *Apéndices a la educación popular*, Parte Tercera, iii-cclx, "Discurso sobre la legislación gremial de los artesanos," a mass of information on the guilds.

with developments in other lands. In France from 1750 projects for guild reform interested the new mercantile element desiring large-scale industrial production, as well as economists and reform statesmen. The monopolistic guilds certainly restricted production and kept prices high, squabbled among themselves, opposed innovations, and failed to do their duty in the training of apprentices or by permitting journeymen easy access to the rank of master. The features for which the medieval guilds may be praised were either no longer operative or were insufficient compensation for the unsuitability of the system in the modern age. Even the brotherhoods organized among guild members tended to waste their funds on celebrations rather than on the provision of succor for the membership. But little guild reform was accomplished in France before the Revolution.[70]

In Spain the Economic Societies were at the forefront of the demand for revision of the industrial system. Valentín de Foronda of the Basque Society wrote that the "natural effect" of the guilds was to raise prices, deprive citizens of the right of employing the craftsmen they wished, and deprive them of the low prices and good quality ensured by competition. To get the simplest work done it was necessary to use men in different guilds, when one worker could do the work.[71] He noted that workers in various foreign countries who enjoyed freedom did not work the worse for it; and in Spain those workers did best who were the least regulated.[72] Foronda's language was a bit more incendiary than that of Campomanes, who in turn was perhaps somewhat more forthright than the general membership of the Economic Societies.[73] Still, the Memorias of the Madrid Society made clear enough the view that the system of competition should be allowed a larger sphere, of operation in Spain by reduction of the guild regulations.

The Madrid Society investigated the guilds because its statutes called for such action, and because ordered to do so by the Council of Castile. The Society's class of arts and crafts took up the task, recognizing that Campo-

---

The ideas of the Madrid and Valencia Societies on guilds sound much like pp. ccx *et seq.* of this "Discurso," where Campomanes summarizes his suggestions for changes in guild regulations. The discourses in Parte Tercera, after the preliminary by Campomanes, deal with the different arts and crafts and are designed to make them more efficient and profitable. They are mostly, perhaps all, by French writers, with Duhamel contributing a number.

[70] Sée, *Economic and Social Conditions in France*, 121-35.
[71] *Espíritu de los mejores diarios*, No. 158 (December 7, 1788).
[72] *Ibid.*, No. 159 (December 15, 1788), and attacking various of the objections commonly made to the project of doing away with the regulations.
[73] Cf. Kany, *Life and Manners*, 169, on Jovellanos' "fulminatory" *Informe sobre el libre ejercicio de las artes* (1785).

manes' study of the popular education of artisans was the only work on the subject published in Spain, whereas they needed much information on the guild ordinances, the instruments and machines used, and a comparison with the crafts of France. The class got from the Madrid guilds information on the number of masters and journeymen, and copies of the ordinances, and were surprised at the small number of crafts and of masters; some essential crafts were lacking entirely, so that goods had to be imported, a situation that might be corrected if the poor of both sexes made these goods. It hoped that the government might correct such decadence as was due to unlawful imports. The masters were charged with not having understood their own interest in limiting the number of journeymen and apprentices, for in countries that understood the matter better, the aspiration had been the largest possible number per master. Though the Society statutes called for "member protectors" of the crafts, they had not been named by 1780 because of the small membership (38) of the class of arts and crafts. They realized that until the guild ordinances were reformed, the "protectors" could do little. Furthermore, to 1780 the class was busy with consideration, on request of the Council, of the ordinances of the woodworking guilds and of the ordinances of guilds outside Madrid.[74]

The Society published in 1780 an extensive study of the ten guilds of artisans of Madrid that worked with wood,[75] dividing it into four parts: (1) an extract of the guild ordinances; (2) general observations on the ordinances; (3) a project of reunion of the ten guilds; and (4) a plan of ordinances. The study showed knowledge of French and English crafts; found that there was too little instruction for apprentices, who tended to be mere servants of the masters; stated that artisans themselves made too little use of instruments; concerned itself with methods of getting costs down;[76] proposed union of some guilds on the ground that the divisions were arbitrary; suggested cutting the heavy gremial costs and giving a good deal of liberty in the exercise of the crafts, for "a just liberty in the exercise of art is that which will animate and sustain its practitioners";[77] and suggested that strangers and foreign Catholics be allowed to exercise their crafts in Madrid. Under no

---

[74] Madrid *Memorias*, I, xxxv-xxxvi, "De la Clase de Oficios"; *ibid.*, II, Memorias of Artes y Oficios, unumbd. pp. at beginning ("Noticia resumida de las actas ..."), and No. I.

[75] *Ibid.*, II, No. V, 45-223. These ten did not include all woodworkers, since some did not have a formal guild or individual ordinances.

[76] *Ibid.*, 224, a folding plan dealing with the wood annually brought into Madrid by guilds of woodworkers, with species, dimensions, prices, etc.

[77] *Ibid.*, 109-10.

pretext would the Society allow formation of a "fixed and exclusive number of masters," or permit new examinations of qualifications of qualified men coming from another place.[78] The proposed new ordinances suggested creation of a pious fund, different from a *cofradía* or brotherhood;[79] and devoted much attention to the need for technical instruction.[80]

The Society in 1780 published a much shorter study of the ordinances of the cutlers and armorers of Toledo. These workers had sent new ordinances to the Council, which passed them to the Society, charging it especially to excise anything tending to monopoly. The report of the Society's class of arts and crafts favored an equal chance of advancement from apprentice to master, opposing discrimination in favor of apprentices trained in Toledo. The report took a gloomy view of other features of the ordinances designed to freeze out strange craftsmen who went to Toledo, considering that a guild test in Madrid was sufficient for exercise of the craft in Toledo. It objected to the sections of the ordinances dealing with festivities, finding they really dealt with a *cofradía* within the guild, and feeling that some such brotherhoods encouraged idleness. The report concluded that: (1) the ordinances for some guilds ought to be reformed throughout Spain; (2) the ordinances ought to make really clear the position and rights of apprentices, journeymen, and masters, and the guilds should erect a *monte pío* to look after orphans, and the sons and widows of masters and journeymen, and to aid education, this pious fund to be supervised by people outside the guild, including the town council and the "member protector" of the guild appointed by the Economic Society; (3) the Society of Toledo ought to spread knowledge of the Basque Society with regard to metals and the making of cutlery; and (4) the Society ought to try to restore the making of swords to its former luster.[81]

In 1782 a memoria found much of the superior economic condition of England due to the willingness of important persons to belong to guilds.[82] Actually, the author was talking about merchant guilds in a country where capitalism had long since commenced the wide transformation of both industry and commerce from the medieval system which clung so stubbornly in Spain. This opinion of the Spanish author contained a kernel of truth, but was also based on a large ignorance and naïveté. By 1787 the editors of the Memorias noted that in examining the gremial ordinances the Societies had found that

---

[78] *Ibid.*, 123.

[79] *Ibid.*, Parte Quarta, Título segundo.

[80] *Ibid.*, Título tercero.

[81] *Ibid.*, No. III.

[82] *Ibid.*, IV, Memorias of Oficios, "Memoria anónima ... sobre el modo de fomentar ... las fábricas de curtidos. ..."

most were directed to fixing monopoly.[83] In the same year the Society published a report on the organization of silversmiths.[84]

In 1777 the Valencia Society noted that good regulation of the guilds was
important for public prosperity, and that the ordinances needed revision
in the light of Campomanes' work, especially to eliminate exclusivistic tendencies that stood in the way of women workers.[85] The Zaragoza Society
showed some interest in guild ordinances.[86]

In summary, the Madrid Society favored more competition, better technical training, reduction of the spirit of routine and adoption of a willingness to accept new methods, an increase in the volume of production, a
lowering of prices, and an improvement of the system of assistance to craftsmen and their families in need. The monarchical governments of 1775-1808
did nothing important about these matters. The Cortes of Cadiz, as in so
many fields, adopted the forward-looking policy of endeavoring to free
industry, but never had an opportunity to implement its policy.

There was nothing unusually interesting about the guild system of Spain.
The Five Major Guilds of Madrid, with their wealth and wide interests,
had counterparts in other lands. The guild system of Spain is of interest
primarily in that it hung on so long and with such influence into a day when
the new capitalism and spirit of competition were broadening opportunity
for large producers, increasing production, and reducing the laborers to an
even worse condition of servitude than was the case with the journeymen
and apprentices of Spain who in the eighteenth century found it difficult to
rise to the rank of master.[87]

---

[83] *Ibid.*, IV, Memorias of Oficios, i-vi, "Resúmen histórico." The Society reported
unfavorably to the Council with regard to a scheme of Oviedo in 1775 for limitation
of the number of artisans there, and for discrimination against goods made outside
the town (*ibid.*, II, Memorias of Artes y Oficios, No. IV).

[84] *Ibid.*, IV, Memorias of Oficios, "Memoria sobre el arte de la platería, y ordenanzas
para el colegio de plateros de Madrid. ..." Nearly 200 pages long, it includes an
extensive examination of the silversmiths of the year 1685, as well as a plan for new
regulations.

[85] *Instituciones económicas*, 46-57.

[86] Sarrailh, *L'Espagne éclairée*, 261.

[87] Ballesteros, *Historia*, VI, 161-62, on guilds in the 18th century; Addison,
Charles III, 118, that removal of restrictions on the corn trade in 1765, and freeing
of all interior trade in 1767 "destroyed the guilds," whereas we have seen that neither
the guilds nor the Economic Societies so understood the matter; García, *Datos
bibliográficos*, No. 130: *Sobre la abolición de ordinanzas gremiales y libre ejercicio de
las artes*, which García describes as an exposition directed to the *Reina Gobernadora*
by the Madrid Society, dated September 28, 1834. Cf. Colmeiro, *Economía política*,
237 *et seq.*

Commerce

The Madrid Society—and probably most others—gave less attention to commerce than to the industrial and agricultural products that might enter into it, although the Society followed Campomanes in appreciation of the connections between the three branches of the economy. It was expected that commerce would improve of itself if production were developed.[88] The Memorias did print views on the value of commerce; its worth to the United Provinces, England, and other nations; its role in augmenting population; the difficulty of separating exterior and interior commerce, since they worked on each other; and the fact that learned men in Spain had tried to persuade the nobility to turn to maritime commerce, but nobles continued to consider it a "species of degradation."[89]

The Madrid Society gave some attention to *libre comercio*,[90] receiving a memoria on the subject which expressed a low opinion of the monopolists of Cadiz, and deprecated emphasis on the mining of precious metals;[91] and another on the commerce of the Indies, pointing out that foreigners got more from a few American isles than Spain from its vast domain;[92] and heard Francisco Cabarrús assert that only the ignorant and the interested opposed free trade, and condemn concentration on the minerals of America when other riches needed attention more.[93]

The Valencia Society in 1777 observed that the nobility should not disdain commerce, that the Basque Society had shown the advantage of commercial

---

[88] Cf. Campomanes, *Apéndice a la educación popular*, Parte Quarta, iii-xcii, "Discurso sobre el comercio activo de la nación," starting with the statement that arts and crafts have an intimate connection with commerce, then pointing out that industry and agriculture will not prosper and profit without commerce to dispose of the products.

[89] Madrid *Memorias*, II, Memorias of Industria, No. IV.

[90] The Council sent the Society the royal decree of February 2, 1778, on free commerce (*ibid.*, II, Apéndice, No. XXXII [pp. 223-306], "Reales decretos, Cédulas, y órdenes relativas a los objetos económicos y aumento del comercio y de las fábricas comunicadas a la Sociedad desde su erección," for a number of items bearing on the Society and commerce, including the cedula on *libre comercio*).

[91] *Ibid.*, III, Memorias of Industria, 255-61, in 1778.

[92] *Ibid.*, 262-81. This author, who had been in America, also hit at the monopolists of Cadiz and Lima, and discussed the possibility of a Panamanian canal.

[93] *Ibid.*, 282-94, in 1778. Cf. for an opinion unfavorable to *libre comercio*, finding that an increase in the number of ports brought disorder, *Espíritu de los mejores diarios*, "Real Sociedad de esta Corte Informe sobre la libertad del comercio, que por particular comisión de la Real Sociedad Económica de esta corte, extendió Don Francisco Xavier de Uriortua, en todo conforme a unas observaciones que presentó él mismo en una junta creado por la Sociedad para aquel objeto," Nos. 147-153 (September 22, 29, October 6, 13, 20, 27, November 3, 1788).

activity by the nobility, that English nobles were in commerce, that in Italy very great people came from commercial families, and that in France, "despite the inclination of the nobles to the glorious career of arms, many dedicate themselves to commerce." Holland was proof that commerce ensured prosperity, since the land did not produce enough itself to maintain a fourth of its population; Louis XIV of France depended on the profits of such ports as San Malo; some of the glories of the history of Spain were due to strength derived from commerce. Commerce did not corrupt, but improved customs. Commerce and manufacturing interacted, and since the latter aided in the relief of idleness and bad habits, then ecclesiastics should promote commerce, as the bishop of San Malo was a member of the Commission of Commerce begun by the Economic Society of Brittany. The Society wondered why Valencia could not trade with America as nearby Barcelona did. It recommended establishment of a Commerce Company, but designed it to promote industrial production rather than commerce as such.[94] The Palma Society intermittently from 1784 to 1802 discussed the commercial development of Mallorca and the creation of a company for trade with the Baltic and with America.[95] The Zaragoza Society as early as 1778 showed its interest in commerce in connection with the famous project of the Canal Imperial.[96]

---

[94] *Instituciones económicas*, xxx-xxxiii, 71-72, 81-83, 108-9, 110-20, 196-206, *et passim*.

[95] Monbeig, "La Real Sociedad Económica," *loc. cit.*, 172; Sarrailh, *L'Espagne éclairée*, 260.

[96] *Ibid.*, 261, citing a Society document of that year.

CHAPTER SIX

Character and Influence of the Spanish Societies

We may cite three eighteenth-century views of the Societies before dealing with the later controversy as to their role and character. Sempere in the 1780's thought the Societies especially useful for Spain, where laws were usually drawn by *letrados*, whose knowledge was too narrowly legalistic, whereas the Societies dealt with all classes of persons, had wider knowledge and better study habits, and greater ability to resist bribes. Also, the Societies gave useful work to nobles and *hacendados*, who were inclined to sloth; and inspired a taste for reading "useful works," spread ideas of political economy, and improved the style of writing and speaking on subjects different from those taught in schools.[1] Cabarrús noted that the Societies, despite their faults, had an incalculable effect on opinion; made possible the discussion of many important questions; "closed the door to many errors"; for, without them, "the great questions of the agrarian law, of the entailed estates, and of the Pious Funds, of the liberty of the crafts, and others . . . would not have been ventilated."[2] Bourgoing found the Societies admirable, producing a "fermentation . . . générale," and considered that "the citizens who composed them occupied themselves essentially with the progress of the arts, agriculture, and industry of the provinces." He observed that the enemies of the Societies charged that the members talked too much and dealt with unim-

---

[1] *Ensayo*, V, 140-42.
[2] García, *Datos bibliográficos*, No. 25: *Elogio ... que en junta ... celebrada por la Real Sociedad Económica ... 1785 leyó ... Cabarrús ...* (Madrid, 1786; 97 pp.). García discusses it at some length.

portant matters; but he found much to praise, although conceding that the Societies had not done all that they might.[3]

Diversity of Judgments on the Societies

This diversity has six main sources. First, judgment must be largely qualitative, though more quantitative judgment might be attempted with profit. Second, activities of the Societies had multiple sources of inspiration and usually aimed at more than one result—to the confusion of some later critics. Third, the effects of the actions of the Societies often were not just those aimed at, ostensibly or in fact. Fourth, some critics have so disliked the objectives or the fundamental ideas or the possible ultimate implications of the activities of the Societies that their judgment was thereby distorted. Fifth, some critics are contemptuous of study and of talk and find it hard to see connections between ideas and physical action, so that for them the Societies were wind without substance. And sixth, some judgments are warped by defective understanding of the function of the Societies. The first three must hamper the efforts of all scholars; the others are avoidable. A few examples of the latter may be noted.

Menéndez y Pelayo, a student of literature, was influenced by distaste for the materialism and secularism of the Societies. He found them animated by many worthy hopes, but sometimes introducing revolutionary ideas; precipitate in their actions, satisfied with "artificial results"; and sometimes afflicted with an irreligious spirit.[4] This view that the Societies were un-Catholic, or very radical in other ways, is an exaggeration and misleading, save for conservatives so rigid as to consider all change unholy.[5]

The anti-intellectual prejudice against the Societies appeared early. Sempere noted a French jibe that the Societies merely jabbered, that vigor comes to individuals from nature and cannot be induced by small prizes, and that individuals in all fields do the big things while institutions merely talk. Sempere objected that to understand the usefulness of the Societies it was necessary to know the condition of Spain, for since the early years

---

[3] *Nouveau voyage*, I, 91, 266-69, including the comment that their funds were modest, "mais le gran point étoit de réveiller leur patrie de son engourdissement, d'offrir un stimulation aux talens des artistes, aux travaux des cultivateurs; d'aiguillonner a la fois leur vanité par la perspective de la gloire, et leur intéret par l'espoir du profit."

[4] *Heterodoxos*, VI, 264-66. Cf. Salvador de Madariaga, *The Rise of the Spanish Empire* (New York, 1947), 215-17, for distaste for the utilitarianism of the Societies.

[5] The present writer bases this view on the examination of some thousands of pages of the publications of the Societies and their members. Cf. Sarrailh, *L'Espagne éclairée*, 268-69, that generally in the Society publications he examined (a considerable number, including many not seen by the present writer), he did not see "un esprit 'novateur,' dangereux pour la tradition nationale espagnole ou la religion catholique."

of the century the government had spent great sums on agriculture, industry, and other economic matters, but largely failed due to lack of knowledge of political economy. Sempere thought the Societies could spread these ideas.[6] Desdevises du Dezert criticized the garrulity of the members, discovered other evidences of vanity, inefficiency, pretentiousness, and bad taste, as in the seals and emblems of the Societies; and declared the meetings often puerile, ridiculing an occasion in 1805 when the Madrid Society conferred on a child of four a prize for Christian doctrine, reading, and knitting. He did, nevertheless, consider the Societies centers of study and experience which tended to reduce the isolation of Spain.[7]

It is not odd that Society members were sometimes vain and verbose; this was inevitable, given a miscellaneous membership, encouraged to express its views. The Societies certainly were "inefficient," but they were voluntary organizations without financial or political responsibilities; they did not have to show a profit or please officials. The esthetic quality of the seals and symbols of the Societies was feeble; but it is as mistaken to demand it there as in the devices of American business clubs. Of course there was dilettantism in the Economic Societies; but that surprises only those who regard them as similar to national academies of science. Finally, the frivolity of the Societies can no more be assumed from the gift of prizes to children, than American universities can be charged with forsaking their vocation by conferring degrees upon men whose achievement is nonacademic.

Estimates as to the Role of the Societies

All the important contentions as to the role and influence of the Societies may be reduced to four categories of judgment. First, it is said that the function of the Societies was to align Spanish with European thought or to reduce ignorance.[8] A second claim is that the Societies were political in their effect,

---

[6] *Ensayo*, V, 143-51, also explaining that the Frenchman disliked academies and literary bodies because of personal difficulties with them in France. Cf. Swinburne, *Travels*, II, 203, for a charge of empty verbalism against the Societies, dismissing them with the comment that they "undertake many things and finish nothing." Swinburne knew little of the Societies, and had small sympathy for things Spanish.

[7] *La Richesse*, 91-92. Cf. Ballesteros, *Historia*, VI, 145, that in some Societies the members occupied themselves with vain symbols; and he sneers at the emblems of the Tudela Society. Young, *Travels in France*, 24, 98-99, 146, 170, 262, 283, condemning French agricultural societies for impracticality.

[8] Ortiz, *Hija cubana*, 15, quoting Aranda, asserts this as the real aim of the Societies; Altamira, *Historia*, IV, 259, that they played a part in the campaign on the part of the few enlightened against ignorance; Labra, *El instituto*, 205, that the reformed universities, the Economic Societies, and the *Ateneo* of Madrid (1820) were the most important factors in bringing Spain into intellectual harmony with the rest of contemporary civilization.

stimulating controversy between sections of the populace, performing their work with the enthusiasm characteristic of revolutionary movements, playing a part in toppling the old regime. This line of argument is confused by praise of the Societies for their work in attempting to reduce class feeling.[9] Third is the claim that the principal function and interest was either economic, or social, or intellectual, or some other one thing. Most of this confusion stems from divergent notions as to the content of the adjectives involved. It would seem to be a perversion of fact to deny that most of the activities of the Societies revolved in one way or another around economic factors; although this says nothing about definitions of economics, or about the purposes of economic action. It is fairly easy to discuss in other than economic terms some of the actions of the Societies, but difficult to ignore the prosaic aspects of the drawing schools, the spinning, the pictures of plows, the discussion of mules and oxen, the commercial hopes, the manufacturing interest, the fertilizer, the new crops. It is especially misleading to assert that the main interest was in education, without adding that it was education to improve industry and agriculture, even though partly for moralistic or philanthropic reasons. Fourth, the influence of the Societies in their early years was due largely to the absence of other institutions able to fulfill their functions. Their decadence in the nineteenth century coincided with the appearance of such bodies as the Ministries of Public Instruction and Public Works, the provincial commissions of those ministries, the Ateneos and other centers of culture and of industrial and economic propaganda, the Chambers of Commerce, Agricultural Federations, and Workers Centers.[10]

The effect of the Spanish Societies on the overseas colonies has been little studied, so there is no controversy on the question. The varying judgments noted above must be expected of organizations with so many interests as the Economic Societies. The Societies accomplished too much to suit some, too little for others.

Summary of Character and Influence

The Societies were founded upon the dual basis of interest in Spanish problems —chiefly economic—and in the ideas of the Enlightenment. They focused

---

[9] For variations on this theme see Ladra, *El instituto*, 216, 320-21, 324; Ferrer del Río, *Carlos III en España*, III, 236; Lafuente, *Historia*, XV, 114, finding it a great merit in Charles III and his ministers to have permitted the Societies, which a less enlightened government might have looked on askance; Montoro, "Historia de la Sociedad Económica," *loc. cit.*, 5-6, that they showed their "true character" in efforts to promote public education, the periodical press, and communications, and helped topple the old regime.

[10] Labra, *El instituto*, 253, 317.

current European thought upon local problems of ancient date. Second, they spread rapidly, which suggests they must have filled a crying need or desire. Third, the membership of all the Societies may not have totaled five thousand in the year 1800, while the active members were but a part of the whole. The members joined quickly after the foundation of each Society; additions thereafter were not numerous. The members represented a small minority even of the upper and middle classes. The paternalism of the Societies was inevitable, given the social structure of Spain, and quite in accord with the spirit of enlightened despotism. The smallness of the middle class and the paucity of economic interest or knowledge among the aristocracy meant that the Societies could not hope to develop an interest capable of overriding the fears of the conservatives. Neither the aristocracy nor the peasantry nor the small middle class could lead Spain closely in the wake of England and France into the age of the bourgeoisie. The French-style salons of Madrid at the end of the eighteenth century[11] indicated that some of the celebrated stiffness of Spanish aristocratic social life was breaking down, but it no more proved the readiness of Spain for the capitalistic economy than did the mixed companies of blue-stockings in England in the eighteenth century. But in the one case the society was passing into the control of the bourgeoisie, and in the other it was not.

Fourth, the Societies helped promote new ideas and freer discussion. How much is another matter; to what effect, yet another.[12] The Societies certainly showed a strong interest in science in general, as well as in its applications to economic activity.[13] They certainly believed in the study of economic matters. They even showed some prejudice in favor of study for its own sake. It is, however, an exaggeration to say that the Societies in the eighteenth century were interested in education as such. They were not interested in all kinds of education.

Fifth, the financial resources of the Societies were slender for the accomplishment of the objectives outlined in their statutes.[14] As a result, they

---

[11] Desdevises, *La Richesse*, ch. vi, sec. iii, "Les Academies et les Cercles."

[12] Gil de Zárate, *Instrucción pública*, I, 44-45, for the view of a liberal educator of the 19th century that the Societies "produce a communication of ideas, a spirit of discussion, a scientific enthusiasm to which Spaniards are not accustomed."

[13] Cf. Valencia *Instituciones económicas*, No. IV, for an example of the scientific interest.

[14] Cf. Carrera Pujal, *Economía española*, III, 522-23, for criticism of the belief of Campomanes that all the small villages of Spain could be converted "by the art of magic" into manufacturing communities, and for considering the Economic Societies as " a panacea for everything" in so converting them, without other aid than the resources of the members; in short, that Campomanes was mistaken in believing that private effort, stimulated and guided by the Societies, was sufficient for the industrial-

depended on the techniques of propaganda and education. The Valencia Society said in 1777 that its function was to stimulate and suggest, not to participate in economic activity itself.[15] In any case, as the Madrid Society recognized, experience was bound to show that the Societies could not work quite as they were set up in their statutes.[16] The textile schools of the Societies were probably their largest physical accomplishment, and they only affected a few women.

Sixth, it may be said that the Societies—especially the Madrid in 1775-1808— provided a very limited and highly restricted sort of popular access to the machinery of government. If this is too strong a fashion of putting the matter, it can at least be agreed that it encouraged one type of unofficial consideration of legislation. That this sort of interest could be dangerous to the colonial system as then constituted was shown by the dubiety of officials in America with regard to the Economic Societies there.

Seventh, the main interest of the Societies was economic. The question of the intent of the members—moral, or political, or economic—is chiefly important in making clear the inevitable cleavage in the ranks. The effects of their activities were as important as their intent. These activities usually dealt with economic questions, whatever the reasons for indulging in such action. The members were rationalists; their interests were chiefly secular; they were utilitarians.[17] The royal order approving erection of the Valencia Society mentioned its economic functions without reference to moral or beneficent interests.[18] The editors of that Society's first publication stated its main interest to be in *economía política*.[19] A man may speak of silos for storage of grain underground,[20] hoping to elevate morals, but some of his auditors will build silos for other reasons.

Eighth, the Societies were hurt by the fact that many members were not active, were enrolled merely to be fashionable, and were in any case ignorant of economic matters and too lazy to improve their knowledge. Some of the projects, views, and hopes of the members were chimerical from the economic point of view. Some essays in the Madrid Memorias reveal the most romantic

---

ization of Spain. *Ibid.*, IV, 14, lack of funds and other resources the Societies' greatest problem.

[15] *Instituciones económicas*, No. VIII, and noting that "the Society is not a Literary University," and its function was not to teach directly, but to stimulate learning.

[16] Madrid *Memorias*, I, xx-xxii, "Análisis del sistema y establecimiento de la Sociedad."

[17] Altamira, *Historia*, IV, 260, they were "oriented in practical directions."

[18] *Instituciones económicas*, No. III.

[19] *Ibid.*, xlv-xlix.

[20] Jovellanos, *Obras escogidas (Clásicos castellanos)*, III, 161 *et seq.*

—or optimistic—notions of human motivation. It was clearly an impractical suggestion which Floridablanca, in the name of the government in 1788, sent to the women's section of the Madrid Society that they try to cut down the luxury of female dress by designing a uniform national costume; and the Countess of Montijo, president of the women's section, recognized its quality by putting her name to a learned and blistering reply.[21]

Ninth, the Societies caught on for a time because of the absence of other institutions to deal with their interests. Some other things may be said about the Societies. They were not equally active. Their operations sometimes were marked by a verbalism which can scarcely be called excessive since it need not in itself have ruined the hopes of the Societies. The functions and interests and influence of the Societies could not possibly be entirely confined by regulations. There is no way of knowing how much the often highly critical essays of members and other contributors represented the opinions of the full membership, since the editors of the published versions no doubt played a selective role. Further, they probably received little material from persons who disapproved of the Societies. The Societies helped, some, to align Spanish thought with that of England and France, but they were not so successful in changing Spanish practice. It may be that they helped, a bit, to reduce ignorance in Spain, or at least to promote new ideas in a very narrow though important circle. In the Societies some men of position managed to consider a little the rectification of the deficiencies of Spanish economic life. But this group was unrepresentative in that it lacked the generally fine sensitivity to threats to their position of the privileged orders in the Spanish world. They helped create that confusion of the Spanish spirit in contemplation of the new age which has been so apparent in modern times.

Influence in America

Some residents of America were on the published membership lists of Spanish Societies. We have some record of Americans in Spain carrying knowledge of the Societies overseas. News of the Spanish Societies arrived in America in Spanish periodicals. The *Gazeta de Madrid* carried notices of the activities

---

[21] Méndez Bejarano, *Afrancesados*, 140-43, printing both letters, wondering who composed the one bearing the signature of the Countess; and (p. 112, n. 1) describing the project for uniform dress as "infantil." The Countess was wife of a man who in the time of Godoy was to be a well-known freemason, but in the period following 1808 a strong monarchist and enemy of democratic tendencies, thus well illustrating the blend of intellectual liberalism and political conservatism found in many members of the Economic Societies.

of the peninsular Societies, and was widely read in America.[22] The Societies founded overseas, are, however, the best evidence of influence there.

We may, in addition, suppose that the Spanish Societies affected America by way of their effect in Spain, since the general intellectual and material condition of the metropolis was reflected overseas. The Societies certainly influenced the ideas and actions of some of the officials sent to America. We are entitled to assume that the Societies had an influence by way of the movement in America of Spaniards other than officials, this being probably true of merchants and of the less numerous scholars and scientists. We can only assume that the Societies influenced many creoles who visited Spain, even when they left no record of the fact.[23] The Spanish Societies must have exercised influence overseas by way of their publications. These showed an overriding concern with peninsular problems,[24] but did refer to America, and in any event promoted the rational examination of economic problems, proposed changes in legislation, and advocated the study of foreign literature. The discourse on popular industry of Campomanes, so influential with the Spanish Societies, dealt mostly with Spanish problems, but it would—when read in America—encourage the reading of foreign authors, and did refer to the land problem in the Indies.[25]

There must have been references to the Societies in private letters passing between Europe and America. The Madrid Society had at least a few connections with America through official channels, receiving from the governor of Santo Domingo some cotton produced there,[26] and persuading the government to order the officials of America to collect samples of gums and resins.[27] We have seen that in 1807 the Havana Society sent a man to study the Pestalozzian instruction which the Madrid Society was promoting. In 1819 the Cadiz Society wrote the town council of Guatemala about a system of mutual instruction.[28]

---

[22] *Infra*, 221, the *Gazeta* carries news of the Madrid Society to Guatemala; *infra*, 220, the *Correo mercantil* of Madrid and the Guatemala Society, and the *Seminario de agricultura y artes* of Madrid carrying to America news of the Royal Aragonese Society.

[23] *Infra*, 239, Belgrano and the Spanish Societies.

[24] García, *Datos bibliográficos*, lists nothing about America till No. 285, a publication of 1870.

[25] *Industria popular*, 118, n. 26.

[26] Madrid *Memorias*, II, Memorias of Industria, No. XI. In 1776 Campomanes presented to the Society the governor's letter and the cotton.

[27] *Ibid.*, III, Memorias of Agricultura, "Informe sobre las gomas, resinas, y gomoresinas." The Society thought that those of America were as good as those of Arabia and Senegal, so in 1779 wrote the king, and received a reply from Floridablanca, informing them that José de Gálvez had been instructed to send orders to America.

[28] José María Gutiérrez de la Huerta, Srio. de Actas e Int. de Correspondencias,

The many members of the Basque Society resident in America have been noted. Probably no other Society had nearly so many there. The Valencia Society for all its activity seems to have had no members in America, but we have observed that it bewailed its lack of trade with that region.[29] Some members of the Madrid Society had such connections with America or American affairs that some of them must have carried or sent some of their knowledge of the Societies to America.[30] The S. Cristóval de la Laguna Society enrolled members who resided in or had a connection with America.[31]

---

to the Ayuntamiento of Guatemala, Cadiz, January 7, 1819—AGG, A1.2-5, leg. 2835, exped. 25310. He sent copies of a "Practical Manual" for mutual instruction.

[29] *Extracto de actas 1786*, 52-64, listing the members, most of whom resided in Valencia; *Extracto de actas 1787-91*, 214-24, the same pattern of residence.

[30] The members in 1780 included: several councillors of the Indies; the director of the Caracas Company; a number of merchants; the bishop of Nicaragua; Josef Gálvez, Secretario del despacho universal de Indias; Manuel Josef de Ayala, of the secretariat of the ministry of the Indies, and first secretary of the Economic Society; Jacinto Sánchez de Orellana, sargento mayor de milicias de Quito; and a merchant of Cartagena de Indias (Madrid *Memorias*, II, Memorias of Artes y Oficios, Apéndice, 307-18). The members in 1787 included: a judge of the audiencia of Mexico, admitted in 1775; another officer of the Mexican audiencia; a lieutenant colonel of the militia of Cochabamba; and a judge of the Manila audiencia (*ibid.*, IV, 364-76 of Apéndices).

[31] Members in 1779 included: Cor. Francisco de Mesa Ponte y Castilla, Marqués de Casa-Hermosa, Corregidor de la Prov. de Guailas, en Reyno del Perú; Manuel de Urrutia Albárez-Franco y Manuel, Oidor honorario de la Audiencia de Santo Domingo, Auditor de Guerra y Marina del Dpto. de la Habana, Juez de Apelaciones del nuevo Orleans, y Provincia de Luisiana; Juan de Guisla Boot y Larrea, Capitán del Reg. Fixo del Número de la Ciudad de Lima; Matías de Gálvez, Coronel de los Rles Exércitos, 2º Comandante, y Ten. de Rey de estas Islas (*Estatutos*, 29-38, "Lista de los socios").

PART TWO

History of the Ultramarine Societies
(1781-1821)

CHAPTER SEVEN

The Colonies in the Eighteenth Century

When the first Economic Societies were formed overseas in the 1780's, Spain had begun a revision of her trading system. But the reduction of restrictions on commerce within the empire did not alter the fact that Spanish production was insufficient to supply American needs, so that foreign and Spanish merchants and creole consumers obstinately continued to conduct business according to its own ethic and in violation of law. A partial commercial reform did not satisfy colonial economic grievances, reinforced increasingly by political and social complaint; intensified by the critical attitude fostered by rationalistic literature; stirred by news of the Anglo-American revolt of 1775, and the French upheaval after 1789; and taking finally the form of a creole self-consciousness expressed in adoption of the name of American.

The great French wars after 1792 complicated Spanish problems by disturbing traffic overseas. When the French invaded Spain in 1808, some creoles found it an opportunity as well as a problem, stating that with Joseph Bonaparte enthroned in Madrid, and the legitimate monarchs the gulls and prisoners of Napoleon, the constitutional link between colony and Crown had been fractured; so that America should form its own interim regimes rather than accept the resistance governments (Junta, Council, and Cortes) of southern Spain. Nor did these creoles feel that the irregular Spanish bodies offered them their due share of power. Thus, before the restoration of Ferdinand VII in 1814, a fair segment of creole America either enjoyed or desired autonomy, if not independence. Neither was offered by the uncompromising Ferdinand, whose policies drove ever deeper the wedge between "patriot" and "servile" in America. And before long the blood of the slain cried out against a return to the ancient system.

So creole views in the year of crisis, 1808, had been in preparation for some time, and however unready creoles were ideologically for political action, they were better prepared than their forebears. This preparation can be seen in the history of the ultramarine Economic Societies, showing officials in Spain and America with fluctuating, discriminatory, and arbitrary views on the colonial Societies; displaying differences between enlightened creoles and Spaniards in America and conservatives dubious of novelty as a threat to easy continuation of the old regime; and giving evidence on the state of the economy and on creole and peninsular views on the deficiencies thereof.

In the 1780's four colonial Societies—Manila, Santiago de Cuba, Mompox, Vera Cruz—were formed or suggested. The Havana, Lima, Quito, and Guatemala Societies were formed early in the next decade. Early in the new century Societies were suggested for Buenos Aires and Bogota; the Havana Society continued; the Guatemala was suspended on orders from Spain; the Lima and Quito were extinguished by the governments there; those of Santiago, Mompox, and Vera Cruz were dead; the Manila was sleeping. By then the wars had sadly damaged connections between Spain and America, and the great events of the times, as well as the spread of revolutionary ideas, had altered the climate of opinion in Spanish America.

After the imposition of Joseph Bonaparte as king of Spain in 1808, the creation of Spanish resistance governments in the south, and the swift growth of political aspiration in America, Societies were formed in 1810 at Caracas and 1812 at Buenos Aires, but were political bodies, unlike the *amigos* of Campomanes. The Havana Society continued, and the flush of liberalism emanating from Cadiz reanimated the Guatemala Society and created a Society in Puerto Rico.[1] Between the restoration of Ferdinand VII in 1814, soon followed by a policy of reaction, and 1822, when most of America was independent, only one new Society was set up, in Chiapas in 1819. The Guatemala Society declined in vigor in those years and was dead by 1821; the Havana had its most fruitful period, under the guidance of Alejandro Ramírez.

Politico-Economic Conditions

By 1790 the population of Spanish America was perhaps fifteen or sixteen million, half again as large as Spain's, and it included Spaniards, creoles, mestizos, mulattoes, Indians, Negroes, and a variety of breeds. It dotted a

---

[1] *Supra*, 61-62, on the Cortes and the Societies.

territory immensely larger than Spain, and some of the regions had so little connection that Mariano Moreno of Buenos Aires in 1810 could claim with some plausibility that the austral area had no more relations with Mexico than with Russia or Tartary.[2]

The people of America were even farther removed from governmental processes than were the people of Spain. The former had nothing like the *fueros* of the Basque provinces, and not even the moribund parliamentary tradition of Castile and Aragon. No city of America had the sense of actual and historical purpose and peculiar quality that belonged to Barcelona. The administrative system of America was staffed by Spaniards, especially in its upper reaches; and the economic system was constructed with the advantage of Spain in mind. For these reasons the creoles complained that: "The Spanish Americans are not as near the throne as Europeans; here is the main reason they are not equally listened to."[3]

The main governmental changes for America during the century were: (1) financial-administrative; and (2) in the trading system. Although fiscal-administrative measures and the considerable relaxation of the trading laws did help improve revenues,[4] and increased trade between Spain and America,[5] they did not end monopolistic practices,[6] nor could they cancel out the basic deficiencies of Spanish production.[7] Contraband traffic not only continued but increased.[8]

---

[2] Ricardo Levene, *Introducción a la historia del derecho indiano* (Buenos Aires, 1924), 300. Some provinces, of course, had close relations (cf. Eduardo Arcila Farías, *Comercio entre Venezuela y México en los siglos XVI y XVII* [Mexico, 1950], 19-20, *et passim*).

[3] *Gazeta de Guatemala*, April 3, 1797, 62-63.

[4] Bailey W. Diffie, *Latin-American Civilization* (Harrisburg, 1945), 436, citing Humboldt, that the royal revenues from New Spain rose from some 3 million pesos in 1712 to over 20 million in 1802.

[5] Clarence H. Haring, *The Spanish Empire in America* (Oxford University Press, 1947), 342, that in 1778-88 the value of trade between Spain and Spanish America may have increased 700 per cent; Altamira, *Historia* (4th ed.), IV, 294 *et seq.*, that trade rose but should have increased more, being hurt by contraband, monopolies, etc.

[6] Cf. Earl J. Hamilton, "The Role of Monopoly in the Overseas Expansion and Colonial Trade of Europe before 1800," *American Economic Review*, XXXVIII, No. 2 (May, 1948), 33-53, for the view that Spain's policy toward the commerce and industry of American was relatively liberal, but that one of the chief creole complaints at the end of the colonial era was against monopolistic practices.

[7] Herbert Priestley, *José de Gálvez, visitador-general of New Spain 1765-71* (University of California Press, 1916), 388 *et seq.*, that eighteenth-century changes in the system were not fundamental, and that their effects represented the last improvements that could be wrung from the old arrangements; Carlos Pereyra, *Historia de América española* (8 vols., Madrid, 1920-27), II, 268, arguing, without clearly acknowledging it, that the prime problems were low Spanish production and the poor distribution system.

[8] Canga Argüelles, *Diccionario*, "Amiens," a report (1802) on the sad state of

The causes of the deficiences of the American economy were complex. Not all were the result of Spanish policy, and even when they were, it is not now thought proper to indiscriminately blame Spain for her actions. Spain was not unique among nations in desiring to use colonial resources for metropolitan advantage. Spanish policy makers had to consider the needs of the empire as a whole,[9] while creole critics could be more parochial in their views. Spanish policy protected some American agricultural producers, while it hurt others, possibly unavoidably since so many provinces could compete in the production of tropical crops.[10] Spain permitted and even encouraged some American industrial production. Low productivity and low purchasing power in America were due to creole affection for the aristocratic dispensation as well as to Spanish policy, and in any event a drastic revision of these matters would have required an effort and knowledge beyond the powers of any nation on earth at the time. Much of Spain's difficulty resulted from the military action and aggressively illegal commercial policies of other nations. Creole criticism of Spanish policy not only often was parochial, but obviously

---

Spain's economy, and statistics showing she had less American trade than foreigners; Carlos Calvo, *Anales históricos de la revolución de la América latina* (5 vols., Paris, 1864-67), I, p. CXXVII, value of trade between Spain and America, amount of foreign goods, and (p. LV) that all the revenues of Spain were less than those of Spanish America in 1810; Priestley, *Gálvez*, 35, a Spanish committee reported in 1765 that of the total Spanish American production (largely precious metals) of some 35 million pesos annually, only some 19,500,000 reached Spain, and most of the rest went to English possessions for Negroes and flour; A. P. Whitaker, "The Commerce of Louisiana and the Floridas at the End of the Eighteenth Century," HAHR, VIII, No. 2 (May, 1928), 190-203, stating that Spanish merchants would have lost even more of the American trade except for the remoteness of most of the colonies, the monopolistic laws, and the scarcity of good ports (which made it easier to control contraband); Vera Lee Brown, "Contraband Trade: A Factor in the Decline of Spain's Empire in America," HAHR, VIII, No. 2 (May, 1928), 178-89; Altamira, *Historia* (4th ed.), IV, 303-11; Pereyra, *Historia de América española*, II, 260 *et seq.*; Haring, *Spanish Empire*, 328 *et seq.*, on contraband; Hussey, *Caracas Company*, 226 *et seq.*, changes in the trading system and other reforms; Víctor Andrés Belaunde, *Bolívar and the Political Thought of the Spanish American Revolution* (Baltimore, 1938), 54-55, breaking the Peruvian trade monopoly did not satisfy Buenos Aires, since Spain could not absorb Platine products or supply its needs; R. A. Humphreys, "The Fall of the Spanish American Empire," *History* (October, 1952), 213-27, that what stimulated the colonial economy in the 18th century was not so much imperial economic reforms as European search for markets and demand for American products; Harry Bernstein, *Origins of Inter-American Interest 1700-1812* (University of Pennsylvania Press, 1945), 99-101, Yankee trade with Spanish America.

[9] Arcila Farías, *Comercio entre Venezuela y México*, 13, 18, 27, *et passim*, for extensive exposition of this thesis, and the judgment that the result often was beneficial to America.

[10] *Ibid.*, 35, on Barinas tobacco growers who wanted Spanish protection against cheaper Caracas tobacco, whereas Caracas growers interpreted protection as oppression.

was political and selfish.[11] When all the above has been said, however, it remains true that Spanish industrial production was inferior—and progressively more so—to that of her rivals, and insufficient for American needs and desires.[12] The Spanish revisionists—some of them in peninsular Economic Societies—recognized this, and outlined the steps required to increase production.

The American Societies also worried—from the early 1780's to 1821— about the basic deficiences of production rather than about small methods of tinkering with the unsatisfactory production then available. This was one difference between the American Societies and the Consulados: although the latter had some interest in production, it was subordinate to the mercantile interest. Of course, the members of the Societies, as well as other Spaniards and creoles, tended to overestimate the riches of America, partly by failing sufficiently to appreciate the relationship between natural resources and cultural capacity to exploit them. Although the Societies had a considerable understanding of this problem, and saw the connection between education and economic production, they underestimated the difficulties involved.

Agriculture in the Indies, as in Spain, was the largest field of economic activity.[13] But if agriculture was in sad case in the metropolis, as the Economic Societies there insisted, its condition was worse in America. The land was at least as unevenly divided as that of the Peninsula, so that it was difficult in America, a land of vast spaces, to get good land of the proper sort in

---

[11] *Ibid.*, 32, for an example of this, and the reproachful comment of the author that creoles were interested only in their own economic concerns rather than in the total interest of the empire.

[12] Cf. Sergio Bagú, *Economía de la sociedad colonial* (Buenos Aires, 1949), for a recent summary of arguments critical of Spain's economic policies and their effects on America. For a contrary opinion see Juan Agustín García, *La ciudad indiana* (Buenos Aires, 1937 [1st ed. 1900]), 218, for the misleading statement that the seventeenth- and eighteenth-century chronicles give an impression of "abundance and wealth, of easy life," and 229, that the "erroneous" impression of poverty in the Plata region is due to an official documentation that is "a perpetual lament," but is contradicted by private documents. See Ricardo Levene, "La política económica de España en América durante el siglo XVIII y la revolución de 1810," in *Anales de la Facultad de Derecho y Ciencias Sociales*, 2d ser., vol. 4 (Buenos Aires, 1914), 594-719, at 597-98, that the seventeenth-century decadance was primarily economic, and 699-719 for the late colonial dispute between the monopolists and the new ideas, some of which were being put into legislation.

[13] Cf. Diffie, *Latin-American Civilization*, 396, citing Humboldt, that at the end of the 18th century the annual value of agricultural produce in New Spain was 30 million pesos, minerals 25 million, manufactures 7 to 8 million; *ibid.*, 350, that the relative value of agriculture was even greater in other areas; Lillian E. Fisher, *The Background of the Revolution for Mexican Independence* (Boston, 1934), 150, 171, on the comparative value of agriculture and industry in New Spain at the beginning of the 19th century; Haring, *Spanish Empire*, 260-61.

desirable locations, but, even so, more good land lay unused than in Spain. Nor was the land of America better tilled than that of Spain. The great technical improvements in agriculture, which the Spanish Societies wished to import into Spain, especially from England, were not being applied to either metropolis or colony. If the Madrid Society could lament the use of mules rather than oxen in the tillage of Spanish soil, Americans might have lamented even more loudly the stick and hoe culture prevailing in most colonial areas.[14] But the dominant minority in Spanish America was little interested in improving the agricultural techniques of small farmers, many of whom were Indians.[15] Although Spanish law for America provided land and other rights for the Indians, implementing the laws was another matter.[16]

Mining was important in America, and sometimes stimulated both agriculture and craftsmanship, but it also resulted in serious distortions of economic practice and public policy. It was a common revisionist view—in Spain and America—that there had been an overemphasis on mining.[17] Although mining in New Spain at the end of the colonial period enjoyed one of its most prosperous periods,[18] that prosperity did not compensate for the deficiencies of the economy as a whole. Furthermore, not all mining areas enjoyed prosperity at the end of the colonial era.[19]

Manufacturing and craftsmanship in America were hampered by Spanish laws governing colonial fabrication, by the emphasis on mining, by monopolistic guild practices, by shortage of capital, poor transportation, low pur-

---

[14] Ward, *Proyecto económico*, Parte I, ch. xx, favored teaching the Indians to cultivate; Campillo, *Nuevo sistema*, Parte Primera, ch. vii, advocated giving the Indians land; Fisher, *Background*, 154 *et seq.*, on bad land division and other agricultural difficulties at the end of the colonial era; *supra*, 49, for Campomanes' opinion in the *Industria Popular* on the land problem in the Indies; Diffie, *Latin-American Civilization*, 363; Conde de Revilla Gigedo, *Instrucción reservada que ... dió a su succesor ...* [1794] (Mexico, 1831), 102, that "the division of lands in these realms is much less equal than in Spain"; *Gazeta de literatura de Mexico* (2d ed.), I, 30 *et seq.*, for an opinion of 1788 on the "decadence" of agriculture and stockraising.

[15] Cf. Ricardo Cappa, *Estudios críticos acerca de la dominación española en América* (26 vols., Madrid, 1889-97), Pt. III, vol. VI, 294-302, *et passim*, for a defense of Spain's agricultural regime in America, ascribing much of the cause of low production to "natural" causes rather than to Spanish policy.

[16] Cf. Vicente Gay y Forner, *Leyes del imperio español* (1924), for a discussion of rights assured to the Indians by law; and a rigorous defense of Spanish virtue, going to the length of emphasizing the provision of early colonial days for representative government in America—which was never implemented.

[17] Cf. Fisher, *Background*, 107, citing a "Project" by Antonio de San José Muro, Mexico, 1787, which stated that countries with products to export were enriched, those with only mines were miserable.

[18] Cf. Howe, *Mining Guild*.

[19] Cf. Arthur P. Whitaker, *The Huancavelica Mercury Mine* (Cambridge, 1941), on the decline of mercury production in Peru.

chasing power, and by other difficulties. The value of goods fabricated in America was much less than that of agricultural products, and, since Spain could not meet the demand, much manufactured stuff was bought illegally from foreigners, directly or indirectly. Craftsmen in America worked chiefly in their own huts or in small shops, and production was puny from the point of view of supplying American needs of many types of goods, or of capacity to compete with foreign fabricators. The Spanish Bishop Manuel Abad y Queipo of Michoacán, "the principal intellectual mover" of early dissatisfaction in the Independence period in New Spain,[20] in 1805 claimed that the clothing industry of New Spain could not dress and shoe one-third of the population; and while the manufacture of cotton textiles was forbidden, Mexican shops were full of contraband cottons.[21] Abad y Queipo's ideas were much like those of the majority of enlightened conservatives who belonged to the Economic Societies in America. He had progressive economic ideas, favoring free commerce, the abolition of old restrictions which had hindered colonial development, the division of the large landed estates, and stimulation of cotton and wool textile manufacturing; but his political views were conservative, for while he believed that colonials should have all the rights of inhabitants of Spain, he objected to innovations in government in periods of agitation, thus opposing both the Cortes in Spain during the French invasion and the idea of a junta of government in New Spain, which he considered an act of rebellion, itself contrary to natural law, the rights of the people, and the laws of God and of society.[22]

Much of the difficulty in the industrial field did stem from the mercantilist policy of Spain, which, if it did not inhibit colonial practice quite so much as is sometimes claimed, was on the whole not a stimulant to industry overseas.[23] The effects on America of the policy of restriction in favor of the

---

[20] Mariano Cuevas, *Historia de la nación mexicana* (Mexico, 1940), 382, and stating that Abad y Queipo expounded "the four social ulcers of our *Patria*, sores that ancient Spain was far from able to cure: economic disorder, oppression of the native races, administrative abuses, and abuses against the Church by the *Real Patronato*."

[21] Fisher, *Background*, 165; cf. *ibid.*, 167, for the view of Antonio de San José Muro—who had connections with the Guatemala Economic Society (*infra*, 210-11)—in 1787 that since foreign imports were the worst enemy of a country, the colonies should be encouraged to manufacture goods that Spain did not supply, and that spinning was the best craft to encourage; *ibid.*, 169 *et seq.*, on encouragement of industry.

[22] Lillian E. Fisher, *Champion of Reform : Manuel Abad y Queipo* (New York, 1955), 65, 70, 78-79, 109-10, *et passim*.

[23] Cf. Gregorio Funes, *Ensayo de la historia civil del Paraguay, Buenos Aires y Tucumán* (3 vols., Buenos Aires, 1816-17), III, 220 *et seq.*, approving the freeing of trade but raving against prohibitions on colonial manufacturing; Altamira, *Historia* (4th ed.), IV, 293, that the industrial life of America was sparse, and this largely

metropolis were aggravated, furthermore, by a vacillating and arbitrary application by colonial officials. Bernardo Ward was an example of a European student of political economy who had some liberal and sensible ideas,[24] but who nevertheless favored restriction of textile production in America, so that Spain, in approved mercantilist fashion, might do the cloth manufacturing for the Spanish world. Ward thought that Indian women might make thread which could be sent to Spain for manufacture into cloth.[25] This was a notion likely to be costly, and difficult to impose upon the affections of colonials who were under no divine obligation to revere a policy directed to the profit of Spaniards.[26]

If agricultural and industrial conditions were less than blooming, the financial structure in America was hardly more healthful. The confusion of the Spanish coinage was compounded by the issuance of paper money in 1779 and succeeding years, although the issues did not depreciate badly until after 1793. Spanish efforts to reform the coinage in the second half of the eighteenth century were failures, merely adding new coins to exist alongside the old. There was a paucity of capital for economic development in America. The scarcity of money in circulation was a severe handicap to business. Merchants in Mexico issued tokens for change. Since the tokens were acceptable only to the issuing agent, they were scarcely a model medium of exchange. Other problems stemmed from such practices as Charles III's secret debasement of the coinage, and from serious difficulty with clipping,

due to Spanish restrictive laws; Haring, *Trade and Navigation*, *passim*, for many comments that Spain's economic policy with regard to America was mistaken and damaging; Priestley, *Gálvez*, ch. i, a strong condemnation of the colonial system, especially in its commercial and public revenue aspects; Hamilton, "Role of Monopoly," *loc. cit.*, 41-43, for Spanish encouragement of industry in America; Demetrio Ramos Pérez, *Historia de la colonización española en América* (Madrid, 1947), 186-88, ascribing the poor industrial development of America to lack of an industrial tradition—Indian or Castilian, lack of industrial facilities and iron and coal, lack of transportation, due in part to interference with traffic by Spain's enemies, and lack of American markets, due to piratical interference with the transfer of goods between American provinces, and to the fact that only the European stock in America had purchasing power, and this demand was largely satisfied by contraband; Fisher, *Background*, ch. iv, a good discussion of industry in New Spain, calling it "unprogressive," and manufacturing the most backward; Cappa, *Estudios críticos*, Pt III, vol. VII, 195 *et seq.*, 283 *et seq.*, vol. IX, 322-62, on decay of Peruvian industry in the 18th century.

24 *Supra*, 9.
25 Fisher, *Background*, 166.
26 Cf. Luís Cháves Orozco, *Historia económica y social de Mexico. Ensayo de interpretación* (Mexico, 1938), 59-64, on some industrial difficulties in New Spain late in the colonial era; Diffie, *Latin-American Civilization*, 388, on Viceroy Revillagigedo's view in 1794 that an extension of manufacturing in New Spain would be damaging to the dependency of colony on metropolis.

sweating, and counterfeiting of coins. Finally, taxes were poorly used from the American point of view, and were quite high, especially when one calculates with them the forced loans to which the government had resort and for which creoles had as little affection as others who have endured such shotgun levies.[27]

The Spanish tradition in the industrial field was hardly the best guide in the new age. In America as in Spain the intellectual-social climate was ill suited to large-scale industrial effort.[28] The affection for science and its practical applications, though increasing, was too much blocked by politico-religious considerations. The middle class was small, and grew little in the face of the aristocratic dispensation which permeated every aspect of thought and action in the world of the dominant minority. The liberals and conservatives of this minority differed on some questions, but no doubt agreed on even more.

This was partly because class distinction in America was reinforced by racial discrimination, made rigid by the fact that the European minority had that fear of mass action by Negro or Indian that such a minority must always display, in British India or in South Carolina or in New Spain.[29] So the Indian's status in such areas as Peru and New Spain and Guatemala displayed some of the marks of caste. Indian blood was hardly an asset, often a liability. Most creoles considered the Indian an inferior creature, as the creole himself was thought inferior by the sons of such celestial areas as Guipúzcoa and Andalucía.

The resulting economic—to say nothing of social—waste is indicated by Campillo's treatise of 1743—published in 1789—on a "New System of Economic Government for America," suggesting that the Indian be given land, noting that the law in America seemed to give him property, but that in practice he was not secure in it. Campillo had wit enough to understand

---

[27] Earl J. Hamilton, "Monetary Problems in Spain and Spanish America, 1751-1800," *Journal of Economic History*, IV, No. 1 (May, 1944), 21-48; Fisher, *Background*, 185, and ch. v.

[28] For a recent expression of this common view, see Sergio Bagú, *Estructura social de la colonia* (Buenos Aires, 1952), 105 *et seq.*, on "Idea y posibilidad de progreso," pointing out that the eighteenth-century European idea of material progress was not widely held in feudal and Catholic Latin America.

[29] Cf. Ortiz, *Hija cubana*, 61, that the condition of the laborer was worse in the colonies than in Spain because of slavery and race, which tended to extend the mark of this vile condition to all who labored, and citing instances of discrimination of all sorts in Cuba; Felipe Barreda Laos, *Vida intelectual del virreinato del Perú* (Buenos Aires, 1937), 377 *et seq.*, the colonial government reduced the Indian intellect to inertia, and encouraged rivalry between *castas*, so no feeling of solidarity might be built up; Cappa, *Estudios críticos*, Pt. III, vol. VIII, 7-19, 29-30, on the difficulties, including a racial problem, of developing fabrication in America.

that the Indians had shown considerable talent before their conquest by Europeans,[30] and felt that the view that the Indian lacked capacity resulted from the malice or ignorance of the Spaniards who repeated it. He wanted the Indians to wear Spanish-style clothes and speak the Spanish language. He knew that creoles would object that this program would encourage rebellions, but he dismissed the argument as nonsense.[31] Dishonest many of the creole arguments may have been, but it is not clear that they were nonsense, since they were in large measure dedicated to the creoles' interest. The creoles showed the same capacity for rationalization that is a feature of the social history of all groups of *homo sapiens*. In any event, such discrimination was a fact. It is interesting to observe that when an Economic Society of Friends of the Country was founded at Caracas in 1834, long after the Independence era, with its propaganda for equality, a broadside was issued to exclude *pardos* from the new organization.[32] So even then *amigo* was a term that crossed racial lines with some difficulty.

Thus class distinction in America was rigorous and the source of an incalculable amount of mistrust, hatred, and inefficiency.[33] The masses had even less sense of identity with the classes than in Spain, for they had even more obvious reasons for detesting them, nor was the natural conservatism of the peasantry bolstered as in Spain by so large a sense of security and continuity. The peasant culture of Spain was less insecure and less drastically different from that of the upper classes than in America. The peasantry of Spain, for all the difficulties of its position, was not subject to as massive a system of semivoluntary and absolutely forced labor, often promiscuously applied. If the peasantry and middle class of Spain could not unite against the privileged orders, it was still less possible for those classes in America to do so.

Perhaps if the creoles had become highly prosperous, they might have remained more nearly quiescent, but this is by no means certain;[34] it might

---

[30] *Nuevo sistema*, Parte Primera, chap. vi.

[31] *Ibid.*, chap. ix. *Infra*, 297-300, for discussion of clothing the Indians.

[32] Laureano Vallenilla Lanz, *Cesarismo democrático* (Caracas, 1919), 109-10. Cf. Antonio Arellano Moreno, *Orígenes de la economía venezolana* (Mexico, 1947), 432-33, for evidence of the influence of economics on the creole attitude toward slavery and class.

[33] Fisher, *Background*, 408, is of this opinion. For a discussion of the economic effects of class pride in Mexico as displayed in the novels of José Fernández de Lizardi (1776-1827), see Jefferson R. Spell, *The Life and Works of José Joaquín Fernández de Lizardi* (University of Pennsylvania Press, 1931), 73 *et seq.*

[34] Cf. Fisher, *Background*, ch. iii, that eighteenth-century economic improvement just stimulated desire for independence in Spanish America, that Spain clung more than other countries to mistaken economic ideas, and that America received the gift of Spain's own deplorable economic conditions.

have made them even more self-assertive, as happened in Anglo-America. And the creoles had other than economic grievances, during the eighteenth century complaining increasingly about political, social, legal, and other matters.[35] The criticism of domestic institutions, however, which distinguished the writings of Spanish revisionists, had less force in America than in Spain. For one thing, the censorship was somewhat stricter for America. For another, Spanish revisionists were more interested in peninsular problems than in encouraging colonials to forget their proper sense of subordination. In the third place, intellectual life was less well organized and its product less brilliant than in Spain. There was in America no such center of intellectual influence as Madrid. In the fourth place, creoles of talent could not easily rise in the king's service in America by the route of Campomanes and Jovellanos in Spain, to develop learned and exhaustive treatises on problems of political economy, which they might even hope would affect administration and legislation. The vigor, depth, power, and impressive magnitude of the studies of the two Spaniards came from long service, with access to the best records, and the aid of friends and officials of learning, experience, and influence. Creoles had less opportunity to combine government experience with critical analysis of the political-economic order.

The result of all this was that works on political economy by authors of the Spanish tongue that were read widely in America in the eighteenth century were chiefly by Europeans writing about Spain; and when the Spanish political economists did discuss America, they usually emphasized trade between metropolis and colony. Whereas Spaniards could read works by their own people on a wide range of Spanish economic problems, creoles could find relatively little printed material that dealt with the American economy as a whole. Campillo and Ward said something about America— from the Spanish point of view—but the more voluminous, learned, and influential works of Campomanes and Jovellanos dealt mainly with Spain. In recognition of this, a work published by the Guatemala Society in 1798 complained that while Spanish writers neglected America, the work of Ward and Campillo was admired, "although experience teaches that it erred in

---

[35] Cf. Levene, *Derecho indiano*, ch. xvi, asserting that Americans had more ability than was generally supposed, and including (p. 302) a proposal of 1797 for legal reforms, separation of the judicial from other powers, appointment of creoles as *oidores;* Enrique Ruíz Guiñazú, *La magistratura indiana* (Buenos Aires, 1916), ch. ix, blasting those who condemn the system of justice in the colonial era, but Guiñazú did not deny that the creoles thought, or affected to think, that they had a grievance in this connection; Herbert I. Priestley, *The Mexican Nation, A History* (New York, 1938), 194, that "the judicial system was indeed a lack of system . . . during the entire colonial epoch"; Luís Galdames, *La evolución constitucional de Chile* (Santiago, 1925), 48 *et seq.*, for a good discussion of the poor administration of justice.

many things."[36] To be sure, the works of Spanish economists had an important effect on economic thought in America, even when they dealt with Spanish problems.[37]

Of course, a fifth reason for the relative lack of forceful criticism of domestic institutions in America was the fact that some colonial practices most needful of change were supported by the creoles themselves. This had always been true of the harsh treatment of the Indians, who were more abused by colonials or by local officials on their own initiative than by the laws of the Indies. And a sixth difference between creole criticism of the local political economy and Spanish criticism of such problems in the Peninsula was that any American complaint about economic conditions, sometimes harking regretfully to a lost golden age even as did Spaniards, was almost certain to include a complaint against Spain. Scapegoats available to Spanish critics of the peninsular economy had a narrower usefulness, and the critics were driven to admission of domestic shortcomings.

There was, to be sure, a great deal of discussion of economic affairs in America, and many documents on economic matters were produced, by Spaniards and creoles. The influence of this activity was important, but more largely confined to the localities where it occurred, than in the case of printed materials. An example of a Spanish official of revisionist tendency in America is Ramón de Posada, a partisan of Jovellanos' suggestions for agrarian reform, who wanted freer (but not free) trade, and believed in a "natural order" that was nearly equivalent to laissez faire, and required that the State intervene relatively little in the national economy.[38]

Altering the powers of the House of Trade and of the Council of the Indies, creating a Ministry of the Indies, setting up the intendancy system in America, increasing the number of captaincies general—such administrative reshuffling, when unaccompanied by a gift of offices, could not be expected

---

[36] *Utilidades y medios de que los indios y ladinos vistan y calzen a la española. Memoria que mereció el accesit ... Antonio de S. José Muro ...* (N. Guatemala), 4.

[37] Cf. Eduardo Arcila Farías, "Ideas Económicas en Nueva España en el Siglo XVIII," *El Trimestre Económico*, XIV, No. 1 (April-June, 1947), 68-82, for the effects on economic thought in America of Physiocracy, mercantilism, and peculiarly American institutions; and for the judgment that Campillo and Jovellanos were the two Spanish thinkers who most influenced American economic thought. See E. del Valle Iberlucea, *Los diputados de Buenos Aires en las Cortes de Cadiz y el nuevo sistema de gobierno económico de América* (Buenos Aires, 1912), 143-70, for a competent, traditional survey of a few well-known examples of Spanish revisionist thought and activity as they related to America.

[38] Arcila Farías, "Ideas Económicas en Nueva España," *loc. cit.*, 75-76, 78-81, also citing an *Informe* of 1778 of the Consulado of Mexico which spoke of an *órden natural*.

to instil in creoles an ungovernable enthusiasm.[39] The discrimination against those of Spanish blood and culture born in America was a part of the system of control, and became finally one of the most important sources of dissatisfaction, and a well-spring of the fight for independence. Well known are the comments of Juan and Ulloa that it was "sufficient to have been born in the Indies to hate Europeans,"[40] and of Alexander Humboldt that the most miserable and uneducated European was thought superior to whites born in the new continent, and that the latter preferred the "denomination of Americans to that of creoles."[41] Nor did it matter that according to law all white creoles were Spaniards, since the laws were abused.[42] So, late in the eighteenth century, the creoles spoke more and more of America rather than of the Indies, and of themselves as Americans.[43] And they railed at the notion that the colonial stock was or ought to be treated as inferior to that of such centers of culture as Galicia and Extremadura.

An example of Spanish-creole conflict occurred in Guatemala in 1796 at the death of the Marquis of Aycinena, prior of the Consulado and town counsellor, when the essentially European Consulado wanted two representatives of each corporation to carry the body to the sepulcher; but the town council, a creole body, demanded an exclusive privilege to carry this creole corpse. The captain general finally had to decree that the occasion did not allow extended pleadings and that the view of the Consulado must prevail.[44] Since members of both these bodies belonged to the Economic Society, it may be guessed that some friction carried over into the latter.[45] While creoles at large developed a strong sense of grievance against

---

[39] Cf. Funes, *Ensayo*, III, 225, complaining that ecclesiastical and civil offices went to Spaniards.

[40] Jorge Juan and Antonio de Ulloa, *Noticias secretas de América* (2 vols., London, 1826), Part II, cap. vi.

[41] *Essai politique sur le royaume de la Nouvelle-Espagne* (2 vols., paged continously, Paris, 1811), 114.

[42] *Ibid.*, 115. Cf. Gregorio Torres Quintero, *Mexico hacia el fin del virreinato. Antecedentes sociológicos del pueblo mexicano* (Mexico, 1921), 45-48, "Los Criollos según los Españoles"; 51-54, "Los Criollos según ellos mismos."

[43] Humboldt, *Nouvelle-Espagne*, 114-15, commented that the distinction between American and Spaniard as words became especially marked in the 1780's, and even more after 1789. Cf. *Gazeta de literàtura de Mexico* (2d ed.), I, 1-4, for 1788 use of the phraseology "nuestra Nación Hispano Americana."

[44] Jph. Domás y Valle to the Ayuntamiento, April 4, 1796, Libro de Actas del Cabildo de Guatemala año 1796—AGG, A1.2-2, leg. 2183, exped. 15724.

[45] Cf. R. S. Smith, "Origins of the Consulado of Guatemala," HAHR, XXVI, No. 2 (May, 1946), 150-61, for information on friction between Consulado and Ayuntamiento, even though some members of the latter were merchants.

Spain,[46] the younger men tended to succumb also to belief in representative government—by a minority, in which they would play a conspicuous part—and in liberty in the conduct of their own affairs; and to turn the light of rationalism on a governmental system ill-equipped for defense against such an attack.[47] Some Spaniards were aware of the danger. José de Abalos, first intendant of Venezuela (1777-1783), warned of the possible loss of the colonies, not for the sentimental and ingenuous reasons of the influence of English propaganda and of encyclopedism, but because of fundamental dissatisfaction with the politico-economic regime of Spain in America.[48] And Count Aranda in 1793 informed the king that "it may not be supposed that our America is as innocent as in past centuries."[49] While it is true that some Spaniards realized the necessity of concessions to America, more opposed the idea. In addition, the system itself was inflexible and yielded but slowly to suggestion.

Intellectual Conditions

The new ideas penetrated Spanish America at an ever faster rate in the eighteenth century, first scientific-philosophical ideas, then sociopolitical. The barriers to this penetration are sometimes exaggerated, and most of

---

[46] Cf. Funes, *Ensayo*, 225-26, accusing Minister of the Indies Gálvez of trying to destroy historical sources and leave Americans in ignorance of their rights.

[47] Belaunde, *Bolivar and Political Thought*, 124-25, divides the new political philosophy of Spanish America at the end of the 18th century into the progressive or reforming, and the revolutionary; Fisher, *Background*, 349-50, notes that in New Spain all the abuses of sovereign power of which the English colonists of Virginia and Massachusetts complained were duplicated, and to them others were added, while the admirable laws were not enforced, and the Bourbon reforms came too late; Antonio José de Irisarri, *El Cristiano errante* (Santiago, Chile, 1929), 13, 104-5, 175, 187, 302-3, *et passim*, for the restless travels of a young creole late in the colonial era, his interest in new ideas, and his Spanish merchant father's connection with Spaniards and creoles of advanced views in Guatemala.

[48] Eduardo Arcila Farías, *Economía colonial de Venezuela* (Mexico, 1946), 303 *et seq.*, and printing (315-19) a letter of Abalos to Gálvez from Caracas in 1780 warning of the possible consequences of the loss of that part of America. This sensible official displayed the usual penchant of his times for overestimation of the riches of America. Cf. Arellano Moreno, *Orígenes*, for extensive discussion of connections between economics and the independence movement; Sofonías Salvatierra, *Contribución a la historia de América Central* (2 vols., Managua, 1939), II, 114, objecting to overemphasis on the importance of the French Revolution on the political history of Central America, and stating that it really was determined by "the desire for liberty of commerce [and by], misery, hunger, and ignorance."

[49] Miguel Luís Amunátegui, *Los precursores de la independencia de Chile* (3 vols., Santiago, 1909-10), III, 273-74. Cf., for further information on Count Aranda's opinions on the problem of America; A. P. Whitaker, "The Pseudo-Aranda Memorial of 1783," HAHR, XVII, No. 3 (1937), 287-313; A. R. Wright, "The Aranda Memorial: Genuine or Forged?" HAHR, XVIII, No. 4 (November, 1938), 445-60.

the men supposedly persecuted for advanced views were actually restricted for political reasons. Even the lethargy that made diffusion of the Enlightenment difficult at first, later stood in the way of effective opposition to it. So far as scientific ideas were concerned, by the end of the colonial era the cultural lag between European discovery and American knowledge had virtually disappeared.[50] The scientific side of the Enlightenment came chiefly through Spain, and the Spanish government itself, through scientific expeditions and otherwise, encouraged this development.[51] Not only was the Enlightenment in the Spanish world weighted in the direction of "useful" knowledge, but even novel philosophical ideas came in the form of a modern eclecticism rather than in a doctrinaire guise.[52] For these reasons the politically and socially conservative in the Spanish world could support the Enlightenment.[53] Although Spain tried to keep doctrinaire sociopolitical ideas from America, it could not. The influence of Rousseau is prime evidence of that fact; once Rousseau penetrated Spanish literature there was no way to keep his influence from America.[54] The creoles evinced a growing interest in the liberalism of England, France, and finally the United States, which indicated that in this direction the colonials had become more advanced than the Spanish.[55] In any event, the impossibility of keeping creoles just a little bit ignorant may be seen in the views of the *Gazeta de Guatemala* on "Ancients and Moderns," listing the great dissimilarities, scientific and technological, political and intellectual, social and commercial, between contemporary and earlier times.[56]

The new ideas came to America by many routes. They came with Spanish officials, ecclesiastics, merchants, and scientists, who had adopted them in Spain,[57] often through connections with Economic Societies of Friends of

---

[50] John T. Lanning, "The Reception of the Enlightenment in Latin America," in A. P. Whitaker (ed.), *Latin America and the Enlightenment* (New York, 1942), 71-94, with calculation of the relative speed with which America picked up the ideas of Descartes, Newton, and Lamarck.

[51] Cf. Howe, *Mining Guild*, for the new mining technology in Mexico, and for the work there of Fausto D'Elhuyar, sometime teacher in the Seminary of Vergara.

[52] J. T. Lanning, "The Last Stand of the Schoolmen," in *University of Miami Hispanic-American Studies*, No. 1 (1939), 33-49, on this intellectual conservatism.

[53] Cf. A. P. Whitaker, "The Dual Role of Latin America in the Enlightenment," in *Latin America and the Enlightenment*, 3-21.

[54] Spell, *Rousseau*, 217-22, a good survey of the introduction of the new ideas in Spanish America; *ibid.*, 232 *et seq.*, the influence of Rousseau in Spanish America in the late 18th and early 19th centuries.

[55] Fisher, *Background*, 84-85, advances this idea vigorously.

[56] *Gazeta*, January 18, 1802.

[57] Cf. Belaunde, *Bolivar and Political Thought*, 75, *et passim*, on "the close connection between reformist thought in Spain and in America."

the Country. Some of the later viceroys and other civil officials in America held liberal views, especially on education and the new science. Some higher ecclesiastics approved a portion of the new thought. A number of these Spanish officials and clerics, together with Spanish merchants and men of learning, helped found and operate the Economic Societies of America. But it must not be supposed that most Spaniards in America were much attached to new ideas; and even less can we suppose any large number of politically liberal Spaniards in America, even among those attracted to the new science or political economy.[58] It could not be expected that many Spaniards would go further than Bishop Abad y Queipo, who favored economic changes of some magnitude, but condemned Rousseau's version of social origins, and considered insurrection against an existing government a sin.[59] This last was a doctrine of dubious apostolic sanction, but favored by the government, which in the reign of Charles III ordered metropolitans in the Indies to teach submission to authority.[60]

Spanish publications carried the new ideas to America. Many Spanish authors assimilated and Hispanicized the ideas of the Enlightenment, serving them up in a form endurable if not entirely palatable to the censorship.[61] Jerónimo Feijóo was much read in America, and his strictures on superstition and his dedication to the rational method did nothing to bolster affection for the old regime.[62] The liberal Madrid periodical *Espíritu de los mejores diarios* was current in the colonies late in the eighteenth century. The influence of the treatises of Campomanes was important. A Cuban periodical in 1800 quoted from his discourse on popular education to the effect that "Spain in the illusion of prosperity, and in the chimerical intent of appropriating to herself exclusively the riches and productions of the New World," prohibited all trade with foreigners and even hindered traffic within her own dominions.[63] The *Gazeta de Guatemala* printed the opinion that "Spain owes more Enlightenment to the little books of Señor Campo-

---

[58] Cf. Arcila Farías, *Comercio entre Venezuela y Mexico*, 27-30, on a Spaniard at Vera Cruz in the 1790's who resolved the conflict between his *nacionalismo* and his liberal economic views in favor of the former, declaring undesirable the prosperity of one American district if it hurt the economy of another, thus permitting his interest in the "unity of the empire" to override his "modern" prejudice against what he considered outmoded mercantilism.

[59] Spell, *Rousseau*, 242-43; *ibid.*, 130, for the judgment that liberals in high clerical posts were the exception.

[60] Barreda Laos, *Vida intelectual*, 362-63; this doctrine was preached in the cathedral of Lima, December 6, 1780.

[61] *Supra*, 17.

[62] Spell, *Rousseau*, 129, *et passim*, Feijóo helping spread Rousseau's ideas in America from an early day.

[63] *Lonja Mercantil de la Havana*, No. 13 (December 5), 97.

manes than to all the fat volumes written in two centuries, that are little read and studied less."[64]

In the third place, the new ideas were carried to America by creoles who had lived or traveled in Spain or other parts of Europe. This was notably the case with young men sent to round out their education. Many prominent leaders of the wars for independence formed their taste for the new thought while in Spain. Francisco de Miranda was sent to Spain in 1771; Manuel Belgrano, in the 1780's; Simón Rodríguez to Europe in the same decade; José Baquíjano arrived there in 1773, and became acquainted with Olavide and Jovellanos in Sevilla; Bernardo O'Higgins was in England and Spain in the 1790's.

A fourth way in which the new ideas came to America was by illegal reading materials. Another was via foreign travelers and merchants and residents in Spanish America.[65] All these routes of influence were important, and they were the more influential in that the censorship, as in Spain, was somewhat relaxed, though it remained stricter than in the metropolis.[66] It remained an annoyance, and at the very end of the colonial period men were still prosecuted for owning and reading prohibited books, though an ever larger amount of nominally prohibited reading matter was openly or surreptitiously imported.

The new ideas were spread in America by *colegios*, universities, and other institutions. The universities of America, like those of Spain, resisted change, but nevertheless began to succumb to the new philosophy. Sloughing off some of their ancient subservience to Aristotle and scholasticism, their cloisters became corrupted with Cartesianism and natural science, with rationalism and the spirit of skeptical inquiry.[67] The new "Carolingian Col-

---

[64] T. III, No. 144 (February 17, 1800), 168.

[65] Fisher, *Background*, 73, *et passim*, for radical Frenchmen in New Spain.

[66] A delicate question, often mixed with emotional defenses of "latinism," and with the question of whether Spain gave America all she had, or held something back for exclusively peninsular use. Desdevises, *La Richesse*, 207, considered control of thought and reading stricter in the Indies than in Spain; Vicente G. Quesada, *La vida intelectual en la América española durante los siglos XVI, XVII y XVIII* (Buenos Aires, 1917), 60, 65-66, found restrictions more rigid for America than for Spain; Cayetano Alcázar Molina, *Los virreinatos en el siglo XVIII* (Barcelona, 1945), xi, a Spanish apologist, in a sketchy book in a well-publicized series, says that the cultural life of the minority in America became in the 18th century not inferior to that of Spain, which proves Spain gave America all she had; Bernard Moses, *The Intellectual Background of the Revolution in Spanish America 1810-1824* (New York, 1924), ch. ii; José Torre Revello, *El libro, la imprenta y el periodismo en América durante la dominación española* (Buenos Aires, 1940), 70, *et passim*.

[67] Cf. John T. Lanning, *Academic Culture in the Spanish Colonies* (London and New York, 1940); Caracciolo Parra Pérez, *Filosofía universitaria venezolana 1788-1821* (Caracas, 1934), pursues the war against Aristotle in Caracas, and even finds (p. 50)

leges" became centers of scientific study and of the rational attitude in general, with that of Charcas displaying a marked taste for revolutionary ideas.[68] The *Academia de San Luís*, founded at Santiago, Chile, in 1797, taught arithmetic, geometry, and drawing, "representing there the same thing as in Spain the schools and courses of the Economic Societies . . . that is, a center of popular technical education, open to the poorest classes."[69]

The new ideas were also spread by American periodicals. The two decades before 1808 saw the establishment of a number of journals of an enlightened character. These were not simply official gazettes. The difference between the first *Gazeta de Goathemala* (1729-1731) and the second (1797-1816) was the difference between two worlds. The scientific matter in the new journals was alone enough to bespeak the remaking of the Spanish American mind. The *Gazeta de Guatemala* in 1802 reprinted from the *Aurora de la Havana* praise of the Spanish interest in natural science, pointing up the work done in America by such men as Mutis, Ruíz, and Pavón, noting the value to economic life of instruction in chemistry and botany, and observing that they ought not be part of universities which taught only theology and law.[70]

These periodicals also contained some discussion of economic matters, a bit of miscellaneous news, and some notable essays on socio-intellectual questions. The *Aviso* of Havana showed this broad interest early in the nineteenth century, carrying items on commerce, science, vaccination, meteorological observations, a bit of foreign news, hygiene, longevity, customs, differences of opinions, social organization, and the Economic Societies.[71] But perhaps even more important than their subject matter was their critical attitude, however attenuated in some cases.[72] They might not be permitted to discuss politics, but they could indirectly criticize the sociopolitical structure in essays on education. In any event, the use of the rational attitude, even in connection with natural science, led to an increase of its application

---

a document he can compare with the *Aldeanos Críticos* of Peñaflorida; Barreda Laos, *Vida intelectual*, 294 *et seq.*, on the opposition to scholasticism in Peru by way of *probabilismo*, promoted by the Jesuits.

[68] Belaunde, *Bolivar and Political Thought*, 40 *et seq.*, "The Pedagogical Reform."

[69] Altamira, *Historia*, IV, 342. *Infra*, 349, on Salas of Santiago.

[70] *Gazeta de Guatemala*, March 15, 1802.

[71] *El Aviso Papel Periódico de la Havana*, scattered issues from No. 7 (June 16, 1805) to No. 169 (June 29, 1806).

[72] Alzate's *Gazeta de literatura de Mexico* (1788-95) was a good example of the new scientific attitude (e.g., in the 2d ed., I, 223-30, an article against Aristotelianism in 1789). Cf. Clement G. Motten, *Mexican Silver and the Enlightenment* (University of Pennsylvania Press, 1950), 29, 34-35, comparing Alzate with the "amigos del país" of Spain. Alzate was a corresponding member of the Basque Society.

to other fields. The Economic Societies of Havana, Quito, Guatemala, and Puerto Rico all established or had close connections with periodicals.[73]

The new periodicals did a good deal, directly and indirectly, to promote Americanism. The *Gazeta de Guatemala*, closely allied to the Economic Society there, was notably bold.[74] It praised an equality of treatment for Spaniards and Americans,[75] in 1797 printing a letter by "Guatemalófilo" declaring that in order to confute the "system of climates" it was only necessary to live in America, "in those countries unknown to Montesquieu, and of which no European can form an idea in his cabinet."[76] And another letter said:

> Before Montesquieu forced upon climate his opinion of the different governments, already the opinion that there are certain climates privileged for the sciences and arts had many partisans. Bodin, Chardin, and after them Fontenelle had said that the torrid Zone, and the two Glacial were not suited to the sciences. . . . Diodoro of Sicily had the same opinion much before Bodin. But it takes more brilliant men than these four to sustain such a theory. This system is against the spirit of religion and that of humanity.[77]

The new ideas could scarcely be spread in cafés or in anything resembling salons, since social life was not well organized in America.[78] At the end of the colonial period, however, there was an upsurge in the spirit of associationalism. The Nariño group at Bogota in the 1780's discussed the new ideas and flirted with treason. Freemasonry spread into Spanish America, bringing its bias in favor of liberalism.[79] The Economic Societies of America were an even more striking evidence of the spread of this spirit of associationalism, for they were entirely legal and were founded on a Spanish model and were usually promoted by Spaniards and included both Spaniards and creoles in the membership.

A good part of the penetration of the Enlightenment in America was summed up in the defense of Antonio de Nariño in the case brought against

---

[73] *Infra*, 159 *et seq.*, on *Mercurio Peruano;* 240 *et seq.*, on *Telégrafo Mercantil* of Buenos Aires.

[74] And cf. Barreda Laos, *Vida intelectual*, 369, for an extreme view on the timidity of the colonial press in Peru; and *infra*, 165 *et seq.*, for evidence that the Peruvian authorities nevertheless found it worrisome.

[75] *Infra*, 212.

[76] April 3, 1797, 58.

[77] I, No. 3 (February 27, 1797), 18-20.

[78] Fisher, *Background*, 71-72, on Revillagigedo's thought in 1790 to keep out cafés where periodicals might be read and discussed, and his realization that private houses were not dangerous because there was so little social life; *infra*, 162, on cafés in Lima.

[79] But not just by the agency of Jews and Frenchmen, as in the highly colored work of Salvador de Madariaga, *The Fall of the Spanish Empire* (New York, 1948), 257 *et seq.*

him for having printed in New Granada the French Declaration of the Rights of Man and of the Citizen.[80] It also showed the creole sense of Americanness growing from the grievance regarding discrimination against colonials.

Nariño claimed the publication merely showed the errors of the National Assembly of France, for to read of polytheism in mythology was not to promote polytheism, and besides the gazettes of Spain had printed accounts of events in France.[81] He quoted from the *Espíritu de los mejores diarios* of Madrid an article on the decision of the Society of Philadelphia to promote the abolition of slavery, an article full of talk about the equality of man.[82] He quoted from the same periodical an article on colonies which spoke in the strongest terms against despotism over colonies by a metropolis,[83] in another place quoted a passage on the "fatherland of Franklin, Adams, Washington, and Hanconk [sic]."[84] He could even point to a fiscal of the audiencia of Bogota who had published in the *Espíritu de los mejores diarios* a discourse condemning excessive celibacy in a nation.[85] Nariño claimed that impartial justice demanded that if a minister of the audiencia of Bogota could publish such things, then a citizen of the same town should be allowed some freedom. The defense was able, but beside the point, for the old regime was not interested in justice so much as in self-preservation. The fiscal was no doubt a Spaniard interested in new ideas, perhaps even in reform, but not in the breakup of the empire, which it was feared that Nariño desired. Persecution was the perfect method of furthering such a desire,[86] but the Spanish government was not the first or last to help throw away what it wished to keep.

Thus by the death of the somewhat enlightened despot Charles III in 1788 and the French Revolution of the following year, the Enlightenment was influencing men in America as well as in Spain. The growing intellectual animation of the younger creoles could not be confined to "safe" channels. Invitation to speculative endeavor in science, medicine, philosophy, and law, led to affection for speculation and dubiety as techniques and as good in themselves. In colony as in metropolis the new ideas were admired for their supposed rational excellence and because they appealed to interests—

---

[80] *Proceso de Nariño; fiel copia del original* ... (Cadiz, 1914), 89-104, for Nariño's statement of October 19, 1795.

[81] *Ibid.*, 99-100.

[82] *Ibid.*, 103.

[83] *Ibid.*, 111-12.

[84] *Ibid.*, 114.

[85] *Ibid.*, 118-22.

[86] *Ibid.*, 167-68, "Carta num. 36 de D. Nicolás de Azara, Embajador de España en París a D. Francisco Saavedra," July 25, 1797, on Nariño's arrival in Paris, and his activities there and in London to promote a rising in America.

usually in change of various sorts—whose genesis had no necessary direct relationship to the new currents of thought.

As in Spain, a very small minority was being reached by the new notions, nor would the social structure easily allow of another arrangement. The difference between the England in which Richardson and Fielding were producing novels, and finding a large audience for them, and the world of Spanish America was vast. The Inquisition in Guatemala late in the colonial era found copies of Fielding's *Tom Jones*,[87] but it is difficult to imagine it appealing widely or having much effect in that place. No Guatemalan had ever lived a life remotely similar to that of Tom Jones. Further, the privileged class as a whole in America could no more be expected to embrace learning than such a phenomenon could be expected of a similar group elsewhere. Not all the wealthy and well-born of Attica were philosophers, and Mexico and Havana, to say nothing of Caracas and Mompox, were a far cry from Athens. As for the general population of America, it had no more access to education than had the general population of Spain—or the rest of the world. Thus, in both parts of the empire, much of the privileged class and virtually all the unprivileged were ignorant of book-learning. Of course the Spanish world was not unique in this regard, though the educational picture was better in some places than in the Spanish world.[88]

As in Spain, not all that portion of the privileged group that swung over with enthusiasm to at least some of the newest thought had examined the implications for its own position of such notions as the rational approach to government and to the sociopolitical order. As in Spain, some of these fashioanble partisans of the new ideas, these faddists and dilettantes, found upon reflection—after 1789, and especially after 1810—that the new ideas were at bottom iniquitous, un-Catholic, and apt to turn things quite topsy-turvy. But, in any event, by the end of the colonial era the Enlightenment in America was changing ideas and stimulating the spirit of critical analysis.[89]

---

[87] Martín Mérida, "Historia crítica de la Inquisición en Guatemala," BAGG, III, No. 1 (October, 1937), 5-157, at 140, two copies of "Fom [sic] Jones o el Espocito," published at Madrid in 1796, condemned for "doctrinas lascivas, heréticas, contrarias al Gobierno y suversivas;" *ibid.*, 146, vol. 4 of "Fom Jones."

[88] Cf. Basterra, *Navíos*, 277 *et seq.*, for a typical defensive view, making Bolívar the representative of the enlightened spirit of the reign of Charles III, and neglecting to give credit to the Enlightenment at large; or *ibid.*, 282, where Basterra seems to find it remarkable that Bolívar had eighteenth-century ideas in the 18th century.

[89] Altamira, *Historia*, IV, 339-47, a well-balanced sketch of intellectual change in America late in the colonial era; Fisher, *Background*, chap. ii, a good account of intellectual life in the decades before independence; Amunátegui, *Los precursores*, I, chap. vi, "La ilustración en los dominios Hispano-Americanos," chap. vii, "El Aislamiento de los dominios Hispano-Americanos," a bitter attack on what he considered the policy of keeping America in ignorance.

The Economic Societies of Friends of the Country in America contributed to this process by their insistence on rationalism, their demand for exact information, their adoration of progress, their largely secular objectives, their thirst for wealth, and their at least mild lust for change.

CHAPTER EIGHT

The First Economic Societies Overseas

This chapter covers the Manila Society, founded in 1781; those of Mompox in New Granada, Santiago de Cuba, and Vera Cruz in New Spain, all created or suggested in the 1780's; the Society proposed for Mérida de Yucatán in 1791; and those of Lima and Quito, formed early in the 1790's. Later chapters deal with the Havana Society, founded in 1791; the Guatemala, created in 1794; and the Societies either proposed or actually set up early in the nineteenth century at Buenos Aires, Santa Fe de Bogotá, Caracas, and in Puerto Rico, and Chiapas.

These dates show that the Basque Society found no imitators overseas in the decade between its foundation in 1765 and the formation of the Madrid Society. The circular of the Council of Castile in 1774, recommending to peninsular officials the discourse of Campomanes on popular industry, and suggesting foundation of Economic Societies, was not sent to America. Nor did the references to Economic Societies in the free trade regulation of 1778 have an immediate effect in America.[1] In colony, as in metropolis,

---

[1] José María Zamora y Coronado, *Biblioteca de legislación ultramarina en forma de diccionario alfabético* (6 vols., Madrid, 1844-46), I, 247, notes the *reglamento* called for cooperation of Consulados and Economic Societies; *ibid.*, V, 468-83, "Sociedades Económicas," that Charles III promoted Econome Societies in America through the *reglamento*, which asserted that Consulados and Societies should promote prosperity. But the passages of the *reglamento* quoted by Zamora show that it was referring to Spain; and Zamora's statement that "with this powerful stimulant" the Societies produced in Guatemala and other parts of America "increibles ventajas" is both an exaggeration of the value of the Societies, and apparently misleading, since the present

the Societies were interested both in the improvement of local conditions—mainly economic, but also social—and in certain of the ideas of the Enlightenment. But the American Societies were different from the Spanish in that their membership was composed of both Spaniards and creoles; the physical environment they wished to exploit was different; the masses they wished to influence were not just like the artisans and peasants of Spain; and the place of America in the governmental system was not the same as that of the European provinces.

The Manila Society

The first ultramarine Economic Society was erected at Manila in 1781, sixteen years after the Basque Society, and six after the Madrid. It was created in the hope of improving an economy that had been disrupted by the British occupation of Manila during the Seven Years' War and by subsequent alterations in international trade. After the British withdrawal in 1764, some of the foreign merchants who had gone to the islands under British protection continued their connections, under special permit or in contravention of law, in either case breaching the monopolistic trading system with Spain via Acapulco. And Manileños were unenthusiastic when in 1766 Spain authorized direct communication with Spain via the Cape of Good Hope, fearing it meant suppression of the Acapulco line and injury to their vested interests. But the new system was not a success and died in 1783.[2]

A report on the condition of the islands after the war by the Fiscal Francisco Leandro de Viana, began by declaring that "there is no greater misfortune in the world than poverty; all have contempt for it, and all regard it with displeasure." The poverty of the Spanish kept the natives from respecting them. The natives, on the other hand, did not properly work the naturally rich land, and were too attached to gambling, banqueting, and sumptuous dress. Viana went on to explore the relationship of industry and commerce to national power; condemned the practise of permitting foreigners to bring goods to the isles, even if from Spain itself, for many ostensibly Spanish commercial houses at Cadiz were fronts for foreigners; and noted the advantages of allowing trade with Spain via the Cape of Good Hope. But it was a Philippine trade company he wanted most, noting that there had been one,

writer finds no evidence that the foundation of American Societies was directly stimulated by the *reglamento*.

[2] William Lytle Schurz, "The Royal Philippine Company," HAHR, III, No. 4 (November, 1920), 491–508; William C. Forbes, *The Philippine Islands* (2 vols., Boston and New York, 1928), I, 43–44; Hussey, *Caracas Company*, 50, 203–4.

formed in 1732, and that many foreign trading companies had done well. He knew that while Ustáriz had disapproved of commercial companies for Spain and America, he had thought an exception might be made for the Philippines. Viana proposed that the company carry goods from China to the Philippines, for such traffic would give Spaniards the profits foreigners had been getting, and it would build up the Spanish merchant marine. As for the objections to such a scheme by the Spanish merchants at Cadiz, they would in large part be forgotten when the merchants became shareholders in the Philippine Islands Company.[3]

Not only had the British occupation damaged the economy;[4] it had created divisions within the ruling class in the islands, and when Simón de Anda y Salazar, who had been auditor at the time of the invasion, and an opponent of collaboration with the English, became governor in 1770, he considered that Archbishop Rojo and other influential persons had acted in collusion with the enemy. Because of this conflict, and because of the continuing economic depression, the regime of Anda (1770-1776) was stormy.[5] Also turbulent was the regime (1778-1787) of Governor José Basco y Vargas, a naval officer, who permitted the Chinese to return to Manila in July, 1778, and, when opposed by the audiencia, arrested some of its members and some military officers, charged them with conspiracy, and shipped them to Spain in 1779. Basco established the tobacco and powder monopolies, improved schools, tried to control banditry, reorganized the armed forces, and founded the Economic Society of the Philippine Islands.[6] While it seems fair to describe him as "the most genuine interpreter of the reforming and progressive

---

[3] "Memorial of 1765," MS. dated Manila, February 10, 1765, in Emma Helen Blair and James A. Robertson (eds.), *The Philippine Islands 1493-1801* (55 vols., Cleveland, 1903-9), XLVIII, 197-338, at 197-98, 227 *et seq.*, 242 *et seq.*, 262 *et seq.*, 272 *et seq.*, 278, 287 *et seq.*, 313-14, 315-16, 318-19, 320-21. The Council of the Indies prohibited publication of Viana's memorial.

[4] Damage done agriculture by the war was investigated by a committee which Spain in November, 1765, ordered the governor to appoint (Charles H. Cunningham, *The Audiencia in the Spanish Colonies as Illlustrated by the Audiencia of Manila 1583-1800* [Berkeley, 1919], 186).

[5] Blair and Robertson, *Philippine Islands*, L, 10-11 of "Preface."

[6] Blair and Robertson, *Philippine Islands*, L, 11, XV, 299; Cunningham, *Audiencia*, 280-81; W. E. Retana, *Epítome de la bibliografía general de Filipinas*, in *Archivo de bibliófilo* (5 vols., Madrid, 1895-1905), I, No. 61, a *bando* of Basco, Manila, October 9, 1782, "dando instrucciones sobre la compra-venta de carabaos," which Retana says consists of 25 articles showing Basco's well-known interest in Philippine agriculture. Cf. Eduardo Malo de Luque, *Historia política de los establecimientos ultramarinos de las naciones europeas* (5 vols., Madrid, 1784-90), V, 374, on a memoria presented to the Manila Economic Society in 1783 favoring importation of Chinese; 354, 375, comments by Malo de Luque on the debate on Chinese.

spirit of Charles III,"[7] that quality did not make him universally admired by his contemporaries.[8]

A royal decree of August 27, 1780, ordered Basco to convene all the learned or competent persons in the colony, "in order to form an association of selected persons, capable of producing useful ideas." But when the decree arrived, Basco already had founded the Economic Society.[9] The governor's connection with the project dated from his "Economic Plan" of 1779, which was accepted by his partisans as the basis for creation of the Society. A session of February 7, 1781, in the hall of the Consulado of Manila, agreed to the establishment. At this time eleven members of the Consulado were enrolled in the Society, and two appointed to draw up its statutes. These statutes were presented to the governor March 6, 1781, and at the same time the Consulado made an annual subscription to the Society of 970 pesos, the value of two *toneladas* assigned it in the lading of the Acapulco galleon. On April 20, Basco approved the project, after it had been agreed to by the corporations and cabildos of the islands,[10] and promised it government protection. The first session of the Society was on April 26, 1781.[11] Governor Basco delivered an address at the formal inauguration of the Society on May 6,[12] in which he bewailed the "decadence" of the Isles; invoked "patriotic love" for the promotion of "public felicity"; argued that although funds might be insufficient to carry out all the great projects of the Society, the important thing was to initiate those measures that would make the Philippines

---

[7] W. E. Retana, "Noticia de Dos Escritores Filipinos: Manuel de Zumalde, Luís Rodríguez Varela," *Revue Hispanique*, LXII, No. 142, 376-439, at 396.

[8] *Ibid.*, 398 *et seq.*, printing extracts from the libellous "La Bascoana," an attack on Basco by Zumalde, written in 1779 and circulated in MS. Zumalde was the son of Guipuzcoans, but himself born in Manila in the 1740's. He went to Spain as a boy, returning to Manila in 1772, seven years after the Basque Society had been founded. Cf. Malo de Luque, *Historia*, V, 319-20, for objection by residents of Manila, who were content with the Acapulco trade, to Basco's efforts to improve agriculture and promote industry.

[9] *Amigos del País* did not appear in the title, though some not entirely satisfactory evidence that the phrase was used in 1783 is offered in Angel Pérez and Cecilio Güemes, *Adiciones y continuación de "La Imprenta en Manila" de J. T. Medina ó rarezas y curiosidades bibliográficas filipinas* ... (Manila, 1904), No. 668.

[10] "Fundación de la Sociedad," *Revista de la Real Sociedad económica filipina*, Año I, No. 1 (May 1, 1882), 8-17, at 6; Cunningham *Audiencia*, 186-87, n. 59; J. Montero y Vidal, *Historia general de Filipinas desde el descubrimiento de dichas islas hasta nuestros días* (3 vols., Madrid, 1887-95), II, 291-92, and n. 1 on 291.

[11] "Fundación de la Sociedad," *loc. cit.*, 7. At this session the *oidor* Ciriaco González Carbajal was named director, Lieutenant Colonel Mariano Jobías was made censor, Alonso Chacón secretary, and as treasurer Francisco David.

[12] Malo de Luque, *Historia*, V, Anexa No. I, is the text of Basco's address.

the "Pearl of the Orient," since the area was potentially rich, requiring only proper development, for

> If sugar alone has enriched Havana and created the sources of many thousands of pesos of income, what are we not able to hope when all our beings are put in movement and action under the wise rules of the Society?

This was the usual cry of the Economic Societies that the land was rich but poorly used—that wealth only awaited proper effort.[13]

The statutes, published in 1781,[14] declared the purposes of the Society to be the improvement of agriculture, industry, and commerce. Four commissions were provided: natural history, manufacturing, internal and external commerce, industry and popular education. This might have been a Spanish Society, though we have encountered no division of natural history in a European body. Juntas and officers were provided as in the Spanish statutes, with officials given designated seats at meetings, but other members to sit as they chose. If the juntas lacked business, they were to read useful Spanish works, as the *Educación popular* of Campomanes, and the "political books" of Ustáriz, Ulloa, Herrera, Moncada, Leruela, Navarrete, Deza, Argumosa, and Zavala; these, the statutes stated, might be expected to indicate "practical and experimental actions" for trial in each province. The income for all this was to come from the Consulado contribution and from yearly dues of five pesos per member.

The Society was active during the governorship of Basco, which ended in 1787.[15] It fostered the production of indigo, cotton, cinnamon, pepper, and the silk industry. A parish priest taught his parishioners to prepare the indigo, presenting to the Society the first specimens. In 1784 the first ship-

---

[13] Cf. *ibid.*, 334-39, *et passim*, for a contemporary argument that development of the Isles would greatly benefit Spain.

[14] "Estatutos de la Sociedad Económica de las Islas Filipinas," in *Revista de la Real Sociedad*, Año I, No. 1, 9-15, the original statutes of 1781. Pérez and Güemes, *Adiciones*, No. 307 bis, list them for 1781; W. E. Retana, *La imprenta en Filipinas. Adiciones y observaciones a la Imprenta en Manila de J. T. Medina* (Madrid, 1897), No. 171, relies on the reproduction in the *Revista de la Real Sociedad* of May 1, 1882; J. T. Medina, *La imprenta en Manila desde sus orígenes hasta 1810* (Santiago, 1896), No. 316, listed it as of 1783, but confessed he had forgotten his source, and in his *Adiciones a la imprenta en Manila* (Santiago, 1904), No. 533, put it down for 1781, taking his information from Retana. Pérez and Güemes, *Adiciones*, No. 772, for a reimpression ostensibly of 1820, which they thought probably was of 1829. In any case, there seem to be no examples of the original printed statutes.

[15] A catalogue of members was published at Manila, probably in 1782, according to Pérez and Güemes, *Adiciones*, No. 662: *Catálogo de los individuos de la Real Sociedad Patriótica de Manila en las Islas Filipinas ... a fines de Enero de 1782.* These Augustinian bibliographers note only that the members included nine Augustinians, three Dominicans, four Franciscans, and two Recolets.

ment of indigo was made to Europe.[16] "Patriotic schools" were established, and the members were enthusiastic about their success, at least in the beginning. In 1785 the Society was sustaining schools in five pueblos.[17] In 1781 the Society proposed prizes for cotton culture,[18] and the next year tried to promote industry and popular education among the natives.[19]

Also in this period, a connection was established between the Society and the second Philippine Company, which received its charter in March 1785. Four per cent of the profits of the Company were to be used for *fomento*, that is, "stimulation of the internal development of the isles."[20] In this the Company was ordered to work with the Society, and "the designs of both organizations reflected the enlightened spirit represented in Spain by Campomanes."[21]

The Society declined rapidly after the departure of Governor Basco in 1787. Governor Aguilar (1793-1806) was especially opposed to the Society. It will be recalled that the Societies of Spain also were having their troubles in this period. The Philippine body paid for the republication at Manila in 1793 of Campomanes' treatise on popular industry,[22] the *vade mecum* of the Spanish Societies. Despite this action, the Society scarcely existed in 1787-1820; its meetings may have been suspended in 1787;[23] in 1797 it was nearly dead, and the Society's 6,000-peso treasury was deposited with

---

[16] Blair and Robertson, *Philippine Islands*, L, 52, citing Montero y Vidal; Malo de Luque, *Historia*, V, 333, 354, on the Society and silk.

[17] Pérez and Güemes, *Adiciones*, No. 668, summarizing a broadside, probably of 1783, on the state of the Society's schools; Encarnación Alzona, *A History of Education in the Philippines, 1565-1930* (Manila, 1932), 45-46, that the Society began its educational activities in 1823, which cannot be strictly but may be substantially true; Evergisto Bazaco, *History of Education in the Philippines* (Manila, 1939), 164-65, 168, some remarks on the educational work of the Society, but disdaining chronology, to state that "the country owes to this Society a great part of its economic, artistic and intellectual progress since 1781 . . . until 1890."

[18] Pérez and Güemes, *Adiciones*, No. 659: *Aviso al Público*.

[19] *Ibid.*, No. 663; cf. *ibid.*, No. 671, more prizes offered to natives in 1784.

[20] Schurz, *loc. cit.*, 503.

[21] *Ibid.*, 504; Malo de Luque, *Historia*, V, Anexa No. II, for the cedula of erection of the Philippine Company, ch. LXXXIX of which provided for representation by the Patriotic Society on the directive junta of the Company in Manila. Cf. Blair and Robertson, *Philippine Islands*, LIII, "Bibliography," 362, listing eight documents of the Archivo de Indias bearing on the Society in its first years, including: Carta [of the Society] al rey dando cuenta de su establecimiento, May 15, 1781; Carta tratando de premios, July 9, 1786; Carta de los directores [of the Society], December 31, 1795.

[22] Pérez and Güemes, *Adiciones*, No. 592.

[23] Blair and Robertson, *Philippine Islands*, LII, 308, on the basis of Fernández Moreno, *Manual del viajero en Filipinas* (Manila, 1875).

the Consulado.[24] The Society was extinguished in 1809, and though royal orders for re-establishment were issued in 1811 and 1813, it was not re-formed until 1819, with the first session persided over by Governor Mariano Fernández de Folgueras (1816-1822), in December, 1819. At that time only two members of the original Society remained.[25]

The Society met again in January, 1820, with sixty new members.[26] Its capital now was over 30,000 pesos. In 1820 the Society attracted as a member a man of the new ideas in Luís Rodríguez Varela, Conde Filipino, born at Manila in 1768, and at this time a corregidor.[27]

The scale of operations of the Manila Society does not appear from the available records. Tomás de Comyn, writing of the evil economic situation of the islands in 1810, said the Society was from the beginning interested in planting mulberry trees, hoping to naturalize the silk industry and even-tually fill the needs of Mexico. Although it gave the first impulse to this work, and Governor Basco sent Col. Charles Conely on a mission to the province of Camarines to plant trees, these were later allowed to die on the benevolent grounds of relieving the natives of the labor of tending them.[28]

Equally unsatisfactory was the discussion in 1821 by the government and the Society of a plan to establish a school of agriculture, for although the Society offered to pay the salary of the professor, the school did not open until 1889, on the basis of a royal decree of 1887.[29] The organization and interests of the Society seem to have been much like those of the Spanish bodies, with variations of emphasis due to a different local situation. The Society continued to engage sporadically in various activities until 1890.[30]

Santiago de Cuba Society

In 1783 the governor of Santiago de Cuba informed the government in Spain of a request for approval of an Economic Society by Dr. Francisco Mozo de la Torre, dean of the cathedral, and by the town-councilmen Francisco Griñán and Pedro Valiente. Already sixty persons were involved in the organ-

---

[24] *Ibid.*, "Preface" to LI, 38, n.

[25] *Ibid.*, LI, 38, 52; Zamora y Coronado, *Legislación ultramarina*, V, 483.

[26] *Ibid.*, LI, 39.

[27] Retana, "Noticia de Dos Escritores," 435, *et passim*, describing him as a man influenced by the encyclopedic spirit of the age though remaining a good Catholic, a description suitable to most members of the Spanish Societies.

[28] *State of the Philippines in 1810*, trans. William Watson (London, 1821) from the Spanish edition (Madrid, 1820), in Austin Craig (ed.), *The Former Philippines through Foreign Eyes* (New York, 1917), 357-458, at 362.

[29] Alzona, *Education in the Philippines*, 44.

[30] Cf. Appendix.

ization.[31] The request moved slowly,[32] but approval was finally given in 1787. The statutes of the Society said its purposes were to increase the population, establish schools for children, give occupation to the idle, assist the needy, and produce memorias to improve agriculture and commerce. It was to allow no preference in the seating at juntas, and avoid factionalism, since "obstinate disputes were ever an initiator of disunion and lukewarmness in organizations. . . . Union and controversy are incompatibles. . . ." The usual provisions were made for officers, publications, a library, commissions, three types of membership, and prizes. "Patriotic schools" were to be founded since "methodical instruction is that which most contributes to the improvement of industry." But in creating schools the Society was not to infringe on the authority of such other corporations as the town councils, but to act only as a "diligent father of families." These schools were for instruction in reading, writing, and reckoning, Christian doctrine, spinning and sewing. The motto of the Society was "Rise and Work."[33]

Pedro Valiente,[34] main promoter of the Society, and José de Granda in 1788 sent to Spain an account of the Society's labors in that year, together with a paper delivered by Valiente at its junta of April 6.[35] Valiente described the Society as a school teaching things not provided by the university. Its object the "common felicity," it was to study the augmentation of the population, establish schools, and aid agriculture, commerce, and popular industry. Valiente wished to provide work for the idle females of Santiago. This was part of his strong plea, citing Campomanes' *Industria popular*, for the necessity of labor. In addition, he wished to increase the population and labor force by reducing infant mortality and investigating the proportion of marriages among Santiago's 14,000 inhabitants.

He advocated neither a purely active nor a purely passive trade, but a

---

[31] Zamora y Coronado, *Legislación ultramarina*, V, 469.

[32] *Catálogo de los fondos Cubanos del Archivo General de Indias* (2 vols., Madrid, 1929-30), t. I, vol. 2, No. 1271-12, and No. 1298-5, for actions of the Consejo de Indias in 1786 and 1787.

[33] Zamora y Coronado, *Legislación ultramatina*, V, 468-74, includes a summary of the cedula of September 13, and the statutes.

[34] Ortiz, *Hija cubana*, 31, calls him *un intelectual*, who had founded a Colegio de Humanidades at Santiago; Carlos M. Trelles y Govín, *Bibliografía cubana de los siglos XVII y XVIII* (2d ed., Havana, 1927), 77, describing him as a Cuban and "Administrador de Correos y Contador de Hacienda," and putting the establishment of the Colegio de Humanidades in 1790; Jacobo de la Pezuela y Lobo, *Ensayo histórico de la isla de Cuba* (Nueva York, 1842), 330-34, has the Santiago Society founded under the "protection and influence" of the Marquis of Sonora.

[35] Valiente's essay is in *Memorias de la Real Sociedad Económica de Amigos del País de la Habana*, série IX, Año XXX [1882], 115-30; and reprinted in Ortiz, *Hija cubana*, 42-54.

decent balance; and balance also in production, for both agriculture and industry must be developed, since "a people of peasants only is always a miserable people," Santiago being good testimony of this, as one of the poorest cities of Cuba. The way to augment the value of Cuban products was to manufacture or refine them, for if the Society while perfecting agriculture did not see to the perfection of industry, the former would be worth nothing. In proof, he stated that the Basque provinces, by fabricating articles instead of exporting bar-iron, had greatly increased the value of their trade; and Malta, by manufacturing a bit of inferior cotton developed a large commerce. He favored schools for artisans, using all the instruments and machinery necessary; and concentration on new products, some of which could be sent to the Consulado of Barcelona for an estimate of their value. He was especially optimistic on the use of cotton in popular industry. By combining that "prodigious discovery" the spinning wheel with the 3,500 idle women of Santiago, Valiente provided statistics showing a nice valuable lot of cotton thread.

He hoped for little from tobacco, a government monopoly, and noted that very few vessels carried it from Santiago to Cartagena and Havana. The local sugar was not well regarded, partly because of poor refining. Hides and wax had but a small market. Woodcutting was expensive, and those owning the necessary oxen preferred to use them otherwise. But the Society could turn to such things as fish, gums and resins, ginger, rattan, fruits, medicinal herbs, pitch, and indigo. This diversification should be aided by a "physical-political-geographical history of this jurisdiction with an exact account of the three kingdoms, mineral, animal, and vegetable." Other studies were to see if the necessities of life were sufficient and low enough in price, and if the roads to bring them to the city were adequate. He opposed traditional agricultural methods, and advocated the use of science, the improvement of crops and livestock, and the opening of good roads to seaports.

Though the Santiago Society published nothing,[36] and may have had only a nominal existence, the Havana Society did know of its existence,[37] wished to cooperate with it, and engaged in at least a small amount of corerspondence with it.[38] In any event, the Santiago Society was not very influen-

---

[36] The town had no press until 1792 (Pedro José Guiteras, *Historia de la Isla de Cuba* [2d ed., 3 vols., Habana, 1927-28], III, 311).

[37] Although the *Papel Periódico de la Havana* in 1791, lamenting that Mompox had an Economic Society while Havana did not, failed to mention the Santiago Society (issue of September 4, reprinted in Fernando Ortiz, *Recopilación para la historia de la Sociedad Económica Habanera* [5 vols., Havana, 1929-43], I, 282-84).

[38] The Havana Society in 1793 received a letter from José Fernández Granda of the Santiago Society, in which was inserted the Valiente paper of 1788, described

tial.[39] Letters were sent in 1817 by the Director of the Havana Society to the archbishop, the governor, and the intendant of Santiago, trying to persuade them to "re-establish" there the Society, "whose ephemeral existence only lasted from the year 1787 to that of 1792."[40] Juan Bernardo O'Gabán, member of the Havana Society, but native of Santiago, in 1817, commenting on the "lethargy" of the eastern part of the isle, asked what had happened to the Santiago Society, whose rules served as a model for the Havana statutes, and recommended that the Havana Society try to stimulate the towns of eastern Cuba to form Economic Societies.[41] A *diputación* of the Havana Society was formed at Santiago in 1832.[42]

Mompox Society

Although New Granada had enlightened viceroys in Manuel Guirior (1773-1776) and Archbishop Caballero y Góngora (1782-1788), both favoring advances in education and economic life, its first Economic Society was organized at Mompox in 1784 without government aid or inspiration. On July 14 the members communicated with the viceroy at Santa Fe, asking license for operation; and he approved by decree of August 17, 1784. An "extract" of the Society's work in September-December was printed at Bogota the next year.[43] The first junta was held sometime before the general

---

above (for receipt of the letter see *junta ordinaria*, July 4, 1793, of Havana Society, in *Colección de Actas de la Real Sociedad* ... [Havana, 1880], 31). On correspondence cf. *ibid.*, 6-7, junta of January 17, 1793; *ibid.*, 16-17, in junta of April 4, 1793, the Havana Society heard a reply from the Santiago Society to the Havana suggestion that the Societies correspond on mutual objectives; *Memorias 1793*, 22. The Havana Society considered sending to the Santiago a project for a Provincial Dictionary of the island, for the assistance of the latter body (Havana *Memorias 1795*, 113); "Junta ordinaria," March 5, 1795 (Havana *Memorias y Anales 1864*, 314-15), decided to send Havana publications to the Santiago.

[39] Cf. Trelles y Govín, *Bibliografía de siglos XVII y XVIII* (2d ed.), 234: "Real Orden desaprobando los dos arbitrios propuestos por la Sociedad Económica de Cuba para crear escuelas de niñas. Abril 17 de 1790." There is no mention of the Santiago Society in the long "Informe Presentado a S. M. por el Ilmo. Sr. Dr. D. Joaquín de Ozes y Alzua ...," archbishop of Santiago, November 30, 1794 (Havana *Memorias 1880*, 107-18, 179-87), which deals with the economy of eastern Cuba, the obstacles to its development, and the need for new economic policies. Emilio Bacardí y Moreau, *Crónicas de Santiago de Cuba* (2 vols., Barcelona, 1908-9), I, 226, 231, mentions creation of the Society, and the establishment of its first primary school, in 1788, then does not mention the Society again.

[40] Havana *Memorias 1817*, 427-28.

[41] *Memorias 1818*, 19-23.

[42] *Acta de las Juntas Generales ... Celebrados ... 1833* (Havana, 1834), 28-29.

[43] *Extracto de las primeras Juntas, celebradas por la Sociedad económica de los amigos del país en la villa de Mompox. ... 12 de Septiembre, hasta 19 de Diciembre de 1784. En Santafe de Bogota. Por Don Antonio Espinosa de los Monteros. Ympresor Real.*

junta of September 12, 1784, the latter being in the house of Lieutenant Colonel of the Royal Armies, Colonel of Militia don Gonzalo Joseph de Hoyos, who was elected perpetual director of the Society. The statutes, which dealt especially with the cultivation of cotton, were agreed to in a junta of September 19. In October proxies (*apoderados*) were named in various cities, and corresponding members were elected, including J.C. Mutis, the famous scientist. In November they decided to write to the viceroy and convey what had been accomplished and ask permission to print the account at Santa Fe.[44]

The existence of the Mompox Society was known at Havana in 1790, where it provoked the *Papel Periódico* to taunt its citizens with their backwardness in comparison with what it called the obscure pueblo of the mainland. Six years later Antonio de San José Muro of New Spain in an essay prepared for the Guatemala Society noted the existence of the Mompox Society.[45] Still, the latter cannot have been very active, since the *Relaciones* of the viceroys of New Granada covering 1782-1803 carried abundant interest in learning and in economics, and that of Mendinueta mentioned the Bogota Society of the early nineteenth century, but they did not mention a Society at Mompox.[46] Viceroy Mendinueta in his *Relación* of 1803 recorded his wish to establish an Economic Society, "unknown in the *Reino*."[47] And when the suggestion had been made in 1801 for the creation of an Economic Society of Friends of the Country in New Granada, the advocate did not mention any such body at Mompox, presumably because he had never heard of it, or because it was dead, or was of no importance.[48] It seems likely it

---

So listed in Eduardo Posada, *Bibliografía bogotana* (2 vols., Bogota, 1917-25), I, 60-62, giving date of publication as 1785, and a resumé of its 50 pages, indicating that a copy is in the Biblioteca Nacional. Cf. José Toribio Medina, *La imprenta en Bogota, 1739-1821* (Santiago, 1904), No. 12.

[44] Posada, *Bibliografía bogotanà*, I, 60-62. The perpetual secretary was the royal accountant Francisco Antona; the treasurer was Captain of Militia Ramón del Corral. The notion long has been current that the first Economic Society in New Granada was that of Bogota. Posada notes that Gredilla in his biography of Mutis claimed that the Bogota Society of 1801 was the first.

[45] *Infra*, 215.

[46] *Relaciones de Mando* (Bogota, 1910 [*Biblioteca de Historia Nacional*, VIII]), Archbishop Góngora, viceroy 1782-88, José de Ezpeleta, 1789-97, Pedro Mendinueta, 1797-1803; *Relaciones de los virreyes del nuevo reino de Granada, ahora Estados Unidos de Venezuela, Estados Unidos de Colombia y Ecuador* (ed. José Antonio García y García, New York, 1869).

[47] *Relaciones de mando*, 488.

[48] Jorge Tadeo Lozano, "Sobre lo útil que sería en este reino el establecimiento de una Sociedad Económica de Amigos del País," in *Correo Curioso de Santafé de Bogotá* (1801), as reprinted in *Periodistas de los albores de la república* (Bogota, 1936), 29-34. *Infra*, 236, for discussion of this proposal.

would have been mentioned more frequently had it attained any notable strength.[49]

Vera Cruz and Mérida de Yucatán Societies

An Economic Society apparently existed briefly—and probably not very effectively—at Vera Cruz in the 1780's. Its existence was known in several American provinces.[50] It established a "Patriotic School,"[51] but possibly did nothing else.[52] Since there was no press at Vera Cruz until 1794, a Society would have operated under difficulties.[53]

It appears that the captain general of Yucatan in 1791 sufficiently despaired of the economic situation there to propose formation of an Economic Society. It probably was never established.[54] The Guatemala Society believed that its suspension by order of 1799 was in part due to its influence in persuading some citizens of Mexico to ask permission to found a Society there.[55] Subscribers to the *Gazeta de Guatemala* in New Spain could read in it about

---

[49] It is not mentioned in José Manuel Groot, *Historia eclesiástica y civil de Nueva Granada, escrito sobre los documentos auténticos* (3 vols., Bogota, 1869-70). It does not seem to be mentioned even once in all the volumes of the *Boletín de Historia y Antigüedades* through the year 1944 (Bogota, 1902-). There is nothing in the *Obras de Caldas* (Bogota, 1912: *Biblioteca de Historia Nacional*, IX), though he has much to say of the new learning, but the economic interest was lacking in Caldas. Alcázar Molina, *Los virreinatos en el siglo XVIII*, 288, notes that Viceroy Mendinueta protected the philanthropist of Mompox, Pedro Martínez de Pinillos, founder of numerous beneficent institutions, but Alcázar does not mention an Economic Society at Mompox.

[50] The *Papel Periódico* of Havana in 1790 used the asserted existence of a Vera Cruz Society to spur Habaneros to the creation of one of their own (Ortiz, *Recopilación*, I, 96-97). Antonio de San José Muro of New Spain in 1796-97 mentioned a Society at Vera Cruz (*infra*, 215). On the other hand, articles in the *Gazeta de Guatemala* in 1799 proposing a Society for New Spain did not mention the existence of any in that realm (*infra*, 215-16); but cf. *infra*, 241, for mention of a Mexican Society in the *Telégrafo Mercantil* of Buenos Aires in 1801.

[51] Manuel B. Trens, *Historia de Veracruz*, t. II (Jalapa, 1947), 538, citing the *Gaceta de Mexico*. This single comment Trens makes in a section on education; presumably the group either did none of the characteristic economic work of the Societies, or if it did Trens had no information on it.

[52] There is no mention of a Vera Cruz Society in Manuel Rivera Cambas, *Histora ... del estado de Veracruz* (5 vols., Mexico, 1861-71), though its discussion of the 18th century is fairly extensive; or in Miguel Lerdo de Tejada, *Apuntes históricos de la heróica ciudad de Vera-Cruz* (3 vols., Mexico, 1850-58), though the character of the work suggests that it would have been included had it attained any stature.

[53] Joaquín Díaz Mercado, *Bibliografía general del estado de Veracruz*, t. I, 1794-1910 (Mexico, 1937), lists the publications of nineteenth-century economic organizations, but no Economic Society.

[54] Desdevises, *La Richesse*, ch. i, sec. iv, 59, citing a document in the Archivo de Indias, and commenting that the captain general did not say where he was going to find people with enough learning to operate an Economic Society.

[55] *Infra*, 215-16.

the Guatemala Society. In addition, travelers between Spain and Mexico must have carried news of the Havana Society to New Spain. But an Economic Society was not established at Mexico City until after the declaration of independence.[56] Though there may have been somewhat more freedom of thought and speech tolerated in Buenos Aires than in Mexico,[57] we can scarcely ascribe the failure to establish an Economic Society at Mexico City to this factor, since the one suggested at Buenos Aires was not allowed, and relative liberalism is difficult to measure.

Lima Society

The Academic Society of Lima was not a true Economic Society in organization or function, since it simply acted as an editorial group for the *Mercurio Peruano;* but it somewhat resembled the Societies in interests and attitudes. When the Society was created, Lima had a population of some 52,000, including 17,000 *españoles* (peninsular and creole). Of the total population, nearly 5,000 either were religious or lived in religious communities. The city had fewer than 400 merchants, 60 *fabricantes,* 1,027 *artesanos;* and 2,900 free servants of mixed blood and 9,200 slaves.[58] Into this large town on the rim of the Occidental culture-area, with its population drastically compartmentalized by race and status, the Enlightenment came by the usual routes to complicate the lives of the dominant minority. Viceroy Amat as early as 1771 signalized the broadened intellectual interest of the age of Charles III by converting a college of the outlawed Jesuits into the Convictory of San Carlos, which proceeded to allow some freedom in philosophical studies. Lima by the end of the century held a lively group of men eager to promote the new learning, although most of the dominant minority probably still clung to scholasticism.[59]

A leading creole intellectual was José Baquíjano y Carrillo, son of the first Count of Vistaflorida. In Spain in 1773-1777 (and again in 1793-1797), where he knew Olavide and Jovellanos at Sevilla, he brought back to Peru

---

[56] Cf. Appendix for the Society of Iturbide's day. Economic Societies were not mentioned in the *Instrucción* (1789) of Viceroy Manuel Antonio Flores to his successor (*Instrucciones que los vireyes de Nueva España dejaron a sus sucesores* [2 vols., Mexico, 1873], I, 626-53), or in that of Revillagigedo in 1794 (*ibid.,* II, 5-527).

[57] Spell, *Rousseau,* 241, makes a point of this.

[58] *Mercurio Peruano,* No. 10 (February 3, 1791), for "Plan Demostrativo de la Población Comprehendida en el Recinto de la Ciudad de Lima, con distinción de clases y Estados," executed under the direction of José María de Egaña. This issue of the *Mercurio* claims that things are not so bad in Lima as some people say, that in relation to population Lima surpasses Madrid in hospitals and in students.

[59] Barreda Laos, *Vida intelectual,* 301 *et seq.,* 314-15; cf. Jorge Guillermo Leguía, *Lima en el siglo XVIII* (Lima, 1921), for a sour judgment of the creole nobility.

the works of prohibited authors. At Lima, Baquíjano in the spirit of the Enlightenment gave battle to scholasticism at the university. His most striking blow was an address of welcome to Viceroy Jáuregui in 1781, in terms so critical and radical, denouncing servile customs in the university, condemning cruelty to the Indians, citing such deplorable authors as Marmontel, Montesquieu, Raynal, and the Encyclopedia, that it was suppressed.[60] Two years later the "reform" party tried to make Baquíjano rector of the university, but the proponents of scholasticism seated their own candidate.[61] Sometime before 1788 Baquíjano had become a member of the Basque Society of Friends of the Country.[62] He was one of the founders of the Lima Society, became its president, and for several years wrote for the *Mercurio* which it directed. In 1793, on his second trip to Spain, he stopped at Havana and was made a member of the new Society there.[63]

As early as 1783 some young men of Lima were associated in an *Asamblea literaria* for the promotion of the new learning.[64] The Academic Society came out of a similar group, the *Mercurio* in 1791 ascribing the origin of the Society to a private association that began meeting in 1787, and soon assumed the name *Academia Filarmónica*. According to the *Mercurio*, the members bore classical pseudonyms and passed their time in an idyllic contemplation of literary and philosophical matters. Although the group soon broke up, four of the members, on reading the *Análisis* of Jayme Bausate announcing publication of his *Diario Curioso*, decided to publish a periodical of their own. These four associated some others in their enterprise, and the new association took the name of Friends of the Country.[65] The history

---

[60] José Toribio Medina, *La imprenta en Lima 1524-1824* (4 vols., Santiago, 1904-07), No. 1503, for discussion of the address, with documents on the suppression and collection of the item; Barreda Laos, *Vida intelectual*, 318-19, on Baquíjano, and that the speech was received with apathy and animosity.

[61] *Ibid.*, 307-9; Spell, *Rousseau*, 135-36; Manuel de Mendiburu, *Diccionario histórico-biográfico del Perú* (11 vols., Lima, 1931-35), II, 351-72, on Baquíjano.

[62] Medina, *Imprenta en Lima*, No 1663: *Alegato que en la oposición de la Cátedra de Prima de Leyes ... de la ... Universidad ... de Lima dixo el Dr. D. Joseph de Baquíjano ..., Socio de la Sociedad Vascongada ...,*" April 29, 1788.

[63] Mendiburu, *Diccionario*, "Baquíjano." He returned to Peru in 1797; went to Spain again in 1812; was excluded from the court by Ferdinand VII and confined in Sevilla until his death in 1818.

[64] *Mercurio Peruano*, No. 163 (July 26, 1792), "Discurso pronunciado el 21 de abril de 1783, por un Socio de la Asamblea literaria que comenzaron a formalizar algunos jóvenes estudiosos baxo el nombre de Academia de la Juventud Limana." Although, as the editors of the *Mercurio* observed in a footnote, it is difficult to extract the meaning from the verbiage of this discourse, the young man hoped to demonstrate the value of useful studies as opposed to the aridities of scholasticism.

[65] *Ibid.*, I, No. 7 (January 23, 1791), 49-52, "Historia de la Sociedad Académica de Amantes de Lima, y principio del Mercurio Peruano." Cf. Medina, *Imprenta en Lima*, No. 1735, printing two representations of Bausate to the government in 1791,

of this group is inseparable from that of the *Mercurio Peruano*.[66] The Society edited the *Mercurio* and did virtually nothing else.

The "Prospectus" (1790) of the *Mercurio* noted the importance of printing to the spread of learning in the modern world, and tied the creation of the periodical press to the "epoch of enlightenment of nations," mentioning its effect in England, Spain, Italy, France, and Germany. Peru needed more news: data on active and passive commerce; mining; arts; agriculture; fishing; manufactures; literature; fine arts; botany; mechanics; religion; and public decorum; also information on current events pertaining to "our nation," as well as "the Canadian, the Lapp, or the Musulman," but with the main emphasis on occurrences in Peru. The editors professed to see no reason why the *Mercurio* and the *Diario* should not work together to the advantage of Peru, without plagiarism or antagonism.[67] The *Mercurio*'s first issue declared that the principal object of its foundation was to make Peru better known; and it asserted enthusiastically that "enlightenment is general in all of Peru."[68]

The statutes or "constitutions" of the Academic Society were not formed till 1792, by Baquíjano, Dr. José Unánue, Jacinto Calero, and José María Egaña, being presented to the authorities in March. The viceroy on October 19 approved them provisionally, pending royal confirmation.[69] They stated that the Society was founded to "illustrate" the history, literature, and "public news" of Peru. These aims were almost identical to those of the *Mercurio*. They also declared that patriotism, humanity, and philosophy had been the agents of the establishment of the Society, and that religion and authority were to be respected by the members. Of the thirty "academic members," elected by a plurality of votes, twenty-one were to be Limeños.

---

asking aid so his *Diario* could continue, and claiming credit for having inspired the *Mercurio*.

[66] *Mercurio Peruano de historia, literatura y noticias públicas que da a luz la Sociedad Académica de Amantes de Lima* (12 vols., Lima, 1791-95). Cf. "Informe del doctor don Hipólito Unánue ... Secretario de literatura de la Sociedad Académica ..., sobre los varios 'Establecimientos literarios' de esta capital, dirigido al virrey fray don Francisco Gil de Lemos," Lima, October 13, 1794, in *Obras científicas y literarias* of Unánue (3 vols., Barcelona, 1914), II, 332-41, that the *Mercurio* began publication under Jacinto Calero "in the name of a Society of literary men."

[67] *Prospecto del Papel Periódico Intitulado Mercurio Peruano ..., que a nombre de una Sociedad de Amantes del País, y como uno de ellos promete dar a luz Don Jacinto Calero y Moreira* (Lima, 1790).

[68] *Mercurio Peruano.* January 2, 1791, 1-7, "Idea General del Perú."

[69] "Progresos y Estado Actual de la Sociedad de Amantes del País por el Señor Oidor, Presidente de ella, Don Ambrosio Cerdán y Pontero," *Mercurio Peruano*, X, No. 329 (February 27, 1794), 136-42; No. 330 (March 2), 143-50; No. 331 (March 6), 151-58; No. 332 (March 9), 159-65. The university and a censor had found them acceptable. A *Juez de Imprentas* was to supervise the Society.

Académicos were to dedicate their efforts to writing for the *Mercurio*, and ability as a writer was a condition of membership. Provision was made for "consulting," "honorary," and "corresponding" members. Something was included to prevent the influence of rank from entering the fraternity, but the clauses on this were less direct than in the Madrid statutes.[70] These statutes lacked an expression of the economic interest of the Spanish Societies, had no division of members for working purposes, and did not mention popular industry or patriotic schools. Royal approval before long enabled the group to change the name to *Real Sociedad de Amantes del País*.[71] As a result of the viceroy's authorization of October, 1792, the Society celebrated its first public session, January 5, 1793.[72] The viceroy also conceded some assistance to the Society.[73]

Dr. Unánue, secretary of the Society, in compliance with the regulations, now drew up a plan showing the subjects pertaining to the interests of the *Mercurio*. Unánue (1755-1833), a creole doctor of medicine and student of science, was to be the most active editor of the *Mercurio*. He was an enlightened upper-class creole, in love with modern learning, and a partisan of strong government and desirous of proceeding slowly with social change.[74] He was chosen by Viceroy Gil de Lemos to write his *Memoria* (1796) for his successor, one of the most extensive and best such memorials produced in the colonial era. He was to gain international fame for his work on the climate of Peru and its influence (1806).[75] In the period of constitutional crisis, he favored the Constitution of Cadiz, and was elected deputy to the Cortes, going to Spain in 1814, returning to Peru in 1817. A few years later, with the coming of the liberating army of San Martín, Unánue became an important conservative political figure in independent Peru.[76]

Unánue's plan for the *Mercurio* was long and ambitious, with twenty main divisions and seventy-five subheads. The main categories were: Ancient History, Modern Civil History, Geography, Ecclesiastical History, Peruvian

---

[70] These *constituciones* were printed in the before-cited article in the *Mercurio* on "Progresos y Estado Actual," 137-42.

[71] *Ibid.*, 164.

[72] José Valega, *La gesta emancipadora del Peru 1780-1819* (3 vols., Lima, 1940-43), I, 137.

[73] *Ibid.*, 138.

[74] His address at the inauguration of the anatomical theater in November, 1792, showed a large knowledge of the history of medicine, and was full of high praise of a government that promoted the progress of science (*Obras*, II, 3-36, "Medicina. Decadencia y Restauración del Péru. Oración inaugural del Anfiteatro ...").

[75] *Ibid.*, I, contains this work.

[76] Benjamín Vicuña Mackenna, in *Obras* of Unánue, I, ix-xxiv; Barreda Laos, *Vida intelectual*, 347-49. Cf. Appendix for Unánue as vice-president of the Patriotic Society of 1822.

Literature, Politics (with slavery the only subhead), Moral Education, Public Economy, Agriculture, Commerce, Physics, Chemistry, Mineralogy, Botany, Anatomy, Practical Medicine, Natural History, Belles-Lettres, Poetry, Public Notices.[77]

The Lima Society did little during the two years of its formal existence except edit the *Mercurio*.[78] It published the first, not the other, volumes of Unánue's famous guides to Peru.[79] But the Society was not even mentioned in the first guide. The *Mercurio* did note some of the juntas of the Society, which apparently were dull affairs, and certainly not like those of the Economic Societies. In 1794 the Society could list the king as protector, the viceroy as his deputy, and Juan del Pino Manrique of the audiencia as vice-protector and *juez de imprentas*. There were twenty-one "academic members," including Friar Diego Cisneros as censor and secretary, José María Egaña as secretary of correspondence, Toribio Rodríguez de Mendoza, rector of the College of San Carlos, and three men who were also members of the Basque Society; six "foreign members," including José Pérez Calama, ex-bishop of Quito, whom we shall meet presently in the Quito Society; and seven honorary members. This total of thirty-four members compared with 247 subscribers to the *Mercurio* for the same year, representing Spanish America from Mexico to Buenos Aires, with a few from Europe. Subscribers included the Patriotic Society of Quito, by this time near the end of its short history; J. C. Mutis of the Royal Botanical Expedition of New Granada, whom we have noted as a member of the Mompox Society; and Governor Luís de las Casas of Cuba, who in 1791 had approved the Havana Society.[80] A correspondent in Cuzco criticized the restricted membership of the Society, observing that the first five issues of the *Mercurio* seemed from a single pen, and inquiring "where are the other individuals of this *numerous* Society?"[81]

Unánue's suggestions for economics in the *Mercurio* were brief, and submerged by the mass of his other proposals. Considerable economic material appeared in the periodical, nevertheless, together with literary and philo-

---

[77] "Progresos y Estado Actual," *loc. cit.*, 152-60.

[78] *Ibid.*, 161-62, for some other interests, including the suggested establishment of academies of civil and canon law.

[79] *Guía política, eclesiástica y militar del virreynato del Perú* (4 vols., Lima, 1793-96).

[80] *Mercurio Peruano*, No. 335 (March 20, 1794), "Lista de los Individuos de la Sociedad de Amantes del País: Año 2° de su formal erección, y 4° de la publicación del Mercurio"; "Lista de señores subscriptores al Mercurio Peruano," 13 unmbd., pp. at back of t. XII of the Yale University file. Cf. Valega, *Gesta emancipadora*, I 139-42, on two foreign members of the Society; D. E. McPheeters, "The Distinguished Peruvian Scholar Cosme Bueno (1711-1798)," HAHR, XXXV, No. 4 (November, 1955), 484-91, an honorary member of the Lima Society.

[81] *Mercurio Peruano*, No. 17 (February 27, 1791).

sophical; but there was no direct political discussion, and little on international relations. The Society editors, as members of the dominant minority, certainly did not want to promote social disturbance, and they deplored *murmuraciones* and the spirit of faction in *cafées*, an institution they regarded with some dubiety.[82] The *Mercurio* yearned mildly—it was always mild— for the old days before 1771 when the first *cafée público* was opened in Lima, for the earlier day when men took *maté* at home. But with a little help from Malpighi, Reaumur, Duhamel, Newton, and Leibnitz, the *Mercurio* managed to find some good in cafes if properly conducted.[83] Most of the material on customs has a literary flavor, and is naive by twentieth-century sociological standards. Of course, the editors were much hampered by the censorship.[84]

The interest of the Society in learning was displayed in the considerable astronomical and meteorological data in the form of tables in the *Mercurio*. The usual interest was manifested in machines;[85] in the scientific description of plants; in metallurgical methods; and in the new anatomical amphitheater of Lima. The *Mercurio* also printed many articles describing areas of the viceroyalty, though the purpose of these was as much improvement of the economy as the advancement of learning.

The single best—and longest—article on political economy was by Baquíjano, early in the life of the *Mercurio*.[86] Baquíjano had the rationalist's respect for good statistics, and included a goodly number despite his observation that they were hard to come by. His opening words might have been penned by the students of political economy he had known in Spain, for he wanted an "exact idea" of the country, to know "analytically" the resources of the land that would make for its "felicity." A flourishing commerce he found necessary to "the opulence of nations," repeating after Campomanes and the Economic Societies that Holland despite her poor soil had attained wealth by mercantile activity, to which England also owed much of her prosperity. But Peru by preference was "nearly exclusively dedicated to the exploitation of mines." Mines should be cared for, as the basis of Peru's wealth, but in addition commerce and agriculture should be improved. Peru might well promote the production of various natural products, as

---

[82] No. 4 (January 13, 1791), "Idea de las diversiones públicas de Lima"; and cf. Barreda Laos, *Vida intelectual*, 369, on the timidity of the colonial press.

[83] No. 12 (February 10, 1791), "Rasgo Histórico y Filosófico sobre los Cafées de Lima."

[84] Cf. No. 19 (March 6, 1791), that they received an admirable letter on the falsity of Platonic love, but thought it best not to publish it.

[85] No. 50 (June 26, 1791), "Máquina de Ayre, de Guillermo White," for use in torrid climes; t. XII, for notice of a machine for milling sugar.

[86] In Nos. 23-31 (March 20-April 17, 1791), signed "J. B. Y. C."

cotton, cinnamon "not inferior to that of Ceylon," *bálsamos*, cochineal "equal to that of Oaxaca" that was being used as a dye in the interior provinces of Peru, and wax that ought to be able to compete with that of Louisiana. He did not discuss industry, but divided his study into an examination of the products of the viceroyalty for internal and external commerce, an examination of external commerce, the causes of the "decadence" of that commerce, and remedies for its "restoration and increase."

He made many observations on the obstacles to economic growth, especially natural obstacles, finding deficiencies in the soil, climate, labor supply, and transportation. He did refer, however, to artificial obstacles, finding in the writings of Floridablanca authority for freeing the economic life of Peru, and quoting from Campomanes' treatise on popular education that Spain "in the illusion of prosperity, and in the chimerical design of appropriating to herself exclusively the wealth and production of the new world," had prohibited trade with foreigners and inhibited it between the inhabitants of America.

He quoted Josiah Child of England to the effect that to know the wealth of a country it was only necessary to know the rate of interest there; if it was high, commerce languished; if low, it flourished. Nowhere was it lower than in Holland and England, being regularly one per cent. Baquíjano pointed out that the discovery of the treasure of America quickly lowered interest in Spain from ten per cent in 1500 to four per cent. He cited Hume on the reduction of interest by means of banks, public funds, and bills of credit, declaring that experience proved the value of the Englishman's opinion, as seen in the experience of the "Colonias Anglo-Americanas" in the use of bills of credit.[87]

Baquíjano considered lack of population a great obstacle to the Peruvian economy, for her "population compared with her immense territory . . . forms a true desert." He ascribed the sparse American population to the racial problems consequent upon mixture, to the climate, and to the harsh conditions of Negro slavery. He had the view we have seen in the Spanish Societies that the population of Spain had declined greatly, from fifty-two million [sic] in the time of Julius Caesar; and he quoted Bernardo Ward to the effect that little of the land of Spain, the richest in Europe, was currently cultivated.

Discussing the poor state of transportation, Baquíjano noted that producers would not work hard if there appeared to be no market for their produce. The trouble was, he observed, that England and France could easily get their products to the sea, either because of short distances and easy topography,

---

[87] He brought Raynal and Montesquieu to the support of other views.

or via rivers and canals, whereas Peru had great distances, unnavigable rivers, and no hope of large investment in public works, so that here products could not compete in price.

Such material on political economy as appeared in the *Mercurio* was largely descriptive and speculative, whereas Peru—and all Spanish America— also needed practical advice and effort for specific economic improvement.[88] While the *Mercurio* did not display quite the passion for statistical information seen in the publications of the Madrid, Valencia, and Segovia Societies, it must be remembered that Lima did not offer so large a useful membership, the statistics for Spain were better, and the American Societies were subjected to more restrictions on their opinions than were the peninsular bodies. The *Mercurio* did print many commercial notices, and several statistical studies of the trade of Peru with Spain. A table on imports from Europe via Cape Horn in 1791 showed that in a total value of about four million pesos, somewhat more than half was to be ascribed to foreign rather than Spanish goods.[89] Another table showed trade between America and Cadiz in 1793.[90] The last thing in the last volume was a table showing that the trade of Lima with Spain was less in 1790-1794 than in 1785-1789, but that imports from Spain had fallen off much more drastically than exports from Peru to the Peninsula.[91] Finally, a great deal of information of value for economic planning was contained in *Mercurio* articles describing various regions of Peru.[92]

The interest in mining was of course prominent in the periodical, but there was also considerable interest in the promotion of agriculture. Other evidences of interest in economics included a project for augmentation of the population,[93] several discussions of the miserable tracks that passed

---

[88] Cf. César Antonio Ugarte, *Bosquejo de la historia económica del Perú* (Lima, 1926), 40, on the weakness of the practical side of education in colonial Peru; 49-51, summary of the causes of the poor economic condition of the region.

[89] No. 19 (March 6, 1791).

[90] No. 370 (July 20, 1794), breaking it down by American ports.

[91] T. XII, bearing title: "Estado en que se manifieste la general importación y exportación de los caudales, manufacturas y frutos con que Lima ha hecho su Comercio con la Península."

[92] Cf. "Peregrinación por el Río Hullaga hasta la laguna de la grand Cocama ... en el año ... de 1790" (Nos. 59-61); "Descripción Histórica y Corográfica de la Provincia de Chichas y Tarija" (No. 37, and carrying on for several issues); "Descripción sucinta de la provincia o partido de Caxatambo, en que se trata por incidencia de la decadencia de las Minas, y de las causas de la despoblación del Reyno" (Nos. 162-63); and others in later issues.

[93] Nos. 32-33 (April 21, 24, 1791), "Proyecto Económico sobre la Internación y Población de los Andes de la Provincia de Guamalíes, propuesto y principiado por D. Juan de Bezares [a Spanish merchant of Lima]."

as roads in Peru,[94] a discussion of the debts of European nations,[95] and some discussion of the relationship of racial and class divisions to the state of the Peruvian economy.[96] The Society did not show in the *Mercurio* the interest of the Spanish Societies in the foundation of technical schools, the promotion of popular industry, the techniques of production, or the regulation of guilds.

The Society had no effect on the Peruvian economy; it is doubtful how much effect it had on opinion, or how much it influenced scientific and literary studies. We may agree with the view that it was nonpolitical, not preparatory to independence, that it printed but two items to which can be attributed an "intention of social regeneration," that it was chiefly a scientific and literary organ, whatever revolutionary ideas some of the members may have privily entertained.[97]

Mild though the *Mercurio* and the Society were,[98] they did represent a tendency toward acceptance of the criteria of rationalism and toward the development of interprovincial communication. The *Mercurio* boasted that in

> only one year we have seen our vigilance confirmed with imitation. Santa Fe, Havana, Quito progressively have adopted our thought [and] it will always be the glory of the *Amantes de Lima* to have published the first literary periodical seen in our America. . . . May the beneficent influence of literature with which it has begun to experiment, extend its well-arrayed advancement through all the other civilized (*cultas*) cities of this vast continent.[99]

---

[94] Cf. No. 74 (September 18, 1791), "Propuesta de unos premios para las disertaciones en que se proponga el método más económico, fácil y permanente para majorar los caminos del Reyno." This article noted that navigation and roads were the two main arteries of circulation; learned men in various lands had considered the matter; Charles III and Floridablanca deserved praise for opening good roads; the roads of the interior of Peru must be as bad as any in the world. The prize was a medal.

[95] Nos. 365-66 (July 3, 6, 1794), 'Ensayo sobre las deudas de las naciones de Europa, y sobre las ventajas que España puede procurarse liquidándolas."

[96] Cf. "Carta Remitida a la Sociedad, que publica con algunas notas," No. 344 (April 20, 1794), 255-62, No. 345 (April 24), 263-67, No. 346 (April 27), 271-74; and "Apéndice a las anotaciones sobre la carta anterior," No. 346, 274-80. The letter assigned much of America's lack of prosperity to such divisions; but the editors denied this, and claimed that the divisions in any case were not due to legislation but to nature, and that the suggested union of the elements was impossible because of their different character and because the *castas*—mulatto, Negro, mestizo—disliked each other. The editors also argued that the charge that the low opinion in which manual labor was held hurt the economy, by asserting that this opinion would only change when enough Europeans had to exercise crafts in America; and they agreed with the letter writer that it would be useful to have "classes intermediate between the nobility and the plebians," but did not believe it would be easy to arrange.

[97] Barreda Laos, *Vida intelectual*, 310.

[98] Lanning, "The Reception of the Enlightenment," 87, calls the *Mercurio* a "model of correctness," and notes that it published "ever increasingly banal material" (p. 88).

[99] T. III, No. 103 (December 29, 1791), 305-6.

The *Mercurio* started out to celebrate liberal tendencies in nearby Quito, but soon dropped all reference to it. It carried enthusiastic accounts of Bishop Calama of Quito in early issues. In December, 1791, it printed an account of the foundation of the Quito Society and of the periodical of that body. In January, 1792, it published Bishop Calama's discourse at the opening of the Quito Society in November, 1791, with editorial comment on the new Society to the north. But thereafter the *Mercurio* never mentioned the Quito Society. This cannot have been an accidental oversight.

One thing the authorities undoubtedly found dubious about the *Mercurio* was the prominence of creoles in its direction, whereas the *Diario Curioso* (1790-1793) was founded by a newly-arrived Spaniard, and the short-lived *El Semanario Crítico* (1791) was the work of a Spanish Franciscan, Father Juan Antonio Olavarrieta, who came to Lima in 1791 as chaplain of the frigate "Dolores" of the Royal Philippine Company. The Society members and the good father detested each other. The *Mercurio* greeted the announcement of the *Semanario* by sneering at Olavarrieta's project for correcting the defects of Peruvian life. It laughed at the pretentiousness of Father Antonio in pretending to deal with an extensive list of complicated matters, and noted that he in fact intended to put forth his best efforts on public diversions, theatrical poesy, and the theater in general. It suggested ironically that he realized that European methods of criticism were scarcely applicable to America. Nor did the *Mercurio* fail to emphasize the father's very recent arrival in America. This first attack ended with the ironic suggestion that with three periodicals in Lima they might now fear that yet another author would come forward, with a project for an "Espíritu de los mejores Papeles Periódicos de Lima."[100]

Two weeks later the Society returned to the attack with a nine-page blast entitled "Justificación de la Sociedad, y del Perú." The *Mercurio* quoted the statutes of the Society to show that it was obligated to defend both itself and the hemisphere against the attacks of outlanders. It objected to the "sarcasmos groseros" of the *Semanario*, found Olavarrieta "full of the blackest venom," described him sarcastically as "this famous reformer of cafés and comedies." The Society responded to his charge that the *Mercurio* copied its materials on commerce, natural history, and industry, by stating that it required more than the mere testimony of the good father to demonstrate the fact. Then in a fine blend of intellectual snobbery and of condescension it proceeded to point out the literary errors committed by their "P.[adre] mío." But one suspects that the members of the Society were

---

[100] No. 46 (June 9, 1791).

most outraged by Olavarrieta's description of Peruvians as "recently conquered savages."[101] The stubborn father obtained the suppression of this issue of the *Mercurio*—though copies had escaped—and counterattacked with yet more mention of the conquest of Peru and with further comments on the quality of its civilization. He may have aimed "to criticize public customs with the principles of moral philosophical reason,"[102] but he was as poor an ambassador as Spain could have found.

A similarly fine perception of the interest of Church and Crown led Archbishop Juan Domingo González de la Reguera to fight creole liberalism. The archbishop had for some years been at odds with the liberal rector of the Convictory of San Carlos, Toribio Rodríguez de Mendoza. The latter had been named to his post in 1785 with the aid of Father Diego Cisneros, opponent of the Inquisition and of intellectual oppression generally, owner of prohibited books which he passed to friends, and possessor of a shield in the fact of his former position as confessor to Queen María Luisa. Rodríguez as an educator promoted the ideas and methods of Descartes, Newton, Gassendi, and Leibnitz, and started the study of experimental physics, astronomy, and mechanics. In 1788 the Holy Office looked into his operations, and for a time the Convictory was suspended on the grounds that it secretly taught natural law even after the archbishop had obtained from Spain an order prohibiting such instruction.[103] The archbishop cannot have been reassured about the Society and the *Mercurio* when Rodríguez and Cisneros became prominent members of the former and editors of the latter. The archbishop was also right about the Convictory, since in the course of time it became a center of sentiment for independence from Spain. It has been suggested that it was at the request of the archbishop that the government in Spain in 1792 asked for copies of the *Mercurio*. He did withdraw his own subscription to the periodical.[104] How much this form of pressure affected the editors is open to speculation; it was not immediately fatal. The Spanish government wrote the viceroy in June, 1793, that it had received the copies of the *Mercurio* he had sent; and it enjoined the editors to work hard at improving the periodical. The viceroy in January, 1794, sent a copy of this communication with a note of his own, to the Academic Society. These

---

[101] No. 50 (June 23, 1791).

[102] Ella Dunbar Temple, *Periodismo Peruano del Siglo XVIII. El Semanario Crítico* (Lima, n.d., reprinted from *La Revista "Mercurio Peruano,"* vol. XXV, No. 198), dealing with the controversy chiefly from the point of view of the *Semanario*.

[103] Barreda Laos, *Vida intelectual*, 131-32, 140-44, 301 *et seq.* Cf. for this period Sebastián Lorente, *Historia del Perú bajo los Borbones, 1700-1821* (Lima, 1871); Carlos Weisse, *Historia del Perú* (4 vols., Lima, 1937-41), II-III; M. Nemesio Vargas, *Historia del Perú independiente* (9 vols., Lima, 1903), I.

[104] Lanning, "Reception of the Enlightenment," 88.

two documents the Society heard at its general junta of academic members, employees, and counsellors.[105]

In October, 1794, Unánue answered a request of the viceroy for information about the "literary establishments" of Lima,[106] in which the creole claimed that the experience of all the globe showed the value of periodicals, for they helped reduce idleness and promote commerce; claimed that the *Mercurio*, aided by the Society, had been much praised; and noted that the eleven volumes issued to date had printed *gratis* the royal orders and other official documents sent to the editors. But, he said, publication of the *Mercurio* was suddenly abandoned due to lack of funds. When the viceroy inquired the reason of the Society, the latter informed him, and asked for aid. Unánue concluded, sarcastically, that since a year had now passed since this request, it must be assumed that publication was at an end. In 1796 Unánue wrote much the same in the report he composed for the successor of Gil de Lemos.[107] In this report he also mentioned the request of Spain for copies of the *Mercurio* as though it showed an encouraging interest on the part of the government, and asserted that the royal order of January 10, 1794, had noted with approval receipt of the copies.[108]

Volume XII of the *Mercurio* was printed in 1795, but no longer was under the protection of the Society and the viceroy.[109] So far as the pages of the *Mercurio* tell the story, the Society of Lima was most interested in the new science and philosophy, and in the economy of Peru, and was strikingly American or creole in its point of view.

Quito Society

The Quito and Lima Societies were suggested and founded concurrently but independently. The Lima originated in a private association of 1787; the Quito was suggested by an individual in 1786 and succeeding years.

---

[105] *Mercurio Peruano*, No. 332 (March 9, 1794), on January 20.

[106] *Obras* of Unánue, II, 332-41, "Informe del doctor ... Unánue ... sobre los Establecimientos literarios ... dirigido al virrey. ..."

[107] Segunda Parte, cap. v, "Historia literaria," of the *Relación de Gobierno del ... Virrey ... Gil de Taboada y Lemos ... año de 1796*, in *Obras* of Unánue, III.

[108] This is a scrambled reference to the communications noted above. At this time Unánue also recorded that the missionary Father Diego Cisneros had succeeded him as editor of the *Mercurio* and intended to bring out vol. XII at his own expense, but had not managed to do so. Cf. Valega, *Gesta emancipadora*, I, 138, that the Society disbanded at the end of 1794.

[109] The title of vol. XII said it was "dado a luz por uno de los individuos de la Sociedad," whereas I-XI were titled *Mercurio Peruano ... que da a luz la Sociedad Académica*. And whereas the issues of I-XI came out regularly every few days, those of XII carried no dates, and presumably were not distributed separately. Barreda Laos, *Vida intelectual*, 311, guesses that the viceroy withdrew protection on orders from Spain.

Both were organized at the beginning of the next decade, the Quito Society holding its inaugural meeting November 30, 1791.

The socioeconomic condition of Quito was even unhappier than that of Peru. The *Mercurio Peruano* noted that the towns of the presidency of Quito had risen and fallen, that prosperity had been succeeded by decay, that the city of Quito itself had once been opulent and flourishing, but had been decaying since the end of the seventeenth century, being now but a skeleton of its former self. But this was not the fault of the inhabitants, who continued to work hard, and had lately redoubled their efforts "to reanimate that dying realm: every place patriotism has commenced to ferment, and from the year 1789 Quito has experienced its advantageous effects."[110]

The most important individual in the history of the Quito Society was Francisco Javier Eugenio de Santa Cruz y Espejo (1747-1795), born at Quito, son of an Indian in the service of a medical friar of the Quito hospital and of a mother with some Spanish blood. Espejo graduated as a doctor of medicine, and became a licentiate in both laws. He became acutely aware of the deficiencies of the Quiteño economy, and finally radically dissatisfied with the political system. He has been called, with deliberate ironic anachronism, "the most terrible 'bolshevic' of the colony."[111] There is no doubt that Espejo frightened those entrusted with preservation of the status quo.

Espejo, in 1792, stated that in 1786 he had announced the "utility and necessity" of a Patriotic Society, though no one accepted the idea.[112] This is a clear reference to the "Representación de los Curas de Riobamba," a notorious satirical attack on the views of an official of the audiencia, in which Espejo ostensibly was defending the clerics. The reference of 1792—coupled with the recommendation of Societies in the 1786 Representación—alone is nearly sufficient to dispel the small doubts that have been expressed as to Espejo's authorship of the "Representación."[113] In any event Quito can

---

[110] No. 103 (December 29, 1791), 300-306, "Noticia de una Sociedad Patriótica, y de un Papel Periódico nuevamente establecido en la Capital de Quito." Cf. Pío Jaramillo Alvarado, *La presidencia de Quito; memoria histórico-jurídica de los orígenes de la nacionalidad ecuatoriana y de su defensa territorial* (2 vols., Quito, 1938-39, paged continuously), 134-37, on economic conditions and the formation of the Society, apparently following González Suárez.

[111] Enrique Garcés, *Eugenio Espejo, médico y duende* (Quito, 1944), chap. xxiii; cf. on the Indian father of Espejo, Federico González Suárez, "Estudio biográfico y literario sobre Espejo y sus escritos," in *Escritos del doctor Francisco Javier Eugenio Santa Cruz y Espejo* (3 vols., Quito, 1912-23), I, ix-lxxii, at xi.

[112] *Primicias de la Cultura de Quito* (facsimile edition, Quito, 1947), No. 7 (March 29, 1792), 53-56, "Anécdotas Concernientes a la Historia."

[113] Cf. Homero Viteri Lafronte, "Al lector," ix-lvi in t. III of *Escritos de Espejo* on Espejo's authorship of the item; Roberto Andrade, *Historia del Ecuador* (7 vols., Guayaquil, 1934-37), I, 164-65, expressing some doubt as to Espejo's authorship.

scarcely have boasted two persons with such an impressive talent for satire and such ability to pack irony into a phrase; to say nothing of such intellectual stamina—for the satirical picture of the curates of Riobamba was a long book, not an essay.[114] Espejo's picture of life in the highlands of Quito plainly reveals the author as a child of the Enlightenment. But the author was not just prating of culture in the sense of book-learning, but was convinced that the economy needed overhauling. He suggested that what was needed was more work and fewer holidays and fiestas,[115] declared that agriculture "amounts to no more than the planting and harvest of potatoes, wheat, and maize";[116] and in considering manufacturing found it necessary to mention Robertson, Raynal, and D'Alembert, and opined that the few small textile *obrajes* turned out cloth fit only for the very lowest class.[117] He said that there was nothing in the province that could be called by the name of commerce, which could not exist without manufacturing and agriculture, and he had shown that they scarcely existed.[118] In the light of these conditions, the king should have Patriotic Societies established in all his American dominions, benefiting them as they did the metropolis.[119] There was a clear implication here that Spain did not do as well by her American as by her European provinces. The work was obviously that of a man lacking in servility, with a talent for the cutting phrase, and determined to criticize his own society.

Espejo was jailed in 1787 as the alleged author of a satire attacking such exalted figures as Charles III and José de Gálvez.[120] From jail Espejo wrote the president of Quito in bitter terms, condemning the ignominy of his arrest in "broad daylight," the use of fetters, the racket with which he was seized, "which gave to Riobamba, Ambato, Latacunga and Quito the idea that I was an enemy of the state, about to be executed." He noted that his enemies had told the president that they had been hurt by his pen "en la

---

[114] *Representación de los Curas del distrito de Riobamba hecha a la Real Audiencia de Quito, para impedir la fe que se habia dado a un informe que contra ellos produjo don Ignacio Barreto*, in *Escritos de Espejo*, III, 1-233, dated at end "Riobamba, December 6, 1786."

[115] *Ibid.*, 54-55, citing Feijóo, Ustáriz, and Diego de Saavedra.

[116] *Ibid.*, 159; cf. 158-63 for more on agriculture.

[117] *Ibid.*, 163-72, on manufactures.

[118] *Ibid.*, 172-73; cf. *ibid.*, 192, that "Commerce is in this *reino* an imaginary entity."

[119] *Ibid.*, 193-94; and cf. *Escritos de Espejo*, I, 167-99, "Voto de un ministro de la Audiencia de Quito," Quito, March 7, 1792, composed by Espejo for Judge Fernando Cuadrado, containing discussion of the products of Quito, suggestions for economic improvement, and observing that Spain could not supply herself with fabrics, much less America.

[120] Cf. Antonio Montalvo, *Francisco Javier Eugenio de Santa Cruz y Espejo* (Quito, 1947), 43-103. The satire was titled *El Retrato de Golilla* and circulated in MS.

representación de curas,"[121] but denied authorship of the satire, saying that the process of reasoning used to attribute it to him could also be used to prove him author of *The Prince* of Machiavelli and Rousseau's *Social Pact.* Furthermore, his works had been directed to "the felicity of this country," which was "for the most part barbarous," and had received "the approbation of the impartial literary men of Europe and Lima." And Espejo declared that his sins were his frankness in following the truth, his energy in expressing it, and the "vigorous but reverent spirit with which I have supported it in the presence of my illustrious and very wise (*prudentes*) superiors."[122]

President Villalengua considered the satire on the magistrate cruel and seditious, and meant to banish Espejo, but the latter sent complaints to Madrid against the president himself, and the Crown decided that the case should go to the viceroy at Santa Fe.[123] Espejo's advanced views were probably reinforced by his association at Santa Fe with such kindred spirits as Antonio Nariño and Francisco Antonio Zea.[124] While there, Espejo wrote, at the urging of his friend and fellow Quiteño the Marquis of Selva Alegre, a discourse on a School of Harmony (*Escuela de la Concordia*), which was to be the basis for foundation of the Quito Society. Espejo recorded of himself and the marquis that "the two members (*socios*) surveyed the economic constitution of Quito on the verge of ultimate ruin," also found the spiritual state of the realm unsatisfactory, and felt that the ideas of the century in which

---

[121] Apparently an open confession of authorship of that work by Espejo. Cf. *supra*, 169.

[122] *Escritos de Espejo*, I, 203-16, "Representación de Espejo al Presidente Villalengua Acerca de su Prisión. Cárcel de Corte y Octubre 27 de 1787," claimed by the editor to have been inedited previously. Espejo also said that he meant to dedicate his *Nuevo Luciano de Quito* to Campomanes, "first savant of the Nation, and perhaps a unique judge of universal literature."

[123] Cf. Guillermo Hernández de Alba, "Viaje de Espejo, el precursor ecuatoriano a Santa Fe," *Boletín de la Academia de Historia* [Quito], XXV (January-June, 1945), 102-5, printing from the Archivo Nacional of Bogota an official summary of the case against Espejo, dated Quito, March 18, 1789; González Suárez, "Estudio biográfico de Espejo," xvi, n. 1; Andrade, *Historia del Ecuador*, I, 170-71; Garcés, *Eugenio Espejo*, 216-20.

[124] Andrade, *Historia del Ecuador*, I, 172, says so, without citing evidence, and claims he was involved in a conspiracy there; Raimundo Rivas, *El andante caballero Don Antonio Nariño* (2d ed., Bogota, 1938), 59, asserts that the *Arcano Sublime de la Filantropía*, a secret society, welcomed Espejo; Hernández de Alba, "Viaje de Espejo," uses Rivas to claim that Espejo got his idea for the Patriotic Society in New Granada, whereas we have seen he favored a Society before going to Bogota; Roberto Botero Saldarriaga, *Francisco Antonio Zea* (Bogota, 1945), 52, has Espejo a member of the Nariño circle, but without citation of source of the statement; José M. Vargas, *La cultura de Quito colonial* (Quito, 1941), 184, states, without adducing evidence, that in Santa Fe Espejo's idea of liberation for America was clarified in conversations with Nariño, Zea, and others.

they lived were being ignored.[125] Selva Alegre, like Espejo, had seditious tendencies.[126]

The discourse on the School of Harmony was printed at Santa Fe in 1789.[127] That the discourse came to the attention of Quiteños seems to be indicated by the fact that they started to organize the Society before Espejo returned from Santa Fe. Espejo himself printed the discourse in 1792 at Quito.[128] The School of Harmony was to promote science, art, commerce, industry, and economy. Espejo lamented that Europeans thought Americans ignorant, that De Pauw "dared to say that Americans are incapable of the sciences... that the University of ... Lima never produced a learned man."

> But (Oh! Immortal God if you hear favorably my supplications) the Society is that which in the *School of Harmony* will perform these miracles: will effectively renovate the face of all the Land, and will make Marriages blossom, and the Population, the Economy, and the Abundance, Learning, and Liberty, the Sciences, and Religion, Honor, and Peace, Obedience to the Laws, and the most faithful subordination to Charles IV.

Europe would then see "what until now it has not seen, or has feigned not to see," an America possessed of cultivation rather than "barbarity." It

---

[125] *Primicias de la Cultura*, 53-56. This account by Espejo in 1792 explained that no one had accepted the idea of a Society when he forwarded it in 1786. The account was well sprinkled with respect for "la razón natural."

[126] Juan Pío Montúfar (b. Quito 1759), son of a Spaniard who was president of Quito (1753-61). Humboldt and Bonpland in Quito in 1802 were received by Selva Alegre; Humboldt later spoke well of him. Selva Alegre was in the Quito revolt of 1809, imprisoned when it failed, later exiled to Spain (Isaac J. Barrera, *Próceres de la independencia* [Quito, 1939], 61-70; Gustavo Arboleda, *Diccionario biográfico de la república del Ecuador* [Quito, 1910], 108-9; Manuel de Jesús Andrade, *Ecuador. Próceres de la independencia* [Quito, 1909], 257-63). President Molina in 1810 wrote to Spain on the revolt, noting that Selva Alegre and his family were the heirs of the seditious schemes of Espejo (González Suárez, ' Estudio sobre Espejo," xviii and n.; Barrera, *Próceres*, 63).

[127] Hernández de Alba, "Viaje de Espejo," that Selva Alegre came to Santa Fe in November, 1789, on personal business, and while there paid for the printing of a "pequeño folleto" which issued from the press of Espinosa in 1789 as this celebrated discourse of the Ecuadorian precursor; José Toribio Medina, *La imprenta en Quito 1760-1818* (Santiago, 1904), 73, has it "impreso en Santafé"; Medina's *Imprenta en Bogota* does not list the item.

[128] *Primicias de Cultura*, No. 4 (February 16, 1792), 31-35; No. 5 (March 1), 35-37; No. 6 (March 15), 41-44; No. 7 (March 29), 49-53. He gave the title as "Discourse Directed to the very illustrious and very loyal City of Quito: Represented by its most Illustrious Town Council ... and to all the Members Provided for the erection of a Patriotic Society upon the necessity of establishing it then, with the title of School of Harmony." Medina, *Imprenta en Quito*, 73, has the title *Discurso sobre la necesidad de establecer una Sociedad de Amigos del País*. The *Mercurio Peruano* praised the discourse highly, and quoted from it in its issue of December 29, 1791 (t. III, 302-3), indicating that knowledge of the discourse printed at Santa Fe had reached Lima, before it was reprinted in the *Primicias* at Quito.

"will give the lie to" Hobbes, Grotius, and Montesquieu, and show a cultivated "nation" that is "American." Lord Chatham, speaking of England's
American colonies, said they might break with the metropolis when they
had the key to such action, which, Espejo said, was something Quiteños
might well ponder. The discourse was hardly likely to endear Espejo to the
authorities, or to make them regard the Society sympathetically.

The discourse did not result in the immediate creation of a Society, and
Espejo complained that its appearance should have induced "so spirited
and active a nation as ours [i.e., Quito]" to form a Society. This did not
happen "because Providence permitted to dominate in that year one of those
influences adverse to the public felicity," which endured through 1790.
So "the most zealous patriots" despaired, but then President Múñoz y
Guzmán finally ordered it established.[129]

The *Mercurio Peruano* assigned to the Count of Casa-Gijón an influence
in the creation of the Quito Society, noting that he brought "the unhappy
situation of his compatriots [of Quito]" to the attention of Spain.[130] Ascribing
Quito's condition to the "ruin or backwardness of its *fábricas* and other industrial divisions that in another time had flourished," he wanted to send to
Quito from Spain "money, laborers (*operarios*) and artisans." But the efforts
of this "learned patrician" did not bear fruit, though he deserved praise,
since "his designs ought to be considered as the germ of the public felicity
and even by itself to have promoted erection of a Patriotic Society that
would be realized in the future." From that time, said the *Mercurio* (not
indicating the time), patriots in Quito thought of association for the common
good, and thus, "quickly were seen united in a spirit of patriotism twenty-
seven enumerated members and twenty-two supernumerary," who created
"an Economic Society under the title of *School of Harmony*." The alleged
role of Casa-Gijón appears but vaguely in this account.[131]

Some role in forming the Society must have been played by Bishop José
Pérez Calama, who had assumed his post in February, 1791, and who later
in the year was made director of the Society. Calama favored enlightenment

---

[129] *Mercurio Peruano*, December 29, 1791, printing a letter of November 4, 1791,
to the Lima Society from the secretary (Espejo) of the new Quito body. Espejo also
said that two members of the Quito body (Espejo and Selva Alegre) were in Bogota
in 1789 when they stimulated foundation of the organization with a *Discurso*.

[130] December 29, 1791. The *Mercurio* said the count was well known at the Spanish
court for his enlightenment and services, citing vol. I of the Memorias of the Economic
Society—presumably meaning the Madrid Society. The Madrid *Memorias* do not
refer to the count, however.

[131] Cf. Andrade, *Historia del Ecuador*, I, 173-74, n. 1, for emphasis on the role
of Espejo, and objection to giving credit to Casa-Gijón. Andrade ascribes the error
to Dr. Pablo Herrera, and notes that Herrera was in part copied by Pedro Ceballos.

for the clergy,[132] was interested in the study of political economy, and promoted university study with a *Plan de Estudios* (1791) which, though it gave first place to theology and canon law, also made provision for science, and recommended the study of Castillian grammar and belles-lettres, and favored the teaching of philosophy in Spanish rather than Latin.[133] He was much praised in early issues of the *Mercurio Peruano*. It printed a pastoral edict in which he offered to have printed the best "scientific memorial" submitted in Spanish by the regular or secular clergy on the value of having a separate place in each house for answering the calls of nature, considering the matter from the points of view of utility for modesty, for Christian decorum, for corporal health, and for enlightened civility and order.[134]

Calama, in a letter to the Lima Society acknowledging receipt of copies of the *Mercurio*, and noting the printing of his edict, hit hard at the scholastic system, bewailing the time he wasted with the *ergotistas* in his youth, when scholasticism was a "universal epidemic," and expressing his sorrow that it was still to be found in Spain and the Indies. He not only praised the *Mercurio*, but the *Papel Periódico* of Bogota as well.[135] Later in 1791 the *Mercurio* printed other evidence of the bishop's enlightenment.[136] It seems unlikely that he could have been in Quito from the beginning of 1791 and not played a role in creation of the Economic Society.

The "adverse" influences of 1790 mentioned by Espejo gave him time to return to Quito before the Society was formed.[137] In November, 1791,

---

[132] González Suárez, *Historia general del Ecuador*, VII, 50-51.

[133] *Ibid.*, 52-53. This question of university studies became involved in a continuing controversy between the university and the Dominicans for control of certain studies, and by 1803 the university faction was pointing out that some knowledge was then available to which St. Thomas had not enjoyed access (John Tate Lanning, "La oposición a la ilustración en Quito," RBC, LIII, No. 3 [May-June, 1944], 224-41).

[134] No. 28 (April 7, 1791). Calama also offered prizes to bakers, and called for essays by the clergy on a number of sound Christian subjects.

[135] *Mercurio Peruano*, No. 50 (June 23, 1791), "Carta escrita a la Sociedad por ... Joseph Pérez Calama ... Obispo de Quito," Quito, May 18, 1791.

[136] No. 77 (September 29, 1791), "Extracto de una oración gratulatoria, y de tres edictos pastorales del Illmo. ... Joseph Pérez Calama ...," printing pronouncements of Calama directed to the promotion of the education of the clergy of Quito, and indicating the Lima Society's admiration for the prelate; No. 103 (December 29, 1791), "Edicto del ... obispo de Quito relativo a la abertura de un nuevo camino," in which Calama showed strong interest in the problem of communications, and praised the poor curates of his diocese for contributing money to the construction of this road.

[137] Cf. Pedro Fermín Ceballos, *Resúmen de la historia del Ecuador desde su orígen hasta 1845* (2d ed., 5 vols., Guayaquil, 1886), II, 357-58, that Espejo was made secretray in his absence, but returned in 1791, but with no indication of when in that year, and without citation of source for any of his statements; González Suárez, "Estudio sobre Espejo," xvi, n. 1, that December 2, 1789, Espejo obtained in Bogota complete

he was named head of the first public library, which had been opened at Quito in May. The inaugural session of the Society was celebrated November 30, 1791, at the new Royal University, formerly the Jesuit college. Present were the president of Quito, Múñoz de Guzmán; the judges of the audiencia as enumerated members of the new Society; Bishop Pérez Calama as director; the subdirector Joaquín Estanislao de Andino; the nobility of both sexes; and, on orders of Múñoz de Guzmán, the principal artisans or masters of guilds; and "all the public with the spirit of Patriotism." The ecclesiastical chapter cooperated, plans were laid for financial support of the Society, and the bishop-director offered it three hundred pesos.

Director Calama gave an address that began by bewailing the poverty of the area, which he claimed to have noted in his edicts to the clergy of the diocese and in *informes* to the king. He pointed out—as the members of the Spanish Societies often did—that Holland was rich without means other than agriculture, the arts, and maritime commerce. Nor should Quito be poor, since it had an abundance of grain and everything necessary for the manufacture of wool and cotton. The cause of Quito's "decadence" was plain: its "lack of active commerce, internal and external." Its "frutos naturales" were not being properly circulated, nor were they being used for industrial production, and from this "by necessary consequence depopulation" flowed. The realm was "prostrated" by "political ills," which the learned people there ought to study. For all the poverty of the region, he felt that if men of learning united they could solve almost any problem, so he called for the "resurrection of this our moribund *patria*" by the method of cooperation. And he pointed to the value of the Economic Societies of Spain, protected by the king and his ministers, declaring that the "progress" of the Quito Society of Friends of the Country could only be impeded by "envy, discord, and lack of application," and deploring the abundance of contentiousness which he said had existed in Quito.[138] It can be imagined that this was pretty strong fare for some of his more conservative and timid auditors.

The Quito Society in 1792 published a periodical under Espejo's direction. The announcement of its publication, in 1791,[139] declared that history showed

---

liberty to return to Quito and to reside where he liked (citing documents in the Archivo de Ministerio de Estado, Quito).

[138] The above account of the inaugural junta is based on the accounts in *Primicias*, No. 1 (January 1, 1792); and *Mercurio Peruano*, No. 112 (January 29, 1792), including 'Discurso Pronunciado por el Ilustrísimo Señor Doctor Don Joseph Pérez Calama, Obispo de Quito, como Director de la nueva Sociedad Económica, en la primera Junta preliminar celebrada el 30 de Noviembre de 1791."

[139] *Instrucción Previa*: printed in the facsimile edition of the *Primicias de Cultura*, 5 unmbd. pp.; also in Medina, *Imprenta en Quito*, No. 33.

man handicapped by his ignorance, while if he used his talent, conditions—including religious conditions—would improve. Quito, however, was ready to use the "dawn of her rationality," and from this "infancy of her enlightenment it is that Quito wishes to make known to the literary world" what she had done. Quito was to have *papeles periódicos* as Europe and other parts of America, although the title "First Fruits of the Culture of Quito" was adopted out of modesty—so Espejo said. These *Primicias* were to promote letters, a university, a new police plan, a Patriotic Society, and a civil reform, for "the press," he pronounced, "is the despository of intellectual treasure."

Any inhabitant of the realm could be an enumerated member of the Society if he contributed "with the light of his talent," and paid the fees.[140] The Society was to meet weekly; annual fees were eight pesos; the Society's main object was to improve and advance the colony, through four commissions: agriculture, sciences and arts, industry and commerce, and politics and belles-lettres. All the parish priests of the capital, the dean of the ecclesiastical chapter, and the oldest canon were enumerated members. The only religious not invited were the friars.[141] The project of the statutes of the Society was done by Espejo, and approved February 24, 1792, by President Múñoz de Guzmán.[142]

The *Primicias*, the only monument and apparently the only accomplishment of the Society—or rather of Espejo—lasted but seven issues, in the first three months of 1792.[143] There is no reason to believe that the Society lasted longer.[144]

One scholar feels that the "violent separation" of Bishop Calama from his bishopric was one of the main reasons for the destruction of the Society. In any event, Calama, who apparently had requested relief, received authorization soon after the foundation of the Society, and seems to have been speeded on his way by President Múñoz de Guzmán.[145] The extinction of the Society has been ascribed to the "inconstancy" of Quiteños, supposedly a "characteristic quality" of the populace of that city.[146] This is of course

[140] *Primicias de la Cultura*, No. 1.

[141] All this on the authority of González Suárez, *Historia general del Ecuador*, V, 372-73, finding the failure to include the friars surprising.

[142] *Ibid.*, 372.

[143] In addition to the items we have noted above, the 72 pages of the *Primicias* contained an article on literature, dealing with intellectual endeavor, and not touching on economic questions; and another on public education.

[144] Montalvo, *Espejo*, 74, quotes (without citation or date) a royal cedula stating that the Society had not received royal permission and was to cease operations at once.

[145] González Suárez, *Historia general del Ecuador*, V, 374-75, and asserting that the Society endured two years (V, 372).

[146] *Ibid.*, V, 373.

a phrase that begs the issue. It would seem more sensible to suppose that the temper of the dominant conservative group was opposed to the operations of the Society, especially with Espejo acting so energetically in behalf of the new organization. Espejo had powerful enemies not likely to forget his offenses. No doubt the disputatious spirit of the Quiteños mentioned by Bishop Calama would see to that. In any event, it was not long before Espejo was jailed once more, in January, 1795, apparently for evolving a plan for the independence of Quito. He was kept incommunicado, without writing materials, and seemingly without reference to legal forms preliminary to a trial. A rumor circulated that he was accused of the impieties of the French Revolution. He became ill in prison, was moved to his home, and died there in December, 1795.[147] There can be no doubt that an influence disturbing to the authorities had been removed.[148]

[147] González Suárez, "Estudio sobre Espejo," xiv, xvi n. 1; Andrade, *Historia del Ecuador*, I, 177, 181-82.

[148] Cf. Andrade, *Historia del Ecuador*, I, 120 *et seq.*, for an account of Espejo's writings, and the ambiguous statement that it was remarkable that an Indian had the idea of "the merits (*merecimientos*) of man"; Garcés, *Espejo*, 155-59, ascribes his radical views primarily to his understanding of the relationship between proper alimentation and culture; Alcázar, *Los virreinatos*, 325, would have it that the Quito Society's "acción cultural fué grande, análoga a las Económicas fundadas en España," claims credit for Spanish enlightenment, says the Society quickly ended because of the death of its most important partisans and because of the inconstancy of the others —all of which is misleading at best.

CHAPTER NINE

The Havana Society (1791-1821)

The Havana Society was organized in 1791, and still exists, the only ultramarine Economic Society to endure into the twentieth century. Some of its best work was done after 1821.

Cuba in the Eighteenth Century

The prime economic interest of the hacienda owners who founded the Society was in the booming sugar industry. Interest in sugar also was strong among merchants, who, with the hacendados, dominated Cuban economic and social life. These groups generally agreed in favoring a *Cuba grande* based on a monocultural export economy rather than a *Cuba pequeña* of diversified agriculture; but they did clash bitterly—especially after 1800—on various matters of economic policy. The hacendados who dominated the Economic Society were little interested in radical political ideas, partly because economic opportunity took the edge from dissatisfaction and directed criticism to those features of the colonial system which threatened their economic prospects.[1] In any event, creole political radicalism was inhibited by the presence of overwhelming Spanish military force.

---

[1] Friedländer, *Historia económica*, 103, quoting Humboldt on his visit of 1800 that one reason for local prosperity was " 'the intimate union between the *ingeni* owners and the merchants of Havana.' " But cf. José Antonio Portuondo, "La evolución cultural," in *Curso de introducción a la historia de Cuba* (Havana, 1937), 25 that 1762-1823 was "a fecund period of creole ascension."

The economic development of Cuba appears in rising export-import values—from 2,060,000 pesos in 1770, to 16,670,000 in 1790;[2] and in the increase of the public revenues from 163,000 pesos in 1760, to 532,000 in 1770, and 1,200,000 in 1782.[3] Contributing to this favorable economic development after 1765 were not only the increase of commerce, but stimulus from public works, the building of fortifications, naval construction, and the maintenance of troops.[4]

The sugar industry grew fairly steadily after the end of the Seven Years' War in 1763, with a notable setback in 1783-1789.[5] Cuban sugar boomed in 1790-1795, when the slave revolt in Haiti ruined the sugar industry there just as wartime European demand was increasing. In these years the price of sugar rose from four reals a pound to 28 to 30 reals.[6] And the sugar industry was aided by the easing of Spanish trade restrictions during wartime. Sugar exports rose from 480,000 *arrobas* in 1765 to 1,100,000 in 1790,[7] doubled the latter figure by 1800, rose another 66 per cent in 1800-1820, and grew even faster thereafter.[8] The number of sugar factories grew from about 120 in 1765 to nearly 600 in 1792,[9] but they remained small.[10] Their methods were improved also, although steam power was scarcely tried.[11] The greatest number and the largest *ingenios* were in the Havana district.[12] We will see that the Economic Society ascribed this concentration to bad transportation.

Tobacco from the middle of the eighteenth century had been the most important Cuban export. It was raised by small white farmers—*vergueros*—who had to deliver their crop to the Factory of the Tobacco Monopoly, and accept its prices. Deliveries to the Factory rose from 27,000 *arrobas* in 1765 to 200,000 in 1789. Production declined quickly after 1790, for reasons that are not entirely clear, although the great sugar boom and the influence

---

[2] Friedländer, *Historia económica*, 96, citing Pezuela.

[3] *Ibid.*, 83, 100. Revenues fell in the period of sugar depression in the 1780's, to 400,000 pesos in 1786, but were up to 973,000 in 1790.

[4] *Ibid.*, 100.

[5] *Ibid.*, 123. This setback was due in part to Spain's return to commercial restrictions following the war of American independence.

[6] *Ibid.*, 112.

[7] *Ibid.*, 83; but on 105 puts 1790 exports at 1,246,000 *arrobas*.

[8] *Ibid.*, 151, 545: exports rose 500 per cent in 1820-50.

[9] *Ibid.*, 83, 87.

[10] *Ibid.*, 87, doubts the estimate of Le Riverend in 1940 that the average number of slaves at Cuban ingenios was 100, and thinks it much lower. Cf. Fernando Ortiz, *Cuban Counterpoint* (trans. Onis, New York, 1947), 49: the average plantation in Matanzas in 1827 was only about 167 acres of cane, and some 750 acres in wood and pasture land; and (p. 50) the great growth of the sugar centrals awaited the railway.

[11] Friedländer, *Historia económica*, 197, very little even in 1827; Ortiz, *Counterpoint*, 49, introduced in 1820.

[12] Friedländer, *Historia económica*, 119.

of the sugar hacendados on the government had something to do with it. Production was down to 37,000 *arrobas* in 1803, and tobacco had to be imported from the United States.[13]

Coffee production was not important before the end of the eighteenth century. Decisive to its growth was the destruction of the coffee production of Haiti by the slave revolt, and the immigration to Cuba of many experienced cultivators. Only 7,000 *arrobas* were exported in 1790, and although exports grew thereafter, the sugar boom prevented the development of much interest among the hacendados of the Havana area. There was more interest in eastern Cuba, where the greatest expansion occurred after a great number of French arrived in 1801-1802. Exports of coffee were 70,000 *arrobas* in 1805, 400,000 in 1810, 900,000 in 1815.[14]

No other crops were important exports, and subsistence agriculture was poorly organized, so that large quantities of food were imported.[15] Industrial and craft operations were of little consequence, save as connected with sugar.

The supply of Negro slaves was an important question for the sugar hacendados and the merchants, who before 1790 complained of a serious undersupply. Import was facilitated by the Spanish decree of February 28, 1789, authorizing free commerce in Negroes for two years; and later extensions to 1816. Between 1792 and 1815 some 122,056 were imported.[16] The Spanish-English treaty of 1817 for extinction of the slave trade was not immediately effective, and many slaves were taken to Cuba thereafter, about 85,000 in 1816-1820 alone.[17] By that time so many Negroes had been introduced that even some former proponents of mass slave imports—like Arango—thought that perhaps the process had been carried too far. The development of the sugar industry certainly increased the Negro element in relation to the white, and the numerical preponderance of the *razas de color* continued in Cuba to the middle of the nineteenth century.[18] Population rose from 171,620 in 1774 to 553,033 in 1817; but the whites declined from 56 per cent to 43 per cent of the total, while the Negro slave group grew

---

[13] *Ibid.*, 63, 83, 91, 93-94, 112, 123, 124-27. Cf. Manuel Mariano de Acosta, *Memoria sobre la ciudad de San Felipe y Santiago Bejucal*, in *Memorias de la sección de historia de la Real Sociedad Patriótica de la Habana* (Habana, 1830-31), 379-441, for an account of what happened to the small white tobacco farmers with the great rise in the number of Negroes in the late 18th century.

[14] Friedländer, *Historia económica*, 105, 121; and cf. 122 for controversy as to the amount of profit involved in the coffee business.

[15] *Ibid.*, 96: among the most important imports in the years before 1790 was flour—30,000 barrels in 1769, 40,000 in 1770, 50,000 in 1790.

[16] *Ibid.*, 106-9, 110.

[17] *Ibid.*, 156.

[18] *Ibid.*, 110.

faster than the free Negro population.[19] This was one of the most important effects of the emphasis on sugar.[20]

The economic gains of hacendados in the years before the Economic Society was founded stimulated them to demand fuller realization of their prospects, which were clouded by various difficulties besetting the sugar industry. The industry required large amounts of capital—especially since the Cuban hacendados both grew and processed their cane—which could be had only at high rates of interest from financiers (*refraccionistas*) who were largely Spanish-born merchants. Negroes were in short supply, and new ones had to be trained. Cuban methods of cultivation and processing were antiquated. Spanish trade regulations sometimes hurt sugar traffic. And from 1793 to 1815 Cuba had to deal with wartime conditions.[21] During this period an increasing conflict developed between the commercial importers, who wished to maintain the prohibitionist system, and the hacendados, who wanted freer trade.[22]

The creole complaint was summarized in 1792 by Francisco Arango y Parreño (1765-1837), creole son of the local oligarchy, with a mind and education considerably above the average, who had studied law in Spain and been the agent there of the town council of Havana. His long and distinguished career, involving many public posts, was to be marked by a concern for political economy, in its practical rather than theoretical aspects, and chiefly from the point of view of the hacendado. He returned from Spain in 1792 and presented to the government his "Discourse on the Agriculture of Havana and Means of Improving It," compounded in large part of those economic ideas we have encountered in Campomanes and Jovellanos, but directed to the problems of the large landowner in Cuba. Arango noted Cuban difficulties as compared with the colonies of France, England, and Portugal: she was deficient in slaves and in technical equipment and knowledge,

---

[19] *Ibid.*, 84, 110: free Negroes rose from 18 per cent of the total population to 21 per cent, but slaves from 26 to 36 per cent. Cf. Ramón de la Sagra, *Historia física, política y natural de la Isla de Cuba* (13 vols., Paris, 1840-62), I, 148 *et seq.*

[20] Cf. Ortiz, *Counterpoint*, emphasizing that "tobacco is liberal," and "sugar is conservative" (p. 56); "sugar spelled slavery; tobacco, liberty" (p. 60); sugar in Cuba has never been controlled by Cubans, but by absentee and almost always unknown foreigners, while tobacco has always been more Cuban (pp. 69-70); in Cuba "sugar represents Spanish absolutism, tobacco the native liberators" (p. 71); "sugar has always preferred slave labor; tobacco, free men" (p. 81).

[21] Cf. Friedländer, *Historia económica*, 113-19, for a good discussion of the main problems of the sugar industry—labor, better cultivation and processing, agricultural credit, transport, use of wood for fuels.

[22] Cf. Julio le Riverend Brusone, "La Economía Cubana durante las Guerras de la Revolución y del Imperio Franceses, 1790-1808," *Revista de Historia de América*, No. 16 (December, 1943), 25-64, at 25-26.

suffered from a stricter system of commercial and revenue control, and was oppressed by higher rates of interest.[23] Arango, like most of the merchants and hacendados, favored economic freedom at least for the operations of the dominant minority.[24]

The intellectual interests of the dominant minority broadened considerably in the second half of the eighteenth century. This development was mostly in Havana, a town of some 48,000 in 1791;[25] but with over 80,000 by 1817.[26] New ideas penetrated in the usual ways, and some additional influence may be attributed to the English occupation of Havana during the Seven Years' War, and to visits by French fleets after creation of the Family Compact between Spain and France. These last, however, were unimportant compared to the carriage of new ideas by Spanish civil officers and ecclesiastics and merchants, by creole visitors to Spain, and to the influence of Spanish and foreign authors and periodicals.

The intellectual condition of educated Cubans after 1790 was similar to that of other creoles. If the intellectual life of Cuba had no historic focus to compare with the universities of Mexico, Lima, or Guatemala, that did not hamper acquisition of new ideas, since the latter were not spread primarily by universities. The poor quality of Cuban educational facilities did not prevent Cubans from studying, in Spain or America, the works being perused by their fellows on the mainland. It notably did not handicap Cubans in the field of political economy. Arango had few equals in other realms of Spanish America.

One sign of a quickening intellectual temper was foundation of the *Papel Periódico de la Havana*, first issued October 20, 1791, and designed to print articles of utility and opinion, a novelty in Cuba where the only other periodical was devoted largely to official notices.[27] The *Papel Periódico* was the

---

[23] *De la factoría a la colonia* (Havana, 1936), 21-113, for text of discourse. Cf. "Elogio" of one-time intendant of Havana, José Valiente, a student of political economy and an experienced administrator, who in the 1790's was deliberately lax in enforcing the commercial laws at Havana (Havana *Memorias 1842*, 321-51).

[24] Cf. Friedländer, *Historia económica*, 136-37, on Arango's quarrels with the *vergueros* and the officials of the Factory,, both of which opposed the rapid development of sugar; and with engineers of the Royal navy, who claimed a monopoly of woods, needed in the processing of sugar.

[25] Santiago had 14,000; the other towns were very small.

[26] "Estado de la población de la plaza de la Habana ...," in Havana *Memorias 1820*, folding table at beginning, showing 84,675 in and around the city, including 24,341 Negro and mulatto slaves, 21,372 free colored persons, and 37,885 whites; in addition there were 10,567 military, bringing the total near 100,000.

[27] Cf. José Toribio Medina, *La imprenta en la Habana, 1707-1810* (Santiago, 1904), 70-77; Antonio Bachiller y Morales, *Apuntes para la historia de las letras y de la instrucción pública en la isla de Cuba* (3 vols., Habana, 1936-37), II, 207.

first Cuban periodical to deal with the problems of the country[28] and, like the other new periodicals of Spanish America in the last three decades of the colonial period, provided some public notice of the new rationalistic and secular spirit.[29]

Foundation of the *Papel Periódico* was favored by Captain General Luís de las Casas y Aragorri (1745-1800), who shortly thereafter also approved foundation of the Economic Society of Havana and of the Consulado. Las Casas was a native of Guipúzcoa, who had served at the Spanish court, then proceeded to a military career in Europe, Africa, and America. His administration at Havana (1790-1796) was marked not only by the favor shown the three institutions mentioned, but by his generally sympathetic attention to the economic needs of the island, even to the extent of non-compliance with Spanish regulations when they seemed detrimental to the interests of Cuba.[30]

Foundation and Early History of the Havana Society (1791-1795)

Twenty-seven Habaneros of the creole landholding group in 1791 requested formation of an Economic Society, "in imitation of others," thanking the Crown for past favors, especially the free introduction of Negroes, but pointing out that the rich land of Cuba would be more prosperous if its inhabitants were not so idle.[31] Governor las Casas approved the idea, and sent the request to Spain, with the proposed statutes of the Society.[32] Habaneros were disgusted that "the miserable pueblo of Mompox" had a Society, while the great island of Cuba still awaited the fertilizing effects of such a body,[33] thus ignoring the feeble efforts of the Society of Santiago de Cuba, formed a few years earlier. Las Casas was seconded in his support of the

---

[28] Cf. Juan Remos y Rubio, *Historia de la literatura cubana* (3 vols. [Havana?], 1945), I, 91-92, for this view.

[29] For an excellent indication of the contents of the *Papel Periódico* to 1805, see Fermín Peraza y Sarausa, "Indice del 'Papel Periódico de la Havana,' " RBC, in many issues in 1943 and succeeding years.

[30] José Manuel Pérez Cabrera, "Don Luís de las Casas ...," in Ortiz, *Recopilación*, I, 132-54; *Elogios fúnebres del excelentísimo ... Luís de las Casas. ... Hechos y publicados por la Real Sociedad Económica ... por el Tribunal del Consulado ...* (Havana, 1802).

[31] *Estatutos de la Sociedad patriótica de la Habana. Aprobados por S. M. Año de 1793* (Havana: Impr. de la capitanía general), incorporated in the cedula of approval, and also giving information on the foundation of the Society.

[32] *Memorias 1793*, 6.

[33] *Papel Periódico de la Havana*, September 4, 1791, reprinted in Ortiz, *Recopilación*, I, 95-97.

proposed Society by the Intendant of Havana, José Pablo Valiente y Bravo, who in later years was to be connected with the Sevilla Society.[34]

The *Papel Periódico*, promoting the Society while awaiting news from Spain, noted that Cuba had many resources, but also many erroneous ideas, a situation that might be corrected by an Economic Society that would examine ideas, detect errors, and spread enlightenment. In such a fraternity men would be forced to reorganize their ideas. It should inquire into idleness and false poverty, false education, and "the presumptuous and belittling etiquette of the powerful who look over their shoulder at the Artisan, the Laborer, and the Merchant, from which follows the backwardness of the Arts, Agriculture, and Commerce."[35] The periodical also gave an account of the origin and foundation of the Lima Academic Society and the *Mercurio Peruano*, emphasizing their unselfish purpose and spirit of community service.[36]

The Crown approved the Society in 1792;[37] Governor Las Casas convoked an inaugural session of sixteen men at the government place in Havana, January 9, 1793;[38] and the first *junta ordinaria* met January 17.[39] The statutes[40] covered points common in the statutes of Spanish Societies: purposes, membership, dues, officers elected by secret ballot for two-year terms, publications, prizes, special committees, weekly "ordinary juntas," annual general juntas, and patriotic schools. The Society was to promote agriculture, commerce, stockraising, popular industry, and the instruction of youth. Membership was available by secret majority vote to residents of Cuba, twenty-five years of age, who were vassals of the king or naturalized foreigners, and if fit for the work of the Society—this last being the usual clause to restrict membership to the "enlightened." Seating at meetings was by order of arrival rather than by antique rules of precedence. The director,

---

[34] Havana *Memorias 1818*, 127-76, for two biographical items on Valiente, who had a strong interest in political economy and assertedly applied Spanish commercial law laxly while at Havana in the 1790's.

[35] September 4, 1791, *loc. cit.*

[36] Issues of October 13 and 16, 1791, in Ortiz, *Recopilación*, I, 98-105. This is a reprint from the *Mercurio Peruano*'s account of the origin of the Lima Society.

[37] *Estatutos;* and cf. *Acta de las Juntas Generales de la Real Sociedad ... de 1833* (Havana, 1834), 20. It was erected by decree of June 6; the statutes approved by cedula of December 15. It was sometimes called Sociedad Patriótica, sometimes Sociedad Económica.

[38] "Primera Junta" of that date, in *Colección de Actas* (Habana, 1880), 3-4; *Memorias 1793* 6.

[39] *Colección de Actas 1880*, 5-6.

[40] Printed at Havana in April, 1793. The projected statutes of 1791 were published in *Memorias 1793*, 84-104. Sent with the statutes were copies of the regulations of the "Escuelas patrióticas" of Madrid and Santiago de Cuba.

as usual in Spain, was to be chosen with care, to be "hardworking, unencumbered, free of prejudices and systems of singularity," and, if possible, to know languages, since he would have to correspond with foreign members. The cedula of approval made small changes, avowedly to bring the statutes into line with those of Madrid, but obviously indicating Spanish nervousness about an American Society, the main reservations being: (a) that commerce was regulated by law (i.e., was not to be tampered with by the Society), and (b) that the Memorias would require government license for publication. Also, the Crown made some special recommendations on education, stipulated that the director was to be appointed without prejudice to the ex-officio presidency belonging by law to the *Jefe Político*, and ordered the Society to meet in the quarters of the town council.

There was some difference of opinion in Havana as to the value of Economic Societies. Early in 1793 Friar Pedro Espinola printed a celebration of the Havana foundation, displaying considerable knowledge of the Spanish Societies, which he said played a part in the "happy revolution" Charles III had worked in the sciences, arts, agriculture, and commerce. Espinola wrote that the Havana Society, conceived by "patriotic zeal" and dedicated to the "common felicity" had initiated useful projects, in a spirit of harmony and reflection.[41] On the other hand, so notable a figure as Arango y Parreño did not share this optimistic view of Economic Societies, in his discourse on agriculture in 1792 questioning their value for Cuba, and pointing out that the Spanish Societies were not accomplishing all they might, being without authority or funds, or the means of making their members really work. Why, he inquired, should one do better in Cuba? He did not oppose formation of a Society, but thought its efforts could only be auxiliary to other more important reforms.[42] Although Arango became director of the Society in 1795—and was one of the Society's editors of the *Papel Periódico*—it was not important in his remarkable labors in behalf of the Cuban economy. His connection with the Consulado, erected in 1794 partly on his recommendation, was more important. He agreed with Society objections to economic monopoly and restriction, while not being a simple convert to laissez-faire economics, but desiring government intervention for the encouragement and development of economic growth. He was like most creole members of the Society in remaining loyal to the connection with Spain. He disagreed with some of the

---

[41] *Establecimiento de la Sociedad Patriótica en la Havana para su pública utilidad* (Habana, 1793), as reprinted in Ortiz, *Recopilación*, I, 90-94. For an even rosier view see the "Oración de gracias, que dixo en la Real Sociedad ... Fray Juan González ...," reprinted from the *Papel Periódico* of January 16, 1794, in Ortiz, *Recopilación*, I, 109-11.

[42] *Loc. cit.*, 66-67.

Society's interests, however, and notably that of agricultural diversification, pushed by Ramírez in the 1816-1820 period, since Arango favored concentration on sugar production. The work of the Society was too diffuse, too impractical, too much touched with philanthropism and unrationalized economic schemes to appeal to a man dedicated to the immediate improvement of the economic position of the hacendados.[43]

Nor did the subsequent history of the Society perfectly justify the optimism of Friar Espinola in 1793. The Society's activity oscillated markedly between 1793 and 1820. An initial period of enthusiasm and activity lasted from 1793 through 1795, was followed by a long period into 1816 when the Society did less, then from 1816 into 1820 it was notably active again, only to fall into another period of quiescence in 1820. These periods are illustrated by the published Memorias, a good indication of vacillating vigor and effectiveness, since the Society's objectives, organization, methods of work, and limited resources made it likely that it could accomplish little without publication. Memorias were issued for the years 1793-1795, then suspended until those for 1817 (including 1816 materials) were brought out, followed by those for 1818, 1819, and January-March, 1820, after which publication was again suspended, until those for 1823 were issued.[44] The history of the Society's educational labors shows the same pattern as the Memorias.

The ebb and flow of activity was partly due to fluctuating interest on the part of the members, partly to the encouragement given the Society during their administrations by Captain General Las Casas (1790-1796) and Intendant Alejandro Ramírez (1816-1821). And the attitudes of ecclesiastical

---

[43] Cf. the introduction by Paul Maestri to *De la factoria a la colonia;* R. Cabrera, *Cuba y sus jueces* (7th ed., Filadelfia, 1891), 275-76; W. W. Pierson, Jr., "Francisco Arango y Parreño," HAHR, XVI, No. 1 (November, 1938), 451-78; D. C. Corbitt, "La introducción en Cuba de la caña de Otahiti, el árbol del pan, el mango y otras plantas," RBC, XLVII, No. 3 (May-June, 1941), 360-66, for the trip of Arango and the Count of Casa-Montalvo for the Consulado to gather agricultural information in England, Portugal, Barbados, and Jamaica; Friedländer, *Historia económica*, 141; Francisco J. Ponte Domínguez, "Don Francisco de Arango y Parreño, Artífice del Progreso Colonial de Cuba," *Revista Cubana*, XXIV (January-June, 1949), 284-328.

[44] Cf. *Memorias 1895*, 129-31, that those of 1793 were actually not published till 1795; those of 1794 not distributed to the members till 1796; those of 1795 in February, 1799, were given to a member to edit, but he did not complete the task till 1804; he was to edit the 1796 materials, but did not. This history of delayed publication suggests that the contrast between 1793-95 and later years might be somewhat exaggerated because of the lack of evidence that may simply be inedited. But all students of the Havana Society agree that its activity slackened in the last years of the 18th and the first of the 19th centuries. Montoro, "Historia de la Sociedad," *loc. cit.*, divides the early history of the Society into 1793-1814 and 1814-23, which is certainly justifiable, although he does not give much evidence for making 1814 the dividing date. *Infra*, 193, for *Tareas* of 1815.

officials varied. Vicar General Luís de Peñalver helped found the Society and became its first director.[45] But Bishop Félix José de Trespalacios did not join the Society,[46] and opposed its operations in the 1790's, believing that Cuba did not need the additional schools proposed by the Society.[47] Trespalacios also clashed with Governor Las Casas and Dr. Tomás Romay, a prominent member of the Society, with regard to the censorship of a discourse by Romay.[48] On the other hand, Trespalacios' successor, Juan José Díaz Espada, who became bishop of Havana in 1802, favored both an expansion of education and the labors of the Society, serving as Society director for several years.[49] His liberalism involved Bishop Espada with the Inquisition, which began proceedings against him in 1815 for heresy and freemasonry.[50] The different views of the Spanish ecclesiastics, Trespalacios and Espada, illustrate the division of opinion of the day.[51]

The members, drawn from the upper stratum of society, especially from the creole hacendado class, numbered 126 in 1793, and 163 by December, 1795;[52] there were few more in the 1816-1820 period. Most members were residents of Havana—113 of the 126 members in 1793. Branches of the Society were set up at various places beginning in 1803, but the Havana contingent was always the heart of the Society.

For working purposes, the members were divided into four classes: sciences and arts, agriculture, popular industry and public ornament (*hermosura del pueblo*), and commerce. Some classes performed more regularly and on a larger scale than others; in the early years, that of agriculture was

---

[45] *Memorias 1793*, 72 *et seq.; ibid.*, 82-83, ex-director Peñalver writes the Society from Louisiana, where he had moved as bishop. Arango succeeded him as Society director.

[46] He was not listed in the catalogues of members for 1793-95.

[47] Cabrera, *Cuba y sus jueces*, 119-21.

[48] "Junta ordinaria," October 2, 1794 (in *Memorias de la Real Sociedad Económica y Anales de Fomento* [Habana, 1864], 56-57); "Junta ordinaria," October 23 (*loc. cit.*, 61-62); "Junta ordinaria," October 30 (*loc. cit.*, 119-20); "Discurso Pronunciado por el Dr. D. Tomás Romay, en Junta ordinaria de la Sociedad ... 31 de julio de 1794" (*Memorias 1838*, 281-82), and "nota" of the editors (p. 283) explaining that the Society in 1794 tried to get the discourse printed in the *Papel Periódico*, but encountered censorship difficulties with Bishop Trespalacios, and asserting that the bishop did not want it printed because it contained praise of Las Casas. Cf. Ortiz, *Hija cubana*, 66; Pezuela, *Ensayo histórico*, 346, 351-52.

[49] Francisco G. del Valle, "El Obispo Espada," in Ortiz, *Recopilación*, I, 161-69; Cabrera, *Cuba y sus jueces*, 309-10, biography of Espada.

[50] Ortiz, *Hija cubana*, 64-65.

[51] *Ibid.*, 17-18, commenting on the persecution of Espada, and later of Varela and Saco, observing that it sadly damaged the influence of the Economic Society.

[52] Catalogues of members in *Memorias 1793*, unnumbered pages at end, and *Memorias 1795*, 153-58.

most active.[53] Some important activities were not carried on by the classes, but by special committees (*diputaciones*), such as those for the Casa de Beneficencia and for the *Papel Periódico*. Each December in 1793-1795 the Society held three-day *juntas generales* to hear reports of the year's work, elect officers, offer and confer prizes. The classes understood their functions to be those of examination, education, recommendation, persuasion, and publicity[54]— that is, followed the pattern of the peninsular Societies; in any case, their meager finances would permit little else.

The chief methods were the meetings and studies of members, a program of publication, educational work, the creation of a public library, and offers of prizes. The three volumes and over 500 pages of the Memorias for 1793-1795 recorded the labors of the Society in all these fields, and propagated the Society's ideas. The *Papel Periódico* was put under the direction of the Society in 1793 on the suggestion of Governor Las Casas. The editors promised to print all papers received, but the primary interest of the Society showed in an expression of special interest in articles on agriculture, commerce, and the arts.[55] The Society also took over direction of the annual *Guía de Forasteros*.[56] The first prizes offered were for essays on the state of Cuban agriculture and means of improving it, on the usefulness of better roads, and on brick and tile for Havana. But only four essays were submitted in 1793, so the prizes were withheld.[57]

The common yearning for material advancement was the lodestone drawing Habaneros to the Society, as revealed in the first words it printed: that the bare necessities of nature were not enough for man, who must reach out for

---

[53] *Memorias 1794* (reprinted in condensed form in *Memorias 1843-44*), 103-6. That of popular industry did not hold a junta till August, 1793 (*Memorias 1793*, 39, and did little in 1794, many of its 21 members being at their haciendas much of the time, or otherwise busy, so that the juntas admittedly were not satisfactory (*Memorias 1794, loc. cit.*, 110-11). The commerce class held but three juntas before December, 1793 (*Memorias 1793*, 41). That of sciences and arts began meeting in August, 1793, but accomplished little that year (*Memorias 1794, loc. cit.*, 102-3).

[54] Cf. *Memorias 1793*, 26-43; "Junta ordinaria," July 18, 1793 (*Colección de Actas 1880*), 33-35. Not only were statements to this effect recorded, but the actions of the Society demonstrated the thesis.

[55] *Memorias 1793*, 63-71, "Papel Periódico. Su objeto y utilidad." The *Revista Bimestre Cubana*, long under Society direction, and still well known, was not published till 1831.

[56] *Memorias 1794, loc. cit.*, 436, two members appointed to handle it; *Memorias 1863*, 4ª ser., t. VIII, 310, record of junta of January 9, 1794, the deputation on the *Guía* submitted a subscription plan; Peraza y Sarausa, "Indice," RBC, LVI, 70, the *Papel* issue of June 1, 1794, in which the "socios diputados" for the *Guía* asked that notices be sent them.

[57] *Memorias 1793*, 73-80; *Memorias 1794, loc. cit.*, 437, for six prizes offered in December, 1794.

more by means of study, and should be interested in agriculture, commerce, and the arts, which are the "three agents of the felicity of peoples"; and declaring that it was a common desire of governments to wish to promote economic improvement, that England had established economic societies, and that Cuba because of its resources was in a good position to follow the example of Spain.[58] And soon the thirst for prosperity found voice in the cry that agriculture was better developed in neighboring foreign isles, and that "we shall never be rich unless the land is used better, and unless finally good doctrines, sustained by systematic education" are assisted by the purposes of the government and the efforts of the Economic Societies.[59] These two statements incorporated much of the motivation of the Society: the mingled optimism and dissatisfaction, the belief that study—principles, doctrine, techniques—was a necessary basis for enrichment, the conviction that proper government assistance and policy were indispensable to the multiplication of fortunes, and the equating of "felicity" with material well-being.[60] Although the statement was often made that the main object of the Society was to promote "public enlightenment,"[61] its interest in education was primarily that learning might improve the island's economic condition.[62]

Although the Society declared that it wanted to work on all elements of the economic system,[63] agriculture was by far its strongest interest.[64] Commerce and industry were little considered, save in connection with agriculture. The class of commerce was the least active of the four classes,[65] presumably because commerce was being handled daily by the Consulado of Havana. The Society showed much less interest in cottage industry in 1793-1795 than did the peninsular or the Guatemala Societies. This was partly because Cuba had no great and ancient handicrafts to revive; partly a reflection of the overriding interest of the hacendado-dominated Society in sugar culture; and partly due to the fact that cottage industry was scarcely to be thought of in connection with the large slave population. So flax and hemp and

---

[58] *Memorias 1793*, 1-6, "Orígen de las Sociedades Económicas." This lead article in the first volume of Memorias gives not only a good idea of the interest in economics, but of the Society's liberal intellectual attitude.

[59] *Memorias 1794, loc. cit.*, 421.

[60] *Infra*, 273-74, for discussion of the Havana Society's interest in material prosperity.

[61] Cf. *Memorias 1795*, 11.

[62] Cf. *Memorias 1793*, 179-80, for a good picture of this in a report by the Society secretary.

[63] *Memorias 1794, loc. cit.*, 419.

[64] *Memorias 1793*, 30 *et seq.*: agriculture is the origin of "our wealth," a sentiment often repeated in the Memorias.

[65] *Memorias 1795*, 49 *et seq.*

cotton, though considered, received less attention than in Spain or Guatemala. The problem of craft guild ordinances was considered, but not vigorously. In this period the Society displayed little interest in agricultural diversification;[66] it did display much interest in better roads, especially in the Havana area, and although this was of interest to sugar growers, the Society wished also to bring other produce into Havana so as to improve the incomes of small cultivators and expand export trade in other lines than sugar.

The prime interest of the Society in sugar was expressed in one of its first actions, considering a machine for pressing sugar that assertedly would eliminate the need for oxen and reduce the number of slaves required.[67] Other machines were considered with some care by the Society, and it contracted with an inventor for the construction of a mill, sixteen men subscribing a total of 2,700 pesos to finance the work. There was even some small thought given in 1795 to the use of steam power in the sugar industry. The members knew that methods were superior in the neighboring English and French isles, and proposed to translate French works on sugar growing and processing. A Society member was selected to prepare a description of the methods used in Cuba.[68] The Society proposed to establish the study of chemistry and botany, primarily for their usefulness in connection with sugar. The demand for an increase of slaves served the hacendados, who knew that the shortage of such labor was another disadvantage of Cuban sugar in comparison with Haiti and Jamaica.[69]

Prominent interests of the Society in 1793-1795 were in the education and care of orphaned girls, and the succor and reform of indigent women. The Society opened its library to the public, making it the first public library in Cuba, and one of the earliest in the entire Spanish world. A member surveyed Havana's primary schools, rendering a pessimistic report in 1793,[70] describing most of them as little more than poorly run tutorial groups. The Memorias of 1795 declared with equal pessimism that the local schools did not offer enough variety, and "from this it resulted that many talents descended to the sepulcher without ever being useful."[71] The Society felt

---

[66] Cf. *Memorias 1794, loc. cit.*, 24-27, a committee report on means of improving eastern Cuba: a tobacco factory for Santiago; better roads; ending copper imports from Lima by working the deposits of east Cuba; encouraging immigration of Canary islanders and Catholic foreigners experienced in stockraising, mining, and agriculture.

[67] *Memorias 1793*, 8-10.

[68] *Memorias 1793*, 119-47, "Exposición ... del método observado en la isla de Cuba, en el cultivo de la Caña dulce y la elaboración de su Xugo," a strictly practical essay, notably detailed with regard to methods, machinery, etc.

[69] *Infra*, 310-11, 324-25, on the Society's interest in sugar.

[70] *Memorias 1793*, 161-75.

[71] *Memorias, 1795* 3-10, "Introducción."

that Cuba needed a new educational system, with emphasis on science. It was interested in a Provincial Dictionary to define technical terms used in Cuba. A committee prepared a general plan for the government of Havana's primary schools. Other members were assigned to form a "genealogical tree" of all knowledge important to science, and to describe the subject of political economy.

The efforts of the Society in 1793-1795 to improve or expand instruction had small practical result. It proposed a free school of chemistry, but failed to set it up. It showed interest in botany, produced a plan for a botanical garden, and sent a young man to study with Martín Sesé of the Royal Botanical Garden of Mexico; but since funds were lacking, the Havana garden was not created. From the beginning, the Society recommended changes in medical education, but accomplished nothing in this period. Frequent suggestions for classes in political economy bore no fruit for many years; the same was true of talk about instruction in drawing. Various other Society suggestions came to naught.

Although the strictly educational schemes of the Society bore little fruit in 1793-1795, it did provide some instruction for philanthropic reasons. A girls' school, the *Casa de Educandas*, was opened in 1793 and soon taken over by the Society. The girls—twenty-seven of them in 1793—were required to be "white, poor, orphans," seven to ten years old. They were inoculated against smallpox, and taught religion, reading, sewing, spinning, and other household arts. The beneficent—rather than simply educational—motive involved in the Casa de Educandas was indicated by its position as part of the *Casa de Beneficencia*, or poorhouse for women, proposed by some local gentry in March, 1792, but taken over by a committee of the Society in January, 1793. In 1794, when the Casa de Benificencia's new building was completed, the thirty-one *educandas* were moved there, but the orphan girls were kept separate from the indigent women who were cared for and instructed in simple tasks in the Casa de Beneficencia proper. By 1795 there were fifty-one girls in the Casa de Educandas and seventy-three poor women in the Beneficencia.[72]

The Society Quiescent (1796-1815)

The Society was relatively inactive in 1796-1815. No Memorias were published. The Society later lamented that its "unhappy decadence" in 1804 led the Baron Humboldt to assert that although the Society protected arts and sciences, these progressed very slowly in a country where the inhabitants

---

[72] *Infra*, 292-94, on this institution.

were occupied exclusively with the production of *frutos coloniales*.[73] The
hacendados who had founded the Society were busy with their estates,[74]
or with the political problems arising from the French invasion of Spain
in 1808, or absorbed in the work of the Consulado, which helped improve
the sugar industry in these years.[75] The Consulado was the focus of the most
important activities of such Society members as Andrés Jáuregui, Nicolás
Calvo (died 1801), and Arango, who in the last years of the century was
director of the Society and *Síndico* of the Consulado (1796-1810). The
Consulado continued its efforts throughout its history, whereas the Society's
work was seriously interrupted in 1796-1816.[76]

Some Society work was done in 1796-1807,[77] including agitation for the
building of a cemetery outside the city, for sanitary reasons,[78] with Bishop
Espada, elected Society director in 1802, especially active in this campaign.[79]
In 1804 the *juntas generales* of the Society received twenty-five memorias
in a contest for a prize offered by the Consulado and the town council of
Havana on the best means of developing the cultivation and processing of
good tobacco, but none of them was thought good enough for the prize.[80]
The Society continued to edit the *Papel Periódico* (called *El Aviso* after
1805), and promoted its economic interests through this medium, as in 1798
printing an announcement by the Consulado of the shipment to Cuba of
Tahitian sugar cane.[81] The library of the Society remained open. An anatomy
class met briefly in 1797. The Casa de Beneficencia continued, but in 1796
the Society began to share direction with representatives of the town council,
the ecclesiastical chapter, and the Consulado. The Casa turned more and
more to poor relief as opposed to the education of orphans. The physical
plant was not expanded. A branch of the Society was set up at Sancti-Espíritu

---

[73] *Memorias 1817*, 429-30, in the secretary's report for 1817.

[74] Friedländer, *Historia económica*, 255, citing José Ricardo O'Farrill as an example.

[75] *Ibid.*, 115, 117-19, on roads, woods, the proposal for a canal from Güines to the
sea; 131 *et seq.*, on the Consulado in these years.

[76] *Ibid.*, 133, emphasizes this point.

[77] Cf. *Memorias 1839*, 105-23, on beehives in 1796; *ibid.*, 344-57, eulogy of Las
Casas in 1801; indications of Society activity in 1798, 1804, and 1805, in the *Papel
Periódico*, as shown in Peraza y Sarausa, "Indice," RBC, LI, 455; LII, 139; LXIV,
180-84; LVII, 178, 182; LXVII, 188.

[78] "Memoria sobre las Sepulturas fuera de los pueblos. La escribió ... Romay ...
1805 ...," in *Memorias 1845*, 235-46.

[79] "Descripción del cementerio general de la Habana. Por ... Romay. Año de 1806,"
in *Memorias 1845*, 307-14. Espada was director in 1802-8, and supported the Society
for many years thereafter (F. G. del Valle, "Espada," *loc. cit.*). Captain General
Ruíz de Apodaca became Society director not long after Espada.

[80] *Memorias 1817*, 361-80.

[81] *Memorias 1845*, 362-63. *Infra*, 257, for *Periódico* and Society in these years.

in 1803. A vaccination junta was created, and was working even before the arrival in May, 1804, of the Royal Expedition on vaccination. Dr. Tomás Romay was active in this work, and in 1804 read to the Society a paper on the subject.

In the brief liberal period of constitutional crisis, from the French invasion of Spain in 1808 to the restoration of Ferdinand VII in 1814, creoles had exceptional opportunities to back their views. A notable instance was an article in 1811 in the *Diario de la Havana* favoring a marketing combination of sugar and coffee producers to obtain better prices. The Spanish party denounced it as a plan of the creole producer against the Spanish merchant— which it was.[82] But while Cuban hacendados might agree with similar groups in other parts of America on this question of creole producer versus Spanish merchant, the Cubans—and Arango, their deputy in the Spanish Cortes— would not agree with creoles from other parts of America who advocated the abolition of slavery.[83]

The Economic Society helped elect Cuba's deputy to the Cortes of 1810, by choosing eight of the sixteen persons who met with the *regidores perpétuos* of the town council of Havana to select him.[84] The Society in 1811 had a communication from the reactivated Guatemala Society. Branches of the Society were erected in 1813 in Puerto-Príncipe and Trinidad.

In 1815 the Society printed an account of the history of the beeswax industry in Cuba.[85] There was enough other Society activity in 1815 to justify a short published review, the first since that for 1795.[86] It contained only a sketch of Society work by the secretary, and reports on finances, the *junta de vacuna*, and the Casa de Beneficencia. The secretary noted that if they were not accomplishing much, their intentions remained good; that Cuba, though "large and not poor," had to import products it could grow itself; and indicated the continuing interest in economic development. Society finances were much as they had been earlier; the Casa remained the same size, with sixty-two orphan girls, and sixty-one indigent women; and the

---

[82] Guerra y Sánchez, *Manual de historia de Cuba*, 226.

[83] Cf. José Antonio Saco, *Historia de la esclavitud de la raza africana en el nuevo mundo* ... (4 vols., Havana, 1938), III, 90 *et seq.*, for discussions of abolition in the Cortes early in 1811, and immediate instructions to Arango from the town council, Consulado, and Economic Society of Havana to oppose the measure.

[84] Montoro, "Sociedad Económica," *loc. cit.*, 25 *et seq.*, with the view that the Society was a stabilizing influence in Cuba during those years of turmoil.

[85] *Sucinta noticia del ramo de la cera en la isla de Cuba, a fines de mayo del año de 1815* (Habana: Arazoza y Soler [1815]); 10 pp.; written by Pablo Boloix, and published under Society auspices. It was later reprinted in Havana *Memorias 1880*, 34-41.

[86] *Tareas de la Real sociedad patriótica de la Habana en el año de 1815* (Habana: Oficina de Arazoza y Soler, 1816; 26 pp.).

junta de vacuna, after twelve years of labor, still was encountering opposition.

A controversy in these years that illustrated the division of opinion regarding the Societies arose from the fact that the Society, with financial aid from Bishop Espada, in 1807 sent to Europe to study the Pestalozzi educational system a creole cleric and Society member, Juan O'Gabán, a teacher of philosophy in the Seminary of San Carlos.[87] O'Gabán visited several countries, and returned to Cuba in December, 1808. His report, approved by the Society, and printed in the *Aviso* the same month, praised the Pestalozzi system but judged it too expensive for Cuba.

The report was reprinted the next February in the *Diario de Mexico,* and denounced a month later by the Inquisition of New Spain. O'Gabán defended himself, while denying the jurisdiction of the Inquisition of Mexico. He claimed he could not be censured under the Index rule prohibiting honorific epithets for authors outside the Church, since he had not described such authors as "good, virtuous, pious." He said he left the religious and moral order to one side and dealt only with such authors' notions of human understanding and the generation and progress of ideas; that the Index did permit giving heterodox authors epithets belonging to certain sciences "because these are gifts . . . that God is in the habit of communicating even to those who are outside the Church"; that the Inquisition had violated the law in publishing a condemnation without giving him a hearing; that Feijóo cited heterodox authors; and that it was immaterial that Francis Bacon was a heretic, so long as he was not cited in connection with religion. O'Gabán adduced instances of the citation of heretical authors by famous Catholic writers, and went so far as to assert that Locke and Condillac opened the door to the Pestalozzi system, hence their work would have to be considered in connection with the latter.[88] O'Gabán's defense is an excellent illustration of the danger to the old regime inherent in Feijóo's work and the determination of liberals in the Societies to make use of such authors. The Society's interest in Pestalozzi no doubt showed a willingness to reduce the competence of the Church, which the latter was bound to protest, but it did not represent an organized or closely pursued effort to push secular education or heterodox ideas.

---

[87] *Memorias 1894,* 124 n.1.
[88] *Memorias 1894,* 120-22, 129-33, 150-53, "La Sociedad Patriótica y el Santo Oficio de Méjico. Representación justificativa del Ldo. Pbro. D. Juan Bernardo O-Gaban dirigida a la Real Sociedad Patriótica de la Habana. ..." And continued in *Memorias 1895,* 27-34, a reprint of the article that caused the trouble, and 39-46, the various documents pertaining to the affair.

The Ramírez Period (1816-1821)

The Society was revivified in 1816,[89] primarily because of strong support from its new director, recently arrived Intendant Alejandro Ramírez (1777-1821), an admirer of the works of Jovellanos, and one of those moderate liberals who wished to save the empire by improving its economy. Born in Spain of poor parents, he showed talent as a young student, and was befriended by former Bishop Lorenzana of Mexico, and by Jacobo de Villaurrutia, an official of the university town of Alcalá de Henares. Ramírez went to Guatemala in 1795 in the wake of Villaurrutia, who in 1793 took up residence there as a judge of the audiencia. Ramírez, remaining in Guatemala until 1813, did much of the editing of the *Gazeta de Guatemala*—a notably outspoken periodical—during its early years, and was secretary to the Consulado and the captain general. He was a member of the Guatemala Economic Society, founded by Villaurrutia. In 1799-1801 Ramírez traveled for the Consulado of Guatemala to the Windward Isles, Mexico, Cuba, and the United States, gleaning agricultural and industrial ideas, and carrying exotic plants back to Guatemala. During the period of constitutional crisis, the Council of Regency, on the advice of Ramón Power, appointed Ramírez as first intendant of Puerto Rico. He took up his functions there in February, 1813, and one of his first acts was to create an Economic Society.[90] He was transferred to Havana in 1816.

Ramírez desired agricultural diversification for Cuba, with especial attention to the small cultivator. This was indicated in the material in Society Memorias. The experience of the Havana Society at this time, however, was not typical of the colonial Societies in the earlier years: most of the American Societies were dead; and much of America was in fact independent of Spain. Thus the activity of the Havana Society in 1816-1820 has a Cuban rather

---

[89] *Infra*, 260, Ramírez described the Society as "new regenerated." Lack of interest in the Society, and its lack of resources, were shown in 1816 by the fact that the government in Spain was considering a request of the Society for aid in collecting the eight peso dues of members (Archivo general de Indias, *Catálogo de los fondos cubanos* [*Colección de documentos inéditos para la historia de Hispano América*], t. I, vol. 2, Nos. 2151-17).

[90] Manuel Isidro Méndez, *El Intendente Ramírez* (Havana, 1944); Eduardo Neumann Gandía, *Benefactores y hombres notables de Puerto-Rico* (2 vols., Ponce, 1896-99), I, 357-70; Paul G. Miller, *Historia de Puerto-Rico* (Chicago, 1937), 241-44; Tomás Blanco, *Prontuario histórico de Puerto Rico* (2d ed., San Juan, 1943), 61; *Relación histórica, concerniente a la junta pública general de la Sociedad económica de Guatemala, celebrada en 25 de abril de 1852* (Guatemala [1852]), 26 *et seq.*; Batres Jáuregui, *América Central*, 527-28; Vela, *Literatura guatemalteca*, 119; Rodriguez Beteta, *Evolución de ideas*, 70, 79.

than a general American significance, although many of the ideas of the members were of course carried over from earlier years.

Society membership was somewhat larger in this period, but not in relation to the larger population of Havana. There was the same difficulty in getting members to participate in the work of the Society.[91] Most members still were residents of Havana, and representatives of the hacendado class. By this time, however, the influence of radical political thought on the younger members was somewhat greater than twenty years earlier, though this influence was far from dominant in the Society. Untypical was the young creole cleric Félix Varela (b. 1788), founder of the first cabinet of experimental physics at the Seminary of Havana, who joined the Society in 1817. Elected to the Cortes in Spain in 1821, he voted to dismiss the king, and when the latter returned to power Varela was condemned to death, but fled to the United States, where he had a long career as a journalist and priest.[92] Untypical also was José Antonio Saco (b. 1797), who became active in the Society in 1820, and was to have a long and distinguished intellectual career, within and without the Society.

There was no important change in the finances or methods of the Society, although in 1816 it began maintaining a deputation in Spain to keep in touch with the Madrid Society,[93] but nothing seems to have come of this before 1820.[94] The working classes of members evidently had been abandoned, since in 1816, on Ramírez' suggestion, the members were divided into classes of education, agriculture, popular industry, and commerce.[95] The Society still directed the periodical (now the *Diario*), as it had for over twenty years,[96] and maintained its library. The deputation of the Society at Sancti-Espíritu, founded in 1803, was by 1817 inactive;[97] the deputations at Puerto-Príncipe and Trinidad were alive.[98]

---

[91] *Memorias 1817*, 418-19, showing that at least Ramírez was working hard.

[92] Cabrera, *Cuba y sus jueces*, 311-13; Fernando Ortiz, "Felix Varela, Amigo del País," RBC, VI, No. 6 (November-December, 1911), 478-84; Rafael Montoro, "El P. Félix Varela. Oración Pronunciada," RBC, VI, No. 6, 485-97; Enrique Gay-Calbó, "Varela revolucionario," RBC, LI (1943), 73-110.

[93] *Acta Juntas Generales 1833*, 21-22, with list of members of the deputation in Spain in 1833. *Supra* 63, for the royal order on such deputations.

[94] The Society in 1817 printed praise of the aims and achievements of the Economic Societies, quoting Campomanes, and especially praising the Basque, Madrid, and Valencia Societies (*Memorias 1817*, 131-51, "Discurso sobre la utilidad y ventajas ... de las Sociedades Económicas").

[95] *Memorias 1817*, 416-17. Thus the class of sciences and arts of the earlier period was dropped. Ramírez became president of the class of education.

[96] *Memorias 1817*, 143.

[97] *Memorias 1817*, 273 et seq.; ibid., 427, that it "ha decaido enteramente."

[98] *Ibid.*

Memorias were published once more for 1817-1819 and January-March, 1820. They were, however, considerably different from those of 1793-1795. They were much longer (1,352 pages for 1817-1820 as compared with 551 for 1793-1795), carried a great many government documents dealing almost entirely with economic matters, and presented a notable amount of statistical information, often in the form of tables. These features made the 1817-1819 Memorias much more similar to the Madrid Memorias than to the Havana of 1793-1795 or to any of the Guatemala Society's printed *Juntas Públicas*. The 1817-1819 Memorias were different also from those of 1793-1795 in their subject matter, in that there was less attention to sugar and more to white colonization and to the crops that these small farmers might grow. The Memorias of 1817 went not only to the 217 Havana members of the Society but 45 copies were sent to members of the Sancti-Espíritu branch, 54 to the Puerto-Príncipe branch, and 40 to the Trinidad; another 54 copies went to subscribers who had no connection with the Society.[99]

It cannot be said that the fundamental ideas and methods of the Society were different, but the emphasis had changed. There was the same desire to improve the economy by means of education and the adoption of new techniques, the same belief that the rich land of Cuba entitled its inhabitants to prosperity, the same interest in roads, chemistry, and vaccination. There was more interest in political economy as a formal subject, more in steam power, a trifle more in crafts, a great deal more in white colonization and crops suitable for small farms—flax, hemp, tobacco, coffee, indigo, beeswax, and wood. Further, the Society was not content with the changes in Spanish economic law which had been enacted since 1796, and the Memorias both implied and stated that errors in legislation should be corrected. By 1819 the Society was bluntly condemning the government's restrictions on commercial enterprise, while pointing out that liberty of commerce in itself was insufficient to ensure prosperity, since capital was needed and ought to enter freely. In this period the Society considered a scheme for a bank supported by hacendados and stockraisers.

The Society continued its educational interests, and added to them. A class of education was created in 1816, and became more active than the other working divisions.[100] It continued to inspect schools; supported primary schools—seven by 1820, including one Lancasterian, with a total of 415 pupils;

---

[99] *Memorias 1817*, 133-38.
[100] In 1817 members scarcely attended sessions of the divisions of agriculture, industry, and commerce, and only that of education worked constantly (*Memorias 1817*, 416-17). Cf. *Memorias 1823*, 113-17, that only the class of education had done well.

took more interest in primary education in the interior; planned, but failed to establish, a school for deaf-mutes, and another of navigation. The specialized education the Society had so long advocated finally got under way, with the establishment of a school of chemistry, a botanical garden, a chair of practical anatomy, and classes in political economy. The Society continued to operate the Casa de Beneficencia. The Society declined in the early 1820's, primarily because after the death of Ramírez in May, 1821, it received less official support. Ramírez' fatal illness is sometimes ascribed to the bitter attacks on him in 1820-1821 by the Spanish party in Cuba, which objected to his identification (for example, in the Economic Society) with the interests of the creole hacendados. After the January-March, 1820, Memorias, none were published till those of April, 1823-April, 1825, after which none were published till those of 1835.[101]

[101] See Appendix for Society in later years. Cf. *Memorias 1823*, 113, for the editorial observation that although the Society had 272 members, scarcely 20 were cooperating in its work.

CHAPTER TEN

The Guatemala Society:
Foundation and Early History (1794-1800)

Guatemala in the Eighteenth Century

The captaincy general of Guatemala included territory extending 1,200 miles from Chiapas to Costa Rica,[1] with an unevenly distributed population of perhaps one million, about half living in the provinces of Guatemala and San Salvador. Whites (creole and peninsular) and *ladinos*—the local term for mestizo—were possibly one-tenth of the population; most of the rest was Indian. A few widely scattered towns held the persons of European or largely European race and culture. The city of Guatemala, created on a new site after the partial destruction of Antigua in the earthquake of 1773, had by 1794 some 20,000 inhabitants, and perhaps 25,000 six years later. No other town approached this size. The towns were situated in the interior, there being no seaport settlement of consequence because of the heat and endemic fevers of the coast, which also was subject to raids by pirates and foreign warships, and offered neither the best land nor the best Indians for labor.[2]

---

[1] With the *de facto* exception of an area around Belize claimed by Britain. Spain's hold on some other areas was not strong, and her sovereignty in the Caribbean coastal area of Mosquitia had only been conceded by Britain in 1786.

[2] There were few Negroes, many mulattoes, some zambos (Indian and Negro). The evidence is poor and confusing. *Ladino* sometimes meant any mixture with some white blood, and *pardo* stood for all persons with nonwhite blood in mixture; but the terms were used loosely. Antonio Larrazabal, *Apuntamientos sobre la agricultura y comercio del reyno de Guatemala* (Nueva Guatemala, 1811), 10, 105, 109, 110, noted

Official business moved slowly because poor communications isolated the city of Guatemala—seat of captain general, audiencia, and archbishop—from the outlying provinces.[3] The intendancy system, installed late in the century, had little effect both because it was applied so late and because the ills of the area would not yield to mere administrative reform.[4] The town councils were with few exceptions not vigorous; by 1800 some were inoperative due to the difficulty of finding qualified men to serve. The ayuntamiento of the capital was by all odds the most important; in it some of the most influential creoles spoke for the interest of the local elite. While the councillors were a politically exclusive and socially conservative group, they were aware that their interest did not always coincide with that of the Crown.[5]

The military force was scanty. The militia, nominally numerous, were of problematical value. The fortified posts (*castillos*) of San Juan, San Felipe,

the confusion of population figures, but ventured an estimate of one million (646,666 *Indios;* 313,334 *pardos y algunos negros;* 40,000 *blancos*). The census of 1803-04 gave a total of 1,037,421, of which 578,236 *Indios*, 318,370 *ladinos*, 140,815 *Españoles* (BAGG, VII, No. 3 [April, 1942], 166). Cf. Alejandro Ramírez on 1804 census in Biblioteca Nacional de Guatemala copy of José del Valle, *Instrucción sobre la plaga de langosta* ... (Nueva Guatemala, 1804); Domingo Juarros, *Compendio de la historia de la ciudad de Guatemala* (3d ed., 2 vols., Guatemala, 1936), I, 61, 66-67; *Gazeta de Guatemala*, April 26, 1802, for the census of 1779; Francisco de Paula García Peláez, *Memorias para la historia del antiguo reyno de Guatemala* (3 vols., Guatemala, 1851-52), III, 179 *et seq.*; J. Antonio Villacorta, *Historia de la capitanía general de Guatemala* (Guatemala, 1942), 439; Salvatierra, *Contribución*, II, 121.

[3] Salvatierra, *Contribución*, II, 171-72: the first monthly mail between Guatemala and Granada was established in 1753, and took eight days from Guatemala to León via San Salvador; from Granada mail went to Cartago; the post from Spain to Guatemala usually came via Veracruz and Oaxaca, and its infrequent arrivals caused a sensation in the isolated city; a monthly postal service between Guatemala and Peru was established in 1809. Cf. *Gazeta de Guatemala*, February 18 and November 13, 1809, on mails; Guatemala, Comisión de límites, "El esfuerzo de Guatemala para canalizar el río Motagua y el dominio indisputado que sobre el mismo ha ejercido desde el siglo XVIII" (Guatemala, 1928, No. 6 of *Publicaciones de la Comisión de límites*), describing the miserable state of communications from the capital to the ports of Izabal and Trujillo; Irisarri, *El Cristiano errante*, ch. vii, *et passim*, for travel in late colonial era.

[4] Juarros, *Compendio*, II, 38-40; Villacorta, *Capitanía general*, 78 *et seq.*; "Guatemala, hace ciento catorce años. Informe ... del Ministro Tesorero de las Reales Cajas de Guatemala, acerca del estado deficiente del Erario antes y después de 15 de septiembre de 1821.—Madrid, 11 de marzo de 1824," ASGH, XII, No. 1 (September, 1935), 3-28, on the deficiencies of the revenues in the late colonial period.

[5] Juarros, *Compendio*, II, 40-43; Ramón A. Salazar, *Los hombres de la independencia* (Guatemala, 1899), 190-93. And cf. in the *Archivo General* of Guatemala the following *expedientes* dealing with the role of the ayuntamientos in sending deputies to the Junta Central and to the Cortes, in 1810-13, and incidentally revealing the poverty of the municipalities: A1-1, leg. 37, exped. 4360; A1-1, leg. 38, exped. 4364; A1-1, leg. 26 exped. 761; A1.2-5, leg. 2835, exped. 25293.

and Omoa had in 1778 a total population of only 1,046.[6] The ancient port of Trujillo, on the Gulf of Honduras, was repopulated by royal order, beginning in 1789, and had two war vessels assigned to it. But even at the start of the nineteenth century the town had but eighty or ninety Spanish householders and 300 Negroes, while the military commandant had available but 200 men of the "fixed," or permanently established, regiment of the realm.[7]

The captaincy general was preponderantly agricultural in its economic life. Climatic conditions and agricultural potential varied according to altitude and other local factors. Most of the labor was done by Indians who were in a subordinate legal-social position. Methods were primitive, and this, rather than a shortage of land, was the cause of the general agricultural poverty of the realm. After its formation in 1794, the Economic Society tried to promote new techniques, but with such a bias in favor of export and industrial crops as nearly to ignore the problem of foodstuffs. In any case, the suspicious and conservative temper of the Indian cultivator stood in the way of any rapid change of method. Most of the cultivated land was dedicated to subsistence crops, the essential elements of the diet being maize and beans. Other plants were cultivated, but the production of wheat was small and sporadic. The most important export crops were indigo and cacao. By the late eighteenth century trade in cacao was badly depressed as compared with its earlier condition, and after 1790 the indigo industry was crippled by the disruption of maritime transport during the great French wars.[8]

Mineral production, never important in the area, was by the end of the eighteenth century almost nil. Memory of earlier exploitation had not been lost, but grew more golden with the years. The absence of important mineral resources led both Spain and other nations to look upon Guatemala with less interest than upon New Spain and Peru.[9]

Various arts and crafts were widely practiced, but the product was disposed of internally and largely according to the terms of a barter economy. The bulk

---

[6] Juarros, *Compendio*, II, 66-67; Villacorta, *Capitanía general*, 74-76.

[7] Juarros, *Compendio*, I, 34; cf. García Peláez, *Memorias*, III, 86-94, on the military resources of Guatemala.

[8] Antonio Batres Jáuregui, *La América Central ante la historia* (3 vols., Guatemala, 1916-49), II, 379 *et seq.*; Chester Lloyd Jones, *Guatemala Past and Present* (University of Minnesota Press, 1940), 185-86, 197 *et seq.*; Larrazabal, *Apuntamientos, passim.*

[9] Batres Jáuregui, *América Central*, II, 384; but cf. the optimistic Patrick Colquhoun, *A Treatise on the Wealth, Power, and Resources of the British Empire* . . . (London, 1814), 367-68, for the view that "Guatimala has always ranked as mong the first of the Spanish trans-Atlantic possessions, being extremely rich in many valuable articles of export."

of it was cottage production for the use of the fabricator, though in the towns, and especially the capital, small shops catered to the urban population. The production of cheap textiles was the most important activity of this category, but there were also smiths, carpenters, candlemakers, masons, and other artisans. Guilds regulated some trades in the capital and, as in Spain, acted as a restraint on production. Complaints of the indolence and inefficiency of artisans were common, though the Economic Society felt that the native abilities of the local craftsmen were so considerable as to justify an attempt to improve their production by the introduction of better techniques.[10]

Coin always was scarce in the realm, and though by 1790 a royal mint was located at the capital, it did little to correct the situation. An unfavorable balance of trade, as the Economic Society explained, drew currency out of the area. Some members of the Society were hard pressed to find cash for payment of the annual dues of eight pesos. Foreign trade was poor—despite some increase in indigo and cochineal traffic since mid-century—and by 1790 Pacific ports had no importance, those on the Atlantic almost none. Export and internal commerce both were handicapped by bad transport, by mule train or porter over primitive tracks. No streams were important commercially. This not only increased prices, but raised a barrier to effort since it seemed a market was not available for local produce. So the commercial community was small, and the merchant guild, the Consulado, erected in 1794, could not increase the volume of trade. Early in the nineteenth century there were only thirty or thirty-five commercial houses in the entire captaincy general.[11] Since commerce was small, Spanish trade restrictions were not a major source of discontent in Guatemala.[12] The monopolistic practices of the merchants, however, were still causing trouble late in the colonial era.[13] Guatemalans certainly wanted a larger commerce, but their interest was primarily in the produce that would enter into the commerce.[14]

[10] Salvatierra, *Contribución*, II, 118-20, 213, noting that textile making was widespread but small-scale, and poorly developed due to "egoistic interests," especially the commercial monopoly, which would not let weaving machinery in; Villacorta, *Capitanía general*, 171-87; Juarros, *Compendio*, I, 61, on virtues and defects of the populace, including the judgment that "tienen bastante ingenio y buena disposición para las artes, como lo prueba la multitud de Menestrales de todos oficios."

[11] Larrazabal, *Apuntamientos*, 17 *et seq.*

[12] F. M. Stanger "National Origins in Central America," HAHR, XII, No. 1 (February, 1932), 18-45, at 26; cf. R. S. Smith, "Origins of the Consulado of Guatemala," *loc. cit.*, for the size and character of the commercial interest.

[13] Salvatierra, *Contribución*, II, 97-98, 100-102.

[14] Cf. on commerce, Juarros, *Compendio*, I, 156-57; Villacorta, *Capitanía general*, 156; García Peláez, *Memorias*, III, 94 *et seq.*; Jones, *Guatemala*, 235, 282; Salvatierra, *Contribución*, II, 92 *et seq.*; Larrazabal, *Apuntamientos*, 98-104; Hubert Howe Bancroft,

The Enlightenment came to Guatemala by the usual routes. The university at the capital, which traditionally had trained a few men in theology, scholastic philosophy, and law, in the last quarter of the eighteenth century showed the influence of the new science, especially as it related to medicine.[15] The press, from 1660 until the middle of the eighteenth century, mainly issued novenas, sermons, funeral orations, pastoral letters, lives of saints, university theses, patents for religious brotherhoods, works on or in native languages with basically a religious purpose, and miscellaneous other religious items.[16] But when the censorship relaxed in Spain, and the new ideas spread ever more quickly throughout the Spanish world, the output of the Guatemala press gradually broadened. In 1769 it published the defense of a thesis upon "experimental physics" by Friar José Antonio de Liendo y Goycoechea,[17] a young creole destined to be a prominent exponent in Guatemala of the new learning in its scientific aspects, and a founder of the Economic Society there. In the 1780's he visited Spain, examining libraries, the botanical garden, and the natural history exhibit; assisting at meetings of academies and societies and inspecting the educational system.[18] He returned to Guatemala with books and scientific instruments. [19] Other items printed before 1790 indicate some diversification of intellectual activity on the side of applied science.[20]

A growing impatience with regulation was shown in 1787 by the petition

---

History of Central America (3 vols., San Francisco, 1883-87), III, 663-64, including some statistics on the small Pacific traffic with Peru, and the small Caribbean trade with Cuba; "Varias noticias del Río de San Juan, Yslas y Adyacentes de la costa de los Mosquitos, provincias y partidos que tiene el reyno de Guatemala," in *Relaciones históricas y geográficas de América Central* (*Colección de libros y documentos referentes a la historia de América*, VIII, Madrid, 1908), 287-328, at 310, for exports for Cadiz in register ships via the Golfo Dulce de Honduras in 1798-1802.

[15] Lanning, *Academic Culture*, 134 *et passim*; Villacorta, *Capitanía general*, 242-50; Ramón A. Salazar, *Historia del desenvolvimiento intelectual en Guatemala* (Guatemala, 1897), 39 *et seq.* Cf. Lanning, *The University in the Kingdom of Guatemala* (Cornell University, 1955), 300 *et seq.*, on the sad state of the university at the end of the colonial period.

[16] José Toribio Medina, *La imprenta en Guatemala 1660-1820* (Santiago, 1910), *passim*. Few other things were printed. A not very striking exception was the *Gazeta de Goathemala* (1729-31), a government organ containing chiefly local news of an official or religious character (*ibid.*, 76).

[17] *Ibid.*, No. 357; Juarros, *Compendio*, I, 248; García Peláez, *Memorias*, III, 232-33; Salazar, *Historia intelectual*, 103; Max Henríquez Ureña, *El retorno de los galeones* (Madrid, 1930), 150.

[18] García Peláez, *Memorias*, III, 233.

[19] Microscope, barometer, telescope, thermometer, and pneumatic and electrical devices (José Mariano Beristain de Souza, *Biblioteca hispano americana setentrional* [2d ed., 3 vols., Amecameca, 1883]), II, 34.

[20] E.g., on the processing of silver ore (1772); a translation of a French work on inoculation (1780); a supposed specific for cancer (1782); and (1788) a method of performing caesarian operations (Medina, *Imprenta en Guatemala, passim*).

of a Guatemala printer, Ignacio Beteta, suggesting elimination of some of the regulatory functions of the government. The suggestion was not well received.[21] But the expansion of publication became more evident from 1790 to the imperial crisis of 1808. The amount of expansion is clear: 408 items published in the 123 years from 1660 to 1783, and 504 printed in the next sixteen from 1783 to 1799.[22] Even more important was the qualitative change, and most important in this respect was the project for a *Gazeta*, conceived by the printer Beteta in 1793, after he had seen the prospectus of the new *Mercurio Peruano*. Beteta was three years obtaining the necessary authorization, since the authorities had misgivings about the enterprise.[23] In the meantime the Economic Society of Guatemala was founded. The connection between the Society and this, the second, *Gazeta de Guatemala* was to be intimate.

Though the literate group became aware of the new learning and attitudes by legal means, it also read widely in prohibited literature.[24] Thus a small but influential minority in Guatemala was shedding its intellectual passivity and seeking answers to questions scarcely discussed earlier. The Economic Society was a focus of some of this activity.

Foundation of the Guatemala Society

In 1794 some men sympathetic to the new learning began to hold discussions at the house of judge of the audiencia Jacobo de Villaurrutia. The latter had been born in Santo Domingo, son of a judge of the audiencia there; soon moved to the mainland when his father was transferred to Mexico; received his early schooling in Mexico, then went to Spain in his teens with ex-Archbishop Lorenzana of Mexico, who had an interest in the Economic Societies of Spain. Villaurrutia attended several universities in Spain, became a lawyer, and in 1787 was named *corregidor* of Alcalá de Henares and of the sixty-four pueblos of its *partido*. He performed not only the ordinary functions of his office, but interested himself in education, was friendly with liberal professors at the University of Alcalá, and assisted in the direction of the periodicals *El Correo de los Ciegos* and *Correo de Madrid*. There is no evidence of direct connection with the Economic Societies of Spain, but he certainly returned

---

[21] *Ibid.*, lxxvii-lxxviii.

[22] *Ibid., passim.* Medina is not complete, but the additions in Gilberto Valenzuela, *La imprenta en Guatemala. Algunas adiciones a la obra que con este título publicó en Santiago de Chile el ilustre literato don José Toribio Medina* (Guatemala, 1933), do not alter the basic picture here established.

[23] Medina, *Imprenta en Guatemala*, lxi, 322 *et seq.*

[24] Martín Mérida, "Historia de la Inquisición," *loc. cit.*, contains much information on this.

to America with a good knowledge of their operation. Appointed judge of the audiencia of Guatemala through his father's influence, Villaurrutia arrived there in 1793, and remained until promoted to Mexico in 1805.[25]

In August, 1794, Villaurrutia as host of the above-mentioned group was considering establishment of an Economic Society. His companions were Antonio García Redondo, José Flores, José Sierra, Juan Ignacio Barrios, and Francisco Barrutia.[26] García Redondo was an ecclesiastic, born in Spain, who as a young man had come to America in the train of a prelate proceeding to Nicaragua. He received a doctorate at the University of San Carlos de Guatemala, and developed a strong interest in mathematics and astronomy. His later work for the Economic Society demonstrated an essential impatience with the intellectually incurious. He became a frequent contributor to the *Gazeta de Guatemala*, and subsequently was identified with the creole faction.[27] Flores was born in Chiapas in the 1750's, but early in life went to Guatemala for his education. His spirit was essentially that of the new experimental science, with a primary interest in medicine, and he was the most prominent figure in the destruction of the old method of medical instruction at the university, being the first to engage in the dissection of cadavers there. In 1793 he was named chief medical inspector of Guatemala. Three years later he journeyed to Spain, via the United States, where he visited the scientist Joseph Priestley at Philadelphia. Receiving official position in Spain, Flores left to the University of Guatemala his library of over 600 volumes, two electric machines, and his anatomical and surgical instruments.[28] Sierra was a Spanish captain of engineers who soon used his specialized training to supervise the school of mathematics established by the Economic Society.[29]

This group of enlightened Spaniards and creoles spoke of its meetings as "patriotic conversations," which label and motive duplicated the practice of the Spanish Economic Societies, and by this date may have been in part a shield against suspicion of being frenchified. The group spent the rest

---

[25] *Octava junta pública de la Sociedad Económica de Amantes de la Patria de Guatemala* (Guatemala, 1811), No. 1 of "Notas" at back; Batres Jáuregui, *América Central*, II, 464, 527; David Vela, *Literatura guatemalteca* (Guatemala, 1943), 175, 199; Virgilio Rodríguez Beteta, *Evolución de las ideas* (Paris, 1929), 65; Méndez, *El intendente Ramírez*, 26; *Relación de la junta general 1852*, 19 et seq. In 1817 Villaurrutia returned to Spain as judge of the audiencia of Barcelona, dying there in 1820.

[26] García Peláez, *Memorias*, III, 263; Salazar, *Historia intelectual*, 261, without citation of source; Vela, *Literatura guatemalteca*, 168, without citation.

[27] Batres Jáuregui, *América Central*, II, 465, 528; Rodríguez Beteta, *Evolución de ideas*, 215-17.

[28] Salazar, *Historia intelectual*, 32, 84 et seq.; Batres Jáuregui, *América Central*, II, 521; Flamenco, *La beneficencia en Guatemala*, 201-202; *Gazeta de Guatemala*, May 22, 1797, 123-25.

[29] Batres Jáuregui, *América Central*, II, 465.

of 1794 discussing the project of a Society. Several documents were submitted to the captain general to be forwarded to Spain, which he did February 28, 1795, giving the group provisional authority to operate. The documents included a project for the statutes, followed by a plan for creation of several schools, signed by Villaurrutia, October 15, 1794; and a petition, November 20, 1794, signed by Antonio García Redondo, José Flores, José Antonio Goycoechea, and Juan Manrique, detailing their conviction that the foundation would benefit the entire realm of Guatemala, and asking that the statutes and other documents be sent to Spain. José Sierra, December 7, 1794, submitted a plan for a school of mathematics, formation of which he thought proper for a learned body, much needed, sure to be beneficial to the public and the state, and useful to such practical crafts as carpentry. He offered his services to the school, and suggested a four-class division including such studies as arithmetic, geometry, algebra, statics, hydraulics, optics, astronomy, and geography. Pedro Garcí-Aguirre, director of the Royal Mint of Guatemala, December 2, 1794, presented a plan for an Academy of the Three Noble Arts of painting, sculpture, and architecture. He proposed adaptation to the needs of Guatemala of the arrangements of the Royal Academies of New Spain, and of Madrid, Valencia, and other places in Spain. The king was to be protector of the academy; the Economic Society as vice-protector would name a secretary for the school. The proposal noted that there was not a sufficient number of qualified teachers in Guatemala to staff the academy properly, but asserted that this could be taken care of until more men were trained.

The fiscal of the audiencia approved the Society project in a long opinion, February 28, 1795, as one of the "means that can contribute powerfully not only to prevent the decadence and even the total ruin to which these provinces move," but even to put them in "the state of abundance and felicity of which they are certainly susceptible." He also thought the Society would teach the ignorant, stimulate the indolent, and aid the destitute. It would even be enough if it found honest means of sustaining the masses of idlers who were flooding the capital. It might contend with the current total corruption of customs, which included the saddling of women with the whole weight of marriage, raising the children, managing the household, and gaining food and clothes for the entire family. The fiscal thought, however, that drunkenness and other vicious habits would be difficult to modify after enduring for three centuries. While the fiscal found the idea of the Society good, he made two suggestions. One was regulation of the crafts, many of which had no general ordinances, while those that did were in no better state since they failed to observe them. This resulted in bad training and poor work, since men became masters without an apprenticeship. So the Society should propose guild reforms to the government. The fiscal's other suggestion concerned the lottery projected for partial support of the Society, and asked that the royal portion go to the local Hospital de San Juan de Díos, at least until other means of succoring the indigent might be found.[30]

The Society apparently commenced its labors in March, 1795;[31] on April 25 some of the members met at the house of Villaurrutia to subscribe funds for a school;[32] at a meeting of May 17 the projected statutes and the memorial to the king were read.[33]

On this provisional basis dues were collected for the year 1795, and the treasurer rendered a report for the period March 4, 1795, to February 12, 1796, listing ninety-one members, including thirteen already in arrears in their dues. The Society had launched a spinning school, was renting a building, buying cotton, and purchasing equipment. Members from outlying parts of the captaincy general were solicited and accepted in 1795. The Society was well enough launched to be able to hold a public junta for the distribution of prizes, November 4, 1795.[34]

These actions showed awareness of the necessity of change; they also showed considerable cooperation between educated Spaniards and creoles for the purpose of improving life—especially economic life—in America. Such attitudes were not suddenly assumed in 1794, but must have existed for some time. The energy with which the Society was planned and put into operation is only less interesting than its easy acceptance by the authorities in Guatemala and the promptness with which they passed the project on

---

[30] AGG, A1.5-6, leg. 51, exped. 1279 (other copies of same in A1-1, leg. 259, exped. 5721) contains the above-mentioned statutes and other documents prepared by the Society members, the opinion of the fiscal, the captain general's approval, and a number of documents relating to the lottery.

[31] The first entry in the accounts was so dated (Quenta de cargo y data que presenta Don Juan José Barrutia como Tesorero Interino de la Escuela Patriótica, corrida desde 4 de Marzo de 1795 hasta 12 de Febrero de 1796—AGG, A1.6, leg. 2006, exped. 13801).

[32] En la concurrencia general de los Yndividuos subscriptores para el establecimiento de la Sociedad Económica. ... Nueva Guatemala 26 de Abril—AGG, A1.6, leg. 2008, exped. 13844. The title of the expediente has no relationship to the document, which is now filed after a treasurer's report for January 1-December 31, 1799.

[33] Vela, *Literatura guatemalteca*, 168.

[34] Quenta de cargo y data ... de ... Marzo de 1795 hasta ... Febrero de 1796, *loc. cit.*; *Junta Pública de la Real Sociedad Económica de Amantes de la Patria de Guatemala, Celebrada en 12 de Diciembre de 1796* (Guatemala, 1796?), 5; Comprobantes de Data de la cuenta de la Escuela Patriótica de Guatemala desde 4 de Marzo de 1795 hasta 12 de Febrero de 1796—AGG, A1.6, leg. 2006, exped. 13802; Don Juan Francisco Candina to Juan Ortiz de Letona, Sonsonate, July 25, 1795—AGG, A1.6, leg. 2267, exped. 16450.

to Spain. More interesting yet is the quick incorporation of nearly one hundred members. The Society did not rely on this success, but hired a legal representative in Spain to assist in getting it approved.[35]

The Society to the Suspension of 1800

The Society was approved by cedula of October 21, 1795, acknowledging receipt of the documents on formation of an institution to promote agriculture, industry, arts, crafts, and education; to banish idleness and give occupation to the natives; and to promote all classes of spinning, especially of cotton. The cedula noted that the statutes conformed with those of other Economic Societies, with the sole difference that they were arranged to suit the country. Most of the proposals of the founders and some of those of the fiscal were accepted. The Academy of the Three Noble Arts was declared a useful idea, but "not suitable" for the present, so the Society was to establish only schools of drawing and mathematics.[36]

The cedula was received by Captain General Domás y Valle on March 14, 1796, passed through the hands of the proper officials, and on March 31 arrived at Villaurrutia's house, where some members of the Society were gathered. By this time the group had been active a year.[37] Godoy, as head of the Spanish government, in an official letter of February 10, 1796, to the captain general, expressed pleasure with the work the organization had done during the provisional period to November 4, 1795.[38] With official approval secured, the Society met in its first "ordinary junta" April 12, 1796, to elect regular officers.[39]

The statutes, resembling those of the Spanish Societies and of Havana, put the aim of the Society as the improvement of agriculture, industry, arts, and crafts, in all the realm, but especially in the capital and its provinces. This was to be accomplished by discourses, demonstrations, prizes, and other methods employed, the statutes said, by the Societies of Europe. The Society was also to improve public education and to banish idleness. Its arms bore the legend: "United Zeal Produces Abundance." Like the Spanish Societies, a division into classes was provided (agriculture, industry, arts

---

[35] Salvatierra, *Contribución*, II, 179.

[36] Copies of the cedula in AGG, A1.5-6, leg. 51, exped. 1279; A1.6, leg. 2006, exped. 13798; A1-1, leg. 259, exped. 5721. The money lottery was approved, and was to follow the rules of a Mexican lottery. The jewelry lottery was not allowed; instead, the Consulado was to contribute funds to the Society.

[37] This appears in the certification of the messenger on the margin of the cedula delivered to Villaurrutia.

[38] *Junta pública December, 1796*, 5.

[39] *Ibid.*, 6.

and crafts), officers were elective, the membership was not limited, and the personal status of members was not to be reflected in any sort of preference within the organization. Points of government not covered by the statutes were to be decided in conformity with those of the Madrid Society, "insofar as they may be adaptable to the circumstances of the country."[40]

The Society was active till 1800. The first public junta following receipt of the royal approval was held December 12, 1796, in quarters of the town council, presided over by Captain General Domás y Valle, as the new body's vice-protector.[41] Villaurrutia delivered the opening discourse, in which he declared that the Society wanted to arouse the zeal of all good citizens to work for the good of the fatherland.[42] A dicourse by Antonio García Redondo emphasized patriotism in opposition to "egoism" and "epicureanism," which were contrary to the common interest; mourned the loss of Guatemala's once-flourishing trade; demanded revival of the cacao industry; and declared that effort was needed on the part of rich and poor, educated and ignorant, politician and artisan.[43]

Subsequent public juntas met at the prescribed six-month intervals through 1799. These eight semiannual meetings were attended by the most important men of the capital (and their ladies), who thus received a running report on the activities of the body, were reminded of its objectives, and were harangued as to the great future in store for the captaincy general if only the vices of egoism and idleness were eliminated.[44]

The Society also held at least 101 private meetings by 1800.[45] At these

---

[40] The statutes are in the above-mentioned *expedientes*, containing papers upon the erection of the Society. They have been printed in BAGG, III, No. 2 (January, 1938), 186-201; and appeared contemporaneously as *Estatutos de la Real Sociedad Económica de Amantes de la Patria de Guatemala, aprobado por S. M.* (Impreso por D. Ygnacio Beteta, 1796). A copy of this last, the printed version, is in AGG, A1.1, leg. 2817, exped. 24903.

[41] *Junta pública December, 1796*, 1.

[42] *Ibid.*, 1-4.

[43] *Ibid.*, 23-34.

[44] *Segunda junta pública de la ... Sociedad ... 9 de Julio de 1797* (Guatemala, 1797); *Tercera junta pública ... 9 de diciembre de 1797* (Guatemala, 1798); *Quarta junta pública ... 15 de julio de 1798* (Guatemala, 1798); *Quinta junta pública ... 16 de diciembre de 1798* (Guatemala, 1799). The printed "segunda" was actually the third, if that of November, 1795, be counted. Two public juntas were held in 1799 but acounts of them were not printed. One met in July, 1799 (Cuenta de los gastos ... la Junta Pública de la Sociedad el día 14 del presente mes ... —AGG, A1.6, leg. 2008, exped. 13851). This was the sixth, according to the organization's own system of numbering. Since the "Octava" occurred in 1811, and was the first after re-establishment, the seventh probably took place toward the end of 1799.

[45] So it appears from the printed *Junta general no. 102 que para su restablecimiento celebró la Sociedad ... el sábado 19 de enero de 1811* (Guatemala, 1811).

the work in progress was discussed, and new labors projected. A "corresponding junta" was formed at the port of Trujillo,[46] and corresponding members were accepted in other areas. The membership catalogue of 1799 listed eighty-six *socios asistentes*, residents of the capital, and sixty-three *correspondientes* from widely scattered places ranging from León and Granada in Nicaragua, to Puebla, Mexico City, Jalapa, and Vera Cruz in New Spain, and to Cadiz in old Spain.[47]

The work of the Society in this period included creation of three schools —spinning, mathematics, and drawing; attempts to expand the production of such industrial crops as flax, hemp, indigo, and silk; the importation of seeds; preparation and submission to the government of a guild reform; prizes given to the authors of essays and to deserving artisans. Above all, it performed its primary function as a stimulant and publicity agent. And it found itself always in need of funds.

The Society was aided by the *Gazeta de Guatemala*, first issued February 13, 1797, and in part edited and written by such Society members as Villaurrutia, Goycoechea, and Alejandro Ramírez.[48] The last, whom we met in the Havana Society, did much of the editing of the *Gazeta* in its early years. He had arrived in 1795, following his friend Villaurrutia from Spain. He was secretary to the captaincy general, and to the Consulado, traveling for the latter in 1799-1801. In 1801 he was elected to the American Philosophical Society of Philadelphia but did not hear of the honor until 1817 when intendant of Cuba. He went to Puerto Rico as its first intendant in 1813.

With what amounted to interlocking directorates, the *Gazeta* was available for circulation of the ideas and activities of the Society both within and without the captaincy general. When Director Villaurrutia declared at the public junta of December, 1797, that the essay of Friar Matías de Córdova on Indian dress represented the introduction into Guatemala of the ideas of political economy and of the encyclopedists, he knew that the *Gazeta* would report his remarks.[49] When the Society received an essay from Friar San José Muro of New Spain on "the usefulness of the permission conceded to neutrals to engage in direct commerce with our ports in the present

---

[46] Cf. *Gazeta de Guatemala*, August 27, 1798, 225-27, for an account of the Junta de Correspondencia of Truxillo, and quotation from an eloquent address delivered there.

[47] *Catálogo de los individuos que componen la Real Sociedad* ... (colophon: "Nueva Guatemala 1 de Marzo de 1799. Sebastián Melón Ex Secretario").

[48] Salazar, *Historia intelectual*, 316 *et seq.*; Batres Jáuregui, *América Central*, II, 513-14.

[49] *Tercera junta pública*, 15-16; *Gazeta de Guatemala*, I, No. 46 (December 18, 1797), 366-68.

circumstances, against some who have attacked it more out of selfish interest than out of proper zeal," it could decide to extract from it for printing in the *Gazeta*.[50] And the Society subsidized some of the publication costs of the *Gazeta*.[51]

The *Gazeta* publicized the Society in almost every issue, stating that this was necessary because it reached a wider public than the Society's publications.[52] *Gazeta* subscribers included most of the influential men of Guatemala City; others in many outlying places in the captaincy general; some in Oaxaca, Puebla, Mexico (more than thirty), and Vera Cruz; and several in Spain.[53] The material on the Society in the *Gazeta* was as varied as the work of the former. Letters to the Society were printed: one from Dr. Flores, who was traveling abroad to perfect his scientific knowledge, and sent news of things he had noted in Havana as of use in Guatemala;[54] one from Dr. Calisto Valles-Hondo of Havana, who had learned of the Society from the *Gazeta*, and praised the periodicals and Economic Societies of both cities;[55] letters from bishops in New Spain who had been invited to become honorary Society members.[56] The periodical was notably useful in spreading word of the prizes offered by the Society for literary or other accomplishments. In dealing with such a Society activity, the editor, who was probably a member of the Society interested directly in its projects, was likely to express the quality of the Society interest in the matter. Thus an essay contest on the value of surveys by officials of the subsistence of the populace received from the *Gazeta* an extended discussion, observing that Jerónimo Feijóo had touched but lightly on the matter in his *Teatro Crítico*; that indeed no complete discourses on it existed; that this sort of survey was especially suitable for large territories, such as the American, where frequent censuses could not be taken.[57]

The *Gazeta*, intimately linked to the Society, is thus a prime source for

---

[50] *Quinta junta pública*, 15.

[51] Cf. bill of the printer Beteta, January 29, 1800, for paper and labor for a supplement to the *Gazeta*, July 15, 1799, dealing with the Society's work with flax—AGG, A1.6, leg. 2008, exped. 13845.

[52] T. II, No. 84 (October 22, 1798), 291-92.

[53] "Subscriptores a este tomo," n.d. Subscriptions in the captaincy general came from Santa Ana, San Salvador, Sonsonate, San Vicente, San Miguel, Comayagua, Tegucigalpa, Truxillo, León, Masaya, Granada, Managua, Cartago, Masatenango, Quesaltenango, and Ciudad Real de Chiapa.

[54] T. I, No. 22 (May 22, 1797), 123-25. A type of cheap shoe, beehives, cistern water.

[55] T. I, No. 34 (September 25, 1797), 268-70. He thought the Guatemala Society had been created in imitation of that of Havana.

[56] *Infra*, 216.

[57] T. II, No. 50 (February 26, 1798), 15-16.

the ideas of the members of the latter, and for the temper of the times in Guatemala. Economics was one of its chief concerns, and it inquired at the beginning of its history,[58] as to what had happened to the ancient manufactures of Spain, to the greatness of the nation to which all Europe once was tributary. Money was now more plentiful than in the past, and the dominions of the Crown vast, but it was not these things but industry that made a nation powerful. The proper policy, the article said, was for the Spanish government to protect industry which produced commerce and commerce which produced industry. The article praised the removal of the unjust "hindrances which for so many years have impeded the progress of its [America's] commerce"; praised equal treatment for America and Spain as a policy serving the interest of both; asserted that Americans must not suppose that their true riches were in precious metals, but should turn to the products of their fertile soil, which would provide them a lucrative commerce. Speaking of the advantages of commerce in general ought not, however, leave men

> indifferent to the country in which we write. In it till now it is to be said that it has not had a truly active commerce. But the protection which our government gives to all its colonies, the erection of a Consulado in this capital [and] an Economic Society . . . all give us a favorable auspice, all make us conceive the agreeable hope that some day this country will offer to the world the rare but agreeable prospect of wealth and felicity, sustained by agriculture, by the arts, and by commerce.

To its economic interest the *Gazeta* added such matters as science, education, and current events. But more important than its subject matter was its avowedly critical attitude. It opposed the egoism of sloth in the same terms used in the publications of the Economic Society. And it carried the attitude into other fields, so that it stimulated controversy throughout the captaincy general and into New Spain. This critical attitude occasioned a brief suspension of the *Gazeta* by the captain general in 1798. Ignacio Beteta, printer of the periodical, appealed to Spain on the grounds that the shortage of paper adduced by the captain general as the reason for suspension was but camouflage for his objections to the critical part of the *Gazeta*, which Beteta declared was its very heart.[59]

---

[58] April 10, 1797, 65-68, "Commerce," including quotations from Martínez de la Mata and Ustáriz, and from Campomanes' *Apéndice* to the *Educación popular*.

[59] Medina, *Imprenta en Guatemala*, xli, 331, 333; Archivo General de Indias, *Independencia de América; fuentes para su estudio* (1st ser., 6 vols., Madrid, 1912), Nos. 672-73; Laudelino Moreno, "Independencia de la Capitanía General de Guatemala," ASGH, VI, No. 1 (September, 1929), 8; *Gazeta de Guatemala*, February 19, 1798.

The Society in 1799 decided to take over direct operation of this critical journal, but could not secure the permission of the captain general. This is not surprising in view of the fact that he already disapproved of the *Gazeta*, nor was he reassured by the nature of the suggestion from the Economic Society. The "Regulation" for the *Gazeta*, drawn by Alejandro Ramírez, Mariano López Rayón, and Ignacio Beteta, proposed to use anonymous articles if their contents were suitable, and proposed to plough back the income of the *Gazeta* into improvement of its quality, using illustrations, increasing the number of supplements, bringing suitable books and periodicals from Europe, and "entering into correspondence for this purpose with their authors or editors." It did suggest that these novelties would have to wait till subscriptions passed 500 and until the price of paper became stabilized. Nor was there any reason for the captain general to be reassured by the statement of López Rayón, at a Society meeting, that the scheme was "the best means for spreading economic-political learning (*luzes*) which is one of the first objects of the institution [and] without which its other [objects] would not progress."[60]

The above helps explain why, although the Society had received official approval without difficulty, it had not secured universal approbation. A number of the speeches delivered at the public juntas of the Society betrayed fear of opposition, though they did not reveal much about the sources of that fear. The discourse of Friar Mariano José López Rayón, prefect and ex-provincial of the Order of Mercy, at the junta of July 9, 1797, was really a plea for continuation of the Society.[61] He first dwelt on the hope of great prosperity founded upon education and common effort on the part of all citizens; then noted that some citizens disliked the Society, and were infuriated by its very successes; and stated bluntly that the royal protection given the Society merely stimulated these critics to plot its ruin. But he declared that such persons would destroy themselves in destroying the Society, because it worked for the benefit of all. The latter part of his discourse was so strong and even passionate a plea for continuation of the body, that Rayón must have had some definite reason to fear its suspension, due either to causes then operating or to ancient interests likely to oppose it.

Other evidence of opposition to the Society appeared in an April, 1798, issue of the *Gazeta*, defending the organization against an attack which apparently had been printed in an earlier issue.[62] And in October the same

[60] Govierno. Yndiferente. 1800. La Real Sociedad económica de Guate. sobre qe. se le permita encargarse de la formación y publicación de la Gazeta de esta Capl.— AGG, A1.5-6, leg. 51, exped. 1282.

[61] *Segunda junta pública*, 34-42.

[62] T. II, No. 56 (April 9), 59-60.

year the *Gazeta* noted that the Society had "opponents and enemies for the same reason that of Manila had them, and the first economic bodies (*Cuerpos económicos*) of Spain."[63] This was about as far as the editors could go under the censorship.

In February-April, 1799, the Society submitted the plan to direct the *Gazeta* to the captain general, and he replied by requesting a list of the members of the Society, their offices, and their assignments. The Society sent him a catalogue of the members, and informed him that information on the commissions they held within the body could be found in the printed *Juntas Públicas*. If he insisted, they would prepare a list of the commissions being undertaken by everyone in the Society. At the same time, it was pointed out that Captain General Domás y Valle was himself vice-protector of the Society, had followed its work, and had presided at the public meetings. The officers of the Society enumerated its services, asserted these deserved publicity, and mentioned that they had been sending information on them directly to the ministers in Spain. Finally, they stated that they had believed he would be pleased at the prospect of an improvement in the directorate of the *Gazeta*.[64] One can imagine the frustration and exasperation of the officers of the Society on the one hand, and on the other the irritation and vague fear of the captain general and those influencing him.

The *Gazeta* in May, 1799, printed an article setting forth the importance of the Society, and fears for its future:[65]

> Outside the *reyno* [of Guatemala] some people believe, and thus some had written from various places, that the matters that the Society of Guatemala treats are only useful for this small precinct, as peculiarities to it. This results from its acts not having been sufficiently made known. The following notice . . . will show the generality and importance of the aims, and also in passing will so guide impartial persons, who hear indistinctly, and until now have not manifested their opinion, that they may refrain from giving it, and may not be determined by categorical reports, whether for or against; because the Society as it has very fervent admirers, has also open and secret enemies, in the manner that these have had in other places.

As late as the middle of 1799 the government in Spain was content with the Society. A cedula of July 15, 1799, acknowledged receipt from Director Villaurrutia of the printed accounts of its third and fourth public juntas. The Crown stated that "the zeal of the members has merited my royal approbation," and directed the administration in Guatemala to find funds

---

[63] T. II, No. 84 (October 22), 291-92.

[64] La Real Sociedad ... sobre qe. se le permita encargarse de la formación y publicación de la Gazeta, *loc. cit.*

[65] T. III, No. 106 (Mai 27), 37-39; continued in No. 107 (June 3), 41-42.

for the body to carry on its work.[66] Only four months later, however, November 23, 1799, the Spanish Minister of Justice and Ecclesiastical Affairs, José Antonio Caballero, ordered Villaurrutia to end all the Society's activities. The order was not received in Guatemala until the summer of 1800. In the meantime, on January 27, 1800, the Society founded a School of Sculpture.[67]

Caballero did not clearly explain the grounds of the suspension, although his order indicated a general reason by mentioning receipt in June of an essay by Friar Antonio de San José Muro on the usefulness of dressing Indians and *ladinos* according to the Spanish mode.[68] This work had won the second prize in an essay contest run by the Society in 1796-1797. Both the winning entry by Friar Matías de Córdoba and that of San José Muro were printed by the Society. The latter had sent in his entry after reading about the contest in the *Gazeta de Mexico*. He was forthright in his belief that America was too little understood, and that Spanish economic policy required alteration. Noting the existence of the Economic Societies of Mompox, Vera Cruz, and Cuba, he bewailed the small number of such "patriotic bodies" in America. After dealing extensively and critically with commerce, trade, and production in America, Friar Antonio finally admitted that he was not on the subject proposed for the contest, but excused himself on the grounds that he had studied America for forty-two years and was interested in what it needed most. He approved of dressing Indians and *ladinos* in Spanish style, but thought that at the same time it was absolutely necessary to give them "means of subsistence, and physical, moral, civil, and scientific education." The volume containing San José Muro's essay also contained extracts from some of the other entries in the contest, most of them critical of the current politico-economic dispensation in America.[69]

Apparently not only the critical content of the San José Muro essay was suspect, but also the fact that the author resided in Mexico, as did at least one other entrant in the contest. This was considered evidence of an excessive zeal to expand the Society's influence, according to the Society at a later date, for its rapid progress made some citizens (*ciudadanos*) of Mexico ask royal license to found a similar body there. But since the Ministry of Justice

---

[66] *Gazeta de Guatemala*, III, No. 142 (February 3, 1800), 157, printing the cedula.

[67] *Relación histórica 1852*, 12-13; *Gazeta de Guatemala*, III, No. 142 (February 3, 1800), 162.

[68] Copies of Caballero's order in AGG, A1-1, leg. 259, exped. 5721; A1.3-8, leg. 1904, exped. 12573. The order speaks of "el socio de mérito Fr. Antonio Muro." Salazar, *Historia intelectual*, 265, citing Lucas Alamán, asserts that it was the essay of Matías de Córdoba that caused the suspension. Villacorta, *Capitanía general*, 452, cites Salazar to the same effect.

[69] *Utilidades y medios de que los indios y ladinos vistan y calzen a la española. Memoria que mereció el accesit ... Antonio de S. José Muro ...* (N. Guatemala, 1798).

and Ecclesiastical Affairs was in the inept hands of Caballero, the Mexican solicitation only resulted in closure of the Guatemala Society, for what were called "just causes and considerations."[70] This tendency to expand its influence certainly was promoted by the *Gazeta*, copies of which went to subscribers in New Spain and spread news there of the Society's activities, to say nothing of disseminating the often highly critical views of the editors who were prominent in the Society.

The Society decided that since it was the only one on the "continent," and in conformity with its statutes, the Director should invite as honorary members the viceroy of New Spain, the archbishop of Mexico, and the bishops of the archdiocese of New Spain, "in order to give luster to the body and to fix its endurance (*afianzar su permanencia*) on the most solid bases."[71] So copies of the statutes and of the printed accounts of the public juntas were sent, with invitations to accept honorary membership. The bishops of Michoacán, Guadalajara, Nuevo León, and Antequera (Oaxaca) wrote in 1798, acknowledging receipt of the publications and the invitation, and expressing approval of the aims of the Society. The bishop of Antequera sent fifty pesos, promising to continue the subsidy each year. The Society in dealing with this prelate made use of its connection with José Mociño of the Royal Botanical Expedition to New Spain. The Society also corresponded with the archbishop of Mexico, who refused honorary membership, politely, but without offering a clear reason. Villaurrutia wrote in reply to this refusal that the Society was "unique in this continent," and politely said that important personages did, and should, support the Society, but that they respected the wishes of the archbishop. Finally, Villaurrutia determined in 1798 by correspondence with the Count of Alcanaz that the viceroy of New Spain, the Marquis of Branciforte, would accept an honorary membership, and the Marquis was accordingly informed by Villaurrutia that the Society was honored to accept his membership.[72] The *Gazeta* carried news of this recruitment of members in New Spain,[73] thus no doubt further demonstrating the unfortunate Guatemalan tendency to reach out across provincial lines.

---

[70] *Octava junta pública*, 3-5.

[71] *Quarta junta pública*, 15.

[72] Copies of 11 letters between Villaurrutia and the above-named individuals, all in 1798, and one from the bishop of Chiapas to Society secretary Melón, from Ciudad Real, December, 1798, expressing thanks for the printed accounts of the public juntas, in AGG, A1.6, leg. 2007, exped. 13839; *Quinta junta pública*, 17, catalogue of honorary members, augmented with names of the viceroy of New Spain, Miguel José de Azanza, and the bishops of Nuevo León and of Guadalajara; *Quarta junta pública*, 15, acceptance of membership by the viceroy and bishops of Oaxaca and of Michoacán, but the archbishop of Mexico and the bishop of Puebla excused themselves.

[73] T. III, Nos. 123, 125, 128 (September 23, October 7 and 28, 1799).

Captain General González of Guatemala, in re-establishing the Society in 1810, attributed the suspension "to the baneful influence of a stupid member of the family of the favorite [Godoy]."[74] The secretary of the Society in 1811 ascribed the suspension to the fact that "the imbecility of the court could not bear American enlightenment," and to Branciforte for inciting Caballero to destroy the Society.[75] And another member of the Society at that time characterized the suspension as due to the "barbarous caprice of a bastard politics."[76] These words were uttered, of course, in the brave but brief days of liberalism when the irregular government at Cadiz was considerably more enlightened than the Crown either before 1808 or after Ferdinand's restoration in 1814.

The Society held its last session on July 14, 1800, and decided to obey Caballero's order, but to send a representation to the Crown setting forth the aims of the Society. This plea was drafted by Friar Ventura Villagolín, Friar Matías de Córdoba, Rafael Trullo, and Antonio Juarros. The Society also decided to attempt to continue the drawing school, as a separate body, under the government, and a representation to this effect was signed September 7, 1800, by José Bernardo Dighero, José Simeón Cañas, Juan Manrique, and Miguel de Arteaga y Olózaga. The captain general did not forward this document to Spain until February, 1802.[77] In August, 1803, an order from Spain to the captain general insisted that none of the labors of the Society be permitted to continue.[78]

The Society had begun liquidating its operations immediately after the meeting of July 14, 1800.[79] Winding up the various enterprises, disposing of property, and paying debts, took the rest of the year.[80] Among their other troubles, the ex-members must have been irked at being compelled

---

[74] *Junta general no 102*, 1-8.

[75] *Octava junta pública*, 9; *ibid.*, 3, assigns the "mysterious" causes of suspension to the "irreconcilable and gratuitous ill will" of Branciforte, "capital and notorious enemy of American *ilustración*."

[76] *Octava junta pública*, discourse by Fr. Antonio Carrascal, unmbd. pp. at end.

[77] By Antonio González Mollinedo, who had replaced Domás y Valle (Salvatierra, *Contribución*, II, 184, for these actions of July 14 and September 7, 1800, and the captain general's delay—all without citation of source); cf. *Gazeta de Guatemala*, May 19, 1800, for its last mention of the regular operations of the Society, though it continued thereafter to mention the Society itself.

[78] Salvatierra, *Contribución*, II, 185.

[79] Real Sociedad año de 1800. Esquela de Hilados. Cuenta final. ...—AGG, A1.5, leg. 2008, exped. 13851.

[80] Cuenta de gastos del Escritorio de la Real Sociedad Económica. ...—AGG A1.6, leg. 2008, exped. 13852. Signed by the secretary, Antonio Juarros, in August, 1800, and by the second secretary and by Villaurrutia in mid-December. *Gazeta de Guatemala*, V, No. 167 (July 28, 1800), 302, advising creditors of the Society to apply to Villaurrutia.

at this time to refuse the bequest of a woman who wished the Society to promote the production of flax and cotton.[81]

The suspension was unreasonable, and clumsily handled, as the members were to say after the re-establishment a decade later. It was discriminatory, since the Economic Society of Havana was still in existence, and several score Spanish Societies remained at least nominally operative. The order certainly was arbitrary, as the members were given no explanation of the reasons for it. The order was foolish, for while the individual members were not punished, they were left to reflect upon their grievance without let and without legislative compensation designed to promote the aims of the now defunct Society.

---

[81] Salvatierra, *Contribución*, II, 185.

CHAPTER ELEVEN

The Guatemala Society:
Suspension and Re-establishment (1801-1821)

Suspension and Re-establishment (1801-1810)

The order suppressing the Society remained in effect from July, 1800, until December, 1810; apparently no attempt was made to secure its withdrawal after the rebuff of 1803.

The drawing school continued in operation, under the auspices of the government in the capital, which led the *Gazeta* to declare with some irony that although the academy had lost its "true mother," the Royal Society, it had found a "powerful father" in the government. Pedro Garcí-Aguirre remained as director of the school, but a new supervisory committee was headed by the senior judge of the audiencia. The school's public junta of August 25, 1801, was attended by the same persons who had attended the juntas of the Economic Society, from the captain general down the social scale. On this occasion Garcí-Aguirre declared in an oration that simplicity of spirit meant simplicity of performance, especially to be deplored in those practising the arts, which could be corrected by making use of the "artificial passions" excited by the noble art of drawing, for

> Since the human spirit is always cowardly and indolent in the face of great enter-
> prises, it is necessary to search out means of exciting it, perhaps by honor, or by
> means of inducement, so that the heart may be animated and take the proper
> course in the pursuit of glory.[1]

---

[1] *Gazeta de Guatemala*, V, No. 220 (August 31, 1801), 545-53. Most of the number was devoted to the *Academia de Dibujo*.

The Consulado contributed to the support of the drawing school, but in 1804 the merchants resisted a suggestion that they also underwrite a school of mathematics, stating that the 250 pesos donated annually for drawing was sufficient outlay for education, especially since no other American Consulados were supporting arithmetic classes. The 3,000 pesos asked yearly for the new purpose was said to be out of the question in view of the damage done to commerce by sixteen years of war between 1779 and 1801, especially since indigo had been compelled to contend also with a plague of locusts. While it would be useful to have instruction in mathematics, the merchants said, the city was in its infancy, having moved not many years before, a process which had hurt the fortunes of many.[2]

The *Gazeta* continued to publicize the drawing academy, constantly spoke in the spirit and upon the subjects to which the Economic Society had devoted itself, printed news of the Spanish Societies, and found occasion to mention the extinguished Guatemala Society. In 1801 the *Gazeta* reprinted from the *Correo Mercantil* of Madrid some enthusiastic praise of the zeal of the Economic Society of Guatemala, describing it as an association with no other interest than the public felicity, able to combat the enemies of useful reform. The *Gazeta* sarcastically headed this section of its issue "Incentive to Merit."[3] The Guatemala Society had been nonexistent for a year by this time.

The *Gazeta* observed that a road opened by the *alcalde mayor* of Suchitepéquez had been promoted originally by the Economic Society to improve communications between highlands and coast. The *alcalde mayor*'s report (1801) to the captain general stated that the former's labors proved that the natives would work well if set the proper example, and that his example was "first and unique of its sort in all this *reyno*." The report was examined by several officials, including Judge Villaurrutia, founder of the defunct Economic Society.[4] On another occasion, the *Gazeta* reprinted from the Spanish *Semanario de agricultura y artes* a notice of the coming opening in 1800 of schools of mathematics, chemistry, civil economy and commerce, agriculture, and botany, by the *Real Sociedad Aragonesa*. The article was an attack on the universities on the grounds of impracticality and failure to deal with real (that is, economic) problems.[5] The same year the *Gazeta*

---

[2] Ynforme relativa a la erección de una escuela de Matemáticas, que por falta de fondos no se realize—AGG, A1.3-8, leg. 1904, exped. 12588.

[3] T. V, No. 211 (July 6, 1801), 509-10; reprinting also from this Madrid issue of April 21, 1800, an ana'ytical extract of the memorial of Garcia Redondo on the promotion of cacao culture and other phases of agriculture.

[4] August 16, 1802, 189-92, including a two-page map by Garcí-Aguirre.

[5] January 11, 1803, 2-3.

gave notice of a series of prizes offered by the Economic Society of Madrid. Since it gave the official gazette of the court as its source, the Guatemala journal made doubly clear the policy of discrimination against America.[6] Two years later the *Gazeta* printed an article on "Philanthropy" which urged the foundation of *cuerpos patrióticos*.[7] And the *Gazeta* not only kept alive the memory of the Society, and of the policy of discrimination against it, but promoted interests as liberal as those of the Society, if not as disturbingly organized. The periodical in these years ranged rather widely, from economic periodicals in Spain, to the geography of Guatemala, Galvinism, the Royal Academy of History of Spain, venereal disease, Mociño's "Noticias de Nutka," the construction of silos, Marshall's *Life of Washington*, the work of Humboldt and Bonpland, the battle of Trafalgar, and the Treaty of Amiens.[8] The *Gazeta* did go too far in an article, March 16, 1803, ridiculing the celibacy of the clergy, and the Inquisition banned the article;[9] but the *Gazeta* was allowed to continue publication.

In 1808 Guatemala learned of the abdications of Charles and Ferdinand, the imposition of a Bonaparte as king of Spain, and the acts of French troops in the Peninsula. The *reyno* hailed Spanish resistance to these actions, and all important individuals and institutions quickly declared loyalty to Ferdinand.[10] Early in 1809 allegiance was sworn in the captaincy general to the Central Junta of Sevilla, formed to govern in the name of Ferdinand.[11] The *Gazeta* soon printed the decree (January 22, 1809) of the Central Junta declaring the American provinces "integral parts of the monarchy," and calling them to send representatives to Spain to sit with the Junta.[12] The election of the delegate was a process that involved municipalities of the entire captaincy general in an experience without precedent in their history.[13]

---

[6] T. VII, No. 302 (May 2, 1803), 103-204 [i.e. 104].

[7] November 21, 1805.

[8] Scattered issues in 1802-05.

[9] Mérida, "Historia de la Inquisición," *loc. cit.*, ch. xviii.

[10] Cf. *Guatemala por Fernando séptimo el día 12 de diciembre de 1808* [Guatemala, 1809], for the culminating avowals, a description of the *jura*, and other documents relating to the current political situation; Enrique Sobral, "La Jura de Fernando VII," ASGH, I, No. 3 (January, 1925), 238-56.

[11] Cf. BAGG, III, No. 3 (April, 1938), 325 *et seq.*, "Documentos acerca de la cooperación de Guatemala en la Independencia de Centro América," for text of the documents of this period; Villacorta, *Capitanía general*, 456-59.

[12] T. XII, No. 58 (a "Suplemento," issued between May 1-15, 1809), 429-32, reprinting the entire decree, and an account of the action taken by the government upon its receipt in Guatemala.

[13] Ramón A. Salazar, *Historia de veintiún años. La independencia de Guatemala* (Guatemala, 1926), 117-19; Villacorta, *Capitanía general*, 133-34.

In those days of constitutional crisis, reform, complaint,[14] and rumor of French designs, a creole reform faction in Guatemala favored broad alterations in the imperial system to give them more authority and economic opportunity. The strength of this group centered in the town governments. In 1809 the ayuntamiento of Guatemala wrote the Central Junta in Spain that tyrannical government in America ought to end, and the "scepter of iron be put aside";[15] and it clashed with the civil censorship in Guatemala, protesting to the Central Junta that the censors would not allow the ayuntamiento to publish a patriotic proclamation.[16] In June, 1810, the *Gazeta* capped the climax of creole excitement by printing the proclamation of the Council of Regency declaring the colonies possessed of the same rights as the metropolis, and their inhabitants now elevated to the dignity of free men.[17]

The town council of the capital expressed its ambition in mid-1810 by supporting the aims of the Tribunal of Fidelity, created by the captain general to prevent espionage by French agents, but by requesting that one-half the members be "creole-Spaniards or Americans."[18] The new creole opinion also was expressed in the "Instructions" on the "fundamental constitution of the Spanish monarchy," furnished by the town council of the capital to Antonio Larrazabal, its deputy to the extraordinary Cortes scheduled for Cadiz in 1810.[19] The instructions were drafted by town councillor José María Peinado, an officer of the Economic Society before its suppression, and an example of what might be called the "conservative reform" faction. That is, he was a member of the creole elite who controlled the

---

[14] Cf. "Los Pasquines y la Junta de Censura," BAGG, IV, No. 1 (October, 1938), 3-12, for official action in Guatemala early in 1808 prohibiting the circulation of lampoons damaging to honorable persons.

[15] Laudelino Moreno, "Guatemala y la Invasión Napoleónica en España," ASGH, VII, No. 1 (September, 1930), 3-17.

[16] *Independencia de América*, No. 1614. A year later the ayuntamiento made an additional protest (*ibid.*, No. 2012). By this time the French had driven the Central Junta to Cadiz, where it surrendered (January, 1810) its powers to a Council of Regency, which in June disapproved the action of the Guatemalan censor (*ibid.*, No. 2214).

[17] José Antonio Villacorta C., "Guatemala en las Cortes de Cadiz," ASGH, XVII, No. 1 (March, 1941), 5.

[18] Villacorta, *Capitanía general*, 465; *Independencia de América*, No. 2343; Bancroft, *Central America*, III, 6, n. 15. The council also wished to change the name to "Tribunal of Protection and Vigilance," which would presumably have weakened the semantic tie with the mother country. The Tribunal was suppressed in 1811 on orders from Spain.

[19] In 1810 the town councils of the captaincy general elected deputies on the basis of one each for the *partidos* of Guatemala, Ciudad Real, San Salvador, Comayagua, León, and Granada.

unrepresentative town council, favored some form of constitutional monarchy, and feared radical social change. He was alarmed by the activities of Hidalgo and Morelos in Mexico, and in 1811 helped the strong-handed Captain General José de Bustamante put down revolt in San Salvador.[20] The instructions severely indicted Spanish government, law, and customs; demanded a constitution that would prevent despotism by the executive by defining the limits of his authority; and included a "Declaration of the Rights of Man," copied from the French. The proposals were conservative in many respects, but did transfer some authority from the imperial administration to the colonial elite. They were accepted for their own deputies by the other five *partidos* of the captaincy general, but three members of the town council of the capital would not approve the document. The liberal majority of the council, however, continued to send instructions to Larrazabal, condemning the sale of offices, demanding the "free" administration of justice, and advocating improved educational facilities.[21]

In this time of rivalry between creole and European,[22] Captain General González wrote the Council of Regency, November 5, 1810, proposing re-establishment of the Society.[23] He did not wait for a reply, but by his own decree, December 12, 1810, relying on a proclamation of the Council of Regency that establishments dedicated to public instruction were one of the principal interests of the Crown, authorized resumption of the Society's operations.[24] In this long decree González called the suspension of 1799 "ministerial, without expression of cause, which until now is not known with certainty," though it had been attributed to the personal venom of a courtier, and

the stupid spirit of rivalry, and of puerile pride, an insensate vengeance, an offshoot of the bastard or traitorous politics that interceded to make tributary and slave

[20] Salazar, *Veintiún años*, 128-30; Bancroft, *Central America*, III, 9, 14.

[21] "Instrucciones para la constitución fundamental de la Monarquía española y su gobierno," ASGH, XVII, Nos. 1, 2, 5 (March, June, 1941; March, 1942), 7-25, 136-47, 333-51; for the "poder" given Larrazabal, and other instructions, see BAGG, III, No. 4 (July, 1938), 479-84; *Apuntes instructivos que al señor … Larrazabal diputado a las Cortes … por el Cabildo … dieron sus regidores … Isasi, … Melón, … González y … Aqueche* (Nueva Guatemala, 1811).

[22] Cf. *Gazeta de Guatemala*, XIV, Nos. 185-187, special issues entitled "Diálogos Patrióticos " between November 10 and 17, 1810, issues. Reprinted from Mexico; highly cr'tical of Hidalgo revolutionary movement; confused effort to determine whether due to creole-European rivalry, and whether such rivalry reasonable and justified; somewhat favored European point of view, but apparent intent of dialogues defeated by weighty arguments permitted the creole partisan in debate, and by excessively legalistic character of some of the European arguments.

[23] *Independencia de América*, No. 2675; cf. Medina, *Imprenta en Guatemala*, No. 1650.

[24] *Junta general no. 102*, 1-6, printing González' permission in full; cf. Salvatierra, *Contribución*, II, 186.

to other nations that which has most title to command respect and exact homage; such were without doubt the secret motives of that mysterious order which enveloped Guatemala in mourning.

Thus ascribing the suspension largely to Godoy, González also noted that he had himself attempted to persuade the government in Spain that the Economic Society was absolutely necessary, and that without it "would be useless always the intent and the forces of the government and the passive influence of its officials." Putting the re-establishment upon a patriotic basis, as indispensable to the enrichment of the monarchy and the unity of the dominions of the Crown, he declared:

> Moved by these considerations, and others derived from them, paying attention to the fact that the Economic Societies, whose general utility no one denies, exist in Spain, and in other parts of America; that that of this *Reyno* was ordered suspended, but not extinguished or abolished, being intended for a limited period and for ephemeral motives, which at present do not exist.

So he ordered it re-established, asserting that there was no doubt that Ferdinand VII would approve, and in his name the Council of Regency. The captain general was not only a sensible man, but an optimist as well.

The Society, by the terms of this decree, was to be governed by the statutes approved in the cedula of October 21, 1795, and to receive back its furniture and records. The captain general named the officers for the next period; promised to order the proper institutions to name their ex-officio members; decreed that the old members might attend meetings; and recommended special attention to the school of drawing, the common lands of the Indians, and methods of populating the ports and littoral of the area.

González was the type of enlightened official who favored the application of reason and knowledge to the problems of the empire; and he welcomed participation by colonials, declaring that combined action was necessary for solution of important problems. His reliance on the approval of Ferdinand, assuming it to have been sincere at a time when Ferdinand was not reigning in fact, was no more mistaken than other men's early hopes for that unprincipled and untalented Bourbon.

The Period of the Cortes (1810-1814)

The importance of the re-establishment was emphasized by celebration of the first "general junta" at the house of the new director, José de Ayzinena, January 19, 1811. The director addressed the thirty-six members attending, with protestations of loyalty to Ferdinand and to the Cortes, not yet so impossible a coupling as it would be a few years later. He suggested honorary memberships for González and for Villaurrutia, founder of the Society, by this time resident in Mexico. Corresponding juntas were to be created, and Larrazabal, deputy to the Cortes for Guatemala City, was to receive a letter asking him to secure approval of the re-establishment. Ayzinena also proposed the naming of commissions on the drawing school, on artisans and textiles, on the grain shortage, on Society finances, and on the suggestions made by González. Nor did he fail to complain of the suspension of 1799 by a "purely ministerial Royal Order."

The junta approved the membership applications of fifty-eight men; and decided to restore the old officers of the Society insofar as possible. Present as officers were such mainstays of the earlier period as Alejandro Ramírez and Antonio Juarros. The junta also decided to promote the spread of enlightenment in the provinces by making ex-officio members of the intendants of Chiapa, Comayagua, San Salvador, and Nicaragua, and of the governor of Costa Rica. The Society wanted approval from Spain, and favored a blanket law by the Cortes encouraging Economic Societies in all America; in the meantime, however, it wanted specific sanction for the Guatemala body.[25] Whatever else may have been the effect of the years 1801-1810, they had not destroyed interest in the Society.

In mid-March, 1811, Captain General González was replaced by José Bustamante y Guerra, a native of northern Spain, and a naval officer who had been on the scientific voyage of Malaspina in 1789-1794, who had recently been active in combating the "independents" of Montevideo, where he had defended the city against the British. Within three weeks after his arrival, Bustamante instructed the Tribunal of Fidelity to proceed against the secretary of the town council of the capital for expressing opinions injurious to the nation and to authority.[26] He proved an energetic executive, though it is not certain that his vigor did not do more harm than good to the cause of Spain. He adhered to much of the letter of the liberal legislation of the period, but always was in opposition to its spirit. His opposition to liberalism related to political matters, however, and the Economic Society continued throughout his term.

The first of the semiannual public juntas after the restoration was held in August, 1811. It condemned the suspension of 1799, attributing it to the Society's attempts to promote a similar body in Mexico, thus rousing the enmity of Viceroy Branciforte, "notorious enemy of American enlightenment." It flatly charged the Spanish court with a policy of keeping America in ignorance. It several times noted approvingly the freedom of the press

---

[25] All this from the printed account: *Junta general no. 102.*
[26] Laudelino Moreno, "Independencia de la Capitanía General," *loc. cit.*, 14; Navarrete, *Opúsculos*, II, 209-17, "Don José de Bustamante y Guerra."

established by the Cortes, one speaker stating that the Cortes would not make the mistakes of the old government, but would understand that a nation must have industry, which the Economic Societies could develop, and for this reason the Cortes would protect them. The Society had picked up the threads of its earlier effort; information was offered on such familiar subjects as flax, cochineal, textiles, the drawing school, and primary education; there was an expanded interest in mining; a new class of "Public Enlightenment" had been provided; a new class of consulting members had been created, to forge intellectual links with distant regions.[27]

The Regency, on application of deputy to Cortes, Larrazabal, approved re-establishment of the Society, in an order of November 23, 1811, noting that Captain General González had re-formed it under the urging of many of the most distinguished persons of the captaincy general, and directing him to aid the Society.[28] Larrazabal wrote the Society at once, word reaching the Society in the spring of 1812.

In February-March, 1812, José Cecilio del Valle was head of a Society committee preparing a class in political economy, "the science of civil societies," which would prevent the wastage of effort in frivolous endeavors.[29] Del Valle, son of a well-to-do family of Honduras, had studied philosophy and law at the University of Guatemala. From 1811 to the declaration of Central American independence in 1821, Valle was one of the most active members of the Society, and he was a prime mover of a revived Society in the republican period after 1821. He had a strong interest in intellectual matters, and thought of the Society mainly as a learned society. His political position was conservative, both before and after Independence, but it must be remembered that the nature of conservatism was changing in those years.[30]

Director Ayzinena made an interesting political use of the Society in San Salvador, where he was sent at the end of 1811 to deal with a creole disturbance apparently aimed at seizure of local authority but not at immediate

---

[27] *Octava junta pública. ... Primera después de su restablecimiento* ... (Beteta, n.p., n.d.); *Gazeta de Guatemala*, XV, No. 226 (July 3, 1811), 274; Fr. Juan de Santa Rosa Ramírez to the Society (AGG, A1.6, leg. 2008, exped. 13855). Men appointed to consulting membership included a resident of Puerto-Príncipe in Cuba and three scientists in Mexico.

[28] *Novena junta pública de la Sociedad ... 5 de abril de 1812* (Por Beteta, n.p., n.d.), 3-4, 20-22, reprinting the order of the Regency in full.

[29] *El Amigo de la Patria*, I, No. 23 (April 12, 1821), 437-45. He referred to such authorities as Galiani, Necker, Jovellanos, Condillac, Locke, Hume, Adam Smith, Sully, Colbert, and the Encyclopedia. He is not to be confused with the two men named José del Valle who belonged to the Society earlier.

[30] Ramón Rosa, *Biografía de Don José Cecilio del Valle* (Tegucigalpa, 1943), *passim;* Batres Jáuregui, *América Central*, II, 533-34.

independence from Spain.[31] As interim governor, Ayzinena quieted the province without much trouble. In February, 1812, he incorporated most of the conspirators into a "corresponding junta" of the Guatemala Society. Previous members of the body were drawn in at once, and others added. The first members were José Matías Delgado, Francisco Aguilar, Juan Miguel Bustamante, Mateo Ybarra, José María Villaseñor, Manuel José de Arce, and Julián González. The recent conspiracy had been hatched at the house of Delgado. Arce was to be perhaps the most noted of Salvadoreño political figures in the early years of the republican period. Ayzinena reported to the Guatemala Society that, unless corresponding juntas were established in all the principal towns of the captaincy general, that "illustrious body" would be unable "to extend its liberal and beneficent ideas" throughout so large a territory. So he had erected the junta of San Salvador "to inspire in the spirits of its inhabitants the purest patriotic sentiments." But at the same time, some of the conspirators had been imprisoned. To expand the work of the San Salvador junta, twenty-one additional members were quickly admitted.[32] Presumably what Ayzinena meant by "purest patriotism" was agitation and labor for an improved life by other than political means. And at this time he also meant loyalty to the imperial connection. His description of the Economic Society as "liberal" must be understood here to mean liberal in its views on intellectual and economic activity rather than on political action.

The Society celebrated a public junta at the capital on April 5, 1812, the date being selected to announce a letter from Larrazabal, deputy to the Cortes, giving notice of the order of November 23, 1811, approving re-establishment of the Society.[33] Captain General Bustamante and Archbishop Casaus attended. The latter, a rigid *españolista*, opponent of free thought, and champion of the political status quo, gave 200 pesos to the Society after the celebration.[34] Before the junta, the members went to church,[35] and heard a sermon by the Society member Tomás de Beltranena, who supported the Society with Roman Catholic history and belief, condemned indiscriminate charity, approved the doctrine of work, and declared that poverty was the source of sedition since men of property supported government because it protected their interests. He considered education the instrument by which the current corruption of the captaincy general could be corrected, and that

---

[31] Villacorta, *Capitanía general*, 472-75.

[32] Sobre erección de la junta de Correspondencia de San Salvador, verificada en 5 de Febrero—AGG, A1.6, leg. 2008, exped. 13856; *Novena junta pública*, 24.

[33] *Novena junta pública*, 3.

[34] *Ibid.*, 8; Salazar, *Veintiún años*, 147-50.

[35] And took honored seats, though at their own meetings they scorned distinction or etiquette (*Novena junta pública*, 3).

the efforts of the Society to improve economic conditions would advance the chances of peace.[36] Beltranena did not mention social or political grievances as causes of sedition, or the fact that sedition was more likely to be the work of persons of moderately good circumstances, but ambitious of social and political advancement, than of the impoverished, brutalized, and usually apathetic lower classes. He may have been aware of these facts and chosen to ignore them, or have believed that the recent Hidalgo rising in Mexico was a spontaneous movement of poor Indians.

A speech at the junta by Luís Pedro Aguirre found that Spain under Ferdinand VII would flourish as Rome under Trajan, and that the Cortes and Regency ruled in his name in conformity with the desires of his heart—which was either optimism, policy, or grievous error. Aguirre sketched the history of the Economic Societies of Spain, noting that they totaled sixty-four; called Villaurrutia the "Campomanes of Guatemala"; criticized the suspension of 1799 only to demonstrate that when the nation recovered its "rights" the Economic Society received the protection it deserved; and praised the voluntary feature of the Society's operations, and said that nature and the "social pact" required that men labor for their mutual benefit.[37] The man was evidently far gone in corruption.

Secretary Juarros, a hold-over from the 1795-1800 period, declared that the Society was now on a new basis as "a political body auxiliary to the government,"[38] as radical a statement on the function of an Economic Society as the present investigator has seen. Juarros also referred to what he called the unjust suspension of the Society in 1799, indicating that approval of the Cortes had been sought lest the Society again succumb to its enemies.[39] This harping on opposition to the Society suggests fear, and it also suggests that opinion as to the role of the organization was divided. Some individuals were bound to feel that such all-embracing studies as were contemplated by José Cecilio del Valle must affect political opinions, even if they understood that he wished to combine a critical intellectual life with political conservatism.

In September, 1812, at a general junta of the Society, José del Valle spoke on political economy, which he seemed to consider a mixture of all the sciences,

---

[36] *Ibid.*, 8-17.

[37] *Ibid.*, 48-54.

[38] *Ibid.*, 19.

[39] *Ibid.*, 20. Juarros' report showed that the interests of the Society had been expanding since the re-establishment some 15 months earlier, although agriculture still was not noted as a separate class of endeavor. The concern with textiles was still notable. It was still hoped that mining might be "revived." As always, the secretary could complain that the Society's ideas were better than its capacity to implement them.

physical and social.[40] The address was primarily that of a man of learning praising the utility of knowledge acquired in the study, rather than in the field, the market place, or the arena of public affairs. He declared that the useful work of the Spanish Cortes was the result of the labors of savants in their studies. But he praised the division of the three powers of government by the Cortes, a note indicating how dead was the old colonial system in the eyes of conservative but intelligent creoles.

In the same month the liberal Spanish constitution of 1812 was proclaimed in Guatemala, and in November the authorities there pledged allegiance to it. The town council, though some members were to lose hereditary privileges under the constitution, congratulated its deputy to the Cortes; and also suggested creation of a board to advise the Cortes on legislation pertaining to Central America.[41] The town councillors and other perpetual municipal officials were superseded, and all citizens, regardless of origin, made eligible for position on the new constitutional ayuntamientos. Elections to the reformed council at Guatemala City were held late in 1812.[42] Restrictions on the suffrage and on office-holding, however, confined the reform to a small proportion of the population. Nevertheless, the local nobility, the imperial officials, and the upper clergy were not pleased, feeling that their interests and position were threatened.[43] The captaincy general also began in 1812 the process of electing deputies to the Spanish Cortes of 1813.[44]

All did not proceed smoothly under the new dispensation. Early in 1813 the reformed town council of Guatemala complained to the Regency in Spain that Captain General Bustamante had not complied with the constitution and wished to prevent installation of the Provincial Deputation,[45] control of which was crucial, since it was to supervise the expanded functions of the town council.[46]

In October, 1813, the town council petitioned the appointment of Antonio Juarros to an intendancy, praising not only his general qualities, but his work for the Economic Society, noting that he had been secretary of the Society from its re-establishment to the end of 1812, when he was elected

---

[40] *El Amigo de la Patria*, I, No. 2 (October 6, 1820), 11-13.

[41] Bancroft, *Central America*, III, 10-11.

[42] Salazar, *Veintiún años*, 162.

[43] Villacorta, *Capitanía general*, 489.

[44] The area was allotted 12 seats, compared with 6 in the 1810-12 Cortes, and but one member of the Central Junta before that.

[45] Salazar, *Veintiún años*, 162, citing "Acta del Ayuntamiento, January 2, 1813."

[46] The Deputations were chosen by the same electors who named the town councils, and the Deputation in each province had joint jurisdiction with the chief civil officer (Bancroft, *Central America*, III, 8, 10 n. 23).

director. The petition praised all his labors in this regard, but especially that relating to "public enlightenment and the education of youth, source of the estate (*los bienes*) of societies."[47] Juarros, as a member of the old, unreformed town council of Guatemala, had signed without protest the liberal *instrucciones* to deputy to the Cortes Larrazabal.[48] For this, in 1815 during the reaction after the restoration of Ferdinand VII, he was barred from public office. On the other hand, another ex-secretary of the Economic Society, Sebastián Melón, did not come under the ban, because he had signed the *instrucciones* only under protest.[49]

In June, 1814, Bustamante had word of the restoration of Ferdinand; and later in the year published the royal decrees abrogating the constitution of 1812, which Ferdinand had with regal honor so recently sworn to uphold. The constitutional freedom of the press was abolished, the recently expanded powers of the town councils were contracted, and orders issued and executed for the public incineration of the *instrucciones* the town council of Guatemala had issued to its deputy to the Cortes. Larrazabal, himself, was imprisoned in Spain as a representative of a radical province to a radical assembly which had now been extinguished.[50] Extinguished also, of course, was the Spanish empire, the more rapidly for the mistakes of the Cortes and the uncompromising character of the regime of Ferdinand VII.

Bustamante could thereafter proceed against sedition with the backing of the metropolitan government. Before this time he had indeed been vigorous in handling revolts in Granada in 1811 and 1812, a conspiracy in the convent of Belén late in 1813, and a really serious disturbance in San Salvador early in 1814. These had resulted in a few executions and a number of imprisonments. But Bustamante could not continue indefinitely to deal drastically with rebels without the support of a determined home government, and while the Cortes opposed American independence, it did give the colonies privileges which stimulated demand for yet more reform. Now in 1814 Bustamante entered upon a policy of "thorough," established a close censorship, made arbitrary arrests, and was successful in preventing further open sedition. All this while the Plata region, Chile, New Granada, and Venezuela were either virtually independent or torn by insurrection aimed at independence. Bustamante managed at any rate to keep dissatisfaction from public expression.

---

[47] Cabildo of Guatemala to Sermo. Sor., presumably meaning either the Council of Regency or the Cortes—AGG, A1.2-5, leg. 2835, exped. 25296.
[48] *Supra*, 222-23.
[49] Salazar, *Veintiún años*, 184.
[50] Salazar, *Veintiún años*, 181-82; *Independencia de América*, No. 4755; BAGG, IV, No. 1 (October, 1938), 13 *et seq.*, printing some of the documents relating to these events.

The Society Under Ferdinand VII (1815-1821)

During the reaction the intellectual cooperation between enlightened Spaniards and creoles declined. The *Gazeta de Guatemala* appeared irregularly in 1815, and in 1816 suddenly expired. The Economic Society met in August, 1814, to hear José del Valle deliver a funeral elegy on Goycoechea, praising the co-founder of the Society for his intellectual accomplishments, and contrasting them with the lethargy of the captaincy general at the time of Goycoechea's birth. No mention was made, of course, of the direct and indirect effects of his stimulation of intellectual life on the political opinions of fellow creoles.[51]

The Society was in existence in 1815 but apparently not very active. The formation of a library was begun.[52] The Society long had wished to bring a mineralogist from Mexico and had entered into negotiations in 1812; in 1815 it still was attempting to raise funds for his compensation. The captain general, town council, and the Consulado all professed themselves unable to assist, either because of poverty or because of the illegality of the use of public funds as suggested by the Society. The Society itself was able to gather only 1,300 pesos of the 3,500 required.[53]

The oft-discussed project of a periodical published by the Society was, however, finally realized in 1815, under the editorship of José del Valle. It was issued every fifteen days from May 1, 1815, to April 15, 1816, when it died for want of sufficient subscribers.[54]

Archbishop Casaus was now director of the Society,[55] a circumstance alone sufficient to ensure the continued divorce of the Society from political reality, since Casaus was perhaps the bitterest opponent of independence in the *reyno*.[56] In March, 1818, Carlos Urrutia y Montoya succeeded Bustamante as captain general. By this time a good part of Spanish America was well on the way to independence. The captaincy general was quiet for the

---

[51] *El Amigo de la Patria*, I, No. 16 (February 19, 1821), 263-78; García Peláez, *Memorias*, III, 229-33; Francisco Fernández Hall, "Antonio de Liendo y Goicoechea, Poeta," *Boletín de la Biblioteca Nacional* [Guatemala], V, No. 1 (May, 1936), 40-43.

[52] *Relación de 1852*, 17, in mentioning the library of that later date, said it was begun in 1815.

[53] *Infra*, 342-44, on mining.

[54] Medina, *Imprenta en Guatemala*, No. 2157, calling it purely scientific.

[55] So identified in Bustamante to the Audiencia, January 26, 1815—AGG, A1-1, leg. 261, exped. 5757.

[56] In 1821 Casaus attended the meeting which decided on independence for Guatemala, but opposed the act and departed in protest (Villacorta, *Capitanía general*, 221).

next two years, though ships manned by South American revolutionists appeared at some of its ports.[57]

Although the Economic Society met in a general junta, October 25, 1818, the address of the director indicated that it was moribund. He said he was determined "to break the silence in this general junta" and turn it to its original purpose of the encouragement of the industrial arts, without which the state was weak and agriculture itself languished.[58] It is not clear when the Society ceased functioning, but it was apparently sometime previous to the declaration of Central American independence in September, 1821. In January, 1819, the Economic Society of Cadiz in Spain wrote to the town council of Guatemala about a system of mutual education, and sent copies of a "Practical Manual" to assist in encouraging it.[59] This suggests that the Guatemala Society was either inoperative or unknown to the Cadiz Society, or was not considered a useful agent for the encouragement of mutual education.

In March, 1820, word came to Guatemala of the liberal revolt of 1820 in Spain. Ferdinand VII again promulgated the constitution of 1812; and convoked a Cortes, in which Guatemala was accorded two temporary representatives until members could be elected in America. Freedom of expression was again established.[60] In Guatemala a new periodical with the significant name of *El Editor Constitucional* appeared July 24, 1820, edited by Pedro Molina, one of the first to have received the new medical education established at the university by Dr. Flores. The *Editor* became the organ of the party favoring independence from Spain.[61] The dying censorship made a futile attempt to prosecute Molina for *lèse majesté*, but he was absolved.[62] Another periodical, *El Amigo de la Patria*, begun October 16, 1820, under direction of José Cecilio del Valle, was in some measure the spokesman of more con-

---

[57] *Ibid.*, 81.

[58] *El Amigo de la Patria*, I, No. 10 (December 23, 1820), 118-22. Cf. Medina, *Imprenta en Guatemala*, No. 2214: Fr. Antonio López, *Instrucción para cultivar los nopales. ... La da a luz la Real Sociedad Económica de Guatemala. Reimpresa a expensas del Real Consulado. ...* (Beteta, 1818).

[59] José María Gutiérrez de la Huerta, Srio. de Actas e Int. de Correspondencias, to the Ayuntamiento of Guatemala, Cadiz, January 7, 1819—AGG, A1.2-5, leg. 2835, exped. 25310.

[60] Decreed by Cortes, October 22, 1820 (*Colección de los Decretos*, VI, 234-46).

[61] Alejandro Marure, *Bosquejo histórico de las revoluciones de Centro América. Desde 1811 hasta 1834* (2d ed., Guatemala, 1877-78), I, 20; Carlos Gándara Durán, *Pedro Molina. Biografía* (Guatemala, 1936), 94-96, *et passim;* Medina, *Imprenta en Guatemala*, 634; Salazar, *Historia intelectual*, 96-97, 321-22; Salazar, *Veintiún años*, 204-5.

[62] Pedro Zamora Castellanos, *El grito de la independencia* (Guatemala, 1935), 97.

servative opinion in opposition to the *Editor*, but its main aim was the discussion of scientific and other intellectual matters.[63]

The *Amigo de la Patria* in 1820 and 1821 carried a number of notices of the work of the Economic Society in earlier years.[64] Evidently nothing current required comment.[65] Very likely the Society was dead. The overriding concern of Valle's periodical with knowledge for its own sake led a historian many years later to declare that it was "infatuated with the pride of learning."[66] Its "Prospectus" of October 6, 1820, stated that it would offend no one, but would confine its work to the improvement of knowledge without which all prosperity was impossible, for "enlightenment is the fount whence flows wealth, the prime beauty of political societies, the greatest ornament of peoples."[67] And in its initial number the *Amigo*—that is, José del Valle —led off with:

> In the scale of being, man is first. In the scale of man the savant is the greatest. The savant is he who most nearly approaches divinity: he who gives honor to the species, and knowledge (*luces*) to the land.[68]

Both before,[69] and after,[70] independence Valle supported the conservative position. In other words, the political attachment of the creole Valle was less to Spain than to the conservative dispensation which he thought the imperial connection bolstered. He was like the members of the privileged minority in Spain who worked for some economic and intellectual liberalization by way of the Economic Societies, but who feared social and political change.

The *Editor Constitucional* from the beginning attacked the "serviles" in strong terms, and demanded that all officials support the constitution of the monarchy, by which it meant the document of 1812, not the ancient hash of

---

[63] Medina, *Imprenta en Guatemala*, 634; Salazar, *Historia intelectual*, 323-24.

[64] T. I, No. 2 (October 26, 1820), No. 10 (December 23), No. 12 (January 20, 1821), No. 16 (February 19), No. 23 (April 12); t. II, No. 4 (May 29, 1821).

[65] *Infra*, 249, for the *Amigo* and the Economic Society of Chiapa.

[66] Salazar, *Historia intelectual*, 323; cf. Virgilio Rodríguez Beteta, "El Amigo de la America," *Centro América*, X, No. 4 (October, November and December, 1918), 232-74.

[67] *El Amigo de la Patria. Prospecto* (Guatemala, 1820).

[68] T. I, No. 1 (October 16, 1820), 1, Valle confessed that this was from one of his own unpublished works.

[69] *Ibid.*, I, 97, contrasting the moderation of the *Amigo* with the material appearing in the *Editor*.

[70] The *Amigo* suspended publication briefly at the time independence was declared, but resumed in November, 1821, appealing to tradition, reviewing the laws given by Spain to America, dividing the 300 years of colonial history into three periods— under the monarchy, without a "fundamentel law"; under the constitution of 1812; and the period in which the constitution was annulled, 1814-20 (*ibid.*, II, 191-93).

forgotten practice that some men of Spain insisted was the constitution of the nation. The *Editor* found that life in Guatemala was less happy than it might be because of the "egoism" of many of its inhabitants.[71] This was a complaint the Economic Society had made. The *Editor* in an early number made a direct appeal for the "re-establishment of the Patriotic Society which was put on such a good foundation in the year [1]810." For one thing, this letter by "A True Patriot" asserted, an Economic Society would promote the production of cotton textiles.[72]

Thus both these periodicals were interested in the re-establishment of the Society; but it was not accomplished till 1829.[73]

---

[71] T. I, No. 6 (August 17, 1820), 44-46.
[72] No. 7 (August 21, 1820), Supplement.
[73] See Appendix for the Society after 1821.

CHAPTER TWELVE

Last of the Economic Societies Overseas

During the first two decades of the nineteenth century, Societies were founded or projected at Bogota, Buenos Aires, Caracas, in Puerto Rico, and Chiapas. The Society of Havana continued in existence; that of Guatemala was suspended from 1801 to 1810, was revived from 1811 to 1814, weakened and died after the latter date; the Manila Society was not active. Dead by this time were the Societies of Lima, Quito, Vera Cruz, Mompox, and Santiago de Cuba.

The Bogota Society

A Bogota Society did not issue from the foundation of the Mompox body in 1784 or from the visit of Espejo to the city later in the 1780's. If Espejo's discourse advocating a Society for Quito actually was printed at Santa Fe in 1789,[1] some of his acquaintances there may have seen it. And they must have heard of the formation of the Quito Society a few years later. In any event, it was presumably as feasible to form such a body at Santa Fe as elsewhere in America.

New Granada enjoyed a considerable stir of intellectual activity in the later eighteenth century. José Celestino Mutis of Cadiz was by the 1760's lecturing on mathematics and astronomy in the *colegio* of Rosario. Viceroy Manuel Guirior (1773-1776) suggested educational and economic improvements, including the distribution of spinning wheels. Archbishop Caballero

[1] *Supra*, 172.

Góngora as viceroy (1782-1788) promoted education, especially the natural sciences, and saw to the organization of the famous botanical expedition under Mutis. During the term of Caballero Góngora the mineralogical expedition under José D'Elhuyar—sometime teacher in the Seminary of Vergara—arrived, and the Economic Society of Mompox was formed and its *Extractos* printed at Bogota.[2]

Viceroy José de Ezpeleta (1789-1796) was interested in the culture of the Enlightenment, saw to the foundation of schools of primary instruction, and —like Caballero Góngora—proposed establishment of a university. Ezpeleta, who came from the governorship of Cuba, brought with him the writer Manuel Socorro Rodríguez, who soon founded the first Bogota periodical, *Papel Periódico de la ciudad de Santa Fe de Bogotá*, which began publication in February, 1791.[3] The *relación* (1796) of Ezpeleta to his successor gave a good deal on the sad state of culture and of economic life, but nothing on an Economic Society.[4] It was in 1794 during Ezpeleta's term that the creole Antonio Nariño printed a Spanish translation of the *Rights of Man and of the Citizen*.[5] Nariño planned to found a club on the model of associations of the learned at Venice, to discuss learned subjects, and read the better dailies and foreign gazettes and other materials. This was the origin of *El Casino*, ostensibly a literary but actually a political club.[6]

Viceroy Pedro Mendinueta y Múzquiz (1797-1803), being asked by some prominent citizens, including José Celestino Mutis, for license to establish an Economic Society, conceded it in November, 1801, sending Mutis a letter, November 25, informing him of the decision and enclosing a copy of the decree. The license permitted the members to hold a junta to name persons to form the statutes, with Mutis named as director of the junta, which was to be held at his residence.[7] The society was promoted in the new periodical *Correo Curioso de Santafe de Bogota*, by Jorge Tadeo Lozano, one of its editors. Lozano, born at Bogota in 1777, and educated at the *colegio*

---

[2] Cf. *Relación* (1789) of Caballero Góngora to his successor, giving a good deal on the condition of the realm but not mentioning an Economic Society (*Relaciones de Mando*, vol. VIII of *Biblioteca de Historia Nacional* [Colombia]). José M. Pérez Ayala, *Antonio Caballero y Góngora, virrey y arzobispo de Santa Fe, 1723-1796* (Bogota, 1951), does not mention the Mompox Society, but (p. 289) notes some Basque Society publications in the library Caballero gave to the archbishopric of Bogota in 1788.

[3] A *Gazeta de Santafé* had in 1785 a very brief life (José T. Medina, *La imprenta en Bogota 1739-1821* [Santiago, 1904], No. 13).

[4] In *Relaciones de Mando*.

[5] *Supra*, 141-42, on Nariño's imprisonment and defense.

[6] Botero Saldarriaga, *Francisco Antonio Zea*, 51, quoting a Nariño MS.

[7] Gredilla, *Mutis*, 225, prints the letter from Mendinueta to Mutis, and 225-26 the copy of the license sent to the latter by the former.

of Rosario, was interested in the new science, and like so many young men of the creole elite had traveled in Spain, where he also saw military service. Returning to New Granada, Lozano worked for the Botanical Expedition.[8] In the *Correo* in 1801 Lozano asserted that New Granada had as many advantages as Peru and Mexico, but that the latter were rich, while the former was decadent; and none of the methods used to improve the economy of the region had succeeded, despite "the fertility of the land" and "the marvellous variety of climate." New Granada needed a

> patriotic body which would be dedicated to the reform of customs by means of good education, and to introduce a good appreciation of industry and the arts. . . . The country in which the arts do not flourish, is not capable of being less than crowded with beggars and corrupt people. . . . More contemptible is the noble who passes his days in shameful idleness, than the artisan who professes however humble a craft.

A Society of Friends, he continued, should promote arts, agriculture, and industry; also, drawing, and public education in various kinds of work, so as to reduce idleness. In Lozano's opinion, these bodies worked well where they had been tried.[9] This combination of hope, frustration, and envy, we have seen in one Economic Society after another. From Madrid to Quito and Guatemala the members thought, or affected to think, that their own areas were peculiarly decadent.

In compliance with the decree of the viceroy, the first junta was held at the residence of Mutis, December 10, 1801. Mutis delivered a talk in which he said that this was a preliminary junta to form the constitutions of the organization, on the model of the peninsular Societies. He hoped that the example of the capital would lead other towns in the viceroyalty to establish Societies. The Santa Fe Society was to deal mainly with the region around the capital, with the chief branches of agriculture, stockraising, and the crafts. But it would occasionally have to deal with the obstacles due to the "enormous literary and civil difference" between the colonies and the mother country. He hoped that a great trade would flow between Spain and America, and the Society would try to promote it. There is not a hint that the Spaniard Mutis, who had spent so many years in America, feared that such a Society might cause friction between metropolis and colony. Mutis wrote the viceroy, December 11, 1801, informing him of the decisions at the above meeting,

---

[8] *Periodistas de los albores*, 6. He was shot by the Spanish in 1816, during the wars or independence.

[9] Lozano, "Sobre lo útil que sería ... una Sociedad Económica ...," *loc. cit.*

[10] Gredilla, *Mutis*, 226-27, printing the speech.

including the naming of four men to fashion the statutes of the Society.[11] There were twenty-three members of the group.[12]

The committee drew up the statutes and they were approved by the Society and by the viceroy early in 1802. The intention was to set up a veritable Economic Society, on the Spanish model, for the statutes asserted that the main interests of the body were: (1) agriculture and stockraising; (2) industry, commerce, and *policía;* and (3) the useful sciences and liberal arts. The statutes resembled those of the other Societies with regard to membership, dues, the publication of memorias, and the emphasis upon useful education.[13]

The Society never became operative. Viceroy Mendinueta in his *Relación* (1803) to this successor, at the end of his chapter on "La Población y la Policía" said a word on guilds of arts and crafts, pointing out that European economists had sufficiently discussed the guild organization. He wanted the government to do what it could to remedy the poor state of the arts and crafts in New Granada, though noting that government must depend on the aid of citizens of enlightenment who were *amantes del país.* And so he "desired the establishment of a Patriotic Economic Society . . . in this capital." But the papers on "the statutes of this Body, unknown in the *Reino*" had not yet been approved. Mendinueta expressed the hope that his successor would feel with him that "an Economic Society is useful and necessary in the *Reino.*" In view of the fact that the next chapter of Mendinueta's *Relación* dealt with "literary education," it would seem plain that he thought of an Economic Society in terms of economics and not of intellectual development.[14]

Just a few years later the periodical *Semanario del Nuevo Reino de Granada*, edited by the distinguished creole member of the Botanical Expedition, Francisco José Caldas, mentioned the project for a Society. This was in an article noting that agriculture and commerce required closer attention in the realm, peasants needed to depart from the old routine and employ new methods. If the best methods and devices were brought from Europe, then America would flourish and become prosperous. And proper attention would also improve commerce. But it was noted that the project for erection in

---

[11] *Ibid.,* 229-30, printing the letter.

[12] *Ibid.,* 229 n., calling them *subscriptores* and listing them, as taken from the paper of Mutis. One of the members was Jorge Lozano.

[13] *Ibid.,* 230-52, of which 232-52 are the statutes. But Gredilla drops his discussion of the Society abruptly after printing the statutes, with no indication as to whether the Society was ever really operative.

[14] "Relación del estado del Nuevo Reino de Granada, presentado por el Exmo. Sr. Virey D. Pedro Mendinueta a su sucesor el Exmo. Sr. D. Antonio Amar y Borbón. Año de 1803," in *Relación de Mando*, 411-588, at 487-88.

Santa Fe of "a patriotic company of commerce," announced in 1801, still had not been realized, though such a foundation "would be able to dissipate the darkness that surrounds us, and distribute the enlightenment necessary in this important matter."[15]

The *Semanario* carried other evidence of interest in economic development, pointing out the value of maps to business men,[16] and asserting that all else awaited the building of roads, for those of Antioquia were "entirely abandoned," and it was "incredible" that in two centuries a good road had not been constructed to link its towns with the Magdalena River, and

> The years and the generations have been heaped one on another, governors have succeeded governors, and nothing more has been thought of than wrangles and profits, neglecting entirely the happiness of the people.[17]

But Caldas was a scientist, and his other writings displayed almost no interest in the study of political economy, that vital fluid of the Economic Societies.[18]

The Buenos Aires Society

When the young creole Manuel Belgrano returned from his studies in Spain to become secretary of the Consulado of Buenos Aires, he brought in "his appreciable intellectual baggage" a knowledge of political economy gleaned in part from the writings of Campomanes and Jovellanos.[19] In a Consulado session, June 15, 1796, Belgrano presented a paper on economic development, pointing out that it was common practice for governments to aid the economy, Spain being no exception, for "few are the cities and towns of our Peninsula that do not have an Economic Society." Belgrano's suggestions as to how the Consulado of Buenos Aires could improve its own region indicated that

---

[15] Reissue of the 1808-10 periodical (3 vols., Bogota, 1942), II, 198 *et seq.*, "Memoria descriptiva del país de Santa Fe de Bogotá en que se impugnan varios errores de la de Mr. Leblond sobre el mismo asunto, leída en la Academia Real de las Ciencias de París, por D. José María Salazar, Abogado de esta ciudad," referring (p. 221, n. 22) to the *Correo Curioso* of Bogota as having examined the project.

[16] *Ibid.*, I, 51-54.

[17] *Ibid.*, I, 243 *et seq.*, "Ensayo sobre la geografía. Producciones, industria y población de ... Antioquia ..., por el Dr. ... Restrepo, abogado de la Real Audiencia de Santa Fe de Bogota," at 272.

[18] Cf. *Obras de Caldas* (Bogota, 1912), and *Cartas de Caldas* (Bogota, 1917), for hundreds of pages of evidence of his interest in science and lack of concern for economics.

[19] Ricardo Levene, *Ensayo histórico sobre la revolución de mayo y Mariano Moreno* (2 vols., Buenos Aires, 1920-21), I, 8-9. And see his: "Significación histórica de la obra económica de Manuel Belgrano," ch. xiii of t. V, sec. I of the *Historia de la Nación Argentina;* and, *Investigaciones acerca de la historia económica del virreynato del Plata* (2 vols.; La Plata, 1927), II, 109 n., on Belgrano's belief in the mutual dependence of agriculture, industry, and commerce—a main point in Campomanes' *industria popular*.

he would have been right at home in an Economic Society.[20] His memoria of the next year on the cultivation of flax and hemp also would have suited the Spanish Societies.[21] At a junta of the Consulado in June, 1798, he presented more ideas on political economy, advocating a great expansion of education; noting that England was first to form societies to deal with agriculture, the arts, and commerce, followed by France, Italy, Switzerland, and others; and that "our Peninsula is full of economic societies," working and studying industriously for improvement of the economy.[22] But no Economic Society was founded as a result of his remarks.

In 1800, however, a Spaniard, Francisco Antonio Cabello y Mesa, who had worked for the periodical press in Lima, asked permission at Buenos Aires to establish a Patriotic Literary Society, and the city's first periodical, the *Telégrafo mercantil*.[23] In the *Telégrafo* he at once praised the work of the periodicals and the *Sociedad de Amantes del País* of Lima, whence he had recently come, and said that since there were "hundreds of men of profound erudition" in the cities of the viceroyalty of La Plata, it too should have a *Sociedad de Literatos*.[24]

Although the *Telégrafo* received considerable support,[25] it began with an editorial complaint about trouble with people who did not care for the idea of the periodical, and lashed out at them as neither "sabios Argentinos" nor "ilustres Ciudadanos y verdaderos patriotas," but "certain pusillanimous spirits" who did not understand the utility of Cabello's projects. It was asserted that the *Telégrafo* would continue and the Patriotic Literary and Economic Society would soon be established.[26]

---

[20] *Documentos del archivo de Belgrano* (7 vols., Buenos Aires, 1913-17), I, 57-80, a MS. entitled: Medios Generales de Fomentar la Agricultura, Animar la Industria, Proteger el Comercio en un País Agricultor. ...

[21] *Ibid.*, I, 80-98.

[22] *Ibid.*, I, 99-115.

[23] *Telégrafo mercantil; rural, político-económico e historiógrafo del Río de la Plata* [April 1, 1801-October 17, 1802] (2 vols., Reimpresión facsimilar, Buenos Aires, 1914-15), I, 5-8, the "Censura del Señor D. Benito de la Mata-Linares," October 31, 1800, and the "Licencia del Superior Gobierno," November 6, 1800.

[24] *Ibid.*, I, 9-12, "Análisis"—of the periodical. Cf. Carlos Ibargurén, *Las sociedades literarios y la revolución argentina 1800-1825* (Buenos Aires, 1937), 13-14, on the probability that Cabello y Mesa exaggerated his role as a *periodista* at Lima.

[25] *Ibid.*, I, 23-29, "Lista de los señores subscriptores al Telégrafo," with 145 subscribers in Buenos Aires and another 100 outside, mostly in other parts of the viceroyalty; the Consulado, as "Protector de la Sociedad y el Telégrafo," was down for 21 copies. The issue of April 4, 1801, printed the Consulado's acceptance, March 30, 1801, of Cabello's request that the *Telégrafo* and the Society be taken under its protection.

[26] No. I (April 1, 1801). Cabello also attacked the "barbarous opinions of Scholasticism," a subject no partisan of the Enlightenment could resist.

Cabello printed a long article on Economic Societies in general, and the one he was proposing in particular. He quickly surveyed Societies within and without Spain, and said he meant to base his statutes on those of Vera, Benavente, and Medina de Río Seco in Spain. His Society would beware of admitting evil doers, nor would it take Negroes, foreigners, mulattoes, Chinos, Zambos, Quarterones, or Mestizos. After this expression of sound conservatism, he declared that the main aims of his Society would be the enlightenment of the country in science and literature. It would have twenty-one enumerated members, also corresponding members, and student members (*Caballeritos Alumnos*). He wanted an annual grant from the Consulado to support a library, as Catherine aided that of the Free Economic Society of St. Petersburg; and funds for prizes, noting that Charles III in 1775 ordered funds for the Madrid Society. Cabello said bluntly that he wanted not formal, "sterile" protection, but real help.[27]

Cabello wrote the Minister of the Indies from Buenos Aires, August 22, 1801, asking royal protection for the Society he wanted to found on the model of those "erected in Mexico, la Habana, and Huatemala [sic], to banish idleness and beggary, preparing boys for the crafts, and girls for all types of spinning," and declaring that the important corporations and people of Buenos Aires approved it. The statutes he sent along, suggesting that the Society be called the Royal Universal Society of Argentina, with its main objects agriculture, commerce, and the crafts, were not much like those of the Societies of Havana, Guatemala, or Madrid. He also proposed the membership of the Society's directive board, with himself as director; all the other officers were important *porteños*, including as secretary Manuel Belgrano.[28]

Hipólito Unánue, once active in the by then defunct Lima Society, wrote to Cabello from Peru in March, 1802, in praise both of Cabello's previous work with Lima periodicals, and in commendation of his "erudito Telégrafo."[29] But a royal order the next month, while approving the *Telégrafo*, did not favor the Society.[30] The periodical was suppressed

---

[27] *Telégrafo mercantil*, No. 2 (April 4, 1801), "Orígen de las Academias Literarias y Sociedades Patrióticas. Idea general de la que el Editor de este Periódico intenta erigir en esta Capital; y estado en que hoy se halla su establecimiento." He noted that his request for approval of the Society was in government channels.

[28] Documents in José Torre Revello, *El libro*, Apéndice No. 92, "Expediente relativo a la fundación del periódico 'Telégrafo Mercantil ...,' y de la Sociedad Argentina, patriótico-literaria y económica ...." Cf. Ortiz, *Hija cubana*, 38-39, for a letter of Cabello to a friend, discussing the Society.

[29] *Telégrafo mercantil*, June 13, 1802.

[30] The order, Aranjuez, April 12, 1802, to the Consulado of Buenos Aires, approving the latter's aid to the *Telégrafo*, but not to the Society, is in Torre Revello, *El libro*, Apéndice No. 92.

by the viceroy the same year,[31] and the Society probably never was organized.[32]

The *Semanario de agricultura, industria y comercio* of Buenos Aires, published from 1802 to 1807, while not mentioning Economic Societies, did display interests similar to those of the Societies. The material was contributed by men interested in science, commerce, and education. An article on education found fecundity and a large and robust population insufficient to ensure prosperity, for in America men in fertile regions with large populations were nonetheless poor; but only education could improve the situation, it being especially unfortunate that there was no agricultural school to serve this "purely agricultural people."[33] The arts and crafts in America should be confined exclusively to free men; not only should slaves be barred from crafts, but the slave traffic should be ended, since it not only caused misery to the slaves, but helped perpetuate poverty in America by making the arts and crafts unenticing. Whereas the real wealth of a state lay in the dedication of the population to work, the arts and crafts were not enough exercised in the Plata area, where the population would be too small for "six centuries"; nevertheless, much of this could be made up by hard labor.[34] Later numbers of the *Semanario*, in 1806-1807, increasingly dealt with international affairs and politics, being full of the reconquest of Buenos Aires, and of documents signed by Santiago Liniers. No population could read this sort of material without being stimulated by the flow of great affairs. This political development was one reason why the later Patriotic Society was not a body on the model of the Economic Societies proposed by Campomanes.

The Patriotic Society of 1812 seems to have come out of a radical group

---

[31] Ricardo R. Caillet-Bois and Julio César González, "Antecedentes para Explicar el Proceso de la Clausura del Telégrafo Mercantil, el Primer Periódico Impreso Bonaerense," *Revista de Historia de América*, No. 12 (August, 1941), 99-120; Juan Pablo Echagüe, "El Periodismo," ch. ii, in t. IV, sec. 2 of *Historia de la nación Argentina*. José de Bustamante y Guerra, then military commandant of Montevideo, played a part in the suppression of the *Telégrafo. Supra*, 225 *et seq.*, for his role in Guatemala a decade later.

[32] Ricardo Rojas, *La literatura argentina, Los Proscriptos*, ch. iv, "Primeras Asociaciones Literarias," claims that the first laical corporation at Buenos Aires was organized by Cabello and that its most important work was the periodical *El Telégrafo*, but he says nothing about the Society; and in the same work, *Los Coloniales*, ch. xi, "Orígenes del Laicismo Porteño," Rojas calls the *Telégrafo* the official organ of the Sociedad patriótico-literaria. Cf. Torre Revello, *El Libro*, Apéndice No. 93, for several documents of 1807-08, on Cabello's solicitation from Coruña of license to return to Extremadura, adducing his American services in proof of merit, including the plan for the Society of Buenos Aires.

[33] *Reimpresión facsimilar* (5 vols., Buenos Aires, 1928-37), No. 155 (September 4 1805), No. 157 (September 18).

[34] *Ibid.*, No. 184 (March 25, 1806), No. 186 (April 9).

that met in 1811 at the cafe of Marcos and indulged in inflammatory discussions against Spain, with much use of Raynal, Robertson, and Rousseau, a triad dear to the dissatisfied in America.[35] The inaugural address of Bernardo Monteagudo in January, 1812, did mention the need of education, but the heart of the discourse was in the denunciation of tyranny, and in such phrases as: "Sovereignty resides only in the people and authority in the laws."[36]

The Caracas Society

Caracas did not have a veritable Economic Society of Friends of the Country in the colonial era. The Guipúzcoa Company no doubt carried news of the Basque Society to Venezuela after 1765; it did not result in formation of an American body. The Basque Society itself only sent propaganda to Venezuela at a relatively late date.[37] The fact that a Society was not formed in Venezuela has not prevented speculation that the Basque Society must have exercised a unique influence there.[38] In any event, the Spanish Societies were founded only ten years after the Basque, and might well have inspired a Society in Venezuela. Certainly the interest in new ideas that was one source of enthusiasm for the Societies was present in Caracas, where the quarrel between the new science and scholasticism went on in the eighteenth century as in the rest of Spanish America.[39]

The Patriotic Society of Caracas was formed at a time when politics was becoming the main concern of the day. In April, 1810, an extraordinary cabildo of Caracas formed itself into a supreme junta and compelled the reputedly pro-French captain general to step down. The junta soon expelled the captain general and some other royal officials from the colony, and proceeded to rule in the name of Ferdinand VII who was the prisoner of Napoleon. The Regency at Cadiz thereupon declared Venezuela in a state

[35] Rojas, *Los Proscriptos*, ch. iv, 322-26, noting that the club of Marcos is poorly documented, and that there were similarities and differences in the two; cf. Juan Canter, "Las Sociedades secretas y literarias," ch. ix in t. V, sec. 1 of *Historia de la nación Argentina*, 274, claiming it had connections with masonry.

[36] "Oración inaugural pronunciado en la apertura de la Sociedad Patriótica la arde el 13 de enero de 1812," in Bernardo Monteagudo, *Escritos políticos* (Buenos Aires, 1916), 161-78.

[37] *Supra*, 45.

[38] Cf. Basterra, *Navíos*, 230 *et seq.*, for an inflated view of the cultural role of the Guipúzcoa Company in America; *ibid.*, 248-53, for the notion that the title of the Patriotic Society of Caracas of 1810 showed indebtedness to the Basque Society, and other rhetorical and uncritical attempts to show Basque influence while completely ignoring the Spanish Economic Societies; *infra*, 346 n., for other views of this author.

[39] Cf. Caracciolo Parra Pérez, *Filosofía universitaria*, 46 *et seq.*, for documentary evidence of this development.

of rebellion and proclaimed a blockade of its ports. This, together with the news of the bloody suppression of the revolutionary junta of Quito in August, 1810, drove the radical wing of the creole group yet further toward independence. By December, Miranda was back in the country and in command of the revolutionary army; by March, 1811, the congress of the American Confederation of Venezuela had met; in July it signed the declaration of independence; and by July, 1812, the counterrevolution had triumphed, Miranda was in irons, and Bolivar in flight.

In Caracas, August 14, 1810, the still nominally loyal supreme junta, in a decree noting the need of aiding agriculture, commerce, beneficent institutions, and the "public education of the youth of both sexes," provided for formation of a "patriotic society of agriculture and economy," which had for its main end "the improvement of all the branches of rural industry of which the climate of Venezuela is susceptible," and was to extend its investigations to whatever else might be thought patriotic.[40] So far as can be judged from the language of the decree, the purpose of the Society was economic progress. The same day the junta also abolished export taxes and extinguished the slave trade.[41]

The Society was not formed until April, 1811, by which time the political education of the creoles had proceeded a good deal further. It was a political club from the time of its establishment.[42] In June, 1811, appeared the first number of the organ of the Patriotic Society, the *Patriota de Venezuela*, which disseminated novel political ideas.[43] Spanish General Pablo Morillo reported in 1815 that the Patriotic Society had been a radical political body, which at first admitted only "true patriots and white persons," but after the declaration of independence (July, 1811), admitted "all classes and estates, white persons, mulattoes, Negroes, and Indians"; and allowed women to attend the evening meetings, after which the entire mixed crowd scandalously paraded the streets.[44] Clearly, the organization was not an Economic Society on the model of Campomanes.[45]

---

[40] *Gaceta de Caracas* (6 vols., Paris, Reproducción fotomecánica, 1939), II, No. 114.

[41] J. F. Blanco and R. Azpurua, *Documentos para la vida pública del libertador* (14 vols., Caracas, 1875-78), II, 587: "Tres grandes medidas dictadas por la suprema junta de Caracas en Agosto de 1810.—Abolición de la Trata.—Est° de una Sociedad Patriótica.—Libertad de Derechos de Exportacion."

[42] José Gil Fortoul, *Historia constitucional de Venezuela* (2 vols., Berlin, 1907-09), I, 195, that it was formed on April 19, 1811, "in imitation of the clubs of the French Revolution," and was revolutionary itself.

[43] W. S. Robertson, *Life of Miranda* (2 vols., Chapel Hill, 1929), II, 105.

[44] Morillo to Secretaro de Estado, Caracas, 1815, in *Boletín de la Academia Nacional de la Historia*, VII, No. 14 (November, 1920), 288-90.

[45] Cf. Lino Duarte Level, *Cuadros de la historia militar y civil de Venezuela desde*

In July, 1811, Bolivar briefly addressed the Patriotic Society in strictly political terms.[46] The same month, Dr. Miguel Peña defended the Society, asserting that the "metropolis had never permitted public enlightenment in its colonies," and that the Society had been formed at Caracas because of abuses, and because of the political situation in Spain. He spoke at length on tyranny and independence, and the revolution of the English colonies of North America.[47] In other words, he uttered the usual cry of the independence period that Spain had deliberately kept her colonies in ignorance, but his interest was in the current political implications of the quarrel with the metropolis.[48]

This Patriotic Society disappeared in the succeeding years of warfare. The later Economic Society founded at Caracas in 1829 was not built on that of the independence period.[49]

The Puerto Rico Society

The Puerto Rico Society was unique among those of America in that it was ordered founded by the government in Spain—the brief, liberal resistance government of Cadiz during the period of constitutional crisis.

Puerto Rico long had been in an evil economic case. In 1765 royal commissioner Alejandro O'Reilly reported on contraband trade there, the inadequacy of the armed forces, and the numerous vagabonds, including sailors who found it easy to exist in that climate without working.[50] The connections of the island with Spain were poor, especially after the beginning of the great French wars, no correspondence at all being received from the mother country in 1805. There was, however, some scientific and intellectual advance in these years, with vaccination being introduced from Danish St. Thomas

---

el descumbrimiento y conquista de Guayana hasta la batalla de Carabobo (Madrid, 1917), 256, for comment on the change of interest from economics to politics in the Society. Arellano Moreno, *Orígenes*, 445, suggests that two societies were formed in 1810—one of "economy and agriculture," which was "distinct from the Patriotic Society."

[46] Blanco and Azpurua, *Documentos*, III, 138-39.

[47] *Ibid.*, 139-43.

[48] Cf. Robertson, *Life of Miranda*, II, 105-6, 112-13, on the operations of the Patriotic Society, considering it a group with simply political interests, and more radical than the Congress; Francisco González Guiñán, *Historia contemporánea de Venezuela* (15 vols., Caracas, 1909-25), I, 24, calls the members "ardent democrats, propagandists for absolute independence"; and the subject is covered with a wealth of citation to back up the political character of the Society in Harold A. Bierck, Jr., *Vida pública de Don Pedro Gual* (Caracas, 1947), 45-48.

[49] See Appendix on the Caracas and other Venezuelan Economic Societies of 1829 and thereafter.

[50] Cayetano Coll y Toste, "Historia de Puerto Rico. Conferencia 24ª Segunda Mitad del Siglo XVIII. Rectificaciones Históricas," BHPR, XII (1926), 129-39, at 133.

in 1803, before the Royal Spanish vaccination expedition under Balmis arrived at Puerto Rico; and the press was introduced, also from St. Thomas, with the *Gaceta de Gobierno* commencing in 1806.[51] Furthermore, however poor the economic situation may have been, the population grew steadily, from about 44,000 in 1765, to some 93,000 in 1785, and more than 220,000 in 1815 or 1820.[52]

An Economic Society was suggested for Puerto Rico by Bishop Juan Alejandro de Arizmendi, in a representation to the king in 1801, mentioning the "felices efectos" of such bodies in other places, including Guatemala;[53] but this suggestion seems to have had no result.

A few years later, Puerto Rico elected Ramón Power y Giral (1775-1813) its representative, successively, to the Central Junta, the Council of Regency, and the Cortes in Spain, where he became identified with the liberal group of American deputies.[54] "Instructions" for Power were drafted by the town council of San Juan and by the towns of Arecibo, Aguada, and Cosmo. The San Juan instructions declared that while "education is the primordial base of the state," in all the island there were but three schools of primary letters, three classes of Latin, two chairs of philosophy and theology, and one of the "exact sciences." They asked a university, instruction in science and the humanities; a hospice where the mechanical arts could be practiced, since idleness was bad for a society; a charity hospital; permission to trade freely with friendly foreigners; and the formation of guilds in the hope of improving the quality of goods.[55]

---

[51] Coll y Toste, "Historia de Puerto Rico. Conferencia 26.ª—Principios del siglo XIX hasta la implantación en la isla de la constitución de Cadiz, en 1812. Rectificaciones históricas," BHPR, XII (1926), 277-84.

[52] Iñigo Abbad y Lasierra, *Historia geográfica, civil y natural de la Ysla de San Juan Bautista de Puerto Rico* (Nueva edición, anotada ... por José Julián de Acosta y Calbo, Puerto Rico, 1866), 306; Lidio Cruz Monclova, *Historia de Puerto Rico (Siglo XIX). T. I (1808-1868)* (Puerto Rico, 1952), 93. Cf. George Dawson Flinter, *An Account of the Present State of the Island of Puerto Rico* (London, 1834), 1-3, on the poor economic condition of the island before 1815, and 114, a table of "Amount of Imports and Exports from 1803 to 1830."

[53] Cruz Monclova, *Historia de Puerto Rico*, I, 66-67 n. 124, quoting the representation from the Archivo General de Indias.

[54] Neumann Gandía, *Benefactores de Puerto-Rico*, I, 343-54; Coll y Toste, "Historia de Puerto Rico—Conferencia 26.ª," *loc. cit.*, 282, 284. Power, born in Puerto Rico of a Basque father and Catalan mother, in 1787 went with his brother to study at the Seminary of Vergara, later studied in France, and then entered the School of Marine Guards at Cadiz in 1792, and was in 1811 a frigate captain when elected Puerto Rican representative to the Central Junta.

[55] "Instrucciones y Poderes dados al diputado don Ramón Power por el Ayuntamiento de San Juan y las villas de Arecibo, Aguada y Cosmo," BHPR, X (1923), 102-38. The instructions are dated 1810.

The Council of Regency in November, 1811, ordered the creation of an intendancy for Puerto Rico, with the intention of promoting the prosperity of the island, and on the advice of Power selected for the position Alejandro Ramírez, then resident in Guatemala. The Regency's order, showing the great value it put upon the Economic Societies, also directed Ramírez:

> Ultimately, with the view of planting and fixing an instructive and solid method in the administration of this isle, to aid industry, to put in practice all the best possible, to make its labor and agriculture flourish, and to propagate useful knowledge, the same intendant will take care to create and organize an Economic Society of Friends of the Country, under the rules and statutes with which those of Spain were established, with the differences, which the diversity of countries and the variety of ends dictate, making in due time a regulation, and sending a copy [to Spain].[56]

Ramírez, leaving his membership in the Guatemala Society, and his other interests there, traveled to his new post via Campeche and Havana, and took over his functions in February, 1813. He drew up statutes for the Economic Society the same year;[57] they were approved by the government in Spain by the middle of 1814, and published in the *Diario Econômico de Puerto-Rico*, itself a creation of Ramírez in collaboration with José Andino.[58]

The statutes said the Society was created, "like the others of its class," to advance agriculture and industry, to circulate light and knowledge in those fields, "which are the fundament of the public felicity," and to introduce new methods suitable to the island. Four permanent "commissions," with three to five members each (a modest enough membership) were provided: (1) The commission on agriculture would collect seeds, instruments, and machines; cultivate an experimental field; give prizes; and issue sheets explanatory of new techniques. (2) The industrial commission would try to find means for occupying the idle of both sexes; import new techniques; give prizes; and create a school of drawing. (3) The commission on population

---

[56] "Real Orden de 28 de noviembre de 1811 ...," in Zamora y Coronado, *Legislación ultramarina*, III, 619-20; and for an assertion that the Regency ordered, December 11, 1811, formation of an Economic Society at San Juan, cf. *Acta de Junta pública celebrada por la Sociedad Económica de Amigos del País de Puerto Rico el día 27 de Junio de 1844* (Puerto Rico, 1844), as reprinted in BHPR, VII (1920), 354-72, at 355. *Supra*, 61-62, for the attitude of the irregular governments of Spain toward the Societies in the period of constitutional crisis.

[57] "Fundación de la Sociedad Económica de Amigos del País ...," in BHPR, I (1914), 295-96; Alejandro Ramírez, Primer Intendente of Puerto Rico, to the Gobierno Superior, Puerto Rico, August 27, 1813, in *ibid.*, VI (1919), 212.

[58] "Fundación de la Sociedad," *loc. cit.*; "Estatutos de la Real Sociedad Económica de Puerto Rico, Aprovados por S. M. en Real Orden de 2 de Julio de 1814, por el Ministro Universal de Indias," BHPR, VII (1920), 56-62; José Toribio Medina, *Notas bibliográficas referentes a las primeras producciones de la imprenta en algunas ciudades de la América española ...* (Santiago, 1904), 69.

would regularize local police regulations; import laborers and find them work. (4) The public instruction commission would push primary letters, without prejudicing the work of the town councils in that field; try the Lancasterian method of mutual instruction; establish a circulating library and a periodical paper "destined to economic matters, accommodating them to the common intelligence"; give literary prizes; and at opportune times found classes or schools of mathematics, experimental physics, chemistry, botany, practical agriculture, and civil economy.

The statutes listed as ex-officio members all parish priests, and most other influential persons, including the town councils, the ecclesiastical chapter, the merchants, and the military. Anyone could be a member who applied to the director with the proper display of public spirit. But while *socios de número* could include anyone voted in by the membership, they had to be Spanish (that is, not a foreigner or a Negro), a *vecino* or resident of the capital, of good conduct, and with a decent occupation. Except for a few of the officers, the members were to take their seats at the juntas in the order of their arrival, "without ceremony or etiquette." No elections were to be by acclamation, and all re-elections required two-thirds of the votes. Presumably these last were devices to forestall the gravitation of the offices permanently into the hands of men prominent in the community.

Ramírez became the first director of the Society, but there was little activity before he left, in 1816, to assume the superintendency of Havana. The government of Ferdinand VII, after his restoration in 1814, apparently reposed no immediate great hopes in the Society.[59] A general junta was held in 1821, but it is not clear that any were held earlier.[60]

The Chiapas Society

Chiapa (today the Mexican state of Chiapas) was the northernmost province of the captaincy general of Guatemala. Communication between that area

---

[59] Cf. Real cédula de S. M., la que contiene el reglamento para la población y fomento del comercio, industria y agricultura de la isla de Puerto-Rico, August 10, 1815 (*Apéndice a los tomos I, II, III y IV de la obra decretos del rey d. Fernando VII ...* [Madrid, 1819], 45-54), which grants quite extensive privileges to Puerto Rico for the improvement of its economy, but does not mention the Economic Society.

[60] For a suggestion that the Society did not exist in 1815, see Zamora y Coronado, *Legislación ultramarina*, II, 239-40. Cruz Monclova, *Historia Puerto Rico*, 118, has it organized in Ramirez' time, without specifying date, and notes (p. 148) that it received a new impulse from the constitutional regime instituted in Spain in 1820, having scarcely existed before then. Richard J. and Elizabeth Van Deusen, *Porto Rico. A Carribbean Isle* (New York, 1931), 87-88, 257, can cite no Society activity in 1813-20. See Appendix for the Puerto Rico Society in 1821-98.

and the capital was difficult. Its ties with New Spain were close. Its isolation was presumably one factor in the creation in 1819 of the Economic Society of Friends of the Country of Chiapa. The founder was a native of that region, Friar Matías de Córdoba, whom we have encountered as winner in 1798 of the Guatemala Society's essay contest on dressing and shoeing Indians and *ladinos*. He had gone as a boy to the city of Guatemala, where he studied at the convent of Santo Domingo and at the university, and received the tonsure as a Dominican. His biographer declares that Córdoba could not stomach Aristotelianism and had recourse instead to modern philosophers. In 1800 he returned to Ciudad Real, Chiapa, to teach in the Dominican house there. Together with some other members of his Order, he conceived the idea of separating this province of the Dominican Order from that of Guatemala, in order to improve its administration. This at least was the ostensible motive.

Córdoba journeyed to Spain for this purpose in 1802 or 1803, and received permission for the division. He was in Madrid in 1808 when the French entered, whereupon he fled to Cadiz, and arrived back in Chiapa early in 1810. There he established a primary school, wrote a book for instruction in rhetoric, and became provincial of his Order in 1815. When news of the Mexican autonomist Plan of Iguala arrived in Chiapa in 1821, Córdoba declared at once in favor of independence from Spain. He would have preferred continuation of the attachment of Chiapa to Guatemala, but topography, local opinion, and the superior strength of Mexico moved the territory into the jurisdiction of that country as it became independent.[61] As late as May, 1821, the Economic Society of Chiapa was reporting to Guatemala its efforts to open roads in the north and urging the latter to do the same.[62]

---

[61] Flavio Guillén, *Un fraile prócer y una fábula poema* (*estudio acerca de fray Matías de Córdoba*) (Guatemala, 1932), 15-16, 19, 24, 51-52, 67-68; Vela, *Literatura guatemalteca*, 211-20; Batres Jáuregui, *América Central*, II, 523-24; "Fray Matías de Córdova. Homenaje de la Sociedad de Geografía e Historia de Guatemala," ASGH, VIII, No. 1 (September, 1931), 3-78; *Acta de instalación de la Sociedad Económica de Amigos de la Patria de Chiapa. Celebrada ... 1819* (Guatemala: Beteta, n.d.).

[62] *El Amigo de la Patria*, II, No. 4 (May 29, 1821), 27-32, printing letter from Córdoba, as director of the Chiapa Society, Ciudad Real, May 8, 1821, including a list of merchants of Campeche who contributed to the road.

PART THREE

Aims and Activities of the Colonial Societies

CHAPTER THIRTEEN

Organization and Method

This chapter deals with the methods of the overseas Societies, their relationships with other institutions, their membership, and their finances.

Methods of the Colonial Societies

Their methods were those of the Spanish bodies, though only the Guatemala and Havana put them to much of a test. The main reliance was on the collection and dissemination of information by the members, serving in part as "an intermediary influence" between the savant and ordinary folk.[1] The chief methods were: division into working groups, regular meetings, preparation of papers, publication, prizes, public juntas, schools and classes of instruction, and collection of books, seeds, instruments, and other materials. The methods were well suited to the character and resources of the Societies. They could influence the small but important literate class, and possibly the government; they could scarcely reach the bulk of the populace or immediately and fundamentally alter the economy. It was for this reason that "patience" was enjoined upon the members of the Guatemala Society.[2] They set great store in the promotion of the spirit of emulation.[3]

Organization followed the Spanish model. Some officers were chosen by

---

[1] Havana *Memorias 1793*, 4.

[2] *Quarta junta pública*, 26.

[3] E.g., Havana *Memorias 1793*, 23-24, on a proposal to erect statues of distinguished men, a project pursued in later years.

secret vote, an uncommon procedure in Spanish America.[4] This principle
of equality appeared also in a deprecation of etiquette and precedence. Even
the Academic Society of Lima inclined to this notion. In Guatemala the
members were said to be simply "citizens,"[5] and places were assigned only
to four officers, and the statutes forbade other "preference" of seats. This
principle of Peñaflorida and Campomanes, making the Economic Societies
congregations of peers, was the more striking in America in that it somewhat
contradicted the ancient assumption of creole inferiority.

Since accurate data were necessary for sound economic planning, the
Societies were interested in practical descriptive and statistical information.
The Guatemala and Havana Societies printed a fair amount of this type of
information, and the latter in 1817-1820 published it in great quantity.[6]

Methods of disseminating knowledge included gifts of spinning wheels
and seeds; promotion of new crops and plants; introduction of industrial
devices, as cotton gins and a fulling-mill in Guatemala;[7] and naming corresponding, meritorious, honorary, and consulting members, which had the
further advantage of committing important personages to the Societies.

Assignment of members to working divisions was usual in America as in
Spain. Three or four was the common number, and agriculture, industry,
and arts and crafts the essential categories. Several Societies included
commerce in the title of a class; others included science, public ornament,
politics, belles-lettres, enlightenment, natural history, and education.

All the Societies provided for discussion and study in regular—usually
weekly—meetings, but, as in Spain, attendance was light, with perhaps
twenty or thirty men ordinarily at the meetings of the Havana and Guatemala
Societies.[8] These meetings permitted an exchange of ideas with a minimum

---

[4] *Infra*, 340, for voting in the Guatemala Society's guild regulation. The administration fell largely on the secretaries and treasurers. The officers of the Guatemala
Society held preparatory juntas to plan activity. The Guatemala secretary was especially
active in handling the correspondence with members outside the capital.

[5] "Puros ciudadanos" (*Novena junta pública*, 51).

[6] Examples in Guatemala included inquiries concerning cotton culture and weaving,
and the work of its commission on cacao plantations. The tables in the Havana
Mémorias of 1817-19 contain data on taxes, duties, white colonization, population,
commerce, and other subjects.

[7] *Infra*, 340, the Guild Regulations of the Society calling for the import of machines.

[8] Attendance at the first 28 ordinary juntas of the Havana Society (January 8-
July 11, 1793) ranged from 15 to 46 members, with 27 the average; at many of the
meetings later in 1793 and in 1794 even fewer attended, and only a very few with
any regularity ("Actas" of the first 81 juntas, January 9, 1793-July 24, 1794, in
Memorias 1880, 3-57, 66-104). The Guatemala Society from 1795 to 1800 held more
than 100 "ordinary juntas" on Saturdays, to which the full membership was invited,
but to which a minority came (cf. AGG, A1.6, leg. 2007, exped. 13852, the secretary

of supervision. Both the membership and the range of interest were broader than in the Consulado, town council, or university. But as was inevitable in organizations of the character of the Economic Societies, considerable time was consumed by innocuous discourses that served a fraternal or social end.

The annual or semiannual public juntas were sometimes gatherings of the local elite of both sexes. This was notably the case in Guatemala; apparently not so in Havana. Plebians might be invited: artisans were summoned to the inauguration of the Quito Society; eighty master-craftsmen attended a public junta at Guatemala in 1797. At public juntas in Guatemala there might be a preliminary discourse; the secretary's report; an intermission for music and inspection of exhibits by artisans, or of products from the Society's vocational schools, or of materials sent in from the provinces; and then, more discourses. At one junta some thirty exhibits included flax from a member's hacienda, minerals from León and Segovia in Nicaragua, Bayal flax-plant from Vera Paz, a variety of textiles, porcelain, images of saints, and an English-style piano.[9] While the sweep of the Guatemala Society's interest early aroused government suspicion, it must be supposed that the social motive in such a provincial town was as strong with many of the gentlemen members and their ladies as the desire to promote the aims of the Society. The annual *juntas generales* at Havana were business meetings, not ceremonial occasions for the public.[10]

Prizes were commonly offered. The Lima Society offered a medal for an essay on the improvement of roads, and even the abortive Bogota Society proposed three prizes each in the categories of agriculture, industry, and literature. The Havana Society offered prizes in 1793-1795 for essays on Cuban agriculture and means of improving it, on the value of good roads, on tile and brick;[11] the six subjects for 1794 were largely economic.[12] No one volunteered to win the prizes offered in December, 1794, within the next year.[13] Prize contests in Guatemala, as in Spain, fell in two categories: econo-

---

attests the election of officers in November, 1798, by only some 30 members). This makes the provision of the statutes that the classes of members meet on different days, so that individuals might attend all, seem optimistic.

[9] *Novena junta pública*, 5-6; cf. *Octava junta pública*, note at end, for inventory of items at the junta.

[10] Cf. "Juntas Generales" of December 9-11, 1794, in Havana *Memorias*, ser. 5.ᵃ, t. IX (Habana, 1864), 187-92, showing 43 members the first day attending to routine.

[11] *Memorias 1793*, 72-73.

[12] *Memorias 1794*, loc. cit., 437.

[13] *Memorias 1795*, 83. Cf. Peraza y Sarausa, "Indice," RBC, LI, 455, for contest of 1798 on slave labor; LII, 139, for prize essay on the advantages of fairs (*ferias*) for Cuba; LXIV, 180-84, prizes for good teaching.

mic production, and literary merit. The first category embraced such matters as spinning and weaving, and flax, cotton, and cacao culture; the second, such questions as the state of literature in Guatemala, the desirability of educating Indians, the usefulness of persuading Indians and *ladinos* to wear European-style clothes, and methods of improving the commerce of the region. Some of the essays were printed by the Society and either distributed gratis or sold. The prizes were chiefly small sums of money, medals, spinning wheels, or membership in the Society. But it was hard to persuade many people to enter the contests,[14] and the results of such competition were unimpressive. It could not be expected that gold medals distributed to Indians by priests to stimulate flax culture would have much effect. And literary contests could not deal with serious matters too seriously—especially if the essays were printed—without alarming officialdom, as happened with the contest on Indian dress.

A program of publication was the single most promising method open to the Societies, but also the most likely to arouse the fears of government. Only the Havana and Guatemala Societies managed much in this field, and their work suffered serious interruptions. They did almost nothing in the way of reprinting European works: the Guatemala Society in the 1790's published a tract on guilds, taken from the *Semanario erudito;* and the Havana in 1819 an extract from Say's treatise on political economy. The Havana Society in 1794 took over direction of the *Guía de Forasteros*.[15] Their other publications were directly related to their own labors, consisting chiefly of accounts of public juntas or memorias on various subjects or reports on Society activities. The separate publication by the Guatemala Society of some of the essays submitted in its contests falls essentially into this category.[16] Even the abortive Bogota Society meant to print memorias containing information on economic and scientific questions, including "cálculos políticos sobre el comercio."

Memorias similar to those of the Spanish Societies were published by the Havana Society for 1793-1795, and for 1817-1819 and part of 1820. The Guatemala Society published shorter accounts of public juntas in 1796-

---

[14] Guatemala *Quinta junta pública*, 14: only one essay had been submitted on the "utilidad de que los Magistrados tengan constancia de los medios con que subsisten los individuos del Pueblo."

[15] "Junta ordinaria," December 19, 1793 (*Colección de Actas 1880*, 63-64); *Memorias 1794, loc. cit.*, 436; *Memorias 1895*, 121-25, on the *Guía*, published by the Society from 1795 to 1868; *Memorias 1863*, 4.ª ser. t. VIII, 310; Peraza y Sarausa, "Indice," RBC, LVI, 70, *Papel Periódico* (June 1, 1794) reference to Society and *Guía*.

[16] Cf. also Havana *Memorias 1795*, 85, the report of the deputation on the Casa de Beneficencia was ordered printed in 400 copies for public information.

1798 and 1811-1812.[17] Although the Havana and Guatemala publications of this class in 1793-1798 totaled only 708 pages, this did not compare too badly with Spanish Societies, since even the Madrid did not bring out its *memorias* regularly. The American materials did represent an innovation for that area, and gave public notice of local aspirations and discontent.

More of the Societies promoted periodicals. The Academic Society of Lima, though unlike the Economic Societies in most respects, did publish the *Mercurio Peruano*, disseminating thereby some of the ideas held by the other Societies. The Havana Society directed the *Papel Periódico* (renamed *Aviso* in 1805 and *Diario* in 1810), using it to publicize the Society,[18] and its profits were used to support the public library of the Society. It had 196 subscribers in 1793; other copies were sold at the press. The Society proposed, "if it were possible and permitted," to subscribe to foreign, as well as Spanish and American, periodicals.[19] The Guatemala Society favored "public papers,"[20] and maintained close relations with the *Gazeta de Guatemala*, though refused permission to take it over entirely.[21] Later, when the Society was given its second lease on life, during the liberal period of the Cortes of Cadiz, it decided it needed a periodical of its own, to deal only with *ilustración*. The Society claimed that Havana published ten *papeles* of this class. Although the Guatemala Society linked this venture with the recent decree of the Cortes on liberty of the press,[22] it was not until 1815-1816,

---

[17] The Havana *memorias* for 1793-95 totaled 551 pages (and 5 tables); those for 1817-20, totaled 1,352 pages (and 28 tables), and much more nearly resembled those of the Madrid Society, with many government orders and much statistical data. The Guatemala *juntas públicas* for 1796-98 totaled 157 pages; those of 1811-12 (including the *Junta General No. 102*) totaled 115 pages. Both Societies published *memorias* in later years (see Appendix). Cf. Havana *Memorias 1895*, 129-31, that the *memorias* for 1793 and 1795 were issued in editions of 200 copies each.

[18] Cf. Havana *Memorias 1795*, 79, for a decision to print a discourse in the periodical.

[19] *Memorias 1793*, 63-71, on the Society's early connections with the *Periódico*, the importance it assigned to it, the emphasis on economic questions; later *memorias* contained reports on it. *El Aviso*, No. 65 (October 29, 1805), announcing that the Society had set tariffs for notices, with one real the rate for sale of a slave, flunkey, mule, or other chattel; *Aviso*, No. 13 (June 30, 1805), No. 14 (July 2, 1805), No. 19 (July 14, 1805), No. 33 (August 15, 1805), No. 42 (September 5, 1805), for more on the Society and the periodical. Cf. Peraza y Sarausa, "Indice," RBL, LVII, 74; Emilio Roig de Leuchsenring, *et al.*, *El sesquicentenario del Papel Periódico de la Havana* (Havana, 1941).

[20] *Quarta junta pública*, 6-7, favoring them for the promotion of agriculture; noting that Godoy sent the prospectus of a *Semanario de agricultura, artes, y oficios*, to the archbishop of Guatemala, and the latter sent to Spain for copies for the Economic Society.

[21] *Supra*, 213-14.

[22] *Octava junta pública*, 30-31, for the proposal for the new periodical, and reference to the decree; and the last page (unnumbered) for a strong statement regarding the advantages of free expression.

during the reactionary period under Ferdinand VII, that it brought out its short-lived *Papel Periódico de la Sociedad Económica.*

Cabello y Mesa in founding the *Telégrafo Mercantil* of Buenos Aires coupled it with a scheme for a Society, having observed in Lima the link between the Academic Society and the *Mercurio.* The short-lived Quito Society supported the even shorter-lived *Primicias de la Cultura de Quito.* The statutes of the Puerto Rico Society called for a popular economic periodical, and were themselves printed in the new *Diario Económico de Puerto Rico,* of which Ramírez, promoter of the Society, was a founder. The new *Correo Curioso* of Bogota favored establishment of a Society.

These periodicals, whether or not directed by Economic Societies, did disseminate news of their activities. But such notice was not a complete substitute for regularly issued publications dealing solely with Society interests. On the other hand, though the Societies might have spent more on publications, it is not clear how large the return would have been. The Guatemala Society in the first three and one-half years of its existence spent less on printing than on furniture, but it could not dispose of the items it did print, even though it distributed them free and tried to sell others through an agent in Mexico. The account of the first public junta of the Society was printed in 212 copies, but in more than a year the Society only managed to distribute three-fourths of so small an edition.[23] And at the time the Society was suspended in 1800 its printer and bookseller still had on hand many copies of Society items.[24]

The American Societies did not do much in the way of research for government, which is not surprising in the colonial realm, and it will be remembered that in Spain this function was important only with the Madrid Society. In the 1790's the Guatemala Society did undertake a study of guilds on royal order, and the captain general did direct the Society to a study of locusts; but the secretary of the Society was optimistic in declaring in 1812 that it was newly become a "political body auxiliary to the government." The Havana Society in 1817-1820 began to function in close collaboration with

---

[23] AGG, A1.6, leg. 2007, exped. 13836, Quaderno de los muebles y alhajas ..., of late 1798. Of the 212 copies, 54 were undisposed of, including 12 with Society member José Mociño in Mexico; also on hand were 25 copies of the second *Junta pública* (including 12 with Mociño), 133 copies of the third Junta, and 132 of the fourth; also, 86 copies of Córdoba's essay on Indian dress, 145 copies of Goycoechea's essay on mendicity, and 308 of the Society statutes.

[24] Including 8 of Goycoechea on mendicity; 245 of the statutes; and 300 of the *Memoria de Jiquilite,* which had just been printed—AGG, A1.6, leg. 2008, exped. 13854, Cuenta ... rendida por Dn. Ygnacio Beteta; August 6, 1800.

Intendant Alejandro Ramírez,[25] but his successor did not encourage the Society.[26]

Relations with Other Institutions

The American Societies had virtually no relations with each other or with the Spanish Societies. What they knew of each other came from the travels of individuals or from reading; there was no institutional interchange. The Quito Society subscribed to the *Mercurio Peruano*, and the latter commented favorably on the foundation of the former, but both were suppressed before a relationship developed. A few men belonged to more than one Society,[27] but this had no important effects. A few efforts were made to get in touch with Spanish Societies;[28] nothing of consequence resulted therefrom. The Havana Society tried to develop a relationship with the Santiago body, but the latter was virtually dead, so nothing developed. The Havana Society in 1816 had a deputation in Spain to keep in touch with the Madrid Society; apparently it did little before 1820.[29] The Guatemala Society was the most anxious to widen its field of vision and action. It had in its archives in 1798 a copy of the Havana statutes.[30] Its effort to extend its influence into Mexico was a factor in the government decision to order its suspension in 1799. After the Society had been re-established a decade later, Antonio Juarros of Guatemala wrote the Havana Society that all the Economic Societies had a common object, and that those of Havana and Guatemala should cooperate.[31] Nothing came of this suggestion.

---

[25] Cf. Havana *Memorias 1817*, 3, for his comprehensive idea of what he would like published in a "papel periódico científico." His influence is seen in the mass of statistical data in the tables in the Memorias, and in the many public documents.

[26] See chaps. XIV-XV for educational and charitable methods of the Societies.

[27] Jacinto Calero of the Lima Society was admitted to the Havana when he stopped in Havana en route to Europe ("junta ordinaria," June 20, 1793, in *Colección Actas 1880*, 27). Baquíjano belonged to the Basque, Lima, and Havana Societies. Juan Ortiz de Letona of the Truxillo corresponding junta of the Guatemala Society was also a member of the Havana. José Julian Hernández, a royal official of Comayagua, belonged to the Havana and Guatemala Societies. Dr. Florencio Pérez y Comoto of Mexico was a member of the Havana Society and a consultant of the Guatemala.

[28] The Guatemala Society provided in its guild regulation that help be sought from Spanish Economic Societies. The Havana Society in 1793 decided to get information on educational methods from the Madrid Society ("junta ordinaria," February 28, in *Colección Actas 1880*, 10-11); it also wanted to get the *informes* of the Madrid Society on hospices (*ibid.*, 16-17, "junta ordinaria," April 4, 1793).

[29] Cf. *Memorias 1863*, 4ᵃ ser., t. VIII, 127, correspondence between the Society and Guatemala in 1793, before there was a Society in the latter place.

[30] AGG, A1.6, leg. 2007, exped. 13836, Quaderno de los muebles. ...

[31] The Juarros note, dated April 3, 1813, was written on a copy of the printed *Manifiesto de la Sociedad Económica de Guatemala sobre su restablecimiento*, being the decree of Captain General González, with the title in manuscript. The Havana Society

Although the Havana and Guatemala Societies existed long enough to have established relations with organizations outside the Spanish world, they did not. Despite their location in America, they did not match the relationship between the Valencia Society and the American Philosophical Society of Philadelphia.[32] There was one feeble connection with the latter, through the Spaniard Alejandro Ramírez, the only resident of Spanish America admitted to the Philadelphia Society before 1822, although between 1784 and 1805 it admitted thirteen residents of Spain.[33] The Havana Society would seem to have been especially well placed for communication with Philadelphia,[34] but that Society remained nearly as isolated as the others.

The case of Ramírez is a striking illustration of the isolation of the American Societies. He was admitted to membership in the American Philosophical Society in 1801, while a resident of Guatemala, but did not receive confirmation of his election until nearly two decades later, when he was intendant at Havana.[35] From Havana, March 28, 1817, he wrote to John Vaughn at Philadelphia, in English with a Spanish postscript:[36]

> As I have lived for many years past in very remote parts of South America, my communications with the P.[hiladelphia] S.[ociety] were very difficult. I was as yet entirely ignorant whether I was really a member of that respectable Body; no more than a simple insinuation having received thro Mr. Yard [?] about my election in 1801.

Thanking them for receipt of his certificate of membership, Ramírez now hoped to be able to do something both as a member of the Philosophical Society, "and as President of the new regenera [ted Society of this?] Island [. . .] small proof of my wishes to take the liberty to send you the first three Nos. of our monthly memoirs." And he noted that

> The Gazeta de Guatemala was, I can say, one of my first literary Essais. I was too young, and think them little worthy your notice, except only as a rarity from an

---

heard the Juarros' note in its junta of July 30, 1813—Biblioteca de la Sociedad Económica de la Habana, Archivo, No. 4, leg. 14.

[32] *Supra*, 59.

[33] *The American Philosophical Society Year Book 1949* (Philadelphia, 1950), 432-44, "Former Foreign Members." No members for Spain were admitted in 1806-21, and no residents of Latin America before Ramírez in 1801, or thereafter until a Brazilian was so honored in 1822.

[34] Cf. Harry Bernstein, "Some Inter-American Aspects of the Enlightenment," in Whitaker, *Latin America and the Enlightenment*, 57: in 1801 the American Philosophical Society "entrusted care of its periodic Spanish shipment to José de Arango" of the Havana Society.

[35] *Early Proceedings of the American Philosophical Society. . . . From the Manuscript Minutes of its Meetings from 1774 to 1838* (Philadelphia, 1884), January 16, 1801, for the election of Alex. Remerez [sic], First Secretary to the Junta of Guatemala.

[36] Archives of the American Philosophical Society, Philadelphia, for the original.

unknown Country. Something more interesting has been printed there the late years. I'll take care to procure it for your library, together with a set of the Mercurio Peruano, the Santafe de Bogata Semanario. . . .

Veo que Um. entiende y escribe el Español que Yo el Inglés. En adelante me tomaré la satisfacción de hablar a U. en mi lengua.

The Philadelphia Society duly noted in 1817 and 1818 contributions to the library by Ramírez.[37]

The isolation of the American Societies was remarked by Friar Antonio de San José Muro of New Spain in 1797 in connection with a contest of the Guatemala Society he had learned of in the *Gazeta de Mexico*:[38]

> It is a shameful thing how few patriotic bodies we are acquainted with in the Americas, and it ought to make us blush that their aims (such as they may be) are not known even by those most inquisitive and well disposed toward the country. Nothing comes here about the activities of the Societies of Manila, of Mompox . . . , Vera Cruz, and Cuba; but although the periodicals of Havana tell us something, it is far from the merit which that of Guatemala has acquired simply by the stroke of patriotism which the Gazeta of Mexico announces.

It remains to comment on the relations of the Societies with Church, government, and organized merchants. Churchmen were divided, both aiding and opposing the Societies. Relations with government were few, aside from permission to carry out operations, or orders to cease them. Although the relations of the Societies with town councils were more important, some conflict was almost inevitable. The statutes of the Puerto Rico Society recognized this by directing it to promote education without prejudicing the work of the town councils. We will see the Guatemala town council little pleased by the Society's invasion of the bullfighting field; and in 1798 it objected to the Society's projected revision of the guild system, supervision of which was an ancient prerogative of the municipal government.[39] The town councils were directed by the statutes of Havana, Santiago, and Guatemala to aid the Societies, but did little but assign them space in the municipal buildings.[40]

---

[37] *Early Proceedings from Minutes*, February 17, March 21, May 16, 1817; July 17, 1818. The Havana Society still was isolated in 1844, confessing it did not know the state of the Puerto Rico Society, or whether the Manila Society was alive; it hinted at the existence of Societies in Mexico, Venezuela, and Chile, and seemed to know of the eighteenth-century Lima Society; but it did not mention the Guatemala Society, which had more life before and after 1820 than the others vaguely mentioned by the Havana author (Havana *Memorias 1844*, t. XIX, 62-63, of an article on "Sociedades Económicas").

[38] *Utilidades y medios*, 6.

[39] *Infra*, 269-70, 341. Cf. *Novena junta pública*, 40-42, that Society work with guilds was supposed to be done without affecting the rights of the ayuntamiento.

[40] Cabrera, *Cuba y sus jueces*, 122, that as late as 1824 the Havana Society was able to obtain from the ayuntamiento only with some difficulty a monthly loan of 100 pesos

The town council of Guatemala claimed it was financially unable to aid the Society, and doubtless it had little income to spare. The enthusiasm of the "constitutional ayuntamiento" of 1813 for the services to the Society of Antonio Juarros, as a recommendation for his requested appointment as an intendant, was an exceptional reflection of the liberalism of the short-lived reformed municipality.[41]

Relations between the Societies and the Consulados were not always close, for although they had some common interest in general economic development, not all their specific and immediate interests coincided. The concern of the Societies for reduction of economic privilege and monopoly sometimes conflicted with the monopolistic interest of the Consulados. The Spanish merchants in Guatemala could scarcely have been entirely pleased by the Society's desire to increase the production of textiles there, or by its "buy Guatemala" slogan of 1811.[42] On the other hand, some creoles were much more interested in immediate commercial development through the Consulados than in the rather academic Economic Societies, many of whose interests were in entirely unproved schemes for diversification of production. Arango y Parreño of Havana and Manuel Belgrano of Buenos Aires are examples of creole sympathy for the Societies, but preference for the Consulados. Thus, while some men were members of both institutions,[43] they did little to support each other. The Manila, Havana,[44] and Guatemala Societies did receive minor aid from the Consulados, and Cabello y Mesa persuaded the Consulado of Buenos Aires to become protector of his projected Society there. The Guatemala Consulado, ordered to aid the local Society, did almost nothing.

Members of the Colonial Societies

Perhaps 600 or 700 men in the years from 1793 to 1820 were members of the Societies of Havana, Guatemala, Quito, Lima, Santiago de Cuba, Mompox,

---

for the support of schools, and exclaiming with his usual passion against the old regime, "Con estos recursos exiguos se preparaba el porvenir y la civilización cubana!" Cf. "junta ordinaria," February 13, 1794 (*Colección Actas 1880*, 78-79), for some exchange of information between the Havana Society and the town council.

[41] AGG, A1.2-5, leg. 2835, exped. 25296, cabildo of Guatemala to Sermo. Sor., October 11, 1813.

[42] *Infra*, 336-37.

[43] Cf. "junta ordinaria" of the Havana Society, July 23, 1795 (in *Memorias 1865*, 360-61), after hearing a memoria at a Society meeting, Francisco Arango got permission of the Society to take a copy for use in his post as Síndico of the Consulado.

[44] Cf. Havana *Memorias 1795*, 83, for a decision in 1794 to ask the Consulado to provide funds for prizes; *Memorias 1817*, 4-5, the Society proposed to coordinate its views on white colonization with the Consulado and Ayuntamiento; *ibid.*, 99 n., financial aid from the Consulado.

and Bogota.[45] Of these, the Santiago, Mompox, and Bogota might be said to have had almost no life; the Quito lasted about a year; the Lima, four years at best. The perhaps 400 to 500 men in the Havana and Guatemala Societies had a fuller experience of the work of such bodies than the 200 members in the other cities.[46]

As in the Spanish Societies, most of the potential members joined quickly; the Societies did not grow much thereafter. Most of the members were drawn from the upper class, thus including, as was said of the Guatemala, "the most selected persons of the *reyno* with illustrious personages from outside."[47] Guatemala had the typical attitude of the Spanish Societies on membership, admitting by a plurality of votes men who were "honorable, decent, of good conduct," either religious or secular, capable of being "useful by reason of their enlightenment, knowledge, or talents." This confinement to the upper-class educated element is illustrated by the fact that nearly all the sixty-odd corresponding members in 1799 were clerics, officials of the royal government, members of town councils, or merchants. Although the Havana and Guatemala Societies accepted all men able to contribute to the work, the Lima and projected Buenos Aires Society of 1800-1802 limited the membership strictly.

Although the majority of the members was creole, a large and important minority consisted of Spanish civil, ecclesiastical, and military officials. This does not seem to have caused friction, since men opposed to the Societies did not have to join them or participate actively in their affairs. Spaniards and creoles who were interested in the aims of the Societies were united by their belief in economic progress by this method. Of course, this did nothing to eliminate the fact of Spanish-creole friction outside the Societies, as could

---

[45] Incomplete contemporary data list well over 500. Left out of this calculation are the Manila Society; the Vera Cruz; the Puerto Rico, planned in 1813, but perhaps not operative till 1821; the Chiapa, organized in 1819; the Caracas of 1810, a political body; the Buenos Aires of 1800-02, proposed but never organized.

The only exceptions to the all-male membership were three ladies made "meritorious members" at Lima (*Mercurio Peruano*, January 23, 1791). A correspondent at Cuzco suggested that Lima probably contained more than three enlightened ladies (*ibid.*, February 27, 1791).

[46] The Havana Society had 126 in 1793, 130 in 1794, 162 by 1796, 217 in 1817, 262 in 1823; the Guatemala had some 60 in the capital in 1795, in 1799 had 86 in the capital and 63 corresponding members, in 1811 after a period of suspension it had 93 in the capital, many of whom had been members before 1800; the Quito had 49 at the beginning—27 enumerated, 22 supernumerary; the Lima in 1794 had 34— 21 academic (resident in Lima), 6 foreign, 7 honorary; Santiago de Cuba, 60 in 1783; the Bogota was organized by 23 men in 1801; the Mompox probably involved no more than 20, though it named 19 proxies in other towns and several corresponding members.

[47] *Novena junta pública*, 50-51.

be seen in the provision of the Guatemala Society's regulation for the guilds, which ruled that the Guild Directorate have hacendados representing the town council and merchants representing the Consulado, that is, creoles and Spaniards. The Spanish Society members in America were, of course, conservatives on most questions, especially political matters, but liberal in their attitude toward intellectual development, and toward relaxation of commercial restriction.[48]

Among Spaniards who helped found ultramarine Societies were Governor Las Casas of Cuba, Governor Basco of the Philippines, and Intendant Ramírez of Puerto Rico. Villaurrutia, founder of the Guatemala Society, was a first-generation creole, but a member of the Spanish governing group as a judge of the audiencia. Captain General González of Guatemala supported the Society in the strongest terms. Also strong supporters of Societies were Vicar-general Peñalver and Bishop Espada of Havana, Archbishop Villegas in Guatemala, and Bishop Calama in Quito. Of course, there is an even longer list of viceroys, captains general, bishops, and archbishops who either opposed the Societies, or were lukewarm regarding them.

Creole members came largely from the upper reaches of the local society, including some of the local nobility and town councillors; but included also some of the poor but learned, especially numerous parish priests and friars. The sixteen men called by Governor Las Casas to the inaugural session of the Havana Society were of the creole upper-class element: nearly all were natives of Havana, numbering among them occupants of important positions in city government, Consulado, and Church, and six holders of American titles of nobility.[49] Later membership lists showed the same pattern, with the addition of civil officials of the royal government, and of military officers from the large Havana garrison.[50] Upper-class creoles in the Society were radical only in desiring some improvement in the economic and social position of creoles.[51] Social change was not desired by such learned creole

[48] E.g., the important Spanish official José Pablo Valiente y Bravo, at Havana in the 1790's, a member of the Society there, and a partisan of further relaxation of the commercial regulations; who after the French invasion of Spain was a liberal in favoring a Cortes, but as a member for Sevilla found it too radical, and opposed its attacks on Crown and Church ("Elogio" of Valiente, in *Havana Memorias 1842*, t. XIV, 321-51).

[49] Havana *Memorias 1896*, 22-28, "Socios fundadores de la Real Sociedad Económica," for biographies of the men attending, January 9, 1793.

[50] Cf. *Memorias 1794, loc. cit.*, 120-27, "Catálogo general ... de los individuos de la ... Sociedad ..., con espresión de los empleos, oficios que en ella ejercen y lugares donde residen"; *Memorias 1795*, 153-58, "Catálogo ... de los individuos ...," listing 163 names (including 3 defunct), including 9 counts and 10 marquises, 1 bishop, 9 friars, 12 presbyters.

[51] There were frequent complaints to the Havana Society that the members were absent from the city for long periods on their haciendas (cf. *Memorias 1795*, 84, three

members of Economic Societies as Baquíjano of Lima, Arango y Parreño of Havana, and José Cecilio del Valle of Guatemala. Some others were more liberal, but the activities of the Societies were not designed to promote social change.

The Guatemala Society can illustrate the elements likely to be drawn into the Societies. Clerics included ex-officio members from the ecclesiastical cabildo and from four local religious houses; ex-officio members from the university were no doubt sometimes religious; the archbishop of Guatemala and several bishops in New Spain were honorary members; doctors of theology, canons, and priests for the capital were numerous, with parish priests among the corresponding members. Civil officials included the captain general as vice-protector of the Society; the judges and fiscal of the audiencia, and the *Contador mayor de cuentas* as ex-officio members; and about two dozen other officials in capital and provinces. The mercantile interest had two ex-officio members from the Consulado. Other members with a mercantile tie included Alejandro Ramírez, secretary of the Consulado; Francisco Andrés de Sarralde, a representative of the Five Major Guilds of Madrid; and ten of the sixty-odd corresponding members in 1799 were identified as merchants. Representatives of the Spanish military among the corresponding members included José Salvador, Colonel of the Army and governor-intendant of the province of León; Salvador de Jabalois, captain of infantry; Carlos Pinzón, captain of the royal corps of artillery and director of the royal works of Truxillo; the captain of His Majesty's *goleta* "La Isabela," berthed at Truxillo; the colonel commandant of the port of Truxillo; and the second officer of "La Isabela."

While probably most of these civil officials, merchants, and military were Spaniards, many of the religious must have been creoles. And the creole element was represented by two ex-officio members from the town council. In 1799 four other members of the town council also were members. The membership lists identify local nobles and militia officers, and the large number of unidentified members must have been largely creole.

Most members lived in the city where a Society was formed. This was in most cases the capital of a major administrative division, so most of the ex-officio members lived there. It was the center of mercantile activity and of learning, containing the largest concentration of persons of means who had some access to the education necessary for participation in the work of the Society. Corresponding members outside the capital were commonly desired, but only became a significant proportion of the membership in Guatemala

presidents of the class of commerce had to be elected to make sure one would be in the city).

—in 1799 having 86 members in the capital, and 63 corresponding members, mostly in other parts of the captaincy general.[52] The membership of the Havana Society was concentrated narrowly in the city,[53] and the smaller Societies were like Havana in this.

Poor communications made it difficult for corresponding members to contribute to the work of the Societies. A possible remedy was branches or separate Societies in provincial towns. The Bogota Society hoped other towns would establish Societies. Three branches (*diputaciones*) of the Havana Society, operating under the same statutes as the latter were established before 1820: Sancti-Espíritu (1803),[54] Puerto-Príncipe and Trinidad (1813).[55] The branches had enough contact with the Havana body to serve much of the purpose of corresponding members. The Guatemala Society in the 1795-1800 period had a corresponding junta at the little port village of Truxillo. It died with the suspension of the Society in 1800, and was not revived with the central body in 1810. Never consisting of more than fifteen men, the corresponding junta's modest work in that isolated hut-cluster on a tropic coast must have done something to relieve the tedium of existence there. The *Gazeta de Guatemala* declared that the *reyno* would be happy if in each of its pueblos, or at least in its capitals, such a junta was formed.[56]

In 1811 some residents of Tegucigalpa decided to create a corresponding junta of the Guatemala Society, but there is no evidence they did so. The same year, the Guatemala Society formed a corresponding junta at San Salvador, not as the result of local demand, but as a device imposed by an

---

[52] Truxillo, 12; Comayagua, 7; León, 6; San Salvador, 4; San Miguel, 3; San Vicente, 3; Santa Ana, 3; 5 from as many places in New Spain; and 20 others scattered through the area of present-day Guatemala, El Salvador, and the Mexican state of Chiapas. Apparently there were no corresponding members in the distant, poor, and thinly populated province of Costa Rica, but the influence of the Society was felt there (cf. AGG, A1.6, leg. 2267, exped. 16453, Dn Josef Vásquez y Telles to Seban. Melón, Cartago, November 3, 1796, acknowledging receipt of notices on the Society's Indian dress contest).

[53] The only exceptions in 1793 were a member each for Río-Blanco, Guanabacoa, and Santiago; in the first two years, several residents of Spain, two persons at New Orleans, and one in Comayagua.

[54] *Memorias 1817*, 273-82, "Establecimiento de una diputación de la ... Sociedad ... en ... Santi-Espíritus." The process was begun under the auspices of a local official of the royal administration. Twenty-seven of the most prominent men of the town applied for admission.

[55] The Trinidad and Puerto-Príncipe branches were still alive in 1817, but the Sancti-Espíritu was badly decayed. The Trinidad died sometime before 1827, and had to be re-established that year. Cf. Havana *Memorias 1817*, 283-90, on the Puerto-Príncipe deputation in 1817; *Memorias 1818*, 19-23, for an assertion of December, 1817, that the Havana Society was getting cooperation outside the city only in Puerto-Príncipe.

[56] *Gazeta*, May 20, 1799, 36.

agent of the government in Guatemala sent to deal with a political disturbance. Presumably it was hoped that the junta might turn the demand for reform into other than political channels. There is no reason to believe that it did, since the membership of the San Salvador junta included several men later conspicuous in the independence movement. One member of this group, Matías Delgado, had been a corresponding member of the Guatemala Society in the earlier period, but the events of 1808-1810 had aroused in him political as well as economic aspirations.

Finances of the Colonial Societies

The financial resources of the Societies were slender. No great sum could be raised from annual dues of eight pesos, unless the Societies found huge numbers of members, and that was impossible since educated men suitable for the work were not numerous. Lacking much government financial support, they therefore depended in large measure on contributions of time and money, not a sound basis for a program of economic development. The Guatemala Society marveled that it had done so much with funds that were small as compared with those English societies had for the development of the arts, commerce, and industry; and that it had done more proportionately than the Dublin Society which awarded so many prizes.[57]

The work of the Havana and Guatemala Societies was sizable enough to give an indication of the financial resources available to such bodies in America.[58] The Havana collected eight pesos dues, made a profit on sale of the *Papel Periódico*, and in 1793-1795 raised over 25,000 pesos for a foreign teacher of chemistry and laboratory equipment, in the hope of improving the sugar industry.[59] In 1795 the Society received some 25,000 pesos—just over 1,200 in dues, while the rest consisted of contributions to the chemistry teacher's fund (300), the Casa de Beneficencia (10,127), to the Casa de Educandas (11,198), and to the library (1,785).[60] This did not provide much financial basis for new activity. And in the period of reduced activity from 1796 to 1815[61] the Society's finances appear not to have improved, for in

---

[57] *Novena junta pública*, 52.

[58] The Lima Society's *Mercurio* was of some consequence, but was the only activity of the Society, so the need for funds was limited. The moribund Manila Society in 1797 deposited its 6,000-pesos treasury with the Consulado.

[59] *Memorias 1795*, 15 et seq.

[60] *Memorias 1795*, chart at end: "Estado General que manifiesta la entrada, salida y existencia de Caudales a disposición de la Sociedad Patriótica. ..."

[61] *Tareas 1815*, 7-9: 10,620 pesos on hand, December 1, 1814; 28,944 collected in the next twelve months.

1816 it asked the Spanish government to help collect its dues. The situation did improve a bit thereafter, partly because the Crown conceded the Society some government revenues in 1818, on the recommendation of Ramírez.[62]

The resources of the Guatemala Society appear smaller than those of the Havana only because the latter had large sums for its beneficent institutions; for other purposes, Guatemala was about as well provided. The Society, however, was not satisfied with its revenues. Some of its problem was due to heavy initial outlays, including rent, and the purchase of houses;[63] but even more to the poverty of the region.[64] The dues of eight pesos were hard to collect, because cash was scarce in many areas.[65] The fact was that members in Guatemala City paid the dues with some reluctance, while members in the outlying areas scarcely paid at all in some periods. This reflected the concentration of most of the limited liquid capital of the area in the city, while the provinces were exceedingly poor. Moreover, the taxgatherer competed for the sparse resources of members, as the Society recognized in creating a commission to investigate its financial problem.[66] Income from dues was greatest the first year—1,736 pesos—and inability to increase income from this source was chiefly a reflection of the static number of members, though also the result of nonpayment.[67] By 1799 the Society was removing eight men from the membership rolls, in some cases at their own request, in others because of failure to pay dues. At least one man declared frankly that he could not pay,[68] and no doubt this was true of others, especially in

---

[62] *Memorias 1819*, 26-27; *Memorias 1820*, 17-18, that by December, 1819, the Society had received 31,920 pesos in government funds; *Acta Juntas Generales 1833*, 29-33, for Ramírez' financial aid, and note that beginning in April, 1820, the bishop gave 30 pesos a month to the Society. Cf. *Memorias 1817*, 14-19, that on December 1, 1816, the treasury held 10,889 pesos, and in January-November, 1818, another 48,313 pesos were collected; *Memorias 1819*, 25-26, complaining that the Society needed more funds for its prizes, schools, and classes; *Memorias 1820*, 48.

[63] AGG, A1.6, leg. 2006, expeds. 13799, 13802, 13803; leg. 2007, exped. 13836, all contain information on the buildings; *Segunda junta pública*, 20-30, report of the acting secretary, noting that the two houses bought, which were used for the schools of spinning and of drawing, only called for an immediate outlay of 1,000 pesos by the Society.

[64] Cf. *Quarta junta pública*, 17-18, "Donativos," noting the need of more funds, and acknowledging gifts. The small size of the gifts suggests the limited resources of inhabitants of the captaincy general.

[65] *Novena junta pública*, 46-47, "Fondos," making both these points.

[66] *Octava junta pública*, 32-33, "Fondos," asserting that in Guatemala "todo se costea con arbitrios."

[67] Information on the accumulation of unpaid dues and entrance fees in AGG, A1.6, leg. 2006, expeds. 13799, 13801; leg. 2007, expeds. 13830, 13831; leg. 2008, exped. 13844. In 1799 the corresponding members had almost ceased paying dues.

[68] AGG, A1.6, leg. 2008, exped. 13842.

the provinces, if we may judge by the letters to the Society from the member at Truxillo, who in 1798 suggested to the corresponding junta there that they hold a meeting on the matter, but had to report that for "algunos motibos" it was not held.[69]

The Society also had income from lotteries, bullfights, gifts, loans, sale of publications, and from disposal of fabrics resulting from its textile operations. Though the dues were in the long run the only regular source of income, some of the other sources were valuable. This was true of lotteries, conceded by the king and leased by the Society to a concessionaire.[70] Lotteries and dues provided some 80 per cent of the Society's income in 1795-1798.[71] The other 20 per cent came from gifts, a loan, sale of works printed by the Society, and from disposal of the products of the spinning school. Sale of publications and textile products brought little. The latter were few and of low quality; and the publications moved very slowly.

The Society publicized its poverty in 1798, offering medals for suggestions.[72] Finding an average annual income of 2,460 pesos unsatisfactory,[73] the Society applied to the government for relief. Among other aid, it secured late in 1798 permission of the captain general for twelve bullfights. Villaurrutia applied to the town council for permission for the Society to use the Old Plaza, and for exemption from contribution from the profits to the municipal treasury.[74] The town council gave permission promptly,[75] but informed the captain general that while it was willing to aid the Society, the condition of Church and State did not seem to justify such disposal of revenue.[76] The Society agreed that it was generous of the town council to make such a concession when its own revenues were decayed, and informed it that the box

---

[69] Thomás Ordíñez to Sebastián Melón, Truxillo, April 20—AGG, A1.6, leg. 2007, exped. 13839, and containing letters on the same subject from dues collectors in other parts of the captaincy general.

[70] The Society had various difficulties with both money and jewelry lotteries (cf. *Junta pública 1796*, 21-22; *Segunda junta pública*, 30-33; *Tercera junta pública*, 13; and many notices in the *Gazeta de Guatemala* in 1797-1800).

[71] In March, 1795 to December, 1798, the lottery yielded 4,452 pesos, while dues came to 2,952 pesos. Lotteries and dues provided all but 1,834 of the 9,237 pesos gathered by the Society from all sources in this period.

[72] *Gazeta de Guatemala*, October 15, 1798, 282-88.

[73] *Quinta junta pública*, 30, "Estado que manifiesta los fondos ...," noting income of 4,150 pesos for the first 20 months, 2,047 the next year, 3,040 the next.

[74] Villaurrutia to the M. N. Ayuntamiento, Nueva Guatemala, December 10, 1798 —AGG, A1.2-5, leg. 2835, exped. 25287.

[75] Libro de Actas del Cabildo de Guatemala, 1798: Cabildo ordinario, December 14, 1798—AGG, A1.2-2, leg. 2813, exped. 15725.

[76] Ayuntamiento to captain general, December 14, 1798—AGG, A1.2-5, leg. 2835, exped. 25287.

provided for the *Alcaldes ordinarios* next to the captain general's would be expanded to provide for all members of the town council.[77]

A concessionaire within a few weeks paid the Society nearly a thousand pesos as rent for the plaza; of this the Society had to give 10 per cent to the Hospital of San Juan de Díos. The bullfight income, together with thousand-peso gifts from Archbishop Villegas of Guatemala and the bishop of Michoacán in New Spain were largely instrumental in swelling the Society's revenues to 5,822 pesos in 1799.[78]

The financial condition of the Society was even less satisfactory after the suspension of 1800-1810. In August 1811 the secretary reported that the Society was receiving funds only from initiation fees and dues.[79] Soon thereafter Archbishop Casaus gave 400 pesos to the Society. It did not, however, recover strength sufficiently to operate as a veritable Economic Society in the style of Campomanes, as it had in 1795-1800.

---

[77] Jacobo de Villaurrutia to the Ayuntamiento, Nueva Guatemala, December 22, 1798—AGG, A1.2-5, leg. 2835, exped. 25287; cf. *Quinta junta pública*, 17-19, "Fondo," for summary of the bullfight concession.

[78] Cuenta corriente de cargo y data de los fondos de la Sociedad ..., January 1, 1799-December 31—AGG, A1.6, leg. 2008, exped. 13844.

[79] *Octava junta pública*, 32-33.

CHAPTER FOURTEEN

Aims, Ideas, and the Problem of Poverty

Aims and Ideas

Poverty and prosperity were the central interests of the Societies; so most of their aims and ideas related directly, or not too indirectly, to economic questions. They also had interests in science, not always closely tied to economics, as in Guatemala's Cabinet of Natural History,[1] or Havana's concern for medicine; and in learning and literature. Further, some of the interest in primary education was philanthropic only. The members had a certain prejudice in favor of "modern" ideas, as opposed to those "innumerable prejudices and errors, which, as a dense haze, had obscured the interests of the Fatherland," before the Spanish discovered they had them, "when at the beginning of the last century Enlightenment dawned in Europe, and spread its rays through all the continent."[2] This prejudice in favor of modern ideas was certainly stronger with some members than others; not all were as learned as Villaurrutia, who when he called "patriotism" the distinguishing feature

---

[1] *Infra*, 303. But cf. A1.6, leg. 2007, exped. 13839, Alejandro Ramírez to Sebastián Melón, Nueva Guatemala, December 23, 1798, noting that a discourse on a method of describing plants, sent by Vicente Cervantes, professor of botany in Mexico, was of limited utility from the point of view of the Society. Even science, in the Societies, usually was meant to serve economics.

[2] Havana *Memorias 1795*, 3. Cf. Havana *Memorias 1793*, 2, on these venturesome times, when philosophy has "opened the dikes which impeded the free circulation of the sciences and arts," and reduced the sphere of scholasticism.

of the Economic Societies,[3] used the term in the sense of loyalty to the Enlightenment.[4]

American and Spanish Societies aired like views on production, the exchange of goods, technical education, and the relief of poverty. Both desired "felicity" for society, and saw the way thereto through the principles of political economy. Both glorified "useful" knowledge and techniques, including statistics, and science in such practical applications as machinery. Both attacked certain natural and artificial restrictions on the economy, which they wished to develop by directing change in accordance with their own views. Both believed in the utility of ideas, and in the value of cooperative effort by the enlightened, displayed in the hopeful motto of the Guatemala Society that "United Zeal Produces Abundance."

One notion of the Spanish Societies did suffer a serious sea-change in the Atlantic passage: the emphasis on local problems. This pointed up the conflict between Spanish and American interests, so the Societies at least mildly stimulated and gave some voice to an Americanism antedating their foundation but becoming vociferous in precisely the years of their existence. They had this effect even though a fair number of the members were Spaniards, and most creole members were not the most radical of that community.

MATERIAL PROSPERITY

Although material prosperity was the pivotal concern of the American Societies, the interest was not simply in improvement of the local economy and personal fortunes, but in the social consequences of poverty, in the decay of "good customs." The members had some interest in maintaining the strength of the Spanish world, and some distaste for contributing to that of its rivals.[5] This could be linked with political conservatism, as when a member of the Guatemala Society in 1812 declared that poverty led people to crime in Guatemala; but, worse than that, "indigence is the nearest disposition to insurrection," for the poor have nothing to lose; and a prosperous vassal is loyal because "his possessions are the guarantors of his

---

[3] Guatemala *Quinta junta pública*, 1. Cf. Havana *Memorias 1793*, 181, that the Society was a "Sanctuary of Patriotism," promoting enlightenment and the common felicity.

[4] Cf. Crane Brinton, *Ideas and Men* (1950), 375, for this characteristic eighteenth-century use of the term, especially in voluntary groups.

[5] Cf. a statement in 1811 by Fr. Antonio Carrascal of the Guatemala Society that they had "under a mistaken calculation begged manufactures from foreign countries," but that a "sane politics" could build economic life, and stop the drain of gold and silver into foreign hands (*Octava junta pública*, "Discurso" in unnumbered pages at end).

fidelity."[6] As additional reasons for interest in material improvement, the members had their prejudice in favor of "progress," and an interest in secular learning, especially political economy and science.

Thus, although the records of the Societies abound in expressions of charitable intent, many were platitudinous; the philanthropic interest sometimes seems perfunctory, the economic never. The Society contests were on economic questions. The economic interest is very clear in the educational activities of the Societies; and it is plain in the manner of organization, statutes, and history of the Societies. This is true of the abortive or short-lived Societies at Lima, Quito, Bogota, Mompox, Santiago de Cuba, and Chiapa, of the Puerto Rican, and the Society suggested for Buenos Aires. It is even clearer in the Manila, Havana, and Guatemala Societies.

With obviously strong feeling the Societies bewailed local economic "decadence," envied Dutch and English wealth, and lamented that other American provinces were more prosperous than their own. The frequent use of the term "utility" to connect matters with economic development is significant.[7] Even the many comments on "felicity" tended to occur in discussions of economic deficiencies.[8] The economic motive not only showed sometimes in charitable activity, but this activity stimulated attention to economic questions in order to reduce the need for charity. Further, the benevolent desire to succor the poor could not be separated from the conviction that the latter ought to be aided to produce goods, as when the Guatemala Society in 1811 discussed the problem of "good customs," that sound Catholic interest of all the Societies.

The production of goods—crops and manufactures—was, indeed, the prime concern of the Societies. They inherited the emphasis on production from Campomanes and from the statutes of the Madrid Society on which their own were based. They inherited also from Campomanes, and from other currently influential political economists, the specific repudiation of bullionism, the axiom that money is not wealth,[9] and the hope that an increased commerce would flow from an improved production of crops and goods. They inherited also the deprecation of emphasis on mining. This was in

---

[6] *Novena junta pública*, 14-15. *Infra*, 326-27, the same idea expressed by Letona.

[7] Havana *Memorias 1817*, 21, "Utilidad de la Botánica," 24, "Utilidad de la Química."

[8] Havana *Memorias 1793*, 3, that "all governments are dedicated" to aiding "the three agents of the felicity of peoples, Agriculture, Commerce, and Crafts."

[9] Cf. Havana *Memorias 1818*, 427, that a nation is made rich not by money, but by capital, i.e., by production. By this time the influence of Say and Smith was considerable in Cuba; but indications of understanding that money is a medium of exchange appeared in earlier years.

turn reinforced in the American Societies by the fact that they were located in areas of no apparent great mineral potential—except in Peru, and here even Baquíjano, while recognizing the importance of mining for Peru, yearned for other forms of economic activity too. This chiefly economic interest of the Societies was evident, finally, when they considered the quantity and quality of the labor force, although this also tended to involve moral judgments, especially concerning the asserted laziness and bad habits of the poor.

Thus it was that while the philanthropic interest was strong in the Guatemala Society, it did not yearn primarily for the advancement of the City of God, but for progress toward at least a modest Rome of the Western world. Its many published statements on progress or improvement more often than not meant advancement of economic life, however coupled with hope of a better intellectual and moral climate.[10] And the interests of the Havana Society were no less heavily weighted in the economic sector. It was hardly philanthropic impulse that led the latter to declare that the bare necessities of nature were not enough for man, who must reach out for more by means of study of all the branches of economic life; or a charitable motive that led it in 1794 to call for the enrichment of Cuba by better use of the land, and by better education, aided by the government and the Economic Societies. It was hardly Christian benevolence that inclined it to the view that the poor of Cuba grew products of so little value that they provided no surplus for the enrichment of the state;[11] or made it publish an attack on the theory that there was a fixed fund of colonial wealth and that all that could be done was to alter its distribution.[12] The Havana Society not only believed that wealth could be increased, but it also demanded a certain level of prices for produce, for "the lack of value with abundance is not wealth."[13]

[10] Cf. the offer in 1812 of prizes by a corresponding member: in writing and Christian doctrine to a child, to masters and journeymen for hard work and production, to Indians and mulattoes for wheat production—AGG, A1.6, leg. 2008, exped. 13856. A member in 1811 wanted to show the world that the Spanish people were not barbarous and inert, but learned and active, and a "breeder of inventions" ("Discurso" of Carrascal, *Octava junta pública*, unnumbd. pp. at end). See ASGH, III, 105, for reproduction of the shield of the Guatemala Society, the principal element of which is a cornucopia being held by two hands, of different men, signifying cooperation, in the sky over a mountainous country, and issuing from the horn plants enriching the country. While this device did not contain as many elements as some of those of Spanish Societies (*supra*, 75, 113), it was as simply directed to economic development.

[11] *Memorias 1794, loc. cit.*, 420.

[12] *Ibid.*, 422 n.

[13] *Ibid.*, 425 n. 8. Cf. *Memorias 1819*, 44 *et seq.*, "Discurso leído en ... la real Sociedad Patriótica, por D. Wenceslao de Villa-Urrutia ...," on the subject "Lo que es la Habana, y lo que puede ser," the main theme of which was economic, the author yearning for the enrichment of the city.

PHILANTHROPY AND CHRISTIAN CHARITY

Although the philanthropic or humanitarian interest was often mixed with economic hopes, this was not always the case. The charitable motive was naturally strong in bodies with so many members from the religious, one of whom in the Guatemala Society called it a *cofradía de piedad*,[14] which they were not. Charity was the motive for the connection of the Havana Society with the Casa de Beneficencia. The charitable motive dominated the report (1796) of the Guatemala Society's commission on a hospice for the poor, poverty being considered largely as a moral-ethical rather than an economic problem.[15] The charitable impulse in this Society was tempered by dubiety as to the utility of indiscriminate charity, which might encourage the undeserving poor in their faults.[16]

The mixture of charitable with other motives was natural enough in such Societies. The Guatemala encouraged weaving to aid the public, to increase commerce, and to cut contraband. Friar Luís García in 1797 declared that the same Society's plan of guild regulation would stimulate manufactures, which would free Guatemala of reliance on foreign countries, increase the circulation of money, and cure evils of poverty similar to those of ancient Rome. And the essays in the Society's contest on Indian dress showed not only a mixture of economic and charitable motives, but secular humanitarianism as well, one entry calling on the "abstract sciences" to show the unity of mankind. Another entry demanded both more economic production and more education to cut the terrible infant mortality of America, declaring it the result of poverty and ignorance; and asserted that too few citizens thought seriously about the general welfare, whereas they should gain internal satisfaction by aiding their fellow creatures who were in a "pitiful human condition" in America. The very terms of the contest showed a mixture of interest, calling for consideration of the physical, moral, and political advantages of dressing Indians *a la española*.[17]

OPTIMISM REGARDING ECONOMIC IMPROVEMENT

Much optimism in the American Societies was based on a belief in "progress,"[18] a part of the current faith that man's problems would yield to his reason. Villaurrutia, Spanish founder of the Guatemala Society, was

---

[14] *Novena junta pública*, 12.

[15] *Infra*, 295 et seq.

[16] *Quarta junta pública*, 21.

[17] *Infra*, 297 et seq.; and 339, for the social welfare aspect of the Guatemala Society's guild regulation; 326, feeding the poor.

[18] E.g., Havana *Memorias 1793*, 2.

strongly antipessimistic, scornful of what he called "faint-hearted spirits."
He thought that "everything proclaims that a happy period is coming for
this *reyno* [of Guatemala], though nearsighted politicians may not recognize
it."[19] And to the general optimism of the Enlightenment, the members
added the three reasons of the Spanish Societies for supposing the economic
situation improvable. First, they hoped for economic advantage from improved legislation and educational facilities. Secondly, they had some notion
of a golden economic age in the past, from which they had fallen into "decadence"; a potent and frequently expressed idea, even though probably not
so vivid a dream as in Spain. Nevertheless, Baquíjano of Lima spoke of the
decadence of commerce. Letona of Truxillo declared that long years before
that area had been prosperous.[20] García Redondo of the Guatemala Society
stated that although fertile provinces had been reduced to "deserts," they
could be made to flourish once more. He repudiated the notion that this
condition was due to colonial "sloth," for "the character of a nation never
varies, though circumstances may vary and change its customs."[21] The
colonials could not, however, link the golden age of the American economy
with a golden age of America as a great power, so that Spanish argument
was not available overseas.

Thirdly, the American Societies felt that their resources promised economic
success if properly worked. It seemed to the secretary of the Guatemala
Society that the "excelentes proporciones" of Guatemala would again make
it prosperous, if well used;[22] and to a member of the Truxillo junta that
Comayagua's many resources and its available labor and fertile land ought
to give the port a lucrative commerce, as in the previous century.[23] Bishop
Calama certainly was optimistic in stating that Quito ought not to be poor
because it had an abundance of grain and everything necessary for the
manufacture of wool and cotton. The Havana Society was equally certain

---

[19] *Quinta junta pública*, 3.

[20] *Gazeta de Guatemala*, August 27, 1797, comparing it with Havana's export
trade of former years, but neglecting to state that Cuban sugar production had been
very much smaller then.

[21] *Junta pública 1796*, 28; cf. *ibid.*, 24, for an eloquent statement of the decline
of the economy from a former state of prosperity; *infra*, 328, on "decay" of cacao in
Guatemala.

[22] *Quarta junta pública*, 3.

[23] *Ibid.*, 14; *Gazeta de Guatemala*, August 27, 1798, printing extracts from the
speech at Truxillo, which included an impressive list of the products of the province,
despite which it was largely unexploited, unpopulated, and presented "a picture
of the most unhappy misery." Cf. for other expressions of puzzlement and depression
in contemplation of the contrast between the fertility of the land and the inability
of the residents to achieve prosperity, in *Segunda junta pública*, 35; *Quinta junta
pública*, 3-4.

that fertile land and good ports promised great prosperity to Cuba,[24] that things were about to become wonderful as men worked more, and used economic science, aided by the Society, with everything announcing "a brilliant fortune, the greatest prosperity."[25] Nor did Americans fail to reject the ancient theory of climate that imputed an inherent inferiority to the American natural scene, the Lima, Quito, and Guatemala Societies all condemning the notion. The American Societies did not, however, share the notion of the Spanish Societies that they had economic advantages in both hemispheres. In Spain, the thought of American resources stimulated hope, while in America the thought of Spanish poverty induced dismay. The American Societies more than once stated their understanding of Spain's economic weakness.[26]

The belief that wealth from these resources required better exploitation meant understanding that various hindrances prevented it. Baquíjano in 1791 noted the obstacles to economic growth in Peru, concentrating on natural obstacles, but also condemning Spain's restrictive policy with regard to American commerce. Bishop Calama told the Quito Society that the realm was "prostrated" by "political ills." Everyone in the Guatemala Society seemed to assume that economic change was both desirable and possible, but that it was retarded by law, chance, laziness, bad habits, war, and bad government in Spain. The last, in the earlier period, meant Godoy, who could be criticized without implicating the sovereign.[27] The *Gazeta de Guatemala* carried the same theme, sometimes in strong terms. Mutis told the Bogota Society of the obstacles to economic development due to the "enormous literary and civil difference between Spain and America." The Havana Society in 1819 declared that the island had obtained from nature a right to prosperity, but this right had encountered "obstacles," due in part to "ignorance of the true principles of political economy," so that foreigners "bringing their manufactures and mercantile stuffs came to steal gold and not to produce it."[28]

---

[24] *Memorias 1793*, 5.

[25] *Ibid.*, 36-38. Cf. *Memorias 1794*, *loc. cit.*, 420, sugar could be more profitable, not due to soil infertility, but to poor cultivation; *ibid.*, 421, could improve other cultivation, imitating neighboring isles; *ibid.*, 422, resources good, exploitation poor; *Memorias 1817*, 40, soil and situation destine Cuba to economic greatness; *ibid.*, 431, because of her advantages, Cuba "is called to occupy the most distinguished place among the American possessions"; *Memorias 1818*, 304, resources and location should make Cuba "uno de los puntos mas comerciales del mundo"; *Memorias 1819*, 49, dreaming of how rich Cuba could become, linking wealth, power, and *ilustración*.

[26] *Supra*, 170, n. 212.

[27] *Infra*, 328, on political restrictions on cacao culture.

[28] *Memorias 1819*, 4. Cf. Havana *Memorias 1794*, *loc. cit.*, 418, that they needed to destroy errors; *Memorias 1817*, 97-99, an editorial note that protection for the crafts

MEANS OF ECONOMIC IMPROVEMENT

The most important demands were for: (1) descriptive and statistical data on the local economies, and study of the principles of political economy; (2) improvement of economic techniques; (3) diversification; (4) expansion and better use of the labor force; (5) better transport. Little was said about credit facilities. The undoubtedly widespread desire for reforms in legislation was little publicized, although a Guatemalan in 1798 did prepare a memorial calling for political action to remove government restrictions on the cacao trade, and the Society there decided that the high cost of labor inhibiting cacao culture in the east coastal area was a problem for government. Of course, the Spanish Societies were similarly circumspect, only the Madrid waxing vociferous in demands for legislation to remove political obstacles, so much emphasized by Campomanes and Jovellanos.

(1) Knowledge was the tool of the Societies, and they thirsted for data and respected accuracy.[29] Collecting information was part of Espejo's intent in declaring that Quito would use the "dawn of her rationality" to improve conditions in the area. The *Mercurio Peruano* printed much factual information. The proposed statutes of the Bogota Society would have it get information on the viceroyalty by enrolling corresponding members in all the towns. Valiente of Santiago demanded a "physical-political-geographical history" of the area, with attention to the animal, vegetable, and mineral kingdoms. The Havana Society printed a memorial which quoted Bayle in praise of dictionaries in proposing a "Provincial Dictionary of the Island of Cuba," to serve as an aid to agriculture.[30] We have noted the interest of the Havana Society in machinery, foreign methods, and the chemistry of sugar. And it printed the opinion that the progress of English agriculture was due to the "indefatigable constancy" of English "investigations."[31] The statistical material in the 1817-1820 Memorias was quite voluminous.

The Guatemala Society gathered considerable information from members

---

raised the long debated question of whether ordinances governing industry that entered into commerce were prejudicial to that commerce, and asserting that liberty, the principal base of industry and commerce, was incompatible with ordinances and regulations, though the latter had use in certain cases and circumstances.

[29] E.g., Havana *Memorias 1794, loc. cit.*, 101, on correcting lunar tables in the *Guía de Forasteros.*

[30] *Memorias 1795*, 106-14.

[31] *Memorias 1793*, 35. Cf. *Memorias 1795*, 132-36, tithes collected in the diocese of Havana in 1789-96; "Discurso sobre ... la tierra Bermeja para cultura de la caña de azúcar. ... Por ... Antonio de Morejón y Gato, en la Real Sociedad económica ..., 1797" (Havana *Memorias 1842* [t. XIV], 401-18), an example of strictly practical economic discussion, here of soil types.

in the provinces. It especially wanted regional information, to give an understanding of the characteristic constitution of the district served by the Society, its resources, and its inhabitants.[32] And it not only demanded information as a basis for action, but insisted that this information not be exaggerated in the reporting, but consist only of the bare facts. Goycoechea asserted that the worst impediment to public felicity was ignorance, citing the Carib Indians as proof of his contention.[33] López Rayón told the Guatemala Society that the youth of the land was capable of acquiring any kind of knowledge, and that from this acquisition Guatemala would become a land of milk and honey.[34] Luís Pedro Aguirre, honorary judge of the audiencia, described the Society as a "committee of rational beings."[35] José del Valle in 1812 praised "the spirit of observation."[36] Villaurrutia was demanding study and knowledge when he declared that the Society had "discovered the most expeditious road to civilization, and the felicity of a prodigious multitude of rational beings," whose misery was contrary to the spirit of government and the sovereigns, as well as to the wisest and most human legislation.[37]

The American Societies—like the Spanish—did little to establish the formal study of political economy. The Havana Society early suggested such study,[38] but did nothing about it. It heard strong support of the thesis that English agricultural progress was due to "indefatigable constancy . . . in all investigations,"[39] and asserted the need of the study of agriculture in Cuba, but thought "the proofs of practice" should be added to theory.[40] The class in political economy formed many years later was not a Society project,[41] but the Society supported it strongly.[42]

The Guatemala Society's secretary in 1798 said that the return of prosperity depended on knowledge of political economy, for

> The economic science is studied in countries where only less than a century ago began the penetration of the first arts and the first rudiments of everything. The northern nations have advanced prodigiously their agriculture and industry,

---

[32] *Segunda junta pública*, 4.
[33] *Quarta junta pública*, 25.
[34] *Segunda junta pública*, 37-38.
[35] *Novena junta pública*, 48.
[36] *El Amigo de la Patria*, April 12, 1821, 439, quoting his work of ten years earlier.
[37] *Quarta junta pública*, 1-2.
[38] *Memorias 1793*, 25, calling it *ciencia económica*.
[39] *Ibid.*, 35.
[40] *Memorias 1794*, *loc. cit.*, 419-20.
[41] *Memorias 1817*, 17, chair of political economy being formed at the *Colegio Semanario*, without any Society connection.
[42] *Infra*, 312-13, on the class in 1818 and thereafter.

simply by the publication by their Societies and Academies of useful papers and memorials. . . . By this means general opinion is formed.[43]

Villaurrutia thought that "the truths of political economy" would help bring the captaincy general to a flourishing condition again.[44] The Society, however, did not establish classes in political economy in 1795-1800, but tried to improve knowledge of spinning, drawing, mathematics, and reading and reckoning. In the later period the Society directed José Cecilio del Valle to plan classes. His report in 1812 argued the value of study, advancing the idea that some men should be retired from the world to consider useful ideas; and quoting Jean Say to the effect that learned men "are not an unproductive and sterile class but cooperate in the production of wealth." All the sciences were useful: chemistry could discover dyes; a fossil, considered in the light of mineralogical science, might aid mining; and the reptilian anatomy should provide lessons for medicine. The government ought to protect these sciences, but not play favorites by neglecting political economy. But the Spanish, he said, had been in Guatemala three centuries without thinking of teaching the subject, although political economy was "the science of civil societies, which gives governments principles of beneficent administration, and gives peoples lessons in prosperity." The great aim of the subject was analysis of the problem of why some countries were rich and others poor. The political economist was to be a discoverer of truths, for

> Newton contemplating the physical universe in order to describe the general principle of the movement, equilibrium, and harmony of the spheres that form it, is a sublime genius worthy the notice of the heavens. The Economist considering the political world in order to discover the origin of the wealth and felicity of peoples, appears a Divine Being worthy of the adoration of gratitude.[45]

(2) The demand for the improvement of economic techniques was general in the American Societies, as was the interest in machines, and new instruments and crops. The Guatemala Society showed this interest,[46] and emphasized the need of skill in the use of spinning wheels and machines.[47] The Havana Society showed much interest in machines, especially for the sugar industry, but also for rice and some other food crops; and it examined

---

[43] *Quarta junta pública*, 3.

[44] *Quinta junta pública*, 1-4.

[45] *El Amigo de la Patria*, I, No. 2 (October 26, 1820), prints the report of 1812; *ibid.*, No. 23 (April 12, 1821), 437, quotes from it.

[46] Cf. chap. XVI for Guatemala interest in new plants, a hydrostatic device, a horse drawn machine of New Orleans, spinning wheels, a seed separator, and guild regulations and marketing methods.

[47] *Quarta junta pública*, 26.

models, built pilot examples, and studied plans.[48] The Bogota Society's statutes suggested a motto like "instruye y fomenta," and provided for student members, young men "distinguished by their birth or application," a provision reminiscent of the Basque and Valencia Societies. The interest of the Societies in technical education was another phase of this demand for improvement of techniques.[49]

(3) Even the smaller American Societies paid some lip service to the Spanish belief in the organic nature of the economy, requiring improvement of all its parts—agriculture, industry, and commerce. We have seen the Havana and Guatemala Societies a number of times printing views reflecting some aspect of this notion. José Cecilio del Valle in 1812 made an especially eloquent statement that the Society was to

> foment and protect the industrial arts, those arts without which States can have neither power nor splendor, without which agriculture cannot recover from the langor to which it inclines in such fertile lands as our own; without which commerce so bold and enterprising becomes apathetic and timid, or to put it better, weakens and dies for lack of nourishment or food.[50]

Cuba was chiefly interested in agriculture and commerce, as Valiente of Santiago indicated, though showing some interest in other crops than sugar and in fabrication. In Havana, it was natural that the hacendados should mainly be interested in sugar cultivation and export. At the end of our period that Society, while supporting free trade, noted that this alone would not ensure prosperity; capital was needed, not for its own sake, since modern economists did not consider money the only source of wealth, but for the expansion of commerce and industry.[51] And in that period dominated by Intendant Ramírez, the Society did emphasize diversification, but without the support of most hacendados. Only the Guatemala Society had a full share of the Spanish interest in the connections between agriculture and textile fabrication; and, like the Havana Society, it insisted on the relationship between agricultural production and mercantile activity.

(4) Interest in labor included a desire to put a larger proportion of the

---

[48] *Memorias 1794, loc. cit.,* 27-28, 28-31, 429, 429-30 n. on dynamics of machines, 430, 431; "juntas ordinarias" of January 2, February 13, May 1, 1794, in *Colección Actas 1880,* 66-68, 78-79, 90-91; *Memorias 1817,* 6, a hydraulic machine; *ibid.,* 101-2, prizes for rice cleaning machines; *ibid.,* 417, on harrows; *ibid.,* 419, Society offered prize for memoria on "a simplified sugar mill"; *Memorias 1818,* 275-80, a thermometer for sugar processing; *Memorias 1819,* 21, Society considering steam engines; Boloix, *Sucinta notica del ramo de la cera,* 9, citing Jovellanos on technical manuals on agriculture in language understandable to peasants.

[49] *Infra,* ch. xv.

[50] *El Amigo de la Patria,* December 23, 1820, printing a talk of 1812.

[51] *Memorias 1819,* 4, 9-10, 44-45.

population to work; a belief in the need for a larger population; and considerable glorification of effort (and even of labor), and condemnation of idleness as not only conducive to vicious habits but detrimental to production. A larger proportion of workers meant, for one thing, providing work for women. The Societies at Havana, Santiago, and Guatemala had hopes of doing this.[52] The desire for a larger population stemmed from the belief that some of their economic ills were due to underpopulation, an idea much favored in Spain also. Baquíjano of Lima thought underpopulation one of the great difficulties faced by the economies of Spain and America. The statutes of the Puerto Rico Society included as one of the four divisions of the membership a commission on population which was to import laborers. The Havana Society had some thought that wealth in itself was likely to bring with it an increase in the population, that this in turn would lead to more wealth.[53] The Society at the time of its creation thanked the Crown for the increased supply of slaves. This was an important preoccupation of the hacendados who dominated the Society. But in later years the Society reflected some of the Cuban alarm at the revolt of the Negro slaves of Haiti and at the frustrated rebellion of José Antonio Aponte in Cuba in 1812. The Society did show some interest in increasing the white population even before that time.[54] In 1811 and 1816 the Society joined with the town council and Consulado of Havana to advocate augmentation of the white population.[55] Arango y Parreño, as an individual, in the same way moved from demand for, to fear of, more Negroes.[56] In 1817-1820 the members of the Society gave a great deal of attention to the problem of adding to the white population of the island.[57] This was a part of Ramírez' interest in

---

[52] Cf. Guatemala *Novena junta pública*, 54, for comment on "this half of our population," a phrase frequently appearing in Spanish Society memorias.

[53] *Memorias 1794*, *loc. cit.*, 424.

[54] *Ibid.*, 25, that families be brought from the Canaries to eastern Cuba and given land, also foreign Catholics who understood the cultivation of various crops, stockraising, beekeeping, and mining.

[55] Montoro, "Historia Sociedad Económica," *loc. cit.*, 26-27.

[56] Cf. J. A. Portuondo, "La evolución cultural," *loc. cit.*, 261.

[57] *Memorias 1817*, 4, on Ramírez' interest in increasing the proportion of whites; *ibid.*, 39-57, a discourse in a contest on what would be best for Havana, arguing that augmentation of the white population was the answer, pointing out that Ramírez had experience with colonization in Puerto Rico, that Cuba had many vacant areas, that population was needed to cultivate tobacco, coffee, sugar, that the proportion of whites to colored was 2 to 3 in some places, 1 to 3 in others; *Memorias 1818*, 97-102, "Real Cedula para la abolición del tráfico de negros ... 1817"; *ibid.*, 103-27, documents on augmentation of whites; *Memorias 1819*, between 84-85, two tables: (a) report on funds collected to finance new white colonization, some coming as gifts, but most of it from government funds; (b) showing 944 colonists arriving to date, the 517 men being shown by nationality and occupation, with 320 farmers, 62 carpenters, 23 masons,

agricultural diversification involving encouragement of small white farmers and less emphasis on large-scale sugar production.

There were two sides to Society doctrine condemning idleness and glorifying effort—one for the upper and one for the lower class. There were three influences at work here, often in the same individual: the interest in production, the religious view that work promoted good customs, and the general view of the Enlightenment that effort was necessary for the attainment of progress, which could be secured by reason operating on knowledge. In any event, it was obvious that unemployment or underemployment were serious problems in Spanish America,[58] and views on the subject were explicit or implicit in many of the statements and actions of the Societies. Even those Societies that died aborning left a trace of their interest in this matter: Lozano of New Granada, in calling for a Society there, condemned idleness; the Quito Society condemned the egoism of sloth; and the motto of the Santiago de Cuba was "Rise and Work," a slogan that might have found a place in *Poor Richard's Almanac*.

The more voluminous records at Havana and Guatemala contain more data bearing on attitudes toward idleness and labor. The Havana Society considered it essential that men work, declaring that Holland by work became prosperous.[59] The Guatemalans said even more, the *Gazeta* finding in the population of one million some 160,000 men and boys between 16 and

---

and other classifications with fewer numbers; 207 of the 209 Spanish men were farmers, all but one of the carpenters were non-Spanish (French, English, Irish, Anglo-American, etc.); *ibid.*, 159-81, the problem of land for the new white colonists; *ibid.*, 287-302, on colonization; *ibid.*, 326-38, a discourse on augmentation of the white population asserting that all nations have had to pay attention to population problems, and advocating Canary islanders; *ibid.*, 343-51, a memoria on hygiene problems in connection with colonists brought to east Cuba, especially to give care to yellow fever victims, and on the land and other aid to be given colonists; *Memorias 1820*, 65-70, government actions on white colonization, asserting that the 100,000 population of Havana was out of proportion to the rest of the isle; *ibid.*, 74-84, population statistics; *ibid.*, two tables at end: (a) showing colonists entering December 1, 1818 to November 30, 1819, by nation and occupation for men—of 1,332 men, there were 416 Spaniards, 389 French, 65 English, 126 Anglo-Americans, 59 German, 136 Irish, 55 Italian, 54 Swiss, and fewer Portuguese, Dutch, Swedish, Polish, and Danish— only one-half the French were farmers, less than one-fourth of the Anglo-Americans, but all the Spaniards; the 1,332 men included 722 farmers, 266 carpenters, 79 masons, 30 bakers, 25 coopers, and fewer than 20 in each of the other 22 classifications. Cf. Duvon C. Corbitt, "Immigration in Cuba," HAHR, XXII, No. 2 (May, 1942), 280-308.

[58] Cuban sugar planters in the Havana Society needed more hands, but Guatemalan landowners had no such profitable crop, or need for hands (cf. *Gazeta de Guatemala*, IV, No. 126 [June 23, 1800], 280-81, for a survey of the labor force and unemployment).

[59] *Memorias 1794, loc. cit.*, 164.

50 available for labor; 780,000 youths, ancients, and women subsisting in idleness; and 70,000 ecclesiastics, judges, officials, and sick and crippled who were nonworkers. The editors judged the officials and ecclesiastics essential, but thought it necessary to put the 780,000 women, youths, and ancients into productive enterprise.[60] The Society published a work that deplored the fact that men "vegetated" in hammocks while women worked. We have seen a member delivering a sermon glorifying work and the accumulation of property as the best safeguard against sedition, since it tied the holder to the status quo. Another member, an honorary *oidor* of the audiencia, stated that even if religion did not demand it, "nature and the social pact oblige each one of us to compensate as much as he can for the benefits he incessantly receives from his compatriots."[61] And the student of political economy, José Cecilio del Valle, in 1812 stated that "labor is the origin of all wealth . . . , the first in the immense scale of values."[62] One member stressed another interest by tying the question directly to Christianity, and asserting that "virtue has always been the sister of labor."[63] Many others flailed idleness,[64] and the term is almost a refrain in the records.[65]

The class bias of the doctrine was clear in the Guatemala Society. The lower classes were to be kept busy, off the streets, out of trouble, self-supporting, contributing to the national wealth. The upper classes, who possessed the "reason," and could secure knowledge, were to set the example for and direct the lower classes. This effort by the elite the Guatemala Society often called "patriotism," and its opposite "egoism," the pursuit of individual ease, whether through idleness or by attention only to personal interest. Personal interest was expected to give way to community spirit, both because this was the necessary point of view of the patriot, and because reciprocal assistance was indispensable to successful progress, since individuals could not secure it alone. These ideas were implicit in much of what was said and done by members of the Society. Director Villaurrutia stated that only "indolent egoists" would deny the value of the Society, and that this attitude was so strongly rooted in Guatemala that only the greatest effort would reduce its influence.[66] And there were various sorts of egoists:

---

[60] *Gazeta de Guatemala*, IV, No. 162 (June 23, 1800), 280-81.
[61] *Novena junta pública*, 53.
[62] *Amigo de la Patria*, October 26, 1820, 16.
[63] *Junta December 1796*, 33.
[64] E.g., *Novena junta pública*, 13.
[65] Cf. Joseph de Ballesteros y Navas to Secretary Melón, Tonolá, August 30, 1797 (AGG, leg. 2007, exped. 13821), an official in the provinces doubtful that the Society's efforts can prevail against local sloth.
[66] *Quarta junta pública*, 2.

Some harmful because of what they do, and others because of what they fail to do, [and] at the least are useless for the common good. . . . I do not believe that they act because of malignity of spirit, but as myopics through poverty of mind and scarcity of ideas they perceive only that which is near to themselves.

He thought such egoists deserved compassion rather than blame. But the eradication of egoism would result in love of country and in a transformation of the "present miserable *reyno*" of Guatemala.[67]

The "Prospectus" announcing the *Gazeta de Guatemala* expressed much the same idea:

Men of ideas, of whatever birth, of whatever class, you recognize the obligation to be useful to your country, and to devote to it your strength and talents; you look with horror upon the miserable egoism that . . . scorns or abhors all that is not of or for itself.[68]

The *Gazeta*, which was intimately related to the Society, meant intellectual and especially literary labor, which the prospectus stated would draw out hidden talents, foment enthusiasm for literary glory, "without which minds are dead or lethargic, remaining in slovenliness as prejudicial to themselves as to the public."

Discrimination against certain types of labor was condemned by members of the Guatemala Society, a view reminiscent of the work of the Madrid Society on the social equality of occupations. A member of the Guatemala Society argued that distinctions of honor in occupations were artificial growths explicable in historical terms, for the word *mecánica* formerly was honorable and unaccompanied by the idea of dishonor (*vileza*). Differentiation of labor made for wealth, but when some occupations came to be considered dishonorable, many men preferred idleness to an infamous calling; and when this happened, wealth declined and population fell.[69] José Cecilio del Valle in his 1812 eulogy of Goycoechea praised him for writing to the court of Charles IV on the need of honoring classes that exercised the arts and crafts, which "do not prosper when the hands that manage them are dishonored."[70] These pleas, of course, did not indicate belief in a state of nature enjoyed by uninhibited and noble savages, for few creoles or Spaniards in America saw anything in the social and moral life of the Indians to suggest lessons for profitable imitation. They did, however, indicate some willingness to modify, in the interests of greater production, one of the more extreme facets of the prejudice against manual labor.

---

[67] *Quinta junta pública*, 1-2.
[68] *Prospecto de Ampilación* [Guatemala, 1797].
[69] *Quinta junta pública*, 20-22.
[70] Reprint in *El Amigo de la Patria*, No. 16 (February 19, 1821), 375.

(5) Most of the Societies were aware of the crippling effects of bad transport, but the Havana Society especially devoted attention to the question, offering a prize on the subject in its first year.[71]

SOURCES OF IDEAS

The Societies did not leave a detailed picture of the sources of their ideas. We have seen that many members—creoles and Spaniards—adopted new ideas in Spain; and that they were forwarded by changes in American universities, and in new periodicals. Not all the influences flowed from modern sources, of course, although the interests of the Societies made it seem so. The mixture of old and new is suggested by the award of prizes by the Drawing School of the Guatemala Society to representations of Hadrian, Newton, San Pablo, and one of the apostles. But while classicism and religion had obvious uses in sculpture, they had less utility in the field of political economy; and since the latter was the prime concern of the Societies, it is not surprising that the members knew eighteenth-century writers in the field, and favored revisionist literature. It does not require quotation from Feijóo in Society publications to persuade us that the members would approve his strictures on superstition and prejudice.[72] And we can be sure that Jovellanos was read widely even though, as José del Valle said, this "enlightened and zealous protector of cultivators, limited his observations to the agriculture of Spain."[73]

While there is sufficient evidence of American awareness of the existence of the Spanish Societies,[74] it is not clear how much knowledge Americans

---

[71] *Memorias 1793*, 75-80, "Dictámen de la Deputación sobre las Memorias de Caminos." The best essay, in the judgment of the deputation, argued that good roads would lower the price of foodstuffs in Havana, thus aiding the city poor, and that it would also aid the sugar industry. Cf. *Memorias 1794, loc. cit.*, 424-25, bad roads handicapped cultivators, by keeping prices low; *Memorias 1795*, 103-5, "Memorias sobre ... caminos ... por ... Nicolás Calvo y O-Farrill ...," primarily on raising funds through the tithes for roads; *ibid.*, 124-30, suggested financing 80 leagues of roads to a total of 231,000 pesos yearly, with over one-half to come from a head tax on slaves on the grounds that the hacendados could afford it; *Memorias 1817*, 181-95, a memoria of 1795 on roads, recommending that the Church and hacendados finance them, through tithes, and a tax on cattle and slaves; *ibid.*, 419-20, a plan of the Consulado on roads sent to the Society by the captain general; *ibid.*, 57-68, an essay largely on damage caused by bad roads and bridges, with calculation (by weight) of the produce flowing into Havana from the countryside.

[72] Feijóo was cited by Espejo, by the *Gazeta de Guatemala*, and the Havana *Memorias*.

[73] Guatemala *Novena junta pública*, 45. Cf. the Havana Society's *Sucinta noticia ... de la cera* (1815), 9; *Memorias 1817*, 283. Jovellanos' *Ley agraria* was reprinted at Havana in 1813 (Havana *Anales y Memorias*, ser. 4ª, t. VII, 1862-63, 34), the cost being borne by subscription, with the Consulado taking 30 copies.

[74] E. g., *supra*, 44-47, 117-19, 138-39, 170, 175, 196, 214, 220, 221, 239, 241, 259.

had of their labors and publications. Knowledge at least was carried to America by the numerous Spaniards in the American Societies, and by creoles who had been in Spain. More information could be derived from Spanish periodicals and the court gazette. The Havana Society early obtained for its library the Madrid Memorias of 1780-1787; in 1794 made use of Basque Society materials;[75] and in 1817 gave an account of the foundation of the Basque Society, quoted from the latter's *extractos*,[76] and praised the work of the Madrid and Valencia Societies.[77] In Guatemala, Goycoechea in 1797 noted that the Spanish Societies offered prizes on poorhouses; the *Gazeta* in 1798 noted some of the activities of the Madrid Society; and a Society publication the same year mentioned one action of the Madrid Society and cited extracts of the Basque Society for 1793.[78] Cabello y Mesa wrote of the Spanish Societies in his *Telégrafo Mercantil* of Buenos Aires. But evidence of detailed knowledge of the publications and labors of the Spanish Societies is sparse in America.

On the other hand, the American Societies were close to the Spanish in the sense that both took many ideas from the works of Campomanes on popular education and industry, which were instrumental in foundation of the Spanish Societies, and furnished the latter with a large portion of their ideas, both those developed in Campomanes' own language, and those of other authors incorporated in the four-volume *Apéndice* to *Educación popular*. Espejo mentioned the work of Campomanes in glowing terms, Baquíjano cited the *Educación* on the exclusivistic Spanish economic system, Valiente of the Santiago Society cited the *Industria popular*. The *Gazeta de Guatemala* made use of Martínez de la Mata and Ustáriz by way of the *Educación*, and praised Campomanes enthusiastically. The Manila Society recommended study of the *Educación*, and in 1793 paid for a reprinting of the *Industria*. Cabello y Mesa at Buenos Aires, in discussing the "Obgetos Principales" of his *Telégrafo Mercantil*, began by citing Campomanes' discourses on education and industry.[79] José Cecilio del Valle of Guatemala called Campomanes "the first or foremost of those who in the past century summoned to useful

---

[75] *Memorias 1863*, 4.ª ser., t. VIII, 433, record of Society junta, May 15, 1794.

[76] Of the *juntas generales* at Vitoria, 1777 (*Memorias 1817*, 140-43 n.).

[77] *Ibid.*, 131-51, "Discurso sobre ... las Sociedades Económicas." Cf. *Memorias 1842*, 421-22, a discourse of 1795, noting that the division of the Havana Society into four classes was "in imitation of that of Madrid"; "junta ordinaria," April 4, 1793 (*Colección Actas 1880*, 16-17), the Society agreed that it should get a copy of the *Informes de la Sociedad de Madrid y de Murcia sobre erección, dotación y gobierno de Hospicios;* "junta ordinaria," May, 1793 (*ibid.*, 92-94), a member using the statutes of the Basque Society.

[78] San José Muro, *Utilidades y Medios*, 4, 57.

[79] *Telégrafo*, I, 12-16.

objectives those Spaniards who were led astray into frivolous or unimportant studies."[80] The Havana Society quoted and made other references to Campomanes.[81]

The other sources familiar to members of the American Societies were too numerous and miscellaneous for detailed analysis here. The Guatemala reprinted from the Spanish *Semanario Erudito;*[82] the contest on Indian dress was an apparent reflection of the suggestion of Campillo; Campillo and Ward were mentioned by one of the contestants; Ward was quoted in the *Gazeta*. Villaurrutia gave the Society a Spanish translation of Duhamel on woods and plantations.[83] The Havana Society had a few works by political economists in its library, and like the Guatemala Society made frequent reference to such foreign savants as Bacon, Locke, and Condillac.[84] The *Mercurio Peruano* in 1791 cited Malpighi, Reaumur, Duhamel, Newton, and Liebnitz; and Baquíjano coupled Hume on freer trade with Floridablanca and Josiah Child. Espejo cited De Pauw, Hobbes, Grotius, Montesquieu, Robertson, Raynal, D'Alembert, Ustáriz and Diego de Saavedra. These, and other references that could be supplied, indicate that Society members had considerable knowledge of the literature of the past century, foreign and Spanish.

EMPHASIS ON LOCAL PROBLEMS; AMERICANISM

The Societies concentrated on local problems; when they occasionally took a wider view, it was American, so their records refer as little to Spain as those of peninsular Societies relate to America. This localism was encouraged by Society statutes, those of Guatemala providing that neglected points be decided in conformity with the Madrid statutes, "insofar as they may be adaptable to the circumstances of the country." That the circumstances of Spain and America were in fact dissimilar was the plaint to the Guatemala

---

[80] Guatemala *Novena junta pública*, 45.

[81] *Memorias 1793*, quotes from the *Industria Popular* at beginning of volume; *ibid.*, 148; "junta ordinaria," September 19, 1793 (*Colección Actas 1880*, 44-45); *Memorias 1817*, 92-93; *ibid.*, 131. Cf. Pérez Ayala, *Caballero y Góngora*, 289, copies of the *Industria popular* in the archbishop's library at Bogota in 1788.

[82] A political-economic discourse on the influence of guilds. Cf. *infra*, 340, for discussion of this in *Gazeta;* and AGG, A1.6, leg. 2007, exped. 13836, for indication in 1798 that 162 examples of the discourse remained in the Society archives, 106 with the printer in Guatemala, and 12 with Mociño in Mexico.

[83] *Quarta junta pública*, 17-18. Some of the other authors mentioned in Society publications, by members in other places, and by the *Gazeta* were Say, Montesquieu, Hume, Smith, Galiani, Necker, Condillac, Locke, Colbert, the Encyclopedia, Buffon, Sully.

[84] E.g., *Memorias 1794*, 31; *Memorias 1794*, *loc. cit.*, 36, 423; *Memorias 1795*, [2], 108, 110, 129-30; *Memorias 1817*, 424; *Memorias 1818*, 344-406, 413-41.

Society of a flax cultivator whose worst difficulty was in adjusting European methods and recommendations to the climatic conditions of America. A similar view, published by the Havana Society, said it would be guided by the example of other Societies, but would diverge when necessary in the light of local conditions of land, climate, vegetation, and indeed "the constitution and disposition of the residents."[85] The statutes of the Puerto Rico Society were to be based on those of Spanish Societies, "with the differences which the diversity of countries and the variety of ends dictate."

As this quotation implies, the social as well as the natural environment of America differed from that of Spain. Thus the views of the American Societies on Indians and Negroes could hardly be duplicated in Spain, and Society members there could not have the interest of the Havana Society in an increase of the white as opposed to black population; or the interest of the Guatemala Society in the *repartimiento*,[86] or its concern for the problem of dressing Indians and *ladinos* in European style. Reference to the Indians in the last connection as "the major portion of our homeland" represented a note that could have no echo in Europe.

Each Society dealt with the problems of a limited area. The Lima Society focused the attention of the *Mercurio* on the viceroyalty, its resources, population, and the state of learning there. In Cuba the Societies at Santiago and Havana, and the branches of the latter in three small towns, dealt with local problems, or at most with Cuban problems; for Havana this meant mainly sugar; for the others, other agricultural interests. Guatemala adopted a good deal of the interest of the Spanish Societies in popular industry, because of the tradition of clothmaking among the Indians of that area. The Society observed that since dyes from New Spain were expensive, partly due to freight charges, local tints should be developed.[87]

This localism sometimes tended to merge into Americanism, so that the expressions "homeland" or "fatherland" (*país* or *patria*) were sometimes used in a highly parochial sense. A member of the Guatemala Society spoke of his "so admirable land," declaring that he loved his *patria* Guatemala with

---

[85] Havana *Memorias 1794, loc. cit.,* 418; *ibid.,* 420, on the differences between cultivation in Europe and Cuba.

[86] Cf. *Quarta junta pública,* 13: a prize offered for a demonstration of the justice of the prohibition of assignment of *repartimientos* by the *juezes,* and for suggestions as to how to stimulate the Indians to work without compulsion.

[87] Cf. Larrazabal, *Apuntamientos,* 155-56, for an exposition of 1811 on the difference between the mainland and islands of America; the latter had an even, hot climate, slaves, and good agricultural exports, so that their relations with Spain were mutually beneficial; but the mainland had a varied climate, could raise both European and Asiatic crops, its inhabitants were all free, and it could engage not only in agriculture but in arts and crafts.

all his heart.[88] An entrant in one of the Guatemala Society's contests called the Americas—not the Indies—the "most precious stone of the Crown." This affectionate tone combined with a note of belligerent defense against Spain in the Quito Society's *Primicias de la Cultura de Quito*, edited by the bitter creole Espejo, who breathed hatred for years—as did the *Gazeta de Guatemala*—of the European dogma that Americans were inferior to men born in the old country, and even wrote in the *Primicias* of a "Nation" that is "American." This American defensiveness was shown also by the Lima Society in defending Peruvian culture against the attacks of the Spaniard Olavarrieta. Yet another form of this localism was displayed by the Guatemala Society in ascribing the economic depression to contraband, and advocating a local textile industry as the remedy, but also suggesting, in 1811, that people "buy Guatemala," and that "Brittany linen" made from maguey be called "Guatemala" linen, since the terminology was merely a commercial device. None of this could have been reassuring to the textile interests of Spain or to the Spanish government.

CASTE AND CLASS

Members of the Societies were drawn from the dominant minority or its satellites, this class distinction being written into the statutes by provision that members be learned enough to forward the work of study, education, and propaganda. In neither hemisphere did the members intend anything egalitarian by their frequent use of the expression "common felicity." In America the class bias was complicated by caste distinctions arising from the presence of large numbers of subordinate peoples of non-European race. The history of the Societies records the confusion of caste and class distinctions. It was clearly a caste judgment when the Havana Society in 1793 decided that only "white" girls could be enrolled in its new Casa de Educandas, or in 1794 to admit only "white boys and girls" to the two new free primary schools, since the facilities would only accommodate 200.[89] But the views of members on Negro slavery reveal a mixture of motives and interests: to improve the proportion of whites, to get more slaves for the sugar industry, to diversify agriculture by way of small white-operated farms growing crops other than sugar.[90] Cabello's Society at Buenos Aires intended to exclude Negroes, and persons of mixed race. It is not clear what the Guatemala Society intended when, in undertaking a census of cacao plantations, it asked which were Indian and which *ladino*. But clear distinction of class

---

[88] *Segunda junta pública*, 35.

[89] *Memorias 1794 loc. cit.*, 33.

[90] Cf. Havana *Memorias 1818*, 11, referring to "la gente de color y otros bagamundos," for an upper-class view on race.

by economic lines is evident in its offer of prizes for flax culture to poor Spaniards, Indians, or *ladinos*. And the Truxillo junta of the Guatemala Society expressed the interest of the dominant minority in its class position when it advocated improvement of the food situation in order to strengthen the Spanish hold on the lower classes, but indicated caste division by identifying them as *Negros Caribes*. And students in the Drawing School of the Guatemala Society were divided in 1796 into *la gente distinguida* and *el común*. The statutes of the Puerto Rico Society excluded Negroes from membership.[91]

The caste and class questions were strikingly delineated in the 1796 contest of the Guatemala Society on the question of whether the predominantly Indian and *ladino* population was not poverty-stricken and given to unfortunate habits because it was not Europeanized. The precise question was what advantages might flow from persuading them to wear Spanish-style clothes and shoes. The winner of the contest considered that only five per cent of the population dressed thus; that the Indians lived like beasts; and that Spaniards found them unworthy of regard, since, as Buffon averred, it was natural to judge people by their appearance. This contestant considered all races human, but noted that others thought the Indians inherently incapable of complete Europeanization. A second contestant opposed European dress for Indians, considering the hierarchical organization proper for society, for there should be "some that command, and others that obey." This man's motives were strongly economic; he wished to keep down the cost of labor, hence the price of indigo and other products, so they could be marketed at Havana. A third contestant favored the reform as necessary for the security of the state, so Indians and *ladinos* would feel they had a fatherland (*patria*), and be motivated to contribute to its well-being. He called upon history to sustain his argument by observing that the Helots were always a danger to the Lacedemonians.

The judges noted that the winner of the contest showed more successfully the desirability of changing the dress habits of Indians and *ladinos* than how it was to be done—as the contest stipulated—without compulsion. The fact was, as the winner noted, that the Indians were prone to think badly of Spanish motives and were easily driven into obstinacy. Thus, three factors inhibited such reform: cost, upper-class opposition, and resistance by the Indians. The contest had stirred considerable interest, and produced some opinions that seemed dangerously critical to the Spanish government.[92]

---

[91] Cf. Appendix for discrimination against *pardos* in connection with the Caracas Society of the 1830's.

[92] *Infra*, 297 *et seq*., for more on the contest; *supra*, 165 and n., *Mercurio Peruano* and race.

The Problem of Poverty

The Societies were interested—on economic and social grounds—in the problems of poverty,[93] wishing to improve production and succor the deserving poor, but only Havana and Guatemala endured long enough to undertake action.[94]

The Havana memorias carried references to the problem, as the statement that though virtue and poverty might go together, poverty might lead to indigence, then to mendicity, with its attendant evils;[95] and its efforts in 1793-1795 had so little success that in 1817 it noted that there were so many vagabonds of both sexes that perhaps some might be sent as colonists to unpopulated parts of the island.[96]

The Havana Society supervised a hospice which included a Casa de Beneficencia for the succor and training of indigent women, to reclaim vagabonds from the vicious habits of their lives; and a Casa de Educandas for the care and education of orphan girls. This hospice was initiated in 1792 by a group of prominent Habaneros, who agreed that when the Economic Society was approved by Spain it should take over the Casa. The Crown approved the Casa in July, 1792, and the Economic Society in December; in January, 1793, a deputation of the Society took over planning for the Casa de Beneficencia.[97] Construction of its building began in April, 1793.[98] A Society committee in 1793 was charged with drawing the ordinances of the Casa, and presented them to the Society in November, 1794. They had used as a model those of some European cities, but did not copy any, because conditions varied between countries.[99] The Society planned a brotherhood to help finance the Casa.[100]

The Casa de Educandas was installed in a rented house, with two women teachers. Instructions for its government provided a curriculum including

---

[93] *Supra*, 275, on general interest in philanthropy.

[94] The Lima Society printed in the *Mercurio* material on beneficent institutions.

[95] *Memorias 1794, loc. cit.*, 422 and n.

[96] *Memorias 1817*, 50.

[97] The original representation to Captain General Las Casas in March, 1792, was accompanied by a subscription of 36,000 pesos for the projected hospice. A provisional planning junta in 1792 received land from Dr. Luís Peñalver, vicar general of the diocese; plans for the building were drawn by Artillery Captain Agustín de Ibarra.

[98] The foregoing is based on Havana *Memorias 1793*, 44-52, "Constitución y Progresos de la Casa de Beneficencia." The representation of 1792 is reprinted in Raimundo Cabrera, *La Casa de Beneficencia y la Sociedad Económica* (Havana, 1911), 14-16.

[99] *Memorias 1794, loc. cit.*, 423-24.

[100] *Ibid.*, 423; cf. "junta ordinaria," February 19, 1795 (in Havana *Memorias 1864*, 313), on the projected "charity association."

religion, reading, sewing, and such household arts as sweeping, laundering, and cooking, teaching the girls not to disdain this sort of work; the girls were to be "white, poor, orphans," of seven to ten years; and they were inoculated. By December, 1794, there were twenty-seven girls in the Casa de Educandas, including two daughters of a widower who paid a fee.[101]

By the end of 1794 the Casa building was nearly completed, and the Casa de Educandas had been installed in one section in December, thirty-three girls being involved in the move.[102] By December, 1795, there were fifty-one girls, including three paying (*pensionistas*).[103] In 1795 the girls made cotton stuffs, purses, gloves, lace, and some other things.[104] In that year, also, the poorhouse side of the Casa was opened—it was completely separate from the *educandas*—with an announcement on March 5 to the public that the Economic Society would form a charitable association for the sustenance of the poor, and another in May that for the present only women would be cared for. Not many women responded voluntarily, so the Society asked the captain general to collect women found asking alms, which he did in August. By the end of the year the Casa de Beneficencia held seventy-three women, both voluntary and forced inmates; the capacity of that part of the institution was 200. The voluntary inmates were set to sewing, and the involuntary to raveling tow.[105] By May, 1805, it held 226 persons, but only 54 were *educandas*, while 104 were poor-relief cases (*indigentes*), and 54 were slaves.[106]

---

[101] *Memorias 1793*, 52-61, "Constitución y Progresos ...," Havana, December, 1794 [sic].

[102] *Memorias 1794, loc. cit.*, 111-13, " ... la Diputación encargada del gobierno de la Casa de Beneficencia"; *ibid.*, 113-14, " ... de la Casa de niñas educandas"; *ibid.*, 115-17, "Discurso ... con motivo de la translación de las Educandas á la Casa de Beneficencia"; cf. *ibid.*, 118-20, "Estado que presenta todo lo que la casa de Beneficencia ha adquirido desde su establecimiento ...," for finances. After December, 1794, the deputation of the Society ran both the Beneficencia and the Educandas (*Memorias 1795*, 62). In 1796 were united to the deputation of the Society for the Casa a member each of the ecclesiastical cabildo, the town council, and the Consulado, on the suggestion of the Society and agreement of the Captain General (Cabrera, *Casa de Beneficencia*, 51-56).

[103] *Memorias 1795*, 64.

[104] *Ibid.*, 64-65.

[105] *Ibid.*, 66-72. Cf. *ibid.*, 147-49, "Noticia del gasto diario ... de la Casa de Educandas ...," dealing with 41 girls, and 14 slaves, teachers, servants, and a total cost of 13 pesos, 6 reals per day, broken down by items of food, giving a good idea of the diet, and other expenses, which averaged out at 2 reals each per day for the 55 persons in the Casa de Educandas; *ibid.*, 148, same for the Casa de Indigentes, which involved more people and a larger total, but less per capita; *ibid.*, on the clothes issued to the *educandas*, *indigentes voluntarias*, and *correccionarias*.

[106] *El Aviso. Papel Periódico de la Havana*, No. 42 (September 5, 1805), the remainder being: *dependientes* (11) and *correcionarias* (3). Cf. *Tareas 1815*, 20, in

In later years the Casa de Beneficencia derived considerable income from the manufacture of cigars.[107] In December, 1816, there were 187 persons in the Casa;[108] and the women and slaves in the poorhouse cigar shop were producing cigars for the royal lottery; the girls in the Casa de Educandas continued making buttons, purses, and clothes. The 28,443 pesos income of the Casa included 9,000 from the manufacture of cigars, 4,500 from the articles made by the *educandas*, the rest from investment and property and government subsidy, in addition to which the institution received gifts of food, cotton, and other items.[109] In 1817 departures and admissions balanced closely, leaving 189 persons in the Casa at the end of 1817, most of the eighty-two entrances and departures having been among the *indigentes*, as might be expected.[110] The number of persons in the Casa at the end of 1818 was the same as a year earlier. The Casa was in bad condition by 1823, like the Society itself, and in 1824 Captain General Vives began to try to improve both.[112] The Puerto-Príncipe branch of the Havana Society in 1817 was considering foundation of a Casa de Beneficencia on the model of the Havana.[113]

Interest in Guatemala involved the usual mixture of motives. One churchman said that human and divine law required care of the unfortunate, all being sons of God, given by nature an equal right in its fruits and productions; and if the first settlers were not too scrupulous in the apportionment of those fruits, the present residents did not need to imitate them.[114] But another churchman spoke largely in terms of binding the poor to the status quo with property.[115] In any event, the region was inhabited by an Indian

---

November, 1815, it held 178 persons: 62 *educandas*, 61 *indigentes* (*blancas y de color*), 1 *correcionaria*, 13 *dependientes*, 54 slaves.

[107] *Memorias 1817*, 105-12, "Relación de las Tareas de la Casa ...," in 1816.

[108] Being 62 *educandas*, 61 *indigentes*, 13 *dependientes*, and 51 female slaves.

[109] All the above from Havana *Memorias 1817*, 113-15, "Estado de la Casa ... en 30 de noviembre de 1816." Cf. *Tareas 1815*, 16-17, for articles produced by the inmates.

[110] *Memorias 1818*, 73-86, for documents on the Casa in 1817.

[111] *Memorias 1819*, 61-72, finances, operations, work of the *educandas*, etc.

[112] Cf. *Relación histórica de los beneficios hechos a la Real sociedad económica, casa de beneficencia y demás dependiencias de aquel cuerpo por ... Francisco Dionisio Vives.* ... (Havana, 1832); Cabrera, *Casa de Beneficencia*, 57-58, the Casa had a debt of 12,000 pesos and a committee of women began to do something about it; "Real Casa de Beneficencia. ... Su Historia," RBC, VII, No. 4 (July-August, 1912), 292-303, at 297, boys were not admitted until the fall of 1827; Pezuela, *Ensayo histórico* [1842], 344-45, by that time there were in the Casa over 400 *criaturas* of both sexes.

[113] Havana *Memorias 1817*, 151-62.

[114] *Quarta junta pública*, 20.

[115] *Supra*, 272-73, for this man's views; 275, for other indications of confusion of opinion and motive with regard to the problems of poverty and progress.

population that was poor and indolent, largely because it could not hope to improve its lot, but was forced to serve the small minority of whites.[116] The Church was both physically and morally incapable of dealing with the problem.[117] The members of the Society were primarily concerned, however, with the poor of the city. The Hospital of San Juan de Dios gave some care to the sick,[118] but the larger problem was to assist the able-bodied indigent who drifted into town.

The Economic Society turned to this question when asked for advice by a "hospice committee" that was considering creation of such an institution. A Society committee, after study, reported in a memorial by Dr. José Antonio Goycoechea, opposing a hospice and proposing instead a Brotherhood of Charity similar to those of Europe.[119]

The Society accepted Goycoechea's ideas in June, 1796, but directed its censor, Antonio García Redondo, to draft a plan of execution that would correct their impractical features. The Society sent its recommendations to the hospice committee, but at the same time printed, as an aid to discussion of this matter of "the greatest transcendence in the public order," Goycoechea's "Memorial on the Method of Destroying Mendicity and of Succoring the True Poor of this Capital," and García Redondo's "Plan of Execution."[120] Goycoechea commenced with the acknowledgment that

> The destruction of mendicity is a matter that has occupied in all times the attention of legislators, the pens of wise men, and the hopes of all men of good will. . . . It is incredible what forces have been expended by all governments for the abolition of mendicity.

Noting that both Church and civil government had long attempted to deal with the problem, and that Europe, including Spain, had numerous poorhouses, he concluded that unfortunately "beggary was multiplied in the same places where the Hospices were established. Madrid and Mexico constitute a lamentable example." In the Low Countries all such institutions were abandoned. A poorhouse could not care for all the poor of a city, much less of wider areas, as was recognized by the fiscals of the Council of Castile, Floridablanca and Campomanes, in founding a poorhouse at

---

[116] Salvatierra, *Contribución*, II, 149, 186.

[117] *Ibid.*, 149-50, on an archbishop's *visita* to the villages, and his report to the king on the sloth and bad habits of the Indians, noting that the churches were disorganized and did little to aid, the curates usually having one or more women.

[118] Flamenco, *Beneficencia en Guatemala*, 18-19, for figures, from the *Gazeta de Guatemala*, on the work of the hospital in 1792-96, with a breakdown by racial groups.

[119] *Junta pública December 1796*, 15-17.

[120] Published in a single volume in 1797 with the title *Memorias sobre los medios de destruir la mendicidad y de socorrer los verdaderos pobres de esta capital* (Nueva Guatemala: Ygnacio Beteta). The following analysis is based on this volume.

Toledo. Even if a house large enough for all the poor could be built, the effect would be bad, since its products would compete unfairly with those of private workmen, resulting in the creation of more poor. The problem, he concluded, was so urgent that the Societies of Spain since 1780 had been offering prizes for suggestions for avoidance of this difficulty.

Other difficulties were that the mixture of persons in such establishments —as in prisons—resulted in so much sickness that the poor avoided them like the plague; and the mixture of the good with the evil caused the corruption of many unfortunates; and the poor in such places did not marry and multiply and provide the state with useful individuals for its defense.

Goycoechea strongly advocated distinction between the unfortunate poor and the deliberately idle, citing as authority sacred history, scripture, and Spanish law, and rejecting the vulgar belief that all almsgiving was blessed. He felt that with the lazy winnowed out the true poor in the city of Guatemala would amount to less than half the total of those who had a claim to poverty. He suggested as a practice with precedent in Spanish law that parish priests license beggars, if they were unable to work, and had been to confession. This localized control would be furthered by prohibition of almsgiving to any but residents of the city, and by a directive from the archbishop to the curates of the province to keep the poor of their parishes at home.

Having catalogued the faults of poorhouses, and controlled the drift of the indigent to town, Goycoechea proposed caring for the veritable and properly certified poor by means of a Charity Association for the capital, to be served by its most influential people. With funds from this association, and with the aid of the guilds, the poor were to be kept busy in workhouses. Funds were not to be spent on a sumptuous edifice. The administration of the workhouse scheme was tied to the six wards (*quarteles*) and districts (*barrios*) into which the city was already divided for civil and ecclesiastical government. The poor were to be divided into those incapable of labor, and those either unable to find work or not completely self-supporting. Other provisions were that the healthy stay at the workhouses only during the day, thus avoiding a common fault of hospices; that artisans be compelled to take apprentices, and women required to teach girls the "labors corresponding to their sex"; and that the poor be paid for their work, and given alms if necessary (unless they spent their earnings improperly).

The "Plan of Execution" by García Redondo wanted the lists of deserving poor compiled by persons of some practical knowledge, preferably with experience in the offices of *alcalde ordinario* or *alcalde de barrio;* and the collection of the funds for the charity houses supervised by a number of persons, rather than by one or two as suggested by Goycoechea. The other recommendations meant to ensure that the poor were not encouraged in idleness, and that the charity should not be too costly for the charitable.

The *Gazeta* publicized the contest, and advertised the printed memorial for sale at Beteta's bookstore. Further, it announced that the question was of such importance that the *Gazeta* itself would devote some attention to it.[121] In the course of a series of articles on the matter, the periodical noted that in 1779 the Society of Soissons had offered a prize on the subject; and that in 1784 the Madrid Society had published sixteen memorials on it.[122]

This scheme of poor relief was like the guild reform suggested by the Society,[123] in proposing to reduce beggary and idleness by persuading people to work. Both were founded on the view that most of the poor were in such case because of bad habits, thus defining poverty as a moral-ethical rather than an economic problem. The economic problem was discussed, however, in the Society's contest, announced in July, 1796, on the physical, moral, and political advantages that might accrue to the state and to the Indians and *ladinos* if they—the bulk of the population—could be persuaded, without compulsion, to wear Spanish-style clothes and shoes. The Society reported the contest under the heading of "Public Education,"[124] and tried to assure judgment on merit by providing that the authors of entries not be revealed until the awards were made.

Ten essays were submitted, and the winner, announced at the public junta of December, 1797, was Friar Matías de Córdova, "Master of Students" at the Dominican Convent in the city. Seconn prize went to Friar Antonio de San José Muro, assistant general of the Bethlemite order in Mexico. Both men were made "members of merit" of the Society, which had their essays printed in full, together with extracts from the other entries.[125] Beteta's printing shop tried to sell the Córdova essay for three reals,[126] but it moved very slowly.[127]

---

[121] II, No. 50 (February 26, 1798), 9-12.

[122] II, No. 51 (March 5, 1798), 17-18; No. 52 (March 12), 25-28; No. 53 (March 19), 33-34; No. 67 (June 25), 157-59.

[123] *Infra*, 338 et seq.

[124] *Junta pública December 1796*, 19-20; *Tercera junta pública*, 13-14. Cf. *Gazeta de Guatemala*, I, No. 7 (March 27, 1797), calling the problem one of "the greatest importance"; and more news on the contest in I, No. 37 (October 16), 294-95; No. 38 (October 30), 312; No. 44 (December 11).

[125] *Tercera junta pública*, 13-14; *Gazeta de Guatemala*, December 11, 1797, 361-62; June 25, 1798, 153-57, July 2, 1798, 161-63. Seven of the ten entries were declared ineligible either because they arrived too late or because the names of the authors were revealed.

[126] Medina, *Imprenta en Guatemala*, 349.

[127] *Supra*, 258 n.

Córdova's work subordinated political economy to Roman Catholic humanitarianism, arguing that the Indians deserved attention from Spaniards because all races were part of the human race. He began by identifying himself with humanity at large:

Until now it has been believed that if men are seen with philosophical eyes they must excite laughter or tears. Vulgarly authorized by the times, with which I have not been able to agree. No, the profound meditations of the abstract sciences have made me understand that I cannot distinguish myself from man, and that humanity is not a fiction of the classroom, but I myself, [and] the unhappiness of men . . . is my own unhappiness.[128]

He thought that most of the "enlightened men" of Guatemala agreed with him, but since many others did not, he was now prepared to convince them. Guatemala in his view did not enjoy the bond that nature intended when it made men dependent upon one another and required them to engage in an exchange of products. This was because "each Indian, mulatto, mestizo, and even poor Spaniard, needs no more than his woman," who made everything he required. But these requirements could be enlarged, for only five per cent of the population dressed in the European fashion.[129] If Indians and mulattoes wore Spanish-style clothes and shoes they would be stimulated from their idleness and all forms of commerce and industry would benefit.[130]

Córdova went on from this to advocate reform of the common Indian method of tillage, especially in the cacao areas, where the women worked while the men "vegetated" in their hammocks. And ambition was further reduced by the visits of the *alcaldes mayores* to those regions, levying unfair taxes.[131] The result of this idleness was perhaps greatest in the moral realm, for the Indians lived like beasts,[132] and Spaniards considered them unworthy of regard.[133]

Córdova argued that while of course the Indians wanted to dress *a la Española*,[134] it was harder for them to take the step than for the mulattoes, since Indians were held down more by the force of opinion, whereas mulattoes were more often confounded with the poor Spaniards as a class.[135]

---

[128] Reprint in Guillén, *Fraile prócer*, 253. Printed in Guatemala in 1798 by Beteta as *Utilidades de que todos los Indios y Ladinos se vistan y calcen a la Española, y medios de conseguirlo.*

[129] Reprint in Guillén, 255.

[130] *Ibid.*, 253-54.

[131] *Ibid.*, 256.

[132] *Ibid.*, 257.

[133] *Ibid.*, 258.

[134] *Ibid.*, 259.

[135] Córdova apparently used "mulatto" as a synonym of "mestizo" and "ladino." He did use all three terms, but *mulato* almost uniformly with Indian in opposition to Spaniard.

This he considered chiefly due to Indian ignorance of the Spanish language, which he believed should be taught them as a matter of policy. In dealing with Indians, however, Córdova advised caution, since they were prone to think badly of Spanish motives and were easily driven into obstinacy. Further, he advocated a flexible program, for "man is not of the order of a machine to which may be given a fixed and infallible direction." Above all else, he argued, the need was for the destruction of the opinion which still supported the old dress for Indians.[136] He closed with a call for common action by men of honor, to enter into a campaign to favor "this part of the species, and the major portion of our homeland (*patria*)."[137]

Friar San José Muro, who had learned of the contest via the *Gazeta de Mexico*, did not confine himself so closely to the subject. He began with a condemnation of "our writers [who] have regarded with indifference the most precious stone of the Crown, which is their America";[138] and condemned the Royal Madrid Society and the Consulado of Barcelona for having proposed only a few years before the "cruel" destruction of the few looms existing in America.[139]

After an extended discussion of economic life in America, he turned to the subject of the contest, estimating the population of the captaincy general at one and a half million, including one million Indians and *ladinos* requiring European clothing.[140] To derive benefit from the Europeanization of their dress, he thought it would be necessary to improve their "means of subsistence, and physical, moral, civil, and scientific education."[141] He found the Indians and *ladinos* in a miserable state, with a terrible infant mortality rate, which he declared one of the results of poverty, nudity, misery, and ignorance.[142] To correct this and other evils, the quality and quantity of, American production would have to be increased.[143] Industry, agriculture, and internal and external commerce ought to be augmented.[144] Better physical and moral education also were required.[145] And these matters should be the concern of everyone, for

---

[136] *Ibid.*, 259-60.

[137] *Ibid.*, 262.

[138] Antonio de San José Muro, *et al.*, *Utilidades y medios de que los indios y ladinos visten y calcen a la española. Memoria que mereció el accesit* ... (N. Guatemala: Beteta, 1798), 3. Pp. 58-73 are "extractos" from other essays.

[139] *Ibid.*, 4.

[140] *Ibid.*, 13.

[141] *Ibid.*, 40.

[142] *Ibid.*, 31-32.

[143] *Ibid.*, 14-28, a mass of statistics and suggestions.

[144] *Ibid.*, 30.

[145] *Ibid.*, 32 *et seq.*

There are few who think seriously about the obligation which each citizen has of forwarding as much as he can the felicity of the homeland (*patria*), and much fewer those who fatigue themselves with it without hope of profit, and only the internal satisfaction of benefiting their fellow creatures. This pitiful human con dition the Illustrious Society of Guatemala has penetrated very well.[146]

Another entry opposed Spanish dress for Indians, arguing that a hierarchical organization was proper for society, in which "some . . . command, and others . . . obey"; that their native clothes covered the Indians well enough; that they should not be given unfamiliar things. Furthermore, who was to pay for their new wardrobes? Dressing the Indians, who were the laborers, in Spanish clothes would be "injurious to this nation (*nación*)," for it would require an increase in their wages, which would raise the price of indigo and other products so that they could not be marketed at Havana.[147]

Another author estimated that the captaincy general contained 570,000 Indians and some 190,000 *ladinos*, and argued that the fabrication of shoes and clothes for them would give employment to thousands, increase the wealth of the state, reduce pestilence, and improve morality. The author suggested that Indian and Spanish needs were the same, and that the reform was necessary for the security of the state, since Indians and *ladinos* would not feel they had a fatherland for which to work, if they obtained nothing in return. He called upon history to sustain his case by observing that the Helots were always a danger to the Lacedemonians.[148]

The contest showed awareness that consideration of the problem of poverty in Guatemala had to begin with the mass of the Indian and *ladino* population. But it solved nothing, as the judges commented in noting that Córdova had been more successful in demonstrating the desirability of these dress reforms than in showing how to accomplish them without compulsion, as the contest suggested. The contest also revealed the difference of opinion within the small articulate controlling class as to whether the Indian could or ought to be integrated into the European community. That question had not been resolved to everyone's satisfaction a century and a half later.[149]

---

[146] *Ibid.*, 29. Cf. Fisher, *Background Independence*, 167, for some other of San José Muro's ideas, especially spinning; John S. Fox, "Antonio de San José Muro: Political Economist of New Spain," HAHR, XXI, No. 3 (August, 1941), 410-16, for his objections to commercial monopoly.

[147] *Ibid.*, 66-69, in the section of extracts.

[148] Too late for the contest, but printed in *Gazeta de Guatemala*, I, No. 41 (November 13, 1797), 325-26; No. 42 (November 20), 333-34; No. 43 (November 27), 341-45.

[149] Cf. Fisher, *Background Independence*, 166, two Mexican viceroys tried to make people in New Spain wear clothes, starting with the stevedores of the customhouse, and workers in the mint and royal cigar factory.

CHAPTER FIFTEEN

Science, Literature, and Education

The Societies did little with science, literature, and other intellectual questions outside the fields of economic development and education. Their educational interests included vocational, technical, and scientific instruction, fine and applied arts, and primary letters; but most of this bore directly or indirectly on their economic objectives.

Science and Literature

Some of the men attracted to the American Societies already were interested in intellectual matters and favored contemporary ideas. And the Societies were drawn to scientific and literary questions by the connections between these studies and the primary interest of the Societies in economic development.[1] Some of these connections were fostered in Society classes and schools. There were, however, a few other activities that do not fall easily under the heading of education.

The Societies had some interest in medicine,[2] including vaccination, in which the Havana and Guatemala Societies showed an interest similar to

---

[1] Cf. Havana *Memorias 1793*, 28, the censor of the Society at the first junta of the Clase de Ciencias y Artes declared that the fundamentals of the arts and sciences were mathematics, drafting, physics, chemistry, natural history, botany, and anatomy.

[2] Havana *Memorias 1817*, 254-63, "Discurso ... sobre si en el actual estado de la ciencia médica, podrá ser buen profesor de ella quien no posea la botánica y química," describing the uses of botany and chemistry in medicine and concluding that a doctor needed them; *ibid.*, 381, "Memoria sobre la dissenteria ...," by a medical doctor of Madrid, who had observed its mortal effects on Negroes in Cuba; Havana *Memorias*

that of the Basque Society. Pupils in the Casa de Educandas of Havana were inoculated against smallpox. The *junta de vacuna* of Havana, under Dr. Tomás Romay, was vaccinating people, despite some opposition, even before arrival at Havana in May, 1804, of the Royal Expedition on vaccination; and Romay, in December, 1804, read to the Society a report on the work of the junta.[3] The Society continued this interest in later years,[4] and in some other scientific matters.[5] A member of the Guatemala Society, the medical doctor Narciso Esparragosa, during the period of the Society's suspension edited an issue of the *Gazeta* in which notice was given of the arrival in the captaincy general of the vaccinating fluid sent from Spain in the royal expedition.[6]

The Guatemala Society showed further scientific interest when Dr. Esparragosa presented to it men he had treated surgically for cataracts, the first time the operation had been performed in the captaincy general. It was announced at one of the Society's public juntas that Esparragosa would

---

1819, table between 60-61, on the sick admitted, released, and deceased at the royal hospital of Havana in 1818; *ibid.*, 220-40, article by Benjamin Rush of the "Academy of Pennsylvania," Philadelphia, May, 1806, translated by Dr. Florencio Pérez Comoto, on the spleen, liver, pancreas, and thyroid; *ibid.*, 241-45, comments of Dr. Romay on the Rush article; *Memorias 1845*, 235-46, a memorial of 1805 by Romay on the health aspect of burial inside the city.

[3] *Acta Juntas Generales 1833*, 26-27; Horacio Abascal, "Contribución de la Sociedad Económica al progreso de la medicina en Cuba," RBC, XLVII, No. 1 (January-February, 1941), 5-31, at 19-20; Abascal, *loc. cit.*, 19-20; *Memorias 1895*, 64-72, a historical review of the Society's vaccination work in 1802-20; Peraza y Sarausa, "Indice," *loc. cit.*, LVIII, 89 *et seq.*, on vaccination in 1805; Horacio Abascal, "Labor de Romay en la Sociedad Económica," RBC, LXV (January-June, 1950), 126-34.

[4] In 1808 was printed an eight-page *Informe* of that year by Romay to the Society on vaccination (*Anales y Memorias*, ser. 4, t. VII, 20); *Tareas 1815*, 23-26, Romay reports progress, but opposition continues; *Memorias 1817*, 281-82, on the hope in 1806 that a junta de vacuna, subordinate to that of Havana, could be formed at Sancti-Espíritu, where a deputation of the Havana Society had recently been opened; *Memorias 1819*, 89-96, report of Romay on work of the *Junta Central de Vacuna* in 1818, having inoculated 20,177 persons, and also sent the "virus vacuno" to the interior of the isle and overseas; *Memorias 1820*, 91-94, account by Romay of work in 1819.

[5] *Memorias 1794*, *loc. cit.*, 101, 434, corrections for lunar tables; *Memorias 1817*, 116-20, on the value of natural science for parish priests, arguing the value of botany and chemistry for both medicine and agriculture; *ibid.*, 287, the Society working against that ignorance which had damaged the land, and especially the need to work with the exact sciences, and claiming that the latter elevate the soul; *ibid.*, 424, a uranographic machine sent to the Society; *Memorias 1818*, 185-99, discourse in Mexico on botany by Dr. Florencio Pérez y Comoto; *Memorias 1820*, 37-38, map of Cuba drawn by a resident and presented to the Society, the latter noting that the map gave most of its attention to the coast, so it had asked the bishop for data on the interior.

[6] VIII, No. 352 (June, 1804); Salazar, *Historia intelectual*, 92-93.

perform the operation gratis for all the poor who came to him.[7] A Cabinet of Natural History was set up on the advice of José Longinos Martínez, naturalist of the Royal Botanical Expedition to New Spain, who resided for a time in Guatemala. He proposed in July, 1796, that the exhibit be prepared, offering his assistance. For this he was made *socio de mérito* of the Society. The display was opened to the public in December, 1796. Nearly a year later the Society wrote Longinos Martínez in Mexico that the collection was not proceeding well. In answer, the naturalist lamented that the science had too few partisans even in Spain, and suggested offering a medal to the person sending in the greatest number of specimens. These were arriving in small quantity from the provinces.[8] The *Gazeta*, soliciting materials for the Cabinet, declared that the exhibit would be of general utility, and contribute to the well-being of humanity and to the advancement of the natural sciences, "whose study is promoted and protected now with the greatest persistence by our glorious Monarch."[9] José Mociño, doctor of the Royal Botanical Expedition, was present at the opening of the Cabinet, and when some of the collection was later sent to Spain he encountered it there.[10]

The Societies displayed some small interest in literature. The first number of the *Primicias de la Cultura de Quito* was devoted in large part to literature as an intellectual endeavor, unconnected with economics. The statutes of the Bogota Society put one of its main interests as the useful sciences and liberal arts. The Havana Society offered a prize for a chronological summary of the most important events of Cuban history from the discovery to 1800, and important Spanish events affecting Cuba.[11] The Guatemala Society paid small attention to any literature but that of political economy. Its discussions of "literature"—often under that title—had little to do with belles-lettres and much with the economic, moral, and physical conditions. It offered a prize for the best demonstration of the question, "What is the true state of letters in Guatemala and the means of advancing them?"[12]

---

[7] *Tercera junta pública*, 12-13; *Quarta junta pública*, 16; *Gazeta de Guatemala*, I, No. 18 (December 18, 1797), 370, II, No. 68 (July 2, 1798), 167-68, No. 76 (August 27, 1798), 232.

[8] *Junta pública December 1796*, 17-18; *Tercera junta pública*, 12.

[9] *Gazeta de Guatemala*, II, No. 49 (February 19, 1798), 7-8.

[10] Villacorta, *Capitanía general*, 269, noting that from this collection came the specimen of the Quetzal which was studied and classified by the naturalist La Llave and named Pharomacros Mociño; *Quarta junta pública*, 15, by agreement with Longinos, the prize contest extended to the end of the year; Salazar, *Desenvolvimiento intelectual*, 465, the Cabinet was the basis of that "today" (end of 19th century) presented by the Republic to the Medical School.

[11] *Memorias 1817*, 102.

[12] *Quinta junta pública*, 14; *Gazeta de Guatemala*, II, No. 88 (November 19, 1798), 317.

The Guatemala literary interest was indicated by the use made of prizes donated by a corresponding member in New Spain. The Society offered one for a "memorial, dissertation, or apologetic discourse *in favor of American literature*."[13] The *Gazeta* said of this contest that the Society called to its aid "literary skills" that had "the most intimate connection with the principal aim" of the Society, and the prize was offered for the enlightenment of "certain men, insolated in their remote cabinets," who so lightly judged the fortunes of America. This was, of course, the old plaint that Europe did not understand American conditions. The "principal aim" of the Society certainly was economic development, so the purpose of the contest scarcely was esthetic. This is further indicated by the fact that the second contest announced at this time was on the crafts of American workmen. The Guatemala Society's lack of interest in classical learning is suggested by its refusal to permit use of its quarters by a man who had government permission to open a public class in Latin. The censor of the Society thought the room could be used for classes more appropriate to the interests of the Society, and suggested mathematics.[14] The Havana Society, also, considered that the traditionally heavy load of Latin carried by students was inappropriate to the age of science.

Education in the Colonial Societies

The whole purpose and method of the Societies was educational, to destroy error and prejudice and spread enlightenment, believing, as a Guatemalan said, that the worst impediment to public felicity was ignorance.[15] All American Societies referred to education in their statutes, and most left some other evidence of this interest. The Bogota statutes dealt with "patriotic schools," declaring that since "methodical education" most contributed to industry and craftsmanship, the Society should establish schools for both sexes; and that the most important of the commissions into which the members were divided were those of "Protectors of Crafts, and of Inspectors of Patriotic Schools."[16] We saw an interest in education at Santiago de Cuba; in the periodical of the Quito Society; and in "patriotic" schools at Manila. One of the commissions of the Puerto Rico Society was on public instruction, to promote primary letters, the mutual system of instruction,

---

[13] *Gazeta de Guatemala*, III, No. 121 (September 9, 1799), 101-2, the donor being a curate in the bishopric of Puebla.

[14] A1.6, leg. 2008, exped. 13848, the censor's report dated June 1, 1799, and the disapproval of use of the room recorded in the *junta ordinaria* of June 6.

[15] *Quarta junta pública*, 25, citing the Caribs as proof of the statement.

[16] Tit. 15 of the statutes printed in Gredilla, *Mutis*.

and classes in mathematics, experimental physics, botany, drawing, practical agriculture, and civil economy. In 1787 the Vera Cruz Society established a "Patriotic School" to teach Christian doctrine, Castillian and French grammar, history, geography, arithmetic, writing, drawing, and music.[17]

Several of the Societies were interested in libraries,[18] but only the Havana had much success, opening its library, financed with profits from the *Papel Periódico*, in June 1793,[19] and soon making it available to a considerable portion of the reading public,[20] becoming the earliest public library in Spanish America and one of the earliest in the entire Spanish world.[21] By the end of 1794 the library held some 1,500 volumes, nearly two-thirds of them on loan from private collections.[22] The number of volumes grew little for some years thereafter.[23] In 1800 the library was moved to the convent of Santo Domingo, which assertedly put it under strong Church influence.[24] The library endured during the period of quiescence into the Ramírez era after 1816.[25]

THE HAVANA SOCIETY AND EDUCATION

The Society was interested in both primary instruction, and in technical and scientific. The former it thought necessary because of the qualitative and quantitative deficiencies of the Havana schools; the latter, because technical instruction was necessary to economic growth, was lacking in

---

[17] Trens, *Historia de Veracruz*, II, 538, citing *Gaceta de Mexico*.

[18] The Puerto Rico statutes called for creation of a circulating library. The Guatemala wanted a library, but collected few books at first (*Octava junta pública*, 31-32, the intendant of San Salvador sent an inventory of the "parte política" of his library, asking the Society to choose what it wanted, but it took only one book), and did not form a library until 1815 (*Junta April 1852*, 17). Cabello y Mesa wanted a library supported by the Consulado as part of his suggested Society at Buenos Aires. The statutes of the Bogota Society provided for a library to bring together the works of the authors "mas acreditados en los ramos del instituto de la Sociedad," and stated that it would be useful for the members to read and discuss the works in the library (tit. 12 of statutes in Gredilla, *Mutis*).

[19] Havana *Memorias 1793*, 68.

[20] *Memorias 1794, loc. cit.*, 108-10, "Plan para franquear la Biblioteca á las personas que no son miembros de la Sociedad," the librarian, Antonio Robredo, a Spaniard, recommending that it be opened to the regular and secular clergy and to army and navy officers.

[21] The only earlier ones—in Spain—were all of the 18th century (J. de J. Márquez, "Biblioteca Pública. Su historia," in Havana *Memorias 1894*, 58-60, 71-76, 88-104, 117-20, 134-38, 154-56; *Memorias 1895*, 53-54, 81-86).

[22] *Memorias 1794, loc. cit.*, 107-10.

[23] Cf. Márquez, "Biblioteca Pública," *loc. cit.*, it had 417 works (in 1,617 volumes) in 1808, and in 1813 had 1,133 works (in 2,862 volumes).

[24] *Ibid.*

[25] *Memorias 1817*, 2, reported it in good condition in 1816. Cf. Peraza y Sarausa, "Indice," RBC, LII, 140, the library in 1805.

Cuba, and apparently would not be given by the university. In 1793-1795 the Society made clear most of its chief educational interests, and it did considerable preliminary work in the field of primary instruction, but little in the field of technical instruction. In 1796-1815 some of the primary work continued, technical languished still. In 1816-1820 the Society expanded in the primary field, and finally managed to get some technical instruction started. Much of the vigor of the educational activity of the Society in the 1816-1820 period was due to the presence of Intendant Ramírez, who in 1816 became both Director of the Economic Society and President of its newly created Education Section (replacing the original Class of Sciences and Arts).

Since all Economic Societies believed that modern ideas could transform the world (economically and socially), it is not odd that the Havana spent considerable effort on education. Most of it was directed to Havana, but some to the interior of the island.[26] The chief interest was education for the improvement of the economy, but there was some belief in the necessity of education for strengthening the nation, and some desire to keep Cuban boys at home by providing proper educational facilities.[27] The Society believed that the instruction available was deficient quantitatively and qualitatively, requiring expansion of facilities, and reform of method and curriculum.[28] From the current deficiency of education it "resulted that many talents descended to the sepulcher without ever being useful";[29] so that they were beginning in the schools "a . . . revolution in ideas," since economic advance required theoretical knowledge in addition to experience, and the destruction of the servile spirit of imitation in order to expand knowledge.[30] There was criticism of learning by rote and ferule, a demand that students be taught to think,[31] an oft-repeated call for more science and mathematics

---

[26] *Memorias 1818*, 1-13, for expression of interest in this.

[27] *Memorias 1817*, 19-20, on need for a *Colegio de Educación*, with studies not suited to the facilities and purposes of the *Semanario* and University, lack of which led parents to send sons abroad; *Memorias 1818*, 9-10, project for Colegio de Educación proving complicated and expensive; *Memorias 1819*, 25.

[28] Cf. *Memorias 1819*, 247-50, on a Society contract with Luís de Sprangh to instruct teachers in his method of teaching writing; *Memorias 1820*, 35-37, Sprangh's method proving defective, the Society paid only part of the sum promised him.

[29] *Memorias 1795*, 5.

[30] *Memorias 1793*, 175-80, remarks of the Society secretary, March 12, 1793. Cf. *Memorias 1794, loc. cit.*, 421, that prosperity required "good doctrine, sustained by a systematic education"; *Memorias 1795*, 142-46, that the current stagnated education only created wearisome, ignorant, and inactive egoists.

[31] Cf. *Memorias 1817*, 224-34, a discourse of Félix Varela, philosophy professor at the Semanario, on the influence of *ideología* on society, in which he demanded the reform of Cuban primary education, getting rid of mechanical methods, and teaching youth to think.

in the curriculum,[32] a belief that education should be more related to economic and civil life.[33] There was the usual criticism of Aristotle and scholasticism, of old prejudices, and of overemphasis on Latin.[34] The Society showed interest in the recruitment, pay, and training of teachers;[35] and in methods of mutual instruction, opening one mutual school in 1820, another in 1821.[36]

The original project of the statutes of the Havana Society provided that since there were no "patriotic schools" in Havana, the Society would found some, as well as others for education of youth in primary letters and in

[32] On more science see *Memorias 1794*, *loc. cit.*, 102, the Clase de Ciencias y Artes decided to translate the preliminary lessons of Condillac so that teachers in Havana's convent schools and university could use them in teaching natural science; *Memorias 1795*, 25-26, the translation of Condillac was done by Dr. Caballero, but not published because the translation by Valentín de Foronda was received in Cuba at this time. On more mathematics see *Memorias 1794*, *loc. cit.*, 44-45, 433; *Memorias 1795*, 30-31, that none of the public schools of Havana currently teaching mathematics, and the university chair of mathematics not in operation; *Memorias 1817*, 14-15, urging the university rector to revive the chair of mathematics.

[33] Cf. *Memorias 1795*, 5-8, that a new type of education needed, so the Society intended to promote the exact and useful sciences in place of "vain and sterile knowledge"; *Memorias 1817*, 70-93, an essay favoring "a good system of public education" as Havana's greatest need, emphasizing the necessity of education for civil society, its role in the greatness of nations, and ability to overcome such natural disadvantages as Cuba's hot climate.

[34] *Memorias 1795*, 32-33, need of a new curriculum and method, and an end of "illusions, of errors, and of vain studies, inevitable fruits of the antique method." On efforts to improve the teaching of Latin, see *Memorias 1794*, *loc. cit.*, 44-45. On the demand for study of Castillian grammar, see *ibid.*, 102, that Castillian grammar should be taught either before Latin or at the same time; *Memorias 1795*, 27; *ibid.*, 33-35, reform of Spanish language needed in the entire isle; *ibid.*, 95-102, a memoria by a friar on pronunciation and writing of Spanish, pointing out that the students of Latin did not learn the natural and political consitution of the country, or its history, chronology, and geography, and that study of Castillian would improve Latin; *ibid.*, 106-14, a memoria by a friar proposing a *Diccionario Provincial*, helping promote commerce, agriculture, and public instruction by a definition of technical and rural terms used in Cuba; *Memorias 1842*, 422-24, a representation to king in 1795 on Society efforts to improve the teaching of Castillian, which the Society had discovered the director of the Semanario found unnecessary; *Memorias 1819*, 251-85, dispute on methods of teaching Castillian grammar.

[35] But no normal school was founded in Cuba till 1849 (Ofelia Morales, *La evolución de las Ideas Pedagógicas en Cuba hasta 1842* [Havana, 1929], 37-38).

[36] *Memorias 1817*, 11, two translations of the Lancaster system received; *ibid.*, 331-32, reprint from Scottish magazine on Lancaster method; *ibid.*, 332-39, report of a commission of the Education Section on Lancaster method for Havana, favoring it to teach all classes of the population to think for themselves and learn new methods for agriculture and industry; *ibid.*, 339-60, "Plan de Enseñanza que ha formado la referida comision"; *ibid.*, 409-12; *Memorias 1819*, 116-55, "Lecciones de ensenañza mútua ...," a long history and explanation of the method; *Memorias 1820*, 22-28, plans for two schools of mutual instruction; *ibid.*, 54-56, "Instalación de la escuela gratuita de enseñanza mútua ...," opened in January, 1820, with 80 pupils; *ibid.* 57-63, discourse by school director; Morales, *Ideas pedagógicas*, 36.

"useful" branches of mathematics.[37] Preliminary to its other actions, the Society had Friar Félix González make a survey of Havana schools.[38] He reported by *barrios*, giving for each school the name, race, and status of the teacher, the number of pupils, subjects taught, tuition fees, and a comment on the quarters. Of the 39 schools, 32 were taught by women; the total children enrolled in the 39 was 1,731; 600 of the total were boys at the convent of Belén. Actually, most of the schools were no more than primitive little tutorial groups directed by mulatto women. González found the worst defect of the schools to be their poor quarters, especially in that they were cramped, which was dangerous to health in the hot climate; he found this defect irremediable, given the poor pay of the teachers. Another defect was that in the 32 schools taught by women, only three women had followed this occupation since youth and lived solely from it; the others had other occupations, so the children got insufficient attention. Even the school of the padres of Belén was unsatisfactory, because there were not enough teachers. González said that the solution was to pay teachers well.

A three-man committee then drew up ordinances for the projected free schools of Havana, and presented them to the Society in October, 1794. This has been called the first Cuban plan for the organization of primary education.[39] They decided that funds permitted establishment of only two free schools; that available women teachers did not teach writing and reckoning well, so a man should be hired for those subjects; free schools would attract too many pupils, so admission should be limited to 200 white children; and the Society should see that the school followed a fixed method of instruction. The committee declared that it drew on authors on the subject and on the practice in other cities, especially Madrid. The regulation dealt in some detail with the obligations and methods of teachers, and the precise methods of instruction in the various subjects.[40]

The committee that prepared the ordinances noted that the question of funds was the greatest problem, and recommended using some of the profits of the *Periódico*, and requesting Church funds.[41] The Society soon named

---

[37] Tit. XI, in *Memorias 1793*, 87 *et seq.* for the projected statutes of 1791. Cf. "Copia de los Capítulos Catorce de las Escuelas patrióticas de Madrid, y Cuba [Santiago]," appended to the cedula of approval of December 15, 1792, those of Madrid emphasizing spinning and weaving more than the Cuban; "junta ordinaria," March 21, 1793 (*Colección Actas 1880*, 14), reading the chapters on Madrid and Santiago schools.

[38] *Memorias 1793*, 161-75, for his report, August 8, 1793.

[39] Morales, *Ideas pedagógicas*, 17.

[40] "Ordenanzas para las escuelas gratuitas de la Havana," by Dr. Joseph Agustín Caballero, Francisco de Isla, and Félix González, in *Memorias 1794*, *loc. cit.*, 31-44, of which 36-44 are the ordinances proper.

[41] *Ibid.*, 34.

a special two-man committee to consider funds for the schools, lamenting that they could not rescue the ignorant and make them useful to the Fatherland.[42] In 1795 Caballero delivered a discourse on education, which the Society approved and ordered Caballero to make a representation to the king. In these documents Caballero declared the system of public education in Havana retarded the progress of the arts and sciences; the reform should begin in the university, which was full of old prejudices, and gave too much attention to the methods of Aristotle.[43] Criticism of the Church's educational institutions was a natural feature of Society opinion on education.[44] The Society set up committees to visit the primary schools of the Havana area, inspecting their condition, overseeing examinations, and granting prizes. This activity was especially intense in the 1816-1820 period, but it started soon after the foundation of the Society.

The Society continued its interest in primary and general education in the 1796-1815 period,[45] but did more thereafter, as in other fields.[46] By 1823 the Society was supporting seven schools of primary letters, including one Lancasterian, with a total of 415 pupils in all the schools, as well as classes in political economy and *constitución*, and a drawing school with seventy pupils;[47] this in a Cuba which a few years later had but 140 schools, of which

---

[42] *Memorias 1795*, 11 et seq., "Escuelas gratuitas."

[43] *Memorias 1842*, 418-24, three Caballero documents on the subject.

[44] *Memorias 1794*, *loc. cit.*, 433, that the religious educators had given great benefit, but their work was imperfect as compared with the necessities of civil life, teaching too much Latin, too little mathematics; Pezuela, *Ensayo histórico*, 344-45, 348-49, that the Society gave some attention to changes in the university curriculum, but that the governors after Las Casas were not interested in the matter.

[45] J. de J. Márquez, "La Sociedad Económica y la instrucción pública a principio del siglo," Havana *Memorias 1896*, 55-62, including Society efforts in connection with primary education in 1805 and 1808 and after 1816; *supra*, 194, on interest in the Pestalozzian method in 1807.

[46] Morales, *Ideas pedagógicas*, calls Cuban education history before 1794 the "Período Primitivo," when little was done; and 1794-1816 the "Período Preparatorio," when important changes were discussed, largely in the Economic Society; and 1816-24 the "Período de Organización y prosperidad de la educación popular bajo los auspicios de la Sección de Educación de la Real Sociedad Económica." Cf. *Memorias 1817*, 10-15, on commissions to examine schools in the city proper and in the suburbs, and figures on what they found; *ibid.*, 121-31, report on girls schools, finding all but two poor, teachers ignorant, and suggesting reforms, including the European use of normal schools; *Memorias 1818*, 442-45, the Society cooperating with religious, houses to found primary schools under the provisions of the royal cedula of October 20, 1817; cf. Morales, *Ideas pedagógicas*, on this cedula and its effect in Cuba; Peraza y Sarausa, "Indice," RBC, 180-84, Society and education in 1805.

[47] *Memorias 1823*, 175, "Estado de los establecimientos de enseñanza gratuita que costea la Sociedad. ..." The Society provided 7,180 pesos for the primary schools, and 4,920 pesos for other educational purposes.

only 16 were free.[48] The Society in this 1816-1820 period also gave some small attention to music training,[49] and to the education of deaf-mutes.[50] There was some controversy within the Society over educational policy.[51] The Society's educational efforts were badly hurt at the end of the 1816-1824 period by the loss of its government revenues.[52]

The strongest interest of the Society in technical or specialized education was in chemistry and botany for the improvement of the sugar industry; the interest in anatomy and in political economy were developed early; interest in a school of navigation came late and had no result.[53] Although technical education was discussed in the first year of the Society's operations, no classes or institutions were established for twenty-five years.

A school of chemistry and botany was proposed in 1793 in a long memoria, which declared that only sugar produced an abundant product for commerce, that most Cubans lived in its "shade," that Charles IV had aided with the free introduction of Negroes and foreign instruments, and with the foundation of the Economic Society, so that if agriculture was not perfect, it was their own fault, for Campomanes had noted that conducive political provisions were not enough in the absence of physical science. Since ignorant men were running the sugar industry and costing the island huge sums, a chemistry school should be founded, emphasizing sugar, and teaching botany also.[54] This suggestion was adopted; a subscription was raised, amounting to 24,615 pesos by 1795; but efforts to find a teacher and equipment in Spain and England failed, due to difficulties of wartime communications, the scarcity of Hispanic professors of chemistry, and the difficulty of finding foreign teachers.[55] Twenty years later the Society remained convinced of

---

[48] In 1826, according to Cabrera, *Cuba y sus jueces*, 122.

[49] *Memorias 1817*, 17, on the foundation in 1816 of an academy of music, which asked the Society for protection as a part of good education, especially for its influence on the customs of youth; *Memorias 1818*, 8.

[50] *Memorias 1819*, 341, the Society preparing to open a school; *Memorias 1820*, 28, funds had prevented its opening.

[51] Cf. *Memorias 1818*, 344-406, a long discourse on education by Nicolás Ruiz, with ambitious suggestions for expansion of the educational system throughout the isle; *ibid.*, 406-7, a report of a Society commission on the foregoing, sneering at it as unoriginal; Morales *Ideas pedagógicas*, 70-71, for an attempt to ascribe this action to political and personal clashes within the Society.

[52] *Ibid.*, 38.

[53] *Memorias 1793*, 29, a suggestion for schools of mathematics, experimental physics (with a hall of machines), a chemistry school with a laboratory, a cabinet of natural history, a botanical garden, and a school of anatomy.

[54] *Memorias 1793*, 147-60, by Nicolás Calvo. The school was to run five years, managed by the Society.

[55] *Ibid.*, 18-19, money collected in 1793; *Memorias 1794*, *loc. cit.*, 426; *Memorias 1795*, 15-19, "Escuela de Química."

the need, reopened the fund for the purpose; in 1816-1820 struggled to find a teacher and buy equipment abroad, finally getting the latter from France. When the teacher died before the chair could be put into operation, Intendant Ramírez secured the services of Dr. José Taso of the military hospital, and the laboratory was set up at the hospital at considerable expense. The chemistry class finally opened in March, 1820.[56]

A botanical garden was suggested in 1793; in 1794 a plan for it was presented; in 1795 Martín Sesé, Director of the Royal Botanical Garden of Mexico, was in Havana for a time, and the Society sought his advice. Sesé agreed to train a Cuban in botany. The Society selected José Esteves; the Consulado provided funds for his training.[57] In succeeding years the Society maintained its conviction that botany was useful to agriculture, medicine, architecture, veterinary medicine, and other fields, but the botanical garden was not established until 1817, and construction and collection were still being pursued slowly and at considerable cost in 1820.[58]

From the beginning, the Society recommended changes in medical education,[59] and had a class of anatomy in 1797,[60] but it was soon discontinued, whereupon the Society spent several years trying to provide such instruction again. Dr. Tomás Romay was active in this, saying that "the cadaver of man is the immense book" in which physiology and pathology are to be more quickly learned than in printed volumes. A chair of practical anatomy was opened in 1819 at the Royal Military Hospital, with Dr. José Taso, an Italian, as professor.[61]

After long talking of the advantages—in part to economic life—to be derived from a study of draughtsmanship and drawing, the Society and the Consulado finally in 1818 helped establish an "academy of natural drawing."

---

[56] *Memorias 1817*, 24-32, "Utilidad de la Química," declaring most of the arts subordinate to chemistry, each sugar *ingenio* "a laboratory" for the extraction of sugar from cane; *ibid.* 421-22; *Memorias 1819*, 22; *Memorias 1820*, 38-41, 71-73, 85-87. Cf. Luís F. Le-Roy y Gálvez, "Historia de la primera cátedra de química en Cuba," RBC, LXVI (July-December, 1950), 65-93.

[57] *Memorias 1795*, 19-23, "Jardín Botánica."

[58] *Memorias 1817*, 5, 15-16, 21-24, 420-21; *Memorias 1818*, 294-302; *Memorias 1819*, 23-25; *Memorias 1820*, 44-47. Cf. reprint of discourse of Dr. Florencio Pérez y Comoto at inauguration of botany lessons in Mexico in 1811 (Havana *Memorias 1818*, 185-99.

[59] Horacio Abascal, "Contribución de la Sociedad Económica al progreso de la medicina en Cuba," RBC, XLVII, No. 1 (January-February, 1941), 5-31, at 17.

[60] Bachiller y Morales, *Apuntes*, I, 155.

[61] *Memorias 1817*, 423; *Memorias 1819*, 210-19, Taso's discourse at the opening of the chair; *Memorias 1820*, 37, gives 35 students, of which 25 from the hospital, and 10 from the university.

Demand was so great that the second class had sixty pupils.[62] The school was still in existence in 1823.[63]

The Society was always interested in political economy as a subject, believing that "economic science," like all work, required order, for which reason Juan Manuel O'Farrill was assigned to describe it, and Pedro Pablo O'Reilly to form "a genealogical tree of all knowledge whose influence on economic science is most . . . evident."[67] But instruction in the subject was not begun until 1818, at the Semanario, with Justo Vélez as professor. The Society had nothing to do with this foundation, but it enthusiastically approved it.[65] The second class, beginning in October, 1819, had eighteen students, which was fewer than in the first, when the study was a novelty.[66] Intendant Ramírez in 1819 proposed a contest for the students on the practical application of political economy to Cuba, and prizes of the works of Say and Adam Smith were awarded.[67] The class only endured to 1824, when it ceased for lack of funds; it was re-established in 1840.[68]

Vélez compiled his lessons from Say, and they were printed at Society expense,[69] but it was recognized that Say could not be followed blindly, so that the class needed to use the best modern authors, national and foreign.[70] His first lesson, avowedly extracted from Say,[71] made the main points that:

---

[62] *Memorias 1818*, 256-58; *Memorias 1819*, 20-21; *Memorias 1820*, 34-35.

[63] *Memorias 1823*, 175. But another drawing school had to be founded in 1832 (*Acta de Juntas Generales 1833*, 24).

[64] *Memorias 1793*, 25-26.

[65] *Memorias 1817*, 17, that the chair was being formed at the Semanario in 1816, and that the study had been recommended by savants, and royal orders to the Consulados and the Economic Societies.

[66] The Society's judgment to this effect in *Memorias 1820*, 43.

[67] *Memorias 1819*, 246-47, on the subject "To demonstrate what this island may produce and contribute to its Metropolis in the present state of the liberty and privileges of its commerce: what more it could and should render to the same Metropolis, if the security of the national navigation be restored, and what would be the consequences if it were deprived of the commerce it enjoys."

[68] Bachiller y Morales, *Apuntes*, I, 146 *et seq.*

[69] Described in *Anales y Memorias*, 4ª ser., t. VII, 41, as: *Compendio del tratado de Economía Política que escribió Juan Bautista Say, hecho por el Pbro. Ldo. D. Justo Vélez, catedrático de esta ciencia en el Real y Conciliar Colegio Seminario de la Habana, de órden de la Real Sociedad Patriótica* (2 vols., Habana: Oficina de Arazoza y Soler, 1819), noting that it was a "free" extract, with inserted references to Cuba and Spain.

[70] *Memorias 1820*, 41, an account in the juntas generales of the Society, December, 1819, of the Society's activities of the year, and noting that students in the class of political economy were hearing of the great changes in the science due to Smith, and of the great works of Ward, Campomanes, Jovellanos, and other Spaniards; and would consult Ricardo, Sismondi, and other sources.

[71] *Memorias 1818*, 413-41, "Discurso acerca de la economía política, leído en la clase del jueves 15 de octubre por el presbítero Ldo. D. Justo Vélez, catedrático de esta ciencia," delivered the day after the chair was inaugurated.

commerce and manufacturing add to the value of agricultural produce; capital and money are not the same thing; a nation does well what its science and ability fit it for; productive economic operations require the work of man, of nature, and of machines; the more civilized a nation, the more branches of industry it has; Adam Smith notes the value of labor specialization, since with repetition of a few functions hands gain skill; Say points out that value depends on demand; a nation is made rich not by money, but by capital, that is, by production; it is better to concentrate on common articles as opposed to luxuries, as seen in the high price of flour, a necessity, as compared with the low prices of coffee and sugar, which people can do without; and he preferred Switzerland, which had neither ostentation, luxury, nor poor, to Mexico, which had *millionarios*, but also "a nearly Asiatic ostentation and . . . many thousands of beggars."

THE GUATEMALA SOCIETY AND EDUCATION

The Guatemala Society promoted both primary and vocational instruction, so that, as it declared, the populace might acquire knowledge that would contribute to the prosperity of the region. The *Gazeta de Guatemala*, as in other fields, helped stimulate interest in the general education of youth, a considerable proportion of its pages being devoted to the question.[72] That the efforts of both Society and *Gazeta* were needed may be judged from the complaint of the archbishop in 1793 that the capital had but one school of primary letters;[73] and from the fact that in 1816 the response to a royal order on the formation of schools in the provinces showed that few people received instruction. Commenting on the order of 1816, one *alcalde mayor* noted that there were classes in only seven of the pueblos of his *Partido*, and came directly to the root of the matter by stating that this was due to the poverty of the district and the lack of religious communities to furnish teachers.[74] Of course, these fundamental deficiences could not be overcome either by the Economic Society or the *Gazeta;* but they could try to stimulate action by persons of influence.[75]

The Society tried to stimulate interest in the erection of schools of primary letters in the Indian villages, offering a prize for the best essay on the subject,

[72] Cf. a long series of articles in III, Nos. 113-22 (July 15-September 16, 1798), on education, but headed "Sociedad."

[73] Real cédula, Aranjuez, January 18, 1795, in reply to a representation of 1793— AGG, A1.2-4, leg. 2246, exped. 16225.

[74] Real cédula. ... Escuelas ... en todos los Pueblos que se consideren necesarias, November 14, 1816, including reports from officials in the provinces of Guatemala on the state of the schools—AGG, A1-1, leg. 29, exped. 865.

[75] Cf. Villacorta, *Capitanía general*, 256-61, on the poor condition of public instruction in Central America at the end of the colonial era.

and noting at a public junta that repeated royal orders had encouraged such schools for America.[76] The prizes were donated by a curate in New Spain, who was a corresponding member of the Guatemala Society, and who wrote that this objective had a good deal in common with the aims of his parish ministry.[77] But in a year only one essay was submitted, and this judged not worthy of the prize; so the contest was continued.[78] Of course, not all members of the dominant minority favored education for the Indians.[79]

The small but active corresponding junta of the Society at the port of Truxillo, considering a school of primary instruction needed there, undertook to establish one. It received approval from the Society at the capital, and permission to use for the purpose the funds owed by Truxillo members to the Society, and thereafter to apply the annual dues of members to upkeep of the school. The censor of the Society at Guatemala, praising the idea of such a school, stated: "Neither agriculture, nor industry, nor the arts and crafts, objectives by which the Society has been proposing the introduction of felicity into the *reyno*, can ever prosper where education is scarce."[80] The school opened in 1799 with twenty children enrolled.[81]

The most important educational efforts of the Guatemala Society were in vocational or technical instruction, and it spent a good share of its funds on the schools of spinning, drawing, and mathematics. Somewhat related were its unexecuted plan for instruction in political economy, and its attempts to bring a mineralogist from Mexico. Of these, the Spinning School was founded by the Society as its first action after securing tentative approval from the captain general of its own establishment. The school existed from 1795 to 1800, and again after the re-establishment of December, 1810, teaching young women to use the spinning wheel, chiefly working cotton. The motive was both economic and social, to increase the wealth of the realm, and to give women useful occupations to prevent their falling into vicious habits.[82]

---

[76] *Quarta junta pública*, 12-13; *Gazeta de Guatemala*, I, No. 47 (December 25, 1797), 376.

[77] Joaquín Alexo. de Meabe to Secretary Melón, S. Dionysio de Tlaxcalá, September 26, 1798—AGG, A1.6, leg. 2007, exped. 13839.

[78] *Gazeta de Guatemala*, III, No. 102 (April 29, 1799), 21.

[79] Cf. Ramón Salazar, *Historia veintiún años*, 27, citing an article in the *Gazeta* of April 6, 1802, arguing the lack of necessity of giving education to the common people; *Gazeta*, III, No. 111 (July 1, 1799), 57, pointing out that Bernardo War[d] had dealt with this question of primary schools for which the Society was offering prizes.

[80] AGG, A1.6, leg. 2007, exped. 13823.

[81] *Gazeta de Guatemala*, May 20, 1799, 36.

[82] *Infra*, 333-35, for discussion of the school.

The Drawing School served a useful and popular purpose, but although it had practical applications in architecture and the description of mechanical devices,[83] its service to the decorative arts was more emphasized in Guatemala. The school was organized in 1796 by Pedro Garcí-Aguirre, director of the Royal Mint at Guatemala, and was the only part approved by the Crown of his ambitious plan for an Academy of the Three Noble Arts of sculpture, painting, and architecture.[84] His "Regulation" for the school based it on that established by the Academy at Cadiz, and gave the Society nominal, and the "Master Director" actual, control of policy and practice. The director was to serve indefinitely; Society members were to be assigned for limited terms to supervise the school. According to Garcí-Aguirre, all depended on the master-director, who ought to possess extraordinary virtue and an unusual knowledge of drawing; and he should be sought in Spain or Mexico, if not available in Guatemala. Garcí-Aguirre received the appointment. He thought the small knowledge that could be expected immediately of the students would not permit division into classes of painting and sculpture, so the initial separation was only between persons of social consequence (*la gente distinguida*) and common people (*el común*). The regulations as to the physical equipment and operation of the school showed that Garcí-Aguirre knew something of the subject.[85]

Public response to the School of Drawing was enthusiastic. The *Gazeta* devoted considerable space to its activities.[86] In addition to funds provided by the Society, various individuals gave money and furnishings to the school, and a master mason worked more than two weeks without compensation in preparing its hall for use.[87]

The school opened for teaching on March 6, 1797, with accommodations for thirty-two students who had been selected in advance of the date. Additional persons came to the class, however, some bringing tables from home and planting them in the cloak room. This interest prompted the Society to buy permanent and larger quarters, in which the school was established with fifty students by the end of April, 1797. Garcí-Aguirre, reporting this, expressed the hope that in a few years Guatemala would have many good

---

[83] *Quinta junta pública*, 13, stating that it would advance industry, teach knowledge of the arts, and reform customs.

[84] *Supra*, 206.

[85] Reglamento general para el est? de la Escuela de Dibujo, adscrita a la Sociedad Económica Pedro de Garcí-Aguirre, N. Guata. 24 de Octubre de 1796—AGG, A1.1, leg. 2817, exped. 24902.

[86] E.g., on prizes, II (1798), Nos. 53, 57, 61, 77; III, (1799), Nos. 97, 125; V, Nos. 205-7.

[87] *Segunda junta pública*, 25 *et seq.*

artists working with painting, sculpture, architecture, and engraving.[88] Apparently he did not intend to let the royal disapproval of his Academy of the Three Noble Arts restrict his actions unduly.

By July, 1798, the school had seventy-nine students, and still could not accommodate all the prospective students.[89] Garcí-Aguirre asserted that three hundred would enroll if room and funds were available.[90]

Texts on drawing were bought in Spain.[91] Prizes were given, and presentation of the monthly awards was made an occasion for illuminations and fireworks.[92] The works receiving honors represented a variety of interests. On one occasion honors for sculpture were awarded for busts of Isaac Newton and the emperor Hadrian; painting, for a picture of San Pablo; and drawing, for the figure of an apostle.[93] Such a mixture of classical, "enlightened," and religious subject matter may have represented something more than the mere accident of what models had been available for copying or adapting.

Garcí-Aguirre attempted to resign in the autumn of 1798, feeling, or professing to feel, that his services were not properly appreciated. The next year, having received some concessions from the sponsors of the school, he was still head, albeit declaring himself not satisfied with all the arrangements made by the Society.[94] One decision, which pleased him as to its general intent but not in its execution, was a modeling room, for which contributions were being collected in 1798. The room was opened for use in January, 1800.[95]

---

[88] Pedro de Garcí-Aguirre to the Director of the Economic Society, Nueva Guatemala, June 26, 1797—AGG, A1.6, leg. 2006, exped. 13820; *Gazeta de Guatemala*, I, No. 4 (March 6, 1797), 31-32; Juarros, *Compendio*, I, 158-59, the school hours were 7-9 p.m.; Medina, *Imprenta en Guatemala*, No. 908, a broadside announcing the school would open March 6, 1797.

[89] Ansmo. Josef de Quirós Diputo. to Secretary Melón, Guatemala, July 26, 1798—AGG, A1.6, leg. 2007, exped. 13839; *Tercera junta pública*, 11-12, reporting 64 pupils; *Quarta junta pública*, 11, reports 69 pupils.

[90] *Quinta junta pública*, 12; cf. *infra*, 340, for the proposal (never executed) that the guilds help finance the school.

[91] Twelve copies were bought in Madrid in 1797—AGG, A1.6, leg. 2006, exped. 13812.

[92] *Gazeta de Guatemala*, I, No. 42 (November 20, 1797), 337-38; cf. *Gazeta*, II, No. 62 (May 21, 1798), 120, for a painting, sculpture, and drawing contest, with aspirants invited from outside the capital.

[93] *Quinta junta pública*, 12.

[94] AGG, A1.6, leg. 2007, exped. 13826, 13828; leg. 2008, exped. 13850, all contain letters on the subject.

[95] AGG, A1.6, leg. 2007, exped. 13827, 13828; *Gazeta de Guatemala*, No. 142 (February 3, 1800), 162; *Quinta junta pública*, 13, that the subscription for the *sala de modelo* had raised 264 pesos in the capital, 217 in the provinces, which was thought to be enough for the room and equipment.

After the Society was suspended in 1800, the School of Drawing operated under protection of the captain general and with assistance from the Consulado.[96] By 1808 some of the men trained in its classes were able to prepare competent engravings for the printed account of the ceremonies pledging loyalty to Ferdinand VII.[97] The Society in 1811 again took over supervision of the school, with Juan Gualberto González as director.[98] The next year it agreed to organize and assist an Academy of Painting, which had been requested by the guild of painters of the capital. Since an architect was the one person not a painter by profession to be admitted, this academy was presumably a professional body, unlike the School of Drawing.[99]

Creation of the School of Mathematics, proposed in 1794 by Captain of Engineers José de Sierra, was delayed first by his absence on the royal service, and then by his illness. José Antonio Goycoechea and Mariano López Rayón offered to teach in the school,[100] but in the end the task was turned over to Friar Joaquín Galve [*sic*] and Miguel Larreinaga.[101] The Society optimistically ordered in Madrid in 1797 one hundred copies of a text of arithmetic and geometry.[102] Classes began in January, 1798,[103] but before long Larreinaga was reporting that the original large enrollment had fallen off so rapidly after the first lessons that he had suspended classes entirely. The Society hoped to start instruction again, but did not do so.[104] The next year the censor of the Society pleaded for re-establishment of the classes on grounds of utility, but confessed that most people in the captaincy general studied only things contributing immediately to their subsistence.[105] The records do not show any more activity in this period.

The interest of the Society in political economy did not for a long while lead to formal instruction. The speeches and writings of members from 1795

---

[96] *Supra,* 219-20.

[97] *Guatemala por Fernando Séptimo, passim,* for these interesting, if unoriginal, engravings.

[98] *Octava junta pública,* 29-30, and noting that a drawing school had been established in San Salvador under the protection of the intendant.

[99] *Novena junta pública,* 40-42.

[100] *Junta December 1796,* 18-19; *Segunda junta pública,* 25; *Tercera junta pública,,* 10-11.

[101] Fr. Fermín Aleal, prior de Sto. Domingo to Villaurrutia, Nueva [Guatemala], December 4, 1797—AGG, A1.6, leg. 2007, exped. 13821; *Tercera junta pública,* 10-11; Los Guatemaltecos (pseud.), *Noticia biográfica del distinguido literato D. Miguel Larreynaga* (Guatemala, 1847).

[102] Record in AGG, A1.6, leg. 2006, exped. 13812.

[103] *Gazeta de Guatemala,* I, No. 48 (January 1, 1798).

[104] *Quarta junta pública,* 11; *Relación 1852,* 11, saying that the school was often suspended.

[105] *Gazeta de Guatemala,* III, No. 112 (July 8, 1799), 61-62.

to 1800 contained numerous references to the need for knowledge of the subject, but regular instruction apparently was not suggested, hardly surprising in view of the dubiety with which the subject was regarded in Spain. A project for a class of political economy was finally prepared by José del Valle in 1812—that is, during the period of the Cortes of Cadiz, of liberty of the press, and of preparation and promulgation of the liberal Constitution of 1812 which hedged in the monarch with restrictions and declared that sovereignty resided in the people. The Society approved Valle's plan of instruction, but there is no evidence that classes were held. Since Valle in discussing the project had publicly approved some of the constitutional novelties adopted by the Cortes of Cadiz, it may be that during the reaction under Ferdinand VII the class was considered undesirable by Captain General Bustamante.[106] At any rate, Bustamante's view of liberalism is well known.

---

[106] *Novena junta pública*, 44-45; *El Amigo de la Patria* (in Valle and Valle Matheu, *Obras de José Cecilio del Valle*, II, 25-29), I, No. 2 (October 26, 1820), 11-23, No. 33 (April 12, 1821), 437-45.

CHAPTER SIXTEEN

Branches of the Economy

The prime economic hope of the American Societies was an expanded overseas traffic, achieved through increased production, rather than by new methods of distribution. Agricultural production was a strong interest with all; the interest in craft or industrial production somewhat less prominent; the interest in mining feeble, and that branch of the economy even deprecated as having b en overemphasized in America.

Commerce and Capital

The Societies emphasized production rather than distribution partly because of their predominantly creole membership, commerce being controlled by Spaniards; partly because the Spanish Societies emphasized production; and partly because it was expected that the internal and external distribution of goods would naturally increase if production were increased, improved, and diversified. Mutis told the Bogota Society it would try to promote a great trade between Spain and America, but by the method of improving local production. Espejo declared that Quito had no commerce, nor would have until it had a great deal more agriculture and manufacturing. In the Guatemala Society, Dighero's attempt to revive the Pacific port of Iztapa was almost the only interest shown in methods of export.[1] Although some

---

[1] *Infra,* 329.

of the Guatemalans interested in navigation on the Río Motagua were
Society members,[2] the Society itself seems not to have dealt with the question.
Villaurrutia told the Society that a great commerce would grow up between
America and the metropolis, with cacao and other products of "our industry
and shops," by the rivers Motagua, San Juan, and Tulija, to exchange for
Spanish manufactures.[3] Another member said the Society would try to
increase the production of the country, but the Consulado would have to
move the goods.[4] In Havana, too, commercial activity was the business of
the Consulado, and the commerce class of the Economic Society was not
as vigorous as the other membership divisions.[5] Of course, the Havana
Society often expressed its appreciation of royal measures lifting restrictions
on commerce. Late in the period, the Society wished to establish a school
of navigation in cooperation with the Consulado,[6] but nothing was done.
When Baquíjano of Lima and Espejo of Quito lamented the wealth accruing
to Holland and England from commerce, their main concern was in providing
goods for an expanded Spanish and American trade. The Lima Society did,
however, through the *Mercurio Peruano*, show more interest in commerce
relative to production than the other Societies.

Internal commerce, or "circulation," did interest the Societies,[7] especially
taking the form of concern for better roads, having in mind both an increase
of domestic traffic and a reduction in the cost of export. We have noted

---

[2] Beristain, *Biblioteca* (3d ed.), lists: José Ignacio Palomo, *Memorias sobre la navegación del río Motagua* ... (Beteta, 1799), and says the author was a member of the Society; and Alejandro Ramírez, *Memoria sobre la navegación del río Motagua* (Guatemala, 1799). On the beginning of the Motagua project in 1796, and its subsequent history, see Guatemala Comisión de límites, "El esfuerzo de Guatemala para canalizar el río Motagua," *loc. cit.*, 7-10.

[3] *Quinta junta pública*, 3.

[4] *Junta December 1796*, 29.

[5] *Memorias 1793*, 41-43; *Memorias 1795*, 49-52, the class of commerce doing little, and noting that commerce mainly the business of the Consulado; *ibid.*, 88, the commerce class doing nothing; "junta ordinaria," July 25, 1795 (*Colección Actas 1880*, 35-37), the commerce class small; cf. "junta ordinaria," July 23, 1795 (*Memorias y Anales 1865*, 360-61), a memoria from Puerto-Príncipe asserting that the decayed commerce of that place required for its regeneration a *casa de comercio;* Peraza y Sarausa, "Indice," RBC, LII, 139, Society prize of 1805 on the advantages of commercial fairs for Cuba; *Memorias 1817*, 5, on the use of steamships in coastal trade; *ibid.*, 196-224, discourse, and tables, on the commerce and public finance of Britain, dealing with the causes of the current British depression, translated from a Scottish daily; *ibid.*, 234-51, several documents on duties on gold and silver, the remission of the metals to Spain, essentially arguing that the sugar traffic was more valuable.

[6] *Memorias 1819*, 23.

[7] *Supra*, 175, Bishop Calama of Quito demanding more circulation.

many members of American Societies commenting on the miserable land transport of the Indies.[8]

The Societies gave relatively little attention to the availability of capital and to rates of interest, despite the obvious relevance of these matters to the improvement of production, which required the adoption of machinery and the introduction of new crops, both likely to be expensive. We have noted the views of Baquíjano on the advantage enjoyed by Holland and England because of low interest rates, and of the Havana Society that not only commerce but also capital should be allowed to flow freely. In the later period the Havana Society printed a suggestion for establishment of a bank, as a great need for the hacendados and stockmen, who were to subscribe capital. It was to be run by the Society. The editors of the Society publication did not care for the suggestion that these two groups of proprietors be forced to subscribe capital to the bank.[9] No doubt the Societies were somewhat reluctant to deal publicly with the question of usurious rates of interest, since money-lending was a concern of the merchant group. Criticism of their activities in this regard would have led to bad feeling in the Societies, whereas there was probably sufficient friction over the desire of the creoles to increase American manufactures.

Agriculture

The American Societies were more interested in agriculture than in other branches of the economy, since that was the chief creole economic resource in the area where the Societies existed, which made it natural for them to believe that "the fruits and products of the land . . . constitute the true wealth of peoples."[10] They gave scant attention to livestock;[11] the Havana

---

[8] Cf. Havana *Memorias 1794*, *loc. cit.*, 424-25, noting the connection between agricultural prosperity and good transport facilities, and that the roads of Cuba were so bad in the rainy season that goods could not be taken to market. See Sagra, *Historia física de Cuba*, I, 244, on costs of overland transport. Cf. Medina, *Imprenta en Guatemala*, No. 1003, listing: Luís Pedro de Aguirre, *Memoria sobre el fomento de la agricultura y comercio interior del Reino de Guatemala por ———, socio y secretario de la Real Sociedad Patriótica de Guatemala* (Guatemala: Beteta, 1800).

[9] *Memorias 1818*, 303-13.

[10] Guatemala *Quarta junta pública*, 26. Cf. Havana *Memorias 1793*, 3, on the prime importance of agriculture; *ibid.*, 30; Havana *Memorias 1794*, *loc. cit.*, that industry depended on agricultural produce; *ibid.*, 104, that the class of agriculture was the largest; Havana *Memorias 1795*, 41; Havana *Memorias 1817*, 278-80, crafts, commerce, and navigation have to found their growth on agriculture.

[11] Valiente of Santiago wanted to improve the industry; the statutes of the Bogota called stockraising a main interest; Havana *Memorias 1817*, 101, a prize offered for cheese and butter; *ibid.*, 102, prize for duck raising. For efforts of the Havana Consulado in 1797 to promote mule and horse breeding, see *Memorias 1843* (t. XVI), 13-19.

had some interest in wood,[12] and considerable in beeswax,[13] a bit in cochineal.[14] But most of the agricultural interests of the Societies were in industrial and export crops, as sugar, indigo, cacao, flax, and cotton. They were naturally most interested in agriculture from the point of view of the large cultivator.[15]

The prime interest in agriculture was apparent even in the abortive and short-lived Societies. Valiente of Santiago hoped to promote the cultivation of old and new crops by a variety of methods; the Lima Society printed items on agriculture in the *Mercurio;* the Mompox Society wished to promote cotton; and all the others desired to improve agriculture. Their hopes included an increase in the circulation of old crops, by way of roads needed to take them to market; revival of those crops that were "decadent"; discovery of markets for native plants that never had been grown commercially; trial of new crops, even exotic plants from the Orient; provision of labor for an increase in production; and an increase of profits by way of refinement of produce. They had some interest in new methods, but less than the Madrid Society, and much less than the latter in the effect on agricultural production of absentee ownership and idle land resulting from the *latifundium.*

Although the agricultural interest of the Havana Society was concentrated strongly on sugar, it considered other crops, notably in 1816-1820. It had some interest in such crops as hemp, flax, cotton, coffee, tobacco, indigo;[16]

---

[12] *Memorias 1794, loc. cit.*, 26, that trade in lumber of eastern Cuba should be allowed with anyone who could pay for it, and noting that Havana could use more; *El Aviso*, No. 108 (February 6, 1806), a prize for the best work in planting trees over a five-year period; *Memorias 1817*, 264-73, a discourse of 1813 on *jobo* wood, arguing that it could be exploited locally, to cut down the importation of lumber from North America; *Memorias 1819*, 338-41, on planting "useful trees" for various purposes; *ibid.*, 351-62, on planting trees. Cf. Sagra, *Historia física de Cuba*, I, 234, on timber on haciendas.

[13] *Memorias 1794, loc. cit.*, 26, that the wax industry should be promoted, partly as an aid to the poor, but it was sadly decayed due to a law forbidding the use of cedar for hives; a prize-winning essay of 1796 by Dr. Tomás Romay on the obstacles to bee-raising in Cuba, was largely a practical article emphasizing wax (in Havana *Memorias 1839*, 105-23); *Sucinta noticia del ramo de la cera*, 5, Captain General Apodaca fixes attention on wax at a Society junta; *Tareas 1815*, 3. The *Sucinta noticia* (1815) of Boloix was reprinted in the *Memorias 1843* (t. XVI), 19-24, with an editorial note, supported with figures, that the wax industry had not made much progress since Boloix's time; and reprinted again in *Memorias 1880*, 34-41.

[14] Peraza y Sarausa, "Indice," RBC, LVII, 74, the Society and cochineal in 1798; Havana *Memorias 1820*, 31, consideration of the development of cochineal, especially in view of the end of the slave trade.

[15] Cf. Havana *Memorias 1794, loc. cit.*, 420, that conditions in Cuba favored the rich cultivator.

[16] *Memorias 1793*, 34, a member to see if flax, hemp, and other plants could be usefully grown; *Memorias 1794, loc. cit.*, 427-28, interest in whether flax, hemp, and other primary materials were grown in the isle, and mention of a Society member who grew flax and hemp; *Memorias 1795*, 44-47; *ibid.*, 152, flax and hemp; *Memorias*

and a little in food crops.[17] The Society recognized the need for improving the methods of agriculture generally, and it commented that too much land lay fallow,[18] and that cultivators were handicapped by poor roads.[19] Interest in agricultural diversification was especially a feature of the 1816-1820 period, when the Society, under the directorship of Intendant Ramírez, not only pushed crops suitable for small farming, and the settlement of white colonists to develop such crops, but considered in some detail the problem of land for their use.[20] Land titles had long been confused in Cuba, and this

---

1818, 200-211, a discourse by a man who had lived in Louisiana, and thought cotton should be grown in Cuba, being currently unknown there, suitable to rich and poor, if used in industry might give work to a multitude of poor women, and takes less labor than sugar which will be hard pressed with the end of the slave trade, and will affect more people than coffee if a cotton industry is developed; *Memorias 1819*, 17-19, cotton. *Memorias 1817*, 6, a new method of coffee cultivation, acquired in Jamaica; *ibid.*, 163-80, a discourse on a coffee raising method with an adverse judgment by the Society; *Memorias 1818*, 24-43, objection to application of Arabian methods of coffee cultivation. *Memorias 1795*, 43, that Virginia tobacco should be grown because preferred on the African coast in connection with the slave trade; *Memorias 1817*, 299-326, on abolition of tobacco monopoly of that year, with benefits expected to result for poor cultivators, including Intendant Ramírez' strong interest in the matter; *ibid.*, 361-80, Ramírez as director of the Society promoting tobacco culture, with extracts from 25 memorias on tobacco presented to the Society in 1804 and forwarded to the Consulado; *Memorias 1818*, 44-72, "Conversación entre un labrador y un hijo suyo, sobre la vida rural, el cultivo, elaboración y tráfico del tabaco ...," being largely an argument that with the abolition of the monopoly, tobacco should benefit smaller cultivators. *Memorias 1818*, 213-24, documents on indigo, including samples of some grown locally, with instructions on cultivation and processing, and pointing out that its great value by weight was an advantage where transport costs were high, as in Cuba. *Ibid.*, 211-13, decree of Ramírez noting that the laws favored cotton, coffee, and indigo as new crops, free of imposts on themselves and on imported utensils and machines.

[17] "Junta ordinaria," January 2, 1794 (*Colección Actas 1880*, 66-68), a machine for milling maize and rice; "junta ordinaria," May 1, 1794 (*ibid.*, 90-91), the same or another milling device for cereals; *Memorias 1795*, 48-49, yucca from which the bread of the poor was made, was being damaged by an insect; *ibid.*, 137-41, on the yucca insect; *Tareas 1815*, 3-4, wheat and maize; *Memorias 1817*, 100-101, a prize on planting fruit trees; *ibid.*, 101, a prize to the farmer presenting to the Society arrowroot flour (*Sagú*).

[18] *Memorias 1794*, *loc. cit.*, 421.

[19] E.g., *ibid.*, 424, 425. Cf. Peraza y Sarausa, "Indice," RBC, LI, 288, for "Agricultura" in the *Papel Periódico*.

[20] Many documents in the 1817-20 memorias deal directly or indirectly with this subject: e.g., *Memorias 1818*, 314-22, "Extracto del Expediente sobre terrenos realengos y sus denuncias ...,"; *Memorias 1819*, 17, Ramírez and the Junta Superior de real Hacienda trying to assure land to small farmers; *ibid.*, 159-81, "Estracto de espediente sobre promover la división y repartimiento de las haciendas de comunidad," in connection with white colonization; *ibid.*, 182-91, more documents on the same subject; *ibid.*, 192-209, "Apéndice de las reales resoluciones ... sobre terrenos realengos y sus denuncias," covering years 1792-1815; *ibid.*, 315-17, on acquisition of *terrenos realengos y baldíos*.

confusion, together with various sorts of restrictive legislation, and some of the natural predispositions of hacendados, meant that much land lay fallow or was unproductively devoted to stockraising. Efforts to deal with these problems had been intensified in the 1790's, with the aid of the Havana Economic Society and the Consulado, and resulted finally in 1814 in a decree to promote cultivation of *mercedes* (holdings in usufruct), and another in 1815, removing restrictions on timber cutting, originally a means of guarding naval supplies. Intendant Ramírez played an important part in implementation of the 1814 order for the promotion of cultivation, and coupled with it plans for promoting white immigration, which received royal approval October 21, 1817. Under this order an effort was made to break up communal holdings, in order to provide land for prospective white immigrants. A few settlements were set up, perhaps the best known being at Cienfuegos and Nuevitas; but the results were not what Ramírez had hoped, and the land reforms in fact proved of more value to the wealthy landholder than to the poor.[21]

The Havana Society devoted a good deal of attention to the sugar industry,[22] with more emphasis on the question of processing than cultivation, but both will be considered here. The interest in chemistry instruction has been discussed.[23] The Society had a strong interest in machines that would increase, speed, or make less costly the processing of sugar;[24] it knew that

---

[21] D. C. Corbitt, "*Mercedes* and *realengos*: A Survey of the Public Land System in Cuba," HAHR, XIX, No. 3 (August, 1939), 262-85. Cf. Guerra y Sánchez, *Manual historia Cuba*, 250, on piñerista (Spanish) complaints that the new provisions chiefly aided creoles. *Supra*, 282, on white colonization in Cuba.

[22] Cf. *Memorias 1842*, 280-88, a Society memoria of 1797 on sugar, which commences with the usual general assertion of the ancient honor accorded agriculture, but then proceeds to concentrate on sugar.

[23] *Supra*, 310-11. Cf. *Memorias 1793*, 15-17, on the importance of science to agriculture.

[24] *Memorias 1793*, 8-10, the Society built a pendulum-activated machine, supposed to eliminate costly oxen, but it failed; *ibid.*, 11-13, proposals on wind and water mills; *ibid.*, 105-7, report of Society committee on machine that failed; *ibid.*, 107-19, report on wind or water machine of Guillermo Duncan, noting that Cuban mills all driven by oxen, and that the use of wind or water power presented problems in Cuba, though used elsewhere in the Caribbean; *Memorias 1794*, *loc. cit.*, 429, 430; *ibid.*, 27-28, condemning the design of a new machine which ignored the principles of dynamics; *Memorias 1795*, 36-40; *ibid.*, 115-18 contract of Society with inventor to build his machine; *ibid.*, 119, subscribers to foregoing machine; *ibid.*, 120-23, an adverse report on a steam engine, not yet usable in Cuba, for reasons of cost; *Memorias 1842*, 401-18, a Society discourse of 1797 on Cuban soils devoted to sugar cane; *Memorias 1845*, 357, on the first importation of Tahitian sugar cane into Cuba, from the Danish West Indies in 1798; *Memorias 1817*, 6-7; *ibid.*, 99-100, a prize on promotion of small sugar cultivation, and a community mill to process the cane.

methods in foreign Caribbean isles were superior to those of Cuba.[25] Cuban methods were discussed by the Society at some length.[26]

The Guatemala dealt with commercial or industrial crops rather than with foodstuffs and subsistence agriculture. The frequent use of the term "cultivation" must generally be understood in the sense of "promotion" or "stimulation." When members linked the future of Guatemala with the progress of agriculture, it is probable that many of them thought in terms of the moral welfare of the populace, but it is doubtful if they envisaged the enrichment of any but the small class of large landowners or merchants. The Society did, however, offer a prize for essays on the justice of the ban on the *repartimiento* system of forced labor, and the damage that would result from permitting it again; but the essays also were to deal with means of providing the Indians with necessities and stimulating them to labor without compulsion.[27] It is notable that the frequent appeals for improvement of the economic condition of the populace in order to promote morality and the abandonment of habits resulting from poverty were made largely in connection with industrial and commercial agriculture and manufacturing.

While there was some appreciation of the fact that the common Indian cultivation was haphazard,[28] not all the agricultural expressions and efforts of the Society kept this carefully in view. Methods of dealing with agriculture included stimulation of interest by speeches at juntas, the importation and distribution of seeds, searches in the provinces by members for plants that might yield to development, a few experimental plantings by members who sent samples of their crops with reports to the Society, and the promotion of exotic plants unknown or nearly unknown in the area. But the Society did not concern itself with the preparation of the soil, with fertilizer, crop

---

[25] *Memorias 1793*, 13-15, the Society decided to translate two foreigners' works on sugar.

[26] *Ibid.*, 15, José Ricardo O'Farrill was commissioned to describe Cuban sugar methods, so they could be compared with those described in the foreign works being translated; *ibid.*, 119-47, "Exposición que D. Joseph Ricardo O-Farrill hace a la Sociedad del método observado en la Isla de Cuba, en el cultivo de la Caña dulce y la elaboración de su Xugo," pointing out that Cuban sugar needed considerable reform, as did agriculture generally, and dealt with sugar industry from land to cultivation, to harvest and processing, with figures as to production per unit of land, and detailed discussion of processing methods, utensils, and machinery, all in all a notably practical discussion; *ibid.*, 147-60, on establishment of a school of chemistry, for considerable discussion of the problems of the sugar industry. Cf. for some additional agricultural interest, *Memorias 1794, loc. cit.*, 104-5, the Society considered a plan for an "Escuela práctica y gratuita de agricultura," but found it too expensive; *Memorias 1819*, 318-25, on differential export duties favoring importation of technical items used in Cuban economic production.

[27] *Quarta junta pública*, 13; *Gazeta de Guatemala*, II, No. 56 (April 21, 1798), 88.

[28] Cf. Guillén, *Frayle prócer*, 256, for Córdova's statement to this effect.

rotation, or irrigation, though such reforms were being discussed in the Spanish Societies.

The Society did, however, pay some attention to foodstuffs. At the end of the century the intendant of San Salvador reported to the captain general that insects were devouring crops in his jurisdiction. The matter was passed to the Economic Society, which named a committee to study it. Its report (June, 1799) pointed out that grain storage was more difficult in Guatemala than in regions with colder climates, and proposed several remedies.[29] Then in 1804 José del Valle wrote a pamphlet on methods of handling locusts, and of alleviating food shortages, citing a work of Count Rumford on means of stretching out a supply of maize.[30] A few years later, in 1811, when a poor wheat harvest had contributed to a food shortage, a commission of the Society experimented with wheat, maize, and potato flours, finally arriving at an equal mixture of the first two, with which they made an "economic bread" (*pan económico*) and sold it in a bread store opened by the Society.[31] In 1812 prizes for wheat cultivation were offered by the newly created corresponding junta of the Society at San Salvador.[32]

An effort to deal with the fundamental problem of food production was made by the corresponding junta at Truxillo. In July, 1798, it reported plans to offer prizes for the growing of maize in the territory around the port, since the fertility of the land was such that there was no excuse for the current poor production and consequent high prices.[33] Later that month, the junta decided that the question was so troublesome as to require the attention of a paid overseer. The commandant of the port agreed to contribute to this person's compensation, and at the same time asked membership in the junta for himself.[34] In October, 1798, the Truxillo members proposed that an improvement of the food situation at the port would both reduce the outlay of the Crown for maintenance of that vital area, and strengthen the

---

[29] *Gazeta de Guatemala*, July 1, 1799, 58-60; July 8, 1799, 64. Cf. issue of August 26, 1799, 94, for a letter from New Spain the following month, referring to the memorial, and suggesting as a remedy the "silos" used in Naples.

[30] Valle, *Plaga de langosta*, 22.

[31] *Octava junta pública*, 23-24; *Junta general no. 102*, 12. *Supra*, 93, the Spanish Societies and Rumford. Cf. Peraza y Sarausa, "Indice," RBC, LII, 312, on "Sopa Económica" (gelatin from bones) in *Papel Periódico* in 1804.

[32] *Novena junta pública*, 24; Sobre erección de la Junta de Correspondencia (AGG, A1.6, leg. 2008, exped. 13856), the intendant offered fifty pesos to the Indian or mulatto who grew the most wheat.

[33] Junta de Sociedad de Truxillo to the Society of Guatemala, Truxillo, July 30— AGG, A1.6, leg. 2007, exped. 13822. Signed by eight members of the junta, including secretary Juan Ortiz de Letona, Chief Treasury Official of the port.

[34] Account of the junta of Truxillo, June 17, 1798, signed by Letona—AGG A1.6, leg. 2007, exped. 13823.

Spanish hold on the lower classes, the *Negros Caribes*. The corresponding junta wrote:

> Their adhesion to us is deduced [fro⁻ the fact] that youths living in Spanish houses already do not wish to be called Carib, and also from the pleasure that they admit when they see a white going through their section (*barrio*) and the submission that governs them, not forgetting to salute with their hats when they encounter a Spaniard.[35]

But this suggestion regarding maize proved less interesting to the Society in the capital than the concurrent proposal of the Truxillo group for creation of schools of primary letters.

Tobacco did not interest the Guatemala Society, though the value of the local crop was increasing rapidly at the time. Tobacco was sold to the value of 300,000 pesos in 1797, over 400,000 pesos in 1801, more then 500,000 in 1808, and in excess of 800,000 pesos in 1809. The increase seems to have been due largely to the interruption of the indigo trade, which drove cultivators to seek a new source of revenue.[36] Perhaps the Society was not attracted to tobacco under the conditions of government monopoly. In any event, that did not prevent José Cecilio del Valle from becoming royal assessor of tobacco revenues in 1813.[37]

Indigo production was in a depressed condition when the Society was founded, and remained depressed till 1821, due to taxation, excessive regulation, the interruptions of maritime traffic during the French wars, and to locust damage. Cultivation of the jiquilite plant, source of indigo, had expanded greatly in the eighteenth century among the poor, who were badly exploited by merchants in being forced to sell their product at an arbitrarily fixed low price, compelled to pay high prices for articles for their own use, and forced to take commodities they did not want as part payment for their production. A Gratuity Fund, supported by a tax on indigo, was set up in 1783 by Captain General Matías de Gálvez to give some relief. The fund was fought for years by the merchants.[38]

Jose Mariano Mociño of the Royal Botanical Expedition in 1797 wrote the Society from Mexico, suggesting a hydrostatic device for the improvement of indigo production. It proved a failure.[39] The next year he sent a treatise

---

[35] Account of junta of October 4, 1798—AGG, A1.6, leg. 2007, exped. 13823.

[36] Salvatierra, *Contribución*, II, 167.

[37] Rosa, *José Cecilio del Valle*, 29.

[38] Salvatierra, *Contribución*, II, 188 *et seq.*, including figures for indigo production in 1772-1802; El Real Tr[ibun]al del Consulado, sobre fomentar la Agricultura, Industria y Comercio—AGG, A1.5-6, leg. 51, exped. 1273. The expediente is for 1817, but it contains material on the Fondo of the Monte Pío de Cosecheros de Añil for 1814.

[39] *Segunda junta pública*, 8 *et seq.*; *Tercera junta publica*, 5.

on jiquilite culture. The Society awarded it a prize, and in 1799 had it published, with notes added by Dr. Goycoechea. The *Gazeta* was advertising this treatise for sale at its offices,[40] and the treatise was later printed at Manila by the Philippine Economic Society.

The Guatemala Society devoted less attention to indigo than to cacao, once a valuable crop there, but long in decay, at this time suffering from the competition of cheap, though often poor quality, cacao from Quito and Peru. In 1796 the Society announced that a study was being made of the decadence of this once rich crop,[41] and a member pleaded strongly for revival of Guatemala's cacao traffic.[42] In July, 1797, it was reported that the commission of cacao plantations (*cacahuatales*) was concentrating on plantings in three provinces which had formerly been rich, where decadence seemed worst, and where the land seemed destined beyond all in America for the production of cacao.

The Society gathered data by consulting a member who owned a cacao plantation, and it offered prizes to Indians in certain areas for the possession after two years of the greatest number of living cacao trees of a certain minimum height.[43] One official, writing to the Society from the far north of the captaincy general, was frankly skeptical of the possibility of overcoming the "laziness" of the natives,[44] but the cacao commission continued its work until 1798. At that time, the chairman, Antonio García Redondo, prepared a memorial, printed the following year,[45] which analyzed the causes of the decadence of cacao culture in Guatemala, the effects of this on the Indian cultivator, and called for political action to remove the restrictions imposed by the government on the cacao trade, as being the worst cause of the evil state of its culture in the region.[46]

The territories where cacao once had flourished were in the northwest, where the population was Indian or mestizo, and fairly dense. The Society

---

[40] *Quinta junta pública*, 7-8; *Gazeta de Guatemala*, IV, No. 185 (December 1, 1800); Medina, *Imprenta en Guatemala*, No. 989, pp. 363-64.

[41] *Junta pública December 1796*, 14; cf. Salvatierra, *Contribución*, II, 205 *et seq.*

[42] *Junta pública December 1796*, 24-27.

[43] *Segunda junta pública*, 6.

[44] Joseph de Ballesteros to Secretary Melón, Tonalá, August 30, 1797—AGG, A1.6, leg. 2007, exped. 13821. This expediente also contains other letters on the matter.

[45] Medina, *Imprenta en Guatemala*, 361: *Memoria sobre el fomento de las cosechas de cacaos, y de otros ramos de agricultura presentada a la Real Sociedad Económica Por el Socio Dr. D. Antonio García Redondo, Canónigo Magistral de la Metropolitana de Guatemala* (Ignacio Beteta, 1799). Medina says that an "analytical abstract" of the work was published in the *Correo Mercantil de Madrid*, April 21, 1800.

[46] *Tercera junta pública*, 3; *Quarta junta pública*, 4; *Quinta junta pública*, 5-6; García Pelaez, *Memorias* (2d ed.), III, 145-48, 201; Batres Jáuregui, *América Central*, II, 466.

charged the *alcalde mayor* of Suchitepéques with a census of the cacao plantations in that district, indicating which were Indian and which *ladino*. And at the port of Truxillo, the ever-active corresponding member of the Society, Juan Ortiz de Letona, sent some cacao to the capital to prove that it grew well in the eastern coastal region, but complained that the increasing cost of labor made production difficult. The Society took the sample as proof that cacao could be grown in the entire province of Comayagua, which had never been one of the centers of its cultivation. But the Society had no recommendation on the labor problem, considering it a matter for the government.[47] Another attempt to help the cacao industry was the construction of a boat on the Pacific coast by Society member José Bernardo Dighero, in order to give back to Iztapa her "ancient name of Port of Guatemala." He thought of the cacao problem as largely a question of marketing; better ports would reduce export costs.[48]

Flax was given even more attention than cacao, presumably on the theory that although it was a valuable crop elsewhere, it was an untried commodity in Guatemala, and needed to be imposed upon cultivators; and in the hope that it might be subject to fewer restricting conditions than other crops. Another possible reason for this interest is the emphasis on flax in the Spanish Societies. Finally, the king, in an order of March 24, 1796, recommended to the captain general of Guatemala the planting of flax and hemp, and the latter official sent the order to the Economic Society.[49] The Society appointed the usual special commission, and flax seeds were imported from Spain.[50] An attempt was made at the same time to discover whether flax was not already being cultivated in the area, with the result that Indians were located who knew the plant, but grew very little. The problem thus being one of stimulating production, the Society offered prizes for the greatest amounts of dressed flax presented in a year. The hope was for increased work in both agriculture and industry.[51] Gold medals were offered to parish priests who best stimulated in their districts the cultivation, collection, and cleaning of flax by poor Spaniards, Indians, or *ladinos*.[52] Instructions on dressing flax were inserted by the Society in the *Gazeta de Guatemala*.[53] Several

---

[47] Juan Ortiz de Letona to the Economic Society, Truxillo, February 19, 1797—AGG, A1.6, leg. 2006, exped. 13811; *Segunda junta pública*, 6.

[48] *Quinta junta pública*, 24-25, "Navegación del Sur"; Batres Jáuregui, *América Central*, II, 468.

[49] *Junta pública December 1796*, 13.

[50] *Ibid.*, 14.

[51] *Tercera junta pública*, 5-7; Vicente Figueroa to the Secretary of the Economic Society, Sumpango, December 14, 1797—AGG, A1.6, leg. 2007, exped. 13821.

[52] *Quarta junta pública*, 4-5.

[53] Suplemento, No. 57 [April, 1798]; No. 64 (June 4, 1798), 132-34.

men in the provinces at once began to experiment with the crop,[54] and one
reported, after the Society's re-establishment in 1810, that although his
efforts had not been financially encouraging, he did not intend to abandon
them. His worst difficulty was in adjusting European methods and recommendations to the climatic conditions of America.[55]

The meager result of the attempt to stimulate flax culture was duplicated
in the case of cotton. Again the Society asked information from the provinces
as to whether the crop was under cultivation. The answers were not encouraging, but corresponding members of the Society were willing to accept seeds
and set the farmers to work.[56] Prizes were offered for the largest amount
cultivated, but adjudication was several times postponed because of the
lack of sufficient properly qualified contestants.[57] The best work was done
at the port of Truxillo, where by the spring of 1798 five persons of European
stock, as well as an indeterminate number of Indians (*Caribes*) had crops.
Only seventy-four *arrobas* (about 1,850 pounds) of cotton had been harvested.
The corresponding junta of the Society at Truxillo reported that the main
difficulty was scarcity of labor and the need of cotton gins and people capable
of using them.[58]

The interest of the Guatemala Society in textile materials included silk
as well as flax, hemp, and cotton. It was recognized that while silk pertained
more to industry than to agriculture, it could not be separated entirely
from cultivation of mulberry trees. Society member Pascasio Letona proved
that the tree could be grown in Guatemala. With this accomplished, the
Society decided that the work was suited to the character of the population,
so that all that remained was to encourage silk culture by means of prizes.
José María Peynado was commissioned to get silk worms from Oaxaca in
New Spain, and Letona was to distribute them and give instructions.[59]
The *Gazeta* informed the public that this service was available, free of
charge.[60] The worms arrived in 1797 but within a few weeks Letona reported
that only three persons had inquired, whereupon the task was laid upon

[54] *Tercera junta pública*, 7; *Quinta junta pública*, 6-7.

[55] *Octava junta pública*, 13; *Novena junta pública*, 25-26.

[56] *Junta pública December 1796*, 12-13; Agustín Rodríguez de Zea to the Royal
Society, April 2, 1797, and Carlos José Yudice to the Secretary of the Society, March 11,
1797—AGG, A1.6, leg. 2007, exped. 13821. Both clearly from the provinces.

[57] *Tercera junta pública*, 7; *Quarta junta pública*, 4; *Gazeta de Guatemala*, IV, No. 145
(February 24, 1800), 174.

[58] Report by Ortiz de Letona and Roque Eztenaga to the Society, Truxillo. May 4,
1798—AGG, A1.6, leg. 2007, exped. 13823; cf. *Quarta junta pública*, 111-15, reporting
on cotton at Truxillo, and noting that seeded cotton could be sold at Havana for
20 pesos a quintal.

[59] *Segunda junta pública*, 7.

[60] I, No. 43 (November 27, 1797), 346.

a man living in a region where mulberry trees reputedly were abundant.[61] A year later the Society was compelled to confess that the notion of cultivating silk had been received coolly in the capital. It was thought that women should be particularly suited to the work, and it was proposed to have a priest who was a member of the Society teach silk spinning to girls.[62]

Cochineal, like silk, required only a secondary interest in agriculture, since all that was needed was a plant suitable as food for the insect from the female of which the dye was extracted. Nopal, a cactus, was the plant most favored. Antonio Larrazabal, Guatemala deputy to the Cortes in Spain, reported back to the Society that on his trip to Spain via Mexico he had discovered a curate at Tluxtla who was cultivating Nopal and setting the insects to feed upon it. The Society wrote the priest for information and samples, which arrived at Guatemala late in 1811. The Society soon discovered that Nopal had long grown near the capital without any cultivation, and the usual commission was named to foster attention to the cochineal business.[63] Several priests were still trying to promote the industry in 1821,[64] without any important result having been achieved.[65]

The Society had some interest in exotic plants. It reported the dispatch through the provinces by the captain general of some Asiatic rushes (*juncos*), supposedly grown in the latitude of Guatemala in the Orient, and to be used in making such diverse objects as umbrellas and containers. Even if such fabrication were a prime necessity of an improved economy, Asiatic rushes were not needed, for some Indians who were consulted said that similar plants grew in their districts.[66] Another exotic agricultural possibility came to the attention of the Society in the form of some opium extracted by an ecclesiastic of the captaincy general from plants of his own cultivation. The Society received a sample and observed that the Physician in Chief of the Royal Hospitals of Mexico had found it better than the opium of the Levant.[67] But the Society did not encourage opium culture.

---

[61] *Cuenta del costo y gastos de un caxoncito de semillas de gusanos de seda, conducido de Oaxaca acqui, por el correo ...*, Guatemala, August, 1797—AGG, A1.6, leg. 2006, exped. 13803; P[ascasio] Letona to Secretary Sebastián Melón, November 20, 1797—AGG, leg. 2007, exped. 13821.

[62] *Quinta junta pública*, 7.

[63] *Octava junta pública*, 22-23; *Novena junta pública*, 29-30.

[64] *El Amigo de la Patria*, I, No. 12 (January 20, 1821), 137-38.

[65] Cf. also, Medina, *Imprenta en Guatemala*, No. 2214, Fr. Antonio López, *Instrucción para cultivar los nopales y beneficiar la grana fina ... La da a luz la Real Sociedad Económica de Guatemala. Reimpresa a expensas del Real Consulado. ...* (Guatemala: Beteta, 1818; 35 pp.); Valenzuela, *Imprenta en Guatemala*, 63-64, a *Circular Gubernativa* of the 19th century, mentioning the Society's interest in cochineal.

[66] *Novena junta pública*, 42-44.

[67] *Octava junta pública*, 18-21; *Novena junta pública*, 28-29.

A collection of exotic plants brought to Guatemala from North America by Alejandro Ramírez offered yet other possibilities. These plants were at Truxillo in 1799, that climate being considered suitable, and Juan Ortiz de Letona a good man to care for them. The eighteen baskets of plants included two varieties of breadfruit, a Chinese olive tree, an Asiatic pimiento, an Indian mango, and a camphor tree.[68] A discussion of the plants in the *Gazeta de Guatemala* was reprinted in the Spanish *Correo Mercantil.*[69] Letona left Truxillo, and the plants thereafter had no care until 1811 when Dr. Vicente Carranza agreed to care for what remained alive.[70] The plants did not become important to Guatemalan agriculture.

Industry, Guilds, and Mining

INDUSTRY AND CRAFTS

The interest in popular industry, so strong in the Spanish Societies, found its best American reflection in Guatemala. There was some interest in popular industry in the Manila and Bogota Societies. In Quito, Espejo found that industry scarcely existed, except for a few small textile workshops (*obrajes*) for cheap cloth; and the Count of Casa-Gijón thought that Quito was in a sad case due to the bad condition of industries that formerly flourished. Valiente of Santiago believed in the need for both agriculture and industry, since "a people of peasants only is always a miserable people"; favored industrial development, and stated his general interest in the subject of value added to products by refinement or manufacture. He was especially interested in spinning wheels combined with idle women for the production of cotton thread.

The prime industrial interest of the Havana Society was in sugar processing, which we have discussed. Its attention to the cottage production of textiles was relatively weak. References to flax, hemp, and cotton made some mention of manufacture,[71] but nothing was done to promote that manufacture.[72] Other forms of industry received little mention.[73] The work of the one

---

[68] *Octava junta pública*, 35-36. This was not the same Ramírez who was one of the founders of the Society and later connected with the Puerto Rico and Havana Societies (Villacorta, *Capitanía general*, 263).

[69] *Gazeta de Guatemala*, VI, No. 273 (August 23, 1802), 187-90.

[70] *Octava junta pública*, 17-18; Batres Jáuregui, *América Central*, II, 467.

[71] *Supra*, 323 n.

[72] Cf. *Tareas 1815*, 5, under the heading "popular industry," interest in the preparation of sesame oil, and in flax culture and linen fabrication; *Memorias 1818*, 9, a woman wished to establish a school to teach hosiery making.

[73] *Memorias 1817*, 6, preservation of meat in brandy, and extraction of piñon oil; *ibid.*, 47-48, that the need for artisans was proved by the purchase of furniture from

hundred-odd orphan girls and indigent women in the Casa de Beneficencia
in turning out shirts and cigars scarcely promoted Cuban industry.[74]

The Guatemala Society had a general interest in industry, hoping that
local manufacture might be developed by the application of proper techniques
and the blossoming of hidden talents; that this would lower the price of
commodities, reduce unpatriotic contraband, and improve habits by reducing
idleness.[75] But although the Society did a little to encourage work in carpentry,[76] crockery-ware and porcelain,[77] leather,[78] and metalwork,[79] by far
its strongest industrial or crafts interest was in spinning and textile production. It was the only overseas Society to duplicate the characteristic effort
of the Spanish Societies in this field. The preparation of yarn and cloth
was emphasized in the foundation of the Society, and its first act was the
creation of a Spinning School. It not only instructed young women in new
methods in this school; it also encouraged master craftsmen. New fabrics
were suggested, dyes sought, the resources of the captaincy general explored,
and spinning wheels and cotton gins sent into the provinces. Silk, wool,
and maguey fiber were considered, but most of the work was done with
cotton, the manufacture of which was declining.[80]

The first contributions that members made to the newly formed Society
were used to set up the Spinning School in 1795. Spinning wheels were
paid for by the archbishop, the captain general and his family, and several
other persons; a room was rented; and the school put under the direction
of Pedro de Ariza. Twelve to fourteen female students (*educandas*) generally
were handled at a time, being taught in relays of at first one month, and
later three months. Each relay of training was under the supervision of

---

foreigners who used the same wood Cuba exported unworked; *ibid.*, 102, a prize offered
for tile and brick making; *ibid.*, 418, the Industry Section of the Society considering
the question of whether foreign-made articles should be admitted if their manufacture
would be easy in Cuba.

[74] It was clearly recognized that the girls were being prepared as good mothers
of families, not as producers of goods (*Tareas 1815*, 16).

[75] Cf. *Gazeta de Guatemala*, III, No. 121 (September 9, 1799), 102, on a Society
prize for an essay on the arts best for America, both for the good of the state and of
the worker.

[76] *Quarta junta pública*, 12; *Gazeta de Guatemala*, III, No. 126 (October 14, 1799),
122; prize offered to a carpenter.

[77] *Novena junta pública*, 39-40; *Octava junta pública*, note No. 7 at end.

[78] *Segunda junta pública*, 21-22; *Gazeta de Guatemala*, IV, No. 157 (May 19, 1800),
prizes offered for tanning.

[79] *Novena junta pública*, 26, a prize for the work of a smith replacing the stuff
imported from foreigners.

[80] Since the destruction of Antigua in 1773, according to Bancroft, *Central America*,
III, 660 n.

several deputies of the Society, who paid the expenses of the school, and were reimbursed by the Society. Trainees received one real daily for attending. Small money prizes were awarded daily for quantitative and qualitative achievement;[81] other prizes were wheels, spools, and carding equipment.

The progress of the trainees was slow, with no thread produced in the beginning, so that in the twenty-five operating days in January, 1797, no prizes were awarded during the first eleven days. Some days had to be spent in seeding the cotton and carding it in preparation for spinning. The scale of operations may be seen in that ten out of twelve enrollees at the beginning of January, 1797, finished out the month; or the total of eighty-four women receiving training in the period November, 1795-December, 1796; or in the fact that although the thread produced was sold and helped support the school,[82] it did not cover the combined cost of the daily real to the students and the prizes, to say nothing of the rent for the school's quarters, or the cotton used by the trainees, which was the single greatest expense of the school during its operations.

The school was still operating at the end of 1797, but the Society felt that most of its objectives had been achieved: that is, that interest had been stimulated, wheels distributed, and some women trained in their use. Therefore, in 1798 the Society decided that the school was too costly, so the daily wage and prizes were abandoned. Since it was felt that enough women from all parts of the city had been trained to permit of concentration upon their work in their own houses, a new type of prize was established. The original school was given up entirely that year, but four of its graduates were assigned to each of three schools created in different parts of the city, and to these the Society continued to provide equipment and materials. The Society soon decided that the new system worked well, and felt that the continued distribution of spinning wheels was certain to prevent much "vicious beggary." The three classes continued under direction of deputies appointed by the Society, until the summer of 1800, when the order of suspension of the Society went into effect. During the five years, several hundred women and girls had received some training in spinning.

The work of the spinning school was resumed after reactivation of the Society in December, 1810; in 1812 the work was diversified. Of one class of thirteen *educandas* in this period, two were set to spinning silk, two to

---

[81] The prizes were of one-half, one, and two reals. Cf. Medina, *Imprenta en Guatemala*, No. 869, a twenty-four-page pamphlet published in 1796, dealing with the public distribution of prizes at the school, November 4, 1795.

[82] In one period in 1796, 62 pounds of cotton costing a bit over seven pesos produced just over 15 pounds of thread which sold for 24 pesos, 3 reals.

wool, and nine to cotton. The school died soon thereafter with the Society itself.[83]

The introduction of better textile-making instruments into the provinces was attempted by the Society. In 1796 it sent a spinning wheel from the capital to the corresponding junta at Truxillo,[84] and in 1799 a seed separator went to the same place.[85] Both articles were sent to Truxillo via San Miguel and Comayagua, being carried at least part of the way by porter. The bishop of Chiapa in early 1799 acknowledged receipt from the Society of two cotton spinning wheels, one hand-operated, the other pumped by foot.[86] A cotton gin was sent to the bishop of Leon in the southern part of the captaincy general.[87]

The effort to improve yarn production was but part of the Society's interest in textile production. Numerous prizes were offered for fabrics. A prize for dimity (*cotonía*) in 1796 to the master craftsman Marcos Alvarado raised the hope in the Society that the local product would soon be preferred to English fabrics, because of price, quality, and because of patriotic interest in local production.[88] Prizes offered for muslins found no competitors in 1798 and 1799 save Marcos Alvarado, who after one postponement of the award was given the prize.[89]

An attempt was made to increase production of a cheap cloth (*panete*) made in Quesaltenango. In 1798 the director of the Guatemala Society received word that there were but two weavers in that highland town.[90]

---

[83] This account of the school is based on numerous MS. records of the Society, mostly business papers, some for the Escuela de Hilado alone, some for the Society as a whole (AGG, A1.6, leg. 2006, expeds. 13799, 13801-13803, 13805-13807, 13812, 13815-13818; leg. 2007, exped. 13831; leg. 2008, expeds. 13844, 13851); and on the printed *juntas públicas* (*December 1796*, 6-9; *Segunda*, 15 *et seq.*; *Tercera*, 7-8; *Quarta*, 8; *Quinta*, 8-9; *Novena*, 7, 33-34). Cf. *Gazeta de Guatemala*, September 9, 1799, 101, a man gave one pound of cotton thread to the Society, but wanted 1,000 pesos for the secret of its production; *Novena junta pública*, 34-36, on the lack of wool weaving in Guatemala.

[84] Receipts for payment for building it, and for carrying it as far as San Miguel, in AGG, A1.6, leg. 2006, exped. 13803.

[85] Agn. Martí y Heredia to Secretary Melón, San Miguel, February 12, 1799—AGG, A1.6, leg. 2008, exped. 13850.

[86] Fermín Joseph Obpo. de Chiapa to Sebastián Melón, Ciudad Real, January 31, 1799—AGG, A1.6, leg. 2008, exped. 13850.

[87] Financial record in AGG, leg. 2008, exped. 13840.

[88] *Junta pública December 1796*, 10; *Gazeta de Guatemala*, III, No. 108 (June 10, 1799), 48. Cf. AGG, A1.6, leg. 2008, exped. 13840, for acknowledgments in February, 1800, by two weavers of San Vicente of receipt of Society prizes for muslin and dimity.

[89] *Segunda junta pública*, 17 *et seq.*; *Tercera junta pública*, 8. Cf. *Gazeta de Guatemala*, February 24, 1800, 174, the Society offers prizes to the three weavers who present examples by June.

[90] *Segunda junta pública*, 17 *et seq.*

This was highly erroneous, as a report by the *corregidor* of Quesaltenango showed when, in response to a request from the Society, he sent an account of textile production in the area. His calculation indicated that from an annual total of 4,200 *arrobas* (about 105,000 pounds) of wool were made about 100,000 yards of cloth of various qualities. This, it was thought, resulted in a trade of perhaps 33,600 pesos in the provinces of Quesaltenango and Totonicapán, with some 13,000 pesos pertaining to the town of Quesaltenango alone. It was further reported that in the town were thirty master weavers and some 190 laborers serving them. The Society concluded that this wool fabric production in the highlands might be improved by the introduction of machines and the improvement of the dyes used.[91] The next year the Society decided that the perfection of *panetes* depended on the construction of a fulling mill. One of the members in the capital prepared a sketch of such a device, while another was charged with drawing up instructions for its operation. They were to take their information from European books on the subject.[92]

The Society experimented with an English cotton gin, found it slow, so the director designed a new one that worked faster with the local cotton.[93] The Society engaged in weaving operations, under direction of its member José Fernández Gil. This activity was, as usual, tied not only to the hope of aiding the public by increasing work, but to the desire to increase internal traffic and cut down the contraband trade with the enemies of Spain. The Society especially wished to produce cotton goods of fine and medium-fine quality. It was persuaded that the worst cause of the depression of the local economy was the illegal commerce, and that cotton cloth production could close it up, for

> So long as these fabrics of Guatemala are equivalent to the English, and may be sold at more moderate prices, it is not necessary to fear clandestine importations . . . and even when the fineness and perfection of some of them is not comparable, as is so in some cases . . . , the notable difference of price will close the eyes of the multitude of consumers.[94]

The program of domestic production and consumption was pushed again after re-establishment of the Society, and in 1811 the printed version of one of the public juntas declared that

> The true promotion of our fabrics consists in giving them consumption, and this

---

[91] *Quarta junta pública,* 10.

[92] *Quinta junta pública,* 12. Cf. *Gazeta de Guatemala,* July 3, 1811, 274, for Society prizes offered to weavers in May, 1811.

[93] *Quinta junta pública,* 11.

[94] *Ibid.,* 9-11.

is only possible by using and wearing ourselves the goods of the country. This is the great principle that the Society wishes to establish.[95]

Local fabrics were presented at this junta to the captain general by influential people. The account suggested that the members of the Society should not only wear these locally fabricated clothes at the ceremonies of the organization, but daily as well, since it would stimulate local industry; it was better to encourage local workmen than to beg from foreigners and make them rich.[96]

The Society also wished to stimulate the manufacture in Guatemala of silk hose and velveteen. Some hose were made under direction of a Society member. It wanted to import what it called the celebrated horse-driven machine of New Orleans that was reputed to clean cotton of its seeds with great rapidity.[97] Maguey fiber received attention in 1797 when, on a member's suggestion, a deputy was named to make some cloth of it and determine whether it was worth promoting as an industry which might increase the work available to the population.[98] In 1811 an account of "Brittany linen" made from maguey by local men was accompanied by a note suggesting that it would be more proper to call the cloth "Guatemala" than "Brittany," since the latter name, taken from the province of France, was adopted there deliberately as a commercial device.[99]

The Society showed interest in other aspects of the textile business. A concern for dyes went along with knowledge of cochineal and indigo, as well as the hope of improving the coloring of fabrics. For one thing, the colors imported from New Spain were expensive, partly because of the high freight charges. One local dye presented to the Society brought a price in Guatemala of sixteen reals an ounce, whereas an equivalent coloring material brought from New Spain cost twenty-four pesos an ounce.[100] The dean of the church of Leon sent advice on dyes.[101] A member living in San Miguel searched the coast for the murex, applied to the Society, and received advice as to the extraction of the purple tint.[102] A lady of Guatemala City sent the Society a specimen of carbonate of soda purified by herself. The Society noted the industrial uses of the stuff and urged idle males "who vegetate in

---

[95] *Octava junta pública*, note No. 6 in unnumbered pp. at back.

[96] *Ibid.* Cf. *ibid.*, note No. 7, for an inventory of things on display—mostly fabrics—at the public junta.

[97] *Novena junta pública*, 36-39.

[98] *Tercera junta pública*, 7.

[99] *Octava junta pública*, note No. 8 at end.

[100] *Novena junta pública*, 32-33.

[101] *Quarta junta pública*, 10.

[102] *Octava junta pública*, 21-22.

inaction" to observe the example set by a woman.[103] The Society received
some printed fabrics, and was interested in the suggestion that this type
of production be extended.[104]

GUILDS

The Guatemala was the only overseas Society to do anything notable in
connection with guild organization, though the others inherited some of
the interest of the Spanish Societies in artisans. The Lima Society printed
figures on the number of artisans in Lima; the statutes of the Bogota Society
provided for the protection of crafts. It would have been interesting to see
what an Economic Society on the model of Campomanes might have done
about guilds in Mexico City, but no Society was formed there until the time
of Iturbide. The Havana Society's class of "popular industry and public
ornament" was interested in forming guilds of the mechanical crafts, but
wanted first to consult the guild ordinances of Barcelona and other Spanish
cities.[105]

In Guatemala, the fiscal of the audiencia, reporting on the project for a
Society there, suggested a new plan of guild regulation, ascribing much local
idleness to faulty guild organization, the quality of work being poor, and
apprentices improperly supervised by the masters. Only the makers of
fireworks were regulated with some order, according to the fiscal. The royal
order approving establishment of the Society accepted the fiscal's suggestion
that the Society study the problem.[106] The secretary of the new Society
was soon stating that although all the objectives of the body were "useful,
patriotic, and illuminating," the "regulation of the guilds of artisans has
without doubt the greatest political and moral transcendency."[107]

In September, 1796, Villaurrutia wrote the town council of Guatemala

---

[103] *Novena junta pública*, 30-31.

[104] *Segunda junta pública*, 20-21.

[105] Havana *Memorias 1793*, 40; *Memorias 1794, loc. cit.*, 111, they still had not done
it; *Memorias 1795*, 59, the Society still interested in the project of regulating artisans
as a means of public order; *Memorias 1817*, 94-99, a paper advocating for Havana
a *junta protectora de las artes*, a great port deserving well-developed crafts, also guilds
should be formed, with the usual rights to examine and certify craftsmen, the paper's
main notion being that guilds would promote crafts, but an editorial note pointed
out that this brought up the old question of whether guild ordinances governing
industry that entered into commerce were prejudicial to that commerce, and emphasizing that liberty was the principal base of industry and commerce, and was incompatible with ordinances and regulations, and another editorial note emphasized that the
Society did want to promote industrial crafts.

[106] Govierno. Indiferente. Sobre que el. Super. Govierno informe a Su M. la
utilidad qe. se sigue del esto. de una Sociedad Económica. ...—AGG, A1.5-5, leg.
51, exped. 1279. *Supra*, 206-7, for the fiscal's other views.

[107] *Junta pública December 1796*, 14-15.

requesting a copy of the "Ordinances of the Guilds" from its archives, and after some delay the council ordered copies made.[108] But the work of the Society proceeded slowly, partly because Villaurrutia, head of the commission on guilds, was busy with his duties as judge of the audiencia, partly because the conception of what was involved had developed rather broadly. Not only was a regulation for the guilds being drafted, but the commission was working on a plan for a brotherhood to provide succor (*hermandad general de socorro*) for guild members in old age, sickness, and in the event of accidents, so that workers would not have to resort to begging or to the public hospital. In the third place, the commission was designing a regulation of popular public diversions.[109]

Society member Friar Luís García in 1797 declared at a public junta that he had seen the nearly completed plan for the guilds and found it admirable, for it would stimulate local manufactures, which in turn would free Guatemala of all reliance on foreign countries; this would then bring increased circulation of money, which would mean the curing of many ills originating in poverty. Finding Guatemala in as evil a state as Rome, he arrived at the somewhat curious idea that since most of the gambling, murder, and other undesirable practices which had filled the jails were due to idleness, necessity, or lack of population, only the organization of the guilds would aid the situation in Guatemala. He also praised the plan for compelling the apprentices to work every day, and for supervising their play at festival time. This antique idea was coupled with the ancient argument that gambling among the lower classes thus would be stopped and their substance preserved.[110] That is, the interest here was in regulation of the habits of the artisans. This was even more directly stated at a public junta of the Society in 1798, demanding education for all artisans as the first step in aiding the arts and crafts, but declaring that most of all they needed better habits.[111]

The *Gazeta de Guatemala* promoted interest in the guilds,[112] noting that

---

[108] Jacobo de Villaurrutia to the Alcalde de primer voto, Nva. Guatemala, September 17, 1796; Xptoval Ortiz de Aviles to the Ayuntamiento, Na. Guatemala, September 19, 1796; Acta of the Ayuntamiento, October 3, 1796; Villaurrutia to Christoval Ortiz de Aviles, Na. Guatemala, October 4; Aviles to the Ayuntamiento, October 4; Order of the Ayuntamiento for the copies of the guild ordinances, October 11, 1796—AGG, A1.6, leg. 2267, exped. 16452.

[109] *Segunda junta pública*, 2, 22 et seq.; *Tercera junta pública*, 9 et seq. Cf. Juan Bautta. de Yrissarry [to the Society], November 2, 1796, asking to be excused from working on the guild ordinances, because of his large family, and his work as a consul of the Consulado—AGG, A1.6, leg. 2006, exped. 13808.

[110] *Tercera junta pública*, 16-22.

[111] *Quarta junta pública*, 7-8.

[112] Nos. 33, 36-38 (September 18, October 9, 16, 23, 1797), 258-61, 281-83, 290-92, 297-98.

the printer Beteta had issued a reprint of a paper from the Spanish *Semanario Erudito* entitled "Political Economic Discourse upon the Influence of the Guilds in the State."[113] The author of the *Gazeta* piece spent more space on his own notions than on those of the reprint, his chief idea being that Europe gained prosperity in the Middle Ages only after the guilds were formed. He felt that the life of the artisans was very important to the prosperity and strength of the state, but observed that the condition of different peoples in Europe had altered from time to time and that the same would be true of Guatemala.

The "General Regulation of Artisans of New Guatemala" went from the Society's special commission on the matter to the government in 1798, and later in the year was printed by Beteta.[114] It provided for a "Guild Directorate" headed by a superintendent, named by the captain general; two hacendado members, who were not to be merchants, named by the ayuntamiento; two merchants, not to be hacendados, named by the Consulado; and two ecclesiastical members, this last being an addition to the original report of the committee, tacked onto the end of the printed version of the regulation. The Directorate was to settle matters by a plurality of votes; import from Europe books, instruments, machines, instructions, and drawings to aid the arts and crafts; seek help from the Economic Societies of Spain; print the regulations of each craft; and keep a close eye on the artisans, excluding craftsmen for bad conduct, regulating their dress, and prohibiting the entrance of new members when a guild was overcrowded. Bullfights, dances, and other diversions of artisans were regulated.

An Artisans Pious Fund was to be set up, supported by contributions by the masters, at the rate of one real weekly. A workman incapacitated by age or sickness drew one real daily for each weekly real he had put in. The soundness of the fund was damaged by a provision that the Directorate might require a contribution from it to the Academy of Drawing of the Economic Society. Other welfare provisions dealt with a brotherhood (*Hermandad General de Artesanos*) or *cofradía*, to engage in religious observances, and to inter deceased members. Other provisions of the Regulations required the guilds to care for the orphans of former members.

---

[113] This item is listed in Medina, *Imprenta en Guatemala*, No. 892, as a five-page pamphlet, presumably printed in 1797, by the printer Bracamonte, for the Economic Society of Guatemala.

[114] *Reglamento general de artesanos de la Nueva Guatemala, que la junta comisionada para su formación propone a la general de la Real Sociedad* (Guatemala, 1798); *Quarta junta pública*, 7-8; Cuenta de cargo y data de los fondos de la Rl. Sociedad ... November 1, 1797, to October 31, 1798 (AGG, A1.6, leg. 2007, exped. 13830), gives information on the copying and printing.

Each guild was to have a Protector named by the town council, and other officers, including *veedores* who would examine apprentices for promotion to journeyman, and the latter for advancement to master. No master was to have more apprentices than journeymen without the express permission of the Directorate. Masters who received that status outside the *reyno* of Guatemala were to be admitted to that position there without further examination.

The above sketch of the General Regulation indicates that the Society members had adopted some of the liberal economic ideas of the Spanish Societies, in the way of better education for craftsmen, and free passage of masters from place to place without being subjected to examinations to prevent their exercising their craft in new communities. On the other hand, the Regulation provided for control of the size of guild membership, and for a very close supervision of the personal lives of the members, and displayed an interest in charity, self-help, and religious activity that outweighed the concern for the economic questions involved.

While the general study of the guilds by the Society was initially suggested by the fiscal of the audiencia of Guatemala, who was not satisfied with the town council's work, the latter body was not inclined to accept the Society's views. The town council soon decided that the Regulation threatened its own authority over the guilds, and in rather an angry session ordered one of its members to write to Spain requesting that the Regulation not be put into effect.[115] It was not implemented, one reason being the suspension of the Society itself by government order in 1800.

In 1811, after the Society had been re-established, the town council took up the task of guild regulation. Antonio de Juarros, who was both a member of the town council and an officer of the restored Society, was prominent in the project. He declared that the time had come, now that the Cortes in Spain was destroying tyranny, for the artisans to achieve their rights. It developed that in the conception of Juarros these rights included a guild system closely controlled by the government through a licensing system.[116] The government of Guatemala asked the Society to render an opinion on the project. What this opinion may have been does not appear, though the

---

[115] Libro de Actas del Cabildo de Guatemala, año 1798. Cabildo ordinario of October 23, 1798—AGG, A1.2-2, leg. 2813, exped. 15725.

[116] Salazar, *Veintiún años*, 143-46, saying Juarros' Reglamento proposed an anachronistic gremial system, based on privilege and destroying "the liberty of business" by requiring license, and that Juarros and the town council sincerely meant to aid, but were blinded by "prejudices of caste and family." Cf. Medina, *Imprenta en Guatemala*, No. 1752: *Reglamento general de policía de artesanos de Guatemala formado por el ... Ayuntamiento* (Beteta, 1811; 48 pp.).

Society published an opinion to the effect that the artisans of Guatemala, though capable and hardworking, were handicapped by a lack of instruments.[117] In any event, Captain General Bustamante did not approve the town council's projected Regulation.[118]

The paternalistic attitude of the elite of a society with a strong class stratification is apparent in the Society's attitude toward the guilds. On the other hand, the economy of the area would have permitted little success from a radically different attitude, even if social conditions would have made a drastic change feasible. The guild Regulation was a fair representation of actual conditions, social and economic, in Guatemala. The general climate hardly changed in some respects for a century thereafter.[119]

MINING

The American Societies inherited a tendency to deprecate the importance of mining from the Spanish Societies and from currently influential Spanish political economists. Even the *Mercurio Peruano*, though recognizing the importance of mining for Peru, wished to promote other forms of economic activity. The Havana Society had little to say about the subject, though it printed a suggestion for the immigration of Catholic foreigners with a knowledge of ore reduction to work the copper of east Cuba, so as to eliminate the anomalous situation whereby people in western Cuba used copper from Peru.[120]

The Guatemala Society pinned its hopes on importing a mineralogist from Mexico to teach, but this hope was not fulfilled.[121] The territory of Comayagua had once produced minerals, but by the end of the eighteenth century the mines were abandoned. A public junta of the Society in 1798 heard that two corresponding members at Comayagua had sent a description of mineral deposits at Opoteca, lamenting that they were not then being worked because of lack of miners.[122] Ortiz de Letona of Truxillo recorded that more than 160 gold and silver mines had been opened in Comayagua, but due to lack of workers few were functioning; and while copper and mercury were known, they were not mined.[123]

---

[117] *Novena junta pública*, 42.
[118] Salazar, *Veintiún años*, 146.
[119] *Supra*, 317, on the Society and the guild of painters. Cf. Cappa, *Estudios críticos*, Pt. III, vol. IX, 1 *et seq.*, for a Jesuit defense late in the 19th century of the moral and religious value of guilds, ascribing attacks on the guilds in part to freemasons.
[120] Havana *Memorias 1794*, *loc. cit.*, 25.
[121] *Supra*, 231.
[122] *Quarta junta pública*, 15.
[123] *Gazeta de Guatemala*, August 27, 1798, 226.

Revival of the mines of Corpus in the bishopric of Honduras was suggested by Friar Juan de Santa Rosa Ramírez, who once had been stationed in that region.[124] José María Peynado, censor of the Society, reviewed the history of the gold mines of the Hill of Corpus and noted that according to tradition they were richer than the Cerro de Potosí, but he decided that it had never been a very satisfactory operation. He thought that work of this sort was beyond the resources of the Society, and recommended that the friar's suggestion be forwarded to the government.[125] But the Society decided to write to the bishop of Comayagua for more information on the mines.[126] The bishop sent to the Society at the capital a report from the parish priest of the mining region which stated that it had a sparse, miserably poor population, which looked with indifference and fear at the mines, the richness of which was but a memory. The last mine had been abandoned nine years before, at the death of the owner. The priest thought that mining might have continued if the owner had not deliberately used ignorant laborers who could not learn much about his operations. The priest and bishop both suggested that trained men be sent to the region.[127]

In 1811 some residents of the town of Tegucigalpa agreed to create a corresponding junta of the Guatemala Society. At the same time, the town council of Tegucigalpa proposed that a Gratuity Fund be set up to assist miners, and that other aid be given them. The Society at the capital disapproved of such methods, feeling that they would not strike at the root of the problem, which it considered to be a lack of scientific knowledge. This lack was to be remedied by provision of a class in mineralogy and metallurgy. With this in mind, the Society asked Bustamante to write the government in New Spain to permit the consulting member of the Guatemala Society, Andrés del Río, to come to the south.[128] Bustamante seems, even before this, to have hoped for a good deal from the revival of mining, writing the town council of Guatemala that mining should be one of the main sources of prosperity of the region.[129] Upon what he was founding such an opinion

---

[124] Juan de Sta. Rosa Ramírez to the Economic Society, February 8, 1811—AGG, A1.6, leg. 2008, exped. 13855.

[125] Report of May 29, 1811—AGG, A1.6, leg. 2008, exped. 13855.

[126] Junta ordinaria, No. 106, July 4, 1811; Antonio Juarros to Manuel Julián Rodríguez, bishop of Comayagua, Guatemala, July 12, 1811—AGG, A1.6, leg. 2008, exped. 13855.

[127] Cappn. Angl. Franco. de Valle to the bishop of Comayagua, September 8, 1811; Manual Julián, bishop of Comayagua, to the Economic Society, Comayagua, September 10, 1811—AGG, A1.6, leg. 2008, exped. 13855.

[128] *Octava junta pública*, 12-15.

[129] Bustamante to the Ayuntamiento of Guatemala, August 19, 1813—AGG, A1.2-5, leg. 2835, exped. 25296.

does not appear. The Society postponed further work on mining, pending
the arrival of del Río, though it did receive samples of ore from Leon and
Segovia.[130] By 1815 the mineralogist still had not arrived, since the money
for his compensation was not available.[131] The class in mineralogy thus never
functioned.

---

[130] *Novena junta pública*, 26-28.
[131] AGG, A1-1, leg. 261, exped. 5757: a number of documents dealing with the
desires and the financial frustration of Captain General Bustamante, the Economic
Society, the Audiencia, the Consulado, and the *Contaduría de Propios Comunidades*.

CHAPTER SEVENTEEN

Conclusion

Some eighty Economic Societies of Friends of the Country were formed in the Spanish world in the half century before its political fragmentation—seventy in Spain, a dozen overseas. Private bodies enjoying some official support, they enlisted an influential minority of the community—nobles, ecclesiastics, public officials, military men, merchants, scholars, and scientists. With a strong sense of the deficiencies of the Spanish politico-economic system, they veered away from bullionism, defining wealth in terms of agricultural and industrial production and the exchange of goods. Occasionally critical of Spanish intellectual achievement, they disseminated some of the ideas and points of view of the Enlightenment. In America, they magnified the differences between the interest of colony and metropolis. In Spain, they were foci of that hesitant and qualified acceptance of the modern temper which has long distinguished the spiritual and social division of that self-tormented land. Science and rationalism, a secular spirit, and an interest in economics marked the activities of the Societies. Each of these was inimical to the unchanged continuation of the old regime.

The parentage of the Societies involved an indubitable peninsular dam with a sire of foreign—hence questionable—antecedents: Spanish interests wed the ideas of the Enlightenment. Thus the Societies could attract patriotic conservatives, at least timidly experimental with regard to the economic-military state of the Spanish world, though unready to change the socio-political status quo; and moderate liberals whose patriotism was complicated by enthusiasm for rationalism, by a hankering for innovation, and by a desire to bring the Spanish way of life more in tune with the concert of European development. These two groups in the Societies could collaborate because the more liberal element was not militant, because drastic measures were discussed but not executed, because they found common ground in their patriotic regard for the material well-being of the realms and in their philanthropic concern for the poor, and finally because the most conservative element in the Societies was not immediately conscious of the possible implications for Spanish society of its activities. Ultraconservatives outside the Societies, not blinded by enthusiasm for progress, were of course conscious of these implications.

The American and Spanish Societies were alike in being founded on the model of Campomanes and the Society of Madrid,[1] and on the dual basis of interest in the state of the Spanish world—especially local portions thereof —and in the ideas of the Enlightenment; in their thin treasuries; and in their restricted membership, drawn largely from the local elite, with a handful of learned and energetic spirits dominating the thought and labors of each Society. The American Societies were not, however, precise duplicates of the Spanish prototype. Different natural and social circumstances caused members of American Societies to act and think somewhat differently from members of Spanish Societies, just as the Enlightenment itself was used in the colonies for ends not always identical with those which intrigued men of the new day in Spain. Also, formation of American Societies proceeded much more slowly than in Spain, partly because intellectual life was less well organized in America, partly because of division in the American upper class between creole and Spaniard, and partly because Spanish officialdom interfered with the foundation and operation of the American Societies. Finally, the Spanish Societies contributed to this divergence by insisting on the importance of local examination of local problems, which for America meant encouragement to emphasize the fact that metropolitan and colonial interests did not perfectly coincide.

---

[1] Not on the model of the Basque Society. Basterra, *Navíos*, ascribes a vast (if unspecified) influence to the Basque Society. He also states (p. 252) that Venezuela was "the organizer of the Societies of Friends of the Country in America." We have seen no evidence to support this notion. We have seen that Venezuela had no Society in the colonial era. The Societies with which Bolivar later had a connection in Lima and Bogota were not like the Amigos del País of Peñaflorida and Campomanes, or those of Guatemala and Havana founded on the Spanish model, just as the society of independent America in the 1820's was different from that of the colonies a generation earlier.

At least fifteen Economic Societies were suggested in the colonies between 1781 and 1819—one in the Philippines, the others in America—and most of them were at least tentatively organized. Between those dates perhaps 600 to 700 Spanish and creole residents of America, including many of the most influential men of the day, were members of the Societies there.

Few of the colonial Societies endured long and, as in the case of the Spanish Societies, their operations disappointed the founders. The Havana Society existed continuously from 1791. The Guatemala was active from 1794 to 1800, when suspended on orders from Spain; reactivated late in 1810, it soon decayed, and was extinct before Central America became independent of Spain in 1821. The Manila Society was active from 1781 to 1787, then moribund to 1819. The Academic Society of Lima published the *Mercurio Peruano* in 1791-1794, and died of government disfavor. The Puerto Rico Society, created in 1813, was not active before 1821. Six others (Santiago de Cuba, Mompox, Bogota, Chiapa, Quito, and Buenos Aires of 1800-1802) either operated less than a year, or were organized but never became operative. The Vera Cruz Society apparently had a brief unimportant existence. The Society suggested for Mérida de Yucatán probably was not organized. The Caracas Society of 1810 and the Buenos Aires of 1812 were political bodies, not Economic Societies.

This chronology suggests that conditions were more favorable to growth of the American Societies before 1795 than thereafter, a reflection of the growth of conservative fears during the French Revolution and its accompanying wars;[2] that, while the liberal resistance governments of southern Spain during the period of constitutional crisis (1808-1814) favored the Economic Societies, they actually accomplished little in their behalf, in Spain or America; and that the wars for Spanish American independence, beginning in 1810, were fatal to the chances of founding or operating Economic Societies on the model of Campomanes.

Thus, nine of the fifteen colonial Societies were initiated before 1795—four in the 1780's, five in the 1790's; and only six thereafter—two in 1800-1802, two in 1810-1812, one in 1813, and one in 1819. From the middle of the last decade of the eighteenth century, the attitude of conservatives in and out of government was often unfriendly to the Societies, which were thought to be excessively inclined to novel ideas and courses of action. This attitude played a part in the extinction of the Quito Society in 1794, and of the Lima soon thereafter; in the suspension of the Guatemala by a government order of 1799; and in the failure to secure approval for the Bogota and Buenos Aires Societies at the beginning of the new century.

---

[2] *Supra*, 58 *et seq.*, for the same influence on the Spanish Societies.

The resistance governments in Spain gave striking proof of favor for the American Societies. The Council of Regency, in approving reactivation in 1810 of the Guatemala Society by the captain general, praised the fidelity of Guatemala to "the legitimate authorities of the Metropolis, in the midst of the horrible convulsions which have agitated other provinces of Spanish America";[3] and in 1811 it showed the same attitude in ordering the first intendant of Puerto Rico to form an Economic Society there. The new atmosphere led a member of the Guatemala Society in 1811 to hope that the work of the Society would be celebrated by the "Congreso Nacional of our Mother Spain."[4] The June 8, 1813, decree of the Cortes, calling for the foundation of new Societies,[5] presumably applied to all the provinces of the monarchy, American and European. It was sent to Guatemala in July of that year.[6]

But with America in the midst of the "horrible convulsions" of warfare for independence noted by the Regency, the times were not propitious for the creation or operation of Economic Societies. Thus, the Societies created at Caracas in 1810 and at Buenos Aires in 1812 were clearly political bodies. And in any event, by 1808 the Vera Cruz, Santiago de Cuba, Mompox, Quito, Bogota, and Lima Societies were defunct, and no effort was made to resuscitate them. The Manila Society was moribund all through the period of constitutional crisis from 1808 to 1814; and the Havana Society lost some of its vigor.

In the succeeding period (1814-1820) of reaction following the return of Ferdinand to Spain, the temper of the times was hardly favorable to Economic Societies, even in the still loyal areas of America. Even if the royal decree of 1815, encouraging Economic Societies, was meant to apply to America, it could have little effect at that date.[7] Only one new Society was founded, at Ciudad Real in Chiapas in 1819. The Guatemala Society gradually died under the leadership of Archbishop Casaus, a man of rigidly conservative views. The Puerto Rico Society remained an embryo after Ramírez left the island in 1816 to be intendant of Cuba. The Havana Society was exceptional among all those overseas, in being in vigorous operation in 1816-1820, under the tutelage of Ramírez. But even his experience, intelligence, zeal,

---

[3] Guatemala *Novena junta pública*, 21-22, for the order of the Council.

[4] "Discurso" of Fr. Antonio Carrascal, *Octava junta pública*, unnumbered pp. at end.

[5] *Supra*, 62.

[6] John T. Lanning (ed.), *Reales Cédulas de la Real y Pontificia Universidad de San Carlos de Guatemala* (Guatemala, 1954), 295-98, for text of the decree.

[7] *Supra*, 63.

and the prestige of his office were insufficient to carry the projects closest
to his heart, and with his death the Havana Society quickly decayed.[8]

The disparity between the seventy Societies of Spain and the dozen of
America cannot be ascribed solely to the fact that the requisite intellectual
and municipal modes of life were less abundant in the colonies. Some
American towns of tolerable size never enjoyed Economic Societies, while
smaller towns attempted organization. It is almost as difficult to explain it
in terms of variant economic interests among the American towns, though
there may be some significance in the fact that relatively prosperous Mexico
had no Society, Lima's was not a true Economic Society, and there was no
great interest shown in Cabello y Mesa's proposal at Buenos Aires.[9] Certainly
the requirements for a Society were not difficult: a suggestion by an individual,
sufficient town life to provide some income and suitable members, and
permission from the government—first local, then metropolitan.

The fact is that much depended on the accidental presence of a few—or
even only one—prominent men, Spanish or creole, determined to promote
a Society. But not all men with knowledge of the work of the Societies considered them valuable. In America this was true of both Spaniards and
creoles. For example, creoles Baquíjano of Peru, Arango of Cuba, Salas of
Chile, and Belgrano of Buenos Aires, had many similar tendencies of thought;
but while Arango belonged to the Havana Society, he doubted its value,
observing that the Spanish Societies had not fulfilled all the hopes reposed
in them, so he depended rather on the Consulado; Baquíjano helped found
the Lima Society, but it was more a literary than an economic society;
Belgrano favored a Society for Buenos Aires, but did not found one, working
rather through the Consulado; Salas, *síndico* of the Santiago Consulado,
founded the Academia de San Luís to promote the exact sciences, in the
belief that this was the first necessity for the improvement of the local
economy. Salas was in Spain in 1777-1784, and his later writings in Chile
indicate knowledge of the Spanish Societies and their ideas, though he did
not mention them by name. Many of his recommendations and arguments
echoed the sentiments of the Societies, though he apparently was not connected with a project for a Society in Chile until 1821.[10]

---

[8] Cf. Appendix for its later resuscitation.

[9] If this be taken as an indication that Societies appealed most to towns where
the elite was relatively unprosperous, Havana is an exception, and in any event it is
difficult to see how such a suggestion is to be correlated with the creation of Societies
in so many small towns in Spain.

[10] Cf. *Escritos de Don Manuel de Salas y documentos relativos a él y a su familia*

An Economic Society was not indispensable for the promotion of most of the objectives of the Societies. The ideas they favored were being otherwise disseminated by such individuals as Belgrano or Salas; by freemasons; by creole members of Consulados enamored of new economic ideas and hopes; by universities ringing at least softly to new philosophical and scientific views; and by such literary and scientific groups as that of the viceregal palace in Mexico in the time of Viceroy Flórez (1787-1789), or the literary-political club of Nariño in Bogota. The "associative spirit" may not have been as important in Spanish-America as in Anglo-America, but it was promoted wherever the ideas of the Enlightenment penetrated.[11]

Thus, failure to found or successfully operate an Economic Society did not necessarily indicate an important difference between Spanish American towns. The Spanish and creole elite of all American towns had an approximately similar range of ideas and aspirations.[12] Cultural differentiation will not explain the relative success of Economic Societies at Manila, Havana, and Guatemala; and their much lesser success at Bogota, Buenos Aires, and Quito; nor the failure to found Societies at Santiago de Chile, Mexico, Cartagena, Cuzco, and Guadalajara, whereas they were suggested or tentatively organized in such places as Mompox, Chiapas, and Santiago de Cuba. And it would be difficult to explain the different histories of the Societies of Quito, Lima, and Guatemala in terms of the different intellectual backgrounds of men such as Selva Alegre and Espejo, Unánue and Baquíjano, Villaurrutia and Goycoechea.

Not only was the accidental presence of promoters important, but equally

---

(3 vols., Santiago, 1910-14), for abundant evidence of his ideas on political economy e.g.: a statement of 1796 (I, 152) that Chile was "without contradiction the most fertile [province] of America and most adequate for human felicity," and demanding (I, 171) "una academia o sociedad" to train and encourage artisans; I, 208-23, a memoria of 1801, including references to the "fatal egoism" fought by Campomanes, the need of unity among all classes, and their union in *sociedades* to enlighten the public; II, 445-47, "Acta de Constitución de la Sociedad 'Amigos del País,' " Santiago, March 1, 1821, signed by twelve men, including Salas, agreeing to found such a Society, but this is the only reference to an "economic" society in the three volumes. See also on Salas, Amunátegui, *Precursores*, III, 343-58; Jorge Huneeus y Gana, *Cuadro histórico de la producción intelectual de Chile* (Santiago, 1910?), 67.

[11] The Economic Society was one of the few nonecclesiastical institutions Juarros could find to mention in his description of Guatemala at the end of the colonial era. Certainly, "voluntary associationalism" had lesser roots in the Spanish-American than in the Anglo-American colonial area (cf. Arthur M. Schlesinger, "Biography of a Nation of Joiners," *American Historical Review*, L, No. 1 [October, 1944], 1-25).

[12] Basterra, *Navíos*, would not agree, preferring (p. 32) to emphasize the "fact of the sudden directive apparition of Venezuela in American destinies"; and (p. 34) to describe Venezuela as a "Basque land, twin brother of Chile."

so was the attitude of one or two local civil and ecclesiastical officials, to say nothing of the attitude of officialdom in Spain. Official actions and attitudes were responsible for some of the failure to found Societies in the colonies, and for much of the lack of success of many of those that were formed. This can scarcely be described as settled policy, since the official attitude toward the Societies—in Spain and America—was both vacillating and promiscuous. Some of the vacillation was due to understandable fears roused by events, such as the French Revolution; some was due to sheer panic; some to personal venom. An American Society would be founded in a burst of enthusiasm by some prominent creoles and Spaniards, patronized by the captain general or other high official, blessed and perhaps subsidized by the bishop, and joined by the flower of the local society. But soon the old regime would express dubiety as to the objectives of the Society, and in some cases refuse to complete the necessary official permission for permanent operation, as at Bogota and Buenos Aires; in other cases they would be destroyed after a short period of operation, as at Quito, Lima, and Guatemala.

There was not, however, any consistent basis for this sort of action, since one Society in America would be allowed to continue while others were crushed. The operation of this policy of discrimination was seen in the way the Lima Académic Society quickly praised the foundation of the Quito Society, then ignored it completely as the reaction set in. It was seen in Bishop Trespalacios' harassment of the Havana Society. It was seen in the way the imperial government in Lima stood with the Spaniard Olavarrieta against the creoles of the Academic Society. This last is illustrative of what might be called the nearest approach to a Spanish policy with regard to the American Societies: to regard them with perhaps even more dubiety than the metropolitan Societies. Proportionately speaking, the government interfered more with the operation of American than of Spanish Societies. In conclusion we may say that Spain did not give her Societies to America; she allowed some to be established, but without enthusiasm.

This of course created some bitterness in America. Pérez Calama and Espejo of Quito pointed out the value of the Spanish Societies, protected by king and ministers, and thought America deserved them too. Friar San José Muro of New Spain wanted more American Societies. Members of the Guatemala Society were especially bitter about the discrimination against their Society. They made this clear in the *Gazeta de Guatemala*, and in the publications of the Society after its reactivation in 1810. They made it clear by printing a sketch of the history of the Spanish Societies, noting that the latter quickly rose in number to sixty-four, whereas the Guatemala

Society, organized by Villaurrutia, its own "Campomanes," was unjustly ordered suspended in 1799.[13]

The prime aim of the American Societies was the development of the local economy. The members tended to view Spain as weak and poor; America as potentially rich, having fallen into "ruin" and "decadence" from a once flourishing state; and other American areas as more prosperous than their own, although local resources made this unnecessary and correctable. They emphasized agriculture, hoping to improve it with new methods, crops, and roads; tended to deprecate the ancient emphasis on mining, an idea they derived not only from experience, but from Spanish political economists and Economic Societies; showed less interest in industry than the Spanish Societies, save where linked to such local produce as sugar; cared more for the production of goods that might enter into commerce than for commerce itself; and paid little attention to banking and credit. Their efforts to change economic practice were modest; they did not develop the subjects of land reform and freer trade on a scale approaching that of the Spanish Societies; they published few objections to the laws in force.

Related to their localism was their isolation, for the American Societies had almost no relations with each other, or with the Spanish Societies. It was not that they had no knowledge of each other, but that there were no effective connections. Even in 1844 the Havana Society knew little of what the other Societies had been, or the Guatemala currently was.[14]

The Societies pursued their ends by publicity, education, example, and experiment. The members, at public and private meetings, delivered and listened to discourses which often were the fruit of considerable study. They published material to promote interest in new methods, crops, and devices for the cultivation or refinement of produce; imported equipment and botanical specimens; and established vocational schools. The Havana Society tended orphans and vagrant ladies, and the Guatemala tried to regulate guilds and succor the deserving poor.

These methods were well suited to their small resources and membership, neither of which could be much expanded in the current state of illiteracy and limited economic development. Of course, by changing the character of the Societies, an attempt might have been made to use lower-class elements. It is doubtful, however, what the general population might have contributed, and certainly not reasonable to expect the local elite to have been enthusiastic

---

[13] *Novena junta pública*, 49.
[14] Havana *Memorias 1844*, t. XIX, 62-63.

about the putative contributions of the generality. It is nevertheless probably true that the members were not sufficiently aware of the difficulties of improving production in Spanish America.

The Societies did stand for several dangerous tendencies from the Spanish point of view, despite the modesty of their projects. They represented organized opinion and study on an unofficial basis, with a unique program of publication—which threatened the traditionally rigid system of intellectual control. Furthermore, they celebrated new rather than traditional ideas, and were dedicated to rationalism and critical analysis of contemporary problems. They were convinced that the greater part of the ills of humanity "were the result of prejudices and false ideas."[15] Fom this followed their optimism, their belief that human problems would yield to the rational faculty, so that they saw the very origin of the Societies "in the mutual necessity that men have of enlightening themselves."[16] Their intellectual achievements may not have been profound,[17] and they were interested in the moderate rather than the radical side of the Enlightenment, especially in the promotion of useful knowledge, but this intellectual activity could only lead to an expanded and embarrassing criticism of the current state of the Spanish world.[18]

This encouragement of a more dynamic intellectual climate was the more alarming in that the Societies tended to move from parochialism into a world of grand motives and great affairs, and to consider interprovincial affairs, even to promote what amounted to Americanism. Villaurrutia told the Guatemala Society that it "had discovered the most expeditious road to civilization and the felicity of a prodigious multitude of rational beings"; that its services could only be denied by "the indolent egoists who were offended by its existence"; and that it was working for the "good of man and the glory of Guatemala";[19] by means of a few zealous and constant "illustrious patriots," whose work constituted a "happy revolution."[20] And

---

[15] Havana *Memorias 1794, loc. cit.*, 108.

[16] Havana *Memorias 1793*, 180.

[17] Andrade, *Historia del Ecuador*, I, 173-74, ridicules the use of the terms *"eminentes, profundos, sabios"* (his italics) by the literary writer Pablo Herrera in speaking of the members of the Quito Society, for in Andrade's view the colony could not produce men deserving of such terms.

[18] Gredilla, *Mutis*, 220, goes further, asserting that the American Societies helped germinate and spread separatist ideas, to the surprise of such Spaniards as Mutis who were involved in the American Societies. Emilio Novoa, *Las Sociedades Económicas de Amigos del País. Su influencia en la emancipación colonial Americana* (Madrid, 1955), 113-33, for speculation, presented as statements, regarding the role of the Societies in colonial emancipation.

[19] *Quarta junta pública*, 1-2.

[20] *Segunda junta pública*, 1-3.

the secretary of the Guatemala Society said that the Societies should not only aid "economic progress," but had the "sacred role" of embracing all "useful knowledge."[21] The Guatemala Society exerted influence in various parts of the captaincy general and even in New Spain. The *Gazeta de Guatemala* wished to promote foundation of a Society in Mexico. The *Mercurio Peruano* tried to promote relations between men of its point of view in Lima and Quito. The Lima Society turned almost vicious when criticized by the Spaniard Olavarrieta, so that the essentially American Society became embroiled in an outbreak of the old antagonism between Spaniard and creole. The Havana Society displayed some interest in Societies in other parts of America.

The strong practical interest of the Societies was potentially as dangerous to Spain as the theoretical, since so much of it was dedicated to descriptive material. The interest of members was not just the result of reading and cerebration, but founded also on observation. This interest appeared strongly in the Havana and Guatemala Societies, and probably would have become clearer in the others had their operations been more vigorous. This descriptive material did not need to express overt discontent in order to be dangerous; it was enough to assert the "decadence" of the local economy and describe its deficiencies, or the resources lying fallow, such description being a main function of the Societies in all the Spanish world. No matter how colorless the descriptions printed by the Lima Society in the *Mercurio*, they did deal publicly and at length with resources little or poorly used. This points up another characteristic of the Societies: their ignorance of their own localities. Again and again they were moved to inquire whether the commonest crops and economic activities were known in their areas, and obliged to report with some surprise that they were.[22] The publications of the Spanish Societies do not give so clear a picture of ignorance of local conditions.

No doubt the emphasis on local problems was potentially as dangerous to the unity of the empire, especially since provincial economic autonomy and ambition were being stimulated by wartime interruptions of traffic, and by revisions of the Spanish system—especially resulting from *comercio libre*, the intendancy system, and the creation of new Consulados in America.[23] Of course, so long as creoles and Spaniards continued to cooperate in Society,

---

[21] *Quarta junta pública*, 3.

[22] Cf. *Mercurio Peruano*, I, No. 1 (January 2, 1791), "Idea General del Peru," which put the main object of the *Mercurio* as making better known the country they lived in.

[23] Cf. Arellano Moreno, *Orígenes*, 301, 407, *et passim*, for the thesis that Spanish economic policies, and colonial reactions thereto, in the late colonial era stimulated localism and nationalism.

Consulado, and other institutions, this emphasis on the part of the Societies might have tended to unite the upper class in support of a program of local development within the imperial framework.[24]

When all this has been said about the risks involved in encouragement of the American Societies, the fact remains that the old regime exaggerated their radicalism, just as it underestimated the extent of creole dissatisfaction. The numerous Spanish members of American Societies were not promoting revolution, but trying to strengthen the Spanish world: such Spanish founders of American Societies as Villaurrutia and Ramírez wanted to use modern ideas and methods to improve the American economy. The creole members were generally moderate men of property and position, sometimes intellectually "advanced," but socially and politically moderate; many in the coming years of independence were to be conservatives, like José Cecilio del Valle of Guatemala. The publications of the American Societies may have been potentially dangerous to unchanged continuation of the old regime, but they were not inflammatory. At most, this was occasionally a literature of complaint, not of protest.[25]

The fact is, of course, that the nature of man and the state of human society were inimical to the unchanged continuation of the old—or any other —regime. The Economic Societies in America might have been used to help bridge the gap between the old and the new, since reasonable, moderately liberal Spaniards and creoles seemed able to cooperate in such bodies. But the failure to use the American Societies as an instrument for the exploration of the possibilities of cooperation between moderately reformist Spaniards and creoles was inevitable since the directors of the Spanish world could not bring about in Spain itself an accommodation of the views of moderates and reactionaries, a failure which in the long run could only promote the growth of radicalism. Conservative Spaniards were unable to see beyond the willingness of the Societies to promote certain kinds of change. So the American Societies neither brought useful change, nor reinforced the status quo, but helped widen the gulf between points of view already separated by other issues.

---

[24] Cf. Robert S. Smith, "José María Quirós. Balanza del comercio marítimo de Veracruz e ideas económicas," *El Trimestre Económico*, XIII, No. 4 (January-March, 1947), 680-711, at 708, for an 1818 opinion of an official of the Veracruz Consulado favoring Economic Societies.

[25] After the event, the last Spanish treasurer of Guatemala did assert that some creoles in 1808 welcomed the capture of Ferdinand VII by Napoleon, seeing it as a chance to gain independence, and that the germ of this desire was in "the erection of the Patriotic Society" of Guatemala in 1794 ("Guatemala, hace ciento catorce años. Informe ... del Ministro Tesorero ..., Madrid ... 1824," *loc. cit.*, 8).

Later History of the Overseas Societies

Independent America had almost no interest in Economic Societies on the model of Campomanes, but promoted its economy by the agency of its new governments and by private bodies of its own development.[1] Guatemala was an exception; the Society there lasted, with some interruptions, from 1825 to 1881, when its functions were taken over by a government agency. Of the colonial Societies, the Puerto Rico lasted until 1898, the Manila until 1890; and the Havana Society exists today. The nineteenth-century Societies are chiefly of local interest.

Mexico (1822), Lima (1822, 1826), Bogota (1826), Venezuela (1829-1836)

The Societies established at these places in America in the first years of independence were of little consequence. They were promoted by men of good education and social position who were generally of the conservative political persuasion.

In Mexico, a Society was founded by conservatives in the time of Iturbide, when it was not quite clear that the Spanish connection was forever broken. Its statutes, accepted by the Regency in Mexico City in February, 1822, said it was "to promote public prosperity"; to exercise no jurisdiction; have no more than twenty-five members (*socios de número*), elected by plurality of secret votes; have correspondents within and without the empire; have as ex-officio members the chief of state, the archbishop, and a representative each of the *Diputación provincial*, the ecclesiastical chapter, and the town council. The ex-officio members, together with the *Diputación provincial* and the town council, in a junta presided over by Iturbide would name ten *socios de*

---

[1] This account of the Societies after 1821 does not pretend to be exhaustive. *Supra*, 349, n. 10, on the Society planned in Chile in 1821.

número who would be founders of the Society. These, with the ex-officio members, would name in their first junta the other ten *socios de número* and twenty *supernumerarios*. There were to be six commissions—agriculture, *industria fabril*, mining and commerce, *policía interior y exterior de los pueblos*, public education, and statistics and geography. The statutes included the usual list of things the commissions were to do to improve the economy, and provide for care of the indigent, and for education of various kinds.[2] The Society had forty-six members by the time of the *junta ordinaria* of March 11, 1822, which elected officers, headed by Iturbide as director "by acclamation," and José Mariano de Almanza as *director suplente* to actually do the work; and named members to the various commissions.[3]

The Patriotic Society of Lima, promoted by Bernardo de Monteagudo, who had been prominent in that of Buenos Aires in 1812, was approved by San Martín in January, 1822. Ostensibly mainly interested in public instruction and learning, it also served as a political forum for the members, most of whom favored monarchical government for independent Peru.[4] A few years later (late 1825 or early 1826) Bolivar, at Lima awaiting the February 10, 1826, convocation of congress, decreed establishment in Lima of an "economic society, titled 'the friends of the country,' whose object, as the name indicated, was to tend to the prosperity of the state 'in all the principal categories that make up the national wealth.' "[5]

Bolivar, as president of Colombia, suggested, March 18, 1826, the creation of a Society of Friends of the Country in Bogota.[6] He had shown an interest in economic organizations as early as 1821.[7]

A Society founded at Caracas in 1829 lamented the failure of the various laws that had been tried in 1821-1828 to promote these "vehicles of public abundance," which were needed in Venezuela, for it had the resources and position to be rich if affairs

---

[2] *Estatutos para la Sociedad Económico-Mexicana de Amigos del País* (28 pp., Mexico: Imprenta Imperial de D. Alejandro Valdés, 1822), carrying at end: "Mexico, Febrero 9 de 1822. Agustín de Iturbide."

[3] *Lista de los Señores Vocales de la Sociedad Económica Mexicana de Amigos del País* (8 pp., n. p., n. d., but probably 1822).

[4] Bernard Moses, *The Intellectual Background of the Revolution in South America, 1810-1824* (New York, 1926), ch. viii, "La Sociedad Patriótica de Lima." José Hipólito Unánue, who had been a member of the Academic Society of Lima thirty years before, was vice-president of this Society (*Obras de Unánue*, I, ix-xxiv). Monteagudo spoke at the inaugural session to the effect that the Spanish system had prevented the spread of enlightenment in America ("Oración inaugural de la sociedad patriótica de Lima," in his *Escritos políticos* [ed. Mariano A. Pelliza, Buenos Aires, 1916], 279-83).

[5] *Memorias del general O'Leary* (32 vols., Caracas, 1879-1914), XXVIII, 328. At the same time Bolivar issued other decrees for the "benefit of the country," including one for the establishment in each departmental capital of a normal school for Lancasterian education (*ibid.*). Basterra, *Navíos*, 252, dates Bolivar's decree as late in 1825; and states that Bolivar, wanting to remake society in Peru, signed as one of his first decrees in Lima the one to create the Economic Society (p. 93).

[6] Basterra, *Navíos*, 253.

[7] J. M. Rivas Groot, *Asuntos económicos y fiscales* (2d ed., Bogota, 1952), 18-19, his decree establishing juntas of agriculture and of commerce; *ibid.*, 65-66, for order of Bogota government in 1826 that local officials collect economic data.

were properly handled.[8] The Society was created under the provisions of the Organic Law of Public Instruction of March 18, 1826, which provided for the establishment of Economic Societies of Friends of the Country in the departmental capitals, to promote useful arts, agriculture, commerce, industry, and establish schools of drawing, architecture, painting, sculpture, and publish memorias.[9] Under this law, José Antonio Páez, *Jefe Superior* of Venezuela, by decree of October 26, 1829, created the Caracas Society. It held a preparatory junta on October 27, its first session on November 9, and its first general junta on December 27, 1830. It did little in its first year because of lack of funds. Among the pending labors of its commission of agriculture was a memoria on Lucatelo's seed drill.[10] The Caracas body also was interested in a workhouse and *casa de beneficencia*, a Lancasterian school, and a variety of economic matters. The membership of forty-five was divided into five commissions: agriculture (with but three members, and one of those defunct), commerce, population and public instruction, arts and crafts, and finance.[11] This was the usual small membership of an Economic Society, but was not exclusive enough for some members, who in 1834 published a broadside proposing the exclusion of *pardos* from the Society. It soon became an issue in politics.[12]

The Secretary of the Interior of Venezuela sent out a circular in February, 1832, ordering the governors of the provinces to establish Economic Societies in their respective capitals. Societies were founded at Apure, Mérida, Coro, Cumaná, Maracaibo, and Carabobo. But the same official reported to Congress in 1836 that the Societies had done little; that some cantons wanted to found Societies, but permission was denied; and that the Caracas Society had founded classes of drawing, music, stenography, and of the Castillian, Latin, and English languages.[13]

The Caracas Society published quite an elaborate volume of statistics in 1835, asserting that the "statistics of a people has for its object the understanding and comparison of the combined forces of man, animals, and nature applied to the work of agriculture, workshops, and commerce."[14] The present writer has seen no evidence that the Caracas Society or provincial Societies existed after 1836. The economic history of Venezuela suggests that they were not very effective.[15]

---

[8] *Memorias de la Sociedad Económica de Amigos del País de la Provincia de Caracas en 1830* (48 pp., Caracas: Imprenta de Fermín Romero, 1831), 6.

[9] *Ibid.*, 7. Cf. Ramón Hernández-Ron, *La Sociedad económica de amigos del país* (Caracas, 1943), 4 and n.

[10] *Supra*, 97, n. 22, the Madrid Society and this drill.

[11] *Memorias Caracas 1830, passim.*

[12] Vallenilla Lanz, *Cesarismo democrático*, 110 *et seq.* Basterra, *Navíos*, 253-54, describes the Caracas Society as evidence of the continuity of the tradition of Charles III, founders and members being "the remains and vestiges of the Caracas aristocracy."

[13] Hernández-Ron, *Sociedad económica*, 23-31.

[14] *Anuario de la provincia de Caracas de 1832 a 1833. Publicado por la Sociedad Económica de Amigos del País de la misma povincia* [sic] (248 pp., Caracas: Imprenta de A. Damiron, 1835), iii. This is a mass of useful statistics, but has almost nothing on the Society itself.

[15] Hernández-Ron, *Sociedad económica*, mentions nothing later than 1836; he says (p. 24) that the documentation on the provincial Societies is not abundant, but says he infers that they "contributed greatly to the economic development of the regions where they functioned." We may doubt this.

Guatemala (1825-1881)

The Guatemala Society, dead by 1821, was revived in 1825, and survived—with some suspensions—under both liberal and conservative governments until 1881. It had a semipublic character in that the government furnished some of its revenues and assigned some of its tasks. It sometimes cooperated with and received financial aid from the Consulado. It maintained its interest in science; belief in *ilustración* as a means of aiding economic development; and the view that the country would benefit from training artisans. It had schools of drawing, sculpture, and mathematics; and late in its history added other subjects. It continued its publication, sporadically; and an interest in the branches of the economy, emphasizing agriculture. The membership was small, as the Society remained a group of the well educated in a land of illiterates.

After 1820 the Society was dead until the state of Guatemala—part of the new Central American federation—decided in November, 1825, that *corregidores* should promote the "re-establishment" of Economic Societies, "to develop agriculture [and] the arts."[16] The Society had at least nominal existence in 1825, when it was decreed dissolved.[17]

The Guatemala legislature, September 29, 1829, ordered the Society re-established, since the Societies had been useful even "under the oppressive domination of the Spanish government." It was to receive the property of the old Society, maintain relations with other Central American Societies, and name members after the government appointed the first thirty.[18] The legislature in the same year provided tax funds for its support;[19] and gave it paintings and sculptures from extinguished convents, and quarters (with the university) in that of Santo Domingo.[20]

Director José Cecilio del Valle at the inaugural session, November 29, 1829, said that Europe's societies or academies since the seventeenth century had been "one of the most active movers of its prosperity." Learned men and *ilustración* were necessary to prosperity, which was the work of savants, capitalists, and laborers. Guatemala did well in 1810 in stating the rights of liberty and property in instructions to its deputy to the Cortes. But since the production of wealth demanded skilled

---

[16] *Catálogo razonado de las leyes de Guatemala.* ... (Guatemala, 1856), 243. The "Gaceta del Gobierno Supremo de Guatemala," August 30, 1824, published the prospectus of the "Mensual de la Sociedad Económica de Amigos del Estado de Guatemala"; but the first issue of the periodical was not issued till April, 1830 (Valle and Valle Matheu, *Obras J. C. del Valle*, II, 286-87).

[17] Rosa, *Del Valle*, 78: the Society was dissolved in 1825, due to the revolut‍on provoked by Arce, re-established in 1829 because of the liberal victory. Batres Jáuregui, *América Central*, II, 464, has it destroyed in 1825. A MS. in AGG (A1.6, leg. 2007, exped. 13832) headed, Catálogo de los individuos que componen la Sociedad económica de amantes del Estado de Guatemala, lists the "Socios fundadores nombrados por la Asamblea Legislativa," starting with José del Valle as director; the AGG director dates this 1825, but it might be 1829.

[18] *Colección de los decretos y de las órdenes mas interesantes que obtuvieron la sanción, emitidas por la segunda lejislatura del estado de Guatemala. Año de 1830* (Guatemala, 1830?), 8-9.

[19] *Catálogo razonado leyes Guatemala*, 343.

[20] *Colección decretos 1830*, 45-46.

workers, requiring education, Campomanes' idea of the popular education of artisans remained "eternal as reason," although some of his other ideas had been refined in late years. Finally, Valle found slavery economically unsound, for "a worker (*operario, obrero, o jornalero*) is not a servant, he is a co-producer of wealth"; and welcomed European immigrants, who would bring both wealth and learning.[21]

In 1830 the government provided funds for the Society, and accepted its statutes; in 1831 provided that it direct the normal school ordered established by legislative decree, and help found a museum.[22] The *Mensual de la Sociedad* appeared in April, 1830. A new class of mathematics for artisans and the poor was opened, May 31, 1831, and the now aged Antonio García Redondo promised to help.[23] A Society junta in March, 1831, heard that in 1820 Guatemala had 134 master weavers and 637 looms, in 1830 only 73 looms; and it was "a pity to see so many artisans lost," with unfortunate social effects. As a result, a Society commission recommended in May, 1831, that import taxes be used to finance foundation by the Society of a "National Bank of Agriculture, Industry, and Commerce," to build roads between the Atlantic and Pacific, promote agriculture, disseminate machines and tools, and "give all possible protection to those meritorious for industry, application, and honesty."[24] It is not clear that the Society did much in 1832-1839.[25]

The Society was re-established by government decree of September 24, 1840, and legislation in 1843 and 1845 allowed a public lottery for its benefit, increased the Consulado's support of the Society to 200 pesos, and granted it public funds.[26] The Society published a weekly *Revista* in December, 1846-May, 1848, the most important editor being José Milla. Also in the 1840's, the Society held classes in drawing and painting, sculpture, and stenography; and promoted economic development, showing an early interest in coffee cultivation at a time when there were few trees in Guatemala.[27] The Society held a public general junta in May, 1847; then none was held for three years.[28]

In 1850 the Society held a *junta general* (May 19), and published a twenty-three-page account; reopened its school of mathematics;[29] maintained the drawing school, with seventy pupils;[30] and received word from the government that Felipe Molina, *chargé*

---

[21] "Discurso procunciado ... 29 de Noviembre de 1829," in Valle and Valle Matheu, *Obras J. C. del Valle*, I, 168-76.

[22] *Catálogo razonado leyes Guatemala*, 243-44.

[23] Batres Jáuregui, *América Central*, II, 469-70.

[24] Nomina de los Maestros del oficio de Tejedor ... y los telares ..., and the report of the commission, signed by Pedro Molina—AGG, A1.6, leg. 2008, exped. 13857.

[25] Batres Jáuregui, *América Central*, II, 469, has it entering a "new era" in 1831, but says almost nothing about 1830-31, and jumps from 1831 to 1845; Vela, *Literatura guatemalteca*, 174, claims the Society had great prestige in 1831, but political turmoil ended it, and it was re-established in 1840.

[26] *Catálogo razonado leyes Guatemala*, 244.

[27] Batres Jáuregui, *América Central*, II, 470-71.

[28] *Memoria que presentó a la Sociedad Económica en la junta general ... Mayo de 1850, su secretario D. José Milla; Discursos que en ella se pronunciaron; calificación de los objetos presentados; y distribución de premios* (23 pp., Guatemala: Impr. N. de la Aurora, 1850), 2.

[29] Guatemala Society *Relación 1852*, 11, the secretary noting that the school, opened in 1798, often had been suspended in the next half-century.

[30] *Memoria 1850*, 5-6, secretary Milla's report.

in Washington, had forwarded from Matthew Fontaine Maury of the Washington Observatory a plan "to start among scientific corporations, societies, and savants, a universal system of meteorological observations." A Society committee later reported that Guatemala lacked instruments and trained men for this last purpose.[31]

The government provided, October 19, 1851, that the Society's governing junta, with vote of the members and of master craftsmen and artisans certified by the Society, would name two Deputies to the Chamber of Representatives of the Republic.[32] The Society director, in swearing to the constitution of 1851, noted that although fundamental codes heretofore took no note of the Economic Societies, now the Society, with direct representation in the legislature, could do more for "the progress of the laboring classes and to improve the customs and education of youth."[33] Also in 1851 (December) the Minister of Government and the Society director agreed—as in 1831—that the Society would form a National Museum.[34]

The Society held a general public junta on April 25, 1852, the first since May, 1850, and printed a fifty-four-page account of the proceedings.[35] There was an exhibit of products of "rural and urban industry" and the fine arts. Three cabinet ministers attended, and the Minister of Interior said that Guatemala had not attained its proper wealth and power, and charged the Society with some of the responsibility, for it had pushed its "new ideas" too far, trying to change everything and achieve an impossible perfection, and the result was a "complete disappointment." Mistaken ideas of the past, as concentration on agriculture and opposition to the protection of industry, would have to be abandoned. A new road was now opened by the representation of the Society in the legislature, which should mean that the arts, crafts, agriculture, and business "will be objects of a special protection, as they are in all the nations of the world."

The secretary reported that the Society had accomplished little, and was short of funds. In the economic field, he noted that coffee had enriched Costa Rica, and that the Society and the Consulado were trying to promote it in Guatemala. He also reported small attempts to promote handicrafts; an attempt by a coffee planter to grow balsam in the highlands; experiments in food preservation; a woman willing to teach her method of making wax flowers; metal coating by means of galvanic piles; work with beeswax and dyes; pioneer work in lithography; and wine made in Antigua. In education, he noted that the Society was trying to promote instruction of the young; that it had several years before tried, and failed, to start a class in anatomy for sculpture and drawing; the school of sculpture was now in bad condition, with only six pupils; but the school of drawing was flourishing, and had over sixty pupils. In

---

[31] *Relación 1852*, 8, 46-54.

[32] *Catálogo razonado leyes Guatemala*, 357; cf. *ibid.*, 358, decree, June 25, 1852, approving the Regulation for election of deputies "in representation of industry and the arts," submitted by the Society, and a legislative order of January 7, 1853, giving force of law to the Regulation. The Minister of Interior praised the new arrangement (*Relación 1852*, 6). It has been claimed that the representatives were always liberals, as Miguel García Granados and Arcadio Estrada (Batres Jáuregui, *América Central*, II, 471).

[33] *Relación 1852*, 18.

[34] *Catálogo razonado leyes Guatemala*, 358.

[35] *Relación 1852*, 1-6, 8-18, for the following sketch on the junta.

addition, the Society was doing some statistical work for the government;[36] and had subscribed to the *Memorias* of García Peláez for its library, formation of which began in 1815. They wanted to reach the public through this library, recognizing with Campomanes that until good principles were generally adopted, the arts could not be well advanced.

The resources of the Society improved later in the 1850's. In 1853 director José Antonio Larrave y Velasco suggested a new building for the Society; it was built with some aid from Larrave's own funds.[37] By decree of February 27, 1856, the government provided funds from a liquor impost for support of the Society.[38] A few years later the secretary said that the new edifice and revenue had ushered in a new era for the Society.[39]

From the general junta of April, 1852, to that of December, 1861, the Society published nothing.[40] The secretary's report to the 1861 junta noted that the Society still had not done all that it would like to, but the prospects were better than in the past.[41] At this time the schools of drawing, mathematics, and sculpture still existed. The Society members included two *socios beneméritos*, forty-three *socios asistentes* (Archbishop García Peláez and forty-two licenciates, doctors, and priests), and twenty *socios corresponsales*, including the Abate Brasseur de Bourbourg, Jorge Skinner, and Alejandro Ramírez y Villa-Urrutia.[42]

After 1861 the Society seems to have been continuously in operation for twenty years, still attracting important Guatemalans and immigrants to its labors. A memoria in 1867 made an interesting reference to the Society's essay contest of 1797 on dressing and shoeing Indians *a la española*, noting that it was still a problem in Guatemala seventy years later.[43] The Society maintained its economic interest, still emphasizing agriculture, introducing new plants, and distributing seeds. In 1862 Enrique Palacios, Society secretary, presented to it an essay lauding the resources of Escuintla for coffee cultivation, and hoping for foreign capital.[44] In 1862 the Society translated from the French and published A. Laprade's pamphlet on silk in Guatemala. Laprade, a representative of a Lyon house, had come to Guatemala to investigate the possibilities

---

[36] Cf. *Catálogo razonado leyes Guatemala*, 358.

[37] Batres Jáuregui, *América Central*, II, 472-73.

[38] *Catálogo razonado leyes Guatemala*, 358. For January, 1857 to December, 1860, the Society's income was some 24,000 pesos, two-thirds of it from the liquor impost (*Memoria leída en la junta general que celebró la Sociedad económica de amigos del país, el 26 de diciembre de 1861*. ... [23 pp., Guatemala: Imp. de Luna, 1862?], 15-16).

[39] *Ibid.*, 13.

[40] *Ibid.*, 3. The secretary called it a "period of silence." Cf. *Catálogo razonado leyes Guatemala*, 358, for a government order, April 6, 1854, for the Society to gather products of the country to send to Europe.

[41] *Memoria 1861*, 17-18: revenues for 1861 were 7,678 pesos, slightly less than the average for the years 1857-60. Cf. Batres Jáuregui, *América Central*, II, 473: in 1861 the resources of the Society "rose" to this "small sum."

[42] *Memoria 1861*, 15-18, 21-23.

[43] *Colección de memorias y trabajos de esta sociedad* (Guatemala: Imprenta de la Paz, t. I-, 1866-), 9.ª Entrega (January, 1867), 173. This publication of memorias by fascicles began in January, 1866, and carried at least as far as entrega 13 (April, 1868), for a total of 266 pages for that period.

[44] *Memoria sobre el cultivo del café en Escuintla, presentada a la Sociedad Económica*. ... (15 pp., Guatemala: Imprenta de Luna, 1862).

of silk raising.[45] In 1870 the Society established a School of Agriculture under a Swiss agronomist. In 1878 it organized the National Exposition, at which were displayed the natural and fabricated products of the country, and objects of art, science, and literature. It helped promote the Immigration Society. The *Sociedad Zootécnica*, founded in 1880, and dedicated to the improvement of livestock, was affiliated with the Economic Society.

In the educational field, the Society in 1876 let its quarters be used for night instruction of artisans in drawing, reading, writing, and arithmetic, these classes totaling 200 pupils in 1877. It again took up the subject of a public library, agreeing with the government in 1879 to form one in its quarters. In 1880 a free School of Commerce was set up in the Society building, with evening classes in political economy, commercial geography, English language, business correspondence, and other subjects.[46]

The Society was abolished by decree of President Barrios, April 26, 1881, when the government departments were reorganized. The Ministry of Fomento took over its functions, while its edifice was taken for the legislature.[47] Batres Jáuregui, a Society member, said that it fell victim to "the centralizing spirit, and political fanaticism."[48]

Manila (1819-1890), Puerto Rico (1821-1898), Havana (1821-)

The three Societies in colonial areas after 1820 seem to have remained fairly active throughout most of the century, though they had little effect on their areas. The Havana Society was by far the most active, influential, and most nearly successful in promoting its aims.

The Manila Society, having been extinguished in 1809, and re-established in 1819, seems to have lasted until 1890. It apparently was more active in the 1820's and 1880's than in the intervening decades. Its activities in the promotion of education and the advancement of the economy resembled those of the other Societies.[49] In the field of publication, the Society in the 1820's translated and had printed and distributed free a book on Lancasterian education, and printed a work on indigo

---

[45] *La Seda en Guatemala* (86 pp., Guatemala: Imprenta de Luna, 1862). Cf. Julio Rosignon, *Porvenir de la Verapaz en la república de Guatemala. Memoria dedicada al consulado de comercio de Guatemala* (37 pp., Guatemala: Imprenta de Luna, 1861), a pamphlet dedicated to the Consulado, but the author, a Frenchman who came to Guatemala with Belgian colonists, was prominent in the Economic Society, and some years later served as its director.

[46] Batres Jáuregui, *América Central*, II, 473-77, for summary of activities in these years; cf. Vela, *Literatura guatemalteca*, 174-75, on the library.

[47] Jones, *Guatamala*, 399 n., citing *Recopilación ... de 1881*. Cf. Montalbán, *Historia literatura*, 162, that the Society ended in October, 1882; Batres Jáuregui, *América Central*, II, 464, that it ended in 1884.

[48] *Ibid.*, 476.

[49] Cf. Montero y Vidal, *Historia Filipinas*, II, 443, 533, 573; "Economic Society of Friends of the Country," in Blair and Robertson, *Philippine Islands*, LII, 307-22, taken from Fernández y Moreno, *Manual de viajero*, and XLV, 22, 282-83, LI, 38-39, XVII, 301, L, 52; Bazaco, *History Education in Philippines*, 168; Alzona, *History Education in Philippines*, 45 *et seq.*

originally published in Guatemala by a member of that Society.[50] The Society printed a memoria in 1833;[51] some years later it gave a prize to a memoria on agriculture, which was then published;[52] in 1881 was published an account of the Society's activities in the previous decade;[53] in 1886 an account appeared for the next five years;[54] in 1882 the Society began publishing a *Revista*.[55]

The Puerto Rico Society, formed in 1813, apparently was not active until 1821. A record remains of general juntas in 1821 and succeeding years, but it is not clear that any were held earlier.[56] The Society statutes were revised in 1829.[57] In 1844 the Society had 68 members in San Juan, and 91 corresponding members, mostly in other parts of Puerto Rico; and heard at a public junta that although it had not been rich since the Regency ordered it founded in 1811, its spirit was good, and it had always tried to promote education and agriculture.[58] The Society was dissolved in 1898, both because it was inactive and because of long-continued conservative opposition to a body noted for its relative liberalism.[59]

The work of the Havana Society after 1820 was too extensive for much comment here. After the Memorias of January-March, 1820, the next published were April, 1823-April, 1825. Then none were published until 1835, after which date a great many volumes and some tens of thousands of pages were published, until the last

---

[50] José Mariano Moziño, *Tratado del Xiquilite y añil de Guatemala ... con notas puesta por José Antonio Goycoechea. Año de 1799* (A. P. C. Griffin, *A List of Books ... on the Philippine Islands* [Washington, 1903], No. 107; Medina, *Imprenta en Guatemala*, 364).

[51] T. H. Pardo de Tavera, *Catálogo razonado de todos los impresos tanto insulares como extranjeros, relativos a la historia, la etnografía ... de las Islas Filipinas ...* (Washington, 1903), No. 2657; Montero y Vidal, *Historia general*, II, 291 n.

[52] Antonio de Keyser y Múñoz, *Medios que el gobierno y la Sociedad Económica de Amigos del País de Filipinas pueden emplear para obtener el desarrollo de la agricultura en el país ...* (55 pp., Manila: Establecimiento Tipográfico del Colegio de Santo Tomás, 1869). It says nothing about the foundation and early years of the Society.

[53] *Memoria de los trabajos ... en el bienio de 1871-80, leída por el Socio Secretario en la sesión celebrada el día 24 de Marzo de 1881* (46 pp., Manila, 1881)—Pardo de Tavera, *Catálogo razonado de impresos*, No. 264.

[54] *Resúmen de las tareas de la Real sociedad económica filipina de amigos del país durante el período de 1881 á 1885* (176 pp., Manila, 1886).

[55] *Revista de la Real Sociedad económica filipina* (Manila, 1882-87; title varied).

[56] Antonio S. Pedreira, *Bibliografía puertorriqueña 1493-1930* (Madrid, 1932), 233-34, listing a number of Society publications, but nothing earlier than 1821, but noting that there may be others. The Bancroft Library, Berkeley, has several Puerto Rico Society publications for 1823 and later.

[57] "Nuevos Estatutos de la Sociedad Económica de Amigos del País de Puerto Rico, Reformado en 1829," BHPR VII, 158-68.

[58] "Acta de la Junta Pública Celebrada por la Sociedad Económica de Amigos del País de Puerto Rico el día 27 de Junio de 1844," BHPR, VII, 354-72.

[59] Julián Blanco to Dr. Cayetano Coll y Toste, San Juan, December 31, 1898, in BHPR, VII, 319-20, under title "Porqué se suprimió la Real Sociedad Económica de Amigos del País." Cf. "Acta de la Real Sociedad ... de 13 de Noviembre de 1836," BHPR, VIII, 379-80; "Acta de la Junta pública tenida por la Real Sociedad ... en 1859," BHPR, XIII, 243 *et seq.*; Cruz Monclova, *Historia Puerto Rico*, 213, *et passim*, for considerable miscellaneous and unorganized information on the activities of the Society after 1821; Van Deusen, *Porto Rico*, 207, 222, 257.

volume in 1896.[60] According to Rafael Montoro,[61] the history of the Society falls into the periods 1793-1814, 1814-1823, 1823-1839, and several later periods. The voluminous memorias of 1835-1896 have never been fully exploited. The Economic Society of Havana exists today.[62]

---

[60] Cf. Adrián del Valle, *Indices de las memorias de la Sociedad Económica de Amigos del País, 1793-1896*, I (Ortiz, *Recopilación*, III), 5-8, "Introducción," for a list of the ten series of memorias from 1793 to 1896. This volume of del Valle's *Indice* is "Indices por volúmenes," giving a good picture of the changing economic interests of the Society in the 19th century.

[61] "Historia de la Sociedad Económica de Amigos del País de la Havana," in Ortiz, *Recopilación*, I, 1-56.

[62] Cf. Adrián del Valle, "La Sociedad Económica en la era republicana," in Ortiz, *Recopilación*, I, 57-79.

Bibliography

Society publications available for the period to 1821 totaled some 10,000 pages (over 6,000 for Spanish Societies, over 3,000 for American). Manuscript material in the Archivo General of Guatemala provided necessary additional evidence on the Society of that place. A considerable amount of evidence on the Societies was gleaned from non-Society publications of the late eighteenth and early nineteenth centuries. For Spain these were largely the writings of literary figures and government officials, as Jovellanos, Sempere y Guarinos, and Fernández de Navarrete. For America more information was derived from periodicals, as the *Gazeta de Guatemala*, the *Mercurio Peruano*, and the *Telégrafo Mercantil*.

Sources available for the Spanish Societies were a satisfactory sample for the present purpose; much more material is available in Spain. The materials for the American Societies were more nearly exhausted. The most important publications of the Havana and Guatemala Societies were exploited. It is doubtful that much can be added to the small printed product of the other American Societies. Manuscript sources in Spain and America certainly can provide further information on the American Societies, but it is doubtful that such information would seriously alter the picture of the American Societies presented here.

Previous studies of the Economic Societies are of restricted value. There has been no study of any magnitude of all the Societies—Spanish and American—or of all the American Societies. Studies of individual Societies tend to be based on too little evidence, are usually badly organized, and spend much interest on origins, motives, and general attitudes, and relatively little on chronology, statistics, and physical accomplishments to say nothing of a precise and orderly analysis of ideas and objectives.

This bibliography is of works cited. It does not list the many works consulted in vain for Economic Society data,[1] or the many more that deal briefly—and often

---

[1] E.g., Eugenio Larruga, *Memorias políticas y económicas sobre los frutos, comercio, fábricas y minas de España* (45 vols., Madrid, 1787-1800).

inaccurately—with one or another of the Societies. A very few works are cited, but not listed in the bibliography. A very few publications of the Valencia Society are in the bibliography, but are not cited; they were consulted by the author. In a few cases bibliographical works have been listed with contemporary materials, rather than with secondary works or studies. Items cited in the text in connection with the short-lived Vera Cruz and the proposed Mérida Societies are not listed in the bibliography. Items cited only in the Appendix are not listed here. Abbreviations used in the bibliography are those listed in the Preface.

The bibliography is arranged by areas, in the following order: Spain, Colonies in the Eighteenth Century, Havana and Santiagó Societies, Guatemala and Chiapas, Lima, Quito, Mompox and Bogota, Buenos Aires, Puerto Rico, Caracas, Manila. Items containing information relevant to more than one area are listed only once.

Spain

This study is primarily built upon 6,304 pages of the publications of the Basque, Madrid, Valencia, Segovia, and San Cristóval de la Laguna Societies. The Madrid Memorias of 1780-1795 comprise 2,727 pages of this total, and were analyzed intensively; the Basque materials total 1,056 pages; the Valencia publications, 1,548 pages, have been used frugally in this study, to keep the citations within bounds. Considerable other printed contemporary material, aside from the Society publications, was available. Even the best of later day studies of Spanish Economic Societies, when the authors used Society publications and manuscripts, suffer from poor organization and from an unwillingness to analyze the evidence in detail. Sarrailh, one of the best of these, made sufficient use of Zaragoza Society materials to make it clear that its performance was much like that of the Societies on which the present study depends.

CONTEMPORARY MATERIALS

American Philosophical Society. Archives.
    Contains letters of Foronda, Ramírez, Campomanes, and others.

————. *Early Proceedings of the American Philosophical Society. . . . From the Manuscript Minutes of its Meetings from 1744 to 1838*. Philadelphia, 1884.
    Information on members of Spanish Societies who were also members of the Philosophical Society.

————. *Yearbook 1949*. Philadelphia, 1950.
    Contains an article on "Former Foreign Members."

Andrés, Juan. *Orígen, progresos y estado actual de toda la literatura. Obra escrita en italiano por el abate D. Juan Andrés, y traducida al castellano por D. Carlos Andrés*. 8 vols. Madrid: Antonio de Sancha, 1784-99.

Anonymous. "Respuesta de Valentín al Autor de la Apologia," *Revue Basques*, XXIV (1933), 136-37.
    MS. printed as part of "Los Amigos del País y un enemigo anónimo," ed. Joaquín de Yrizar, *loc. cit.*, 134-37. The previously unknown reply to the "Apologia de una nueva Sociedad últimamente proyectada en esta M. N. y M. L. Provincia de Guipúzcoa con el título de los Amigos del Pays," excerpts from which Yrizar prints here, and

which was an eighteenth-century attack on the Basque Society as dealing only with music and poesy, as being frenchified, and a danger to religion.

Bourgoing, Jean François, baron de. *Nouveau voyage en Espagne, ou tableau de l'état actuel de cette monarchie.* ... 3 vols. Paris, 1789.
He admired the Economic Societies.

Cabarrús, Conde de. "Cartas sobre los obstáculos que la naturaleza, la opinión y las leyes oponen a la felicidad pública; escritas por el Conde de Cabarrús al señor Don Gaspar de Jovellanos, y precedidas de otra al Príncipe de la Paz," in *Epistolario Español* (2 vols., BAE, XIII, LXII), II, 551-602.
Written in the 1790's. First published at Vitoria in 1808.

Campillo y Cosío, José. *Nuevo sistema de gobierno económico para la América: Con los males y daños que le causa el que hoy tiene, de los que participa copiosamente España; y remedios universales para que la primera tenga considerables ventajas, y la segunda mayores intereses.* Madrid, 1789.
Written nearly half a century before publication. Of considerable influence with those interested in reforms of the economic system.

Campomanes, Pedro Rodríguez, Conde de. *Tratado de la regalía de amortización, en el qual se demuestra ... el uso constante de la autoridad civil para impedir las ilimitadas enagenaciones de bienes raíces en iglesias, comunidades, y otras manos muertas.* ... Gerona, 1821 [Madrid, 1765].
A good example of his learning and interest in broad economic reform. The volume includes a eulogy (1803) of Campomanes.

————. *Discurso sobre el fomento de la industria popular. De órden de S. M. y del Consejo.* Madrid: En la imprenta de D. Antonio de Sancha, 1774. 158 pp.
Analysis of Spanish economic decadance, especially in the field of industry, and advocating Economic Societies to promote popular industry. The Spanish and American Societies were established largely because of this work.

————. *Discurso sobre la educación popular de los artesanos, y su fomento.* Madrid: Antonio de Sancha, 1775. 22+475 pp. On the gremial system—apprenticeship, training, brotherhoods, etc.—with copious references to earlier Spanish writers on allied subjects; and devoted pp. 284-92 to the role of the Economic Societies in the care of the crafts of the country.

————. *Apéndice a la educación popular.* 4 vols. Madrid, 1775-77. Reprints of Spanish political economists, some not easily available at the time; royal decrees, regulations, etc., mostly of recent date, on economic matters; and nearly 700 pages of discourses by Campomanes. A work of very great influence among members of Economic Societies—and revisionists generally—in Spain and America.

"Ceremonial del Real Semanario Patriótico Bascongado," *Revue Basques*, XIV (1923), 439-41.
A MS. edited by Julio Urquijo, showing the Seminary involved in religious processions in 1782-83. He offers this against the charge that it was laical.

"El Borracho Burlado, Opera-Cómica, En Castellano, y Bascuence. Escrita y puesta en música por un Caballero Guipuzcoano," *Revue Basques*, I (1907), 383 *et seq.*

By Peñaflorida. Forward by the ayuntamiento of Vergara, August 25, 1764, praising Peñaflorida for his learning, and his "admirable Plan de una Academia."

Espíritu de los mejores diarios literarios que se publican en Europa. Madrid, July, 1787-August, 1790.

Some 3,200 pages of a periodical notably liberal on intellectual questions, though of course it could not deal with such political issues as the French Revolution. It did praise Anglo-American revolutionaries. Reprints from European and Anglo-American periodicals. Considerable Economic Society material.

Feijóo y Montenegro, Fray Benito Jerónimo. *Obras escogidas.* Madrid, 1924. BAE, LVI.

Purveyor of the Enlightenment to Spain; enemy of superstition and prejudice; rationalist; an intellectual father of the Economic Societies.

Fernández de Navarrete, Martín. *Colección de opúsculos ... La dan a luz D. Eustaquio y D. Francisco Fernández de Navarrete.* 2 vols. Madrid, 1848.

Several items bearing on the Basque Society, especially (II, 337-74) his "Elogio Póstumo" of Peñaflorida, delivered in 1785.

Floridablanca, Conde de (José Moniño y Redondo). *Obras originales del Conde de Floridablanca y escritos referentes a su persona.* Madrid, 1924. BAE, LIX.

Several important items by a minister of government who supported the Economic Societies.

————. *Gouvernement de Charles III, roi d'Espagne; ou, Instruction réservée transmise a la Junte d'état par ordre de ce monarque; publiée par Don Andres Muriel.* Paris, 1839.

Including Floridablanca's opinions of the Societies, and of economic conditions.

Foronda, Valentín de. *Lógica de Condillac, puesta en diálogo por D. Valentín de Foronda, y adicionada con un pequeño tratado sobre toda clase de argumentos. ...* Madrid, 1794.

An important indication of the enlightened interests of this member of the Basque Society. It had some influence in America.

————. *Miscelánea, ó, Colección de varios discursos. ...* Madrid, 1787.

Including one on the need of correcting errors in Feijóo; and another on the beneficent work of the Basque Society.

————. *Miscelánea, ó, Colección de varios discursos.* 2d ed. Madrid, 1793.

Gaceta de Madrid. 1789, and scattered numbers in 1808-13, 1822.

Contains notices of various Societies.

García, Juan Catalina. *Datos bibliográficos sobre la Sociedad económica Matritense.* Madrid: M. Tello, 1877. 167 pp.

Includes 332 numbered items, in chronological order, including Society publications, with extensive discussion of, and quotation from, some items.

Godoy, Manuel. *Cuenta dada de su vida política por D. Manuel Godoy Príncipe de la Paz ó sean Memorias críticas y apologéticas para historia del reinado del señor D. Carlos IV de Borbón anotadas y comentadas por Ivan Peters.* 4 vols. Madrid, 1908-9.

Apologetics; proclaiming his love of learning, and of the Economic Societies.

Humboldt, Guillermo de. "Diario del Viaje Vasco 1801," trans. T. de Aranzadi, in *Revue Basques,* XII (1922), 614-658; XIV (1923), 205-50.

————. "Los Vascos o Apuntamientos sobre un viaje por el país vasco en, primavera del año 1801," trans. Aranzadi, in *Revue Basques*, XIV (1923), 376-400; XV (1924), 83-137, 262-305, 391-445.

A great deal of information, divided by towns or areas.

Indice último de los libros prohibidos y mandados expurgar: para todos los reynos y señorios del católico rey de las Españas. Madrid, 1790, 1805.

With the supplement of 1805, contains books prohibited, and the rules governing printing, sale, export and import, correction, and possession of printed material. Issued by the Spanish Inquisition.

Isla, Padre Francisco José de. *Obras escogidas.* Madrid, 1918. BAE, XV.

Includes material bearing on his dispute with members of the Basque Society, notably "Los Aldeanos Críticos" of 1758.

Jaudenes y Nebot, José de. *Sobre la excelencia y utilidades del comercio, y las que pueden resultar a Mallorca del establecimiento de una Compañía, Discurso que por comisión de la Real Sociedad Económica Mallorquina, dixo su individuo de número D. Josef de Jaudenes y Nebot, Socio de la de Amigos del País de Valencia, de la Filosófica de Filadelfia ..., en junta general que celebró ... 30 de Julio de 1797, con motivo de leer en público la Real Cedula en que S. M. aprueba el establecimiento de dicha Compañía. ...* Palma: Imprenta real, 1798. [vi], 26 pp.

Jefferson, Thomas. *The Writings of Thomas Jefferson.* Ed. P. L. Ford. 10 vols. New York, 1892-99.

Jovellanos, Gaspar Melchor de. *Obras publicadas é inéditas.* 2 vols. Madrid, 1858-59 BAE, XLVI, L.

Numerous items connected with or bearing on the Economic Societies.

————. *Obras escogidas.* 3 vols. Madrid, 1935-46. *Clásicos Castellanos*, t. 110-11, 129.

Includes 10 letters of Jovellanos to Antonio Ponz, finished sometime after 1790, and bearing on the Societies, and on the Spanish economy generally.

Macanaz, Melchor de. "Auxilio para bien gobernar una monarquía católica, o documentos, que dicta la experiencia, y aprueba la razón, para que el Monarca merezca justamente el nombre de Grande. Obra, que escribió, y remitió desde París al rey nuestro señor Don Felipe Quinto Don Melchor de Macanaz, &c.," in *Semanario Erudito* [Madrid], V (1797), 215-305.

Martínez de Mata, Francisco. "Epítome de los Discursos que ha dado á su Mag. Francisco Martínez de Mata ... en que prueba: como la causa de la pobreza, y despoblación de España ...," in Campomanes, *Apéndice a la educación popular*, I, 433-500.

————. "Ocho discursos," in *Apéndice a la educación popular*, IV, 1-431.

Moncada, Sancho de. *Restauración política de España, y deseos públicos, que escrivió en ocho discursos El Doctor Sancho de Moncada, Cathedrático de Sagrada Escritura en la Universidad de Toledo.* Madrid, 1746 [1619].

Múgica, S. "Un caso curioso de viruela," *Revue Basques*, XVI (1925), 306-20.

Documents showing the attitude in 1791 of different sections of society in the Basque country on smallpox vaccination.

Peñaflorida, Conde de. "Historia de la Real Sociedad Bascongada de los Amigos del País," *Revue Basques*, XXI (1930), 317-33; XXII (1931) 442-82.

Edited by Urquijo from a folio of 116 pages. Most of it is devoted to the organizational meetings of the Society at Vergara, February, 1765. Important for this.

Rousseau, Jean Jacques. *Confessions*. Ed. of the Bibliophilist Society, n. d.

He knew, and discussed in the *Confessions*, the Basque, Manuel Ignacio de Altuna, influential in the intellectual development leading to formation of the Basque Society.

Sempere y Guarinos, Juan. *Ensayo de una biblioteca española de los mejores escritores del reynado de Carlos III*. 6 vols. Madrid: Imprenta real, 1785-89.

Extensive information on various Economic Societies, by a man very favorably disposed toward them and toward the new ideas generally. One of the best contemporary sources, though not a good substitute for Society publications.

Real sociedad bascongada de los amigos del país. *Estatutos aprobados por S. M. para govierno de la Real sociedad bascongada de amigos del país*. Vitoria: T. de Robles [1774]. 180 pp.

Including the approval of the Crown, and 46 pp. of "Catálogo" of the members.

————. *Plan de la colección general de estatutos de la Real sociedad bascongada de los amigos del país, según el acuerdo de sus juntas generales, celebradas en la Villa de Vergara por noviembre de 1770*. Madrid: A. de Sancha, 1772. 36 pp.

————. *Extractos de las juntas generales celebradas por la Real Sociedad Bascongada de los Amigos del País en la ciudad de Vitoria por septiembre de 1771*. Madrid: Antonio de Sancha, 1772. [4], 85 pp.

Only a small part of this, and the other volumes of *Extractos*, is taken up with an account of the annual *juntas generales;* the volumes are a review of the year's activities, and the basic source for the history of the Society.

————. *Extractos ... en la Villa de Bilbao ... 1772*. Vitoria: Tomás de Robles, Impresor de la misma Real Sociedad, n. d. 134, 2 pp.

————. *Extractos ... en la Villa de Vergara ... 1773*. Vitoria: Robles, n. d. 124 pp.

————. *Extractos ... en la Ciudad de Vitoria ... 1774*. Vitoria: Robles, n. d. 158, 1 pp.

————. *Extractos ... en la Villa de Bilbao ... 1775*. Vitoria: Robles, n. d. 220 pp.

————. *Extractos ... en la Villa de Vergara ... 1776*. Vitoria: Robles, n. d. 112 pp.

Sociedad Económica, Madrid. *Catálogo de los libros que forman su biblioteca*. Madrid: Imprenta del Colegio Nacional de Sordo-Mudos y Ciegos, 1870. 260 pp.

————. *Colección de las memorias premiadas, y de las que se acordó se imprimiesen sobre los quatro asuntos, que por encargo particular publicó la Real Sociedad económica de amigos del país de esta corte en suplemento de la gazeta de 14 de agosto de 1781. Tratan del exercicio de la caridad y socorro de los verdaderos pobres, corección de los ociosos, destierro de la mendicidad voluntaria, y fomento de la industria y aplicación*. Madrid: La Imprenta real, 1784. 4 parts in 1 vol. i-xxvii, 395, 17, 55, 17 pp.

A mass of information on habits of work, poverty, and almsgiving and charity generally.

————. *Memorias de la Sociedad Económica*. 5 vols. Madrid: Sancha, 1780-95.

The single best printed source, it has a confusing pagination, the volumes respectively totaling 484, 715, 650, 713, and 265 pages, for a total of 2,727. The first two volumes came out in 1780, the next two in 1787, and the fifth in 1795. More than half of vol. 5 is taken up with Jovellanos' report on the agrarian law.

————. Gabriel Alonso de Herrera. *Agricultura general. Corregida según el testo original de la primera edición publicada en 1513 ... y adicionada por la Real Sociedad Económica Matritense.* 4 vols. Madrid: Imprenta real, 1818-19.
Here primarily of interest for the list of 8 authors who added to the text, the prologue telling of the work on the edition by the Economic Society, and the fact that with the extensive additions the text still scarcely referred to America.

Sociedad Económica, Segovia. *Real Sociedad económica de los amigos del país de la provincia de Segovia. Actas y Memorias. 1785.* Segovia: Antonio Espinosa, 1785. 424 pp.
Including an extract from its *actas* from foundation in 1780 to 1784.

Sociedad Económica, Tenerife. *Estatutos de la Sociedad Económica de los Amigos del Pays de la ciudad de S. Cristóval de la Laguna, capital de la isla de Tenerife, una de las Canarias, con real aprobación, y agregación á la de Madrid.* Madrid: Blas Román, 1779. 38 pp.
Including a list of the members.

Sociedad Económica, Valencia. *Instituciones económicas de la Sociedad de Amigos del País de la ciudad, i reino de Valencia.* Valencia: Benito Monfort, 1777. ii, lxii, 208 pp.
Very useful; considerable material on history of the Society, as well as on its interests.

————. *Real cedula por la qual se aprueban los estatutos de la Sociedad Económica de Amigos del País de Valencia.* Valencia: Benito Monfort, 1785. 54 pp.

————. *Extracto de las actas de la R. Sociedad de Amigos del País de Valencia del Año 1785. ...* Valencia: Benito Monfort, 1787. 37 pp.

————. *Extracto de las actas ... 1786 ...* Valencia: Joseph Tomás de Orga, 1788. 64 pp.

————. *Extractos de las actas ... que comprende desde el principio del año 1787 hasta 13 de noviembre 1791.* Valencia: Benito Monfort, 1792. 224 pp.

————. *Junta pública de la Real Sociedad Económica de Amigos del País de Valencia. Celebrada el día 11 de diciembre de 1799.* Valencia: Benito Monfort, 1800. 194 pp.
The first since 1791.

————. *Junta pública ... 1800.* Valencia: Benito Monfort, 1801. 408 pp.

————. *Junta pública ... 1801.* Valencia: Benito Monfort, 1802. 262, 1 pp.

Spain. *Apéndice a los tomos I, II, III y IV de la obra decretos del rey d. Fernando VII ... años de 1814, 815, 816 y 817.* Madrid: Imprenta real, 1819.

————. *Colección de los decretos y órdenes que han expedido las Cortes generales y extraordinarias desde ... 24 de setiembre ... 1810 ... 1814.* 5 vols. Madrid and Cadiz, 1813-21.

————. *Decretos del rey Fernando VII, T. II (1815).* Madrid: Imprenta Real, 1819.

————. *Diario de las sesiones de las Cortes generales y extraordinarias. Dieron principio el 24 de setiembre de 1810, y terminaron el 20 de setiembre de 1813.* ... 9 vols. Madrid: J. A. García, 1870-74.

————. *Novísimă Recopilación de las leyes de España* [1805], being vols. VII-X of *Los Códigos Espắñoles* (12 vols., Madrid, 1847-51).

Swinburne, Henry. *Travels through Spain, in the years 1775 and 1776.* 2d ed. 2 vols. London, 1787.
Unfriendly to Spain.

Ulloa, Bernardo de. *Restablecimiento de las fábricas, y comercio español: errores que se padecen en las causales de su cadencia, quales son los legítimos obstáculos que le destruyen, y los medios eficases de que florezca.* Madrid: Por Antonio Marin, 1740.
The main theme is the necessity of improving industrial production. Nearly half the volume is devoted to an extract of Ustáriz' great work.

Ustáriz, Gerónimo de. *Théorie et practique du commerce et de la marine.* Hambourg, 1753.
The first edition, in Spanish (Madrid, 1724), and later editions were very influential in Spain among political economists, and had some influence on statesmen.

Ward, Bernardo. *Proyecto económico, en que se proponen varias providencias, dirigidas á promover los intereses de España, con los medios y fondos necesarios para su plantificación; escrito en el año de 1762 ... Obra póstuma.* Madrid, 1779. 400 pp.
A favorite author of members of the Economic Societies in Spain and America. Favored considerable revision of the economic system, including the rules governing American commerce.

Young, Arthur. *Travels in France during the years 1787, 1788, 1789.* 3d ed. London, 1890.
The first edition was 1792. Gives a good account of the agricultural societies of France, which were known to some Spaniards. Unsympathetic toward the theoretical interests of savants in farming.

STUDIES

Addison, Joseph. *Charles the Third of Spain.* Oxford, 1900.

Altamira y Crevea, Rafael. *Historia de España y de la civilización española.* 3d ed. 4 vols. Barcelona, 1913-14.

Aralar, José de. *El conde de Peñaflorida y los caballeritos de Azkoitia.* Buenos Aires: Editorial Vasca "Ekin," 1942.
Considerable material on the Basque Society; well documented in places; very repetitious; much taken up with pro-Basque diatribes against Spanish scholars; only 24 pages devoted to the activities of the Basque Society other than its Seminary, which is the usual procedure in dealing with the Basque Society.

Artíñano y Galdácano, G. de. *Jovellanos y su España.* Madrid, 1913.

Ballesteros y Beretta, Antonio. *Historia de España y su influencia en la historia universal.* 9 vols. Barcelona, 1918-41.

Borrego, Andrés. *Historia de las Cortes de España durante el siglo XIX a partir de la instalación de las generales y extraordinarias de 1810 hasta advenimiento del rey D. Alfonso XII.* 2 vols. Madrid, 1885.

Brinton, Crane. *Ideas and Men. The Story of Western Thought.* New York, 1950.

Brown, Vera Lee. *Studies in the History of Spain in the Second Half of the Eighteenth Century.* Northhampton: *Smith College Studies in History,* XV, Nos. 1-2 (October, 1929-January, 1930).

Buckle, Henry T. *History of Civilization in England.* 2 vols. New York, 1871-73.
Vol. II, ch. 1, is "Outlines of the History of the Spanish Intellect...," which now seems to rest on too little, and too often inferior, evidence.

Canga Argüelles, José. *Diccionario de hacienda, con aplicación a España.* 2d ed. 2 vols. with Apéndice (i.e., supplemental list). Madrid, 1833-34.
First edition was 1826. Author had a long public career, some of it as minister of the Council of the Indies. A mine of information, much of it statistical, on economic conditions in Spain and America. A good deal of historical information, and many comparisons of the Spanish economic situation with that of other European nations. Tends to favor liberalization of the Spanish economic system.

Carrera Pujal, Jaime. *Historia de la economía española.* 5 vols. Barcelona, 1943-47.
Covering 1500-1808, emphasizing economic literature rather than economic life, it is an excellent account of Spanish views of the country's economic woes, but less satisfactory as a description of the economy itself. Carrera is critical of scholars (e.g., Colmeiro) who oversimplify economic history, but he does believe that the weakness of manufacturing was the critical element in Spain's economic failure. He insists on a considerable continuity of Spanish economic thought and action from the 17th century to the 18th, and notes that the revisionists of the latter were not invariably sound in their proposals. Fairly extensive use was made of the publications of Spanish Economic Societies. The study is primarily based, however, upon writings on economic subjects, rather than on government, business, or other types of records.

Castillejos, Fernando de la Quadra Salcedo, Marqués de los. *Economistas vascongados y artículos varios sobre problemas destacados de la economía vizcaína.* Bilbao, 1943.
A collection of short newspaper articles.

Castillo, Andrés V. *Spanish Mercantilism: Gerónimo de Uztáriz Economist.* New York, 1930.

Castro, Américo. "Algunos aspectos del siglo XVIII (Introducción Metódica)," in his *Lengua, Enseñanza y Literatura* (Madrid, 1924), 281-334.

Cejador y Frauca, Julio. *Historia de la lengua y literatura castellana comprendidos los autores hispano-americanos.* 14 vols. Madrid, 1915-22.

Colmeiro, Manuel. *Biblioteca de los Economistas Españoles de los siglos XVI, XVII y XVIII.* Madrid, 1861 (Real Academia de ciencias morales y políticas, *Memorias,* I, 33-212).
The 405 items, annotated, do not cover the ground, but are useful in the early stages of an investigation.

———. *Historia de la economía política en España.* 2 vols. Madrid, 1863.

A general survey, without much detailed information on any one subject. Useful for the general history of economic ideas in Spain.

Dánvila y Collado, M. *Reinado de Carlos III.* 6 vols. Madrid, 1890 (X-XV of the Academy of History's *Historia General de España*).
Deals with the Economic Societies in VI, 400-409.

Desdevises du Dézert, Georges N. *L'Espagne de l'ancien régime.* 2d ed., 3 vols., in *Revue Hispanique: La Société Espagnole au XVIIIe Siècle,* LXIV, Nos. 145-146 (June and August, 1925), 226-645; *Les Institutions de l'Espagne au XVIIIe Siècle,* LXX, Nos. 157-158 (June and August, 1927), 1-556; *La Richesse et la Civilisation Espagnoles au XVIIIe Siècle,* LXXIII, Nos. 163-164 (June and August, 1928), 1-488.
Valuable for the politico-socioeconomic condition of eighteenth-century Spain; based on wide research; sometimes too sweeping in its judgments.

Enciclopedia Universal Ilustrada Europeo-Americana, "Económico"—'Sociedades Económicas de Amigos del País,' XVIII, 2.ª parte, 2832-34.
The confusing picture it gives of the history of the Societies is illustrative of the literature on the subject.

Ferrer del Río, Antonio. *Historia del reinado de Carlos III en España.* 4 vols. Madrid, 1856.
Vol. III, 231-42, is on the Economic Societies; a competent sketch.

Fuente, Vicente de la. *Historia de las sociedades secretas antiguas y modernas en España y especialmente de la franc-masonería.* 3 vols. Barcelona, 1933.

Gigas, Emile. "Un voyageur allemand-danois en Espagne sous le règne de Charles III," *Revue Hispanique,* LXIX, No. 156 (April, 1927), 341-519.
Based on the notes of a Danish functionary in Spain in the 1780's.

Gil de Zárate, Antonio. *De la instrucción pública en España.* 3 vols. Madrid, 1855.
Zárate was Director of Public Education for a time. Rationalist; anticlerical; condemns the lack of technical education in Spain.

Gómez de Arteche, José. *Reinado de Carlos IV.* 3 vols. Madrid, 1893-98? (XVI-XVIII of the Academy of History's *Historia General de España*).

Hamilton, Earl J. "The Decline of Spain," *Economic History Review,* VIII (1938), 168-79.

———. "The Mercantilism of Gerónimo de Uztáriz: A Reëxamination," 111-29 in *Economics, Sociology and the Modern World, Essays in Honor of T. N. Carver,* ed. Norman E. Himes (Harvard University Press, 1935).

———. "Money and Economic Recovery in Spain under the First Bourbon, 1701-1746," *Journal of Modern History,* XV, No. 3 (September, 1943), 192-206.

———. *War and Prices in Spain 1651-1800.* Cambridge, Mass., 1934.

Helman, Edith F., "Some Consequences of the Publication of the *Informe de Ley Agraria* by Jovellanos," 253-73 in *Estudios Hispánicos Homenaje a Archer M. Huntington* (Wellesley, Mass., 1952).
A scholarly study delineating the violent reaction of the Inquisition, and conservatives generally, to the *Ley Agraria.*

Hussey, Roland D. *The Caracas Company (1728-1784)*. Cambridge, Mass., 1934.

Kany, Charles. *Life and Manners in Madrid, 1750-1800*. Berkeley, 1932.

Klein, Julius. *The Mesta; A Study in Spanish Economic History 1273-1836*. Cambridge, Mass., 1920.

Laborde, Alexandre de. *Itinéraire descriptif de L'Espagne, et tableau élémentaire des différentes branches de l'administration et de l'industrie de ce royaume*. 2d ed. 5 vols. Paris, 1809.

Labra y Cadrana, Rafael María de. *El instituto de derecho internacional*. Madrid, 1907.
Much of it is discussions of the origin, history, and functions of the Economic Societies of Spain, without scholarly apparatus or much attention to chronology.

Lafuente y Zamalloa, Modesto. *Historia general de España desde los tiempos primitivos hasta la muerte de Fernando VII*. 25 vols. Barcelona, 1887-90.

McLachlan, Jean O. *Trade and Peace with Old Spain, 1667-1750*. Cambridge University Press, 1940.

Marichalar, Amilio, and Cayetano Manrique. *Historia de la legislación y recitaciones del derecho civil de España*. 9 vols. Madrid, 1861-72.

Márquez, Javier. "Gerónimo de Uztáriz como Economista," *El Trimestre Económico*, XI (1944-45), 471-94.

———. "El Mercantilismo de Saavedra Fajardo," *El Trimestre Económico*, X (1943-44), 247-86.

Méndez Bejarano, M. *Historia de la filosofía en España hasta el siglo XX*. Madrid, 1926.

———. *Historia política de los afrancesados (con algunas cartas y documentos inéditos)*. Madrid, 1912.
Well documented; harsh criticism of the state of education, the economy, etc., at the end of the 18th and beginning of 19th centuries; on the other hand, strong against "frenchification"; information on Economic Societies, including documents.

Menéndez y Pelayo, Marcelino. *La ciencia española*. 4th ed. 3 vols. Madrid, 1915-18.
Independent discourses, not all by Menéndez; lacks plan; clearly the work of a literary man and bibliophile and polemicist. The only usable portion is the "Inventario bibliográfico de la ciencia española" (III, 139-480).

———. *Historia de los heterodoxos españoles*. 2d ed. 7 vols. Madrid, 1911-32.
A great deal of comment on the Economic Societies, by an advocate of Roman Catholic orthodoxy, considering the Societies instruments of materialistic philosophy. Undocumented, biased, repetitious, sometimes absurd, it has had great influence.

Merimée, Paul. *L'influence française en Espagne au dix-huitième siècle*. Paris, 1936.

Miguel, Antonio de. *El potencial económico de España*. Madrid, 1935.

Millares Carlo, Agustín. *Ensayo de una bio-bibliografía de escritores naturales de las Islas Canarias (Siglos XVI, XVII y XVIII)*. Madrid, 1932.
Lists a number of Economic Society items.

Millares Torres, Agustín. *Historia general de las Islas Canarias.* 2d ed., Havana, 1945.

Monbeig, Juliette P. "La Real Sociedad Económica de Los Amigos del País. Une Source de l'Histoire Economique de Majorque au XVIIIe Siècle," *Annales du Midi,* XLV (1933), 163-73.
Based on Society publications and archives.

Morel-Fatio, A. *Études sur L'Espagne.* 2d ed. of 2d ser. Paris, 1906.

Mounier, André. *Les Faits et la Doctrine Économiques en Espagne sous Philippe V: Gerónimo de Uztáriz.* Bordeaux, 1919.

Ramón y Cajal, Santiago. *Reglas y consejos sobre investigación científica (los tónicos de la voluntad).* 8th ed. Madrid, 1940.
By a Spanish scientist. Ch. x deals with different theories as to Spain's intellectual backwardness in recent centuries.

Ramos Oliveira, Antonio. *Politics, Economics and Men of Modern Spain 1808-1946.* London, 1946.
Tries to tie the failures of Spain in the late 18th and early 19th centuries to the later unsatisfactory condition of the country. Rails against the obscurantism of Spanish historical literature.

Río, Angel del. *Historia de la literatura española.* 2 vols. New York, 1948.

Ríos, Fernando de los. "The Social Sciences as Disciplines: Spain and Portugal," *Encyclopedia of the Social Sciences,* I, 295-300.
Points out the importance of the records of the Economic Societies.

Rousseau, Francois. *Règne de Charles III d'Espagne (1759-1788).* 2 vols. Paris, 1907.

Rubío, Antonio. *La crítica del galicismo en España (1726-1832).* Mexico, 1937.

Sarrailh, Jean. *L'Espagne éclairée de la seconde moitié du 18e siècle.* Paris, 1954.
Based on wide research, especially in literary sources. The chapter on the Basque Society, and that on the Spanish Societies, are based on considerable acquaintance with Society publications, and on some manuscript material, notably from the municipal archives of Zaragoza.

Sée, Henri. *Economic and Social Conditions in France during the Eighteenth Century.* Trans. E. H. Zeydel. New York, 1927.

Smith, Robert S. "Spanish Anti-Mercantilism of the Seventeenth Century," *Journal of Political Economy,* XLVIII (1940), 401-11.

————. "Maltusianismo Español del Siglo XVII: *El Arcano de Príncipes* de Vicente Montano," *El Trimestre Económico,* XXII, No. 3 (July-September, 1955), 350-85.

Soraluce y Zubizarreta, Nicolás de. *Real sociedad bascongada de los amigos del País. Sus antecedentes y otros sucesos con ella relacionados.* San Sebastián: Esto. tip. de Juan Oses, 1880. 108 pp.
Contains some information not in Aralar. Based on research in the sources, but is not well documented. Almost no analysis of the work or ideas of the Society. Concentrates on foundation, and on some selected (on an unfathomable principle) interests of the author.

"The Spanish Enlightenment," *The Times* (London) *Literary Supplement*, March 15, 1957.
A stimulating essay on the historiography of the Spanish Enlightenment.

Spell, Jefferson R. "An Illustrious Spaniard in Philadelphia—Valentín de Foronda," *Hispanic Review*, IV (1936), 136-40.

————. *Rousseau in the Spanish World before 1833*. University of Texas Press, 1938.
Valuable for the intellectual condition of the Spanish world. Little on the Economic Societies.

Ticknor, George. *History of Spanish Literature*. 4th American ed. 3 vols. Boston, 1872.

Urquijo, Julio de. "Review" of Basterra's *Una empresa del siglo XVIII* ..., in *Revue Basques*, XVII (1926), 129-32.
Important not only as a review, but for information, including heretofore inedited documents, bearing on the history of the Basque Society. He finds Basterra "más poeta que historiador."

————. "Los Amigos del País y la vacuna," *Revue Basques*, XVI (1925), 321-22.
An interesting, plausible, suggestive, and documented attempt to explain the origins of the legend of the heterodoxy of Peñaflorida and his friends, much noised by V. de la Fuente and Menéndez y Pelayo.

————. *Los Amigos del país (según cartas y otros documentos inéditos del siglo XVIII)*. San Sebastián, 1929.
The author looked at 3,500 inedited documents relative to the Basque Society. The work contains many documents; is especially valuable for the foundation of the Society, for the travels of Ramón de Munibe, for bibliographical suggestions; but it tells remarkably little of the real work of the Society, which an analysis of the *Extractos* published by the Society would make possible.

Valverde, Antonio de. "La Creación de las Sociedades Económicas," RBC, XXI, No. 1 (January-February, 1926), 38-41.

Whitaker, A. P. "The Elhuyar Mining Missions and the Enlightenment," HAHR, XXXI, No. 4 (November, 1951), 557-85.
Some important information on the Basque Society and the Spanish government.

The Colonies in the Eighteenth Century

Many of the items cited in chapter VII are listed in later sections of this bibliography, rather than here; some are listed under Spain.

CONTEMPORARY MATERIALS

Alzate Ramírez, José Antonio. *Gazeta de literatura de Mexico* [1788-95]. 2d ed. 4 vols. Puebla: Reimpresión [with title *Gacetas de literatura de Mexico*] ... á cargo del ciudadano M. Buen Abad, 1831.
The usual creole interest in science and the new learning generally, with considerable attention to economic matters. Alzate was a corresponding member of the Basque Society.

Funes, Gregorio. *Ensayo de la historia civil del Paraguay, Buenos Aires y Tucumán.* ... 3 vols. Buenos Aires, 1816-17.

Humboldt, Alexander. *Essai politique sur le royaume de la Nouvelle-Espagne.* 2 vols., paged continuously, Paris, 1811.

Juan, Jorge, and Antonio de Ulloa. *Noticias secretas de América.* 2 vols. London, 1826.

Proceso de Nariño; fiel copia del original que existe en el Archivo general de Indias de Sevilla. Ed. José Manuel Pérez-Sarmiento. Cadiz, 1914.

Revilla Gigedo, Conde de. *Instrucción reservada que el Conde de Revilla Gigedo, dió a su succesor en el mando, Marqués de Branciforte sobre el gobierno de este continente en el tiempo que fué su virey.* Mexico: C. Agustín Guiol, 1831.

Salas, Manuel de. *Escritos de Don ... y documentos relativos a él y a su familia.* 3 vols. Santiago, 1910-14.
Salas had an interest in an "academia o sociedad" as early as 1796.

Zamora y Coronado, José María. *Biblioteca de legislación ultramarina en forma de diccionario alfabético.* 6 vols. Madrid, 1844-46.
Contains documentary material bearing on American Societies in general, and on the Manila, Santiago, Havana, and Puerto Rico Societies.

STUDIES

Alcázar Molina, Cayetano. *Los virreinatos en el siglo XVIII.* Barcelona, 1945.

Amunátegui, Miguel Luís. *Los precursores de la independencia de Chile.* 3 vols. Santiago, 1909-10.

Arcila Farías, Eduardo. *Comercio entre Venezuela y Mexico en los siglos XVI y XVII.* Mexico, 1950.
A valuable and challenging scholarly work, emphasizing the great problems Spain faced in contriving an economic policy for the entire empire, and demanding a re-evaluation of interprovincial trade, especially that centering on New Spain.

———. *Economía colonial de Venezuela.* Mexico, 1946.
A valuable, scholarly study.

———. "Ideas Económicas en Nueva España en el Siglo XVIII," *El Trimestre Económico*, XIV, No. 1 (April-June, 1947), 68-82.

Arellano Moreno, Antonio. *Orígenes de la economía venezolana.* Mexico, 1947.
Useful for economic thought and development in the late colonial period.

Bagú, Sergio. *Economía de la sociedad colonial. Ensayo de historia comparada de América Latina.* Buenos Aires, 1949.

———. *Estructura social de la colonia. Ensayo de historia comparada de América Latina.* Buenos Aires, 1952.

Belaunde, Víctor Andrés. *Bolivar and the Political Thought of the Spanish American Revolution.* Baltimore, 1938.

Bernstein, Harry. *Origins of Inter-American Interest 1700-1812.* University of Pennsylvania Press, 1945.

Brown, Vera Lee. "Contraband Trade: A Factor in the Decline of Spain's Empire in America," HAHR, VIII, No. 2 (May, 1928), 178-89.

Calvo, Carlos. *Anales históricos de la revolución de la América latina, acompañados de los documentos en apoyo* ... 5 vols. Paris, 1864-67.
   The Introduction (I, pp. V-CXXXVII) has many statistics (not always well certified) on colonial economic life, especially overseas trade, mining, and government revenues.

Cappa, Ricardo. *Estudios críticos acerca de la dominación española en América.* 26 vols. Madrid, 1889-97.
   Father Cappa's work is pro-Spanish, and literary rather than scientific, but contains some interesting information and views on the colonial economy, largely that of Peru, and emphasizing the 16th century.

Chávez Orozco, Luís. *Historia económica y social de Mexico. Ensayo de interpretación.* Mexico, 1938.

Cuevas, Mariano. *Historia de la nación mexicana.* Mexico, 1940.

Diffie, Bailey W. *Latin American Civilization.* Harrisburg, 1945.

Fisher, Lillian E. *The Background of the Revolution for Mexican Independence.* Boston 1934.

————. *Champion of Reform: Manuel Abad y Queipo.* New York, 1955.

Galdames, Luís. *La evolución constitucional de Chile.* Santiago, 1925.

García, Juan Agustín. *La ciudad indiana (Buenos Aires desde 1600 hasta mediados del siglo XVIII).* Buenos Aires, 1937 [1900].

Gay y Forner, Vicente. *Leyes del imperio español. Las leyes de Indias y su influjo en la legislación colonial extranjera.* 1924. (Universidad de Valladolid *Publicaciones de la sección de estudios americanistas*, série primera, número 1).

Hamilton, Earl J. "Monetary Problems in Spain and Spanish America, 1751-1800," *Journal of Economic History*, IV, No. 1 (May, 1944), 21-48.

————. "The Role of Monopoly in the Overseas Expansion and Colonial Trade of Europe before 1800," *American Economic Review*, XXXVIII, No. 2 (May, 1948), 33-35.

Haring, Clarence H. *The Spanish Empire in America.* Oxford University Press, 1947.

————.*Trade and Navigation between Spain and the Indies in the Time of the Hapsburgs.* Harvard University Press, 1918.

Howe, Walter. *The Mining Guild of New Spain and its Tribunal General 1770-1821.* Harvard University Press, 1949.

Humphreys, R. A. "The Fall of the Spanish Empire," *History*, XXXVII, No. 131 (October, 1952), 213-27.

Huneeus y Gana, Jorge. *Cuadro histórico de la producción intelectual de Chile.* Santiago, 1910 (?).

Lanning, John T. *Academic Culture in the Spanish Colonies.* Oxford University Press, 1940.

———. "The Last Stand of the Schoolmen. Philosophical Evolution in Hispanic America," in *University of Miami Hispanic-American Studies,* No. 1 (1939), 33-49.

Levene, Ricardo. *Introducción a la historia del derecho indiano.* Buenos Aires, 1924.

———. "La política económica de España en América durante el siglo XVIII; y la revolución de 1810," in *Anales de la Facultad de Derecho y Ciencias Sociales,* 2d ser., vol. 4 (Buenos Aires, 1914), 594-719.

——— (ed.). *Historia de América.* 14 vols. Buenos Aires, 1940-44.

Madariaga, Salvador de. *The Fall of the Spanish Empire.* New York, 1948.

———. *The Rise of the Spanish Empire.* New York, 1947.

Moses, Bernard. *The Intellectual Background of the Revolution in South America, 1810-1824.* New York, 1924.

Motten, Clement G. *Mexican Silver and the Enlightenment.* University of Pennsylvania Press, 1950.

Novoa, Emilio. *Las Sociedades Económicas de Amigos del País. Su influencia en la emancipación colonial Americana.* Madrid, 1955.
Of no interest to scholars.

Ortiz, *Hija cubana.* See list for Havana

Pereyra, Carlos. *Historia de América española.* 8 vols. Madrid, 1920-27.

Priestley, Herbert I. *The Mexican Nation, A History.* New York, 1938.

———. *José de Gálvez, visitador-general of New Spain (1765-71).* University of California Press, 1916.

Quesada, Vicente G. *La vida intelectual en la América española durante los siglos XVI, XVII y XVIII.* Buenos Aires, 1917.

Ramos Pérez, Demetrio. *Historia de la colonización española en América.* Madrid, 1947.

Ruíz Guiñazú, Enrique. *La magistratura indiana.* Buenos Aires, 1916.

Smith, Robert S. "José María Quirós. Balanza del comercio marítimo de Veracruz, e ideas económicas," *El Trimestre Económico,* XIII, No. 4 (January-March, 1947), 680-711.

Spell, Jefferson R. *The Life and Works of José Joaquín Fernández de Lizardi.* University of Pennsylvania Press, 1931.

Torres Quintero, Gregorio. *Mexico hacia el fin del virreinato. Antecedentes sociológicos del pueblo mexicano.* Mexico, 1921.

Valle Iberlucea, E. del. *Los diputados de Buenos Aires en las Cortes de Cadiz y el nuevo sistema de gobierno económica de América.* Buenos Aires, 1912.

Whitaker, Arthur P. "The Commerce of Louisiana and the Floridas at the End of the Eighteenth Century," HAHR, VIII, No. 2 (May, 1928), 190-203.

————. *The Huancavelica Mercury Mine.* Harvard University Press, 1941.

———— (ed.). *Latin America and the Enlightenment.* New York and London, 1942.

Vallenilla Lanz, Laureano. *Cesarismo democrático.* Caracas, 1919.

Havana and Santiago de Cuba Societies

Most important were 2,885 pages of Havana Society material produced in 1793-1823, and mostly published then. Of this total, 2,233 pages comprise the Memorias of 1793-1795 and 1817-1823 and the Tareas of 1815; independently published Society items in the period total 113 pages; and the other 539 pages were later published in various society Memorias in 1838-1895, and include the records of the *juntas ordinarias* of 1793-1795. Cuban scholars have produced some valuable studies of aspects of the history and labors of the Havana Society. The bibliographical and other materials brought together in Ortiz, *Recopilación*, are a splendid contribution to the study of the Society. Friedländer analyzes in some detail the economic interests and ideas of the Society, but is sometimes confusing. Little contemporary (or other) material is available on the Santiago Society, and most of that is found in Havana Society publications.

CONTEMPORARY MATERIALS

American Philosophical Society. See the list for SPAIN.

Arango y Parreño, Francisco de. *De la factoría a la colonia.* Havana, 1936. 168 pp.
Several of Arango y Parreño's works, with introduction by Raúl Maestri. Politico-economic views in late colonial era of the type of moderately liberal creole prominent in the Societies.

El Aviso Papel Periódico de la Havana. Havana, 1805-7.
Carried numerous Economic Society items. Edited by the Society.

Lonja Mercantil de la Habana. 1800.

Medina, José Toribio. *La imprenta en la Habana 1707-1810. Notas bibliográficas.* Santiago de Chile, 1904.

Ortiz Fernández, Fernando (ed.). *Recopilación para la historia de la Sociedad Económica Habanera.* 5 vols. Havana, 1929-43.
Vol. I contains the original statutes, and a number of other contemporary documents; historical sketches of the Society; several biographies of important members. Vol. II is Ofelia Morales, *La evolución de las ideas pedagógicas en Cuba hasta 1842*, which includes material on the educational interests of the Society. Vol. III is Adrián del Valle, *Indices de las memorias de la Sociedad Económica de Amigos del País, 1793-1896. I. Indice por volúmenes*, which is accurate and highly useful. Vol. IV is companion to the foregoing: *II. Indices por materias y por autores*, which is useful, but not a good index. Vol. V is Fernando Ortiz, *Hija cubana del Iluminismo*, a short (72 pp.), very interesting and useful essay not only on the Havana Society but on the Economic Societies in general.

Peraza y Sarausa, Fermín. "Indice del 'Papel Periódico de la Havana,' " RBC, LI (1943), and many subsequent issues for a decade.

Sometimes includes resumés of material that appeared in this periodical edited by the Economic Society.

Sociedad Económica, Havana: *Memorias de la Sociedad Patriótica de la Havana, Año de 1793.* Havana: En la Imprenta de la Capitanía General. 189 + 10 pp.
Probably published in 1795.

————. *Memorias de la Sociedad Patriótica de la Habana. Año de 1794.* Havana. En la Imprenta de la Capitanía General. Reprinted in condensed form in *Memorias de la Sociedad Económica de la Habana,* tomo XVII (Habana, 1843), 417-38; tomo XVIII (Habana, 1844), 24-45, 101-27.
According to Del Valle the original had 184 + 7 pp. and 3 tables. It was apparently not distributed to the members until August, 1796.

————. *Memorias de la Real Sociedad Patriótica de la Habana. Año de 1795.* Habana En la Imprenta de la Capitanía General. 158 + 3 pp.
Editing did not begin until 1799, and was completed in 1804.

————. *Memorias de la Real Sociedad Económica de la Habana. Colección Primera que comprehende doce números. Correspondientes a los doce meses del año de 1817.* Habana: Oficina del gobierno y de la Real [S]ociedad Patriótica por S. M. 5 + 1 + 446 pp.

————. *Memorias de la Real Sociedad Económica de la Habana. Colección segunda que comprehende doce números, correspondientes a los doce meses del año de 1818.* Habana: Oficina del Gobierno y de la Real Sociedad Patriótica P. S. M. 445 pp.

————. *Memorias de la Real Sociedad Económica de la Habana. Colección tercera que comprehende doce números, correspondientes a los doce meses del año de 1819.* Habana: Oficina del Gobierno y de la Real Sociedad Patriótica por S. M. 362 + 7 pp.

————. *Memorias de la Real Sociedad Económica de la Habana. Colección cuarta que comprehende doce números, correspondientes A los tres primeros meses de 1820 y nueve últimos de 1823 que fué cuando continuó su publicación.* Habana: Oficina del Gobierno y de la Real Sociedad Patriótica por S. M. 94 + 304 pp.
Cited separately in the study as the Memorias of 1820 and of 1823.

————. *Acta de las Juntas Generales de la Real Sociedad Económica de Amigos de este país. Celebradas en los días 17, 18 y 19 de diciembre de 1833.* Habana: Imprenta del Gobierno, Capitanía General y Real Sociedad Económica por S. M., 1834.
Contains material bearing on the earlier period.

————. *Memorias de la Sociedad Patriótica de la Habana Por una comisión permanente de su seno.* Tomo VII. Habana: Imprenta del Gobierno ..., 1838.
Contains an item of 1794.

————. *Memorias.* ... T. VIII. Habana: Imprenta del Gobierno ..., 1839.
Includes a eulogy of one-time Governor Las Casas, read to the Society in 1801; and a memoria on beehives, written in 1796, and published by the Society.

————. *Memorias.* ... T. XIV. Habana: Imprenta del Gobierno ..., 1842.
Contains four Society documents for the period under study.

————. *Memorias.* ... T. XVI. Habana: Imprenta del gobierno ..., 1843.
Documents of 1797 and 1815, though not of Society origin or connection.

————. *Memorias.* ... T. XVII. Habana, 1843.
Condensation of *Memorias 1794*, as indicated above.

————. *Memorias.* ... T. XVIII. Habana, 1844.
Condensation (cont'd) of *Memorias 1794;* and a biographical sketch of an early Society member.

————. *Memorias.* ... T. XIX. Habana: Imprenta del Gobierno ..., 1844.
Includes (pp. 56-65) article on history of the Societies in Spain and America.

————. *Memorias.* ... T. XX. Habana: Imprenta del Gobierno ..., 1845.
Five items of interest for the period under study.

————. *Anales y Memorias de la Real Junta de Fomento y de la Real Sociedad Económica.* Ser. 4ª T. VII. Habana: Imprenta del Tiempo, 1862-63.
Contains information on Society publications in the early years.

————. *Memorias de la Real Sociedad Económica y Anales de Fomento.* Ser. 4ª T. VIII. Habana: Imprenta del Tiempo, 1863.
Some of the numbers are for 1864, despite the title page. Contains the Society juntas from the first, January 9, 1793, to that of August 21, 1794.

————. *Memorias ... y Anales de Fomento.* Ser. 5ª T. IX. Habana: Imprenta del Tiempo, 1864.
Includes the record of some juntas in 1794-95.

————. *Memorias ... y Anales de Fomento.* T. X. Habana: Imprenta del Tiempo, 1865.
Includes records of two juntas in 1795.

————. *Colección de Actas de la Real Sociedad Patriótica de la Habana.* Habana: Imprenta la Antilla de Cacho-Negrete, 1880. 104 pp.
Entirely taken up with the record of juntas from January 9, 1793, through July 24, 1794.

————. *Memorias.* ... Sér. 9ª t. I. Habana: Imprenta la Antilla de Cacho-Negrete, 1880.
Includes several items for the period under study.

————. *Memorias.* ... Sér. 9ª t. III. Habana: Cacho-Negrete, 1882.
Several items for the period.

————. *Memorias.* ... Sér. 10ª t. I. Habana: Imprenta "El Pilar" de Manuel de Armas, 1894.
Several important items for the period under study.

————. *Memorias.* ... Habana: Manuel de Armas, 1895.
Several items for the period under study.

————. *Memorias.* ... Habana: Manuel de Armas, 1896.
Several items on the period under study.

————. *Elogios fúnebres del excelentísimo Señor D. Luís de Las Casas y Aragorri.* ... *Hechos y publicados por la Real Sociedad Económica de la Havana y por el Tribunal del Consulado de la misma ciudad.* Havana: Imprenta de la Capitanía General, 1802. 22, xxiii, xxxi pp.

———. *Estatutos de la Sociedad patriótica de la Habana. Aprobados por S. M. Año de 1783,* Havana: Impr. de la capia. general [1793?]. 2, xxv pp.
Including statutes, and 4 pp. of "Copia de los Capítulos catorce de las Escuelas patrióticas de Madrid, y Cuba."

———. *Memorias de la sección de historia de la Real Sociedad Patriótica de la Habana.* T. I. Habana: Impr. de las viudas de Arazoza y Soler, 1830-31. xvi, 454 pp.
T. I issued in two parts; no more published. Contains Arrate's *Llave del Nuevo Mundo* [1761], of little use here, although the Society's "Notas," pp. 277-347, contain much useful information on the economic history of the island; and Manuel Mariano de Acosta, *Memorias sobre la ciudad de San Felipe y Santiago Bejucal,* which shows the effects of the increasing Negro population in the late 18th century on the small white tobacco farmer.

———. *Relación histórica de los beneficios hechos a la Real sociedad económica, casa de beneficencia y demás dependencias de aquel cuerpo por el Escmo. Sr. Don Francisco Dionisio Vives. Escrita por las comisiones reunidas de ambas corporaciones.* Habana, 1832. 2, 36 pp.
Contains information on the condition of the Society at the end of the period under study.

———. *Sucinta noticia del ramo de la cera en la isla de Cuba, a fines de marzo del año de 1815.* Habana: Arazoza y Soler [1815?]. 10 pp.
Published under the auspices of the Society. Pablo Boloix was the author.

———. *Tareas de la Real sociedad patriótica de la Habana en el año de 1815.* Habana, 1816. 26 pp.

Spain. Archivo General de Indias. *Catálogo de los fondos cubanos del Archivo. ...* 2 vols. Madrid, 1929-30 (*Colección de documentos inéditos para la historia de Hispano-América,* VII, XII).
Several Economic Society items in vol. II.

Trelles y Govín, Carlos M. *Bibliografía cubana de los siglos XVII y XVIII.* 2d ed. Habana, 1927.

———. *Biblioteca histórica cubana.* 3 vols. Matanzas, 1922-26.

STUDIES

Abascal, Horacio. "Contribución de la Sociedad Económica al progreso de la medicina en Cuba," RBC, XLVII, No. 1 (January-February, 1941), 5-31.

———. "Labor de Romay en la Sociedad Económica," RBC, LXV (January-June, 1950), 126-34.

Bacardí y Moreau, Emilio. *Crónica de Santiago de Cuba.* 2 vols. Barcelona, 1908-9.
Bachiller y Morales, Antonio. *Apuntes para la historia de las letras y de la instrucción pública en la isla de Cuba.* 3 vols. Havana, 1936-37. [1859-61].

Cabrera, Raimundo. *La Casa de beneficencia y la sociedad económica (sus relaciones con los gobiernos de Cuba)*. Havana: Impr. "La Universal," 1914. 258 pp.
Carries to 1824 by p. 56. Does not give a good picture of what the Casa accomplished.

———. *Cuba y sus jueces (rectificaciones oportunas)*. 7th ed. Philadelphia, 1891.

Corbitt, D. C. "La introducción en Cuba de la caña de Otahiti, el árbol del pan, el mango y otras plantas," RBC, XLVII, No. 3 (May-June, 1941), 360 66.

———. "Immigration in Cuba," HAHR, XXII, No. 2 (May, 1942), 280-308.

———. "*Mercedes* and *realengos:* a Survey of the Public Land System in Cuba," HAHR, XIX, No. 3 (August, 1939), 262-85.

Friedländer, H. E. *Historia económica de Cuba*. Havana, 1944. 570 pp.
Finds the great Cuban problems during the past 150 years: the alternative between monoculture and agricultural diversification; the composition of the population and labor conflicts; and international economic relations. Well over one-half of the text proper is on 1815-68, and some of the earlier sections are rather sketchy. As compared with many Latin American works, it has an admirable amount of documentation (the author was trained in Europe), fine coverage, praiseworthy depth, and a fine attempt to tie to world developments. It is, nevertheless, in many respects badly organized, albeit most helpful and stimulating. He made a considerable use of Economic Society records.

Gay-Calbó, Enrique. "Varela revolucionario," RBC, LI (1943, Primer Semestre), 73-110.

Guiteras, Pedro José. *Historia de la Isla de Cuba*. 2d ed., 3 vols. Havana, 1927-28 (*Colección de libros cubanos*, I-III). 1st ed. was 1865-66.

Guerra y Sánchez, Ramiro. *Manual de historia de Cuba (económica, social y política)*. Havana, 1938.

Le Riverend Brusone, Julio J. "La Economía Cubana durante las Guerras de la Revolución y del Imperio Franceses, 1790-1808," *Revista de Historia de América*, No. 16 (December, 1943), 25-64.

Le-Roy y Gálvez, Luís. "Historia de la primera cátedra de química en Cuba," RBC, LXVI (July-December, 1950), 65-93.

Méndez, Manuel Isidro. *El intendente Ramírez*. Havana: Impr. "El Siglo XX," 1944. 95 pp.
Composed as a discourse. Thin. Of some value for Cuba, Puerto Rico, Guatemala.

Montoro, Rafael. "El P. Félix Varela, Oración Pronunciada," RBC, VI, No. 6 (November-December, 1911), 485-97.

Morales, Ofelia. See Ortiz, *Recopilación*.

Ortiz Fernández, Fernando. *Cuban Counterpoint. Tobacco and Sugar*. Trans. Harriet de Onís. New York, 1947.
Originally published, in Spanish, in 1940. A fascinating work, of some value for the present study as it deals with monoculture versus agricultural diversification, with the latifundio and the small farm, with economic feudalism and liberalism.

————. *La hija cubana del iluminismo.* See Ortiz, *Recopilación.*
Also printed in RBC, LI, No. 1 (January-February, 1943), 5-72.

————. "Félix Varela, Amigo del País," RBC, VI, No. 6 (November-December, 1911), 478-84.

Peraza y Sarausa, Fermín. *Historia de la Biblioteca de la Sociedad económica de amigos del país.* Havana: Anuario bibliográfico cubano, 1939. 36 pp.
Also in RBC, XLII, Nos. 1-2 (July-October, 1938).

Pezuela y Lobo, Jacobo de la. *Ensayo histórico de la isla de Cuba.* New York: Impr. española de R. Rafael, 1842.

————. *Historia de la isla de Cuba.* 4 vols. Madrid, 1868-78.

Pierson, W. W., Jr. "Francisco de Arango y Parreño," HAHR, XVI, No. 4 (November, 1938), 451-78.

Ponte Domínguez, Francisco J. "Don Francisco de Arango y Parreño, Artífice del Progreso Colonial de Cuba," *Revista Cubana*, XXIV (January-June, 1949), 284-328.

Portuondo, José Antonio. "La evolución cultural [1762-1868]," in *Curso de introducción a la historia de Cuba* (Havana, 1937: *Cuadernos de historia habanera*, ed. E. Roig de Leuchsenring, X), 257-68.

Remos y Rubío, Juan N. *Historia de la literatura cubana.* 3 vols. Havana, 1945.

Roig de Leuchsenring, Emilio, *et al. El sesquicentenario del Papel Periódico de la Havana.* Havana, 1941.

Saco, José Antonio. *Historia de la esclavitud de la raza africana en el nuevo mundo y en especial en los países Americo-Hispanos.* 4 vols. Havana, 1938 (*Colección de libros cubanos*, XXXVII-XL).

Sagra, Ramón de la. *Historia física, política y natural de la Isla de Cuba.* 13 vols. Paris, 1840-62.
    Volumes I-II contain much material, often statistical and factual, even scientific, bearing on economic life. He made relatively little use of the records of the Economic Society, and was little concerned with its activity.

Guatemala and Chiapas

Manuscript materials were indispensable to analysis of the history and labors of the Guatemala Society, since available Society publications for the period under study total only 505 pages. The *Gazeta de Guatemala* provides excellent contemporary data on the Society. Guatemalan scholars have produced relatively little on the Society.

CONTEMPORARY MATERIALS

Manuscripts. Most of the Society material in the Archivo General of Guatemala is in A1.6, legajos 2006-2007, 2267, which contain only Society material; but documents bearing directly on the Society are found in other legajos, e.g., those of the ayuntamiento. A1.6, leg. 2006, expeds. 13798-13820, over 300 sheets of various sizes, of the Society records, etc.; leg. 2007, expeds. 13821-13839, some 250 sheets of Society materials; leg. 2008, expeds. 13840-13857, some 250 sheets of Society materials; leg. 2267, expeds. 16450-16453, some 30 pages of manuscript, including Society correspondence. A1.1, leg. 2267, exped. 16452; leg. 2817, expeds. 24902-24903. A1.5-6, leg. 51, expeds. 1279-1282. A1.3-8, leg. 1904, exped. 12573. A1.2-4, leg. 2246, exped. 16234. A1.2-2, leg. 2813, exped. 15725. A1.2-5, leg. 2835, expeds. 25310, 25287, 25296. A1-1, leg. 259, exped. 5721; leg. 261, exped. 5757.

Acta de instalación de la Sociedad Económica de Amigos de la Patria de Chiapa. Celebrada el día 1.º de Abril de 1819. Guatemala: Beteta. 18 pp.

El Amigo de la Patria. Guatemala, 1820-22.

"Prospecto" issued October 6, 1820; 48 numbers until March, 1822. Edited by José Cecilio del Valle. Contains data bearing on the Economic Society in earlier years.

Beristain de Souza, José Mariano. *Biblioteca hispano americana setentrional.* 2d ed. 3 vols. Amecameca, 1883.

Córdova, Matías de. *Utilidades de que todos los Indios y Ladinos se vistan y calcen a la Española, y medios de conseguirlo sin violencia, coacción, ni mandato. Memoria premiada por la Real Sociedad Económica de Guatemala en 13 de diciembre de 1797.* Nueva Guatemala: Beteta, 1798. 2, 3-22 pp.

"Documentos acerca de la cooperación de Guatemala en la Independencia de Centro América," BAGG, III, Nos. 3-4 (April, July, 1938), IV, Nos. 1-4 (October, 1938; January, April, July, 1939).

El Editor Constitucional. Guatemala, 1820-21.

Edited by Pedro Molina; liberal, republican; praised the Economic Society.

Gazeta de Guatemala. Guatemala, 1797-1816.

A critical creole periodical, sometimes frankly "American"; liberal, especially on intellectual questions. Intimately linked to the Economic Society, to the study of which it is indispensable. There is not a complete file in any one place. The author has seen almost all numbers to 1811.

Goycoechea, Fray José Antonio. *Memoria sobre los medios de destruir la mendicidad, y de socorrer los verdaderos pobres de esta capital.* Nueva Guatemala: Beteta, 1797. 48 pp.

Pp. 1-2 are "Advertencia"; 3-36, Goycoechea's memoria; 37-48, a "Plan de ejecución" by Antonio García Redondo. The memoria was submitted in an Economic Society essay contest.

"Guatemala, hace ciento catorce años. Informe (inédito hasta ahora) del Ministro Tesorero de las Reales Cajas de Guatemala, acerca del estado deficiente del Erario antes y después de septiembre de 1821. Madrid, 11 de marzo de 1824," ASGH, XII, No. 1 (September, 1935), 3-28.

Guatemala (City) Cabildo. *Apuntes instructivos que al señor don Antonio Larrazabal diputado a las Cortes extraordinarias de la nación española por el Cabildo de la ciudad de Guatemala, dieron sus regidores don José de Isasi, don Sebastián Melón, don Miguel González y don Juan Antonio de Aquileche.* Nueva Guatemala: M. de Arévalo, 1811. 7, 67 pp.

Composed by several members of the Economic Society; largely political, but with the economic views often expressed by the Society.

———. "Instrucciones para la constitución fundamental de la Monarquía española y su gobierno," ASGH, XVII, No. 1 (March, 1941), 7-25; "Instrucciones de la Municipalidad de Guatemala a su Diputado a Cortes, escritas en 1811 por José María Peinado," ASGH, XVII, No. 2 (June, 1941), 136-47; "Instrucciones dadas por el Ayuntamiento de Guatemala al Diputado a Cortes, Canónigo D. Antonio de Larrazabal," ASGH, XVII, No. 5 (March, 1942), 333-51.
> Important for the views of the influential creoles who favored retention of the connection with Spain, but changes in the constitution of the empire. This group, with the clerics and Spanish in Guatemala, composed most of the membership of the Economic Society.

———. *Guatemala por Fernando séptimo el día 12 de diciembre de 1808.* [Guatemala, 1809] 166 (i.e., 130) pp.
> Includes engravings by men who had studied in the Drawing School of the Society.

Irisarri, Antonio José de. *El Cristiano errante. Novela que contiene mucho de historia.* Santiago de Chile, 1929.

Juarros, Domingo. *Compendio de la historia de la ciudad de Guatemala.* 3d ed. 2 vols. Guatemala, 1936.
> Originally published 1808-18. Short section on the Economic Society.

Lanning, John T. (ed.). *Reales Cédulas de la Real y Pontificia Universidad de San Carlos de Guatemala.* Guatemala, 1954.

Larrazabal, Antonio. *Apuntamientos sobre la agricultura y comercio del reino de Guatemala.* ... Nueva Guatemala: Arévalo, 1811. 185 pp.
> By one of the key figures of the period. Very useful on many subjects, e.g., Indians, estimates of Guatemalan population, criticisms of the Spanish economic system, and insistence on the regional peculiarities of Guatemala.

Longinos Martínez, Joseph. *Compendio instructivo sobre el modo mas seguro de disponer, juntar, conserbar, y remitir las producciones Naturales, dispuesto por el Naturalista D. Joseph Longinos Martínez para que sirba de instrucción y acompaña a la adjunta carta Circular.* Colophon: Nueva Guatemala y Enero 1 de 1797. 9 pp.
> Directions for collection of mineral, vegetable, and animal specimens by the members of the Economic Society.

Medina, José Toribio. *La imprenta en Guatemala, 1660-1821.* Santiago, 1910.

Mérida, Martín. "Historia crítica de la Inquisición en Guatemala," BAGG, III, No. 1 (October, 1937), 5-157.
> Done in the late 19th century; some of materials used later disappeared. Lists of printed matter seized.

San José Muro, Fray Antonio de, *et al. Utilidades y medios de que los indios y ladinos vistan y calzen a la española. Memoria que mereció el accesit entre las presentadas sobre este asunto a la Real Sociedad de Guatemala.* Guatemala: Beteta, 1798. 73 pp.
> Pp. 3-58, the San José Muro essay; 58-73, "Extractos de las otras memorias que concurrieron al premio ofrecido sobre la materia de la anterior."

Sociedad Económica. *Estatutos de la Real Sociedad Económica de Amantes de la Patria de Guatemala, aprobada por S. M. en R. Cedula fecha en S. Lornzo a 21 de Octubre de 1795.* Guatemala: Beteta, 1796. 16 pp.

————. *Junta Pública de la Real Sociedad Económica de Amantes de la Patria de Guatemala, Celebrada en 12 de Diciembre de 1796.* Guatemala: Bracamonte [1797]. 35 pp.

The first summary of a public junta to be printed by the Society, though it was not the first public meeting held. Two discources, and secretary's summary of work.

————. *Segunda junta pública de la Real Sociedad Económica de Amantes de la Patria de Guatemala, Celebrada en 9 de Julio de 1797.* Guatemala: Viuda de Arévalo, 1797. 43 pp.

Two discourses, and secretary's summary.

————. *Tercera junta pública de la Real Sociedad ... celebrada el día 9 de diciembre de 1797.* Guatemala: Beteta, 1798. 22 pp.

Two discourses, and secretary's report.

————. *Quarta junta pública de la Real Sociedad ... celebrada el día 15 de julio de 1798.* Guatemala: Viuda de Arévalo, 1798. 27 pp.

Two discourses, and secretary's report.

————. *Quinta junta pública ... celebrada el día 16 de diciembre de 1798.* Guatemala: Viuda de Arévalo, 1799. 30 pp.

Two discourses: secretary's report; financial table for the Society from foundation to the end of 1798.

————. *Catálogo de los individuos que componen la Real Sociedad de Amantes de la Patria de Guatemala en el año de 1799.* [Guatemala, 1799] 8 pp.

————. *Junta general no. 102, que para su restablecimiento celebró la Sociedad Patriótica de Guatemala el sábado 19 de enero de 1811.* [Guatemala, 1812] 16 pp.

Contains the Captain General's decree of re-erection, including his condemnation of the suspension of 1800; lists of members; declaration of purpose.

————. *Octava junta pública de la Sociedad Económica de Amantes de la Patria de Guatemala. Fundado por el Sr. D. Jacobo de Villa Urrutia y Salcedo, del Consejo de S. M. Oydor de esta Real Audiencia, &c. Primer después de su restablecimiento Celebrada el día 12 de agosto de 1811.* [Guatemala]: Beteta, n. d. 33, 12 pp.

Discourses; secretary's summary; information on the suspension of the Society in 1799-1800; biography of Villaurrutia.

————. *Novena junta pública. ... Segunda después de su restablecimiento, celebrada el día 5 de abril de 1812.* [Guatemala]: Beteta, n. d. 54 pp.

Discourses and reports; information on the formal approval of re-establishment by government in Spain.

————. *Relación histórica, concerniente a la junta pública general de la Sociedad económica de Guatemala, celebrada en 25 de abril de 1852.* Guatemala: Impr. de la Paz [1852]. 54 pp.

Some information on the period under study.

————. *Reglamento general de artesanos de la Nueva Guatemala, que la junta comisionada para su formación propone a la general de la Real Sociedad.* Guatemala: Beteta, 1798. 48 pp.

Spain. Archivo General de Indias. *Independencia de América; fuentes para su estudio.* 1st ser., 6 vols. Madrid, 1912.
Describes several documents relevant to this study.

Valenzuela, Gilberto. *La imprenta en Guatemala; algunas adiciones a la obra ... de ... Medina.* Guatemala, 1933.

Valle, José Cecilio del. *Instrucción sobre la plaga de langosta; medios de exterminarla, o de disminuir sus efectos; y de precaber la escasez de comestibles.* Guatemala: Beteta, 1804. [5], 32 pp.

———. *Obras.* Comp. José del Valle and Jorge del Valle Matheu. 2 vols. Guatemala, 1929-30.
Many of the items deal with the Economic Society.

"Varias noticias del Río de San Juan, Yslas Adyacentes de la costa de los Mosquitos, provincias y partidos que tiene el reyno de Guatemala," 287-328 in *Relaciones históricas y geográficas de América Central* (*Colección de libros y documentos referentes a la historia de América*, VIII, Madrid, 1908).

STUDIES

Bancroft, Hubert Howe. *History of Central America.* 3 vols. San Francisco, 1883-87.

Batres Jáuregui, Antonio. *La América Central ante la historia.* 3 vols. Guatemala, 1916-49.

Fernández Hall, Francisco. "Antonio de Liendo y Goicoechea, Poeta," *Boletín de la Biblioteca Nacional* [Guatemala], V, No. 1 (May, 1936), 40-43.

Flamenco, José. *La beneficencia en Guatemala.* Guatemala, 1915.

Fox, John S. "Antonio de San José Muro: Political Economist of New Spain," HAHR, XXI, No. 3 (August, 1941), 410-16.

"Fray Matías de Córdova. Homenaje de la Sociedad de Geografía e Historia de Guatemala," ASGH, VIII, No. 1 (September, 1931), 3-78.

Gándara Durán, Carlos. *Pedro Molina. Biografía.* Guatemala, 1936.

García Peláez, Francisco de Paula. *Memorias para la historia del antiguo reyno de Guatemala.* 3 vols. Guatemala, 1851-52.

Guatemala. Comisión de límites. *El esfuerzo de Guatemala para canalizar el río Motagua y el dominio indisputado que sobre el mismo ha ejercido desde el siglo XVIII* (Guatemala, 1928, *Publicaciones de la Comisión de límites*, No. 6).

Los Guatemaltecos (pseud.). *Noticia biográfica del distinguido literato D. Miguel Larreynaga.* Guatemala: Impr. de la Paz, 1847. 5 pp.

Guillén, Flavio. *Un fraile prócer y una fábula poema (estudio acerca del fray Matías de Córdova).* Guatemala, 1932.
Includes (249-62) the text of Córdova's essay on dressing Indians *a la Española.*

Jones, Chester L. *Guatemala Past and Present.* University of Minnesota Press, 1940.

Lanning, John T. *The University in the Kingdom of Guatemala*. Cornell University Press, 1955.
Clearly shows how unsuited the University was for the promotion of the aims of the Economic Society.

Martínez Sobral, Enrique. "La Jura de Fernando VII," ASGH, I, No. 3 (January, 1925), 238-56.

Marure, Alejandro. *Bosquejo histórico de las revoluciones de Centro América. Desde 1811 hasta 1834*. 2d ed. 2 vols. Guatemala, 1877-78.

Moreno, Laudelino. *Independencia de la Capitanía General de Guatemala*. Madrid, 1927. Also in ASGH, VI, No. 1 (September, 1929).

————. "Guatemala y la Invasión Napoleónica en España," ASGH, VII, No. 1 (September, 1930), 3-17.

Rodríguez Beteta, Virgilio. "El Amigo de la América," *Centro América*, X, No. 4 (October, November and December, 1918), 232-74.

————. *Evolución de las ideas*. Paris, 1929.
Apparently based on wide acquaintance with sources, especially the *Gazeta de Guatemala*. Essentially literary in character; rhetorical; interpretative.

Rosa, Ramón. *Biografía de Don José Cecilio del Valle*. Tegucigalpa, 1943.

Salazar, Ramón A. *Historia del desenvolvimiento intelectual de Guatemala desde la fundación de la primera escuela de letras europeas hasta la inauguración del Instituto Nacional de Indígenas efectuada en el año de 1896*. Tomo I, "La Colonia." Guatemala, 1897.
No more published. In some ways still the best thing available, but unscientific in technique and poorly organized.

————. *Historia de veintiún años. La independencia de Guatemala*. Guatemala, 1926.
A serious attempt to deal with the last two decades of the colonial era, marred by poor organization, an overabundance of quotation, and a lack of citations.

————. *Los hombres de la independencia* (Guatemala, 1899).

Salvatierra, Sofonías. *Contribución a la historia de Centroamérica* (*Monografías documentales*). 2 vols. Managua, 1939.
Some of the sections are based on research in Spanish archives, and are valuable contributions, especially to economic history. The eleven-page section on the Economic Society is poor.

Smith, Robert Sidney. "Origins of the Consulado of Guatemala," HAHR, XXVI, No. 2 (May, 1946), 150-61.

Stanger, F. M. "National Origins of Central America," HAHR, XII, No. 1 (February, 1932), 18-45.

Vela, David. *Literatura guatemalteca*. Guatemala, 1943.

Villacorta Calderón, J. Antonio. "Guatemala en las Cortes de Cadiz," ASGH, XVII, No. 1 (March, 1941).

――――. *Historia de la capitanía general de Guatemala*. Guatemala, 1942.

Zamora Castellanos, Pedro. *El grito de la independencia*. Guatemala, 1935.

Lima

This account is written primarily from the contemporary evidence in the *Mercurio Peruano de historia, literatura, y noticias públicas que da a luz La Sociedad Académica de Amantes de Lima. Y en su nombre D. Jacinto Calero y Moreira* (12 vols., Lima, 1791-95, totaling 3,606 pp.). Some valuable information was taken from *Obras científicas y literarias del doctor D. José Hipólito Unánue* (3 vols., Barcelona, 1914), of which vol. III is the *memoria* or *relación* of Viceroy Gil de Taboada, which Unánue wrote in 1796; Ella Dunbar Temple, *Periodismo Peruano del Siglo XVIII. El Semanario Crítico* (36 pp., n.p., n.d.; from *La Revista "Mercurio Peruano,"* XXV, No. 198); José M. Valega, *La gesta emancipadora del Peru 1780-1819* (3 vols., Lima, 1940-43). A small amount of data is in the following: José Toribio Medina, *La imprenta en Lima (1584-1824)* (4 vols., Santiago, 1904-07); D. E. McPheeters, "The Distinguished Peruvian Scholar Cosme Bueno (1711-1798)," HAHR, XXXV, No. 4 (November, 1955), 484-91; and Unánue's *Guía política, eclesiástica y militar del virreynato del Perú, para el año de 1793-96* (4 vols., Lima, 1793-96), of which vol. I was published by the Academic Society of Lima.

Felipe Barreda Laos, *Vida intelectual del virreinato del Perú* (Buenos Aires, 1937), gives considerable background data, but very little on the Society, and nothing that cannot be gleaned from the *Mercurio*. There is no more than a bare reference to the Academic Society in such general works as Sebastián Lorente, *Historia del Perú bajo los Borbones (1700-1821)* (Lima, 1871); and Carlos Wiesse, *Historia del Perú* (4 vols., Lima, 1937-41). Nor is there anything of value on the Society in more specialized works, such as: Jorge Guillermo Leguía, *Lima en el siglo XVIII* (Lima, 1921; 38 pp.); and César Antonio Ugarte, *Bosquejo de la historia económica del Perú* (Lima, 1926). There is very little pertinent in Manuel de Mendiburu, *Diccionario histórico-biográfico del Perú* (11 vols., Lima, 1931-35); and nothing in Manuel de Odriozola, *Documentos históricos del Perú en las épocas del coloniaje después de la conquista y de la independencia hasta la presente* (10 vols., Lima, 1863-77). Rubén Vargas Ugarte, *Biblioteca peruana: manuscritos peruanos* (5 vols., Lima, 1935-47), lists no MSS. that seem likely to help; and his discussion of historiography, *Historia del Perú (Curso universitario) Fuentes* (Lima, 1939), is of no help with regard to the Academic Society.

Quito

Most important for this account of the Quito Society were the *Mercurio Peruano* of Lima; the Quito Society periodical edited by Espejo, *Primicias de cultura de Quito* (facsimile ed., Quito, 1947; 16 + 56 pp.); and the *Escritos del doctor Francisco Javier Eugenio Santa Cruz y Espejo* (t. I-III, ed. by Federico González Suárez, Quito, 1912-23), which includes a reprint of the *Primicias*, a biography of Espejo, a critical estimate of his work, and reprints of his literary works, and documents (some of them previously inedited), making reference to the desirability of an Economic Society for Quito, and discussing the economic and intellectual deficiencies of the area. Little help was had from José Toribio Medina, *La imprenta en Quito (1760-1818) Notas biblio-gráficas* (Santiago, 1904); or Carlos Enrique Sánchez, *La imprenta en el Ecuador* (Quito, 1935). Of some value were Enrique Garcés, *Eugenio Espejo, médico y duende* (Quito, 1944), poorly organized and documented, thought it prints some documents; Guillermo Hernández de Alba, "Viaje de Espejo, el precursor ecuatoriano a Santa Fe," *Boletín de la Academia Nacional de Historia* [Quito], XXV (January-June, 1945), 102-5; and Antonio Montalvo, *Francisco Javier Eugenio de Santa Cruz y Espejo* (Quito, 1947).

There is a poor section on the Society in Pío Jaramillo Alvarado, *La presidencia de Quito; memoria histórico-juridica de los orígenes de la nacionalidad ecuatoriana y de su defensa territorial* (2 vols., paged continuously, Quito, 1938-39). There is considerable unorganized information on the Society in Roberto Andrade, *Historia del Ecuador* (7 vols., Guayaquil, 1934-37); and Federico González Suárez, *Historia general de la República del Ecuador* (2d ed., 7 vols., Quito, 1931). Little or nothing of value on the Society came from: Manuel de Jesús Andrade, *Ecuador. Próceres de la indepen-dencia* (Quito, 1909); Gustavo Arboleda, *Diccionario biográfico de la república del Ecuador* (Quito, 1910); Isaac J. Barrera, *Próceres de la independencia, lecturas biográ-ficas* (Quito, 1939); Pedro Fermín Ceballos, *Resúmen de la historia del Ecuador desde su orígen hasta 1845* (2d ed., 5 vols., Guayaquil, 1886); John T. Lanning, "La oposi-ción a la ilustración en Quito," RBC, LIII, No. 3 (May-June, 1944), 224-41; José M. Vargas, *La cultura de Quito colonial* (Quito, 1941), which devotes 16 pp. to Espejo without illuminating the history of the Society. Cited, though of almost no value for the Quito Society, were Botero Saldarriaga and Raimundo Rivas, bibliographical information on which is to be found under New Granada, below.

Mompox and Bogota

The very small amount of information on the Mompox Society came from Eduardo Posada, *Bibliografía bogotana* (2 vols., Bogota, 1917-25, *Biblioteca de Historia Nacional*, XVI, XXXVI), which gives a resumé of its published Extracto of 1785. The Extracto is listed in José T. Medina, *La imprenta en Bogota, 1739-1821* (Santiago, 1904). The present author has found no discussion of the Mompox Society in scholarly works. Most important for the Bogota Society was A. Federico Gredilla, *Biografía de José Celestino Mutis con la relación de su viaje y estudios practicados en el Nuevo Reino de Granada* (Madrid, 1911), which includes a reprint of the statutes of the Society. Also of value were Jorge Tadeo Lozano, "Sobre lo útil que sería en este reino el establecimiento de una Sociedad Económica de Amigos del País," in *Correo Curioso de Santafé de Bogotá* (1801), as reprinted in *Periodistas de los albores de la república* (Bogota, 1936), 29-34; and the *relaciones* of the viceroys to their successors in *Relaciones de Mando* (Bogota, 1910 [*Biblioteca de Historia Nacional*, VIII]), and *Relaciones de los virreyes del nuevo reino de Granada* (ed. José Antonio García y García, New York, 1869). The Bogota Society was mentioned in the *Semanario del Nuevo Reino de Granada* [1808-10] (3 vols., reprinted at Bogota, 1942).

Of some indirect interest were *Cartas de Caldas* (Bogota, 1917, *Bibl. Hist. Nac.*, XV), and *Obras de Caldas* (Bogota, 1912, *Bibl. Hist. Nac.*, IX); Roberto Botero Saldarriaga, *Francisco Antonio Zea* (Bogota, 1945); Raimundo Rivas, *El andante caballero Don Antonio Nariño. La Juventud (1765-1803)* (2d ed., Bogota, 1938; *Bibl. H st. Nac.*, L);

José M. Pérez Ayala, *Antonio Caballero y Góngora, virrey y arzobispo de Santa Fe, 1723-1796* (Bogota, 1951). Neither New Granada Society is mentioned in the best-known histories of Columbia or in the *Boletín de Historia y Antigüedades* from vol. I (1902) through the year 1944.

Buenos Aires

The *Telégrafo mercantil; rural, político-económico e historiógrafo del Río de la Plata*, 1801-02 (Reimpresión facsimilar, 2 vols., Buenos Aires, 1914-15), edited by Cabello y Mesa, gives a good idea of the latter's purpose in trying to found the Economic Society, the progress he made, and his reaction to the difficulties he encountered. *Documentos del archivo de Belgrano* (7 vols., Buenos Aires, 1913-17), shows Belgrano's interest in a Society for Buenos Aires, some years before Cabello y Mesa's project. There is valuable documentation on Cabello's Society in José Torre Revello, *El libro, la imprenta y el periodismo en la América durante la dominación española* (Buenos Aires, 1940), Apéndice No. 92, "Expediente relativo a la fundación del periódico 'Telégrafo Mercantil ...,' y de la Sociedad Argentina, patriótico-literaria y económica. ..." Valuable on opposition to the Telégrafo is Ricardo R. Caillet-Bois and Julio César González, "Antecedentes para Explicar el Proceso de la Clausura del Telégrafo Mercantil, el Primer Periódico Impreso Bonaerense," *Revista de Historia de América*, No. 12 (August, 1941), 99-120. The *Semanario de agricultura, industria y comercio*, 1802-07 (Reimpresión facsimilar, 5 vols., Buenos Aires, 1928-37), contained nothing on Cabello's Society, but did promote similar economic interests.

Of minor usefulness were Juan Pablo Echagüe, "El Periodismo," *Historia de la nación argentina*, IV, sec. 2, ch. ii, 59-70; Ricardo Levene, "Significación histórica de la obra económica de Manuel Belgrano y Mariano Moreno," *Historia de la nación argentina*, V, sec. 1, ch. xiii, pp. 489-522, and *Ensayo histórico sobre la revolución de mayo y Mariano Moreno* (2 vols., Buenos Aires, 1920-21), and *Investigaciones acerca de la historia económica del virreynato del Plata* (2 vols., La Plata, 1927); Carlos Ibargurén, *Las sociedades literarios y la revolución argentina 1800-1825* (Buenos Aires, 1937). The material in Ricardo Rojas, *La literatura argentina* (2d ed., 8 vols., Buenos Aires, 1924-25), is very general, but valuable as representing the judgments of a well-known scholar, on both the Society of Cabello and that of 1812. The 1812 Society is discussed in Juan Canter, "Las sociedades secretas y literarias," *Historia de la nación argentina*, V, sec. 1, ch. ix, 189-305. The best evidence of the character of the 1812 Society is Bernardo Monteagudo, "Oración inaugural pronunciado en la apertura de la Sociedad Patriótica la tarde el 13 de enero de 1812," in his *Escritos políticos* (Buenos Aires, 1916).

Puerto Rico

The Regency's order to Ramírez to create a Society is in Zamora y Coronado, *Legislación ultramarina*, III, 619-20: "Real Orden de 28 de noviembre de 1811. ..." Other sources for the foundation are: Alejandro Ramírez, Primer Intendente de Puerto Rico, to the Gobierno Superior, Puerto Rico, August 27, 1813, in BHPR, VI (1919), 212; "Estatutos de la Real Sociedad Económica de Puerto Rico, aprovados por S. M. en Real Orden de 2 de Julio de 1814 por el Ministerio Universal de Indias," BHPR, VII (1920), 56-62, reprinting from the *Diario Económico de Puerto Rico*, November 18,

1814; and Cayetano Coll y Toste, "La Propiedad Territorial en Puerto Rico. Su Desenvolvimiento Histórico," BHPR, I (1914), 239-310, of which sec. xxii (pp. 295-97) is subtitled "Fundación de la Sociedad Económica de Amigos del País. Impuestos al Tabaco y al Aguardiente." There is a small amount of useful information on the Society in Lidio Cruz Monclova, *Historia de Puerto Rico (Siglo XIX). T. I (1808-1868)* (Puerto Rico, 1952).

The following were of minor usefulness, most of them having nothing directly on the Society before 1821: Iñigo Abbad y Lasierra, *Historia geográfica, civil y natural de la Ysla de San Juan Bautista de Puerto Rico* [1782] (Nueva edición, anotada ... por José Julián de Acosta y Calbo, Puerto Rico, 1866); *Acta de Junta pública celebrada por la Sociedad Económica de Amigos del País de Puerto Rico el día 27 de Junio de 1844* (Puerto Rico, 1844), as reprinted in BHPR, VIII (1920), 354-72; Cayetano Coll y Toste, "Historia de Puerto Rico. Conferencia 24ª. Segunda Mitad del Siglo XVIII. Rectificaciones Históricas," BHPR, XX (1926), 129-39, and "Conferencia 26ª. Principios del siglo XIX hasta la implantación en la isla de la constitución de Cadiz, en 1812," BHPR, XX (1926), 277-84; "Instrucciónes y Poderes dados al diputado don Ramón Power por el Ayuntamiento de San Juan y las villas de Arecibo, Aguada y Cosmo," BHPR, X (1923), 102-38; George Dawson Flinter, *An Account of the Present State of the Island of Puerto Rico* (London, 1834); José Toribio Medina, *Notas bibliográficas referentes a las primeras producciones de la imprenta en algunas ciudades de la América española* ... (Santiago, 1904); Eduardo Neumann Gandía, *Benefactores y hombres notables de Puerto-Rico* (2 vols., Ponce, 1896-99); Richard J. and Elizabeth Van Deusen, *Porto Rico. A Caribbean Isle* (New York, 1931). There is nothing helpful on the Society before 1821 in José Géigel y Zenón and Abelardo Morales Ferrera, *Bibliografía puertorriqueña* (Barcelona, 1934; written in 1892-94); or Antonio S. Pedreira, *Bibliografía puertorriqueña 1493-1930* (Madrid, 1932).

Caracas

A small amount of source material on the Society of 1810-1811 is in *Gaceta de Caracas* [1808-18] (6 vols., Paris, Reproducción fotomecánica, 1939); and in J. F. Blanco and R. Azpurua, *Documentos para la vida pública del libertador* (14 vols., Caracas, 1875-78), II, 587, "Tres grandes medidas dictadas por la suprema junta de Caracas en Agosto de 1810 ... Esto. de una Sociedad Patriótica ...," and addresses to the Society by Simon Bolivar and Dr. Miguel Peña, III, 138-43. An interesting Spanish view of the Society is given in a letter of Pablo Morillo, Caracas, 1815, in *Boletín de la Academia Nacional de la Historia* [Caracas], VII, No. 14 (November, 1920), 288-90. There is some information on the short history of the Society, and substantial agreement as to its character in: Harold A. Bierck, Jr., *Vida pública de Don Pedro Gual* (Caracas, 1947); Lino Duarte Level, *Cuadros de la historia militar y civil de Venezuela desde el descubrimiento y conquista de Guayana hasta la batalla de Carabobo* (Madrid, 1917); José Gil Fortoul, *Historia constitucional de Venezuela* (2 vols., Berlin, 1907-09); Francisco González Guiñán, *Historia contemporánea de Venezuela* (15 vols., Caracas, 1909-25); W. S. Robertson, *Life of Miranda* (2 vols., Chapel Hill, 1929).

Caracciolo Parra Pérez, *Filosofía universitaria venezolana 1788-1821* (Caracas, 1934), is good for intellectual background. There is nothing pertinent to the subject in José Toribio Medina, *La imprenta en Caracas 1810-1822* (Santiago, 1904). Ramón de Basterra, *Una empresa del siglo XVIII: Los navíos de la Ilustración. Real Compañía*

Guipuzcoana de Caracas y su influencia en los destinos de América (Caracas, 1925), is a mass of assertion without demonstration; incorrectly claims that Venezuela was "the organizer of the Societies of Friends of the Country in America"; and indulges in inflated claim for the intellectual pre-eminence and immense influence of Basques in America.

Manila

Material available on the Manila Society in 1781-1820 was sufficient to establish the outlines of its foundation and history, and to permit a sketchy description of its interests and activities; but was insufficient to support an analysis of its operations. The Society statutes were reprinted as part of an article entitled "Fundación de la Sociedad," in *Revista de la Real Sociedad económica filipina*, Año I, No. 1 (May 1, 1882), 8-17. Eduardo Malo de Luque, *Historia política de los establecimientos ultramarinos de las naciones europeas* (5 vols., Madrid, 1784-90), contains some scattered information on the Manila Society, and considerable information on politico-economic conditions in the Philippines, but is most valuable for the publication in, V, Anexa No. I, of the discourse of Governor Basco at the formal inauguration of the Society in 1781. Some Society items of the period before 1820 are listed in the following bibliographical works: J. T. Medina, *La imprenta en Manila desde sus orígenes hasta 1810* (Santiago, 1896), and *Adiciones a la imprenta en Manila* (Santiago, 1904); Angel Pérez and Cecilio Güemes, *Adiciones y continuación de "La Imprenta en Manila" de J. T. Medina o rarezas y curiosidades bibliográficas filipinas* (Manila, 1904); W. E. Retana, *Epítome de la bibliografía general de Filipinas*, in *Archivo del bibliófilo* (5 vols., Madrid, 1895-1905), I, and his *La imprenta en Filipinas. Adiciones y observaciones a La Imprenta en Manila de J. T. Medina* (Madrid, 1897).

There is not much on the Society before 1820 in Emma H. Blair and James A. Robertson (eds.), *The Philippine Islands 1493-1801* (55 vols., Cleveland, 1903-09); they sketch a bit of the Society's history, relying on well-known histories of the Philippines; they list a few documents in the Archivo de Indias bearing on the early history of the Society (LIII, 362); they of course include documents bearing on the economic conditions of the islands. Some small assistance was had from the following: Encarnación Alzona, *A History of Education in the Philippines, 1565-1930* (Manila, 1932); Evergisto Bazaco, *History of Education in the Philippines* (Manila, 1939); Charles H. Cunningham, *The Audiencia in the Spanish Colonies as Illustrated by the Audiencia of Manila 1583-1800* (Berkeley, 1919), including the information (281 n. 33) that the original *autos* and plans for the Manila Society are in A. I., 106-1-14; Tomás de Comyn, *State of the Philippines in 1810*, trans. William Watson (London, 1821) from the Spanish edition (Madrid, 1820), in Austin Craig (ed.), *The Former Philippines through Foreign Eyes* (New York, 1917); William C. Forbes, *The Philippine Islands* (2 vols., Boston and New York, 1928); J. Montero y Vidal, *Historia general de Filipinas desde el descubrimiento de dichas islas hasta nuestros días* (3 vols., Madrid, 1887-95); W. E. Retana, "Noticia de Dos Escritores Filipinos: Manuel de Zumalde, Luís Rodríguez Varela," *Revue Hispanique*, LXII, No. 142, 376-439; William Lytle Schurz, "The Royal Philippine Company," *HAHR*, III, No. 4 (November, 1920), 491-508. There is some information on the Society in Zamora y Coronado, *Legislación ultramarina*, V.

Index

José Muro, 215; promotion by Cortes desired, 225; praised by Guatemala Society, 226; educational function of, 253; suitability of methods, 253; voting in, 253-54; equality in, 254; interest in statistics in, 254; methods of disseminating knowledge, 254; working classes of, 254; meeting of, 254-55; prizes offered by, 255-56; publications of, 256-58; research of, for government, 258-59; isolation of, 259-60, 261; members of, 258, 262-67; relations with Church, Cabildo, Consulado, 261-62; residence of members, 265-66; branches of, 266-67; finances of, 267-70; interests of, summarized, 271-72; views compared with Spanish Societies, 272; interest in material prosperity, 272-74; interest in philanthropy, 273; interest in "utility" and "felicity," 273; interest in production, 273; views on bullionism, 273; deprecation of mining, 273-74; views on the labor force, 274; philanthropy and charity in, 275; mixture of motives in, 275; optimism on economic improvement in, 275-77; resources of America lauded, 276-77; on hindrances to American prosperity, 277; means of economic improvement in, 278-86; and changes in legislation, 278; desire exact data, 278-79; study of political economy in, 279-80; and improvement of economic techniques, 280-81; and organic view of the economy, 281; views of on labor and idleness, 281-85; and transportation, 286; sources of ideas of, 286-88; localism in, 288-89; problems different from those of Spanish Societies, 289; "Americanism" in, 289-90; and caste and class, 290-91; and the problem of poverty, 292-300; and science, 301-3; and literature, 303-4; and education, 304-18; and libraries, 305; and commerce, 319-20; and capital and interest, 321; and agriculture, 321-32; and industry and crafts, 332-38; and guilds, 338-42; and mining, 342-44; moderate Spaniards and creoles collaborate in, 345-46; compared with Spanish Societies, 346; effects on, of French Revolution and Wars for Independence, 347-48; favored by Spanish governments of 1810-

1814, 348; in 1814-1821, 348; lack of confidence in, 349; locations of, reasons for, 349-51; why fewer than the Spanish Societies, 349-52; their ideas spread by other means, 350; harassed by Spanish government, 351; summary of aims and actions, 352; upper-class character of, 352-53; possible influence on separatist spirit, 353, 355 n; as danger to the old regime, 353-55; radicalism exaggerated by Spain, 355; failure of Spain to use properly, 355. *See also* Bogota; Buenos Aires; Caracas; Chiapas; Guatemala; Havana; Lima; Manila; Mompox; New Spain; Puerto-Príncipe; Puerto Rico; Quito; Sancti-Espíritu; San Salvador; Santiago; Trinidad; Truxillo; Vera Cruz; Yucatan

Economics, study of. *See* Political economy

Economy, decadence of, and Spanish Societies, 77, 79; of Philippines, 148; of Quito, 169, 175; of Guatemala, 206; and American Societies, 273, 276, 352

Economy, hindrances to the, spoken of in Spain, 76, 83, 95, 98; spoken of in America, 163, 212, 237, 277, 328

Economy, organic view of, in Martínez de Mata, 6; Ward on, 9; and Basque Society, 29; and Spanish Societies, 81, 94, 109; and American Societies, 153, 162, 281; Espejo on, 170; in *Gazeta de Guatemala*, 212

El Editor Constitucional, of Guatemala, 232-34

Education, American, and new ideas, 139-40; school proposed by Santiago Society, 154 n; and Vera Cruz Society, 156; lack of work on, in Lima Society, 165; Pestalozzian, and Havana Society, 194; University of Guatemala, 203; and Guatemala Society, 206; Guatemala Drawing School, 219-20; attack on Spanish universities in Guatemala, 220; in mathematics, in Guatemala, 220; Council of Regency favors, 223; improvement demanded in Guatemala, 223; as panacea against sedition, 227-28; as basis of prosperity, 233, 240, 307 n; discussed in Buenos Aires, 242; improvement asked for Puerto Rican, 246; chief function of American Societies, 353; in Havana's *Casa de*

H

M

Macanaz, Melchor Rafael de, and Sociedades Patrióticas, 11, 25; economic ideas of, 11 n

Machinery, and Spanish Societies, 86, 86 n, 97, 100, 100 n; and American Societies, 162, 280-81, 281 n, 310 n, 324, 324 n, 336, 337

Madrid, Economic Society of, foundation of, 51-52; statutes of, 52; hurt by French Revolution, 59-60; and Cortes and Regency, 62; periodical of, 66; *Memorias* of, 67; advice of, to government, 67-68; women members of, 69-71; finances of, 74; and honorable nature of labor, 82; and popular education, 86; and poverty, 90; and cheap meals, 93; and guilds, 106-8; connections with America, 119 n; knowledge of, in America, 173 n, 196 n, 221, 287, 297. *See also* Economic Societies, of Spain

Maguey, fiber of, for textiles in Guatemala, 337

Mallorca, Economic Society of, 54, 65 n, 66, 80 n, 84, 86 n, 87, 101, 110

Manila, Economic Society of, and importation of Chinese, 147 n; foundation of, 148; inaugural address, 148-49; statutes, 149; activities of, 149-50; popular industry and, 150; and Philippine Company, 150; decay of, 150-51; silk and, 151; referred to, in Guatemala, 214

Manrique, Juan, 206, 217

Manufacturing. *See* Industry

Martínez de Mata, Francisco de, 6, 212 n, 287

Mathematics, and Spanish Societies, 86, 87; and American Societies, 206, 304, 310 n. *See also* Education

Medicine, and Basque Society, 37, 42; and American Societies, 193, 245-46, 301-2

Melón, Sebastián, 230

Mendicancy. *See* Poverty

Mendinueta y Múzquiz, Pedro, Viceroy of New Granada, 155, 156 n; approves Bogota Society, 236; asks an Economic Society in his *Relación,* 238

Menéndez y Pelayo, Marcelino, 28 n, 104; on Peñaflorida, 27 n; on French

influence in Basque Society, 40 n, 44 n; on practical nature of Spanish Societies, 76 n; on Spanish Societies, 112

Mercantilism, in Spain, 5, 7, 8; effects on American industry, 129-30. *See also* Government; Laissez faire; Political economy; Trade

Merchants, number of, in Lima, 157; and *hacendados,* at Havana, 178; number of, in Guatemala, 202; in Guatemala Society, 265. *See also* Consulado

Mercurio Peruano, foundation of, 159; Society's plan for, 160-61; subscribers to, 161; economic material in, 161-65; and Enlightenment, 165; and Bishop Pérez Calama, 166; trouble of, with authorities, 166-68; known in Havana, 184; European authors cited by, 288

Mesta, 10, 97

Mexico. *See* New Spain

Military, in Spanish Societies, 32, 71; in Guatemala Society, 265

Mining, deprecated in Spain, 11 n, 109; in America, 128, 201; deprecated in America, 128 n, 162, 212, 342; and Guatemala Society, 231; in American Societies, 342-44

Miranda, Francisco de, 139, 244

Mociño, José, aids Guatemala Society in Mexico, 216; selling Guatemala Society publications in Mexico, 258 n; and Guatemala Cabinet of Natural History, 303; and indigo of Guatemala, 327-28

Molina, Pedro, 232-34

Mompox, Economic Society of, founded, 154; *Extracto* of, 154; statutes of, 155; knowledge of, in America, 155, 183, 215

Moncada, Sancho de, 5-6, 149

Money and value, Sancho de Moncada on, 6; Martínez de Mata on, 6; Ustáriz on, 8; tokens for change in Mexico, 130; money scarce in Guatemala, 212; money said less important than industry, 212; money not wealth, 273; money said less important than production, 313. *See also* Bullionism; Capital

Montalvo y O'Farrill, Juan, at Seminary of Vergara, 47 n

Monteagudo, Bernardo, and Buenos Aires Society of 1812, 243

Monte de Piedad. See Poverty